Reciprocity and Retaliation in U.S. Trade Policy

THOMAS O. BAYARD
KIMBERLY ANN ELLIOTT

with contributions by Amelia Porges and Charles Iceland

Reciprocity and Retaliation in U.S. Trade Policy

Institute for International Economics
Washington, DC
September 1994

Thomas O. Bayard, *Deputy Director and Research Fellow*, was formerly Program Officer for International Economics at the Ford Foundation and Economist at the US Department of Labor. He is coeditor of *Economic Relations Between the United States and Korea: Conflict or Cooperation?* (1989) and author of several articles on trade and adjustment policies.

Kimberly Ann Elliott, *Research Associate*, is coauthor of *Measuring the Costs of Protection in the United States* (1994), *Economic Sanctions Reconsidered* (second edition 1990), *Auction Quotas and United States Trade Policy* (1987), and *Trade Protection in the United States: 31 Case Studies* (1986).

INSTITUTE FOR INTERNATIONAL ECONOMICS
11 Dupont Circle, NW
Washington, DC 20036-1207
(202) 328-9000   FAX: (202) 328-5432

C. Fred Bergsten, *Director*
Christine F. Lowry, *Director of Publications*

Cover design by Michelle M. Fleitz
Typesetting by Automated Graphic Systems
Printing by Automated Graphic Systems

Printed in the United States of America
97 96 95 94   5 4 3 2

Library of Congress Cataloging-in-Publication Data

Bayard, Thomas O.
   Reciprocity and retaliation in U.S. Trade Policy / Thomas O. Bayard and Kimberly Ann Elliott ; with contributions by Amelia Porges and Charles Iceland.
      p. cm
   Includes bibliographical references and index.

   1. United States—Commercial policy.   2. Reciprocity—United States.   3. Competition, Unfair.
   I. Elliott, Kimberly Ann, 1960–   .
   II. Institute for International Economics (U.S.)   III. Title.
   HF1455.B334   1994
   382'.3'0973—dc20   94-22348
                                                                    CIP

ISBN 0-88132-084-6

Marketed and Distributed outside the USA and Canada by Longman Group UK Limited, London

Contents

List of Figures

List of Boxes

Preface

The Institute has conducted extensive studies of trade policy, both globally and in the United States. Those studies have addressed multilateral negotiations, such as the recently completed Uruguay Round; regional efforts, such as the Canada–United States Free Trade Agreement and the North American Free Trade Agreement; and bilateral talks, notably between the United States and Japan. We have also probed the domestic foundations of trade policy in the United States, most thoroughly in I. M. Destler's classic *American Trade Politics* (second edition, 1992).

This new volume assesses the results of the shift toward a more aggressive and more unilateral trade policy in the United States after 1985. It thus cuts across all dimensions of American trade policy: its domestic politics, its efforts with major partner countries, and its impact on the global trading system. In doing so, the volume adopts the case study method employed so effectively by one of its coauthors, Kimberly Ann Elliott, in her previous pathbreaking work with Gary Clyde Hufbauer and Jeffrey J. Schott on the effects of economic sanctions (*Economic Sanctions Reconsidered,* second edition, 1990). The new analysis also reflects the Institute's continuing interest in the interaction between the domestic and external aspects of international economic policy, especially in the United States, dating back to William Cline's 1982 study *"Reciprocity": A New Approach to World Trade Policy?*

The Institute for International Economics is a private nonprofit institution for the study and discussion of international economic policy. Its purpose is to analyze important issues in that area and to develop and communicate practical new approaches for dealing with them. The Institute is completely nonpartisan.

The Institute is funded largely by philanthropic foundations. Major institutional grants are now being received from the German Marshall Fund of the United States, which created the Institute with a generous commitment of funds in 1981, and from the Ford Foundation, the William and Flora Hewlett Foundation, the William M. Keck, Jr. Foundation, the Andrew Mellon Foundation, the C. V. Starr Foundation, and the United States–Japan Foundation. A number of other foundations and private corporations also contribute to the highly diversified financial resources of the Institute. The Chase Public Policy Program and the Alfred P. Sloan Foundation provided partial funding for this study. The Dayton Hudson Foundation provides support for the Institute's program of studies on trade policy. About 12 percent of the Institute's resources in our latest fiscal year were provided by contributors outside the United States, including about 5 percent from Japan.

The Board of Directors bears overall responsibility for the Institute and gives general guidance and approval to its research program—including identification of topics that are likely to become important to international economic policymakers over the medium run (generally, one to three years), and which thus should be addressed by the Institute. The Director, working closely with the staff and outside Advisory Committee, is responsible for the development of particular projects and makes the final decision to publish an individual study.

The Institute hopes that its studies and other activities will contribute to building a stronger foundation for international economic policy around the world. We invite readers of these publications to let us know how they think we can best accomplish this objective.

C. FRED BERGSTEN
Director
August 1994

Acknowledgments

Many people contributed to this study. Our greatest debt is to the many participants and close observers of the trade disputes studied here who agreed to interviews or who commented on drafts of the manuscript. All of those interviews were off-the-record, and most of those we spoke to requested anonymity. Their help was indispensable.

We were blessed to have two very patient and diligent research assistants, Ruth Junkin and Charles Iceland, who combed USTR public files and other sources to collect information and data for the summaries of the 91 section 301 cases summarized in the appendix. We are also grateful for the very able research assistance over the years provided by Janet Daly, Cindy McKowan, Terence Mulligan, Kevin Parikh, and Yuichi Takahashi.

We especially appreciate the detailed and insightful comments on large parts of the manuscript that we received from Judith Bello, Robert Hudec, Douglas Nelson, John Odell, Amelia Porges, and Alan Wm. Wolff. We would also like to thank Marcelo Abreu, Ray Ahearn, Robert Baldwin, Steve Charnovitz, Michael Finger, Marc Levinson, Keith Maskus, Rachel McCulloch, Stephen Woolcock, and the participants in seminars at the American Economic Association, the University of Southern California, the Royal Institute of International Affairs, the National Bureau of Economic Research, and the joint Harvard-MIT seminar on international political economy for their help and advice on various parts of the manuscript. The Institute for International Economics hosted three study group meetings at which valuable input was received. And, as always, we are very grateful for the stimulating dialogue and many valuable suggestions offered by our colleagues at the Institute, particularly C. Fred Bergsten,

William R. Cline, I. M. Destler, Marcus Noland, J. David Richardson, John Williamson, and Paul Wonnacott.

Finally, we would like to thank Christine Lowry, Valerie Norville, Brigitte Coulton, and Faith Hunter for their great patience and skill in shepherding this book through the publications process under trying conditions, Jay Dick for his assistance producing figure 1.3, and Lisa Heredia, Anthony Stancil, and especially Angela Barnes for their careful attention to detail in typing the manuscript.

Introduction

In 1985 the United States adopted a controversial new trade tactic, which Jagdish Bhagwati (1990) has called aggressive unilateralism. The United States became more assertive in demanding that its trading partners reduce real or imagined barriers to US exports and investment and protect intellectual property rights. The new trade stance is aggressive because US demands have often been backed by highly publicized threats of retaliation under the section 301, special 301, and super 301 provisions of US trade law. It is unilateral in two respects. First, the United States frequently, but not always, unilaterally decides a foreign trade practice is unfair. Second, the United States typically requires that its partners unilaterally liberalize without any reciprocal concessions from the United States. Critics have charged the United States with acting as self-appointed judge, jury, and executioner in the pursuit of trade justice.

The traditional postwar US approach to opening foreign markets has been to encourage multilateral negotiations in which many countries exchange reciprocal commitments to lower trade barriers under the auspices of the General Agreement on Tariffs and Trade (GATT). In the eight rounds of global trade negotiations since 1947, the United States has led in pressing for reductions in tariffs and quantitative restrictions and in designing international rules to limit trade-distorting practices such as subsidies, dumping, and discriminatory government procurement practices. In the latest multilateral negotiations, the Uruguay Round (1986–93), the United States was the *demandeur* for reforms of trade-distorting agricultural policies and for new rules to liberalize trade in services, limit restrictions on foreign investment, and guarantee stronger international rights

1

to owners of intellectual property. The United States also pressed hard for an improved GATT dispute settlement mechanism to resolve trade conflicts.

Although average tariffs on industrial goods in the major industrial countries had fallen to around 5 percent by the early 1980s, there was mounting concern in large segments of the US business and policy communities that past trade negotiations had not resulted in a fair and balanced outcome. Notwithstanding significant tariff liberalization under the GATT, many foreign markets were seen as substantially more protected than the US market, with foreign governments relying relatively more heavily on subsidies, administrative practices, and other nontariff barriers. Critics of US trade policy alleged that foreign producers and investors enjoyed easy access to the relatively open US market while US firms were denied equivalent opportunities abroad. This perceived unfairness in the terms of market access led to growing political pressure for some ill-defined form of reciprocity (Cline 1982). If trading partners continued to refuse to give American firms reciprocal access to their markets, many urged, the United States should retaliate by restricting foreign opportunities in US markets.

Successive US administrations have insisted that the new approach of aggressive unilateralism is a complement to, not a substitute for, the traditional multilateral approach to trade liberalization. Many foreign and domestic critics, however, see it as a dangerous departure from multilateralism, and it has provoked considerable controversy.

Hawkish supporters of aggressive unilateralism argued in the mid-1980s that foreign trade barriers must be eliminated because they contribute to the trade deficit, undermine American competitiveness, and cost Americans their jobs. Others argued that foreign "industrial targeting" must be countervailed because it erodes the US technological edge. The "lesser evil" school argued that an aggressive strategy was necessary to sustain a pro-trade political coalition and to force much-needed reforms in the GATT trading system. On the other hand, its critics have charged that aggressive unilateralism is not terribly effective in opening foreign markets or in protecting intellectual property, that it runs the risk of provoking costly trade wars, and that it undermines both the functioning of the global trading system and US leadership in the world economy.

Despite the controversy and much heated rhetoric, there has been relatively little analysis of aggressive unilateralism's actual impact on foreign trade barriers and on the functioning of the global trading system. The best of the initial analyses is Bhagwati and Patrick's (1990) edited volume, *Aggressive Unilateralism: America's 301 Trade Policy and the World Trading System*, many of whose authors are highly skeptical of the new US approach. A more recent study, Patrick Low's (1993) *Trading Free: The GATT and US Trade Policy*, contains a very thoughtful and also quite damning assessment. We owe an intellectual debt to these books in helping us to clarify our own thinking and analysis.

Yet we arrive at a somewhat less critical assessment of aggressive unilateralism's results to date: it has not had the disastrous effects that some feared. But it also has not been as successful as its supporters hoped it might be.

Moreover, now that many of the reforms pushed by the United States have been at least partially incorporated in the new World Trade Organization (WTO), there is less of an argument for aggressive unilateralism. If the United States continues with an aggressive unilateral strategy in defiance of its international obligations and outside a broader multilateral context such as existed while the Uruguay Round was being negotiated, it could face more serious consequences in the future than it did in the past. Up until the end of 1993, the United States could plausibly argue that some aggressive unilateralism was necessary to get the multilateral system back on track. With the successful completion of the Uruguay Round, a continuation of aggressive unilateralism is likely to be rejected as bullying, pure and simple. This is evident in the flood of denunciations poured on US trade policy vis-à-vis Japan in 1994. Thus our principal policy recommendation is that the United States move from aggressive unilateralism to aggressive multilateralism, using the improved dispute settlement mechanism to enforce the WTO rules.

In this study, we address three main questions. First, has aggressive unilateralism been effective in its narrowly defined objective of opening foreign markets, and what factors have contributed to its success or failure? Second, what has been the broader impact of aggressive unilateralism on the functioning of the multilateral trading system and on the credibility of US leadership in that system? Third, with the completion and likely ratification of the Uruguay Round, what role should US demands for reciprocity and threats of retaliation play in the future? In particular, is there still a role for super 301 in US trade policy?

Methodology

The study takes two different but complementary approaches to case-study analysis. Part of our assessment of the efficacy of aggressive unilateralism and of the factors that contribute to its success or failure is based on a statistical analysis of 72 regular, special, and super 301 cases that have been completed since 1975 and that have reasonably clear outcomes. This analysis is supplemented by 12 detailed case studies of individual trade disputes. The broader empirical analysis is useful in assessing the quantifiable trends and general factors that contribute to the outcomes of section 301 actions. The more detailed case studies provide insights into the less quantifiable tactics of negotiations and the *sui generis* factors that influence outcomes.

The reader should be aware of the limitations of our approach. First, the section 301 experience provides a convenient data base for study, but many trade disputes are resolved informally before they reach the status of a section 301 case. Thus, for example, several US negotiators have told us they averted potential disputes simply by telephoning their counterparts abroad and warning of serious consequences if an offending trade measure or practice was imposed or was not removed. It is impossible to know how many conflicts are resolved informally or how important they are because they leave no paper trail. The disputes that become formalized in section 301 or other legal actions such as GATT dispute settlement may be the more difficult ones that cannot be handled with a telephone call or over a drink. In addition, we cannot assess "the dogs that didn't bark"—the potential foreign trade barriers that may have been deterred by the aggressive use of threats in earlier cases. Both of these factors may cause us to underestimate the efficacy of US threats in opening markets or deterring new barriers. It is perhaps most accurate to describe our empirical analysis as focused on one class of aggressive unilateralism—section 301 disputes, which may not be fully representative of the entire range of trade conflicts.

Second, there are also limitations in our use of detailed case studies. There is no such thing as a typical case; every dispute has unique characteristics that often have an important impact on the outcome. This makes it difficult to draw general conclusions that may be relevant to a broader class of disputes. We did, however, find some common themes that ran through a number of case studies—for example, the importance for a successful outcome of a domestic constituency in the target country favoring the changes that the United States demands.

In selecting the cases for detailed study, we tried for balance and representativeness of the known universe of US trade disputes. Thus, for example, we picked cases involving services, intellectual property, agricultural, and manufactured goods because these are all important subjects of trade conflicts. We also tried to represent US trading partners most subject to US threats. Thus, Japan is the subject of five of our case studies because it is a frequent target. We also wanted to be comprehensive in our assessment of super 301, so we studied all of those cases, including the "noncases" of Korea and Taiwan, where preemptive agreements were reached. Overall, we think that our sample of detailed case studies is reasonably representative, but not perfectly so.

Plan of the Book

We will begin our discussion in chapter 1 with a look at the political and economic events that served as the catalyst for the shift toward aggressive

unilateralism—in particular the policy debate over ▬
Trade Act of 1974. Chapter 2 then describes how section
the procedures that currently govern investigations. It also
debate over the 1988 Trade Act and the evolution of the super 3▬
ments. Chapter 3 summarizes what proponents thought aggressive
eralism might achieve and what critics feared it might produce. We
analyze the "truth and consequences" of the 301 policy in the 1980s: wh
we have learned from experience with the actual 301 cases brought since
1975 about the policy's effectiveness in market opening and its impact
on the international trading system. Chapter 4 gives detailed analysis of
the circumstances in which section 301 appears to have been most effective
in opening markets for US exporters.

The second part of the book is devoted to 12 detailed case studies. The
first three chapters analyze super 301 cases involving Japan (satellites,
supercomputers, and wood products), Brazil and India (quantitative
restrictions, services, and investment), and the preemptive agreements
with Korea and Taiwan to avoid super 301 designation. Chapters 8
through 11 include case studies of intellectual property in Brazil, the
oilseeds dispute with the European Union, Japanese import quotas for
beef and citrus, and financial services in Japan and the European Union.

We summarize our conclusions and recommendations in part III, looking first at super 301 specifically (chapter 12) and then more broadly at
the future roles for reciprocity and retaliation (chapter 13).

section

301

dis

mat-

then

at

Section 301 as a Tool of Aggressive Unilateralism

1

U.S. Trade Pressures and Policy in the 1980s

For most of the postwar period, US trade policy rested firmly on two principles: multilateralism and nondiscrimination based on unconditional most-favored nation (MFN) treatment. At US insistence, these principles were embodied in the General Agreement on Tariffs and Trade (GATT), established in 1947 to govern international trade. Since then, the multilateral negotiation of reciprocal trade concessions, from which all GATT members automatically benefit through MFN treatment, has been the major vehicle for significant trade liberalization. In recent years, however, the strong US embrace of these principles, and of the multilateral GATT system itself, has weakened. Exceptions to unconditional MFN have become more important. Among the more important factors in this erosion are the decline in US hegemony, the increase in international economic interdependence, and the fact that many Americans now view the field on which the trade game is played as unfairly tilted against US competitors.

One result of these trends and changing perceptions has been an increased emphasis on using unilateral US trade leverage to "level the playing field." On the import side of the trade balance, the United States increasingly resorted to two measures: countervailing duties to offset alleged foreign dumping and subsidies, and "voluntary" export restraints to directly limit imports. Since 1985, successive administrations have also tried to deflect some of the pressure to restrict imports by aggressively attacking foreign barriers to US exports.

This book examines the shift in US trade policy and the tactics used in individual cases as a basis for assessing both the impact on the international trading system and the effectiveness of US challenges to foreign barriers since 1975. We begin in this chapter by summarizing the political and economic pressures that spawned what has been called "aggressive unilateralism." We also define the term as it will be used in this book. A key tool of aggressive unilateralism is section 301 of the Trade Act of 1974, which authorizes the president to respond to unfair foreign trade practices. This chapter refers occasionally to section 301's role in the policy debates of the mid-1980s, but the detailed explanation of how section 301 works and the story of the evolution of "super" 301 are reserved for chapter 2.

The Role of the GATT

Unconditional MFN under the GATT means that a tariff concession one member offers to another "shall be accorded immediately and unconditionally to the like product originating in or destined for the territories of all other [members]." It requires that, in general, members should not discriminate against one another with respect to trade policy. Reciprocal trade negotiations under this system were expected to result in "a broad balance between the reduction in trade barriers offered by the United States and the liberalization secured from other major trading partners in negotiations, or reciprocity 'at the margin' on a basis of all products considered together" (Cline 1982, 7).

During the 1980s, however, many in Congress and the private sector came to believe that the process of reciprocal liberalization under the GATT was increasingly biased against the United States (if unintentionally so). The seven previous rounds of GATT negotiations had been relatively successful in reducing tariffs but had been less effective in devising disciplines for subsidies and other nontariff barriers. Since many policymakers believed, with some justification, that other countries relied more heavily on nontariff barriers and other industrial policies than did the United States, the result of the GATT negotiations' focus on tariffs had been to leave the US market relatively more open.[1]

These critics of US trade policy began to emphasize reciprocity in *levels* of protection—or comparable market access—rather than just reciprocal

---

1. Low (1993, 76) presents data showing that from 1960 through 1988 both Japan and the European Union spent a higher proportion of national income on subsidies—much higher in the case of the Union. Low also presents data showing that a much higher proportion of Japan's imports are subject to "hard-core" nontariff barriers than those of either the United States or the Union (p. 74). In agriculture, the Organization for Economic Cooperation and Development (OECD) estimates that in the late 1980s, the calculated "producer subsidy equivalent" for the United States was about 70 percent of the OECD average, with the European Union at or slightly above the average and Japan more than 60 percent above the average. Only Australia and New Zealand had lower estimated PSEs than the United States (OECD 1991, chapter 5).

changes in the level of protection (Cline 1982, 7). As the focus shifted from the process of liberalization to the actual outcome, US trade policy became more bilateral and more sector-specific, and threats of market closure, rather than offers of further market opening, became more prominent as a negotiating tool. In addition to the perception that the benefits of past GATT negotiations were not fairly distributed, another important source of the pressure for an aggressive unilateral trade policy was the growing belief in Congress and elsewhere that the GATT system had been ineffective in enforcing the rules. Moreover, as international investment and trade in services grew in importance, GATT was simply irrelevant to an ever-growing share of world trade.

GATT rules recognize that the balance of concessions can tip, whether by intent or inadvertently. GATT Article XXIII is supposed to govern the settlement of disputes among GATT members, and under it GATT members can collectively authorize retaliation to restore balance if no other solution can be found.[2] Article XXIII covers situations in which one GATT member claims that another has either violated GATT rules or has otherwise "nullified" or "impaired" benefits that the complaining country expected to receive as a result of abiding by its GATT obligations.[3] In either case, the plaintiff country must bring its complaint to the GATT, and if consultations do not resolve the dispute, a panel of independent experts will be appointed to review the merits of the case. If the panel rules that a violation, nullification, or impairment by other means has occurred, the members of the GATT—acting by consensus—may authorize the plaintiff country to retaliate against the defendant country.

As discussed in Jackson (1989), the GATT was not originally intended to serve as a formal institution; rather, it was an agreement among "contracting parties." A premium was placed on consensus in decision making and negotiation for the resolution of disputes. Over the years, however—mainly because of US pressure—the process became more legalistic, with an emphasis on adjudicating disputes based on the rules rather than negotiating mutually acceptable solutions. Opposition to the legalistic approach, combined with the inherent vagueness of some GATT rules, led to increasing pressure on the dispute settlement process. Detailed data compiled by Robert Hudec (1993, 287 and 290) show that the number of GATT complaints filed more than tripled, from 32 in the 1970s to 115 in the 1980s. Also, of the 40 cases in the 1980s in which violations were found, 7 resulted in no satisfaction for the plaintiff, up from none in the previous three decades, despite the validity of the complaints.

---

2. Article XXII calls for consultation among members as the first phase of dispute settlement; only if these consultations fail to resolve the dispute are members expected to invoke the more formal dispute settlement process of Article XXIII.

3. See Hudec (1975) for a thorough treatment of the meaning of "nullification and impairment" and its connection to the origins of section 301 of the Trade Act of 1974.

Finally, the limited coverage of GATT rules became a source of growing frustration. When the GATT was founded, services trade other than travel and tourism was practically nonexistent, and foreign investment was a tiny fraction of what it is today. Also, since 1947 the computer and communications revolutions have triumphed, and intellectual property has become an increasingly important component of more and more products. Although the United States was primarily responsible for limiting the GATT's role in agricultural trade—having sought a waiver for its own sins in the 1950s—as agricultural exports increased in the 1960s and 1970s, it repeatedly sought to restrain and roll back foreign restrictions on agricultural imports. Over the years, these gaps in the GATT loomed larger as sources of US frustration with the trading system.

The United States is a major player in the agricultural and services sectors, and its economy is relatively less regulated in most parts of these sectors. Thus, many in Congress and the business community began to look to aggressive unilateralism to protect US "rights" in areas where GATT could not or would not. The Reagan administration had tried at the ministerial meeting in 1982 to get GATT members to agree to launch a multilateral negotiation to strengthen and expand GATT rules but had been rebuffed. In the minds of many in business and policy circles, that left US negotiators with no alternative but aggressive unilateral trade policy to enforce US rights under trade agreements and to pursue liberalization of sectors GATT rules did not cover.

Increasing Pressure on the System

The roots of the pressures reach back at least to the early 1970s. The collapse of the Bretton Woods system for exchange rate management in 1973 and the first oil shock in 1973–74 highlighted increased US dependence on trade (figure 1.1) and its vulnerability to economic events beyond its borders. At the same time, congressional reforms in the wake of the Watergate scandal weakened party discipline and allowed committees to proliferate. These developments had the unfortunate side effect of further undermining the mechanisms for containing protectionist trade pressures that had evolved following the Smoot-Hawley debacle of the 1930s.[4] Finally, perceptions that key trading partners were "free riding" on the international trade system added to the dissatisfaction with US trade policy and performance.

Secretary of the Treasury George Shultz articulated these concerns as early as 1973 in congressional hearings on what became the Trade Act of 1974:

---

4. Destler (1992, chapters 3 and 4) details the increasing economic and political pressures on the US trade policy system in the 1970s and 1980s.

Figure 1.1 US trade dependence

total trade as a share of GDP

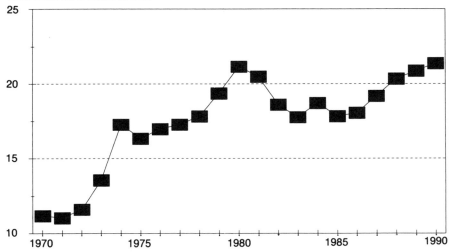

Source: *Economic Report of the President*, 1994.

> Today, economic power is not concentrated in the United States alone as it was thirty years ago. Great centers of wealth have grown up in Europe and Japan. . . . However, along with this diffusion of power has gone a reluctance to remove restrictions that are contrary to the principles of an open world economy. . . . In this changed world of economic equals we need to deal with those restrictions, and we need new rules to assure equality of responsibility. (US House of Representatives, Committee on Ways and Means 1973, 159)

Yet, in the three problem areas cited by Shultz as in need of reform— quotas and other nontariff barriers, agricultural trade restrictions, and preferential trade arrangements—little was achieved in the Tokyo Round of multilateral trade negotiations (1974–79), and the debate over US trade policy intensified.

The cracks in the US commitment to multilateralism and nondiscrimination that appeared in the 1970s widened considerably in the 1980s. President Ronald Reagan took office in 1981 with an economic platform emphasizing free trade, deregulation (including financial markets), and tax cuts. Although Reagan's economic policy also included a commitment to reduce government spending on domestic programs, those cuts were more than offset by large increases in defense spending. Nor did the promised supply-side revenue benefits of the tax cuts appear. Meanwhile, Federal Reserve Chairman Paul Volcker had sharply tightened monetary policy to squeeze out the double-digit inflation sparked by the second oil shock in 1979–80. Loose fiscal and tight monetary policies together yielded large budget deficits and high interest rates, which "crowded in" capital from abroad and put upward pressure on the value of the dollar. At its peak in 1985, the trade-weighted value of the dollar was 50 percent higher than it had been in 1979–80.

The sharp appreciation of the dollar was a major cause of the exploding US merchandise trade deficits in the mid-1980s (Bergsten 1988; Destler and Henning 1989; and Niskanen 1988). The US deficit on international goods and services trade doubled from $24 billion in 1979 to $50 billion in 1983 and doubled again in 1984 to $103 billion. Increasing imports and the recessions in 1979–80 and 1982 hit key industrial import-competing sectors particularly hard. While overall employment in manufacturing declined 12 percent between 1979 and 1983, employment in the auto assembly and steel sectors dropped 33 percent (Bureau of Labor Statistics, *Supplement to Employment and Earnings*, various years). Though the growth in imports slowed during the recession year of 1982, it resumed with the economic recovery in 1983, and US merchandise imports in 1985 were nearly 30 percent higher than they had been in 1981. But US exports remained stagnant because of the still-rising dollar and because growth among US trading partners remained sluggish following the 1982 recession, especially in Europe. The impact on US exports was further exacerbated by the debt crisis in Latin America, a major market for US goods. In fact, US merchandise exports did not regain their 1981 level until 1987 (*Economic Report of the President*, 1994).

Although these macroeconomic shocks were widely recognized as the dominant cause of the deteriorating American trade balance, many believed foreign industrial policies and trade barriers were an important source of the problem. For example, in 1986 Congressman John Dingell (D-MI) circulated a report on "unfair foreign trade practices" to the members of the House Energy and Commerce Committee, which he chaired. The introduction of the report stated:

> The Subcommittee [on Oversight and Investigations] believes a thorough reading of the record ... leads inevitably to the conclusion that the United States is being victimized in the world market. Further, while our trading partners have relentlessly pursued their economic self-interest in determining import and export policies, this country has been hamstrung by a free trade ideology that ignores the realities of the world trading system. (US House of Representatives, Committee on Energy and Commerce 1986, 3)

The report (p. 4) concluded that "tariff and non-tariff barriers to U.S. exports are pervasive among our trading partners" and that "Japan and other countries have made selective barriers to imports the cornerstone of a successful national economic development strategy. . . ."

For those who believed that the US market was more open than those of its trading partners, demands for unilateral trade concessions were justified to "level the playing field." Even many of those who accepted the basic fairness of past tariff-cutting deals increasingly lamented the gaping holes in the coverage of GATT rules, which allowed subsidized European agricultural exports to erode US market shares and left barriers to services and foreign investment untouched. These frustrations were exacerbated by the European Community's blockage of US-backed reforms of agricultural trade policies in the Tokyo Round, as well as its opposition to reform of the GATT dispute settlement process. The holes in GATT rules and its institutional weaknesses raised questions about its relevance in a changing world economy and weakened support for the multilateral approach to trade problems.

The Reagan administration initially responded to the increasing trade pressures with ad hoc import protection for a few select import-competing industries—including autos in 1981, steel in 1982 and 1984, and Harley-Davidson motorcycles in 1983. But neither the administration nor Congress was willing to tackle the underlying sources of the trade imbalance. President Reagan and Secretary of the Treasury Donald Regan even lauded the overvalued dollar as a sign of renewed American economic strength (Destler and Henning 1989, 26).

President Reagan and US Trade Representative William E. Brock did try to deflect mounting protectionist pressures by proposing early initiation of a new multilateral trade negotiation. Reagan strongly urged his counterparts at the July 1981 Group of Seven (G-7) economic summit to hold a GATT ministerial meeting the following year to discuss an agenda for the next trade round. What the president and his advisers could not know was that November 1982, the date of the ministerial meeting, would be nearly the trough of the deepest global recession since the Great Depression. The agenda proposed by the United States—including agriculture, services, investment, and intellectual property—was also unrealistically ambitious for the time. The ministerial turned acrimonious, and the US effort to initiate a new round of multilateral trade negotiations was rebuffed.

Neither before nor for some time after this effort did the administration do much to respond directly to concerns about foreign trade policies inhibiting US exports. Just as it ignored the appreciation of the dollar, the first Reagan administration also did not see foreign trade barriers as a significant problem and pursued a policy of benign neglect in both areas. There were 21 section 301 investigations of alleged unfair trade practices pending during the first Reagan term, but only two were even partially resolved to US satisfaction in that period (see the summary assessment table in the appendix).

Former USTR William Eberle, testifying on behalf of the US Chamber of Commerce before the House Ways and Means Committee in July 1982, lamented the lack of presidential commitment to section 301 and rather tepidly endorsed proposed amendments to strengthen it:

[T]he failure of the United States government to aggressively enforce our rights stems not from a lack of legislative authority, but rather from a lack of will. We are now persuaded, however, that legislation to clarify the coverage of section 301, if that will give more authority in the eyes of certain parties and signal Congress' concern over the lack of full use of existing authority, is appropriate although we do not believe it is entirely necessary. (US House of Representatives, Committee on Ways and Means 1982, 34)

Reluctance on the part of the executive branch to pursue a more activist trade policy, combined with increasing protectionist pressures caused by the macro shocks, threatened the political bargain embodied in the Reciprocal Trade Agreements Act of 1934, under which Congress had delegated day-to-day authority to set trade policy to the executive branch. Implicit in this bargain was the executive branch's responsibility to conduct trade policy so as to reduce constituent pressures on Congress to intervene directly. Congress did not believe that the first Reagan administration was living up to its part of the bargain. As one Senate aide remarked during a round of congressional Japan bashing in the spring of 1985, "The target isn't the Japanese; it's the White House" (quoted in Destler 1992, 124).

Frustrated by both the process and the results of trade policy in the first Reagan administration, Congress increased the pressure on the president to set trade policy priorities and to pursue them vigorously. The Trade and Tariff Act of 1984 required USTR to issue annual National Trade Estimate reports listing and, where possible, quantifying the effects of significant foreign barriers. The 1984 act also encouraged aggressive action against identified barriers by authorizing the US Trade Representative to initiate section 301 investigations without waiting for an industry petition.

After passage of the 1984 act, Congress continued to signal that it would not wait forever for an executive branch response. Using data compiled by the Congressional Research Service, Destler (1992, 81) counted 49 bills that had been introduced in the first nine months of 1985 "whose primary purpose was to restrict trade, and whose primary apparent motivation was to benefit US producers"—a 60 percent increase over the same period two years earlier.[5]

Too Little Too Late: The 1985 Trade Policy Action Plan

The Reagan administration finally got the message and went on the offensive with its international economic policy in 1985. Economically, the

---

5. A more comprehensive count by Ray Ahearn showed that 99 trade bills were introduced in Congress in 1985 that were "significantly and directly protectionist in purpose and effect." Using similar, though not identical, selection criteria, Destler estimates there were an average of 58 bills "whose primary purpose was to restrict trade" in each of the three previous *two-year* sessions of Congress (Destler 1992, 81).

Figure 1.2 US exchange rate and trade deficit

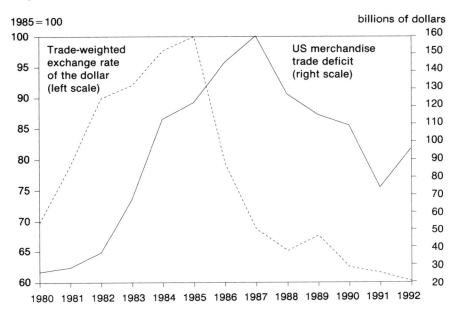

most important policy shift was adoption of an explicit dollar devaluation policy, coordinated with major US trading partners in the G-7 at the Plaza Hotel in New York City.[6] Recognizing, however, that there is a lag before exchange rate changes are reflected in trade flows (figure 1.2), the administration simultaneously adopted an aggressive export promotion strategy to divert attention from the import side of the trade balance. In addition to the symbolic importance of the shift to an activist trade policy, administration officials hoped this strategy would spur more active support of a liberal trade policy from export interests, at least partially offsetting the pleas for protection from import-competing interests.

Primarily for political reasons, but also to spark some support for liberalization, the Reagan administration departed from multilateralism to sign a free trade agreement (FTA) with Israel in April 1985. A year later, the administration entered negotiations toward an FTA with Canada (Schott 1989, 5–6). Simultaneously, the administration renewed efforts to launch a multilateral trade negotiation, finally getting agreement from other GATT members in September 1985 to establish a preparatory committee to decide what the objectives of a new round should be (Oxley 1990, 132–34). The Uruguay Round negotiations were finally initiated a year later in Punta del Este, Uruguay.

---

6. See Funabashi (1989) for a detailed description and analysis of the events surrounding the so-called Plaza Agreement.

Thus, the new trade strategy was multifaceted. J. David Richardson (1991, 21–22) has characterized it as "contingent multilateralism"—"multilateralism where possible, minilateralism where necessary." He identified two distinct strains of minilateralism: preferential liberalization, as illustrated by the free trade agreements with Israel and Canada, and "grievance minilateralism," which is broader than aggressive unilateralism since it encompasses the Market-Oriented Sector-Specific (MOSS) talks with Japan in 1985–86 and the Structural Impediments Initiative (SII) talks with Japan in 1989–90, as well as "section 301 activism after 1985."

In the same month that US trading partners agreed to begin planning a new multilateral round, Reagan abandoned the hands-off attitude toward the value of the dollar and embraced section 301 as a market-opening tool. On Sunday, 22 September, Treasury Secretary James Baker met with his counterparts from Japan, West Germany, Great Britain, and France to decide on a coordinated strategy for dollar depreciation. The following day, the president delivered a speech to members of the President's Export Council, his Advisory Committee for Trade Negotiations, and other business leaders in which he declared that he would "not stand by and watch American businesses fail because of unfair trading practices abroad." In that speech, Reagan announced that he had ordered USTR Clayton Yeutter to initiate investigations into Brazil's policies with regard to the informatics industry, Japan's barriers to cigarette imports, and Korea's restrictions on foreign insurance providers. He also ordered Yeutter to resolve by 1 December two long-running disputes with Japan and the European Community—over leather and leather footwear exports, and canned fruit subsidies, respectively—or to propose appropriate retaliatory action if he could not. A little more than a month later, the USTR office initiated an investigation into Korea's treatment of intellectual property.

In 1987 testimony aimed at heading off further changes to section 301, USTR General Counsel Alan F. Holmer stated that there had been "a watershed change" in the summer of 1985 in the administration's approach to section 301. Holmer offered as proof the five public retaliations, two public threats, and "a whole series" of private threats by USTR under section 301 since mid-1985 (US Senate, Committee on Finance 1987, 28). Figure 1.3 illustrates the increased and more aggressive use of 301 beginning in 1985. It also shows, however, that after an initial flurry of activity—the six cases it initiated in 1985–86—USTR initiated no other cases until after passage of the Omnibus Trade and Competitiveness Act of 1988, though the United States did retaliate twice—against the European Community in a dispute over their ban on beef from cattle treated with growth hormones and a dispute with Brazil over inadequate protection for pharmaceutical patent protection.

Senator Tom Daschle (D-SD) noted his concerns about the durability of the USTR's commitment to an aggressive 301 policy during the debate over what became the 1988 Trade Act: "The frustration that most of us have . . . is the lack of assurance, the lack of confidence that perhaps after you [Yeutter] leave, the same kind of diligence in utilizing 301 will be present as it appears to be now" (cited in Bello and Holmer 1990, 60). Similarly, Senator John Danforth (R-MO) characterized efforts to amend section 301 as seeking to "transform a sporadic, unpredictable, occasional, ad hoc use of Section 301 . . . into a systematic attempt" to address apparently intractable trade problems (cited in Bello and Holmer 1990, 81).

Thus, despite the administration's new aggressiveness, Congress continued to have concerns about the administration's resolve in vigorously attacking foreign trade barriers. Combined with the slow pace of adjustment in the trade balance, especially with Japan, this kept trade policy high on the agenda, and both houses of Congress took up new trade legislation in early 1986. And the heart of what eventually became the 1988 Trade Act was super 301 (Bello and Holmer 1990).

What Is Aggressive Unilateralism?

Jagdish Bhagwati coined the term "aggressive unilateralism" in response to the "super" and "special" variants of section 301 created by Congress in the 1988 Trade Act. As suggested by the discussion above, however, the seeds of aggressive unilateralism were planted in September 1985, when President Reagan adopted the rhetoric of "free but fair" trade and ordered USTR Yeutter to launch an aggressive export promotion policy using section 301.

Of special concern to Bhagwati and other critics of aggressive unilateralism is the use of threats of retaliation and tight deadlines to force countries to change practices that the United States considers "unreasonable"— even when they have not been deemed violations of GATT or any other trade agreement. Bhagwati thus uses the term to denote a double dose of unilateralism: the United States unilaterally determines what is unfair and then demands unilateral trade concessions to rectify the alleged "cheating."

However, in addition to analyzing the consequences for the international trading system, we are also interested in examining the utility of threats in compelling countries to open their markets. Therefore, the definition of aggressive unilateralism as used in this book requires only unilateral demands for liberalization. In other words, in addition to the "unreasonable" practice cases that concern Bhagwati, our definition also encompasses 301 cases that involve GATT violations or practices that otherwise "nullify and impair" expected US benefits under the GATT. In sum, we use aggressive unilateralism to refer to any bilateral trade negotiation in which unilateral demands for liberalization are backed by threats of retaliation.

Figure 1.3   Threats and retaliation in section 301 cases, 1975–92[a]

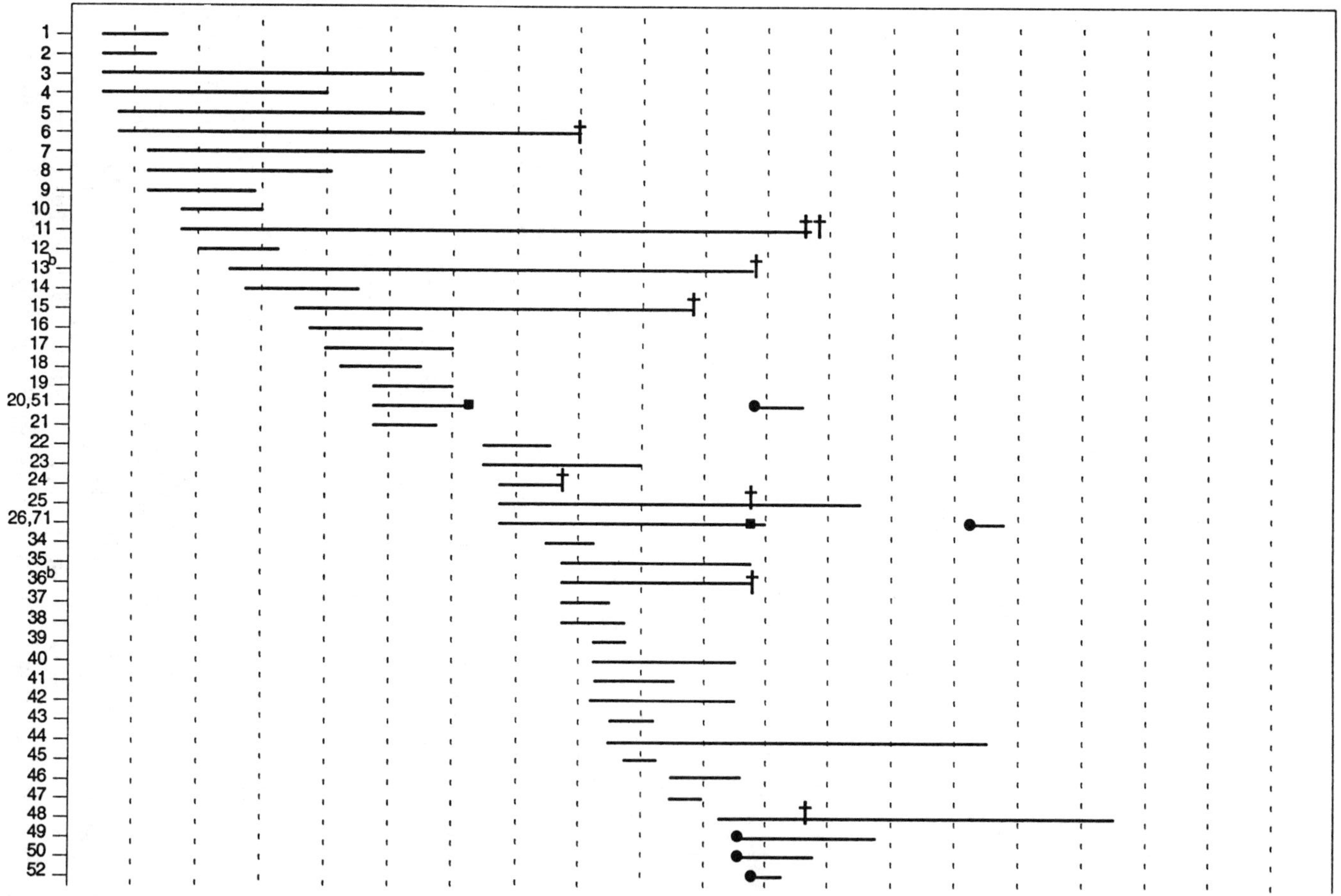

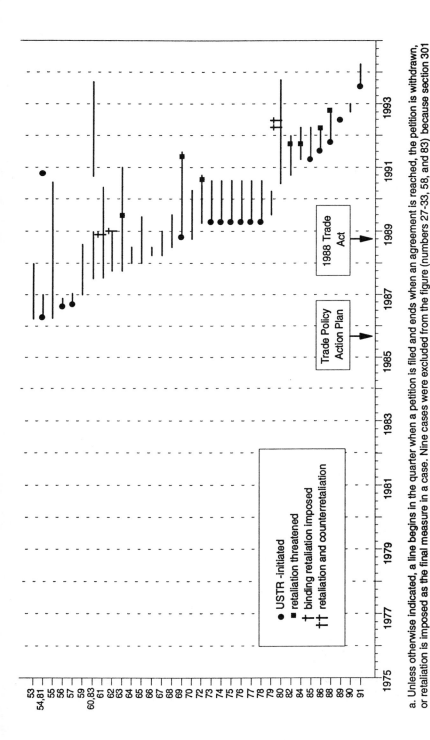

a. Unless otherwise indicated, a line begins in the quarter when a petition is filed and ends when an agreement is reached, the petition is withdrawn, or retaliation is imposed as the final measure in a case. Nine cases were excluded from the figure (numbers 27-33, 58, and 83) because section 301 was not the primary statute used (see the appendix for summaries).

b. No agreement was reached to liberalize the targeted barriers, and US retaliation was accepted by Japan as part of a much larger compensation package to lower Japanese tariffs on other products.

21

Our definition also includes aggressive market-opening tools other than just section 301 in its various forms. Other trade policy tools that could be considered aggressively unilateral include:

- Article 19 of the Merchant Marine Act of 1920, which authorizes the Federal Maritime Commission to retaliate against foreign practices that discriminate against US shipping;

- the US Department of Agriculture's Export Enhancement Program, created in the 1985 farm bill to do battle with the European Community over its agricultural export subsidies;

- the Telecommunications Trade Act of 1988 (in the omnibus trade act), which authorizes retaliatory action against countries that do not open their telecommunications markets to US exporters;

- Title VII of the omnibus trade act, the Buy American Act of 1988, which authorizes retaliation against countries that either are not in compliance with their obligations under the GATT Government Procurement Code or engage in "a significant and persistent pattern of discrimination against the United States" in their government procurement;

- the Primary Dealers Act of 1988 (also in the omnibus act), which authorizes retaliation against countries that discriminate against US financial firms in their government bond markets.

We do not systematically analyze these other tools of aggressive unilateralism, simply because to do so would have added years to the study. However, the Primary Dealers Act is discussed in chapter 11, and others of these provisions come up in the context of some of the section 301 cases.

Of course, there are also any number of trade disputes that never get to the stage of a section 301 investigation. But those negotiations are often informal, difficult to track, and impossible to analyze systematically. Chapter 11, however, does analyze the dispute with the European Community over its proposed Second Banking Directive, which was resolved without the formal invocation of any trade statute. And in chapter 10, Amelia Porges analyzes the negotiations with Japan over its beef and citrus quotas, in which section 301 made only a brief appearance.

We turn now to a detailed and systematic analysis of section 301 as a tool of aggressive unilateralism.

2

Making 301 "Super"

The evolution of super 301 was driven by two closely linked congressional concerns. The first was the perception that the Reagan administration had badly neglected US trade policy in the early 1980s, and even though the White House had adopted a much more aggressive trade stance in September 1985, Congress wanted to ensure that such neglect would not recur. Second, by 1987–88, many members were frustrated by the continuing lack of adjustment in the trade balance, particularly with Japan. The apparent failure of the Japanese surplus to respond to the sharp appreciation of the yen fed the growing body of opinion that Japan's fundamental institutions—its economic and political systems, even its culture—were themselves trade barriers. This view led many in Congress to conclude that negotiations aimed at changing the rules governing trade would not work with Japan. They wanted the administration to make deals that led to increased US exports; they wanted tangible results.

This chapter describes section 301's evolution (see summary in table 2.1), as well as the political debate over "results-oriented" trade that produced the super 301 compromise in the Omnibus Trade and Competitiveness Act of 1988. It briefly summarizes the results of the 1989–90 experience with the original super 301. Detailed treatment of specific super 301 cases is found in chapters 5 through 7, while the assessment of super 301 as a trade policy tool may be found in chapter 12. This chapter concludes with a discussion of President Clinton's renewed super 301, comparing it to the original and to the alternative proposed by Congressman Richard Gephardt (D-MO).

Table 2.1 Evolution of section 301

Law	Presidential authority	Change from previous law
Trade Expansion Act of 1962 (section 252)	Broad discretion to retaliate against "unjustifiable" agricultural barriers; limited authority to retaliate against other barriers	
Trade Act of 1974 (sections 301–302)	Expanded discretionary authority to retaliate against unjustifiable and unreasonable foreign barriers, with no distinction made between agricultural and nonagricultural good	Replaced section 22; extended coverage to services "associated with international trade"; authorized action against foreign export subsidies; required USTR to submit reports to Congress every six months
Trade Agreements Act of 1979 (sections 301–306)	Specified that president should use authority to enforce trade agreements	Clarified applicability of statute to services "whether or not associated with specific products"; established more detailed procedures for investigations, including time deadlines for action; required consultations with foreign trade partners and use of available dispute settlement procedures; allowed postponement of deadlines if dispute settlement ongoing
Trade and Tariff Act of 1984 (sections 301–307)	Discretionary authority unchanged; but USTR now permitted to initiate investigations and recommend action to the president	Explicitly authorized retaliation in the services sector; explicitly included for the first time coverage of intellectual property and direct foreign investment; section 181 required submission to Congress of National Trade Estimate Report
Omnibus Trade and Competitiveness Act of 1988 (sections 301–310)	Authority to retaliate shifted from president to USTR, subject to specific presidential direction, if any; retaliation against unjustifiable practices made mandatory, but with many loopholes permitting considerable discretion	Established super 301, requiring USTR in 1989 and 1990 to identify trade priorities, including designating "priority countries and practices" to be investigated under section 301; established "special" 301 to promote more aggressive assertion of intellectual property rights; established new deadlines for action in cases involving GATT dispute settlement or intellectual property

An Introduction to Section 301

In the US political system of divided powers and checks and balances, the US Constitution gives the Congress sole power to "regulate commerce with foreign nations," including the authority to levy duties. The executive branch has no specific authority to regulate foreign trade other than what Congress explicitly delegates to it. The special interest lobbying and log rolling among members that typically marked the passage of tariff bills in the 19th and early 20th centuries culminated in the highly protectionist Tariff Act of 1930, commonly known as Smoot-Hawley. The retaliation and trade stagnation that followed passage of the Smoot-Hawley bill were widely blamed for deepening the Great Depression and spurred Congress to look for ways to tie its own hands on trade policy.

In 1934, Congress passed the Reciprocal Trade Agreements Act, giving the president the authority to lower tariffs by up to 50 percent in the context of bilateral trade agreements in which the United States also received tariff concessions. With this law, Congress delegated general tariff-setting authority to the president, and the US system "moved decisively from an inflexible, statutory tariff to a 'bargaining tariff.' "[1] As I. M. Destler (1989, 193) describes it:

> The main result was not protection for industry but rather 'protection for Congress'. . . . Or to employ a more flattering description, our national legislature, recognizing its vulnerability to industries seeking import restrictions, opted to exercise 'voluntary legislative restraint.' "

Over time, Congress has extended and expanded the president's authority to lower tariffs through reciprocal negotiations, as well as delegating limited authority to raise or lower trade barriers in response to other situations—for example, the "escape clause," authorizing temporary protection for domestic industries injured by imports.

With the formation of the European Economic Community (EEC) in the 1950s and the implementation of the Common Agricultural Policy (CAP) in 1962, Congress also became increasingly concerned about barriers to US exports that might not be addressed in the traditional tariff-cutting negotiations under the General Agreement on Tariffs and Trade (GATT) or that might "impair the value of tariff commitments made to the United States." In section 252 of the Trade Expansion Act of 1962, Congress for the first time "authorized the President to respond to unjustifiable, unreasonable or discriminatory acts of a foreign government . . . which oppress, restrict or burden U.S. commerce" (Archibald 1984, VII-1).

---

1. Destler (1992) is the definitive account of the development of the US trade policymaking system, including the creation of the "bargaining tariff" in 1934 (chapter 2); Destler (1989) is a much briefer treatment that hits the high spots.

Reflecting US concerns about the CAP, section 252 provided broad discretionary authority to retaliate against "unjustifiable" foreign restrictions on US agricultural exports and more limited authority to act against barriers affecting other US exports. Variable import fees maintained in a "manner inconsistent with provisions of trade agreements" were specifically mentioned as an actionable practice subject to the more limited retaliatory authority. Section 252 was used twice: the first time in 1963 after the EEC imposed variable levies on poultry imports—the so-called chicken war—and the second in 1974 in response to Canadian restrictions on US exports of cattle and meat (Hudec 1975).

Section 252 was succeeded by section 301 of the Trade Act of 1974, which rejected the narrow emphasis on agriculture and elevated foreign subsidies as a source of trade policy concern.[2] The original 301 statute provided that, whenever the president determines that a foreign country or instrumentality

- maintains unjustifiable or unreasonable tariff or other import restrictions which impair the value of trade commitments made to the United States

- engages in discriminatory or other acts or policies which are unjustifiable or unreasonable

- provides subsidies on its exports to the United States or to other foreign markets that substantially reduce sales of competitive US products in the United States or third markets or

- imposes unjustifiable or unreasonable restrictions on access to supplies of food, raw materials, or other products that "burden or restrict" US commerce

he "shall take all appropriate and feasible steps within his power to obtain the elimination of such restrictions or subsidies." This includes the suspension or withdrawal of previous trade concessions, the imposition of duties or other import restrictions only against the exports of the targeted foreign country, or the imposition of fees or restrictions only on the services of that country. The statute also allowed the president to impose retaliation on a most-favored nation (MFN) basis, but that was subject to congressional veto (Hudec 1975, 523).

Section 301 expanded the president's authority to respond to foreign unfair trade practices, relative to section 252, by dropping the focus on agriculture and explicitly including services "associated with" international trade. The new statute also provided an opportunity for private parties to petition the US Trade Representative to investigate complaints

---

2. Useful sources describing various phases of the evolution of section 301 are Archibald (1984), Bradley (1989), and Bello and Holmer (1990).

of unfair trade barriers.[3] In fact, in its original form, USTR was required to investigate *all* formal complaints received, but with no deadlines for action. According to former USTR Associate General Counsel Jeanne Archibald (1984, VII-2), of the 21 complaints filed between January 1975 and December 1979, the president issued a determination in only one, and 14 were still pending at the end of 1979.

In the Trade Agreements Act of 1979, Congress simplified the definition of circumstances "requiring action" under 301 and spelled out more explicitly the authority granted to the president; it also specified procedures that the executive branch should follow in implementing 301. One amendment explicitly authorized the president to enforce US rights under trade agreements. According to Archibald, this authority reflected "congressional intent that section 301 be utilized as a tool for enforcing the international disciplines" on subsidies, government procurement, and other nontariff barriers that had been negotiated in the Tokyo Round (1984, VII-3). The definition of other actionable practices was condensed to those that either violated or "denie[d] benefits to the United States" under any trade agreement or were "unjustifiable, unreasonable, or discriminatory" and "burdened" or "restricted" US commerce.

In other amendments, the 1979 act restored full discretion to apply retaliation on a nondiscriminatory basis, expanded the definition of services to include activities not directly linked to trade (for example, all types of insurance, rather than just marine insurance, as well as other financial services, and broadcasting). It also gave USTR discretion to decide whether to accept a private petition. The 1979 amendments established deadlines for various phases of the investigation but at the same time required USTR to consult with the foreign country and to use international dispute settlement mechanisms under the GATT when appropriate. Allowing deadlines to be waived as long as the dispute settlement process continued rendered them effectively meaningless in many cases.

Section 301 was amended again in the 1984 Trade and Tariff Act. This act expanded the definition of commerce to include foreign direct investment "with implications for trade in goods or services" and for the first time distinguished between practices that should be considered "unjustifiable" and those that were merely "unreasonable." This distinction would gain added importance in the subsequent 1988 Trade Act.

The key change in the 1984 act was that it authorized the USTR to initiate investigations without waiting for a private petition or an order from the president. The president had always had authority to take action under 301 without having received a petition but did not use it until the European enlargement case in 1986, which involved US demands for compensation following the accession of Portugal and Spain (see appen-

---

3. The original version of 301 offered by the president did not provide this opportunity for private parties.

Box 2.1 Mirror, mirror on the wall, who is the unfairest trader of them all?

In 1984 Congress established the National Trade Estimate Report on Foreign Trade Barriers (in section 181 of the Trade Act of 1984, as amended by the 1988 Trade Act) to encourage the president to set US trade liberalization priorities. The USTR must provide an annual report to the president and Congress identifying the following:

- significant foreign barriers to, and distortions of, US exports of goods, services, intellectual property, and foreign direct investment;
- the trade-distorting effects of these barriers and, if feasible, the dollar value of lost trade and investment opportunities;
- section 301 and other actions to eliminate these barriers, or the reason no action was taken;
- US priorities to expand export opportunities.

Many foreign governments are offended that the United States criticizes their trade barriers while ignoring its own. In retaliation, several governments now issue their own reports on US barriers. Taking the offensive may also be good defense. Section 301 allows foreigners to defend themselves against US complaints by showing that the United States has similar trade impediments [section 301(d)(3)(D); also see Hudec 1990a, 22].

The European Community's 1992 *Report on US Trade and Investment Barriers* presents a 96-page catalog of US trade impediments "to redress the impression given by the US National Trade Estimate that trade barriers are primarily a problem encountered by American business abroad, while the US market is essentially open." The European Community broadcast its special displeasure with section 301 by listing it first in its indictment of unfair US trade practices.

A 1992 report by an advisory committee to Japan's Ministry of International Trade and Industry, *Unfair Trade Policies in Major Trading Partners*, cited the United States for unfair trade practices in nine of ten categories surveyed, trailed by the European Community and Korea, with restrictions in six categories.

In releasing Canada's 1992 *Register of United States Barriers to Trade*, Trade Minister Michael Wilson commented: "It is important to point out that the United States also has numerous barriers to trade."

Congress intended the NTE report to encourage the president to attack trade barriers abroad. But by provoking foreign emulation, it held up a mirror to America's home-grown obstructions. The GATT's Trade Policy Review Mechanism, established largely at US urging, takes the mutual education process a step further in providing periodic reviews of all GATT members' trade regimes. GATT members hope that greater policy transparency will encourage reciprocal trade liberalization through multilateral negotiations.

Title taken from Robert Hudec's (1990) wonderfully lucid discussion of the concept of fairness in US trade policy.

dix, case 301-54). Apparently, by authorizing USTR to initiate investigations, Congress hoped that the administration would be more willing to invoke section 301 and more aggressive in prosecuting cases.

The 1984 act also created the annual National Trade Estimate (NTE) reports. This provision required USTR to list and, where possible, quantify the effects of significant foreign trade barriers (box 2.1). USTR was not required to act against these barriers, but it was expected to describe actions taken or to explain why nothing was done. This amendment was intended to encourage the executive branch to set specific trade negotiating priorities and to initiate 301 investigations where appropriate.

Congress amended section 301 even more substantially in the 1988 Omnibus Trade and Competitiveness Act.[4] Expanding on the perceived need for USTR to set priorities and to act on them vigorously, Congress added provisions mandating that USTR initiate cases under certain circumstances and also mandating retaliation in certain cases where the elimination of unfair practices or compensation for them could not be negotiated. As explained below, these "mandatory" provisions were not all that they seemed. Other amendments transferred authority to take action against unfair trade practices from the president to USTR and stiffened the deadlines for taking action, allowing a maximum of 18 months before retaliation might be imposed, even if the international dispute settlement process was not completed. Congress also added section 306, requiring USTR to monitor foreign compliance with trade agreements, including those negotiated as a result of section 301 investigations, and to take action under section 301(a)(1) if a foreign country "is not satisfactorily implementing a measure or agreement. . . ." Figure 2.1 illustrates the sequence and timing of 301 investigations for various types of cases as specified in the 1988 Trade Act.[5]

In the new section 301, Congress directed the US Trade Representative in 1989 and 1990 to identify priority practices, "the elimination of which are likely to have the most significant potential to increase U.S. exports (either directly or through establishing a beneficial precedent)" and to identify "priority foreign countries," taking into account "the number and pervasiveness" of the unfair trade practices and "the level of United States exports of goods and services that would be reasonably expected from full implementation of existing trade agreements. . . ." This is the provision known as super 301. In addition, under section 182(b)—the "special" 301 provision—USTR each spring has to identify priority countries that deny adequate intellectual property protection and then initiate investigations of those practices.

Unjustifiable or Unreasonable Practices and Mandatory Retaliation

Until the Trade and Tariff Act of 1984, the 301 statute did not clearly distinguish between "unreasonable" and "unjustifiable" foreign trade

---

4. See Bello and Holmer (1990) for a detailed discussion of the 1988 amendments to section 301.

5. Once the Uruguay Round results are implemented, more cases will have to be taken through the unified dispute settlement process of the new World Trade Organization, subjecting more cases, including those on subsidies and intellectual property, to the longer 18-month schedule.

Figure 2.1 The section 301 process

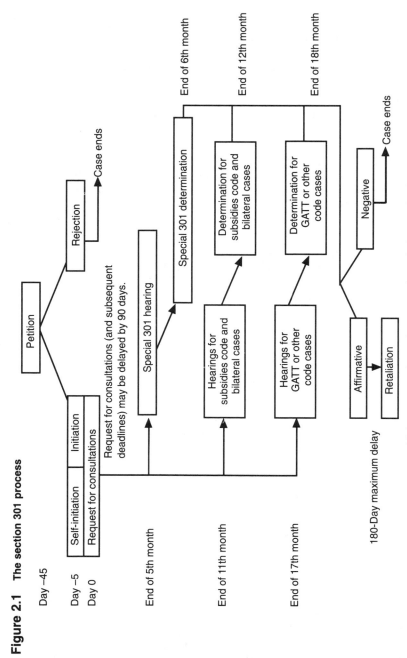

Source: Office of the US Trade Representative.

practices. The 1974 version used the terms interchangeably, but the committee reports on the trade bill cited the GATT concept of "nullification and impairment" as an example of what Congress meant by "unreasonable."[6] The 1979 amendments to section 301 specified that the president should use this authority in three sets of circumstances: to enforce US rights under trade agreements, to respond to any foreign practice that is "inconsistent with . . . or otherwise denies benefits to the United States under any trade agreement," or to respond to other "unjustifiable, unreasonable, or discriminatory" practices that "burden or restrict" US commerce.

The 1984 Trade Act retained this language from the 1979 amendments, but for the first time offered separate, if vague, definitions of unreasonable and unjustifiable. The definition of unjustifiable basically repeated the second standard, which in turn reiterated the first about enforcing US rights under trade agreements (Archibald 1984, 11–13). In other words, unjustifiable practices are usually those that violate the GATT or other trade agreements, or otherwise nullify or impair expected US benefits under those agreements and burden US commerce. "Unreasonable" was defined to cover practices that were "not necessarily in violation of or inconsistent with" US legal rights, but which are "otherwise deemed to be unfair and inequitable." The 1984 act also offered specific examples of practices that could be considered unreasonable, including denial of intellectual property rights (IPR) protection or "opportunities for the establishment of an enterprise."

The 1988 act left these definitions unchanged but expanded the list of foreign practices that might be considered unreasonable. In addition to the IPR and right of establishment clauses from the 1984 Trade Act, Congress added government "toleration . . . of systematic anticompetitive activities by private firms" that have the effect of restricting US access, export targeting, and denial of labor rights, including the right of association, the right to organize and bargain collectively, protection of child labor, and working conditions.

What is more important about the distinction between unjustifiable and unreasonable practices in the 1988 act is the effect it has on USTR's decision whether to retaliate in a given case. Congress made retaliatory action in 301 cases mandatory if the USTR determines that the foreign practice or policy violates or "is inconsistent with" a trade agreement (generally the GATT, but also bilateral trade agreements), causes nullification or impairment, or "is unjustifiable and burdens or restricts" US commerce. In cases involving unreasonable practices, the decision of whether to retaliate is explicitly discretionary.

The action-forcing character of the mandatory provisions should not be overstated, however. The section requiring "mandatory action," 301(a),

---

6. See Hudec (1975) for a full discussion of GATT nullification and impairment and the early meaning of "unreasonable."

also contains a number of loopholes that allow USTR to avoid taking action: if a dispute panel determines that the alleged unfair trade practice does not violate GATT rules or nullify or impair expected US benefits, if "the foreign country is taking satisfactory measures to grant" US rights or offers compensation, if retaliation would "cause serious harm to national security," or "in extraordinary cases," where retaliation "would have an adverse impact on the United States economy substantially out of proportion to the benefits of such action, taking into account the impact of not taking such action on the credibility of the provisions of this chapter. . . ." In a memorable phrase arising from a colloquy between former USTR Robert Strauss and Senator Robert Packwood (R-OR), retaliation under super 301 was described as "mandatory but not compulsory" (quoted in Bello and Holmer 1990, 59, note 58).

The Evolution of Super 301

Despite the Reagan administration's shift to a more activist trade policy in September 1985, Congress continued to push the president and USTR Clayton Yeutter to be more aggressive in using 301. In May 1986, Chairman John Dingell circulated to the other members of the House Energy and Commerce Committee a report on unfair foreign trade practices that had been prepared by the Subcommittee on Oversight and Investigations (which he also chaired). The report concluded:

> U.S. trade policy generally, and policy toward export promotion specifically, has been conducted on an ad hoc basis, addressing problems only after significant political pressure has been applied. . . ." (US House of Representatives 1986, 4)

The report went on to recommend a procedure that would "build on" the National Trade Estimate Report "to develop an aggressive approach to eliminating barriers to U.S. exports," including listing priority barriers, USTR initiation of 301 cases, and "full retaliation if our trading partners refuse to promptly eliminate those barriers" (US House of Representatives 1986, 5).

Although the approach recommended in the Dingell report ultimately won out, the proposal that captured the most attention during the drafting of the 1988 Trade Act was the results-oriented amendment proposed by Congressman Gephardt. The Gephardt amendment, which would have required identification of priority foreign countries based on the size of their bilateral trade surpluses with the United States as well as the "pervasiveness" of their barriers to trade, was not aimed exclusively at Japan. But Japan was the primary target, and the crafting of the amendment reflected the view of Gephardt and many of his colleagues that Japan is different from other countries, that the barriers to trade in Japan were systemic, and that demands for tangible, bottom-line results were the only way to make any progress.

The "Japan Problem"

The notion that the Japanese economy does not behave in quite the same manner as Western capitalist market economies (or, at least, like the Anglo-Saxon variety) became increasingly widespread in the 1970s and 1980s. There is no agreement, however, as to exactly how Japan differs and even less on what to do about it. And of course some experts still disagree with the basic premise, arguing that Japan's unusual trade patterns can be explained by its unusual resource endowments and distance from major markets in the United States and Europe.

Many congressional policymakers were influenced by the more hawkish of the so-called revisionists in the business, academic, and policy communities. The Japan problem as seen from this perspective typically has three key elements.[7] First, these revisionists argue that because of the multidimensional and structural nature of Japanese trade obstacles Japanese markets are not likely to respond to standard market-opening approaches that focus on changing rules. Second, they argue that historically Japan has opened its markets only when confronted with external threats, be they Commodore Perry's black ships, trade retaliation, or international opprobrium as an unfair trading partner. Many trade hawks also believe that Japan's trade barriers significantly restrict US exports and contribute importantly to the trade deficit. They complain that these trade impediments are particularly galling and unfair since Japan enjoys relatively unfettered access to US markets.[8]

A major source of the frustration with Japan and the demands for a results-oriented approach was the alleged systemic or structural nature of many Japanese trade barriers. As summarized by Ahearn, Cronin, and Storrs (1990, 11):

> [R]educing Japanese trade barriers is often compared to the task of "peeling an onion." While negotiations to reduce one layer of barriers to specific products could be successful on paper, another layer of barriers often imbedded in Japan's socioeconomic fabric was often seen as limiting positive results in terms of rising exports. Barriers such as Japan's inefficient and complex distribution system,

7. For examples of revisionist arguments, see Johnson (1982), Prestowitz (1988), van Wolferen (1989), Tyson (1992), and Fallows (1994). Of course, the arguments in these works are more complex than the simplification presented here, and not every aspect of this characterization would likely be endorsed by all of these authors. The intent is simply to characterize in general terms the tenor of the debate in policymaking circles in the 1980s.

8. This view ignores or minimizes the significant US barriers to Japanese exports in the 1980s, including the "voluntary" export restraints on autos, steel, and machine tools. See Hufbauer and Elliott (1994) on US trade barriers.

exclusionary business practices, and lax antitrust enforcement were often cited as the real constraint on increases in competitive exports.

The problem of peeling away the "onion-like" layers of Japanese protection is illustrated by the case of aluminum baseball bats.[9] After several years of negotiations involving, sequentially, technical standards, safety standards, and inspection requirements, US exporters, which had been barred entirely from the Japanese market until the early 1980s, still had only a tiny share of the market. At one point in the negotiations, a Japanese negotiator claimed that American bats were inappropriate because Japanese softballs were different. This echoed Japanese claims in other negotiations that Japanese snow was different and made foreign-made skis inappropriate or that they could not import more beef because their intestines were shorter than those of Americans (Balassa and Noland 1988, chapter 3).

Many US negotiators and businessmen, frustrated by repeated experiences like these, argue that the traditional US approach to opening Japanese markets—negotiating rules for improved market access—was largely ineffectual. A better alternative to the traditional rule-oriented approach to liberalization, in their view, is to require Japan to commit to specific results, preferably those that were readily observable, such as increases in imports. In the words of Clyde Prestowitz (1988, 322):

> Our negotiations should always be for results. To negotiate over the procedures of a foreign culture in hopes of obtaining an unidentified "open" market is to court failure and frustration. . . . We can negotiate anything identifiable and concrete. We cannot negotiate philosophy or perceptions and should not try to do so.

Others, however, are skeptical of the empirical importance of alleged Japanese structural protection and reject the proposed results-oriented approach. Many of the alleged obstacles involve private Japanese consumer or producer behavior rather than government policy. Jagdish Bhagwati, for example, argues that the perceived Japanese reluctance to buy imports may simply reflect differences in tastes, product quality, and the importance of long-term consumer-producer relationships rather than collusion to restrict imports (Bhagwati 1990, 20–24). These sorts of "barriers" are not easily amenable to government policy.

Whether negotiating rules or results, many in Congress and the business and policy communities also interpret the history of US-Japan trade negotiations as justifying a special need for credible threats. One of the few nonculinary Japanese words to enter the American vernacular is *gaiatsu*, the term for foreign pressure. In the opinion of some experts, Japan is a "reactive state" that requires *gaiatsu* to reach internal political consensus to liberalize (chapter 10; Porges 1991). In this view, Japan drags out negoti-

---

9. What follows is drawn from Prestowitz (1988, 96–99), press reports, and interviews.

ations interminably and only makes concessions when faced with irresistible pressure. Moreover, it has been alleged that Japan only abides by trade agreements when faced with credible threats of retaliation. Thus, these analysts conclude that the traditional strategy of negotiating changes in Japan's trade rules will not work. The rules change, but US exports do not increase. Instead, Japan should be compelled to show results—to either import more US goods or face certain retaliation.

These views are by no means universally accepted, however. The debate over the magnitude and source of Japanese trade barriers, which was first characterized by heated rhetoric, eventually generated some analytic light. But despite a burgeoning literature on the issue, there continues to be much controversy over the premises underlying the alleged Japan problem and even more debate over the most effective strategy for dealing with Japan. No consensus has yet emerged, and there will be no attempt to resolve the debate here.[10] What is important for our story is that the revisionists' arguments had a significant effect on many members of Congress, which in turn had an important impact on US trade policy.

Toward a Results-Oriented Approach: From Gephardt to Super 301

In 1985 three influential Democrats—Senate Finance Committee Chairman Lloyd Bentsen, House Ways and Means Committee Chairman Dan Rostenkowski, and Congressman Richard Gephardt—introduced a bill that would have imposed a 25 percent tariff surcharge against countries with "excessive" trade surpluses, most conspicuously against Japan (Bergsten and Cline 1987, 14–15). It was a sign of things to come in the debate over results-oriented trade policy. Despite the administration's shift to a more activist trade policy in mid-1985, Congress resumed its work in 1986 on what eventually became the 1988 Trade Act.

One of the most controversial elements in the House of Representatives' trade bill, passed by the Ways and Means Committee in March 1986, was Gephardt's proposal. The original Gephardt amendment[11] would have required USTR first to identify countries with "excessive and unwarranted" bilateral trade surpluses and then to identify those that "also engage in a pattern of unjustifiable, unreasonable, or discriminatory trade policies or practices having a significant adverse effect on U.S. commerce. . ." (Bello and Holmer 1990, 76). Once priorities were identified

---

10. For a sampling of the positions in the debate, in addition to the revisionists cited in footnote 1, see Golub (1994), Saxonhouse (1993), and Bergsten and Cline (1987). Other analyses addressing elements of the Japan problem include Balassa and Noland (1988), Lawrence (1993), Petri (1991), and Bergsten and Noland (1993).

11. Gephardt continued to pursue results-oriented trade policy in trade debates in 1991 and 1992, when he proposed a bill that focused on the US-Japan deficit in automobile and auto parts trade.

by this formula, USTR would have just six months to negotiate with the targeted countries agreements that would eliminate the unfair practices and reduce the US bilateral deficit "by the amount attributable to the unfair practices."[12] To demonstrate measurable, incremental progress, targeted countries were expected to reduce their bilateral surpluses by at least 10 percent annually for three years. Finally, the amendment mandated retaliation against countries that either failed to reach an agreement with USTR or failed to otherwise achieve the surplus reduction targets.

The Reagan administration adamantly opposed the Gephardt amendment and threatened a veto. The administration and other opponents saw the proposal as conceptually flawed because it focused only on trade barriers when even its author acknowledged that they were not the most important cause of the US trade deficit. Aside from the likely minor impact on the trade deficit, the tactics also raised serious concerns about the possible consequences of putting US trade policy "on automatic pilot" (Bello and Holmer 1990, 77–78).

Some trading partners might find the unilaterally imposed US surplus reduction goals so politically unacceptable that they would refuse to negotiate. Even those that accepted surplus-reduction targets might not be able to meet them due to forces beyond their control, such as appreciation of the dollar or an increase in US growth. Or, it might be easier for the foreign country to enforce the surplus reduction targets by reducing exports than by increasing imports—especially in a case such as Japan, where the barriers are not formal border measures such as tariffs and quotas but allegedly informal, often private, barriers. In this case, compliance would not increase US exports, but it could harm US producers and consumers by reducing access to some imports and raising prices.

If compliance was not forthcoming and the United States raised its own import barriers in retaliation, US consumers again would pay the price. And if foreigners responded to US retaliation with their own counterretaliation, all parties would be worse off. The magnitude of potential US retaliation and foreign counterretaliation in the late 1980s was considerable. Applying the Gephardt formula to Japan in 1989 would have required roughly a $15 billion (30 percent) reduction in Japan's $50 billion bilateral surplus over a three-year period.[13]

Critics viewed the Gephardt proposal as equivalent to adding a blunderbuss to the US trade policy arsenal. It might blast away foreign trade

---

12. Using 1986 trade data, Bello and Holmer (1990, 76) found that Brazil, Hong Kong, Italy, Japan, Korea, Taiwan, and Germany would have met the Gephardt criteria for excessive surpluses.

13. If Japan refused to accept an agreement, USTR would have been required to retaliate in an amount equivalent to the loss in US exports caused by all of Japan's "unwarranted" trade practices. Bergsten and Noland (1993, 189) estimate that Japanese trade impediments restricted US exports by $9 billion to $18 billion in the early 1990s.

barriers, but the collateral damage to overall US interests would likely exceed the benefits. In a number of ways, the Gephardt proposal would have set in motion a dangerous process over which the president had very limited control. House Ways and Means Committee Chairman Rostenkowski (D-IL) criticized the proposal as "too draconian to be effective," while Congressman Jack Kemp (R-NY) questioned how it could possibly work: "[W]hen you have a problem with your neighbor and you pull a gun, do you expect him to carry on a reasonable discussion?" (quoted in Bello and Holmer 1990, 79). The Gephardt amendment did not command overwhelming support in Congress. Most important, the leadership of the key committees did not endorse it, and it was included in the House version as a floor amendment only after much debate and a narrow 218–214 vote (Destler 1992, 92).

Unwilling to accept the risks associated with the Gephardt amendment, Congress settled on super 301 as an alternative. As passed, super 301 required the president each spring in 1989 and 1990 to designate trade negotiating priorities, including priority countries characterized by "the number and pervasiveness" of their unfair trade practices. The intent was to address the alleged systemic unfairness in Japanese trade practices, and the expectation was that Japan would be named a priority foreign country. Proponents of super 301 touted it as preferable to the Gephardt blunderbuss because it was a more controlled, less scattershot policy instrument. Super 301 prevailed because the congressional leadership believed it sent a strong message about trade priorities to the president while allowing him more latitude in implementation than Gephardt did.

This greater latitude was a key reason the Reagan administration reluctantly acquiesced to super 301.[14] Super 301 retaliation was completely discretionary in cases involving unreasonable or discriminatory barriers that did not violate a trade agreement. And as discussed above, there were several waivers that could be invoked even in cases involving violations of trade agreements or unjustifiable practices, where retaliation would otherwise be "mandatory." Super 301 also gave USTR more discretion than Gephardt in determining the appropriate level of retaliation.

So what is so "super" about super 301, and why does it evoke such strong rhetoric from both critics and supporters? Many of those who opposed Gephardt's proposal simply transferred their hostility to super 301 because it also was viewed as an extension of US unilateralism, in which the United States set itself up as judge, jury, and executioner without regard for international trade rules. Similarly, many of those who

---

14. Both Gephardt and super 301 waived retaliation in certain cases, but the super 301 waivers were more extensive and included several conditions—adverse GATT rulings on US complaints and national security—that Gephardt did not. Moreover, the Gephardt waivers were subject to congressional disapproval, and the president had to submit for congressional approval an alternative plan to reduce the bilateral deficit.

liked Gephardt's more aggressive thrust but thought it went too far trans-ferred to super 301 their high expectations for measurable results. Thus, both those who supported super 301 and those who opposed it did so for the same reason: they saw it as a bigger, more powerful version of regular 301.

Carla Hills Wields the Velvet Crowbar

In a 1 March 1989 hearing before the Senate Finance Committee, newly confirmed US Trade Representative Carla Hills spoke of the fine line she must walk in balancing various trade priorities: "The broad choice . . . is 'when to use the crowbar and when the handshake.' " Hills identified the Uruguay Round as a top priority but also said the administration would not "fall into the trap of suspending all actions against unfair trade practices on the ground that they will spoil the atmosphere" for those negotiations. In both 1989 and 1990, the two years for which super 301 was originally authorized, Carla Hills and her team wielded the crowbar deftly. They managed to pacify, if not delight, Congress, while avoiding trade retaliation and collapse of the Uruguay Round (though agriculture blocked the scheduled conclusion at the end of 1990).

During that March 1989 hearing, senator after senator indicated that, unless there was significant progress on bilateral trade issues in the interim, they expected to see Japan on the list of priority foreign countries that spring. Senator Danforth (US Senate Committee on Finance 1989, 14–15) was among the most assertive, stating that "hustling" to conclude an interim agreement in order to avoid naming Japan would be contrary to congressional intent:

> [W]hile Super 301 was designed to be aimed at more than Japan, it was not aimed at anything less than Japan. . . . I would just like to say to you [USTR Hills] that this co-author of [super 301] would really be startled and very disturbed if Japan were not on the list for any reason. . . ."

Selecting Targets, Spring 1989

While action against Japan could not be avoided without provoking an angry congressional backlash, it was not obvious what the overall super 301 strategy should be. Some in the administration suggested naming only Japan, so as to minimize the risk of sparking trade wars. Others suggested naming a long list of targets so as to render the procedure meaningless. Though some hard-core free traders thought Hills should have been willing to confront Congress and not name anyone at all, most observers concerned about minimizing the domestic political fallout while keeping the Uruguay Round on track thought she struck about the right balance (Ahearn, Cronin, and Storrs 1990, 20–21).

On the appointed day, Hills announced the administration's trade liberalization priorities and plans for implementing super 301 (USTR, Statement of Ambassador Carla Hills, 25 May 1989). She emphasized that the administration's top trade liberalization priority was the successful conclusion of the Uruguay Round. Super 301 would be used to support and complement US efforts in the round by focusing on the elimination of specific practices that were indicative of broader concerns in the global trading system. Ambassador Hills identified six priority practices in three priority countries:

- Japanese exclusionary government procurement involving both *supercomputers* and *satellites*, and technical barriers to trade in *forest products*;

- Brazilian *quantitative import restrictions*;

- Indian *trade-related investment measures* that prohibit or burden foreign investment and barriers to trade in services, specifically the closure of India's *insurance* market to foreign firms.

One analysis characterized the practices designated as "ones that the Administration thought were amenable to some kind of negotiated solutions or were emblematic of broader issues being negotiated in the Uruguay Round" and that the administration had "tended to downplay some of the Super 301 statutory criteria that emphasized the choice of practices that had the greatest potential to increase U.S. exports" (Ahearn, Cronin, and Storrs 1990, 2).[15]

Hills did not name Japan as a priority foreign country generally on the basis of "the number and pervasiveness" of unfair trade barriers facing US exporters, as had been expected in Congress and elsewhere. Instead, the president announced a separate Structural Impediments Initiative (SII) to address alleged structural Japanese trade barriers such as rigidities in the distribution system (box 2.2).[16] Finally, Hills reported that super 301 had given her leverage to reach trade liberalization agreements with Korea and Taiwan in exchange for not designating them as priority foreign countries.

Key members of Congress—including Senate Finance Committee Chairman Lloyd Bentsen (D-TX), House Ways and Means Committee Chairman Dan Rostenkowski (D-IL), and Ways and Means Trade Subcommittee Chairman Sam Gibbons (D-FL)—praised the decision, though Bentsen and others adopted a wait-and-see attitude as to whether the SII talks

---

15. Mastanduno (1992) disagrees with this assessment, at least with regard to Japan. He emphasizes strategic trade concerns and the preferences of US industry and Congress over negotiability and multilateral objectives in the selection process.

16. See *Department of State Bulletin* (September 1989, 78) for the text of the announcement.

Box 2.2 The Structural Impediments Initiative

President Bush announced the Structural Impediments Initiative on 25 May 1989, the same day USTR Carla Hills announced the decision to name Japan under super 301. The president directed the USTR and the secretaries of state and the treasury to form a high-level committee with other interested agencies to propose negotiations with Japan on structural impediments to trade and balance of payments adjustment and on anticompetitive practices. The negotiations would take place outside the super 301 framework. Despite the likely intent of Congress that such barriers be tackled under super 301, the administration believed these sensitive matters should be addressed in a less confrontational forum. The Japanese insisted that the talks be reciprocal, addressing American structural problems as well.

Members of Congress were skeptical about the outcome of negotiations that would take place without strict deadlines or the threat of retaliation. Max Baucus, chairman of the Senate Finance Committee's Subcommittee on International Trade, warned that the practices being discussed in the SII talks would be investigated under super 301 if SII failed to produce results. Senator John Rockefeller (D-WV) called SII a "sham."

On 28 June 1990 the United States and Japan reached agreement on an SII joint report. Japan agreed to (1) reduce the saving-investment gap by, among other things, launching a ¥430 trillion public infrastructure plan for fiscal 1991–2000; (2) increase the supply of land available for residential, commercial, and public investment by implementing a number of reform measures; (3) reform the Japanese distribution system through deregulation, strengthened antitrust enforcement, and the improvement of import-related infrastructure in order to improve market access; (4) attack exclusionary business practices through vigorous antimonopoly enforcement, encouragement of nondiscriminatory corporate procurement, faster processing of patent applications and more transparent and pro-competitive government

would be an effective alternative to discussing structural Japanese barriers under super 301. Gephardt and other trade hawks not surprisingly criticized the decision as having "gutted" congressional intentions to strengthen section 301 (Ahearn, Cronin, and Storrs 1990, 20–21). But despite widespread congressional skepticism, the SII initiative—combined with the announced successes with South Korea and Taiwan—helped to defuse more intense criticism of the narrowness of the super 301 decision.

Super 301 Results, Spring 1990[17]

While Carla Hills merely skirted congressional intent in 1989 by not naming Japan as a priority foreign country for having pervasive and systemic barriers, she pushed the limits of congressional tolerance in 1990

---

17. Readers should refer to chapters 5 through 7 for a detailed discussion of the super 301 negotiations with Japan, Brazil, India, Korea, and Taiwan and chapter 12 for an analysis of the results. The outcomes of these cases are only briefly summarized here.

interaction with business; (5) loosen *keiretsu* relationships and make them more transparent to facilitate the entry of foreign goods, services, and investment into the Japanese market; and (6) monitor price differentials between goods sold in Japan and abroad, higher prices in the Japanese market being regarded as indicators of structural barriers to import competition.

The United States agreed to (1) reduce the federal budget deficit; (2) promote productive investment; (3) loosen export controls; (4) increase support for research and development; (5) beef up export promotion programs; and (6) improve work force education and training.

The two countries also agreed on follow-up procedures. The negotiating teams would meet three times during the first year and twice a year thereafter to review each country's progress in implementing its commitments. A joint report would be issued each spring. After three years, the two countries would decide what further monitoring arrangements were necessary.

Japan's efforts to reduce the saving-investment gap and reform the distribution system received praise from Washington. However, there was still substantial disagreement between the two countries about Japan's enforcement of its antimonopoly laws. Washington argued for stiffer penalties and more aggressive enforcement of the laws (and even contemplated using US antitrust law against Japanese companies). Many SII critics, including Senator Baucus, argued that the talks had failed to curb the exclusionary practices of *keiretsu* (*JEI Report* no. 19B, 17 May 1991, 12; *International Trade Reporter*, 18 March 1992, 494; *Financial Times* 24 May 1991; *JEI Report* no. 4B, 1 February 1991, 5).

One Japanese official noted, however, that the United States had not taken concrete action to reduce its budget deficit or promote private saving and corporate investment, as it had pledged (*International Trade Reporter*, 23 January 1991, 103).

US officials have stressed that it will take three to five years for the SII agreement to register in the trade account (*JEI Report* no. 1A, 11 January 1991, 2).

by again citing completion of the Uruguay Round as the administration's top trade priority and refusing to make any new super 301 designations. She did redesignate Indian barriers to foreign investment and insurance imports, since no agreements had been reached, but terminated the investigations in those cases. Hills also refused to retaliate against India, noting that services and trade-related investment measures were the subject of negotiations in the Uruguay Round. Hills's announcement was applauded by those concerned about bringing the round to a successful conclusion in December as scheduled. But even some sympathetic observers questioned whether Hills had gone beyond the most expansive interpretation of the law's requirements (Destler 1992, 132–33; Nanto 1991, 18). Nevertheless, "Congress grumbled, but did nothing more" (Destler 1992, 133).

Wanting to avoid blame for causing a collapse of the Uruguay Round was probably the major reason for congressional restraint in the spring of 1990. Another was that Hills emphasized the positive. She noted that agreements had been reached with Japan to open the public markets for supercomputers and satellites and to liberalize the market for wood products. And she terminated the investigation involving Brazil, citing newly elected President Fernando Collor de Mello's commitment to eliminate most quantitative restrictions and to rely on tariffs as his primary trade policy tool. Thus, four of the six super 301 investigations resulted in agreements that largely achieved US negotiating objectives (table 2.2).

Interestingly, these results are not much different from what had been achieved with regular section 301 after September 1985—60 percent, as compared with a super 301 success rate of 67 percent (four of six).[18] Super 301 proponents often cite the preemptive agreements with South Korea and Taiwan as important evidence of super 301's utility. But those agreements, while helpful in defusing congressional disappointment that Japan had not been named a priority foreign country, do not appear to have produced much else. When examined closely, the promises made look fairly modest, and in South Korea's case they were mostly unfulfilled (see chapter 7).

Nor is it true that super 301 is necessary to address the "Japan problem." According to our assessments, discussed in detail in chapter 4, about two-thirds of regular 301 cases targeting Japan resulted in at least partial achievement of US objectives. If the supercomputer case—which has been the subject of close monitoring and repeated disputes since the agreement was reached—is classified as a marginal failure rather than a marginal success, the super 301 record with respect to Japan is again no better than that for regular 301.

Clinton's Kinder, Gentler Super 301

Efforts to renew and "put teeth into" super 301 began almost immediately after it expired at the end of 1990. Senator Carl Levin (D-MI) introduced legislation in January 1991 to renew super 301 and to restore Gephardt-like quantitative triggers for determining both country and sectoral targets. However, this and a similar proposal, introduced by Gephardt in the fall, were aimed primarily at the US trade deficit with Japan in autos and auto parts.[19] Both proposals required action against designated priority countries if no negotiated resolution was achieved; the Gephardt proposal also would

---

18. See chapters 3 and 4 for details on our definition of success and on the results for all section 301 cases.

19. The Levin proposal would have required identifying as a priority foreign country any trading partner whose bilateral trade surplus with the United States accounted for more than 15 percent of the total US trade deficit. It would also have required identifying as a priority unfair trade practice any practice identified in the National Trade Estimate Report that is "associated with a sectoral deficit . . . of 5 percent or more" of the bilateral trade deficit. A Congressional Research Service report (Nanto 1991, 19) estimated that in 1990, only trade with Japan in autos and auto parts would meet the Levin criteria. The similar Gephardt proposal raised the 5 percent sectoral trigger to 10 percent, still targeting Japanese auto exports.

Table 2.2 Super 301 results

Case	Outcome of negotiations	Estimated annual increase in exports	Assessment	Comments
Japanese supercomputers	Agreement reached	Less than $100 million[a]	Objectives advanced but not fully achieved	US exports increased but results appear to be managed by Japanese government; not clear that public market was liberalized
Japanese satellites	Agreement reached	$150 million[a]	Objectives largely achieved	
Japanese wood products	Agreement reached	$750 million [b]	Objectives largely achieved	Assessment assumes tariff cuts promised in Uruguay Round, ratified and implemented
Brazil import licensing	Agreement reached	$100 million[c]	Objectives largely achieved, but . . .	Outcome primarily due to new government, adoption of new economic program under pressure from international financial institutions, not 301
Indian investment	No agreement	$0	Failure	Hints from India of possible compromise apparently not pursued
Indian insurance	No agreement	$0	Failure	
Korea	Agreement reached preemptively	Little or none	Nominal success only	Although commitments carried out on paper, continuing bureaucratic red tape prevented significant liberalization
Taiwan	Taiwanese plan accepted, no formal agreement	$100 million to $500 million[d]	Some objectives largely achieved	Tariff reductions mostly implemented as promised; reduction of trade surplus targets met; however, adjustment more likely due to appreciation of the new Taiwan dollar and political manipulation than to liberalization.

a. See chapter 5.

b. Level expected by the industry if agreement is fully implemented; results to date are much smaller (see chapter 5).

c. The value of US exports to Brazil increased 9.3 percent in the four quarters after elimination of the quantitative restrictions as compared with the four previous quarters; the two percentage points by which this figure is higher than the annual average for 1987–89 is attributed to the liberalization (*Direction of Trade Statistics*).

d. Based on USTR's estimate of benefits of promised tariff reduction (National Trade Estimate Report 1993, 247).

have given the Senate Finance and House Ways and Means Committees the authority to initiate 301 investigations of priority practices.

In October 1991 Senators Baucus (D-MT) and John Danforth (R-MO) introduced an alternative bill, which mirrored the original version of the Senate super 301 amendment to the 1988 Trade Act, to renew super 301 for five years beginning in 1992, with only modest procedural changes. The Baucus-Danforth bill retained the original super 301 criteria for making designations but extended the period between publication of the National Trade Estimate Report and announcement of the designations from one to six months. Baucus-Danforth also would have allowed the Senate Finance and House Ways and Means Committees to file a section 301 petition by resolution (but did not require initiation of an investigation).

USTR Hills quickly stated her opposition to renewal of super 301. However, the administration as a whole took the position that, while super 301 was unnecessary, the president would not necessarily oppose renewal.[20] No trade legislation was passed in 1992, and following the election in November, President-elect Bill Clinton endorsed renewal, though with no specifics as to form. Shortly thereafter, Congressman Sander Levin (D-MI) predicted that, with a more activist Democrat at the helm, renewal of super 301 would probably be a straight extension of the original version (*International Trade Reporter*, 9 December 1992, 2103; *Inside U.S. Trade*, 11 December 1992, 13).

Early in 1993, Senator Baucus reintroduced the proposal to renew super 301, in slightly modified form, for five years. He initially tried to attach the proposal as an amendment to renewal of the president's "fast-track" negotiating authority in the spring and then to the implementing legislation for the North American Free Trade Agreement in the fall. Each time, administration officials convinced him not to do so, arguing in the first case that it would open the fast-track bill to a host of other unwanted amendments and in the second that it would lose critical Republican votes needed for NAFTA ratification.

Instead, USTR Mickey Kantor promised that the administration would renew super 301 by administrative action (*Journal of Commerce*, 7 January 1994, 1A). After extensive interagency debate over the appropriate timing and content of an executive order to revive super 301, President Clinton finally issued an order on 3 March 1994. The executive order followed the collapse of the latest round of trade negotiations with Japan in February and the reintroduction by Baucus of legislation to permanently renew super 301.

Most observers thought that super 301 would be renewed virtually unchanged from the original, but a last-minute initiative by the Council of Economic Advisers and the Office of Management and Budget con-

---

20. Congressional testimony by Commerce Under Secretary for International Trade Michael Farren, cited in *International Trade Reporter*, 1 May 1991, 660.

vinced the president and his cabinet to make this a kinder and gentler super 301 (Hobart Rowen, "Wall Street's High Anxiety Over Reviving Super 301," *Washington Post,* 27 March 1994, H1). Clinton's version is kinder because, unlike the original, it neither requires nor encourages the labeling of entire countries as unfair traders. Instead, like regular 301, it only cites practices as unfair. The new super 301 is gentler in two respects. First, USTR is not required to designate practices already addressed by US trade law, in bilateral agreements, or in current negotiations in which progress is being made. In addition, the president may direct USTR not to cite a practice that otherwise fits the criteria in the order. Second, the new super 301 is gentler because it gives USTR more time to conduct negotiations before designations are due. Finally, unlike most congressional proposals, which would make super 301 permanent, Clinton's super 301 will expire after the 1995 designations.

Initial congressional reaction to the executive order was favorable. Senator Baucus called it "a bold and historic statement" and observed that super 301 is "the only trade tool that has ever produced market opening" (Office of Senator Max Baucus, press release, 3 March 1994). Congressman Richard Gephardt said: "I support that executive order. I believe it will make a difference. Super 301 has worked" (speech before Economic Strategy Institute Annual Conference, Washington, 10 March 1994, 5). Nevertheless, Senator Baucus continues to support statutory and permanent renewal of super 301, and Congressman Gephardt has introduced yet another results-oriented bill that would set quantitative targets for opening Japanese markets.[21]

It may be useful at this stage to compare the specific procedures under the original Gephardt amendment, the original super 301 of the 1988 Trade Act, President Clinton's 1994 version of super 301, and regular 301 in more detail. The key differences are in the amount of discretion the president retained to set US objectives and to use retaliatory threats. These differences are summarized in table 2.3.

Both Gephardt and the original super 301 of the 1988 Trade Act strongly encouraged USTR to label countries as unfair traders. Both reflected congressional determination to pressure the president to address the Japan problem. In principle, both Gephardt and the original super 301 allowed USTR some freedom to decide which countries to designate. In practice, however, a USTR decision not to designate Japan would have provoked congressional criticism and perhaps a major confrontation. Japan aside, USTR's decision to designate other countries under both Gephardt and the original super 301 was based on a discretionary (and, given the measurement problems, a rather subjective) determination of the magnitude and pervasiveness of barriers to US exports in the target country.

---

21. Senator Baucus's bill is S. 1858, "A Bill to Make Super 301 Permanent," 22 February 1994. Congressman Gephardt's bill is H.R. 3900, "The Fair Market Access Act of 1994," 24 February 1994.

Table 2.3 Comparison of presidential discretion under the Gephardt amendment, the 1988 and 1994 versions of super 301, and regular 301

Provision	Gephardt amendment	1988 Trade Act super 301[a]	Clinton 1994 super 301[a]	Regular 301
Selection of target country and unfair trade practices	Mathematical formula for determination of countries with "excessive" trade surpluses; USTR had some discretion, except for Japan (for political, not statutory, reasons) on determination of whether surplus was also "unwarranted" and hence subject to negotiation or retaliation	USTR had considerable discretion, except for Japan (for political, not statutory, reasons) to select priority countries and priority practices	USTR has considerable discretion, except for Japan, (for political, not statutory, reasons) to select "priority foreign country practices"	Complete discretion on USTR-initiated cases; some leverage to deter or encourage industry petitions
Trigger for investigation or negotiation	Annual determination required	Annual determination required	Annual determination required, but with two large loopholes that allow USTR to avoid a designation if the country in question is engaged in fruitful negotiations or the president directs USTR not to designate a practice	Complete discretion on timing of USTR-initiated cases; some leverage on timing of industry petitions
Time deadline for agreement or retaliation	6 months	12–18 months (6 months for IPR) with additional 6 months delay possible (3 months for IPR)	Same as 1988 super 301	Same as super 301

Results required	10 percent annual reduction in bilateral surplus required for up to three years by complete elimination of all unwarranted trade practices or their adverse effects on US exports	No quantitative results required; USTR required to seek elimination of or compensation for priority practices within a three-year period with congressional expectation that US exports would increase in each of three years	No quantitative results required; practices should be eliminated "as quickly as possible" or compensation should be granted	Same as super 301, except that there is no explicit congressional expectation that US exports would necessarily increase within a specified period
Retaliation required	Mandatory with presidential waivers, which could be disapproved by Congress	Mandatory for unjustifiable practices and violations of trade agreements; discretionary for others; considerable latitude to waive even "mandatory" retaliation	Same as 1988 super 301	Same as super 301
Maximum retaliation	Amount necessary to achieve up to 30 percent reduction in surplus or amount equivalent to burden of all unwarranted foreign practices on US exports	Amount equivalent to the burden of the specified practices on US exports	Same as 1988 super 301	Super as super 301

a. Unless otherwise indicated, super 301 refers to both the 1988 Trade Act version and to the 1994 Clinton executive order.

The 1994 Clinton super 301 does not explicitly designate countries as unfair traders. Rather, USTR is directed to designate "priority foreign country practices." This formulation merges the separate 1988 super 301 provisions for designating "priority foreign countries" and "priority practices." The Clinton administration seems to want to avoid even the appearance of publicly designating an entire country as an unfair trader, the element of the original super 301 that trading partners found so offensive. However, the Clinton super 301 is just as clearly aimed at perceived Japanese structural protection, and it is by no means certain that Japan or any other potential target will appreciate the subtle difference.

Under regular 301, USTR has complete discretion to initiate cases and has substantial latitude to set the terms of these investigations. Typically, such investigations address specific sectoral practices, but as discussed below, a broad spectrum of practices may be targeted, as in the 1992 China case (see chapter 12 for a discussion). The key difference from either version of super 301 is that the president also has complete discretion under regular 301 to decide when to initiate cases.

Both the 1988 super 301 and the Gephardt proposal limited presidential discretion by setting annual deadlines for USTR to name, or not name, "excessive and unwarranted surplus countries" (Gephardt) or "priority foreign countries" (the 1988 super 301). The Clinton super 301 also sets a deadline but gives the president considerable latitude *not* to designate "priority foreign country practices." As mentioned above, designations are not required if US trade law, bilateral agreements, or fruitful negotiations are addressing them, and the president has the unlimited authority to direct USTR not to designate a practice. Once a designation is made, the negotiating procedures for the original and Clinton super 301s are the same as for regular 301, and they give USTR significantly more latitude than Gephardt would have in five areas.

One important difference is in the deadlines required for negotiations. Under Gephardt's proposal, after a country was designated USTR had only six months to negotiate an agreement. The 1988 super and regular 301 give USTR 12 to 18 months for most cases and six to nine months for intellectual property rights cases. The 1994 Clinton super 301 allows six months after the release of the National Trade Estimate Report before priority practice designations are made; the original allowed only one month.

A second difference is in the specificity of results required. Gephardt forced USTR to impose quantitative targets for surplus reduction. In contrast, neither version of super 301 explicitly mandates specific numeric goals. Instead, under the original 1988 super 301 USTR was expected to seek the elimination of, or compensation for, the offending practices within three years. Congress expected but did not require that a super 301 agreement would lead to an increase in US exports in each of the following three years. The 1994 Clinton super 301 exhorts USTR to seek the elimination of unfair practices (or obtain compensation) "as quickly as possible," a less demanding standard than in the original. The Clinton super 301 and regular 301 do not impose either quantitative goals or even an explicit expectation of increased US exports.

A third difference in presidential discretion between Gephardt and super 301 is in USTR's latitude to select specific unfair practices for negotiation. The Gephardt amendment was aimed at all unjustifiable, unreasonable, or discriminatory practices that had a significant adverse impact on US commerce. Both the original and new super 301s allow USTR considerable leeway in selecting specific priority practices. The law gives USTR discretion to select those practices whose elimination has the greatest potential to increase US exports. In practice, under the old super 301 this meant USTR could select practices most amenable to negotiation within the 12 to 18 months allowed. USTR could leave more complex practices (e.g., the distribution system or *keiretsu*) for other forums such as SII, where there were no statutory deadlines.

A fourth difference is in presidential discretion to retaliate. The Gephardt amendment mandated retaliation whenever the surplus reduction goals were not achieved. Both the original and Clinton super 301s and regular 301 require retaliation only when US rights under international law or under a trade agreement are violated. Moreover, compared with Gephardt, the two super 301s and regular 301 give the president more latitude to waive mandatory retaliation.

A fifth difference is in the quantum of retaliation required. Gephardt required potentially massive retaliation against all unwarranted foreign practices or to achieve the surplus reduction targets. Under both old and new super 301s and regular 301, USTR is instructed to impose retaliation for practices it wants to eliminate that is "equivalent in value to the burden or restriction being imposed" on US commerce. Thus, USTR can limit the potential damage to American interests caused by US retaliation and foreign counterretaliation.

Perceptions about super 301 are frequently divorced from reality. The actual language of the original super 301 statute, though subject to misuse or abuse, created neither the demon envisioned by its critics nor the avenging angel its proponents desired. Super 301 neither triggered trade wars nor caused the Uruguay Round to collapse. The 1988 super 301 was useful in reducing congressional pressure on trade policy and in inducing Japan to discuss fundamental structural barriers under the much-maligned Structural Impediments Initiative. Certainly, it was a preferable alternative to the Gephardt proposal. The Clinton super 301 is an even more flexible policy instrument than the original. However, the Clinton super 301 is not necessary to achieve US trade policy goals, is potentially counterproductive, and, as argued in chapter 12, should not be renewed and need not be used.

3

Truth and Consequences

The factors driving increasing support for a more aggressive and more unilateral US trade policy in the 1980s were both long- and short-term. Dissatisfaction with US trade policy and performance built throughout the 1970s as interdependence and competitive pressures on the US economy grew and as the limitations of the General Agreement on Tariffs and Trade (GATT) became more evident. In the first half of the 1980s, unease turned to deep concern when macroeconomic imbalances resulted in unprecedented trade deficits and severe competitive pressures for US industry.

The first section of this chapter explores why some policymakers felt that aggressive unilateralism was not only necessary but was a justified response to these pressures. Next, we examine what policymakers in Congress and the administration in the 1970s and 1980s hoped aggressive unilateralism might achieve and what critics warned the consequences might be. The rest of the chapter explores the actual experience with section 301 since 1975 and what it reveals about the effectiveness and consequences of aggressive unilateralism.

Arguments for and against Aggressive Unilateralism

Many in Congress and industry in the 1980s felt that the United States faced an increasingly uneven playing field in international trade. They further believed that multilateral negotiations under the GATT, which had been based on reciprocal reductions in protection, had resulted in different levels of protection, leaving US markets substantially more open than those in Europe and Japan. In addition, developing countries continued to receive "special and differential treatment," which allowed them to benefit from the tariff concessions of the industrialized countries while they kept their own economies relatively closed. Critics also pointed out that GATT rules—by ignoring foreign investment and services—failed to cover an increasing share of world trade that was especially important to American firms.

What Was Aggressive Unilateralism Expected to Achieve?

Advocates of aggressive unilateralism argued that the inequitable results of past multilateral trade talks justified the US demands for unilateral liberalization. Because past efforts to address these inequities through GATT negotiations and dispute settlement procedures had failed, they argued, the United States had no other alternative in enforcing its rights under trade agreements. Many countries heavily regulated trade in services, products incorporating intellectual property, and foreign investment—all of which had become increasingly important for the American economy. Because US markets tended to be relatively less regulated (except those relying on intellectual property, where more protection was the aim), the GATT's lack of rules governing these areas fed the growing perceptions of unfairness. Moreover, by the 1980s, as the US trade deficit ballooned, many in Congress and the business community became convinced that these inequities were important factors in declining US competitiveness. These advocates' chief aim was to open markets for US exporters. But if that could not be achieved, proponents were willing to correct perceived imbalances by retaliatory closure of the US market.

Policymakers in the Reagan and Bush administrations did not find all of the arguments convincing, but they saw their options as limited. US Trade Representative William Brock had been rebuffed in 1982 when he proposed multilateral trade negotiations to address GATT's weaknesses. At the same time, there was strong pressure for protection from import-competing industries that increasingly cited unfair practices abroad as a major source of their woes (Nivola 1993; Low 1993, chapter 4; Destler 1992, chapter 6). Export interests, an important component of the traditional antiprotection coalition, were demoralized by the impact of the overvalued dollar on their sales abroad and were relatively inactive in this period (Destler and Odell 1987, 41). Meanwhile, the trade deficit continued to rise, and the number and variety of trade-restricting proposals on Capitol Hill proliferated.

The administration felt it had to do something or risk Congress taking matters into its own hands. To address the trade deficit, the administration reached agreement with key trading partners for a coordinated dollar depreciation. To buy time while waiting for the exchange rate changes to affect trade balances, the administration also adopted a more activist and aggressive trade policy using section 301.

Administration officials had several objectives in pursuing an aggressive 301 strategy. First, they hoped to placate Congress by opening foreign markets and increasing US exports. By focusing on exports, the administration hoped to mobilize export interests and at least partially offset the pro-protection lobbying from import-competing sectors. Second, administration officials used section 301 and the threat of even more congressionally mandated aggressive unilateralism to prod trading partners into agreeing on multilateral trade negotiations. The United States wanted both to strengthen dispute settlement procedures so that GATT rules could be more consistently enforced and to fortify and expand GATT rules in areas where they either did not exist or were too weak. US negotiators argued that significant reforms were needed if American support for GATT was to be maintained. And unless and until those reforms were in place, they argued, aggressive unilateralism was justified, both in cases where the GATT dispute settlement system had broken down— GATT legal scholar Robert Hudec's (1990b) "justified disobedience"— and where trading partners blocked negotiations on new rules.

As the decade wore on, the debate over the "Japan problem" also became more heated. The overall trade deficit followed the dollar down (with an 18- to 24-month lag), declining from a peak of $160 billion in 1987 to $115 billion in 1989. But because Japan's exports to the United States were roughly three times as large as its imports from the United States in the mid-1980s, US exports to Japan had to increase three times faster than US imports just to keep the trade deficit from growing (Bergsten and Noland 1993, 33). Thus, even though US exports to Japan grew faster in this period than total US exports, and much faster than US imports, the bilateral deficit with Japan seemed hardly to budge, declining only from $57 billion to $50 billion. This fed perceptions that Japan was different from other countries, won converts to this notion, and provided ammunition for those who argued that unseen, informal obstacles and exclusionary business practices in Japan were important barriers to US exports (see further discussion in chapter 2). Congress once again intensified the pressure on the administration to tackle these barriers.

The Warnings of the Critics

During the 1970s and 1980s, the critics of aggressive unilateralism rejected its underlying premises. They also expressed concerns about its possible consequences, both for global economic welfare and for the institutional framework that has governed international trade for nearly four decades.

First, the critics—and even some proponents who favored an aggressive unilateral strategy for other reasons—repeatedly pointed out that trade policy cannot correct trade imbalances. For instance, if resources in an economy are fully employed, export promotion may affect the composition of a country's exports but is not likely to increase the level of exports. If Country A's economy is not at full employment, or if trade barriers in Country B raise that country's level of saving or reduce its domestic investment, trade policy may raise the level of Country A's exports. But with floating exchange rates, again there will be little impact on the trade balance because Country A's currency will appreciate, causing exports to decrease and imports to increase. Fundamentally, the trade balance is a macroeconomic phenomenon, determined by the balance between saving and investment by government, industry, and citizens, and it is usually not significantly affected by trade policy (see, e.g., Bergsten and Noland 1993, chapter 2). Many economists and others also argue that declining US competitiveness during the 1980s, to the extent they believed it was a problem, was due largely to domestic factors, such as the quality of education and the rate of investment, and that the trade deficits of the early and mid-1980s were largely a temporary phenomenon due to misaligned exchange rates.[1]

The second premise questioned by the critics is the utility of an aggressive unilateral strategy in negotiating market opening. They argued that such a strategy would be more likely to close markets than to open them. William R. Cline, for example, feared that trade tensions in the early 1980s were already so high that "a new approach of aggressive reciprocity by the United States could trigger counterretaliation at least as often as it would achieve foreign liberalization" (Cline 1982, 23). Critics felt that some of the support for an aggressive market-opening policy was disingenuous—that, in fact, some proponents hoped the negotiations would fail and that the United States would have to retaliate, thereby providing increased protection from imports. Even when intentions were honest, critics predicted that aggressive unilateralism would trigger trade wars because foreign governments would refuse to negotiate with a gun to their heads. The United States would then be forced to retaliate, which could cause additional market closure if the foreign government counterretaliated.

Even where this trade war scenario did not play out, critics charged that the dynamics of bilateral agreements reached under the threat of retaliation would tend to produce discriminatory results. First, they argued, it would usually be politically easier for the government in the targeted country to divert trade from other countries to the United States— keeping total imports steady—than it would be to genuinely liberalize and allow the level of total imports to increase. Second, as Nivola (1993, 13) asked, wouldn't targeted countries, "under the threat of retribution,

---

1. The debate over American competitiveness—both its definition and its trend—has been extensive and wide-ranging (see, e.g., Competitiveness Policy Council 1992).

reason that the safest way to ease bilateral tensions was to grease the wheels that squeaked the loudest?" Thus, in Bhagwati's words (1990, 36), "The game is set up . . . in terms of implicit pro-trade diversion bias rules that all parties recognize as political realities."

Critics also rejected the "altruistic rationales" offered for aggressive unilateralism. J. Michael Finger (1991), for example, dismisses the "export politics" argument for aggressive unilateralism, arguing that it actually reduces the incentive of export-oriented interests to oppose protectionist measures. If US exporters previously had supported reductions in US trade barriers as the "price" of market opening abroad, with an aggressively wielded section 301 US exporters could achieve liberalization of foreign markets without having to support reciprocal liberalization of US barriers. Thus the critics feared that section 301 tilted the domestic political balance against removing US trade barriers through broad multilateral negotiations under the GATT.

Finally, and most fundamentally, critics argued that whatever market opening occurred would inevitably be at the expense of the international trading system. Bhagwati (1990, 32–36) dismissed the notion that "the 301 weapon was necessary or instrumental" in launching the Uruguay Round or in keeping it going and even expressed concern that 301 might "undermine efforts to make the Uruguay Round successful." Moreover, despite the weaknesses of the GATT dispute settlement process—which has resulted in only one authorized retaliation in more than 40 years of GATT history (Hudec 1975)—Bhagwati rejected Hudec's "justified disobedience" argument for some cases of aggressive unilateralism. Bhagwati argues that willful disregard of GATT rules breeds cynicism and undermines the long-term sustainability of the system by replacing "the rule of law by the law of the jungle. . . ." Even Hudec pointed to the hypocrisy of the US position, given its own poor record of complying with GATT panel findings against it only after lengthy delays if at all (Hudec 1990b and 1993). Some critics have derided US claims of benign intent in using section 301 to reform the GATT as akin to a US military officer's explanation during the Vietnam War that "we had to destroy the village in order to save it."

The Truth about Section 301 and Market Opening

Before addressing the concerns of critics who believe US unilateralism threatens the international trading system, it seems worthwhile to examine whether the section 301 approach has in fact achieved market opening. The last half of the chapter then addresses the concerns of those who believe that the negative cumulative and systemic effects of aggressive unilateralism outweigh any of the case-by-case results.

Section 301 is just one tool among several available to American trade policymakers for opening markets. But the experience with section 301 since 1975 provides a convenient data base for analyzing at least some of the effects of aggressive unilateralism. First, it provides a reasonably large sample of cases. Second, there is a large, public, and relatively accessible archive for these cases. The US Trade Representative's office has public files on all investigations conducted. These files contain, at a minimum, the petition filed (if applicable) and all *Federal Register* notices regarding actions taken. (USTR also provides a list of all section 301 investigations, briefly summarizing the status of each and any action taken.) The appendix contains brief summaries of each of the 91 cases investigated under section 301 since it went into effect on 1 January 1975 (except the ones that are the subject of detailed case studies in Part II). The table in the appendix summarizes our assessment of the outcomes in each of these cases.

Many of the trade policy experts we interviewed for this project argued that 301 should be regarded as a "residual" instrument—one that is only used when other less formal, less public, perhaps less confrontational means have failed. Thus, by examining only petitions accepted by USTR, the sample may be biased toward the toughest cases. In many more cases, a mere threat by USTR to accept a petition or initiate an investigation may have been sufficient to effect changes in foreign trade policies. Moreover, the ever-present, implicit threat that a country could be the target of US trade retaliation may deter governments from adopting foreign trade policies that otherwise would be the source of disputes.

It is difficult to assess many of these arguments, especially those involving cases of successful deterrence, where the effects of US policies are often unobservable. From a few of the cases that are observable, however, it is not clear that examining only formal 301 investigations necessarily lowers the success rate for US negotiators substantially. For example, USTR twice rejected petitions from the Rice Millers Association—in 1986 and 1988—to investigate the Japanese rice import ban because USTR believed bilateral negotiations would almost certainly fail. These reservations about the potential for drawing conclusions from the set of formal investigations undoubtedly have validity. But we do not believe they negate the utility of this effort. Given the prominence of section 301 as a trade policy tool, it is still useful to draw even narrow conclusions about whether and when retaliatory threats using this tool are effective.

The Experience with Section 301

There is no typical section 301 case. The countries targeted range from Japan to Norway, and the sectors involved range from beef and corn to footwear to insurance and computer software. Table 3.1 shows the distribution of cases by target country and by broad sectoral categories. Just 10 countries (counting the European Union as one) account for 76 of the 84 cases included in the table.[2] Interestingly, the European Union rather than Japan is by far the most frequent target, and not surprisingly agricultural disputes have dominated the US trade agenda with Europe. Just under a quarter of the total number of 301 cases have involved US-EU agricultural disputes, while 40 percent overall have involved disputes over agriculture. A third of the cases sought access for manufactured goods, while the remainder addressed the "new" areas of services and intellectual property.

It is interesting that Mexico, the fourth largest US export market, has never been the subject of a 301 investigation, though it was placed on the priority watch list released in May 1989 under the special 301 provisions of the 1988 Trade Act regarding intellectual property protection. (Mexico was removed from the list the following year.) Argentina, on the other hand, has been a surprisingly frequent target of 301, given that it is a relatively small market for US goods, but three of the five cases against Argentina involved services or intellectual property issues.

Table 3.2 shows the increasing importance accorded intellectual property protection in recent years. In contrast, services trade—the other major "new area" negotiated in the Uruguay Round—has been the subject of investigations less often in recent years than in the late 1970s. The prominence of agriculture on the 301 agenda is consistent across the period studied.

Table 3.2 also provides evidence of the more aggressive trade policy adopted in the second Reagan administration. The number of 301 investigations increased 50 percent in the 1985–89 period relative to the previous five-year period, with intellectual property cases alone accounting for 40 percent of the increase. Even more striking is the sharp increase in the proportion of cases involving public or explicit threats, which include USTR-initiated cases. USTR-initiated cases occurred in two waves—one in 1985–86, when the Reagan administration was trying to influence the debate in Congress over the omnibus trade bill, and the other (with an interim pause) in 1989–1991, when the Bush administration had to implement the super 301 and special 301 provisions included in the 1988 Trade Act.

---

2. Two of the 91 cases—involving imports of subsidized Canadian softwood lumber (nos. 58 and 87)—are excluded from this analysis because section 301 was used only for administrative purposes, not as a negotiating tool. Six more (nos. 27–31 and 33) are counted as one case because they had the same petitioner and involved the same products and issues. Those six complaints, regarding allegedly subsidized steel imports from six European countries, were eventually shifted into a section 201 (escape clause) investigation at the order of the president. The products in the six steel complaints ultimately were wrapped into the "voluntary" export restraint program installed in 1984.

Table 3.1 Section 301 cases by country and type of product, 1975–June 1994

Target country/region	Number of cases initiated[b]	Manufactures[c]	Agriculture-related[d]	Services	Intellectual property
World					
Total	**84**	**29.5**	**35**	**10**	**9.5**
Public threats[a]	41	12.5	13	7	8.5
European Union					
Total	22.5	2.5	19	1	0
Public threats	9	0	9	0	0
Japan					
Total	12.5	7.5	4	1	0
Public threats	8	6	1	1	0
Korea					
Total	8	2	3	2	1
Public threats	4	0	1	2	1
Taiwan					
Total	7	4	2	0	1
Public threats	3	1	1	0	1
Canada					
Total	6	4	1	1	0
Public threats	3	2	0	1	0
Brazil					
Total	6	2.5	1	0	2.5
Public threats	4	1.5	0	0	2.5
Argentina					
Total	5	1	1	2	1
Public threats	2	1	0	1	0
India					
Total	4	1	1	1	1
Public threats	3	1	0	1	1
Thailand					
Total	3	0	1	0	2
Public threats	3	0	1	0	2
China					
Total	2	1	0	0	1
Public threats	2	1	0	0	1
Other[e]	8	4	2	2	0

a. Public or explicit threats include initiation of an investigation by USTR; publication of a presidential determination that an actionable policy or practice exists, including a definite date for taking action, publication of a retaliation "hit list," or imposition of retaliation.

b. Excludes two cases involving Canadian exports of softwood lumber. Includes six steel cases against Austria, France, Italy, Sweden, the United Kingdom, and Belgium that were eventually transferred to a section 201 case, counted here as one case and included under "other"; another case, alleging the 1976 EC-Japan steel agreement burdened US commerce, is split between the European Community and Japan.

c. Includes case brought over Taiwan's customs valuation system, the super 301 case against Brazil for its import licensing system, the super 301 case against India for restrictions on foreign investment, and the general case against China in 1991–92. The Brazilian informatics case, which involved both market-access issues and intellectual property concerns, is split between the manufactures and IP categories.

d. In addition to raw agricultural products, includes processed food and other agricultural and natural resource–based products *if* the issue arises from a subsidy to or protection for processors to offset the high cost of protected agricultural inputs—e.g., pasta, wine, tobacco products.

e. "Other" includes Guatemala, Indonesia, Portugal, and Spain prior to EC accession, and Norway, named in one case each, and those countries named in the steel cases referred to in footnote b, counted as one.

The sharp drop in cases after 1989 is notable. It could be explained by US negotiators' desire to focus on concluding the Uruguay Round. Also, US firms may have hoped that the Uruguay Round end game would produce results without the expense of a USTR petition. It will be interesting to see whether the pace of petitions or USTR-initiated cases picks up again following implementation of the Uruguay Round agreement.

Methodology

Of 91 investigations initiated from 1975 through June 1994, 19 have been excluded for various reasons, leaving 72 cases to be analyzed.[3] The sample includes the six investigations that resulted from the spring 1989 super 301 designations, which are treated here the same as all other section 301 cases. The assessments of these cases are based on information from the US Trade Representative's public files supplemented by press reports, interviews, surveys of US government officials, petitioners, their counsels, and others involved in the cases, as well as examination of trade data.[4]

A "successful" case is defined here as one in which US negotiating objectives—that is, improved market access for US exporters of goods and services, reduced export subsidies by the European Union and others, and improved protection for intellectual property rights (IPR)—were at least partially achieved. For purposes of this discussion, we do not pass judgment on the validity of the negotiators' objectives. It should be noted, however, that USTR has generally been conscientious in using section 301 to reduce obstacles to trade and has avoided any temptation to use it as a protectionist tool. For example, the Reagan administration refused

---

3. As in tables 3.1 and 3.2, the six cases regarding alleged unfair practices with respect to steel exports from six European countries (nos. 27-31 and 33) and the two Canadian softwood lumber cases (nos. 58 and 87) are excluded. In addition, as of June 1994, four cases were either pending or too recently concluded to make trustworthy assessments about the outcome: EC meat packing (case no. 301-83), Chinese trade barriers (301-88), and Taiwanese and Brazilian intellectual property protection (301-89 and 301-91). Four other cases are also excluded because the president issued a formal determination that the practices alleged in the complaints were not actionable under section 301: EC-Japan steel arrangement (301-10), Taiwanese barriers to footwear exports (301-38), EC satellite launching subsidies (301-46), and Indonesian pencil slat subsidies (301-90). Another case, Swiss product marking standards (301-21), is left out because no determination was made, and the investigation resulted in a change in US, not foreign, law. Case no. 32, Canadian subsidies for subway railcars, was handled as a countervailing duty case. Finally, one case, Korean steel wire subsidies (301-39) is excluded because the petition was withdrawn before any formal determination was made, and the outcome could not be determined.

4. We mailed copies of the case summaries from the appendix to either the petitioning firm or group, or to its legal counsel, and to each chair of the interagency committee on section 301 since 1975. We received responses from either the petitioner or its counsel in 32 of the 72 cases and heard from or talked to five former 301 committee chairs. We also solicited comments on the detailed case studies from both American and foreign officials involved and interviewed a number of people involved in these cases as well.

Table 3.2 Change in volume and product distribution of 301 cases over four periods, 1975–93

Target country by period	Total number of cases	Manufactures[b]	Agriculture[c]	Services	Intellectual property
1975–79					
Total	**21**	**5**	**11**	**5**	**0**
Public threats[a]	5	1	2	2	0
European Community					
Total	8.5	0.5	8	0	0
Public threats	2	0	2	0	0
Japan					
Total	4.5	2.5	2	0	0
Public threats	1	1	0	0	0
Other[d]					
Total	8	2	1	5	0
Public threats	2	0	0	2	0
1980–84					
Total	**21[e]**	**11**	**8**	**2**	**0**
Public threats	5	2	2	1	0
European Community					
Total	6	1	4[f]	1	0
Public threats	2	0	2	0	0
Japan					
Total	1	1	0	0	0
Public threats	1	1	0	0	0
Taiwan	3	2	1	0	0
Other[g]					
Total	11	7	3	1	0
Public threats	2	1	0	1	0
1985–89					
Total	**31**	**10.5**	**14**	**3**	**3.5**
Public threats	23	8.5	8	3	3.5
European Community					
Total	6	1	5	0	0
Public threats	4	0	4	0	0
Japan					
Total	7	4	2	1	0
Public threats	6	4	1	1	0
Korea					
Total	5	0	3	1	1
Public threats	3	0	1	1	1
Brazil					
Total	3	1.5	0	0	1.5
Public threats	3	1.5	0	0	1.5
India					
Total	3	1	1	1	0
Public threats	2	1	0	1	0
Others[h]					
Total	7	3	3	0	1
Public threats	4	2	2	0	0

Table 3.2 Change in volume and product distribution of 301 cases over four periods, 1975–93 *(continued)*

Target country by period	Total number of cases	Manufactures[b]	Agriculture[c]	Services	Intellectual property
1990–93					
Total	11	3	2	0	6
Public threats	9	2	1	0	6
European Community					
Total	2	0	2	0	0
Public threats	1	0	1	0	0
Thailand					
Total	2	0	0	0	2
Public threats	2	0	0	0	2
Other					
Total	7	3	0	0	4[i]
Public threats	6	2	0	0	4

a. Public or explicit threats include initiation of an investigation by USTR; publication of a presidential determination that an actionable policy or practice exists, including a definite date for taking action, publication of a retaliation "hit list," or imposition of retaliation.

b. Includes case brought over Taiwan's customs valuation system, the super 301 case against Brazil for its import licensing system, the super 301 case against India for restrictions on foreign investment, and the general case against China in 1991–92. The Brazilian informatics case, which involved both market-access issues and intellectual property concerns, is split between the manufactures and IP categories.

c. In addition to raw agricultural products, includes processed food and other agricultural and natural resource–based products *if* the issue arises from a subsidy to or protection for processors to offset the high cost of protected agricultural inputs—e.g., pasta, wine, tobacco products.

d. Includes two against Canada and one each against Argentina, Korea, and Taiwan.

e. Includes six steel cases against several European countries that were eventually transferred to section 201 case, counted as one here under "other."

f. All filed in 1981.

g. Includes two each for Argentina, Brazil, Canada, and Korea.

h. Includes two each for Argentina and Taiwan.

i. Special 301 designations of India, China, Taiwan, and Brazil.

to use 301 to limit imports of steel from several European countries, ordering the US International Trade Commission (ITC) to open a section 201 (escape clause) case instead. Although the steel industry did eventually win protection, following an affirmative finding by the ITC, the principle of reserving the 301 remedy primarily for tackling barriers to US exports was preserved.

In our view, and in contrast to that of some other observers, conclusion of an agreement is not sufficient to call an outcome a negotiating success.[5]

---

5. Sykes (1992), for example, concludes that 58 of the 83 section 301 cases he examined were successful (70 percent). But in several of the cases he has defined as successes, we have found that the agreements were not stable and have concluded that they cannot be considered as having successful outcomes.

If a case recurs because the agreement was not implemented to US satisfaction, or if it was circumvented in some other way, it is classified as a failure (and called here a "nominal success"). We divided the cases into four categories, illustrated by the following examples:

- Failures are exemplified by three cases challenging EC export subsidies to no avail—barley (case no. 301-5), wheat flour (301-6), and sugar (301-22).

- Nominal successes are cases in which an agreement was reached but not implemented to US satisfaction. These are exemplified, again, by three cases challenging EC efforts to support its agricultural sector—in this case, processed fruit and vegetable producers. USTR challenged border measures restricting imports of canned fruit and vegetable products in the late 1970s—minimum import prices and licensing requirements in 301-4 and an arbitrary method for calculating the sugar content of canned fruit in 301-7. The Community then replaced these measures with production subsidies, which the US negotiators challenged in case 301-26. Negotiations produced an agreement in 1985 on reducing subsidies, the implementation of which the United States challenged in 1989 (case 301-71, which finally appears to be working). Another example is case 301-72, in which the Thai government agreed to remove a GATT-illegal ban on imports of cigarettes but replaced it with a GATT-legal tariff.

- Partial successes are illustrated by two cases challenging Japan's quotas on leather and leather footwear imports (301-13 and 301-36), which Japan converted to tariff rate quotas but was unwilling to significantly liberalize. Instead, Japan offered compensation to US negotiators, lowering tariffs on other imports valued at more than $230 million.

- Successful cases are exemplified by Japan's decision to eliminate its tariff on cigarettes and liberalize marketing regulations, which increased US exports manyfold (301-50), and Brazil's decision to do away with its import licensing system (301-73).

The last case, addressing Brazilian quantitative import restrictions, illustrates one of the many hazards in this exercise. In a previous Institute for International Economics study of foreign policy sanctions, the authors counted as successes only those cases in which there was a positive policy outcome *and* sanctions made at least a modest contribution to the outcome (Hufbauer, Schott, and Elliott 1990). The Brazilian import licensing case is an example of how the failure to make that distinction could inflate the success rate. For the sample studied here, however, it appears to be a distinction without a difference because the Brazilian case is the only one of that type we found.

The hazards in drawing often subtle distinctions between marginal failures and marginal successes are even greater. In drawing the line between success and failure in a particular case, we also occasionally had to draw fairly arbitrary lines between cases. Our assessment of the Japanese semiconductor case (301-48) is one with which many observers will no doubt disagree. The US-Japan semiconductor agreement did increase the sales of US firms, and it did contribute to an increase in foreign market share in Japan, from less than 10 percent in 1986–87 to just over 14 percent by the time the agreement expired in 1991 (see table A.11). But the stated objective of the agreement was a 20 percent foreign market share, and USTR, supported by the petitioners, refused to lift the retaliatory sanctions imposed against Japan in 1987 until a new agreement was signed in 1991.[6] Thus we classify case no. 301-48, encompassing the first semiconductor agreement, as a failure based on the decision to keep the retaliation in place. The second agreement, backed by the threat to reimpose retaliatory duties, appears to have been more successful in satisfying the petitioners' and US negotiators' demands, but it does not appear in our data base because a second 301 case was not filed.

An example just on the other side of the success/failure divide is the Japanese construction case. In the 1988 Trade Act, Congress required USTR to initiate an investigation of discriminatory Japanese government practices in awarding contracts for public construction projects. Building on the Major Projects Arrangement (MPA), concluded in March 1988, USTR negotiated an agreement in 1991 that expanded the list of projects that would be eligible for the special bidding procedures outlined in the MPA. Two years later, however, US negotiators revisited the issue, threatening sanctions but never initiating a 301 investigation, and eventually negotiated an agreement that fundamentally changed the Japanese system for awarding construction contracts above a certain threshold. Although the 1991 agreement might be considered only a "nominal" success, since it was reopened, we concluded that it was a partial success because US firms did increase their involvement in the public Japanese market and because the new agreement seems to have expanded the old agreement rather than simply seeking its enforcement. The two middle columns of table 3.3 list the cases that were closest to the narrow line dividing success and failure and highlight those where the judgments were particularly difficult.

A final caveat: it must be emphasized that this definition of success is a narrow one. For example, the outcome in some cases was improved

---

6. USTR imposed retaliatory duties on $165 million in imports from Japan in April 1987, even though the agreement had been in place for less than a year, because of the Japanese government's "apparent failure . . . to fulfill its obligations" under the agreement, including the understanding that "the expected improvement in access by foreign-based semiconductor producers would be gradual and steady over the period of the agreement" (*Federal Register*, 31 March 1987, 10275).

Table 3.3 Difficulties in classifying section 301 cases that are marginal failures or successes[a]

Nominal successes[b]	Marginal nominal successes[b]	Marginal partial successes	Partial successes
Guatemala, shipping	Japan, cigars	Canada, fish	EC, egg products
EC, canned food	Japan, pipe tobacco	Taiwan, misc.	EC, citrus
EC, canned food	Korea, insurance	Taiwan, beer, wine, tobacco	Japan, leather
EC, animal feed	EC, poultry	Japan, supercomputers	EC, pasta
USSR, insurance	Japan, semiconductors	Japan, construction	Brazil, footwear
EC, wheat			Japan, footwear
Argentina, insurance			Korea, footwear
EC, canned food			Brazil, soybeans
Korea, IPR			Taiwan, rice
EC, meat			Argentina, air couriers
Brazil, IPR			Taiwan, films
EC, soybeans			Brazil, IPR
Argentina, IPR			Argentina, soybeans
Thailand, cigarettes			India, almonds
Norway, toll equipment			Korea, cigarettes
Canada, beer			Korea, beef
Thailand, IPR			Korea, wine
Thailand, IPR			EC, canned fruit
India, IPR			Japan, wood products
China, IPR			EC, enlargement

IPR = intellectual property rights
a. Explanations of nominal and partial success are found in the text.
b. We classify these cases as failures.

access for specific US firms; success in these cases does not necessarily mean the market as a whole was liberalized; market shares may only have been reallocated to benefit US firms at the expense of third parties. In such cases, the result might not be considered a success for US trade policy more broadly defined—improving global welfare or strengthening the liberal multilateral trade system. These are among the issues discussed below.

Section 301 Outcomes: Market Opening or Market Closing?

Section 301 appears to have been a reasonably effective tool of American trade policy, especially when compared with the use of economic sanctions as a tool to achieve noneconomic foreign policy goals. Based on the evidence at hand, we conclude that US negotiating objectives were at least partially achieved about half the time (35 of 72 cases), as compared

Table 3.4 Market-opening results in section 301 cases

Period	Number of successes	Number of failures	Success ratio (percentage of total)
1975–92	35	37	48.6
Case resolved:			
Before September 1985	9	20	31.0
After September 1985	26	17	60.5
Case resolved in:			
1975–79	3	4	42.9
1980–84	3	14	17.6
1985–88	16	5	76.2
1989–92	13	14	48.1
Excluding IPR cases	12	8	60.0

IPR = intellectual property rights

with only about one success in every three foreign policy sanction cases (41 of 120) (Hufbauer, Schott, and Elliott 1990, 93).[7]

Like the US experience with foreign policy sanctions, the success rate has not been stable over the period in which 301 has been employed. But in stark contrast to the foreign policy sanctions, the success rate for section 301 increased over time, nearly doubling after announcement of the president's trade policy action plan in September 1985, from 31 to 60 percent (table 3.4).[8] Given the efforts by Congress over the years to make 301 stronger and more effective, it is interesting to break the results down further, into periods defined by trade laws: the Trade Act of 1974 (1975–79), the Trade Agreements Act of 1979 (1980–84), the Trade and Tariff Act of 1984 (1985–88), and the Omnibus Trade and Competitiveness Act of 1988 (1989–92).

Table 3.4 shows that section 301 had its greatest rate of success prior to passage of the 1988 Trade Act, with its super 301 provisions. In fact, regular 301 as implemented from 1985 through 1988 had a slightly higher success rate, 76 percent, than did super 301, 67 percent (four of six cases—or five of eight, 63 percent, if the preemptive negotiations with South Korea and Taiwan are included; see chapter 12).

Bhagwati (1990, 35) and others worried, however, that "since [section 301] reflects clout and concentrated pressure from the United States, there is a strong likelihood that the targets of the 301 actions will satisfy American demands by diverting trade from other countries (with less political

---

7. These results are higher than those of Patrick Low (1993, 88–89) who found only a 35 percent success rate for section 301 cases. Since Low did not publish his case-by-case assessments we could not determine the source of the difference.

8. There were 81 US foreign policy sanction episodes from World War I through 1990. In the period prior to 1973, the success rate in these cases was just over 50 percent (18 of 35); since then it is only 17 percent (8 of 46) (Hufbauer, Schott, and Elliott 1990, 108).

clout) to the United States, satisfying the strong at the expense of the weak."

In fact, there is very little evidence of discriminatory outcomes in the cases covered by GATT rules. Taiwan, which was not a GATT member at the time, is frequently charged with discriminating in favor of US exporters when negotiating trade deals. The South Korean government actually published lists in the mid-1980s showing exactly which imports and in what amounts they were going to divert to US exporters from other suppliers, mainly Japanese, in order to reduce tensions.[9] But we found no 301 cases involving potential or actual GATT violations where the US demanded discriminatory treatment and none where the formal agreements were on anything other than a most-favored nation (MFN) basis. One reason may be that competing exporters have learned to defend themselves. For example, when the United States filed GATT complaints against South Korean and Japanese restrictions on beef imports, Australia quickly filed parallel complaints to ensure that its interests were protected. In cases for which comparable data are available, there is very little evidence that US exporters have gained market share at the expense of exporters from other countries (see appendix).

The only cases we have been able to identify where US negotiators acquiesced in explicitly discriminatory agreements were in an area where there was no MFN requirement under GATT rules: the IPR agreements with South Korea and China, which provided retroactive patent and copyright protection only for US firms. US officials insist these provisions were inserted over their objections. Even in these cases, however, prospective protection was available to all comers. Moreover, the discrimination was temporary; within a year or two, the Europeans and Japanese were able to negotiate agreements providing similar retroactive protection to their firms. Less explicit discrimination in favor of US firms also appears to have accompanied the reluctant opening by Korea of its insurance market in the early and mid-1980s. Again, over time, as Korea expanded the number of foreign insurance firms allowed to operate there, some were from countries other than the United States.

Finally, contrary to the fears of many, the more aggressive use of section 301 did not result in any major trade wars. The United States retaliated in 15 of 91 section 301 investigations as of April 1994, and only two targets counterretaliated: the European Union (twice) and Canada (once). But in one case, involving Spanish and Portuguese accession to the Community in 1986, the US retaliation was nonbinding, as was EC "counterretaliation." In two other cases, involving Japanese quotas on leather and footwear, the United States raised tariffs on $24 million worth of Japanese leather goods as part of a negotiated compensation package that also

---

9. This trade diversification effort actually had a dual purpose. South Korea was running a large bilateral deficit with Japan that it also wanted to reduce.

Table 3.5   US retaliation under section 301

USTR case number	Target country	Issue	Form of retaliation
6	EC	Export subsidies on wheat flour	Instituted retaliatory export subsidies (EEP); no resolution.
11, 25	EC	Tariff preferences on citrus, export subsidies for pasta	Increased tariffs on EC pasta in retaliation for tariff preferences on citrus, also to offset pasta subsidies. EC counterretaliated. Retaliations were lifted when agreement was reached.
13, 36	Japan	Quotas on leather and footwear	Increased tariff on Japanese leather products as part of negotiated compensation agreement.
15	Canada	Border broadcasting/ advertising	Passed mirror legislation; no resolution.
24	Argentina	Bilateral agreement on hides	Withdrew tariff concession; no resolution.
48	Japan	Barriers to semiconductor exports	Increased tariffs; lifted when new agreement was signed in 1991.
54[a]	EC	Accession of Spain and Portugal	Announced nonbinding quotas on EC exports. EC counter-retaliated with similarly nonbinding restrictions on US exports. No commercial impact. Both retaliations were lifted when agreement was reached.
61	Brazil	Patent protection for pharmaceuticals	Increased tariffs; retaliation was lifted when agreement was reached (though agreement has not been implemented to date).
62[a]	EC	Ban on hormone-treated beef	Increased tariffs; no resolution.
80	Canada	Provincial restrictions on beer sales	Increased tariffs. Canada counterretaliated. Both retaliations were lifted when agreement was reached.
82	Thailand	Copyrights	Some GSP privileges withdrawn.
84	Thailand	Patent protection	Some GSP privileges withdrawn.
85[a]	India	General intellectual property	Some GSP privileges withdrawn.

a. Indicates case was initiated by USTR.

lowered Japanese tariffs on $236 million of imports of interest to the United States. In five other cases, the retaliation was lifted after a short time as part of negotiated resolutions of the disputes. Table 3.5 lists the section 301 cases where retaliation occurred.

In sum, section 301 only seldom resulted in trade-diverting agreements or trade retaliation and no agreement at all. Even rarer were 301-sparked trade wars. And 301 does appear to have resulted in some market opening, usually modest, in half the cases overall and three-fifths since 1985. It is impossible to quantify precisely the amount US exports may have increased because of section 301. Even a rough, order-of-magnitude estimate is difficult to make. Nearly two-thirds of the cases studied (46 of 72) involved total exports to the target country of the product in question of no more than $100 million; 16 involved exports of less than $10 million. The total value of US exports in the successful cases in the year after they were concluded was roughly $4 billion (in current dollars).

One of the biggest gains was US exports of cigarettes to Japan, which ballooned from less than $50 million to more than $1 billion by 1990. Close behind was a $750 million increase in exports of beef to Japan (from $350 million to $1,100 million).[10] Adjusting for the rapid growth of the Japanese market, US sales of semiconductors in Japan also increased by almost $1 billion annually by the end of the agreement negotiated under section 301.[11] Other relatively large export gains were $100 million each in increased exports of cigarettes to South Korea and Taiwan and $100 million in increased exports of beef to South Korea. US industry has predicted that it might increase sales of wood products to Japan by $750 million as a result of the super 301 agreement. To date, however, the gains have been far more modest. The market-access agreement signed with China in 1992 might eventually be worth several hundred million dollars a year if fully implemented. Thus, a reasonable estimate of the increase in US exports due to section 301 might be $4 billion to $5 billion annually as of the early 1990s. This compares with an estimated $30 billion to $40 billion increase in US exports as a result of the Uruguay Round agreements (Schott 1994).

Consequences of Section 301 for the International Trading System

Many defenders of section 301 believe that those who focus on narrow, market-opening results miss the forest for the trees. These usually reluctant proponents contend that the trading system in the early 1980s was close to being broken and that, in the words of Robert Hudec (1990b), US disobedience was "justified" to keep the multilateral system from collapsing completely. Defenders also argue that US aggressive unilateralism was an important factor in launching the Uruguay Round and expanding its agenda to include agriculture, intellectual property, investment,

---

10. This case was not a 301 but was negotiated in conjuction with 301-66, Japanese citrus.

11. For reasons peculiar to this case, the agreement focused on sales of foreign firms rather than exports; see Tyson (1992, chapter 4) for details.

and services, and that it was essential in restraining Congress from passing even more protectionist or Japan-bashing legislation. Critics reject these "altruistic" arguments made in defense of aggressive unilateralism (Bhagwati 1990, 30–33).

The obvious problem in evaluating these arguments is that the counterfactual cannot be observed: we cannot know what would have happened to the trading system in the absence of aggressive unilateralism. Here is what we do know:

- Congress did not pass sector-specific protectionist legislation.
- The Uruguay Round was launched in September 1986 with an expanded agenda.
- Dispute settlement reforms were part of the "early harvest" approved at the round's mid-term review in December 1988.
- The Uruguay Round did not collapse when USTR implemented super 301 in 1989–90.
- The round was successfully concluded, albeit three years later than planned.

Before we discuss the broader context of US trade policy, it is useful to assess the credibility of the US commitment to GATT reform in light of its own behavior. There are two sources of evidence for this analysis. First, how did USTR use 301? Was there any attempt to uphold the spirit, if not the letter, of GATT rules? Second, how did the United States respond when it was the subject of GATT complaints?

Section 301 and GATT Rules

Table 3.6 suggests that the use of section 301 has been neither as aggressive nor as unilateral as the number and volume of the condemnations would suggest. When the US Trade Representative has been aggressive and unilateral, it has often been in agriculture, where GATT rules were especially weak. USTR has been quite restrained with respect to trade in manufactures, where GATT rules are the most effective. USTR has been the most aggressive and unilateral where GATT rules do not apply at all.

In 11 of 22 cases in which a GATT panel was established, the United States acted unilaterally, either issuing a formal finding of unfairness, publishing a hit list, or actually retaliating (table 3.6). But each time the action either accompanied a GATT ruling or followed what Hudec has called "general legal breakdown." While unauthorized retaliation is clearly GATT-illegal, Hudec (1990b, 121) argues:

> The obligation not to retaliate without GATT authority presumes that GATT will be able to rule on the disputed legal claim, and, later, on the request to retaliate. If GATT is, in fact, unable to rule, the complainant may be free to resort to "self-help" in some circumstances.

Table 3.6 Section 301: how aggressive, how unilateral?[a]

	GATT panel established	Potentially GATT-applicable but no panel		GATT not applicable
		Agricultural products	Manufactured products	
Retaliation imposed or publicly threatened	11	4	1	16
No public threat	11	11	10	8

a. Based on the data base described earlier in chapter 3.

Similarly, Chayes and Chayes (1993) argue that the defense of disobedience as a necessary evil "is based on the simple judgment that there are cases where the damage to the legal system caused by inaction in the face of deadlock will exceed the damage caused by some disobedient act trying to force a correction."

In 6 of the 11 cases involving GATT panels, the United States imposed retaliation, subsequently lifted in three. Hudec has noted that retaliation in the Japanese leather cases (nos. 13 and 36) probably would have been approved by GATT had it been asked to do so.[12] Moreover, in these cases increased US tariffs on Japanese exports of leather goods were a minor part of a much larger negotiated package of compensatory tariff cuts by Japan ($24 million out of a total compensation package worth an estimated $236 million). Hudec also suggests that US retaliation in three other cases—involving subsidized EC wheat flour (301-6) and pasta exports (301-25) and EC tariff preferences on citrus (301-11) that discriminated against US exports—was probably justified because they were examples of "legal breakdown" in the GATT. In these cases, the GATT dispute settlement process either was not allowed to operate—as in the pasta and citrus panels, where the European Community blocked progress at various stages—or was not able to come to a judgment, as in the wheat flour case.[13]

There were only five cases potentially subject to GATT rules that provoked US moves toward retaliation in the absence of GATT dispute settle-

---

12. A GATT panel ruled against Japan's quantitative restrictions (QRs) on raw leather in 1984. At a council meeting in July 1985, the United States asked for a ruling on Japan's QRs on leather footwear, which were part of the same program, based on the previous panel report. When the US request was rejected, a separate panel was appointed to consider the issue but was not convened before a settlement was reached.

13. US retaliation in the recent Canadian beer case (301-80) followed multiple GATT rulings against Canada's provincial restrictions on the sale of imported beer, wine, and liquor. Retaliation in this case cannot be blamed on international legal breakdown since Canada accepted the rulings. Instead, the retaliation was triggered by actions at the provincial level in Canada that the United States claimed undermined the integrity of the agreement.

ment procedures. (A case is defined here as potentially "GATTable" if it involves a GATT member and trade in goods—whether agricultural, industrial inputs, or manufactured.) Of those, four involved disputes with Europe over agriculture. Only one of these cases involved manufactured exports to a GATT contracting party: the Japanese semiconductors case (301-48). But in the other 21 potentially "GATTable" cases that were not taken before the GATT, the United States took no unilateral action, other than initiating the investigation.

Critics here and abroad are not so concerned about US retaliation without authorization in cases where there are valid complaints about GATT violations. They may not like it, but they usually recognize, like Hudec, that the system was not functioning effectively in the 1980s. What really enrages foreign governments is when the United States unilaterally determines that a foreign practice that violates no international agreement is "unreasonable," demands unilateral concessions, and unilaterally retaliates if the foreign government does not capitulate. In other words, the rest of the world does not appreciate it when the United States appoints itself judge, jury, and executioner.

Indeed, US negotiators have been aggressive in pursuing unilateral liberalization in areas not covered by GATT rules, either retaliating or threatening to do so in 16 of 24 cases involving non-GATT members or non-GATT issues. Even here, however, in only one of three cases in which section 301 retaliation was imposed did the retaliation violate US GATT obligations. In the Argentine hides case (301-24), the United States abrogated a bilateral agreement with Argentina when the Reagan administration concluded that Argentina was not fulfilling its commitments.[14] And, in the Canadian border broadcasting case (301-15), US retaliation was in the form of mirror legislation limiting the tax deductibility of advertising on Canadian stations by US firms. This legislation did not violate any GATT obligation, since services were not then covered.

The one clearly GATT-illegal retaliation in this area was the United States' raising of tariffs on $39 million worth of imports from Brazil after negotiations to change Brazil's policy on patent protection for pharmaceuticals failed (chapter 8). There were three other retaliatory actions in areas not covered by GATT rules, all involving the withdrawal of some Generalized System of Preferences (GSP) benefits from Thailand (two cases) and India for their lack of intellectual property protection.[15]

---

14. The retaliation involved raising the US tariff from the zero level negotiated bilaterally back to the level bound in GATT negotiations and thus did not violate US GATT obligations.

15. Most observers regard GSP as a privilege granted by the United States to developing countries that can be adjusted or withdrawn at US discretion without violating the GATT. Hudec argues, however, that the enabling clause, through which GATT gives permission for GSP, requires that the preferences be nondiscriminatory for all developing-country markets (personal communication, 7 July 1994).

This record suggests that USTR was aware of the potential systemic costs of violating the United States' existing GATT obligations in the course of trying to extend GATT rules in new areas and that USTR therefore exercised some restraint. In contrast, US behavior as a defendant in GATT disputes, unfortunately, tends to undermine the credibility of the US commitment to GATT reform.

In the context of developing his argument for "justified disobedience," Hudec emphasized that the credibility of US assertions that it is indeed concerned with strengthening the GATT, rather than simply seeking unilateral trade concessions from countries targeted under section 301, depended on its overall behavior. If US unilateralism is not to "spread cynicism" throughout the system regarding the value of GATT commitments (Bhagwati 1990, 35), it must be implemented in a broader context of support for the international system. One element of that support is the willingness of the United States to submit to the international law it is purportedly seeking to reform. In Hudec's view (1990b, 137–38), justified disobedience requires that

> . . . governments acting out of a concern to improve GATT law must necessarily respect that law as fully as possible, even when disobeying it. Accordingly, they must accept the power of the legal process to judge their disobedient behavior, and must accept the consequences imposed by law. In plain terms, the disobedient government must accept a panel proceeding promptly, cooperate in a prompt decision, abstain from blocking the decision, and accept a fair measure of retaliation without trying to punish the plaintiff.

Although US negotiators must be given credit for pushing hard to get the Uruguay Round started, to broaden its agenda, and to strengthen GATT rules, much US behavior in the GATT during the 1980s does not satisfy Hudec's criteria for credible justified disobedience. Hudec has extensively analyzed GATT dispute settlement in the 1970s and 1980s and concluded that, contrary to its self-projected white-knight image, the United States was among the worst offenders in the 1980s in terms of failing to comply with GATT dispute settlement procedures.

Among other things, Hudec found that "the United States is currently the worst offender, or tied for worst . . . [in] . . . blocking panels, blocking Council approval, and blocking retaliation authority" (1992, 33). He also concluded that the United States was responsible for by far the largest number of "negative outcomes" in dispute settlement proceedings. It refused to take remedial action in four cases where GATT panels had ruled for the other party. It imposed GATT-illegal retaliation in another five cases and, despite a legitimate GATT complaint by the victim, removed the retaliation only after arm twisting forced the victim to accede to US demands. Thus, the United States responded negatively to fully half (9 of 18) of the valid complaints brought against it in the 1980s. This record represents nearly two-thirds of all such negative outcomes in the

1980s. And finally, in cases it has lost, the United States has routinely delayed taking remedial action within the section 301 deadlines it expects of others (Hudec 1992, annex 3).

In defense of US negotiators, they did not control the outcomes in all of these cases. Three involved challenges to US retaliation in section 301 cases: Japanese semiconductors (discussions in several GATT Council meetings, but no panel requested by Japan), Brazilian intellectual property rights policy, and the EC hormone-fed beef ban, where each party blocked the other's request for a panel (see appendix). But other cases were political dynamite—such as the challenge by the Sandinista government in Nicaragua when the United States eliminated its sugar quota—or challenged US procedures in administrative trade cases that required legislative change to rectify. The need to pass legislation in order to remove the objectionable practice is another reason that US responses in some cases were so drawn out. Nevertheless, US credibility in its GATT reform campaign would have been considerably enhanced had it done as it wished others to do.

Domestic Politics, the Uruguay Round, and the Effects of Aggressive Unilateralism

The political and economic context in the 1980s must be kept in mind when evaluating the impact of section 301 on the international system. Defenders of 301 argue that aggressive unilateralism was necessary to enforce and strengthen GATT rules as part of the effort to fend off protection at home. Recall first that the GATT dispute settlement system was in severe disarray in the late 1970s and early 1980s (Hudec 1993, chapter 8). And second, the limited coverage of GATT rules made it seem increasingly irrelevant to large segments of the US business community and to many members of Congress. Given the unwillingness of America's trading partners in the first half of the decade to initiate a new multilateral round of trade negotiations to address these issues, US negotiators felt they had no choice but to negotiate the issues bilaterally, in some cases imposing a unilateral solution.

Observing that increased "enforcement" of international agreements is not without cost, Chayes and Chayes (1993, 203) argue that "[t]he US deployment of [section 301] against violators of GATT obligations reflects a unilateral political decision (1) that existing levels of compliance were not acceptable and (2) to pay the costs of additional enforcement." A situation that Chayes and Chayes believe may produce this political commitment is fear that "the tipping point [toward regime collapse] is close, so that enhanced compliance would be necessary for regime preservation" (202).

Several observers have pointed to the contentious 1982 GATT ministerial meeting as symbolic of the erosion of the international trading system, perhaps close to this "tipping point." Former Australian Ambassador to the GATT Alan Oxley (1990) called the 1982 ministerial "the nadir of the GATT." Similarly, Hudec has interpreted the ministerial—and in particular the refusal of the other parties to even consider the US proposal to negotiate rules in the new areas of services, investment, and intellectual property—as an important impetus for increased US unilateralism. Hudec (1990b, 130) observed that the US goal of market opening in these new areas:

> was often pursued in a fairly arrogant manner, but before condemning the entire operation it is worth asking ... [h]ow long would it have taken to persuade governments to accept the proposed Uruguay Round agenda? Indeed, what would happen to the Uruguay Round today if the threat of bilateral retaliation were removed entirely?

Observers as knowledgeable as former GATT head Arthur Dunkel have reportedly credited US unilateralism with saving the GATT, at least temporarily. Bhagwati (1993, 25) says that Dunkel "is supposed to have remarked [that] the best thing that the United States did for the GATT was to start down the 301 and Super 301 road, thus unifying an outraged and alarmed world behind the trading regime."

After President Reagan embraced a more aggressive, export-oriented trade policy in September 1985, it was another year before the Uruguay Round was finally launched. At the same time he adopted the activist trade policy, Reagan also directed Treasury Secretary James Baker to coordinate a depreciation of the dollar with key US trading partners. While recognizing that exchange rates and macroeconomic policy were the key to reducing the US trade deficit and that multilateral negotiations were the preferable forum for trade liberalization, the administration also recognized that those policies take time to work. Aggressive unilateralism helped the administration buy time until the dollar depreciation could affect the trade balance in 1987. In his thorough and careful analysis of US trade policy, I. M. Destler (1992, 131) characterized this "damage-limitation effort" as "at least a qualified success" in ensuring that the trade bill that finally passed in 1988 was one the administration could live with: "In the most unfavorable trade-political climate since 1930, [USTR] Yeutter and his aides had gotten the negotiating authority they needed [to complete the Uruguay Round], and had managed to neutralize—or modify—the most restrictive provisions."

Many critics, however, worried that the administration won the battle but lost the war. J. Michael Finger, for example, argues that section 301 fundamentally changed the internal US politics of multilateral trade negotiations. He suggests (1991, 20) that the more aggressive use of section 301 reduced US exporters' enthusiasm for the Uruguay Round because they no longer needed to support reciprocal reductions in US trade barriers as the quid pro quo for better access to foreign markets:

> The menace . . . of "301" is not that it serves US export interests but that it unchains them from the necessity to oppose US import-competing interests. It arms the US negotiator not with the authority to remove US import restrictions, but with the threat to impose new ones.

Thus, some fear that aggressive unilateralism may have been so successful that many traditional supporters of the GATT system—multinational corporations and other export interests—now feel they have an alternative that may even be preferable to the long, tedious negotiating rounds that typically precede multilateral liberalization.

Given the vigorous lobbying that most of American business is doing to ensure ratification of the Uruguay Round, this criticism seems overblown. There is one potential area for concern, however. Among the strongest proponents of aggressive unilateralism in the 1980s were the pharmaceutical, audiovisual, software, and chemical companies, which desperately wanted patent and copyright protection for their products. Intellectual property was included in the recent GATT agreement, but many of these companies believe the new rules are inadequate. It is possible they will continue to appeal to USTR to use section 301 to push some countries to move further and faster than GATT requires, possibly in violation of the new dispute settlement rules. If the ongoing sectoral market-access negotiations on services do not produce results, some services providers could take a similar tack.

In addition to expanding the agenda to services, investment, and intellectual property, US unilateralism also spurred heightened interest in strengthened GATT dispute settlement procedures. Ambassador Oxley (1990, 85) argued that "[o]ne of the primary interests of the European Community in the Uruguay Round was to secure greater commitment from the United States to use GATT procedures to handle trade disputes rather than resorting to unilateral action under its own trade legislation."

The dispute settlement area seems to be the clearest case of US pressure for reform having an impact on the GATT. US critics of the dispute settlement procedures noted that they permitted countries to delay or block establishment of panels to hear complaints and allowed defendants to block adoption of panel findings and the plaintiffs' requests for authority to retaliate.[16] In response to US and others' complaints, there were various procedural reforms, culminating in the 1988 Montreal Midterm Agreement, that speeded up the early stages of the process but did not resolve the problem of the defendants' veto over adoption of panel findings or authorization to retaliate (Hudec 1993, 231–33).

US negotiators continued to press for far-reaching reform, and by 1991 the parties reached an "understanding" that ". . . converted the GATT

---

16. For a wide-ranging summary of views and an assessment that "the most obvious and difficult issue facing the GATT is its members' lack of political will to cooperate on GATT matters," see US International Trade Commission (1985, 82).

dispute settlement procedure into a thoroughly automatic conveyer belt that took a legal claim from complaint to retaliation without any need to obtain the defendant's consent at any stage" (Hudec 1993, 237). Hudec attributes the dramatic reform in dispute settlement to the fact that:

> The United States had apparently made a convincing case that the US Congress would continue to insist on its new, bellicose, "take-the-law-into-your-own-hands" legal policy unless and until GATT had a legal enforcement procedure that met US standards of effectiveness. Governments [that] preferred a more cautious, more voluntary adjudication system had apparently persuaded themselves that the risk of unchecked US legal aggression was a greater danger that an excessively demanding GATT legal system.

Hudec and some other international law scholars fear that the GATT system and its members may not be ready for the new dispute settlement procedures. There are legitimate doubts about whether the more powerful traders, particularly the European Union and the United States, are truly prepared to subject themselves to the new discipline. There are also concerns about how well a strong dispute settlement system can adjudicate fights over the GATT's still relatively poorly defined trade rules, particularly those governing the new areas of services, investment, and intellectual property.

Overall, it seems fair to credit US leadership—including through unilateralism—with at least a modest role in preventing the collapse of the GATT dispute settlement system in the early 1980s and in prodding US trading partners into agreeing to initiate the Uruguay Round in 1986. To borrow a phrase from French economist Patrick Messerlin (as quoted in Finger and Nogues 1987, 713), one can characterize aggressive unilateralism's impact on the round this way: the United States viewed section 301 as a way to force GATT reform; the rest of the world viewed GATT reform as a way of restraining American use of section 301.[17]

A special meeting of GATT contracting parties was held in February 1989 to discuss unilateralism, with most of the discussion focusing on criticism of US policy. The United States defended itself by arguing that it "believed in the GATT multilateral process and was first among countries trying to strengthen it. [The United States] had been forced to act unilaterally because GATT was not strong enough, nor comprehensive enough, to do the job" (Hudec 1993, 230). Although the new rules negotiated in the Uruguay Round are far from perfect, further progress could be severely undermined if the Clinton administration misreads the lessons of the past. Aggressive unilateralism should continue to be a last resort, and it should continue to be clearly linked to further strengthening of the multilateral

---

17. Messerlin was referring to different US and non-American views on the purpose of the GATT subsidies code: the United States viewed the code as a way of restraining foreign subsidies; the rest of the world viewed the code as a way of restraining US countervailing duty actions.

regime. Otherwise, America's trading partners will view it simply as a bully that has forsaken global leadership to pursue narrow sectoral interests at the expense of global welfare—and its own.

The dangers of this path can be seen in the vociferous worldwide condemnation of US policy toward Japan in 1994 when US aggressive unilateralism was front and center, rather than being part of a broader trade policy pushing for both multilateral and minilateral *reciprocal* trade liberalization, as in 1993. Ultimately, whether these reform efforts pay off in the long run will depend on whether the United States ultimately embraces—for itself, as well as for others—the reforms for which it fought so hard. We return to these issues in chapter 13.

4

When and How Does Section 301 Open Markets?

In chapter 3 we concluded that section 301 had been a reasonably effective market-opening tool in the latter half of the 1980s. In this chapter, we consider some of the factors that contributed to its success. The first part of the chapter uses the data base of section 301 cases described in chapter 3 to draw general and suggestive conclusions about when section 301 is more or less likely to result in market opening. We use a historical approach that is shaped by bargaining theory. We study the pattern of variation across cases with different characteristics and outcomes in order to identify elements that contribute to success or failure. We have not tried to build from scratch a theoretical framework for analyzing the use of threats in trade negotiations. To do that and then to use it to evaluate section 301 would require knowing the counterfactual in each case: what would have happened in the absence of the threat? We believe there is much to learn from a straightforward categorization and cross-tabulation of the cases with respect to behavioral and other criteria. The final section discusses insights from the detailed case studies found in part II that could not be captured by the more formal testing of hypotheses in the first part of the chapter.

Insights from Bargaining Theory

Many trade negotiations involve an effort by all parties to realize joint gains by cooperating in lowering trade barriers. The Uruguay Round of multilateral trade negotiations under the General Agreement on Tariffs and Trade and the North American Free Trade Agreement are two prominent recent examples. The United States has not abandoned its commitment to cooperative bargaining, as demonstrated by its role in bringing the Uruguay Round to a successful close. But, as described chapters 1 and 2, the growing belief that past negotiations had resulted in a playing field tilted against the United States led to pressures in the 1980s to seek unilateral liberalization from US trading partners. John Odell (1993, 233) describes a distributive bargaining process as one in which

> . . . one state seeks actions by another without giving up anything in return, the other either maneuvers to minimize its concessions or counterattacks, and neither makes much effort to formulate new joint-gain arrangements.

Since the United States does not offer reciprocal market-opening concessions when it engages in distributive bargaining, its leverage derives from the threat, implicit or explicit, to close its own market to the target country's exports. The critical elements in the success or failure of these negotiations are, on one side, the value that the target country places on maintaining access to the US market and, on the other, the credibility of the US threat to retaliate. Threats typically "succeed" when the perceived economic and political costs to the target of complying with a demand are lower than the perceived costs of defiance.[1]

The direct costs of defiance for the target depend on the likely size of any US retaliation and the probability that it would actually be imposed if negotiations were to break down. Other, less tangible costs are the potential impact of the dispute on the country's overall relationship with the United States and, if the targeted trade barrier is a GATT violation, the effects of continued defiance on the credibility of the international trading system. The United States may also have concerns about these intangibles, which could undermine its credibility to retaliate in some cases.

The direct economic costs of compliance consist primarily of adjustment costs that would be borne by import-competing sectors if trade barriers are liberalized. US negotiators often argue, as do economists, that the net effect even of unilateral liberalization should in most cases be a welfare gain for the liberalizing country.[2] While negotiators on the other side of the table may privately concede the intellectual validity of this argument, they still must bring home an agreement that their domestic constituencies can ratify. As discussed at length in the trade literature, the perceived

---

1. Analyses of the elements of this calculus may be found in Cline (1982), McMillan (1990), Sykes (1990), and Oye (1992).

2. As discussed in chapter 8, improved protection of imported intellectual property may not improve the welfare of poorer less developed countries, which may be one factor explaining the low success rate in these cases.

political costs of liberalization often determine the outcomes of these debates, while economic logic may be largely irrelevant.

John McMillan (1990, 213) has used game-theoretic models to analyze 301-type negotiations and to identify conditions that, at the margin, can "shift the terms of agreement in the United States' favor." He concluded:

> This shift will be larger (a) the greater the harm to the targeted country from having its access to the U.S. market limited; (b) the smaller the targeted country's ability to harm the U.S. in retaliation; (c) the smaller the costs within the targeted country of complying with the U.S. demands; and (d) the greater the benefit to the United States—in the U.S. negotiators' perception—from the demanded liberalization.

These conditions set the general parameters for analyzing the efficacy of threats in trade negotiations, but as McMillan illustrates, the outcome in any given case relies heavily on each party's perception of the weight that the other side places on various outcomes. Since information is not perfect, interests often are not clearly defined, and the possibility of miscalculation or bluffs always exists, most analyses go on to examine the underlying factors that affect perceptions of cost and benefit, as well as negotiating tactics that might be used to enhance or undermine the credibility of a threat to retaliate.

The tactical mechanisms analyzed in the literature often follow Schelling (1960) in focusing on the role of commitment in making a threat credible (see Sykes 1990; Dixit 1987; Mann 1987). These analyses suggest that the more negotiators can either tie their own hands with respect to retaliating, or convince a negotiating partner that their hands are so tied, the more credible the threat to retaliate will be. The desire to enhance the credibility of US trade negotiators has been an important motivation behind many of the congressional amendments restricting presidential discretion under section 301. Among the tactical mechanisms adopted by Congress to enhance the credibility of section 301 threats are the setting of deadlines and the identification of circumstances that "shall" result in retaliation if satisfactory resolution of trade disputes cannot be achieved through negotiation.

Analyses of these tactics often assume that states act as rational, unitary actors. There is a burgeoning literature, however, on how domestic politics and divisions within countries can affect bargaining outcomes and, in turn, how international negotiations influence domestic political alignments to one party or the other's advantage.[3] John Odell (1993, 255) has formulated two key hypotheses regarding how domestic political configurations can affect bargaining outcomes:

---

3. See the cases in Evans, Jacobson, and Putnam, eds. (1993), especially the ones by Odell and Krauss; Schoppa (1993); and Mayer (1992).

The greater the internal opposition to carrying out a threat within the threatening nation itself, the lower the credibility, and the less likely the target capital will be to comply. Within the target nation, the greater the net internal political cost of compliance for the executive, relative to net internal political cost of no-agreement, the less likely the target government will be to accept agreement on the terms demanded.

In other words, the more united are interests in the threatening country and the more divided are interests in the targeted country, the more likely it is that the *demandeur* will get a more favorable agreement.

As argued in much of the recent literature on what Putnam has dubbed "two-level games," analyses that focus primarily either on the state as the central actor in international relations or on the role of domestic politics in influencing diplomacy will likely produce less-than-satisfying results. Putnam, Odell, and others in this genre are seeking to build a theory that integrates both approaches. We have culled from this literature hypotheses that appear to be particularly relevant to the section 301 experience. The following hypotheses will be examined here:

- The more concentrated the costs of the demanded policy change in the targeted country and the more diffuse the benefits, the less likely agreement will be (Evans 1993, 412–14). This hypothesis leads one to expect that, if an organized constituency already exists in the target country that would benefit from the policy change demanded, then the benefits may also be concentrated, and agreement will be more likely than otherwise.

- If a constituency in favor of change does not already exist in the target country, threats identifying potential targets of retaliation may spur previously inactive interest groups to enter the debate, tilting the political balance toward agreement.

- The more politicized the issue in the target country, the more likely it is that groups that do not care if the outcome is no agreement will enter the debate and constrain negotiators' flexibility (Putnam 1993, 446).

- Side payments may be used to buy off domestic groups that otherwise would oppose the agreement (Mayer 1992, 806–17).

Lessons from the Broad Survey of Section 301 Cases

The 72 cases described in chapter 3 constitute the data base used for the broad survey of section 301 results. Many of the hypotheses discussed above, particularly those dealing with domestic politics, could not feasibly be tested against all 72 cases in the data base. Those not included here are discussed in the section that follows, where lessons are drawn from the detailed case studies in part II of the book. We begin with McMillan's general conditions as to when section 301 is likely to be most effective and then identify a few tactical, political, or other variables that might be expected to affect bargaining outcomes in section 301 negotiations.

In the previous Institute for International Economics study of foreign policy sanctions, the first—and most obvious—variable identified as being potentially important in determining outcomes was the difficulty of the goal: the more difficult the goal, the less likely one would be to expect a positive outcome. In a statistical analysis of the foreign policy sanctions data base, Elliott and Uimonen (1993, 406) confirmed this hypothesis: the variable representing the difficulty of the sanctioner's goal in each case was significant at the 95 percent confidence level and had the expected sign. Attempts to define a similar variable in this study failed to find any consistent patterns in the data, however. This may be because, as some observers argue, only the hard cases ever become section 301 investigations (see the discussion in chapter 3). It may also be that we simply did not hit upon an illuminating definition. Additional research on this question would be useful.

As noted by McMillan (1990), each party's bargaining strategy will also be affected by its perceived vulnerability to retaliation or counterretaliation. In what follows, the target country's vulnerability to US retaliation is represented by the share of the target's GNP that is accounted for by exports to the United States. It is expected that the higher this ratio, the higher the odds of a successful outcome for US negotiators.

Since most US trading partners invoke public retaliatory threats in trade negotiations far less often than has the United States in recent years, the willingness of a country to respond aggressively to US threats seemed to us an important component in measuring US vulnerability to counterretaliation. Japan is a large country and one with which the United States trades extensively. But it rarely threatens to retaliate, rarely even raises GATT challenges to US behavior, and has never come close to actually retaliating. Therefore, a simple continuous variable, such as the size of the target or the proportion of US trade conducted with the target, did not seem adequate to capture US negotiators' likely *perceptions* regarding US vulnerability to counterretaliation. Instead, in this study, we use a dummy variable that is set equal to 1 if the target has ever retaliated against the United States in a trade dispute and 0 otherwise.

The choice of this variable is based on the assumption that these are the only targets to which the United States attaches a positive probability of counterretaliation. In this sample, as it turns out, the dummy is positive only for three targets: the European Union, which is the only US trading partner to counterretaliate in the context of a section 301 case; Canada, which has "retaliated" (taken "compensatory withdrawal" of concessions granted to the United States) in the context of escape clause cases (as has the Union); and China, which counterretaliated in a dispute over textile quotas. All three also regularly threaten to counterretaliate in trade disputes with the United States.

Defining variables to represent McMillan's other two conditions—concerning the relative values that each negotiator places on various outcomes—is much harder since the task would require extensive knowledge about political coalitions in each of the 72 cases. Circumstances affecting the costs of compliance in the target will be explored in the section examining the detailed case studies. From the perspective of the United States, one variable that might be used to proxy for the value to US negotiators of getting an agreement is the bilateral trade balance with the target country. The hypothesis here is that the larger the US bilateral trade deficit with a country, the greater will be political pressure from Congress and the private sector to attack trade barriers aggressively in that country. This might allow negotiators to more plausibly argue that their hands are tied with respect to what constitutes an acceptable outcome and thereby make retaliatory threats more credible.

Tactics also can enhance a negotiator's credibility and increase bargaining leverage. For example, failure to carry out a public threat can have worse consequences for a negotiator's reputation, thus weakening her effectiveness in future negotiations, than not carrying out an implicit or private threat. In the 301 context, announcement of a presidential finding of an unfair practice, with a specific deadline for action, ties the negotiators to some degree and may make the previously implicit threat more credible. On the other hand, as Kenneth Oye (1992) and others have pointed out, making a threat public may also raise the perceived costs of compliance for the targeted government if it fears setting a precedent for future negotiations. Thus in some cases, implicit threats, including the threat to initiate a 301 investigation, may be as effective or even more so than public threats. Unfortunately, private and implicit threats often are unobservable and thus cannot be consistently measured or systematically modeled.

The US Trade Representative's initiation of section 301 investigations (relevant only since 1985) might also have a credibility-enhancing effect by signaling that USTR places a high priority on a case. In the debate over the omnibus trade bill in 1987 and 1988, the Reagan administration argued that making USTR initiation of some cases mandatory would lessen the impact of self-initiation since such cases "currently had clout because they were extraordinary" and signaled to target governments "that the administration meant business" (Bello and Holmer 1990, 83–85). Essentially, making a threat public raises the costs to US negotiators of backing down, because it affects their credibility in future negotiations and may increase the probability that a threat will be carried out if a satisfactory bargain is not struck.

Another of the hypotheses discussed above regarding domestic politics had to do with ways of increasing political participation by groups in the target country that may support the US position in the negotiations. This could be done positively—for example, by publicizing the fact that Japanese consumers pay much higher prices for food as a result of the government's agricultural trade policies—or negatively, by identifying explicitly the products that will be retaliated against if no agreement is reached. An explicit threat makes it clear who will pay the costs of retaliation and raises the costs of defiance for the target country government if those sectors become politically mobilized.

The hypotheses regarding the role of threats in enhancing a negotiator's credibility are tested by creating a dummy variable set equal to 1 if USTR or the president issues a formal finding that an unfair practice exists (with a deadline for action), publishes a retaliation "hit list," or initiates a case; otherwise it is 0. The negative version of the "participation expansion" hypothesis will also be tested separately by creating a dummy variable that takes the value 1 if a retaliation "hit list" was published in a case, and 0 otherwise. The positive version of the "participation expansion" hypothesis is analyzed in the section examining lessons from the detailed case studies (see also Schoppa 1993).

A GATT panel finding of noncompliance with international rules is another means by which a negotiator can try to influence the target country's calculations of the costs and benefits of various outcomes. By adding international opprobrium to unilateral US condemnation or by damaging the country's reputation for abiding by its commitments, a negative GATT ruling can increase the costs of defiance. Use of the GATT dispute settlement process might also lower the costs of compliance by providing domestic political cover for the target country government, allowing a change in policy to be interpreted as fulfilling its international obligations rather than as caving in to US pressure. To test the hypothesis that GATT rules make a difference in determining outcomes, we compare cases in which a GATT panel ruled against a targeted government, at least in part, with those where there was no ruling.

Finally, it might be expected that the likelihood of a negotiated agreement resulting in genuine market opening would be affected by the type of trade barrier being discussed. Traditional border measures—tariffs and import and export quotas on goods—may be relatively easier to negotiate because they are more transparent, objectives are easier to define, and because such barriers are more likely to be clearly GATT-illegal. Transparency may also make agreements to eliminate or reduce such barriers easier to monitor and enforce. Other types of barriers—subsidies, state trading, technical standards—may be less transparent and their impact harder to measure, perhaps leading to agreements that are more difficult to enforce. To test this hypothesis, another dummy variable was created, scored as a 1 if the trade barrier in dispute was a tariff or an import or export quota and 0 otherwise.

General Results

To briefly reiterate the results presented in chapter 3, we concluded that US negotiating objectives were at least partially achieved 49 percent of the time overall (in 35 of 72 section 301 cases). Between September 1985 and the end of 1992, 60 percent of all cases resolved resulted in achievement of some or all of the US negotiating objectives (26 of 43) compared with just under a third from 1975 through the first half of 1985 (9 of 29). The general results with regard to the factors contributing to a successful section 301 negotiation are presented here. The next section discusses the results for the more recent period and possible factors contributing to the increased effectiveness of section 301 since announcement of President Reagan's Trade Policy Action Plan in September 1985.

In addition to doing simple tabulations to see which of these variables appear to be correlated with success, we also used the probit regression technique to establish the relative importance of the independent variables in determining successful outcomes.[4] The results suggest that a successful outcome is more likely the more dependent the target country is on the US market, the larger the US bilateral deficit with the target is, and the more transparent the targeted trade barrier is. There is some evidence that success is less likely if the target has a record of counterretaliating against US exports in trade disputes, but the result is not statistically significant. Surprisingly, neither public nor explicit threats, as we have defined them, appear to affect outcomes in section 301 cases. The cross-tabulations are contained in table 4.1; table 4.2 summarizes the regression results.

The results suggest that vulnerability of the target to US trade retaliation, as measured by its dependence on the US market for its exports, is an important factor in explaining outcomes. The average target-country export dependence in successful cases was 7.5 percent of GNP versus 4.3 percent in failures (table 4.1). In the regression analysis, the coefficient for this variable (TXDEP) was significant at the 95 percent level and robust (model 1 in table 4.2). It is not clear whether US concerns about possible counterretaliation played much of a role in these cases. Table 4.1 shows that cases that targeted the European Community, Canada, or China (countries that have counterretaliated against the United States) generated positive results only about 35 percent of the time, as compared with a success rate of 57 percent in all other cases. But the coefficient for the dummy variable used to represent US counterretaliation concerns (COUNTER), while negative as expected, is not statistically significant.

---

4. The probit technique was chosen because it is more appropriate than ordinary least-squares regression for equations with a dichotomous dependent variable such as success/failure. See Bayard and Elliott (1992) for an amplified discussion of why we chose this technique and Pindyck and Rubinfeld (1981, 274–87) for a detailed description of the probit technique.

Table 4.1 Characteristics of section 301 successes and failures
(number of cases, unless otherwise noted)

	Number of successes (35 cases)	Number of failures (37 cases)	Successes as a percentage of total number of cases
Average target export dependence (target country exports to US as a percentage of target's GNP)	7.5	4.3	
US counterretaliation concern (cases involving EC, Canada, China)	9	17	35
No counterretaliation concern	26	20	57
US bilateral trade deficit with target	$15 billion	$2 billion	
Border measure targeted	19	6	76
Other barriers targeted	16	31	34
Public or explicit threat[a]	20	18	53
USTR-initiated	13	6	68
Other public threats	5	4	56
Retaliation imposed[b]	2	10	17
No known threat	15	19	44
GATT ruling against target	7	6	54
Excluding the EC	5	2	71
No GATT panel convened	24	27	47
GATT not applicable	11	15	42
GATT case involving a border measure	10	3	77
GATT case involving other types of barriers	1	7	13
Cases ending:			
Before September 1985	9	20	31
After September 1985	26	17	60
Other			
Target's exports to US as percent of total			
Greater than 30 percent	20	6	77
Less than 30 percent	15	31	33
Average US exports to target	$110 million	$224 million	
US exports to target			
Less than $10 million	8	10	44
Between $10 million and $100 million	16	12	57
Between $100 million and $1 billion	11	12	48
Greater than $1 billion	0	3	0

a. Subcategories do not add to this total because of overlap among the categories of types of threats.

b. Failures include partial withdrawal of GSP benefits in three intellectual property cases.

Table 4.2 Probit regression results

Independent variable	Model 1			Model 2			Model 3		
	Coefficient	Standard error	T-statistic[a]	Coefficient	Standard error	T-statistic[a]	Coefficient	Standard error	T-statistic[a]
Constant	−0.95	0.35	−2.69*	−0.83	0.37	−2.22*	−0.53	0.43	−1.24
TXDEP	5.08	3.05	1.67**	6.35	3.06	2.08*	6.28	3.22	1.95**
COUNTER	−0.14	0.42	−0.33	0.02	0.46	0.05	0.09	0.46	0.18
TBAL	−0.000055	0.000017	−3.36*	−0.000040	0.000015	−2.62*	−0.000004	0.000002	−2.72*
HITLIST	−0.83	0.46	−1.83**						
TPAP				−1.06	0.46	−2.31*	−1.42	0.53	−2.68*
TBILL							−0.73	0.50	−1.46***
RULING	−0.43	0.58	−0.74	−1.06	0.62	−1.71*	−1.18	0.63	−1.87**
BORDER	1.70	0.45	3.74*	2.09	0.52	4.05*	2.21	0.54	4.10*
Log likelihood	−30.28			−29.10			−27.99		
Percentage of cases correctly predicted	82			83			83		

TBAL = US trade balance with the target
COUNTER = 1 if target has retaliated against US in a trade dispute, 0 otherwise
HITLIST = 1 if retaliation hit list issued in case, 0 otherwise
TPAP = 1 if case ended before September 1985, 0 otherwise
TBILL = 1 if case initiated after August 1988, 0 otherwise
TXDEP = target's exports to US as a percentage of GNP
RULING = 1 if case involved a GATT panel ruling, 0 otherwise
BORDER = 1 if there is a border measure affecting goods (import and export quotas, and tariffs), 0 otherwise

a. Using a one-tailed t-test, * indicates significance at the 99 percent level, ** at the 95 percent level, and *** indicates significance at the 90 percent level.

The size of the bilateral trade balance between the United States and the target country turns out to have strong explanatory power in this analysis. The average US bilateral trade balance in successes was -$15 billion in successes and -$2 billion in failures.[5] The regression analysis confirms that the more negative the US trade balance with a target, the more likely a successful outcome. The coefficient on this variable (TBAL) is significant at the 99 percent level and robust.

The simple tabulation in table 4.1 and the regression results reported in table 4.2 also strongly support the hypothesis that transparent border measures are the more likely type of barrier to be liberalized as a result of section 301 negotiations. Seventy-six percent of cases targeting border measures were successfully resolved versus only 34 percent of other types of cases. The regression results for this variable (BORDER) are also statistically significant (at the 99 percent level) and robust.

The variables we defined to represent the use of threats to enhance credibility or to tilt the political balance in the target country performed less well than expected. The success rate for all cases involving public or explicit threats is barely above 50 percent, as compared with 44 percent when there was no known threat. The variable representing threats generally (including USTR initiation, formal determinations with deadlines, or hit lists) was not close to being significant in the regression analysis, and that result is not even reported in table 4.2. The HITLIST variable was significant at the 95 percent level but unexpectedly had a negative sign.

Cases initiated by USTR did have a somewhat higher success rate: 68 percent versus 40 percent for other cases (table 4.1). So we created a third dummy variable to indicate USTR-initiated cases (INITIATE). Since USTR initiation has only been relevant since 1985, we had to split the sample at that point to run regressions using the INITIATE variable. The sign is positive as expected in this model, but the coefficient is still not significant and the results are not reported in table 4.2.

Closer inspection of the data, however, reveals a few nuances that are worth noting. First, contrary to what might be expected, USTR has not tried to enhance its reputation or popularity with Congress by picking easy cases that it knew it could win. Five of the six USTR-initiated cases that ended in failure involved nontraditional issues—intellectual property, services, or investment—that are anything but easy to negotiate, as demonstrated in the Uruguay Round, but which have been high congressional and private-sector priorities (also see chapter 8 on intellectual property). Second, USTR initiation does appear to have been helpful in negotiations with the European Community. USTR initiation made little difference in non-EC cases. Strikingly, however, the success rate for cases targeting the Community increased from 25 percent to 75 percent if a

---

5. If Japan is excluded from this calculation, the absolute value of the difference is smaller but the relative difference is even greater: − $6 billion in successes and -$77 million in failures.

case was initiated by USTR. Given the cumbersome EU decision-making process, especially with regard to the Common Agricultural Policy (CAP), it may be that high-profile actions such as USTR initiation are necessary to capture policymakers' attention.

Unexpectedly, GATT procedures do not appear to add much leverage: the success rate for cases in which a GATT panel ruled against a target's policies (54 percent) was not significantly different from that for cases in which there was no GATT ruling or GATT rules were not applicable (47 percent). But there is still evidence of some deference to GATT rules in these cases. In every case where a GATT panel found a violation or evidence of nullification and impairment, changes in the offending policy were made. In almost half, however, the target country replaced the illegal trade barrier with another type of barrier or disagreed with the US interpretation of what had been agreed.

Two other aspects of these cases should be noted. First, many GATT rules are not clearly defined. Second, many of these cases attempted to attack EC policies under CAP, reform of which many observers believed would only come about through negotiation, not through legal adjudication (Paarlberg 1986). The success rate for cases involving GATT panels that also targeted border measures is significantly higher (77 percent) than in cases where the panel had to grapple with less transparent barriers (34 percent). Unfortunately, there is no way of determining whether the strong performance of the BORDER variable is due primarily to the transparency of the barrier or to the greater clarity of GATT rules in those cases.

There is also a stronger positive correlation between GATT dispute settlement procedures and success if the European Community is excluded. Cases with GATT rulings, other than those involving the Community, were successful 71 percent of the time (vs. 54 percent overall). Cases involving GATT rulings against the European Community ultimately were judged to be failures on five of eight occasions. Each time the Community changed the offending practice, but it exploited ambiguities in GATT or the bilateral agreements to continue to protect its agricultural producers and processors.

Section 301 since the 1985 Trade Policy Action Plan

Though only a third of section 301 cases were satisfactorily resolved from 1975 to September 1985, three-fifths have been at least partially successful since then. Some observers have speculated that this is because USTR began accepting and initiating more "easy," winnable cases. Consistent with that theory, table 4.3 shows a decrease in the proportion of cases targeting the European Community since 1985 and an increase in the number of cases involving countries against which the United States had the most success even before 1985: Japan, Korea, and Taiwan.

Table 4.3 Effectiveness of section 301 before and after September 1985

	1975–September 1985 (29 cases)		Since September 1985 (43 cases)		Percent change in	
	Percentage of total in each category	Successes/ total in category	Percentage of total in each category	Successes/ total in category	Proportion of cases in each category	Success rate
By target						
EC	34	1/10	23	6/10	−32.6	500
Japan, Korea, Taiwan	28	5/8	37	14/16	34.9	40
Other countries	38	3/11	40	6/17	4.2	29
Tactics						
Public threats	14	0/4	79	20/34	473.3	n.a.
GATT panels	24	2/7	33	9/14	34.9	125
Other						
Border measures	41	7/12	30	12/13	−26.9	58
US share of total target exports greater than 30 percent	28	5/8	42	15/18	51.7	33

n.a. = not applicable

A number of US trade officials we interviewed noted that USTR exercised more careful screening of prospective cases and consulted more closely with potential industry petitioners after 1985. The so-called P-list, which lists section 301 petitions withdrawn or rejected by USTR before any investigation is initiated, supports the notion that USTR screened cases more rigorously after 1985. From 1980 through 1984, only four petitions were filed and then withdrawn or rejected. From September 1985 through 1990, petitioners withdrew 16 petitions, and USTR declined to initiate investigations in seven more. The proportion of petitions filed that USTR accepted declined from 85 percent in the early 1980s to 60 percent in the latter half of the decade. A number of experienced trade negotiators believe that this informal screening improved the quality and timing of cases and thus increased the likelihood of success, not just in cases involving "easy" targets, but overall. It should be noted that the success rate after 1985 rose for all targets and actually rose the most for cases involving the European Community (table 4.3). After all, there is a difference between weeding out "bad" cases and accepting only "easy" cases.

Table 4.3 also provides evidence of the increased aggressiveness in prosecuting 301 cases after 1985. The proportion of cases involving public or explicit threats increased by 65 percentage points. The success rate for cases involving threats also jumped sharply, from zero in the earlier period to 59 percent after 1985. But the success rate for cases with no public threat was even higher—67 percent after 1985 (up from 34 percent). Thus both success rates and the use of public threats increased sharply after announcement of President Reagan's Trade Policy Action Plan (TPAP), but there is little statistical evidence of a causal relationship between public threats and success.

An alternative hypothesis is that, while individual public threats were not significant in determining outcomes, there was a general change in USTR's attitude toward section 301 and the tactics used that improved credibility and contributed to an increase in the odds of obtaining a successful outcome. To test whether the Trade Policy Action Plan, which launched USTR's more aggressive tactics, is correlated with the increased effectiveness of section 301, another dummy variable was created. TPAP is set equal to 1 if a case was concluded before September 1985 and 0 otherwise; a negative coefficient is expected for this variable.[6] As shown in table 4.2 (model 2), the coefficient for TPAP is negative as expected and is significant at the 99 percent confidence level.

---

6. The end date of cases is used for TPAP because several lengthy cases that had been initiated in the late 1970s and early 1980s were concluded only after adoption of the more aggressive strategy in the fall of 1985. In fact, three of those cases—exports to Japan of leather and nonrubber footwear and exports of canned fruit to the European Community— were resolved as part of the action plan, when President Reagan ordered USTR to prepare retaliation hit lists if the cases were not resolved before 1 December of that year.

As shown in table 3.4, however, the effectiveness of section 301 was greatest in 1985–88 and actually declined in the years following passage of the 1988 Trade Act. Another dummy variable, TBILL—set equal to 1 if the case was initiated after the signing of the congressional trade bill in August 1988 and 0 otherwise—was added to model 2. As expected from the results in table 3.4, the coefficient for TBILL is negative. It is also significant at the 90 percent confidence level, but the result is not robust.[7] Nevertheless, these results suggest that, contrary to conventional wisdom, the provisions of the 1988 Trade Act, including super 301, did not improve the chances of achieving a successful outcome relative to the administrative and attitudinal changes adopted in 1985. Whether the decline in effectiveness is reversed probably depends in part on the type of case investigated in the future. As noted in table 3.4, the success rate is a quite respectable 60 percent if cases targeting inadequate protection for intellectual property rights are excluded.

Lessons from the Detailed Case Studies

Two key hypotheses regarding the role of domestic politics in international negotiations have been developed at length in Odell (1993) through studies of the Brazil informatics policy (301-49) and EC enlargement (301-54) cases. The first says that the more united US negotiators and their political supporters, the more credible retaliatory threats will be, and the higher the chances of a successful outcome. The second says that the higher the political costs of compliance in the target country, the lower the likelihood of getting a satisfactory agreement. A subsidiary hypothesis is that when a constituency exists in the target country that would benefit from the policy change demanded, the costs of compliance for the target government will be lower to the extent that sector engages in lobbying activity that partly or wholly offsets the lobbying of the sector that expects to lose from the policy change.

When there is no constituency favoring change for its own reasons, then retaliatory threats by the demanding country to mobilize previously uninvolved sectors in the target country may become more important. There is always a risk, however, that such threats will backfire and so politicize the issue that the target government finds it impossible to conclude an acceptable agreement. Finally, side payments to buy off the constituencies that will suffer from the policy change may also be useful in facilitating an agreement.

Aside from the explicit retaliatory threat hypothesis, the information requirements were simply too extensive to allow us to test the other

---

7. TBILL and TPAP are negatively correlated, and if TPAP is dropped, the sign on the coefficient for TBILL is still negative but is insignificantly different from zero.

domestic-politics hypotheses against all 72 cases in the section 301 data base. But the detailed case studies in part II, along with the case studies by Odell and another on the Japanese semiconductor case (Krauss 1993), do provide support for some of these hypotheses.[8] The cases are arrayed in table 4.4 according to outcome and the general political conditions identified by Odell regarding unity of purpose in both the *demandeur* and target countries.

Table 4.4 supports the hypothesis that a concentrated and vocal constituency for change in the target country improves the odds for US negotiators: all four of the cases where that was true were mostly successful. In the Japanese satellites and financial services cases, the US side was divided to some degree because US firms that had successfully penetrated the Japanese market feared possible retribution if US negotiators pushed too hard for further liberalization (US firms may also have feared losing excess profits gained from operating in a protected market). These divisions were offset, however, by divisions on the Japanese side: NTT, NHK, and other satellite users balked at the government's desire to develop an indigenous satellite production capability because of the greater expense and lower reliability of domestically made satellites, while Japanese security firms opposed the big Japanese banks' efforts to keep the government bond market largely to themselves in the Schumer amendment case (see chapters 5 and 11).

The importance of a strong pro-change constituency in the target country is also illustrated by recent developments in India and Korea. As described in chapter 6, India refused to make any concessions on its foreign investment and insurance barriers when it was designated a super 301 priority in 1989. In South Korea, support for liberalization, outside of the technocratic elite that negotiated the agreement in 1989 to avoid super 301 designation, was both narrow and shallow, and it quickly collapsed when economic conditions soured in 1990. In recent years, however, both countries have elected leaders committed to change who have either undertaken or are trying to implement significant liberalization (particularly in the investment area), without the super 301 sword hanging over their heads. As in Brazil following Fernando Collor de Mello's election in 1990, it is simply easier to push on an open door (chapter 6).

Not surprisingly, no agreement at all was reached in the two cases where there was no sympathetic constituency in the target and the US side was divided. Odell's (1993) study of the Brazilian informatics policy case illustrates how a unified position in favor of retaliation in the demanding country can tilt an outcome in US negotiators' favor. Odell divides

---

8. The oilseeds dispute with the European Union (chapter 9) does not appear in the table because it is complicated by the linkages to the broader agricultural deal in the Uruguay Round.

Table 4.4 Role of political factors in outcomes of 15 case studies

Political factor	Success	Partial success	Nominal success	No agreement
Pro-change constituency in target				
United US position	Brazil super 301 EC banking directive			
Divided US position	Japanese satellites Schumer amendment			
No or weak pro-change constituency in target				
United US position	Japanese beef and citrus EC enlargement	Brazil informatics II Japanese supercomputers Japanese wood products Taiwan super 301	Korea super 301 Brazil pharmaceuticals Japanese semiconductors	Indian insurance
Divided US position				Indian investment Brazil informatics I

this case into two phases. In the first phase (Informatics I in table 4.4), US computer and software firms were divided as to the wisdom of retaliation; as in the Schumer and satellite cases, firms that were already in Brazil opposed the US government position. Brazilian negotiators were aware of this division and refused to make any concessions. In the second phase (Informatics II), US industry came together in support of retaliation, and some modest concessions were garnered from Brazil (thus advancing the case from an outcome of failure to one of partial success; see table 4.4).

Most of the cases fall in the area where there was no organized or only a weak pro-change constituency in the target country but the American side was united. In these cases, with no help from a target country constituency that would benefit from change and that was organized and able to lobby for it, the implicit or explicit threat of American retaliation might be expected to play a larger role. Yet, as in the earlier empirical work, there is scant correlation between the presence or absence of public or explicit threats and the outcomes in these cases.

The US announcement of specific retaliation accompanied by tight deadlines for implementation appears to have contributed to success (without retaliation) in the EC enlargement case. Publication of a specific retaliation hit list, in conjunction with changing private-sector views, may also have contributed to a successful outcome in the second phase of the Brazilian informatics case. But the imposition of retaliation did not move the Brazilian government to change its pharmaceutical patent policy, an issue that often becomes quite politicized (chapter 8). In the Japanese semiconductor case, not only was there no vocal constituency in Japan in favor of liberalization, the main constituency injured by compliance with US demands was often the same group that had to implement the agreement: vertically integrated Japanese firms that both produce and use semiconductors. The US market share did improve following the imposition of sanctions in 1987, but it did not reach the demanded 20 percent level until after the original agreement had expired, and then only after additional threats of retaliation.

The hypothesis in Mayer (1992) that side payments can facilitate agreement also helps to explain the outcomes in the EC enlargement and Japanese beef and citrus cases. In addition to lobbying from sectors fearing possible retaliation in those cases, side payments were provided by the target country governments to ensure that those agreements could be ratified. Side payments of a sort were also provided in the Japanese supercomputer case, where increased government procurement budgets allowed Japanese firms to increase prices (and profits) and still win contracts. The American Forest Products Association has also alleged (in a submission to USTR calling for closer monitoring of the 1990 agreement) that the Japanese government has increased subsidies to the wood products sector, but the data are not definitive on that question.

By contrast, there is no evidence that side payments were even considered in any of the cases in which there was no target-country constituency in favor of change and US negotiators achieved no or only illusory success. All of these cases were highly politicized in the target countries. Thus the governments either chose the no-agreement option, because the political costs of compliance were too high, or miscalculated and concluded an agreement that it was subsequently unable to ratify—whether formally, as in the Brazil pharmaceuticals case, where legislation has not passed the Brazilian Congress, or informally, as in the Japanese semiconductors case, where grudging cooperation from private firms fell short of US expectations.

II

Case Studies of Aggressive Unilateralism

5

Super 301: Japan

Supercomputers and Satellites

The supercomputer and the satellite super 301 cases, launched in 1989, were responses to alleged Japanese "targeting" of high-technology industries in which US producers were very competitive.[1] The United States claimed in both cases that Japan excluded US firms from public procurements to promote its nascent domestic industries.

US concerns were threefold. First, many in the US public and private sectors were anxious to prevent a repeat of Japan's perceived successes in targeting sectors such as steel, autos, machine tools, semiconductors, and electronics.[2] It was believed that the Japanese government had provided these favored industries with a wide array of assistance—subsidies, cheap capital, protection—that helped them grow from inefficient infants into fierce global competitors. This targeting was thought to have undermined US competitiveness and cost the American economy jobs and profits.

Both supercomputer and satellite manufacturers are said to benefit from economies of mass production. Failure to crack the Japanese government

---

1. For the basic conceptual argument on how the United States might respond to foreign targeting, see Krugman (1984a and b; 1987b) and Dixit (1987). Krugman cautions (1984b, 101) that the appropriate US response is an empirical question requiring detailed information about the industry in question and warns that his conceptual arguments can be misused ". . . to defend any and all accusations against foreign countries."

2. See Balassa and Noland (1988, 35–42) for discussion of Japanese industrial policy and Mastanduno (1992) on USTR's decision to select supercomputers and satellites.

procurement market therefore allegedly prevented US producers from achieving maximum cost competitiveness and denied them revenues to finance R&D for future products. Thus, US export promotion of supercomputers and satellites in the short run was also intended to protect these US industries against Japanese competition in US or third-country markets in the longer run.

Second, the supercomputer and satellite industries are considered "strategic" industries because of their very high profits, beneficial spin-offs, and/or linkages to other sectors of the economy.[3] Supercomputers, for example, are thought to enhance US competitiveness because they are used in research, design, and production, particularly in the automotive, aerospace, chemical, pharmaceutical, and petroleum sectors.[4] More generally, research and development in the satellite and supercomputer industries might create knowledge that is useful in other parts of the economy. Thus it was argued that the US government should care about the economic health and size of these two industries, not just for their own sakes, but also because of their broader impact.

A third concern was that the supercomputer and satellite industries were important to US national defense and security, including the Department of Energy's nuclear weapons and NASA's aerospace programs. Both industries owe much of their early development to government purchases and government-financed R&D. It was believed that maintaining the commercial viability of these industries benefited national security by reducing reliance on potentially insecure foreign supply sources, both for these products and other high-technology goods; sustaining civilian production capacity that could be mobilized in time of national emergency; and lowering the cost of government procurement, to the extent that economies of scale or scope existed or costs of R&D could be shifted to the private sector.

The negotiations in both cases led to somewhat improved market access and thus benefited US producers, at least modestly. However, the agreements also set precedents that some US government agencies and industries may find objectionable in the longer run. In both cases, the United States acknowledged the principle of reciprocal market access for Japanese producers in US government procurement. The US government market for both products, although formally open, has been closed in practice to foreign suppliers, primarily on national security grounds. With the end of the Cold War and growing international competition in high-technology industries, Japan and Europe may challenge this de facto exclusion in the future.

---

3. Defense specialists use the term "strategic" to describe industries that produce goods and services for national security purposes. However, we use "strategic" only in the context of competitiveness.

4. On the commercial use of supercomputers, see General Accounting Office (1991).

The satellite and supercomputer cases may have also reinforced the US goal of expanding the coverage of the government procurement code in the Uruguay Round. At the very least, the cases sent a message that the United States was prepared to act unilaterally to force open hitherto closed public procurements. US negotiators took care to ensure that both agreements were consistent with the GATT procurement code and that the markets were opened on a nondiscriminatory basis, although the United States is the dominant supplier of both products.

Supercomputers[5]

US and Japanese Policies

The US government has played the central role in creating and sustaining the American supercomputer industry[6] (box 5.1). Supercomputers were initially developed in the early 1970s to meet national security needs. For example, they are used in the design and testing of nuclear weapons, military ships, and aircraft and in intelligence-gathering activities such as code breaking and analysis of huge masses of information. In the 1980s and 1990s, the government has played a growing role in making supercomputers accessible to the scholarly and business communities to promote scientific and commercial applications.[7] Since the 1970s, the government has provided many hundreds of millions of dollars for research and development of hardware and software and is the largest single buyer of supercomputers themselves, spending several billion dollars over the years. In essence, the United States has an industrial policy that favors the supercomputer industry.

Between the mid-1970s and 1983, only US firms, primarily Cray Research, Inc. and Control Data Corporation, sold supercomputers.[8] In 1983 two Japanese firms, Hitachi and Fujitsu, entered the market, having received substantial Japanese government funding for research and development. NEC entered the market in 1985. Some observers believe that Japanese government support by the Ministry of International Trade and Industry (MITI) and Nippon Telephone and Telegraph (NTT) for very large-scale integrated circuits (VLSI) in the 1970s was "a critical ingredient

---

5. The primary references for this section are the 1991 Office of Technology Assessment study by Marie Anchordoguy (hereafter OTA 1991) and Tyson (1992). Anchordoguy's excellent study is essential reading on the supercomputer dispute, and our debt to it is obvious from the number of times we cite it.

6. For a history of supercomputers until the mid-1980s, see Kozmetsky (1987).

7. The High-Performance Computing Act of 1991 recommends government support for supercomputing of $2.9 billion over fiscal years 1992–96.

8. Control Data Corporation's supercomputer subsidiary ETA entered the market in 1983 and exited in 1989. Cray Research, Inc. spun off Cray Computer Corporation in 1989.

Box 5.1 What is a supercomputer?[1]

There is no generally accepted definition of a supercomputer, except the somewhat frivolous: the fastest machine available at any given time. Three different machines are described as supercomputers: large-scale supercomputers, vector processors, and minisupercomputers. The market for all supercomputers grew by about 30 percent annually in the 1980s.

Large-scale supercomputers are designed for large, complex numerical calculations. They are typically many times faster than a mainframe computer. The definition of fast changes quickly: present-day processor chips in some desktop computers are nearly as fast as the supercomputers of the 1970s. The main producers are Cray Research, Inc., Fujitsu, NEC, and Hitachi. The global market for these machines in the late 1980s was about $1 billion annually. Prices range from a few million to $30 million.

Vector processors are mainframes with the addition of a set of high-speed processors. IBM is the leading producer, and the market in the late 1980s was estimated at $100 million annually. Unit prices range from $1 million to $2 million.

Minisupercomputers are a relatively recent development of the late 1980s. There are two types: smaller, somewhat slower, and much cheaper versions of large-scale supercomputers; and those based on the radically different architecture of "massively parallel processing." The latter are characterized by linkage of more than 1,024 slow, simple, inexpensive processors. There are literally hundreds of firms involved in R&D or production of minisupercomputers, and US firms, particularly Intel Corporation and Thinking Machines, are considered to have the most advanced machines. The world minisupercomputer market of the late 1980s was estimated to be $200 million annually. Prices range from $300,000 to several million dollars.

---

1. This is based on the testimony of Fred W. Weingarten of the Office of Technology Assessment in hearings on *The US Supercomputer Industry* before the House Committee on Science, Space and Technology, 101st Congress, 1st session, 20 June 1989 and US Department of Commerce (1992).

---

in Japan's ability to enter the supercomputer market in the early 1980s" (OTA 1991, 264). VLSI chips are the basic building blocks for supercomputers, and MITI alone provided about $150 million for R&D between 1976 and 1980 (OTA 1991, 264).

A second and more direct source of Japanese government support was MITI's 1981–89 Project for a High-Speed Computing System for Scientific and Technological Uses. MITI's justification for its $121 million contribution to the research consortium of six Japanese firms—Hitachi, Fujitsu, NEC, Mitsubishi, Oki, and Toshiba—was that the project would have ". . . broad spillovers sharply raising the scientific and technological level of every industry . . . thereby contributing to our aim of establishing our nation as a leader in technology" (OTA 1991, 265). It is not clear that the project had many direct commercial results. However, it may have been quite important in stimulating Japanese firms' interest in commercial opportunities. One official at Fujitsu, now the leading Japanese seller of supercomputers, reported that Fujitsu initially did not view the supercomputer market as profitable but participated in the consortium to avoid antagonizing MITI (OTA 1991, 267).[9] It is still not clear whether supercomputers are profitable for the three major Japanese producers: Fujitsu, NEC, and Hitachi.

Hitachi produced the first Japanese-made supercomputer in 1983. Sales of Japanese-made machines had grown rapidly by 1985, with the big three's introduction of supercomputers that were priced competitively with mainframes. By 1986 Japanese producers had installed or received orders for 64 units, more than one-quarter of the total world stock (*JEI Report* No. 46B, 19 December 1986, 10).

Cray and Control Data supercomputers have been widely considered superior to Japanese-made supercomputers, both on price–real world performance criteria and in the all-important availability of software. However, in the mid-1980s US producers had a lackluster sales record in Japan:

> CDC has no units in operation in Japan. Of the six Cray supercomputers installed in Japan just three are owned by publicly funded organizations—the Universities of Nagoya and Tokyo and NTT. (The other three Crays belong to Mitsubishi Research Institute, Toshiba, and Nissan Motor.) Moreover, no government-financed body has ordered a Cray since NTT's X-MP was delivered in August 1984. (*JEI Report* No. 46B, 19 December 1986, 11)

In the mid-1980s, Japanese producers began efforts to enter the US market. US producers were especially disturbed by the sale of an NEC supercomputer to the Houston Area Research Consortium (HARC) (*JEI Report* No. 46B, 19 December 1986, 11). "Probably more than any other single development, this January 1986 contract award transformed supercomputers into a bilateral trade issue since HARC was reportedly planning to buy an American-made system until NEC came in with what Cray and CDC executives felt was an unfairly low bid."

The 1987 Supercomputer Agreement

In response to industry complaints, on 10 December 1986 USTR initiated an investigation under section 305 of the 1974 Trade Act. The fact finding was to include an assessment of Japanese government procurement practices, support for research, and the overseas sales practices of Japanese

---

9. Another project (1981–91) to develop a Fifth Generation Computer, for which MITI provided $333 million, is widely viewed as having failed to achieve its objective of creating a true "thinking machine" but may have contributed to progress in parallel-processing technology. The Fifth Generation project is also said to have stimulated the US government to take a more proactive role in supporting US producers (OTA 1991, 268). See also T. R. Reid, "Japan Ends Computer Project," *Washington Post*, 2 June 1992, C2.

Box 5.2   The MOSS talks: 1985–87[1]

The Market-Oriented Sector-Specific talks were a precursor to super 301 and the Structural Impediments Initiative. They sought to address the allegedly onion-like layers of Japanese protection in four sectors: telecommunications, electronics, medical equipment/pharmaceuticals, and forest products (Tyson 1992, 58–59). In 1986 transportation machinery and auto parts were added as a fifth sector. The MOSS negotiations sought the identification and elimination of Japanese tariff and nontariff barriers in these sectors, without setting specific sales goals or quotas. US business representatives were generally positive about the outcome but noted that they still faced formidable obstacles to increased sales in Japan.

The telecommunications negotiations were considered successful because they eliminated restrictive regulations and harmonized US and Japanese standards in some areas. The medical equipment/pharmaceutical talks eased certain regulatory barriers and made the regulatory system more transparent. Although the forest products discussions produced commitments to reduce tariffs, they did little to eliminate nontariff barriers, particularly product standards and building codes. American industry representatives were satisfied with the progress made but hoped further discussions would lead to more market opening. The electronics negotiations achieved some tariff reductions and established intellectual property rights for certain products, but "lacked the definition and momentum of the other MOSS negotiations."

Semiconductors and supercomputers were eventually handled outside the MOSS framework. The auto parts talks differed from the other MOSS negotiations in that private-sector obstacles (e.g., *keiretsu*), rather than government barriers, were considered the primary impediments to freer trade. The August 1987 agreement amounted to little more than a Japanese promise to provide further information on the Japanese auto market. In mid-1988, GAO noted that "U.S. auto parts makers are . . . generally positive about the Auto Parts MOSS talks, even though they cannot directly attribute any increased sales or specific market share gain to the specific agreements."

---

1. This is based largely on General Accounting Office (1988); all quotes are from the GAO report unless otherwise noted. See also Tyson (1992, chapter 3) and Prestowitz (1988, chapter 10).

---

firms. Simultaneously, USTR announced that it was initiating discussions on Japanese public procurement of supercomputers under the Market-Oriented Sector-Specific (MOSS) framework (box 5.2; *International Trade Reporter*, 17 December 1986, 1520–21).

The section 305 investigation found that US producers were discriminated against in Japanese government procurements. The bilateral discussions on supercomputers were subsequently detached from the MOSS talks and conducted separately under the veiled threat of a section 301 action. Two related issues were discussed: the discrimination against US producers in government procurement and the high discounts that Japanese producers offered to government-financed purchasers, especially academic institutions.

Cray complained that Japanese public procurement procedures lacked transparency and were biased against US machines (Tyson 1992, 76–82). Government entities did not have to give adequate advance public notice of procurement opportunities. The process was also biased in that it was unclear what sort of price-performance criteria were used to award contracts. US producers argued that their exclusion from the Japanese public market hurt their long-run global competitiveness by preventing them from achieving economies of scale and denying them revenues that could be devoted to R&D (Cray Research, Inc. 1990, 2.2–2.4).[10]

The discounting issue was fairly complex (OTA 1991, 272–73). Japanese manufacturers were said to offer discounts of up to 80 percent off list price to certain government-controlled research institutions, primarily public universities and laboratories. Cray argued that such discounts put the sales price below the cost of production. The Japanese supercomputer manufacturers were integrated electronics producers and could subsidize their supercomputer sales with profits from other activities.[11] Cray, by contrast, specialized in supercomputers and could not long afford sales below costs.[12]

Japanese producers argued that they would strongly prefer not to discount so heavily but were forced to by the low procurement budgets of public buyers. In fact, such discounts are a well-established practice in the United States as well as in Japan. The benefits include improving the possibility of replacement or connection sales, training new users who will be future buyers, and feedback from sophisticated users on how to improve hardware or software.

The US administration's approach to the supercomputer talks was initially fairly nonconfrontational—using a low-key section 305 investigation and the MOSS framework rather than initiating a section 301 case. In 1986 NTT made a token purchase of a Cray supercomputer as a goodwill gesture. The atmosphere changed, however, in a 27 January 1987 meeting between MITI Vice Minister Makoto Kuroda, Deputy USTR Michael B. Smith, and other high US trade officials.[13] Kuroda allegedly told the US

---

10. Cray estimated that the total number of supercomputers in Japan would more than double between 1989 and 1993, with the public-sector market accounting for nearly 30 percent of the growth.

11. One potential mechanism for cross-subsidization is the purchase by diversified Japanese supercomputer manufacturers of their own machines for use in other lines of business, such as semiconductor production (OTA 1991, 277). Another potential source of revenue is guaranteed sales to members of the manufacturers' keiretsu. "About 56 percent of all supercomputers sold in Japan through 1990 were sold by one keiretsu member to another" (Department of Commerce 1992, 31).

12. See Michael B. Smith ("Facing the Goliath of Japan in the Supercomputer Market," *Washington Post,* 25 April 1989, A14) for this argument. Smith was deputy USTR and the chief US negotiator of the 1987 agreement.

13. See Stuart Auerbach, "Remark Fires US Campaign to Retaliate Against Japan," *Washington Post,* 26 March 1987, A1. The headline refers to a decision to retaliate against Japan for

negotiators that the United States could not expect to sell supercomputers to Japanese government agencies, regardless of price or quality. He also reportedly said that Cray would have to be nationalized or merged if it were to survive.

Kuroda denied the report, and NTT quickly announced the purchase of a second Cray. Neither NTT purchase was counted by US officials as a public procurement, however, since both machines were resold immediately to the Recruit Corporation, a private Japanese firm. The Japanese government also moved forward with plans for an emergency budget increase to allow Japanese public universities to increase purchases of supercomputers. These efforts were reportedly intended to avert US retaliation over Japan's failure to meet the terms of the 1986 semiconductor agreement (OTA 1991, 274).

The negotiators forged ahead and completed an agreement on 7 August 1987.[14] Japan agreed that it would be implemented in a manner consistent with the GATT Government Procurement Code and would provide nondiscriminatory and national treatment to foreign suppliers. It specified a more transparent procurement process, including advance public notice to potential suppliers. It called for performance, rather than design, specifications wherever practicable. However, these specifications would be based on the undefined concept of "basic need requirements." The agreement did not address the price discounting issue, reportedly because of disagreement among the US negotiators on how the issue should be handled.

Although Ambassadors Matsunaga and Yeutter both emphasized that the agreement did not specify a minimum number of US supercomputer sales or market share in Japan, Yeutter noted that "the proof of the pudding will come in sales" (*International Trade Reporter*, 8 August 1987, 1008).

In October 1987, the Japanese government announced the purchase under an emergency budget of two additional supercomputers from Cray and Control Data by MITI's Agency of Industrial Science and Technology and the Tokyo Institute of Technology. But the 1987 agreement is widely viewed as a failure because, aside from these two purchases, US producers failed to make any additional sales to the public sector in 1988–89 (figure 5.1). Although the bidding was formally open, some observers believe that "the Japanese government made sure that American companies won" (Tyson 1992, 77).

---

alleged violation of the 1986 semiconductor agreement, not to supercomputers. However, the semiconductor and supercomputer conflicts were proximate in time and emotionally linked in US and Japanese negotiators' minds. The text of the State Department's cable reporting on Kuroda's remarks was printed in the *Washington Post*, 28 April 1987, C2.

14. The agreement consists of an exchange of letters between USTR Clayton Yeutter and Japanese Ambassador Nobuo Matsunaga dated 7 August 1987, on file in USTR's public access reading room.

Figure 5.1   United States shares of public and private supercomputer sales in Japan, 1985–94

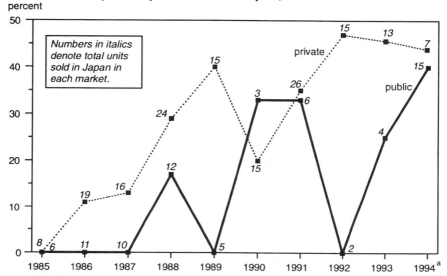

a. 1994 public procurements are through March 1994 and contain the results of spending under the fiscal 1993 regular and supplemental budgets. 1994 private procurements are through July 1994.

Sources: US Department of Commerce, Office of Computers and Business Equipment (personal communication). Private procurement data for 1993–94 are from Cray Research, Inc.

The agreement has been criticized on several grounds (OTA 1991, 274). First, it did not address the discounting issue. There were three reasons it did not: because US officials believed that the discounts were hurting Japanese producers, because IBM was discounting its mainframes to Japanese and US universities, and because Europeans might object to an agreement that eliminated discounts to European buyers.[15]

Second, the agreement failed to establish meaningful price-performance criteria. The notion of "basic need requirements" was so vague that it allowed public agencies to tailor their requirements to Japanese producers' equipment. In practice, this meant that performance could be specified in terms of theoretical peak performance, in which Japanese firms excelled, rather than actual workload performance and software availability, where

---

15. The US negotiators may have been influenced by the GATT case the European Community filed in February 1987 that claimed that aspects of the 1986 US-Japan semiconductor agreement raised semiconductor prices in the Community. The Community won its case but shortly thereafter negotiated its own agreement with Japan to maintain a price floor on semiconductor imports.

Table 5.1 United States and Japan: sales and shares in the international supercomputer market as of September 1989

| | United States | | Japan | | |
Market	Units	Percentages	Units	Percentages	Total
Europe	73	89	9	11	82
Japan	16	17	76	83	92
North America	168	98	3	2	171
Total	257	75	88	25	345

Source: Cray Research, Inc., reprinted in House Committee on Science, Space and Technology, hearings on HR 3131, The National High-Performance Computing Technology Act, 101st Congress, 2nd session, 14–15, March 1990, 46.

the US machines were clearly superior (OTA 1991, 25–58; US Department of Commerce 1992, 18).

Congress was skeptical of the effectiveness of the 1987 agreement and included in the 1988 Trade Act a special section, "The Supercomputer Trade Dispute." Section 1307 expressed concerns about Japan's implementation of the 1987 agreement, the continuation of deep price discounting, and alleged Japanese targeting of the supercomputer industry ". . . with the objective of eventual domination of the global computer market." It concluded with a "sense of Congress" urging USTR to give the highest priority to concluding and enforcing agreements to improve market access for US supercomputers in Japan.

The 1990 Supercomputer Agreement

An October 1988 USTR review of the 1987 agreement found that US producers still faced significant barriers in the Japanese public-sector market. The 1989 National Trade Estimate Report (p. 103) stated that:

> US suppliers find themselves excluded from serious consideration in Japanese government procurements due to technical specifications favoring incumbent Japanese suppliers. Extraordinarily low Japanese government supercomputer budgets effectively require massive discounts of up to 80 percent off list price.

In May 1989, USTR Hills designated Japanese government procurement as a priority practice under super 301 and on 16 June initiated an investigation under section 302 of the 1988 Trade Act (54 *Federal Register,* 7 June 1989, 24440; 21 June, 26137). The central argument in the US complaint was that American producers were highly competitive in all global markets except Japan and particularly in the Japanese public-sector market (figure 5.1 and table 5.1). As of 1989, for example, US producers had sold 89 percent of the machines installed in Europe (table 5.1) and 98 percent of the supercomputers in the United States but only 17 percent of the machines installed in Japan. These low US sales in Japan, notably in the public sector (figure 5.1), were considered clear evidence of Japanese government discrimination against US producers. The exit of Control Data from the large-scale supercomputer business in April 1989, leaving Cray as the sole US producer, may have contributed to USTR's decision to designate Japan (*Washington Post*, 18 April 1989, D1).

Japan formally refused to negotiate under the super 301 threat but immediately began to respond to American complaints. On 28 June MITI announced that it would provide administrative guidance limiting academic discounts to government entities to 50 percent.[16] MITI also pointedly observed that no US government institution had ever bought a Japanese supercomputer and urged the Bush administration to do so (*International Trade Reporter*, 7 July 1989, 874). On 7 July, a Japanese government official announced that the fiscal 1990 budget for public supercomputer procurement would be doubled or tripled (*International Trade Reporter*, 12 July 1989, 912). On 21 July, Tohoku University announced that it would purchase a Cray after NEC withdrew from the bidding, reportedly under Japanese government pressure to reduce bilateral trade friction (OTA 1991, 276).

After four arduous rounds of negotiations, on 23 March USTR Hills announced a tentative settlement of the supercomputer dispute. The settlement came shortly before Hills had to decide whether to cite Japan for a second time as a priority foreign country. American officials were cautiously optimistic about the agreement's potential to open the public Japanese supercomputer market. Echoing USTR Yeutter's statement in the previous negotiations, US officials stressed that the agreement provided no guarantee of quantitative results but noted that "the real test will be when the cash registers ring" (*International Trade Reporter*, 28 March 1990, 427).

On 15 June USTR Hills and Japanese Ambassador Ryohei Murata exchanged letters formalizing the agreement.[17] Unlike the 1987 agreement, the 1990 supercomputer agreement addressed the discounting problem. It required that public-sector buyers base their estimated contract prices and procurement budget requests on actual private-sector market prices, if possible.

It also addressed the US complaint that performance specifications used by Japanese agencies discriminated against US producers. Government entities were required to draw up their specifications in terms of "actual minimum needs" based on "minimally acceptable benchmark results which demonstrate the operational performance of the supercomputers."

---

16. It was alleged by US industry sources that the Japanese manufacturers merely lowered their list prices to conform to the limit on discounts.

17. The letters are on file in USTR's public access reading room.

The inherent bias toward incumbent suppliers was addressed by requiring that replacement or interconnect procurements be specified "in such a way that suppliers can compete effectively against the incumbent supplier."

The agreement also responded to the US demand that the criteria for selecting winning bids be transparent and nondiscriminatory. It required that the evaluation of bids be based on "technical excellence, with overall system performance being of fundamental importance, and cost." This provision was intended to ensure that price–real world performance criteria would be used in evaluating bids—something Cray (1990, 3.10–3.23) had frequently complained the Japanese did not do. In addition, the availability of software, a strength of US producers, was to be included in the evaluation.

Finally, the 1990 agreement contained a detailed complaint settlement mechanism that is described in four single-spaced pages, compared with the one short paragraph in the 1987 agreement. It established the Japanese Procurement Review Board, an independent entity, to consider procurement complaints by potential suppliers. As described below, the complaint process was used for the first time in 1992.

Following the 1989 agreement, in 1990–93 US producers sold four of the fifteen supercomputers procured and installed by Japanese government-controlled institutions. US producers sold six of the fifteen units installed in 1994. We defer our assessment of the agreement until a later section and turn now to the satellite case.

Satellites

US and Japanese Policies

Until the early 1980s, the US government had a monopoly on American space activities, with the significant exception of communications satellites.[18] The space program initially had both national security and scientific goals. The military, for example, spent huge sums on missile launchers and satellites for communications, mapping, and navigation. The intelligence community spent billions on satellites to collect information. NASA was primarily concerned with the advancement of science and knowledge through space exploration. Since the mid-1980s, the US government has given moderately high priority to encouraging the commercialization of space activities by the private sector.

In all US space activities, however, the distinction between national security, science, and commerce is often blurred. Launchers developed for the military or NASA by civilian contractors are sold by those same firms to put commercial satellites into orbit. Much of the technology

---

18. In 1962 the US government established the Communications Satellite Corporation (COMSAT), a private for-profit firm, to promote the commercial development of satellite communications.

involved in communications and mapping satellites was developed for the military by civilian contractors and is used by those same firms to build commercial satellites.[19] Even "the distinction between military and civilian launches is arbitrary to a certain extent, since any satellite can be used for either sector. . . . Communications satellites can carry either military or civilian traffic, and navigation satellites are used by both the military and civilian communities" (Smith 1992, 81). For example, the military's NAVSTAR Global Positioning System of satellites is used by both the military and civilians. NAVSTAR was used to great effect in positioning allied troops during the 1991 Persian Gulf War. However, a shortage of military receivers during the war reportedly led some US soldiers to write home to ask relatives to send the civilian version of the NAVSTAR receivers. The military, in fact, used commercial receivers fairly extensively during the conflict (Smith 1992, 63–64 and 84–85).

The US government space budget was $23 billion to $30 billion annually in the late 1980s and early 1990s, with the Defense Department accounting for more than half of the total (US Department of Commerce, *Space Business Indicators,* June 1992, 29). Although the government has an open procurement policy, in practice most purchases for space activities are from US vendors. In some cases, the government invokes the national security or research exemptions to the GATT Government Procurement Code. In 1990 President Bush issued a Commercial Space Launch Policy requiring that, where feasible, all government payloads be launched on US vehicles (Office of the Press Secretary, White House, "Commercial Space Launch Policy," 5 September 1990, 1). Foreign firms often supply key components to US producers, but generally they are minority subcontractors for US firms that sell the final product to the US government.

The United States played a vital role in the early development of Japan's space activities. A 1969 US-Japan Agreement on Space Cooperation permitted US firms to cooperate with Japan. The agreement was unusual in actively encouraging the transfer of technology, rather than the export of goods, to Japan—while Europe was denied access to that same technology (Mastanduno 1991, 94; Logsdon 1992, 297). Bilateral cooperation focused on Japanese development of both launchers and satellites. In practice, the early transfer of technology involved Japanese firms working as junior partners with US firms, which did most of the actual manufacturing.

Early US-Japan Tensions Over Satellites

By 1978 Japan had developed a sufficient manufacturing base that it could proclaim its goal of an autonomous space program based on indigenous

---

19. For example, the Commerce Department reports that the Strategic Defense Initiative has resulted in "dramatic reductions in the size, weight and cost of many spacecraft parts, and private firms are interested in exploiting these advantages in commercial satellites" (foreword to *Space Commerce: 1992 Review*).

Box 5.3 Organizational structure of Japan's space program

Japan's space program is loosely coordinated by the Space Activities Commission in the prime minister's office and is implemented primarily by two lead agencies: the Institute of Space and Astronautical Science (ISAS) under the Ministry of Education, Science, and Culture and the National Space Development Agency (NASDA), which is under the Science and Technology Agency in the prime minister's office and also receives guidance from the Ministry of Transport and the Ministry of Post and Telecommunications (MPT).[1] ISAS is primarily responsible for basic scientific research and has a budget of roughly $125 million. NASDA's $1 billion budget is devoted largely to practical applications, including research and development with potential commercial application.

1. See recent NASDA annual reports for organizational charts and Wray (1991, 466–67) and Logsdon (1991, 294–96) for discussion. See two Japan Economic Institute (JEI) reports by Susan McKnight for detailed discussions of Japan's space program: *JEI Report* No. 11A, 16 March 1984, and No. 45A, 1 December 1989.

technology (box 5.3; Logsdon 1992, 297). One reason for seeking autonomy was the growing US refusal to export state-of-the-art space technologies and the fact that Japanese launchers developed with American technology could not be used for commercial operations without US permission (Rohrer and Smith 1989, 1). This goal of self-sufficiency was formalized in the Space Activities Commission's July 1983 "Long Range Vision on Space Development," which prohibited procurement of foreign satellites if they would interfere with indigenous development (1989 National Trade Estimate Report, 103–04). Since the late 1970s, the Japanese content of indigenous communications satellites has risen from 24 to 80 percent, and the local content of broadcast satellites has grown from 14 to 83 percent (Wray 1991, 469). Because of the small scale of production, Japanese satellites were considerably more expensive than US-made satellites.[20]

After the commission's 1983 long-range space vision was announced, the United States repeatedly complained about Japanese government discrimination against US aerospace firms.[21] Under US pressure, Japan's Ministry of Post and Telecommunications (MPT) in 1985 was authorized

20. Some Japanese satellites appear to be up to twice as expensive as their US-made competitors (see 4 October 1989 testimony of Deputy USTR S. Linn Williams before Senate Commerce Committee in hearings on the Japanese space industry 1989, 5; and Susan McKnight's informative "Japan's Satellite Development Program Revisited," *JEI Report* No. 45A, 1 December 1989, 6).

21. See Prestowitz (1988, 122–24) for discussion of an attempt by NTT in July 1983 to buy Hughes' satellite technology, which reportedly "sent a shock wave through Washington" and caused the US government to begin examining Japanese public procurement of satellites.

to license private companies that could compete with NTT in providing satellite communications. These firms were given the right to import satellites. Two private telecommunications firms were established: Japan Communications Satellite (JC-SAT), owned by C. Itoh, Mitsui, and Hughes Communications; and Space Communications Corporation (SCC), owned by Mitsubishi. The new firms each purchased satellites: JC-SAT bought two satellites from Hughes; SCC bought two from Ford Aerospace (Mastanduno 1991, 95–96). These satellites were launched in 1989–90.

The creation of a Japanese private sector eager to buy less expensive US satellites did not reduce US pressure to open up Japan's public procurement. In particular, the United States continued to complain that NTT was prohibited from buying US satellites, although NTT was covered by the GATT Government Procurement Code. The issue was raised periodically in the MOSS talks and cited in the annual National Trade Estimate Reports, but Japan's basic policy of indigenous space development remained unchanged. An advisory committee of the Space Activities Commission urged that "the fundamental policy of our country's space development programs should be the development and maintenance of our own technology of international level and the acquisitions of the capability to freely conduct our own activities in outer space" (Space Activities Commission 1987, 90).

The Japanese government steadfastly denied that its space objectives were commercial. Rather, it sought the advancement of science and technology, the exploration of space, and participation in international cooperative efforts in space.

US officials discounted these idealistic Japanese motives and instead argued that Japan was targeting space industries for commercial development. In 4 October 1989 testimony before the Senate Commerce Committee on the Japanese space industry, Undersecretary of Commerce J. Michael Farren asserted that:

> To the Japanese, satellites are not an industry unto itself but a window on the whole space industry for the 21st century. Japan is looking to aerospace as a source for its future growth and prosperity. Our National Aeronautics and Space Administration has pointed out in a recent report that space is a new economic frontier, and that space commerce is directly linked to American competitiveness in the global market. NASA has noted that "a single $100 million launch contract is equivalent in economic terms to the import of 10,000 Toyotas." NASA has published a report linking space technology spinoffs to 46 various industrial and commercial applications ranging from medicine to composites to the environment. The Japanese Ministry of International Trade and Industry has its own version of this report stressing that growth in aerospace leads to growth in other industry areas. MITI's "space industry tree" branches out into the automotive, energy and electronics industries among others. (p. 14)

Despite mounting US government concern about Japan's policy of autonomous space development, the super 301 case dismayed US satellite makers (*JEI Report* No. 45A, 1 December 1989, 1–4). A vice president of Hughes said, "We were surprised . . . we weren't pushing the US government to do this," and General Electric said it also opposed the super 301 designation (*Wall Street Journal*, 15 June 1989, A10).

Some US officials believed that the US industry's reservations were based on fear of jeopardizing current sales to the private sector and occasional emergency sales of satellites or leasing of transponders to Japanese government entities (Mastanduno 1991, 97; Williams 1989, 21). They may have been particularly anxious not to irritate MPT, which licensed imports of satellites and was a strong supporter of indigenous satellites.

The lack of US industry support caused considerable difficulty for the American negotiators. Deputy USTR S. Linn Williams (1991, 27) reports that he was taunted by Japanese negotiators that US firms did not support the case.

In contrast to the lack of industry support, there was unusual consensus within the Bush administration for the satellite case. Even agencies such as the Council of Economic Advisers, which was generally skeptical of all forms of 301, accepted this case because it saw Japanese discrimination as blatant and indefensible. The leading US proponents of the case were Deputy USTR Williams, Assistant USTR Joseph Massey, and Commerce Undersecretary J. Michael Farren. They believed it was important to pre-empt Japanese targeting of an important high-technology industry in which the United States had a strong competitive advantage (Williams 1989; Farren 1989). For example, in 1991 US manufacturers had contracts to build 69 percent of the 84 communications satellites on order worldwide (US Department of Commerce, *Space Business Indicators*, June 1992, 45–46). US producers have consequently been able to achieve significant economies of mass production. Hughes Aircraft alone "employs 9,000 people working on a satellite order book worth about $3 billion. It has the world's only mass production line for telecommunications satellites" (*Financial Times*, 31 July 1992, 13). Global sales of communications satellites were $8 billion in the 1980s and were expected to double to $16 billion in the 1990s.

Williams (1989, 7) argued that the case responded to Congress's intent in drafting the super 301 legislation since it had "the potential to increase US exports significantly, both directly and by setting a precedent." Although the Japanese market for communications satellites is relatively small and intermittent due to the geographical compactness of the country, potential sales were not inconsequential. General Electric's 1989 sale to NHK, Japan's public broadcast corporation, was valued at $88 million, and the sale of two Hughes satellites to JC-SAT was worth over $400 million.

The 1990 Agreement

The satellite dispute was described as "the most difficult of the three super 301 issues because the United States basically was telling Japan that it had to give up its quest to become a competitor in the world market for applications satellites"(*JEI Report* No. 16B, 20 April 1990, 12). The issue was viewed as a matter of high principle on both sides.

Japan argued that it had a sovereign right to an autonomous space program with noncommercial objectives. The super 301 case was viewed as a high-handed US attempt to thwart a high-minded Japanese policy aimed at expanding the frontiers of science and technology. According to a MITI official: "If the U.S. is saying we don't have to develop our own space technology, that has to be considered arrogant" (*Wall Street Journal*, 15 June 1989, A10).

US officials, on the other hand, viewed the Japanese policy of indigenous satellite development as unambiguous protection aimed at promoting an infant industry and a violation of the spirit, if not the letter, of the GATT Government Procurement Code. The clearest example of Japan's commercial objectives, in US minds, was the Japanese CS-4 communications satellite. It was to be jointly developed by the National Space Development Agency (NASDA) and NTT, with NTT covering about 75 percent of the estimated $600 million cost (*International Trade Reporter*, 21 March 1990, 391). Although the Japanese government claimed it was an R&D satellite, US officials believed "the CS-4 is obviously a commercial satellite, developed with commercial capacity and intended to be used for paying customers" (Williams 1989, 5). They cited two facts to support this claim: NTT, a user of commercial satellites, was paying most of the costs, and the MPT refused to license a third private satellite company that could import commercial satellites, on grounds that existing capacity was sufficient. This denial suggested to US officials that "the Japanese government intends to force users to use the CS-4 satellite when it is launched" (Williams 1989, 5).[22]

In early 1989, a few months before the super 301 designations, the Japanese government took two additional actions possibly intended to assuage US pressure. In January, NTT decided to lease 13 of 64 transponders on a Hughes-built satellite, and in February NHK bought a General Electric satellite as an emergency replacement for a Japanese-built satellite that had failed (*Wall Street Journal*, 15 June 1989, A10).

After four fruitless rounds of negotiations, in March 1990 Prime Minister Toshiki Kaifu ordered the two key ministers, Takeshi Fukaya of MPT and Tomoji Oshima of the Science and Technology Agency, to resolve the dispute (*International Trade Reporter*, 21 March 1990, 390–91). A tentative agreement was reached on 3 April, and the final agreement was signed on 15 June (*International Trade Reporter*, 4 April 1990, 460, and 20 June 1990, 895).

---

22. The 1990 National Trade Estimate Report (p. 115) asserts that "... it appears that the market is being reserved for 'research' satellites, while private sector development is regulated and protected to avoid excessive capacity."

In the agreement, the Japanese government committed itself and the entities under its control, including NTT and NHK, to "procure non-R&D satellites on an open, transparent and nondiscriminatory basis, and in accordance with the GATT Procurement Code."[23] The agreement applies to all satellites except R&D satellites, defined as those "designed and used entirely, or almost entirely, for the purpose of in-space development and/ or validation of technologies new to either country, and/or noncommercial scientific research." However, in the Japanese government's view, there appears to be some ambiguity on the definition of R&D satellites. Ambassador Murata's letter suggested the need to elaborate on the definition, perhaps using the Organization for Economic Cooperation and Development as a forum. The agreement also contains a detailed, six-page description of dispute settlement procedures.

To some Japanese observers, the agreement was "in all respects a complete acceptance of American demands" (Wray 1991, 473). It forced NASDA and NTT to scrap the CS-4 project. An MPT official stated that the "severity of the settlement was beyond expectations" because the agreement covered all commercial satellites, not just communications satellites (Wray 1992, 472). Similarly, US trade officials describe the agreement as a significant setback for Japanese commercial satellite development.

In view of the initial hard-line positions on both sides, why did Japan finally accede to virtually all the US demands? One possible reason is that the Japanese space community was not in fact unified in support of autonomous development, and particularly in support of the CS-4 project. It appears that NTT and NHK opposed the policy because of the high cost of domestically built satellites, which were sometimes twice as expensive as technologically superior imported satellites.

Wray (1991, 471) reports that:

> After NTT's privatization in 1985, the Space Agency pressured it to continue to bankroll the [communications satellite] program. By the late 1980s, however, NTT had become more concerned about cutting costs, and resisted this pressure for continued funding. In the end it only reluctantly accepted the brunt of its development cost. NTT's reluctance also stemmed from its analysis of the market in 1989. It reasoned that this new and larger communications satellite could not operate profitably beside the imported satellites. . . . On the other hand, the satellite importers themselves feared competition from the government-supported communications satellite program (CS-4).

Commerce Undersecretary J. Michael Farren (1989, 18) testified that:

> When you talk to NTT officials privately, they will tell you they would very much like to be able to benefit from . . . cost savings. But, given their relationship to

---

23. The agreement consists of several exchanges of letters between USTR Hills, Ambassador Ryohei Murata, and Keiji Shima, chairman of NHK. They are on file in USTR's public reading room.

the Government of Japan, and their interest in continuing in their current positions, it is not likely they are going to go out and purchase an American satellite. . . . I think NHK will be in the exact same position.

NASDA itself may not have been totally committed to even its 25 percent share of the CS-4 program. Wray (1991, 471–73) reports that NASDA's CS-4 expenditures strained its ability to fund higher priority projects such as the Experimental Data Relay and Tracking Satellite, which seeks advances in communications and broadcast technologies.

The first test of the new procurement policy came in June 1991, when NTT invited bids for two N-Star communications satellites worth $500 million. Three US firms and no Japanese firms responded. The NTT contract was awarded in December to Loral Space Systems, which had acquired Ford Aerospace. However, several Japanese firms—Mitsubishi Electric, Toshiba, and NEC—were part of the Loral consortium. Mitsubishi had been the prime contractor on the canceled CS-4 project (*JEI Report* 45B, 6 December 1991, 10). In September 1992 General Electric won a bid to supply NHK with a $70 million broadcast satellite.

In April 1991, MPT reversed its earlier decision and licensed a third private satellite communications firm, Satellite Japan. Hughes Space and Communications Group won a competition against General Electric, British Aerospace, and Aerospatiale to supply two satellites to Satellite Japan (*Space News*, 27 July 1992, 8).

US manufacturers appear to be satisfied with the agreement. One Hughes executive pointed out that it was "not an enormous piece of business. But more importantly, it eliminates the shelter that Japanese firms have enjoyed" (*Los Angeles Times*, 4 April 1990, D2). The agreement appears to have reinforced the already dominant position of US communications satellite manufacturers in the global market, which is estimated at $1.2 billion to $1.4 billion annually, with US firms receiving about 65 to 70 percent of the business.[24]

Assessment of the Supercomputer and Satellite Agreements

Initial Results

In both agreements, the United States appears to have achieved its most immediate objective of opening Japanese government procurement to foreign bidders. Both agreements were carefully written to conform to the GATT Government Procurement Code and thus in principle provide

---

24. Hughes alone has built more than 40 percent of all communications satellites now in commercial use. See General Motors Corporation, "Prospectus," 15 October 1992, 39–44, for discussion of the industry. See also US Department of Commerce, *US Industry Output 1992*, on the US satellite industry.

nondiscriminatory treatment for all foreign suppliers.[25] In practice, the agreements will primarily benefit US producers, since the United States has a very strong global market position in both industries. The potential gains to US producers are modest but not inconsequential.

Cray Research won three of the nine "competitions" held under the supercomputer agreement in 1991–92.[26] The pattern of sales lends some credibility to Tyson's claim (1992, 79) that the Japanese government managed the results. Of the nine procurements, Cray did not bid on four uncontested contracts to upgrade existing Fujitsu machines. It lost two competitions against Fujitsu and NEC (the eventual winner). It won by default on three bids that Japanese manufacturers did not contest. Some observers believe that their government pressured the Japanese firms not to bid on these three contracts, although NEC had previously installed machines at two of the sites and was therefore thought to have an incumbent's advantage. It is too early to determine whether procurements under the 1990 agreement are, in fact, being managed.

However, USTR was sufficiently concerned with the possibility that Japan was not living up to its commitments that in April 1993 it initiated a compliance investigation under section 306 of the 1988 Trade Act.[27] The year-long review focused on purchases made under Japan's fiscal 1993 regular and supplemental budgets. The inclusion of funding for supercomputers in the supplemental budget was interpreted by some observers as a way of assuaging US concerns about the low level of US sales in 1990–92. A total of 15 supercomputers were purchased, six of which came from American firms. USTR acknowledged that the six purchases were a "positive development" but decided to continue the review indefinitely because of lingering concerns about unfairness and discrimination in procurement.[28]

Although Cray Research did not contest USTR's decision not to retaliate, it had several complaints and concerns, particularly regarding the way public agencies made price–real world performance comparisons. Cray objected that the Japanese had lowered their minimum performance specifications and thus had given more emphasis to price over performance in their evaluations. Moreover, five of the six purchases were massively parallel processing (MPP) machines in which US producers—IBM, Maspar, Intel, Thinking Machines, and Cray—were far advanced over Japanese producers. The fact that the Japanese agencies bought one of

---

25. USTR lawyers point out that the GATT code was used as a model for the two agreements.

26. The facts in this assessment are from *JEI Report* No. 28B, 24 July 1992, 13. We are responsible for the interpretation of the outcomes of these competitions.

27. Office of the US Trade Representative, "Section 306 Review of Japan's Implementation of the 1990 US-Japan Supercomputer Agreement," 30 April 1993.

28. "USTR Announces Three Decisions: Title VII, Japan Supercomputers Review, Special 301," Office of the US Trade Representative, Press Release 94-28, 30 April 1994.

each of the leading American MPP supercomputers led Cray to suspect that the purchases were an attempt to learn from and then leapfrog US manufacturers' technologies. Cray and USTR questioned why no US firm had ever won a public procurement in head-to-head competition with a Japanese producer (USTR press release 94-28, 30 April 1994).

Possibly as a result of a reduction in discounting and tight government budgets, the Japanese government procurement market appears to have shrunk from an average of 10 to 12 machines installed annually in 1986–88 (figure 5.1) to 3 to 6 machines since 1989. We estimate that US manufacturers could win one-third to one-half of this smaller market, selling one to three supercomputers worth $10 million to $90 million annually.[29]

A Department of Commerce (1992, 44) review of the 1990 supercomputer agreement reported US government concerns that a smaller public market could work to Cray's disadvantage:

> ... concern was expressed that the reduced number of pending procurements reflected a move to limit first-time supercomputer acquisitions in favor of those agencies seeking to upgrade existing systems. Managing procurements by such a method could effectively block foreign systems, because specifications continue to favor incumbent Japanese suppliers. Finally, delays in supercomputer procurement are favorable to Japanese supercomputer makers, who hope to catch up or surpass US firms with their next generation of systems, but are not yet ready to compete on a performance basis.

The Japanese market for commercial satellites, mainly for communications, is small and not likely to grow rapidly in the near future. Based on recent sales under the 1990 agreement, US satellite producers could sell one or two additional satellites annually, worth anywhere from $100 million to $300 million. Most of these sales will involve Japanese and other foreign subcontractors; thus the value added by US producers will be less than the total sales value.

It is too early to judge whether these super 301 cases advanced the broader US goal of deterring Japanese government targeting of these industries. At the very least, it is likely that denial of a protected market will slow the development of these adolescent Japanese industries into full-fledged global competitors. Similarly, it is early, and may in any event be impossible, to determine if US actions in these two cases have had a broader deterrent effect on foreign targeting in other high-technology

---

29. The low end of this range is based on the assumption that Cray would maintain the 33 percent share of the public market for large-scale supercomputers it captured in 1990–91 and sell machines priced at $10 million each. The high estimate assumes that Cray could capture 50 percent of the public market, which is the share that Cray's then-CEO John Rollwagen expected in the *private* Japanese market (cited in Department of Commerce 1992, 33). These machines could be worth up to $30 million each. Cray estimates that US supercomputer manufacturers could easily sell machines worth $100 million annually in the Japanese public market (statement of John Rollwagen, House Committee on Government Operations, 1 and 8 July 1992, 113–14).

industries. At the very least, the fact that the United States initiated these cases enhances the credibility of its threat to respond similarly to other alleged foreign targeting.

Both agreements contain detailed complaint resolution procedures, modeled on the US government's own procedures, that can be used by bidders to contest public procurement awards. In addition, the two governments will hold annual reviews. US officials hope these procedures and reviews will help to quickly and peacefully resolve future conflicts in these two sectors, but it is too soon to judge whether this is the case. In fact, the satellite agreement's dispute settlement procedures have not yet been invoked.[30]

Thus far, there has been one supercomputer procurement dispute, involving allegations of unfair performance standards. Both US government and Cray officials criticized an October 1992 decision by the Super-computer Procurement Review Board not to overturn a disputed bid.[31] Repeated consultations under the agreement's review procedures failed to resolve the dispute.

Are Supercomputers and Satellites Strategic Industries?

Proponents of the supercomputer and satellite cases insisted that the strategic nature of these industries provided a strong argument for using super 301. They argued that the potential benefits of market opening went well beyond either the deterrent effect or the mere dollar value of increased US exports. This section examines those claims and the evidence.

The claim that supercomputers and satellites are indeed strategic industries is plausible but unproven. To settle the issue would require detailed

---

30. A brief controversy over the 1990 satellite agreement erupted in September 1991 when *Nihon Keizei Shimbun*'s 4 September US edition reported that MPT had formed a consortium with several Japanese firms to establish an environmental chamber to test commercial satellites. Japanese firms reportedly asked for government assistance because, according to Katsumi Osunga, director of MPT's space communications division, "for Japanese markets to develop their own commercial satellites, they have to have a large-scale testing chamber . . . [but] the market is too small because the American satellites are more cost effective" ("Japan Proposes Group to Help Satellite Firms," *Wall Street Journal*, 5 September 1991). According to Hiroshi Hirabayashi, economics minister at the Japanese embassy in Washington, "Maybe because of the expressions of concern from the United States side, the MPT officials have all but abandoned the idea" ("Japan Satellite-Subsidy Plan Dropped After US Pressure," *New York Times*, 19 September 1991).

31. The dispute involved Cray's loss to NEC of a sale to the National Institute of Fusion Science in June 1992. Cray invoked the agreement's complaint resolution mechanism to protest the award to NEC, claiming that the performance tests favored Japanese suppliers, that Cray's superior performance was not sufficiently credited, and that NEC's promised performance had not been demonstrated in tests. The Procurement Review Board rejected Cray's complaint. In April 1993, USTR Mickey Kantor launched an investigation of Japanese compliance with the agreement (*JEI Report* No. 28B, 24 July 1992, 13; No. 39B, 16 October 1992, 8; No. 17B, 7 May 1993, 9–10).

empirical analysis beyond the scope of this book. Instead, we take the more limited approach of using two criteria developed by Paul Krugman and other strategic trade theorists.[32] We find that the evidence on the strategic nature of these industries is, at best, mixed.

Krugman's (1984b and 1987b) first criterion is whether the so-called strategic industry earns or could earn extraordinary profits in global markets.[33] These above-normal profits derive from obstacles to competition, such as import protection, high R&D or capital expenditures, or the cost advantages of scale economies or of learning by doing that accrue to incumbent producers.

The motive for government assistance to highly profitable strategic industries is crassly mercantilist. Governments reason that if any super profits are to be earned in global markets, domestic rather than foreign firms should get them.

It is not entirely easy, however, to identify those industries earning unusual profits (Dixit 1986). Reported rates of return are not necessarily an accurate indicator because some rents may be paid to labor in higher wages and benefits. A second measurement problem stems from the fact that high profits earned by existing firms may not reflect true supernormal *industry* profits if other firms in the industry have exited because of low profits. A third difficulty is in identifying "American" firms.[34] For example, US supercomputer manufacturers buy some of their chips from foreign, often Japanese, suppliers. If the foreign chip suppliers are oligopolists, US supercomputer producers may have to share their profits by paying higher prices for components. Similarly, US satellite producers, especially those selling to Japan, have co-production or subassembly arrangements with Japanese manufacturers. Here, too, extranormal profits may have to be shared with foreigners. Finally, American citizens may not get all the rents because foreigners own interests in US firms or can buy US corporate stocks. Thus, for example, Loral Space Systems, which won the $500 million N-Star satellite competition, is 49 percent owned by a European aerospace consortium.

Recognizing these measurement problems, there is some evidence of superprofits in the supercomputer industry in the 1980s. The leading US supercomputer producer, Cray Research, reports a 22 percent average post-tax return on shareholders' equity between 1981 and 1991 (Cray,

32. See Krugman (1986) for a valuable collection of papers on strategic trade theory and Richardson (1989) for a survey of empirical work.

33. High profits are not to be confused with high value added: the payments to labor and capital. Some industrial policy advocates argue that the US government should promote industries with high wages. Krugman (1987b, 209) notes that this would lower wages and create unemployment in unfavored industries.

34. See Reich (1991) for a lively discussion of the problems of determining "Who is US?"

Annual Report 1991).[35] This compares with a 10 percent return on equity for all US durable goods industries. It also appears to be higher than the return leading mainframe computer manufacturers earned in the 1980s. The Japanese supercomputer producers were reportedly not profitable in the late 1980s at the time of the dispute (OTA 1991, 275).

It is more difficult to estimate the profitability of satellite production since the three leading US manufacturers all have diversified aerospace operations and do not report rates of return separately for their satellite operations. It does not appear, however, that these firms per se are unusually profitable as measured by returns on sales or assets.

A second criterion for identifying a strategic industry is whether it has important linkages or spin-offs to other parts of the economy. Unfortunately, some proponents of supporting strategic industries are excessively expansive on what sorts of linkages they think might justify government assistance for a specific industry. Just because an industry is linked to others does not necessarily mean it deserves special government help.

In assessing interindustry linkages and spin-offs, economists make a distinction between pecuniary and nonpecuniary (primarily technological) externalities—that is, benefits of production that accrue to those outside the producing firm. Both types of externalities cause a cost-saving change or innovation in one industry to be passed on to other industries. The crucial difference is that those who receive pecuniary externalities have to pay for the benefits received whereas beneficiaries of technological externalities do not. In contrast to pecuniary externalities, the benefits of technological externalities are not always appropriately priced and allocated by market forces so as to maximize national economic welfare. The nation may underproduce in externality-laden industries. Consequently, the existence of pecuniary externalities does not argue for government assistance, while the existence of technological externalities may.

Supercomputers or satellites may generate both pecuniary and technological externalities. Some industry analysts refer to supercomputers as "technology drivers," which set the pace for technological innovation in other segments of the computer industry or the economy.[36] However, these analysts could be referring to either pecuniary or nonpecuniary externalities.

The distinction is important for policy purposes. An innovation like massively parallel processing generates a pecuniary externality because it dramatically reduces the cost or increases the efficiency of computing.[37]

---

35. Returns have been falling since 1986–87, and in 1992 Cray announced its first-ever loss. Some observers attribute part of Cray's problems to its lag in exploiting massively parallel processing technology.

36. US Department of Commerce (1992, 7) cites a number of interesting examples of what appear to be nonpecuniary externalities related to supercomputers.

37. An example of a pecuniary externality is the use of minisupercomputers with parallel processing to track consumers' buying patterns, thus allowing retailers to adjust inventory

These cost savings are passed on directly to customers and users in the form of lower prices. To be sure, the advent of lower-cost computing can confer substantial benefits on the rest of the economy. Lower costs of supercomputers make them accessible to more users and encourage new applications that result in new products or cost-saving ideas throughout the economy. However, the market works well in ensuring that the prices of these products fully reflect the benefits they provide to society.

Such pecuniary externalities provide no rationale for government assistance to the supercomputer, or any other, industry because market forces have led to the level of supercomputer production that maximizes the nation's welfare. Of course, the government could subsidize supercomputers or potato chips. But a dollar spent on these subsidies will yield no more than a dollar in benefits to users.

The argument is very different in the case of technological externalities. In this case, an innovation in supercomputers yields benefits to users or others in the economy that they do not have to pay for. One can imagine, for example, an innovation that results from creating the software or the architecture for massively parallel processing that has wider uses in other parts of the computer industry. Some innovations, particularly knowledge and ideas, are not patentable or easily kept secret and therefore diffuse more or less freely throughout society. In this case, market forces do not set a price that reflects the benefits society enjoys from the externality. The fact that the innovator does not get paid by all users of the innovation creates a plausible argument for government support. If innovators cannot always reap the benefits of their creativity through royalties and licensing agreements, they will underinvest in the creation of new knowledge and ideas. Hence, in principle, government should subsidize basic research and development that has widespread application and diffuses freely throughout the economy.

There is a third type of externality, which Krugman (1987b, 244) calls a linkage externality, that looks like a pecuniary externality but acts like a technological externality.[38] It can occur when an imperfectly competitive industry supplying inputs to other sectors benefits from economies of scale.

Supercomputers and satellites may, quite plausibly, generate linkage externalities. Both industries play a vital intermediate role in the production of many goods and services—a role very much akin to basic economic infrastructure such as transportation and communications facilities. Supercomputers, as described earlier, are used in the design and production of other goods and services. Communications satellites provide a fundamental infrastructural service: telecommunications.

---

and purchases quickly (*Wall Street Journal*, 23 December 1992, B1).

38. Krugman credits Ethier (1979 and 1982) with identifying this type of externality.

Both supercomputers and satellites are also said to experience economies of mass production. If so, an expansion in demand will cause their costs of production to fall and benefit the many sectors of the economy that use them.

A linkage externality differs fundamentally from a pecuniary externality because, with scale economies, the real resources used to produce supercomputers or satellites decline as they are produced in larger quantities. For all intents, the users of supercomputers or satellites experience the benefits of a technological externality—they get a lower priced input at no cost to anyone. The free benefit comes from the greater efficiency of the satellite or supercomputer manufacturers operating at higher levels of output.

The possibility of technological or linkage externalities raises a question of great policy importance. Must the nation produce these goods in order to reap the external benefits, or does it merely require access to the goods? Krugman's answer (1987b, 223) is that "if the externality is international in scope, it does not matter how the industry is distributed between domestic and foreign producers." Three hypothetical examples will illustrate this point.

In the first example, the supercomputer industry might generate a technological externality, say an unpatentable idea that has general applicability to the entire computer industry from desktops to mainframes. If the idea flows relatively quickly and inexpensively across international boundaries, the US economy will benefit regardless of whether supercomputers are produced in the United States or Japan. There is no case here for US government support for domestic supercomputer manufacturers. Rather, the best thing government can do is to support the widest and quickest possible dissemination of the idea.

Consider a second example in which it is the use, rather than the production, of supercomputers that generates technological externalities for the rest of the economy. Imagine the development of a solution to a specific software problem that has general applicability to a larger class of software problems and that cannot be copyrighted or kept secret. In this case, public policy should aim to provide improved access to both supercomputers and software, wherever they are produced, so as to maximize the production of generally applicable ideas.

A third example of a technological or linkage externality focuses not on machines or software but on people. Suppose that access to supercomputers and software creates a cadre of sophisticated users who are themselves the source of new ideas that flow freely among users and producers of supercomputers. These users communicate with each other via global computer networks (linked, of course, by satellites), they attend international conferences to discuss new ideas, and they write for learned journals with worldwide distribution. The key points are that they generate valuable ideas through communication with each other and that some of these

Figure 5.2 Optimal subsidies for externalities

Source of Externality	Scope of Externality	
	Global	*National*
Production	Subsidize consumption	Subsidize production
Consumption (or users)	Subsidize consumption (or training for users)	Subsidize consumption (or training for users)

ideas are freely available. Anyone with experience in a research institution will recognize the phenomenon of an international fellowship of professionals who generate ideas by freely exchanging ideas.

In this case, the appropriate role for government in fostering dissemination of externalities should be to nurture the development of sophisticated supercomputer users. Government could support training, subsidized access to supercomputers, and networking of users.[39] If the goal is to create externalities, in this case it does not matter if the supercomputers are made in the United States or Japan. Figure 5.2 summarizes these cases and their policy implications.

As might be expected, there are important caveats to this line of argument. First and foremost, a government should be concerned about maintaining a domestic industry if there is a risk of foreign monopoly or cartelization. If letting a domestic industry succumb to foreign competition would severely restrict competition and cause consumers to face higher prices or restricted access to externality-laden goods, there may be a case for government subsidization of domestic producers. The government's decision to support a domestic industry will probably revolve around whether the potential for new entrants would prevent foreign firms from exercising significant monopoly power.

A second caveat is that it is important to be sure that technological or linkage externalities really do exist. Krugman (1991, 53–54) points out that the problem with technological externalities, being ideas, is that they rarely leave a paper trail. Linkage externalities may be more easily observ-

---

39. It is true that both supercomputer manufacturers and commercial users have a financial incentive to support this cadre because of the ideas they generate and the fact that they are a source of skilled employees. However, the manufacturers and commercial users will underinvest in nurturing sophisticated users because they cannot reap exclusive benefits: the ideas generated circulate freely, and employees can move freely from firm to firm. However, it may be reasonable for government to seek co-funding from the private sector for this type of human capital-building activity. Some observers (see *The Economist's* survey of human capital theory, 26 March 1994, 85–86) argue that workers themselves will invest considerably in their own training if it is not firm-specific.

able, since they are generated by intermediate industries that have scale or learning economies of production. In both cases, however, the onus is on proponents to show that the externality exists.

A third caveat is that the externality must be international, not domestic, in scope; otherwise there may be good reasons to be concerned about whether the good is produced in the United States or abroad. Here, too, there are difficulties in determining whether and how quickly and cheaply technological externalities travel across borders.[40] For linkage externalities, if the good or service is traded, the externality is likely to be international.

It is sometimes argued that users of externality-laden goods must be geographically close to the producers to learn best how to apply the new goods or ideas. Distance may create a lag in the diffusion of ideas. This is particularly problematic if the first users of the good or idea gain an advantage over competitors by being first. If so, there may be a reasonable argument for government support for domestic producers. Alternatively, it may be cheaper for the government to invest in dissemination of information about new products and ideas developed abroad.

Policy Implications

The satellite and supercomputer cases have important policy implications, not just for these two industries, but potentially also for many other high-technology sectors. Proponents of these two cases argued that supercomputers and satellites were especially deserving of government help in the Japanese market because they are vital to US competitiveness and to national security. Unfortunately, the advocates offered merely plausible, not totally convincing, arguments and evidence. Many other high-technology industries could and may eventually make similar arguments. Because government financing is necessarily limited, and to avoid expensive policy mistakes, it behooves government decision makers to provide a defensible rationale and evidence for supporting high-technology industries on competitiveness and/or national security grounds.

Much of the evidence required to make reasoned policy decisions for specific industries, whether high- or low-tech, must come from detailed knowledge of the industry. While there is often a wealth of such information scattered about the public and private sectors, it is not always available in a timely fashion. For example, in high-technology industries, information about alleged externalities is not readily available and could take considerable time to be collected and assessed. Moreover, industry representatives do not always objectively present vital information about their industries so that policymakers can readily assess the pros and cons of policy options.

---

40. See Lichtenberg (1992) for some evidence suggesting that international dissemination of externalities is not complete or instantaneous.

Policies to support specific industries, particularly trade policies, are often made under severe time constraints with inadequate information and analysis. The result is sometimes ineffectual policies or costly mistakes. Many knowledgeable observers have complained that the US government is inadequately structured to collect and assess the industry-specific information needed for sensible policymaking (Competitiveness Policy Council 1992, 33–34; Tyson 1992, 289–95). They recommend that some government agency be charged with collecting detailed information about industry structure and performance. We strongly support creating such a repository of information and analytic capacity within government. Our goal is not to promote industrial policy. Rather, the purpose is to have vital information available when decisions have to be made. Of course, better information does not guarantee good policymaking, but it usually helps.

The congressional Office of Technology Assessment, the General Accounting Office, the Library of Congress, the Departments of Agriculture, Labor, and Commerce, the International Trade Commission, and other government agencies contain valuable industry expertise, as do many private-sector trade and professional associations. To argue for a new industrial information collecting and assessment agency is not to denigrate existing expertise. Rather, it is a plea to draw on these valuable sources to collect information in a comprehensive way, fill in gaps, and make the information more accessible and timely.

Two recent examples of policy toward supercomputers, described in the following two sections, illustrate the need for better information and analysis when issues of competitiveness and national security arise. Both examples have broader implications for US trade and industrial policy toward high-technology industries.

What Role for Retaliation?

The first example focuses on the issue of Japanese price discounting of supercomputers.[41] The 1987 supercomputer agreement was criticized for not dealing with the discounting problem. It was believed that discounting was ruinous for US manufacturers, which could not long survive a price war with their deep-pocketed Japanese competitors. The 1990 agreement, on the other hand, is seen by some knowledgeable observers as "deeply flawed" because the limits it imposed on discounting will strengthen the profitability of Japanese manufacturers and thus allow them to compete more effectively with American producers (OTA 1991, 277).

---

41. The issue is of continuing importance because of ongoing discounting in commercial supercomputer sales ("Megaflops," *The Economist*, 28 November 1992, 79). The issue is more generally relevant to how the US government should respond to foreign government subsidies or private predatory behavior.

Tyson (1992, 81–82) argues that, absent a coherent US strategy to attack Japanese structural protection, a better alternative to the discounting agreement would have been to retaliate by subsidizing US sales to Japanese public institutions. Tyson's proposed export subsidy is not intended to deter Japanese discounting because raising prices would simply help the Japanese producers. Rather, the purpose of the export subsidy would be to allow US producers to compete in the Japanese public market. An export subsidy might indeed be appropriate if the technological or linkage externalities generated by US production diffused mainly within the American economy but not outside US borders—at least not quickly. The benefits to the United States might include lower costs to American users of supercomputers as US producers experience economies of scale or technological spin-offs that are freely acquired by US but not foreign firms.

To be sure, Japanese users would benefit from cheaper supercomputers, and they might even thank American taxpayers for the subsidy. But the real purpose of the US export subsidy is preemptory. It would slow or prevent the development of the Japanese supercomputer industry and thus deny the Japanese economy the benefits of any linkage or technological externalities, which are assumed to be local, not international, in scope.

If, on the other hand, the nonpecuniary externalities are global rather than national, a US subsidy to Japanese consumers is not the best way to improve American welfare (figure 5.2). Rather, the best policy would be to stop worrying about American supercomputer manufacturers and instead to subsidize American users of supercomputers.[42] If externalities are global in scope, it does not matter if American users buy machines made in the United States or Japan. What matters is that there be a supercomputer industry *somewhere* that generates externalities. US users will benefit from the subsidy, and the US economy will benefit from the externality.

A subsidy to American buyers would also be appropriate if the externality is generated by the use, rather than the production, of supercomputers. If the externality is local rather than global, it makes sense to use US tax dollars to benefit the American economy by giving US buyers access to low-cost machines or by nurturing a cadre of sophisticated users. But, here again, it does not matter whose machines American consumers buy, only that they have access to the best available machines.

What Role for Reciprocity?

The second illustration of the policy importance of having good information and analysis is the issue of reciprocity in public procurement. In both

---

42. Similarly, if externalities are global, the US government should not impose antidumping duties on Japanese producers that discount their US prices. If the US government wishes to maintain a US supercomputer industry for national security reasons, it should directly subsidize the US industry rather than restrict US consumers' access to low-cost foreign machines.

the supercomputer and satellite agreements, Japan sought and received an explicit acknowledgment that the US public sector would be reciprocally open to foreign sellers. As a matter of principle, US public procurement is open to foreign vendors as required by the GATT Government Procurement Code. In practice, foreign sellers have not had much access to these public markets for two reasons. First and foremost, US vendors are generally the lowest-cost sellers, albeit in part because they have received significant government financial support to develop their products. Second, foreign vendors have been excluded from certain government procurements, as permitted by the GATT code, when purchases were made for reasons of national security or pure research.[43] In addition, in several highly publicized incidents, the administration or Congress actively discouraged US purchases of Japanese supercomputers (Tyson 1992, 80).

Several observers have pointed to the apparent lack of US reciprocity as a potential problem with the 1990 supercomputer agreement (Tyson 1992, 80; OTA 1991, 277). Japanese supercomputers currently are not very competitive in the US market based on price–real world performance or software availability criteria. However, some observers worry that if Japanese producers do become competitive, their government will seek reciprocity. Reciprocal access to the US government market, which constitutes nearly half of the US supercomputer market, would threaten American supercomputer firms' profitability.[44]

The issue of reciprocity has also caused considerable congressional concern. In July 1991, House Majority Leader Richard Gephardt and Congressman Martin Sabo, in whose Minnesota district Cray is located, introduced an amendment to the High Performance Computing Act that would have restricted foreign access to the US public supercomputer market (*Congressional Record*, 11 July 1991, H5421–23). The amendment was dropped under threat of presidential veto.

In July 1992, Congressman John Conyers, chairman of the House Government Operations Committee and its Subcommittee on Legislation and National Security, held hearings entitled "Is the Administration Giving Away the US Supercomputer Industry?" Conyers was concerned about reports that NASA "was restrained from using the 'industrial mobilization' exemption, in response to the Japanese threat, to protect national security by limiting competition on purchases of supercomputers to US vendors" (House Committee on Government Operations, press release,

---

43. See General Agreement on Tariffs and Trade *Agreement on Government Procurement* (revised text), Geneva, 1988. Article VIII contains the national security exemption. Article V. 16(e) permits single tendering procedures for research and development.

44. Testimony of Arvid G. Larson before the House Committee on Government Operations, hearings on "Is the Administration Giving Away the US Supercomputer Industry?" 1 and 8 July 1992.

7 July 1992, 1). Following the requirements of the GATT Government Procurement Code, in January 1991 NASA requested and received a national security exemption from the General Services Administration for the purchase of a supercomputer for its Ames Research Center. The exemption was based on NASA's belief, with the Department of Defense's concurrence, that it was necessary to restrict the purchase to domestic sources to prevent foreigners from acquiring information on certain aerospace technology deemed important to national security.[45] A US subsidiary of the Japanese supercomputer manufacturer NEC challenged the exemption. The General Services Administration's Board of Contract Appeals ruled that the exemption could not be justified. NASA therefore held an open competition, which Cray won.

In testimony before the House Committee on Government Operations (1992, 113), Cray CEO John Rollwagen complained that some US procuring agencies had misinterpreted the 1990 supercomputer agreement as containing "an implied quid pro quo or reciprocity arrangement. There have been examples in the US where some government agencies have lowered their standards, that is, changed the performance expectations for systems being purchased that enabled Japanese competitors to fit in the specifications."

Administration officials were extremely sensitive to the charge that the 1990 agreement imposed any reciprocal requirement on US public procurement. USTR General Counsel Gary Edson testified that "the 1990 supercomputer agreement with Japan is a one-way street: it imposes obligations only on Japan, *not* on the United States. Indeed, it requires Japan to undertake obligations beyond those imposed by the GATT Government Procurement Code" (House Committee on Government Operations 1992, 209).[46] In fact, USTR Hills's 15 July 1990 letter to Ambassador Murata acknowledges "that it is the policy of the Government of the United States to provide competitive and non-discriminatory market opportunities in the United States consistent with our obligations under the GATT Government Procurement Code. This policy maintains the openness and transparency of the US market for government procurement of supercomputers without regard to the nationality of the manufacturer."

It seems a distinction without a difference to argue that the 1990 agreement imposes no reciprocal obligation on the United States when, as part of the agreement, Japan requested and received an assurance from USTR that the United States was similarly obligated under the GATT code. In any event, the United States is certainly obliged to provide reciprocity, whether under the code or under the agreement.

---

45. See testimony of Edward G. Frankle in House Committee on Government Operations (1992, 184–87) and letter from NASA administrator Richard Truly to Carla Hills (359–61).

46. See also Department of Commerce (1992, 45–46) for a strong denial that the 1990 agreement is reciprocal.

Some members of Congress and federal agencies are clearly uneasy over the reciprocity issue. They worry that opening US public supercomputer procurement will undermine the US industry, which is deemed crucial to US security. Based on NEC's protest of the Ames procurement, it seems likely that Japanese firms will challenge future national security exclusions.

The national security argument for maintaining a domestic supercomputer industry has not been made public.[47] Such arguments generally revolve around the need for secure access to certain goods for two reasons: use by government agencies such as the Defense Department and the intelligence community, and use by the civilian sector to produce war materiel. The need to maintain certain domestic industries for national security purposes is described as the "industrial mobilization" exemption in US regulations, which permit restrictions on procurement from foreign vendors.[48]

It is indisputable that government agencies and the civilian sector need secure access to the best available supercomputers for national security purposes. The fundamental policy issue is whether the government needs to maintain an American supercomputer industry to have secure access to the best supercomputers.

The natural inclination of national security officials is to prefer domestic to foreign suppliers in order to maintain secure lines of supply, reduce the risks of espionage, and to be guaranteed state-of-the-art technology. As Graham and Krugman (1991, 115–16) point out, in the days of US technological preeminence, having the best available technology was almost synonymous with having American technology. This is no longer the case. Foreign firms are increasingly sources of state-of-the-art defense-related technology. The question is whether US security is best served by excluding foreign supercomputers from defense-related procurements. The answer will invariably depend on the characteristics of the specific good in question—hence the need for detailed information and analysis of defense-related industries.

Graham and Krugman (1991, 152) suggest that, in general, the best policy may be to allow foreign vendors to bid on national security-related procurement but require them to maintain production and/or R&D facilities in the United States. This approach has three advantages. First, it maintains secure access to defense-related goods produced under US jurisdiction and limits the potential for espionage. Second, it provides

---

47. For a generic discussion of such national security arguments, see the memo from the Congressional Research Service to the House Committee on Government Operations (1992, 410–15).

48. Code of Federal Regulations Federal Acquisition Regulations System, 48 CFR chapter 1, section 6.302-3 (1 October 1991 ed.), p. 87. See also section 6.302-6, which provides an exemption if disclosure of the government's needs would compromise national security.

both government and civilian users with the best available technology at the most competitive price. Third, it ensures that the American economy reaps the benefits of externalities generated either through the production or consumption of high-technology goods. Any subsidies or government-sponsored research should be available to both American and foreign-owned firms producing in the United States.

Strengthening US competitiveness is the best way to enhance the nation's capacity to mobilize industrial production in time of war. Restricting US access to foreign technology and reducing competition serve neither America's security nor its competitiveness goals.

Wood Products

The wood products case was perhaps most illustrative of how Congress wanted super 301 to be used: to secure a significant increase in US exports by peeling away onion-like layers of Japanese protection. It was by far the largest super 301 case against Japan in terms of potential US export opportunities. Government and industry estimates in 1988–89 of the possible annual export gains ranged from $500 million to $2 billion.[49] As Congress intended, the case addressed the alleged problem of multiple layers of protection. The official US complaint focused exclusively on technical barriers, such as product standards, building codes, and testing and certification procedures. Some of these ostensible nontariff impediments were arguably violations of the GATT's Agreement on Technical Barriers to Trade. In addition, US industry representatives pressed for substantial reductions in Japan's tariffs, which were sometimes quite high but perfectly legal under the GATT. The US industry also sought cuts in alleged Japanese subsidies. Finally, the industry urged discussion of structural issues, such as land use, under the Structural Impediments Initiative (SII) negotiations.

Japan is the largest foreign market for US wood products, accounting for about 40 to 45 percent of US exports. In recent years, about 70 percent of these US wood exports were logs or raw products such as wood chips

---

49. Commerce Department estimates were "clearly well over half a billion dollars, and it may be well over a billion dollars of potential exports" according to testimony by Deputy Assistant Commerce Secretary Allan Dunn before the Senate Finance Committee Subcommittee on International Trade, 101st Cong. 1st sess., 22 June 1989, on Japanese Trade Barriers to Forest Products, S. Hrg. 101-526, Pt. 1, p. 10. Lawyers for the National Forest Products Association used what they characterized as conservative assumptions to estimate a potential gain of $2.1 billion (see "Comments concerning Japanese Restrictions Affecting Importation of Forest Products, Under Section 301 of the Trade Act of 1974, As Amended," submitted to USTR by the law firm of Dewey, Ballantine, Busby, Palmer, and Wood, 18 July 1989, on file in the USTR reading room).

(table 5.2a; US Department of Agriculture, *Wood Products: International Trade and Foreign Market,* March 1994). Although Japan has historically been a major market for US forest products, US government and industry officials have long felt that US exports, particularly of high value-added products, should be much larger.

The super 301 case was the latest in a long-running series of US efforts to open the Japanese wood products market. Since the late 1970s, US producers have complained about a host of tariff and regulatory obstacles, which, they argue, distort the structure of Japan's consumption and trade in wood products.

Japan is the world's largest net importer of wood products, but its per capita consumption is among the lowest in the industrial world (FAO, *Forest Products Annual,* 1992).[50] Japanese imports are strongly skewed toward raw materials rather than finished products. In the mid 1980s, Japan accounted for 40 to 45 percent of world trade volume in logs, but only 10 percent of trade in processed wood products (Australian Bureau of Agricultural and Resource Economics 1988, 253).

There are, of course, several factors other than protection that could explain these patterns of trade and consumption. Japan's small size and mountainous terrain probably account for its comparative disadvantage in wood production and hence its high imports. Low per capita consumption could be due to high transport costs and a preference for building materials less flammable and more earthquake-resistant than wood.[51]

It is more difficult to explain the high ratio of raw to finished imports of wood products without some evidence that Japan is an unusually efficient producer of fabricated products. In fact, US government and industry analysts argue that Japanese wood fabricators are high-cost and inefficient by world standards.[52] They contend that Japan would be a much larger importer of fabricated wood products absent trade and regulatory obstacles.

The US industry has complained particularly about Japan's tariff structure. Most raw wood products such as logs and rough-cut lumber enter Japan duty-free. However, tariffs on wood products rise with the level of fabrication. This escalation of tariffs on finished products leads to high

---

50. The United States is the world's largest gross importer but is also a major exporter of wood products. Per capita consumption is discussed in US Department of Commerce (1989, 5–6).

51. Japanese industry and government officials cite frequent earthquakes, the fact that Japan has one of the highest rates of deaths by fire among the industrial countries, and memories of US firebombing during World War II, as reasons for consumer preferences and building codes that limit wood construction. (US Department of Commerce 1989, 142–45).

52. See US Department of Commerce (1989, chapter 3) for an extensive discussion. The report emphasizes the difficulties of making cost comparisons and shows data that suggest that Japanese mill costs are two to three times US costs.

Table 5.2a United States: wood products exports to Japan, 1980–93 (millions of dollars except where noted)

	1980	1981	1982	1983	1984	1985	1986	1987	1988	1989	1990	1991	1992	1993
Logs[a]	1,659	1,067	1,044	852	797	843	951	1,312	1,586	2,001	1,992	1,815	1,954	2,255
Lumber[b]	230	188	206	202	198	200	311	439	567	694	639	630	631	765
Panels[c]	8	5	7	6	6	5	8	16	23	30	32	38	35	52
Joinery and Carpentry[d]	n.a.	n.a.	n.a.	n.a.	n.a.	5	9	17	26	37	56	54	43	45
FSM[e]	n.a.	n.a.	n.a.	n.a.	n.a.	n.a.	n.a.	n.a.	n.a.	2	4	4	3	9
Total[f]	1,918	1,282	1,276	1,079	1,021	1,068	1,300	1,812	2,241	2,834	2,814	2,616	2,723	3,194
Logs (as percentage of total)	86.5	83.2	81.8	79.0	78.1	78.9	73.1	72.4	70.8	70.6	70.8	69.4	71.8	70.6
Real yen-dollar exchange rate (1980=100)	100	105	118	117	120	121	92	84	78	86	92	85	82	76
Real Japanese GDP growth (percent)	4.3	3.7	3.1	3.2	5.1	5.0	2.6	4.1	6.2	4.7	4.8	4.0	1.3	−0.1
Japanese new residential construction (1980=100)	100	91	90	84	84	87	93	115	112	114	113	98	102	112

n.a. = not available

a. Softwood and hardwood logs and chips

b. Softwood and hardwood lumber

c. Softwood and hardwood veneer and plywood, hardboard, particle board, medium density fiberboard, oriented strand board, and other panels

d. Windows/frames, flush doors, doors/frames, parquet panels, shuttering, shingles, edge-glued lumber, FSM, and builders' joinery and carpentry of wood nesoi

e. Fabricated structural members

f. Total includes some products not contained in the above categories.

Sources: US Department of Agriculture, Foreign Agricultural Service, *Wood Products: International Trade and Foreign Markets, Annual Statistical Trade Issue,* March 1992, 18, 20; and 1993–94 updates; Peter Gold and Dick Nanto, Congressional Research Service, "Japan-U.S. Trade: U.S. Exports of Negotiated Products, 1985–1990," 26 November, 1991 (91-891 E), 38; US Department of Commerce export statistics; Japanese Ministry of Construction (for data on housing construction).

Table 5.2b United States: wood products' export growth per period, 1980–93 (percentage change in dollar values)

Wood product	1980–85 Japan	1980–85 World[a]	1985–89 Japan	1985–89 World[a]	1990–93 Japan	1990–93 World[a]
Logs	− 49	96	137	29	13	− 19
Lumber	− 13	− 31	247	149	20	13
Panels	− 32	− 16	453	176	61	16
Joinery and Carpentry	n.a.	n.a.	590	n.a.	− 20	56
FSM	n.a.	n.a.	n.a.	n.a.	150	64
Total	− 44	− 8	165	100	14	11

n.a. = not available

a. Excluding US exports to Japan.

Note: For definitions and sources, refer to table 5.2a.

effective rates of protection. For example, in the 1980s finished softwood lumber and plywood faced nominal tariffs of 8 and 10 percent, respectively. But, because of the low tariffs on raw wood, the effective rates of protection were 19 and 27 percent, respectively (US Department of Commerce 1989, 132–35). Some US experts believe that, absent these high effective rates of protection, many high-cost Japanese producers would leave the industry, greatly increasing demand for imports. Thus, the US industry gave high priority to reducing Japanese tariffs.[53]

US producers also railed against numerous nontariff barriers (US Department of Commerce 1989, 135–54). Their complaints included:

■ product standards that discriminate against imports;

■ standards based on aesthetic qualities (e.g., appearance) rather than performance characteristics;

■ unnecessarily restrictive building and fire codes;

■ subsidies, including low-cost loans and tax incentives for inefficient producers;

■ government tolerance of cartels and restrictive business practices.

Responding to these complaints, in January 1978 USTR Robert Strauss and Minister for External Economic Affairs Nobuhiko Ushiba issued a communiqué calling for expanded bilateral forest products trade and increased Japanese imports of processed products.[54] In 1979–80 binational

---

53. See the industry's testimony to the Senate Finance Committee, Subcommittee on International Trade, *Japanese Trade Barriers to Forest Products,* S. Hrg. 101-526, Pt. 1, June 1989.

54. See "Statement of the Japan Lumber Importers Association" before the USTR, submitted by the law firm of Mudge, Rose, Guthrie, Alexander, and Ferdon, July 1989, on file in the USTR reading room.

government and industry committees were formed to encourage increased US exports of wood products, particularly processed goods. These committees served largely to exchange information and discuss problems such as product standards and building codes. They did not negotiate over alleged trade barriers, nor did they have much discernible impact on US exports. The value of US wood product exports to Japan declined by nearly 45 percent, from $1.9 billion in 1980 to $1.1 billion in 1985 (table 5.2a), a period of both dollar overvaluation, when total US exports to Japan grew by only 6 percent, and of slightly slower economic growth in Japan, which experienced a drop of 10 percent compared with the previous five-year period. The Japanese housing market went into sharp decline in 1979–85, with wood home construction particularly hard hit.[55]

The MOSS Talks

After several years of bilateral discussions, US trade officials and industry representatives grew increasingly frustrated with Japan's unwillingness to open its wood product markets (Japan Economic Institute Report 23B, 15 June 1984, 5). Following immediately on the successful beef and citrus negotiations (see chapter 10), in the spring of 1984 USTR William Brock criticized Japan's reluctance to reduce tariffs on softwood plywood, veneer, and particle board. Agriculture Secretary John Block announced that Japanese tariff reductions for these products were a high priority because they could yield an extra $1 billion in US exports. US officials pointed out that Japanese consumers and the home-building industry would benefit from these tariff cuts. Japanese officials responded that their wood products industry was in poor economic health and could not accept liberalization.

In January 1985, in a meeting with President Reagan, Prime Minister Nakasone proposed market access negotiations on wood products under the auspices of what eventually became the MOSS talks (box 5.2). The two sides reached a "consensus" (no formal agreement was ever signed) in January 1986 that focused primarily on tariff cuts and included modest but valuable progress on nontariff obstacles.

The Japanese government offered to cut tariffs and to accelerate other reductions previously agreed to in the 1979 Tokyo Round.[56] These tariff reductions, averaging 30 percent, were offered on a number of fabricated products that were high priorities for US exporters, including laminated

---

55. The yen depreciated vis-à-vis the dollar by about 20 percent in real terms in this period. See Yu and McCormick (1992, 41–46) on Japanese housing trends.

56. See "Statement of the Japan Lumber Importers Association" before the USTR, submitted by the law firm of Mudge, Rose, Guthrie, Alexander, and Ferdon, July 1989, p. 9, on file in the USTR reading room.

lumber, softwood plywood, veneer, and particle board (US Department of Commerce 1989, 157). The cuts were phased in over the period January 1986 through April 1988.

The MOSS talks also began to address several US complaints about nontariff impediments. Japan agreed to modify its building code to allow greater use of 4-by-8 panels in construction. This change was important to US exporters that produce these panels in huge volume for the US market, and found it costly to retool to provide the smaller 3-by-6 panels required by the Japanese building code.

The MOSS consensus also allowed establishment of foreign testing organizations (FTOs) in the United States to certify that US products met Japan Agricultural Standards (JAS). The JAS stamp certifies that the product meets a certain level of performance. The stamp is sometimes required under the building code, and it is seen generally as a quality indicator. FTOs save US exporters time and money, since products can be shipped directly to the buyer, thus avoiding lengthy delays for inspection in Japan (US Department of Commerce 1989, 137).[57]

Discussions during and after the MOSS talks resulted in two other changes seen as important by US exporters. First, Japan agreed to accept ponderosa and lodgepole pine, which are abundant in the United States, for use in laminated lumber (US Department of Commerce 1989, 141). Second, among several changes in standards and building codes, the most valuable from US producers' viewpoint was relaxation of building code restrictions on single-family, three-story wood houses. This change was expected to increase demand for wood products over time, because it would permit bigger houses in urban areas where land is often very expensive (US Department of Commerce 1989, 146).

Overall, the US industry viewed the MOSS talks as quite productive (General Accounting Office 1988, 40–42). The US Department of Commerce (1989, xiii) called them a "major factor in increasing US exports." However, both the US government and industry wanted additional progress in liberalizing both tariff and nontariff barriers.

The 1989 Super 301 Case

Between 1986 and 1989, the dollar depreciated by 30 percent in real terms relative to the yen, and average annual Japanese growth accelerated slightly compared with the previous four years. The Japanese housing market recovered in 1986–89, and the total square footage of annual wood housing construction grew by 25 percent.[58] The Congressional Research

---

57. It is estimated that FTOs could save US exporters as much as 7 percent of the landed price of lumber.

58. On Japanese housing construction, see Moffett and Waggener (1992, 57–58 and appendix 6).

Service (Gold and Nanto 1991, 37–38) calculates that US exports of wood products to Japan that were covered in the MOSS and other negotiations grew by about 133 percent, from $340 million to $791 million, between 1986 and 1989. By comparison, all other US merchandise exports to Japan grew by 65 percent in this period (Congressional Research Service 1991, 9; see also tables 5.2a and b for data on aggregate US-Japan trade in wood products).

Despite this growth in wood exports, US government and industry officials continued to press for further market opening. The Japanese government, however, repeatedly refused bilateral talks, arguing that any further negotiations should be conducted multilaterally in the Uruguay Round. The United States viewed this as procrastination since Japan was not then offering concessions on wood products in the round.

The Bush administration faced strong, mounting pressure from industry and Congress to make Japanese wood product barriers a super 301 priority. In March 1989, the National Forest Products Association (NFPA), representing 85 percent of the industry, urged USTR Hills to designate Japan.[59]

There was also strong bipartisan support for a super 301 case in the Senate. The two leading congressional proponents were Senators Robert Packwood (R-OR) and Max Baucus (D-MT), who represent major wood-exporting states. Both senators are influential actors in trade policy: Packwood is the senior Republican on the Finance Committee, which has primary Senate jurisdiction over trade issues, and Baucus chairs the Finance Committee's Subcommittee on International Trade.

In April, the Department of Commerce (1989, 121) released a study, *The Japanese Solid Wood Products Market,* that included a detailed discussion of obstacles facing US exporters. The report concluded that "further [Japanese] concessions without additional [US] initiatives appear unlikely." The Commerce study was commissioned by Senator Packwood, who said that it bolstered his argument for a super 301 case (*Journal of Commerce,* 24 April 1989, 5).[60] On 16 May, 13 senators signed a letter drafted by Senators Baucus and Packwood urging President Bush to launch a super 301 action on wood products. They argued that opening the Japanese market could yield a $1.2 billion increase in US exports and that Congress had drafted super 301 precisely to focus on such major barriers.

---

59. The US forest products industry comprises both very large and very small producers, some of which export both logs and finished products and others that export either raw or finished products. Initially, there are some differences within the industry over whether and how to pursue improved market access. By mid-1989, however, the industry reached an internal consensus and was reasonably unified in its tactics.

60. The industry commissioned a number of technical studies that were used by the Commerce Department and consulted closely with Commerce as the report was being written. The industry reportedly spent about $1 million in studies and legal activities related to the super 301 case.

USTR Carla Hills designated Japanese technical barriers on wood products as a priority practice under super 301 on 26 May 1989. Her designation focused exclusively on those regulations and standards that had discriminatory and trade-restricting effects on US exports in possible violation of Japan's obligations under the GATT Agreement on Technical Barriers to Trade, better known as the Standards Code.[61] The omission of tariffs, which were also a priority for US industry, was intentional. First, USTR wanted to use super 301 in ways at least nominally consistent with GATT rules: high tariffs per se are not a violation of Japan's GATT obligations. Second, it was unclear whether high tariffs were actionable under section 301: they are not "unjustifiable" or "discriminatory," and it is not obvious that they come under even the very broad rubric of "unreasonable" trade barriers.

The NFPA's lawyers recognized this second ambiguity and advised USTR to ignore it and seek liberalization of Japanese tariffs, as well as nontariff barriers.[62] The association complained of an "interrelated web" of Japanese barriers and warned that removal of one might not lead to significant market opening. The US producers therefore sought a combination of tariff cuts, reform of standards and building codes, and discipline on subsidies.

Specific US complaints about Japan's tariff structure included high effective rates of protection on finished products and misclassification of certain laminated wood products into 15 to 20 percent tariff categories when they should correctly be subject to a 3.9 percent duty.

The industry repeated its long-standing complaints about Japanese building codes and product standards, which were said to be unnecessarily restrictive and an unjustifiable violation of the GATT Standards Code. US exporters were particularly eager to obtain revisions in the building code that would permit greater use of wood products in residential and commercial construction. A frequent complaint was that Japanese product standards still reflected design or aesthetic criteria rather than performance criteria, as required by the Standards Code. Moreover, Japan refused to use foreign performance-based test results in certifying some imported products. The industry cited a particularly egregious example—involving a fireproof certification—of why some Japanese standards were unreasonable under US law and a possible violation of the GATT code:

> . . . a wood product was developed with a clear coating which, when heated to a particular temperature, would turn to foam and douse a flame. Japan required, however, that the product be subjected to a flame for a certain period before it

---

61. "Report on Trade Liberalization Priorities Pursuant to Section 310 of the Trade Act of 1974," *Federal Register* 54, No. 108, 7 June 1989, 24438–42.

62. See "Comments Concerning Japanese Restrictions Affecting Importation of Forest Products," submitted by the law firm of Dewey, Ballantine, Bushby, Palmer, and Wood on behalf of the National Forest Products Association, 18 July 1989, on file in the USTR reading room.

could be certified as fire-proof. Since the wood product doused the flame before the time expired, it was not certified. As foreign [test] data are not accepted, although based on performance and quality of materials, this product was not certified.[63]

The industry also claimed that a variety of Japanese subsidies nullified and impaired US rights under the GATT. In addition, some subsidies, reportedly given to win the Japanese industry's acceptance of the MOSS consensus, were in fact used to offset the MOSS liberalization and hence were unjustifiable under section 301.

Finally, the industry listed a number of structural impediments such as anticompetitive practices, the distribution system, and land-use and housing policies. It recommended that these practices be addressed under either super 301 or the SII talks.

The wood products negotiations were politically sensitive for both sides. USTR was under very substantial industry and congressional pressure to reach a satisfactory deal. There was significant bipartisan congressional support for retaliation, particularly among the leadership of the Senate Finance Committee. For example, Senator Max Baucus, chairman of the Finance Committee's trade subcommittee, threatened to submit legislation mandating retaliation against Japan unless the wood products case was expeditiously resolved (*Journal of Commerce*, 7 December 1989, 1A). An array of industry representatives also urged retaliation if the negotiations failed to yield significant Japanese liberalization.[64]

The Japanese government faced political resistance from its industry, which was in economic decline and strongly opposed further liberaliza-tion.[65] The industry, which was rural and scattered throughout many legislative districts, enjoyed substantial political support in the Diet.

The US negotiators attempted to exploit differences between the Minis-try of Agriculture, Forestry, and Fisheries (MAFF) and the Ministry of Construction, which represented somewhat different industry interests. Thus, for example, USTR received some support from the MAFF and from the influential former Minister of Agriculture (and future Prime Minister) Tsutomu Hata for changes in the building code that would permit greater use of wood products, both domestic and foreign-made. The Ministry of Construction (MOC), which had little experience in trade

63. See "Comments concerning Japanese Restrictions Affecting Importation of Forest Prod-ucts," submitted by the law firm of Dewey, Ballantine, Bushby, Palmer, and Wood on behalf of the National Forest Products Association. The same example is cited in Department of Commerce (1989, 153), which refers to a story in a December 1988 article in *Business Tokyo*.

64. Testimony before the Senate Finance Committee, Subcommittee on International Trade, on Japanese Trade Barriers to Forest Products, S. Hrg. 101-526, Pt. 2., 26 February 1990.

65. Japanese industry representatives reported that 657 saw mill factories and 22 plywood factories had closed in 1986–88 (statement submitted to USTR, 17 July 1989, on file in USTR reading room).

negotiations, deeply resented foreign demands to revise the building code in ways that might conceivably undermine safety. There was an office within MOC whose purpose it was to increase the use of 2-by-4 wood products in construction, but MOC was also under considerable pressure from steel and concrete producers not to undermine demand for their products. USTR and the US industry appealed directly to Japanese consumers, who would benefit from safe, lower cost, and more aesthetic wood housing. However, they say that these tactics had, at best, a modest impact on the negotiations.

The most important influence on the outcome was the fact that the Japanese government strongly wanted to avoid being designated for a second time as a super 301 priority country. Redesignation could have led to quite substantial US retaliation over wood products that almost certainly would have targeted Japanese manufactured exports. It also could have led to renewed congressional pressure to designate additional priority practices. It almost certainly would have contributed to a sharp deterioration in bilateral economic, and perhaps political, relations.

The deadline for USTR to announce its new super 301 priorities was 30 April 1990. US negotiators say they used the threat of super 301 redesignation to reach tentative agreements on supercomputers and satellites in late March and early April. However, the wood products deal was not struck until the deadline was imminent (25 April), and it was reportedly a key factor in USTR Hills's decision not to redesignate Japan. To the Japanese government's relief, on 27 April USTR Hills announced that Japan would not be named for a second time as a priority country (Japan Economic Institute Report 18B, 4 May 1990, 13).

The agreement required some compromise on both sides.[66] Japan, which had strenuously resisted further tariff liberalization, promised quite substantial cuts, particularly of its highest rates, on about $100 million of imports. For its part, the United States accepted that these tariff reductions would be negotiated in the Uruguay Round and implemented upon completion of the round. Effective June 1990, Japan also agreed to reclassify certain laminated products into a 3.9 percent tariff category, a huge cut from the previous 15 to 20 percent duties.

Most of the 27-page agreement is devoted to detailed concessions on nontariff measures. Japan accepted that, in principle, building standards should be performance-based. Whenever possible, foreign test data would be accepted when drawing up standards for new products. The certification process would be open and expeditious, proceeding in a number of cases on agreed timetables. Building and fire codes were to be revised to permit the greater use of wood products, for example, in three-story buildings for commercial and residential use.

---

66. See Japan Economic Institute Report 18B, 4 May 1990, 12, for a summary. The agreement consists of an exchange of letters between USTR Carla Hills and Ambassador Ryohei Murata dated 15 June 1990 and is on file in the USTR reading room.

The agreement contains a carefully crafted institutional structure and process intended to sustain ongoing liberalization and resolution of disputes. It establishes a Building Experts Committee and a Japan Agricultural Standards Technical Committee, composed of government and industry experts from the United States, Japan, and other interested countries. These technical committees monitor implementation of the agreement and advise the two governments on ways to harmonize standards, building codes, and testing methodologies. In addition, a Wood Products Subcommittee of the US-Japan Trade Committee, composed of high-level government officials, was created to monitor implementation of the agreement and the work of the two technical committees. The subcommittee was to meet at least twice annually and was expected to resolve any disputes within six months.

The agreement very briefly addressed the subsidy issue. The government of Japan stated its intention to ensure that its subsidies were consistent with the GATT code and the OECD agreement on positive adjustment policies and did not nullify and impair the rights of GATT members. Structural issues such as land prices were left to the SII talks.

Evaluation of the 1990 Wood Products Agreement

The US industry was cautiously pleased with the results of the negotiations. Stephen Lovett, a vice president of the National Forest Products Association, said the agreement "goes a long way towards making up the deficiencies of the MOSS agreement. Even though the Japanese wood products market remains protected in many areas, US government negotiators did an excellent job in achieving a comprehensive package of measures that will eliminate many, but not all, trade barriers."[67] Bob Donnelly, chairman of the forest products Industry Sectoral Advisory Committee to the US government, described the agreement as "a very good one...[that] could help to boost United States sales of value-added wood products in Japan by $750 million annually." He characterized the revisions in the building code, notably those relating to three-story wood buildings, as "major progress in expanding the market."[68] Donnelly pointed out, however, that further progress was necessary both in the Uruguay Round to realize the tariff cuts promised in the super 301 agreement and bilaterally in the two technical committees to make continued progress in removing nontariff obstacles.

Congressional reaction was also quite positive. During the 27 April 1990 hearing of the Senate Finance Committee's trade subcommittee,

---

67. Testimony before the House Ways and Means Subcommittee on Trade, 15 July 1991, 2.

68. Testimony before the Senate Finance Committee, Subcommittee on International Trade, *Super 301: Effectiveness in Opening Foreign Markets,* S. Hrg. 101-995, 101st Cong., 2nd sess., 27 April 1990, 29.

Senator Baucus applauded the entire super 301 process as an "overwhelming success" and said he was "confident that the forest products trade agreement will boost US forest products and create jobs." He cautioned, however, that the super 301 agreements required constant monitoring to achieve what Congress and the US industry expected: results in the form of additional sales to Japan. Senator Packwood gave the agreement a score of 8½ on a scale of 1 to 10, compared with the previous level of market access, which he rated a 3. He described the agreement as "much more than I was hoping for . . . this is great news for Oregon" (Press release, office of Senator Packwood, 25 April 1990). The 1993 National Trade Estimate Report (p. 147) states that "US wood product exports to Japan are expected to increase significantly as a result of the agreement."

Industry officials and government specialists emphasize three features of the agreement that they hope will contribute to its success in increasing US exports. First, the Japanese commitments are spelled out in considerable lawyerly detail and often include specific timetables for implementation. Second, the agreement establishes an institutional structure (the three committees) for ongoing monitoring of its implementation. Third, the agreement is forward-looking in seeking not only to resolve current problems but also to avoid future conflicts by creating a process (via the JAS and Building Committees) to harmonize building standards and ensure that new products can be expeditiously approved.

As of early 1994, US government and industry officials continued to be reasonably pleased with the implementation of the agreement, with the very important exception of the size of Japanese tariff cuts negotiated in the Uruguay Round (described below). They say that the two technical committees are making progress in removing nontariff barriers and speeding the approval of new products. One US government participant on the technical committees praised the detail and specificity of the agreement because it allowed the US side to hold its sometimes unenthusiastic Japanese counterparts accountable for implementation. However, a US government participant also noted that Japanese agencies continue to write building design requirements in ways that intentionally favor Japanese-made products over imported products although there is no apparent technical or safety reason to do so. The United States challenges these discriminatory requirements with some success, albeit slowly and rarely completely, in the meetings of the technical committees.

The agreement appears to have met USTR's goal of using super 301 to strengthen the GATT. It provides improved market access on a most-favored nation (MFN), as opposed to a discriminatory, basis. The eventual tariff cuts will be offered to all exporting countries, although the products specified in the agreement are clearly of greatest interest to North American exporters. The heart of the agreement is the nontariff barriers reduction, which the two technical committees oversee. Participation in these committees is open to all interested countries, although thus far only US and Canadian representatives have attended. The provisions on testing, certification, and standard setting were carefully written to be fully consistent with the GATT standards code.

The agreement's tangible results—the increased US sales that Congress and the industry sought—were disappointing until 1993. Table 5.2 shows that between 1989 and 1992 total US wood exports to Japan stagnated. Exports of logs and lumber declined until 1992, while sales of higher value-added products (panels and fabricated structural members) increased slightly off a very small base.

Several macroeconomic and sectoral trends may explain the weak US export performance between 1989 and 1992. The dollar appreciated vis-à-vis the yen in 1989–90 and was about 5 percent higher in real terms by the end of 1992 compared with 1988. Real growth in Japan slowed to an average of 3.4 percent in 1990–92, compared with an average of 4.5 percent in the preceding five years. In 1992 Japanese growth plummeted to 1.3 percent. Residential construction weakened considerably in 1991–92. There is some debate over whether the widening US export ban on logs harvested from federal and state-owned forests is a factor in the small drop in log exports.[69]

There are grounds for guarded optimism about the potential for growth in US wood exports to Japan. Macroeconomic trends became more favorable as the yen began to appreciate sharply vis-à-vis the dollar in early 1993, and the Japanese government announced a fiscal stimulus to lift the economy out of recession. Residential construction increased sharply in 1993 and early 1994, partly as a result of increased government support for housing loans. It is likely that the combination of renewed Japanese growth, a stronger housing market, a more competitive exchange rate for the dollar, and progress since 1990 in reducing Japanese nontariff barriers will contribute to future US export opportunities in wood products.

US government and industry officials placed considerable emphasis on the eventual impact of the tariff cuts promised in the Uruguay Round. The 1993 National Trade Estimate Report (p. 147), for example, asserted that "satisfactory market access . . . ultimately hinges on the implementation of agreed-upon tariff reductions in the Uruguay Round."

The products on which tariff cuts were promised in the 1990 agreement amount to only about $100 million (1991 values) of US exports. Although tariffs range from 3.5 to 20 percent, the trade-weighted average is only 5.19 percent.[70] The 1990 agreement promises cuts at least as great as those

---

69. See *Japan Economic Institute Report* No. 13B, 9 April 1993, 3–5, for a discussion of Japanese concerns about the log export ban. See also Perez-Garcia (1991). Some US industry participants, however, argue that the log ban both forces Japan to import higher value-added products and makes US exporters of these products more competitive. J. David Richardson (1993, 50–51) argues to the contrary that the log export ban was generally ineffectual, as US exporters simply substituted logs harvested from private lands.

70. This figure is based on trade values for 1988, which was the base year for the Uruguay Round negotiations.

required by the "Swiss Formula" in the previous Tokyo Round. This would imply at least a 33 percent reduction to a 3.45 percent average tariff. The US industry had hoped to achieve the elimination of many tariffs.[71] In the end, however, the Japanese negotiators agreed to cut trade-weighted tariffs by a third.

To calculate the impact of the tariff cuts requires estimates of the elasticity of Japanese import demand for the products in question. We have been unable to locate such elasticities in the literature. An alternative is to calculate what the average elasticity would have to be to produce a doubling of US exports to $200 million. Assuming a 33 percent tariff reduction, the implied elasticity is about 50, which is very high but not totally implausible given the small share of imported fabricated products in total Japanese consumption and the fact that some tariffs appear to be prohibitive. Thus, as an extreme upper bound, we would guess that US exports could increase by as much as $100 million due to the tariff cuts.[72]

A recent General Accounting Office report (1993) suggests that US exporters need to do more to take advantage of the opportunities created by the super 301 and previous wood products negotiations. The report cites a number of complaints from Japanese customers about US exporters' "lack of commitment to and lack of understanding of the Japanese market." Among the problems cited were reliability of supply, customer service, and availability of products (e.g., 3-by-6 panels) designed for the Japanese market. In contrast, Japanese customers claimed that Canadian exporters were more successful in meeting their needs. The report concludes that unless US exporters focus more on consumer needs the US "effort to open the Japanese market will have served to help [foreign] competitors more than the US industry."[73] The US Department of Agricul-

---

71. US industry had strongly urged the complete elimination of all wood product tariffs, and President Clinton called that goal "a high priority negotiating objective" in a letter to Congressman Ron Wyden (D-OR) dated 2 September 1993.

72. Calculations such as this are fraught with uncertainty. Bergsten and Cline (1987), based on perfectly reasonable assumptions, estimated that reductions in Japanese tobacco tariffs and liberalization of the distribution system could cause US exports to double to $200 million. In fact, tobacco exports have soared to well over a billion dollars. It may be that the combined impact of tariff cuts and reductions in nontariff barriers could have substantially greater effects than we hypothesize for the tariff reductions alone. Some US industry observers also suggest that, given high effective rates of protection and the high cost of Japanese producers, even a modest cut in nominal tariffs would drive many Japanese producers from the industry and significantly increase demand for imports.

73. It is difficult to make meaningful comparisons of US and Canadian export performance and still more difficult to discern the reasons for differing performance. In the area of softwood lumber, in which the US and Canada are major exporters to Japan, Canadian exports to Japan grew by 30 percent in 1990–92, while US exports stagnated. The US and Canadian dollars both depreciated by about the same amount (10 to 11 percent) vis-à-vis the yen in this period. Factors other than alleged Canadian marketing prowess could contribute to the difference in performance. These factors include differences in the product mix

ture's Foreign Agricultural Service, the lead government agency for monitoring wood product exports, is reportedly giving more attention to a customer-oriented focus in export promotion.

The wood products agreement illustrates the potential pitfalls of a results-oriented approach to trade liberalization that sets rigid quantitative goals and deadlines for obtaining them.[74] We share the views of both government and industry representatives that the agreement will eventually create fairly substantial export opportunities.

However, for the first three years of the agreement, US exports did not increase, due primarily to macroeconomic factors over which the Japanese government has limited control. Only in 1993 was there substantial growth in US exports, in part because of the yen appreciation and an increase in housing starts, although Japanese growth remained very weak. A results-oriented, quantitative approach could have led to retaliation in the face of such poor results. Clearly, retaliation would have been unjustified and contrary to US interests. In this case, at least, presidential discretion not to retaliate has been the better part of valor.

---

and differences in export prices. Still, the strong difference in export performance suggests that differences in marketing may be important.

74. Congressman Ron Wyden, chairman of the House Committee on Small Business Subcommittee on Regulations, Business Opportunities and Technology, wrote to President Clinton on 11 August 1993 urging him to include implementation of the wood products agreement in the US-Japan framework discussions initiated in July. The congressman complained that the agreement had failed to deliver the expected results. He urged quantitative benchmarks for measuring progress and establishing "deadlines for achieving measurable improvement."

6

Super 301: Brazil and India

Using the super 301 provisions, of US trade law, the United States chose to challenge the trading practices of India and Brazil along with those of Japan for several reasons. First, the administration wanted other countries to be named along with Japan in order to cushion the political impact in Japan. Also, there was merit in the claims: at least until recently, both Brazil and India were widely regarded as abusing the General Agreement on Tariffs and Trade (GATT) principle of special and differential treatment for developing countries to protect their domestic producers with extensive and highly restrictive trade barriers. The attack on Brazil's extensive use of quantitative restrictions signaled US negotiators' impatience with developing-country abuse of the GATT Article 18(B) exemption for balance of payments problems.

US negotiators were also frustrated by the intransigence of India and Brazil on the new areas under negotiation in the Uruguay Round, including services, intellectual property, and foreign investment. US Trade Representative Carla Hills signaled this frustration by naming Indian barriers to foreign investment and the ban on foreign insurance providers as super 301 priorities.

In the spring of 1990, USTR Hills announced mixed results in these cases. She claimed a success with respect to Brazil's quantitative restrictions, which President Fernando Collor de Mello had promised to largely eliminate. But that outcome had far more to do with Collor's election than with the skill of US trade negotiators. Hills could report no progress at all in the discussions with India on foreign investment and insurance. It seems quite possible that no other outcome was anticipated in those cases.

Why Brazil and India?

The starting point for explaining the selection of Brazilian and Indian practices under super 301 was the desire of some US policymakers to diffuse the blow to Japan by designating other countries as unfair traders (Ahearn, Cronin, and Storrs 1990, 18; *Wall Street Journal*, 26 May 1989, A7). These officials wanted to minimize any damage to the broader bilateral relationship. They also hoped that Japan would be less paranoid and more willing to make trade concessions if it were not completely isolated.

USTR officials emphasize, however, that the selections were a logical outcome of the super 301 process. USTR had earlier solicited public suggestions on which countries it should designate. Of 39 comments received, Korea was cited in 20, Japan in 15, India in 10, and Brazil in 7. The US Chamber of Commerce had recommended that those four be named priority countries, based on the number and pervasiveness of their trade barriers and the potential for increasing US exports (US House Ways and Means Committee 1989). In the 1989 National Trade Estimate Report, which was used to identify super 301 candidates, the listing of Japanese trade barriers took 18 pages. Brazil was tied for second place with Canada with 10 pages of alleged barriers. With Japan's designation a foregone conclusion and preemptive agreements with Korea and Taiwan completed, it was at least plausible that Brazil and India would be named.[1]

The number of private-sector complaints against Brazil and India reflects the high trade barriers each has used to protect its domestic market. Brazil was the world's 10th largest economy and the 12th largest US export market in the late 1980s (taking the European Community as a single market), and the US trade deficit with Brazil, which had been rising throughout the 1980s, peaked at $5 billion in 1988 (table 6.1). Brazil had also been the target of four previous regular 301 cases including fractious ongoing disputes over intellectual property rights and trade barriers in informatics, and intellectual property rights for pharmaceuticals.[2] India was a less important trading partner, in part because its domestic economy was even more heavily regulated than Brazil's. For example, according to the 1989 USTR National Trade Estimate Report, the stock of US foreign direct investment in India in 1987 was under $500 million, compared to $10 billion for Brazil.

Finally, some observers saw the super 301 designation as retribution for Brazilian and Indian opposition to US objectives in the Uruguay Round

---

1. USTR officials also say that the European Community was not designated under super 301 because the key trade disputes, especially on airbus and agriculture, were being negotiated in the round or bilaterally. Of course, there was probably also concern about the Community's possible negative reaction—it had reportedly threatened to withdraw from the Uruguay Round.

2. See chapter 8 on the pharmaceuticals dispute and Odell and Dibble (1988) on the informatics dispute.

Table 6.1a   US trade with Brazil, 1980–92 (millions of dollars)

Year	US exports[a]	US imports[a]	Balance
1980	4,344	3,715	629
1981	3,798	4,469	−671
1982	3,423	4,285	−862
1983	2,557	4,946	−2,389
1984	2,640	7,621	−4,981
1985	3,140	7,526	−4,386
1986	3,885	6,813	−2,928
1987	4,040	7,865	−3,825
1988	4,266	9,294	−5,028
1989	4,804	8,410	−3,606
1990	5,048	7,898	−2,850
1991	6,154	6,727	−573
1992	5,751	7,609	−1,858

a. Export figures based on f.a.s. values; import figures based on customs values.

Table 6.1b   US exports to Brazil, 1988–92[a] (millions of dollars)

Commodity	1988	1989	1990	1991	1992
Total all commodities	4,106	4,636	4,876	5,945	5,442
Foods/feeds, beverages	27	80	117	202	113
Industrial supplies and materials	1,220	1,521	1,592	1,858	1,731
Capital goods	2,491	2,455	2,572	3,205	2,683
Automotive	107	148	140	189	311
Consumer goods	173	246	284	291	449
Special category (military)	8	84	51	71	55
Exports, NEC	81	102	120	129	100

a. Excluding reexports, f.a.s.; 1988 data are estimated.

Source: US Department of Commerce.

(see, e.g., Martin Wolf, "US versus India," *Financial Times,* 12 June 1989, 19). When the round was launched at Punte del Este in September 1986, Brazil and India both played leading roles in organizing developing country resistance to inclusion of the "new" issues of intellectual property, services, and investment. The Indian and Brazilian ambassadors to the GATT, Shrirang Shukla and Paulo Nogueira Batista, reportedly "fought tooth and nail to keep the new issues . . . off the Uruguay Round agenda" (*Financial Times,* 16 December 1993, 7). As leaders of the Group of 10, they successfully fought to have services put on a separate negotiating track, which ultimately resulted in the General Agreement on Trade in Services (GATS). As late as the Montreal GATT ministerial meeting in December 1988, there was still Brazilian and Indian opposition to moving ahead in these negotiations, particularly over intellectual property rights. As one USTR official noted, the super 301 designations were "intended as a signal to other countries that if they did not address the issues identified by the United States as high-priority negotiating issues in the

Uruguay Round, they would have to address them in a bilateral negotiating context under 301" (Feketekuty 1990, 92).

Brazil and India were also leading proponents of the view that developing countries deserved special and more favorable treatment in the GATT, notably that they not be required to offer reciprocal liberalization in the round. The United States, by contrast, argued that the more advanced developing countries should be obligated to offer reciprocal liberalization of their trade barriers. The United States also wanted to prevent the extension of the special and differential treatment principle to the areas for which new rules were being negotiated.

Special and Differential Treatment for Developing Countries

The US attack on Brazil's quantitative import restrictions was a skirmish in an ongoing North-South conflict over the issue of "special and differential" treatment for developing countries in the GATT, and the subsidiary question of how and when they should be "graduated" from this preferential status as they achieve higher levels of development.[3] Poor countries have long insisted that their underdevelopment requires that they be treated more favorably under GATT rules and in tariff-cutting negotiations than rich countries. Developing countries argue they should not have to liberalize as much or as fast as advanced countries, because they need import protection to nurture infant industries and to limit balance of payments deficits, but should nevertheless benefit from industrialized country liberalization on a most-favored nation (MFN) basis without making reciprocal concessions. The discrimination in favor of developing countries goes even further than that, with some less developed country (LDC) exports receiving *better*-than-MFN treatment through preference programs such as the European Union's Lomé Convention and the US Generalized System of Preferences (GSP).

Entitled "Government Assistance to Economic Development," Article 18 of the GATT permits the use of import restrictions by developing countries "to raise the general standard of living of their people." Sections A and C provide an infant industry justification for protecting specific industries. Section B allows developing countries to use quantitative import restrictions to maintain adequate balance of payments reserves. It urges that quantitative restrictions (QRs) be relaxed and eventually eliminated as a developing country's balance of payments problems abate. Brazil was, at that time, viewed as a major abuser of Article 18(B).

Academics and policy economists at the International Monetary Fund (IMF), World Bank, GATT, and elsewhere were skeptical that the balance

---

3. See Hudec (1987) for a comprehensive and insightful discussion of the debate.

of payments waiver served any useful purpose.[4] These critiques are two-tiered.

First, trade restrictions are unlikely to be a first-best solution to any but the most temporary balance of payments problem. A chronic balance of payments problem usually indicates a fundamental macroeconomic imbalance: the nation is spending more than its income and finds it difficult to secure external financing for the deficit. Frank (1987, 12) also points out that import protection can worsen a long-term external payments problem if it discourages exports by causing the exchange rate to appreciate or raises the cost of capital goods and intermediate inputs used in export production.

A second argument against Article 18(B) is that it is really a disguised form of infant industry protection. Developing countries rarely invoke the specific infant industry provisions (sections A and C of Article 18), but they frequently have used the section B balance of payments justification. This preference for section B may occur because, unlike sections A and C, section B does not require developing countries to compensate their injured trading partners (Anjaria 1987, 670–71). The fact that QRs tend to be used over long periods to protect specific firms and industries reinforces the suspicion that the real intent has been to nurture infant industries.

The special and differential element of Article 18(B) lies in developing countries' ability to use QRs *indefinitely* for balance of payments purposes. GATT Article 12 allows developed countries to use QRs for balance of payments purposes, but only very briefly and subject to close scrutiny by the Committee on Balance of Payments Restrictions (BOP Committee) assisted by the IMF. In contrast, developing countries are subject to less strict and less frequent surveillance by the BOP Committee.[5] As a result, some poor countries have maintained extensive QR regimes for decades under Article 18(B). GATT legal scholar John Jackson (1989, 277) cites LDC use and misuse of Article 18 as an example of how "many developing countries are able to take advantage of either explicit or implicit exceptions in GATT so as to pursue almost at will any form of trade policy they wish."

From the US government's perspective, perhaps the most compelling argument against special and differential treatment was not economic but political. Policymakers believed that GATT exceptions for developing countries eroded political support in the United States for multilateral liberalization. Acting Treasury Secretary Peter McPherson (1988, 2) noted several months before the super 301 designations that "LDC ability to

---

4. For views critical of Article 18(B), see Eglin (1987) and Anjaria (1987) (Eglin was employed by the GATT and Anjaria with the IMF, but the views are the authors'). Also see Frank (1987) and Hindley (1987), academic economists publishing their own views in World Bank documents.

5. For descriptions of surveillance procedures, see Eglin (1987) and Anjaria (1987).

avoid GATT obligations weakens the political formula of reciprocal concessions and undercuts trade-liberalizing negotiations." McPherson (1988, 5) went on specifically to attack abuses of Article 18(B), noting that it

> ... has allowed indefinite trade restrictions under a BOP [balance of payments] cover. The rationale is BOP correction, but the restrictions actually serve to protect domestic industries, even if that was not the original intent. Fully 85 percent of LDC import quotas notified to GATT are justified under the BOP waiver. Some of these quotas have been in place for decades.

Hindley (1987, 71–72) points out that the nonreciprocity involved in special and differential treatment was not a political problem for rich countries as long as Third World trade was relatively unimportant. But over the years, a number of developing countries had grown to be significant participants in the global trading system. In 1984, eight developing countries ranked among the world's 20 largest exporters. It rankled the United States that these large Third World exporters were not offering reciprocal access to their markets. Moreover, Hindley (1987, 68) argues that Article 18(B) posed a special problem because "potential industrial country partners in the bargain may not be prepared to deal with a party that has the ability to withdraw legally from its side of the bargain, while holding them to their side." Hindley went on to recommend that the industrial countries develop a code in the Uruguay Round that would require the more advanced developing countries to renounce the use of import restrictions for balance of payments purposes.

Indeed, the United States mounted an aggressive challenge to special and differential treatment during the Uruguay Round. The US objective was twofold: (1) to encourage the more advanced developing countries to graduate from special and differential status and begin to offer reciprocal trade concessions in the traditional tariff and nontariff barriers negotiations; and (2) to prevent developing countries from extending the special and differential principle of nonreciprocity to the "new" areas (services, intellectual property rights, investment), where the United States was particularly interested in LDC liberalization. On this line of reasoning, Brazil was a logical target for US efforts to establish the graduation principle for Article 18(B).[6] The designation of Indian barriers to insurance and foreign investment also signaled that the United States expected significant improvements in market access in these areas in the Uruguay Round, or else.

---

6. Alleging misuse of Article 18(B), the United States brought section 301 and GATT cases against not only Brazil but also India (1987) and Korea (1988). Liberalization resulted in both cases, and Korea also renounced future use of Article 18(B). See case summaries in Hudec (1993, appendix, part I, nos. 163 and 173).

Brazilian Quantitative Import Restrictions

The super 301 action against Brazil sought to liberalize the prohibition on imports of roughly 1,000 items and its restrictive licensing which set company and sectoral import quotas. The case aimed to advance US goals in the Uruguay Round by challenging the alleged abuse by developing countries of GATT Article 18(B), which allows for temporary quantitative import restrictions for balance of payments purposes. Brazil did indeed undertake quite significant trade liberalization and ultimately renounced future use of Article 18(B). Moreover, the Uruguay Round made modest progress in controlling the use of quantitative import controls for balance of payments purposes.

Thus US goals were largely achieved, but super 301 seems not to have played a large role in achieving these results. Brazil's liberalization was the result of internal and external pressures for reform that coincided with the super 301 case. US leverage was adroitly applied, but it was far more a case of pushing on an open door than of battering down a barred gate.

The case benefited from good timing and tactics. Clumsy US tactics might have provoked a nationalistic backlash that would have slowed rather than encouraged Brazil's trade liberalization. The case shows the value of presidential discretion in determining the timing, tactics, and content of section 301 actions.

The Case Against Brazil

As in all of its super 301 actions, USTR used the Brazil case to promote its goals in the Uruguay Round, as part of a larger effort to eliminate GATT-inconsistent QRs and licensing restrictions on imports (*Federal Register* 54, no. 108, 7 June 1989, 24438–42). The United States sought "to strengthen and clarify the requirements of Article 18, to ensure that they are used as a temporary derogation from GATT obligations, rather than an open-ended mechanism to protect particular industries with measures that would otherwise be GATT-inconsistent." (*Federal Register* 54, no. 108, 7 June 1989, 24440). The Brazil case was the only super 301 case that explicitly claimed a violation of GATT obligations and thus had a deadline of 18 (rather than 12) months for resolution. (The other possible violation of GATT obligations was the Japanese wood products case; see chapter 5.)

The United States complained that Brazil maintained a 1,000-item list of prohibited imports including meat and dairy products, plastics, chemicals, leather products, electronic items, motor vehicles, and furniture. The licensing regime imposed quotas, by Brazilian company and sector, for imports of office equipment, engine parts and electrical machinery, among many others. Moreover, US exporters complained that the licensing procedures lacked transparency, sometimes appeared arbitrary, and thus created uncertainty.

It is hard to do justice to Brazil's labyrinthine import control system of the 1980s in a brief summary.[7] Brazil's import regime at that time was exceedingly complex, it was operated by officials who had a high degree of discretion and were constrained by relatively few published rules or guidelines, and its restrictiveness varied considerably with the country's current account surplus or deficit.

Brazil's import control regime served two purposes: to alleviate balance of payments problems and to promote growth and development by nurturing favored firms and industries. The heart of the regime in the 1980s was the system for allocating scarce foreign exchange. A license was required for virtually all imports. Access to a license depended on the type of good, the availability of foreign exchange, and reportedly on the importer's working relations with the administering bureaucracy. Some imports were banned altogether, and for others licenses were "temporarily" suspended, often for many years. Each importer first had to negotiate an "import program" with CACEX, the Central Bank's Foreign Trade Department. These negotiations set an aggregate value for the importer's potential entitlement to foreign exchange but gave no guarantee of actual foreign exchange.

In addition, as part of Brazil's overall industrial policy, certain imports had to be approved by the government agencies responsible for promoting specific industries. These controls were designed to protect domestic firms from foreign competition and in some cases, reportedly, to enforce market-sharing arrangements. Thus, for example, imports covered by the Informatics Law (e.g., computers, microprocessors) had to be approved by SEI, the informatics agency. Imports subject to the Law of Similars were denied licenses if they competed too closely with domestic goods. The administering officials had wide discretion to determine which imports were covered.[8] These bureaucrats consulted extensively with the competing domestic industry, and it was apparently common for importers to agree to purchase some import-competing goods or to enter into market-sharing arrangements as the quid pro quo for getting an import license.

The penultimate stage in the licensing process was for the importer to receive approval for its external financing arrangements from the Central Bank. The final stage in the process was the issuance of an import license by CACEX. Approval was not automatic even if all the previous hurdles had been cleared. It depended on the availability of foreign exchange,

---

7. What follows is based on the GATT (1993b) *Trade Policy Review of Brazil* and on interviews with Brazilian and World Bank economists.

8. In principle, the Law of Similars applied only to those goods receiving tariff preferences or other fiscal benefits or being imported by federal, provincial, or local governments. In practice, the administering bureaucracy acted as if all imports were covered by the law.

and thus the import regime was more or less open depending on the expected current account balance.

In the mid- to late 1980s, the Brazilian government faced mounting internal and external pressures to liberalize its import regime as part of a larger market-oriented reform process. The internal pressures for change came from business people and scholars who were increasingly concerned about the deteriorating economy and had growing doubts about the continued viability of the import substitution model.

It is difficult to document the change in Brazilian attitudes toward the protective trade regime. The change was part of a much larger intellectual shift in favor of policy reform by Latin American elites that was impelled by the dire economic circumstances of the early and mid-1980s. Income and living standards were stagnant or falling in most countries, including Brazil (table 6.2), and there was a growing perception that the old development model was inadequate. There was also a widening body of opinion in business, policy, and scholarly circles in favor of significant market-oriented reform.[9]

If anything, Brazil lagged behind other Latin American countries in developing a reform-minded consensus. It was difficult for many Brazilian public and private sector decision makers and scholars to depart from the previous development model because it had performed so well for the 20 years preceding the debt crisis of the 1980s. Abandoning the old model required a leap of faith that a more market-oriented approach would help lift Brazil out of its economic malaise. Part of the Latin American intellectual conversion was driven by the successful experiences in East Asia. Perhaps even more important was a sense that prevailing economic conditions were so bad that there was no alternative but to reform.

The domestic business community was deeply ambivalent about Brazilian industrial policy. Even the more export-oriented firms, which would gain the most from liberalization, were often also beneficiaries of preferential tariffs and subsidies. Many import-competing firms were grossly inefficient and unable to compete without substantial protection. They naturally opposed market opening. Thus while there was growing recognition in some business circles that the current situation was unacceptable, there was no broad-based business lobbying for economy-wide liberalization. It appears that the business community shifted from strong support for the import-substitution model to neutrality or, at best, cautious support for moderate reform.

---

9. The shift in attitudes is mirrored by the fate of the 1986 book, Balassa et al., *Toward Renewed Growth in Latin America,* which had been widely condemned in Latin America for its recommendations favoring market-oriented reform, but which survived to supply what became the conventional wisdom of the late 1980s. Also see Williamson (1990) and Cline (1994, chapter 5) on the change in Latin American growth strategies in the late 1980s and early 1990s.

Table 6.2 Brazil: economic indicators, 1980–92 (billions of US dollars unless otherwise indicated)

	1980	1981	1982	1983	1984	1985	1986	1987	1988	1989	1990	1991	1992
Overall balance of payments[a]	-4	1	-9	-10	-6	-9	-14	-13	-6	-12	-10	-3	18
Current account	-13	-12	-16	-7	0	0	-5	-1	4	1	-4	-1	6
Trade balance	-3	1	1	6	13	12	8	11	19	16	11	11	16
Merchandise exports	20	23	20	22	27	26	22	26	34	34	31	32	36
Merchandise imports	23	22	19	15	14	13	14	15	15	18	21	21	21
Capital account[b]	9	12	7	-3	-6	-9	-9	-11	-10	-13	-6	-2	11
Total debt stock	71	81	93	98	105	106	114	124	116	111	116	117	121
GDP 1985 prices (1985 = 100)	94.7	90.6	91.1	88.0	92.6	100.0	107.6	111.5	111.4	115.1	110.4	111.9	111.0
GDP per capita (1985 = 100)	106.5	99.4	97.6	92.1	94.7	100.0	106.0	107.5	105.2	106.5	100.1	99.5	96.8

a. Excluding reserves, exceptional financing, and liabilities constituting foreign authorities' reserves.

b. Including net errors and omissions, but excluding reserves, exceptional financing, and liabilities constituting foreign authorities' reserves. Figures not exact due to rounding.

Source: IMF, *International Financial Statistics;* World Bank, *World Debt Tables.*

A growing number of academics were coming to believe that import substitution was outdated or had run its course. This was itself a fairly significant shift in opinion because the previous economic model had enjoyed quite widespread scholarly support. Moderate market-oriented economists, many of them from the Pontifical Catholic University and the Getulio Vargas Foundation, took up important advisory and policy-making positions in government and urged outward-looking reforms. Few of these influential academics were ideological free traders. They favored removing the worst excesses of the protectionist past while retaining a significant role for government in industrial policy.

In sum, the change in elite attitudes toward reform was a significant departure from the past, but not a radical break. The greatest pressure came from the deteriorating economy, which forced everyone to rethink past beliefs, if not to agree on new directions. The evidence of success in other outward-looking economies and the entry into positions of influence of reform-minded economists gave impetus to cautious liberalization in 1987 and 1988, as described below.

The external pressure for reform was less nuanced and thus is easier to describe. The leading outside proponents of reform were the international financial institutions, the commercial banks with substantial loans in Brazil, and the US government. To some degree, these actors applied pressure in tandem.

From the onset of the debt crisis, the World Bank and the International Monetary Fund pressed hard for significant trade liberalization as part of a broader package of macroeconomic and microeconomic policy reform to restore Brazilian growth and competitiveness. The World Bank produced a series of (reportedly) strongly worded confidential reports criticizing Brazilian trade policy (see GATT 1993b for citations to certain of these reports).

The commercial banks were most concerned with Brazil's ability to pay its debt service. They did not initially urge trade reform and may even have believed that tighter import controls would free up scarce foreign exchange for debt service. Eventually the banks recognized that far-reaching macroeconomic and structural reforms were necessary to allow Brazil to achieve sustainable growth rates adequate to service its debt. Commercial bank support for fundamental reform become noticeably stronger after Brazil's February 1987 declaration of a temporary moratorium on medium- and longer-term debt service. Pressure mounted through the late 1980s as Brazil and its lenders had a series of disputes over debt servicing. The commercial banks reportedly did not press for any specific reforms, but urged the Brazilian government to take the policy actions recommended by the IMF and the World Bank. Thus after 1985, Brazil's official and commercial lenders all insisted on far-reaching market-oriented reforms to restore Brazilian growth and access to international capital markets.

The US Treasury was prominent in the debt negotiations along with the commercial banks, the World Bank, and the IMF. It strongly encouraged significant trade liberalization as a necessary condition for new lending and debt relief. In November 1987 the United States and other countries reportedly challenged Brazil's QRs in a GATT Article 18 balance of payments review. The United States also supported a Canadian complaint in the GATT about import restrictions under Brazil's Law of Similars (National Trade Estimate Report, 1989, 17).

It is not clear whether this external pressure for change was explicitly coordinated, but all the important external actors did send the same unambiguous message. Given Brazil's need for external financing and its deteriorating economy, its creditors' advice carried considerable weight.

In response to these internal and external pressures, the Brazilian government began to move cautiously but purposefully toward liberalizing its trade regime. At least part of the rationale was to fight inflation by lowering import prices. As was often the case in the past, improvements in 1988–89 in Brazil's balance of payments position made it easier for the government to proceed with modest import liberalization. In contrast to previous episodes, the Sarney government insisted that this opening was a permanent change in course.

One element of the reform process was to replace quantitative restrictions with tariffs and reduce and unify the tariff structure. In 1988 average nominal tariff rates were reduced from 51 to 41 percent. The number of different tariff rates, their dispersion, and the maximum rate were all reduced. The simple average tariff rate fell further to 35 percent in 1989.[10]

In 1988–89, quantitative restrictions rather than tariffs were the binding constraint on imports. These QRs were also reduced. In 1987 CACEX reduced the number of banned items from 4,500 to about 2,400 (CACEX Communicado No. 177, 21 September 1987). In 1988 the number of banned items was further reduced to about 1,200 (CACEX Communicado No. 208, 21 November 1988). In both 1988 and 1989 the value of approved import licenses was increased.

Although the 1989 National Trade Estimate Report noted Brazil's recent liberalization, it was not sufficient to deter the super 301 case. On 25 May 1989, USTR Hills cited Brazil's quantitative import restrictions as a super 301 priority practice.

Brazil responded to its designation by requesting that the GATT Council discuss the super 301 actions against Brazil, Japan, and India at its meetings of 21–22 June 1989. Not unexpectedly, the United States was strongly condemned by virtually every GATT member that spoke. All three super

---

10. For details see GATT (1993b, 103–18). These simple averages do not reflect the fact that many imports were subject to tariff concessions and duty exemptions. The import-weighted average rate calculated on a duties-collected basis actually rose from 7 percent (1987) to 8.1 percent (1988 and 1989).

301 targets said they would refuse to negotiate bilaterally with the United States.

Brazil's representative, Ambassador Rubens Ricupero, cited several blistering editorials in leading newspapers excoriating the United States for undermining the global trading system and the Uruguay Round. He singled out for special criticism the "new and grave precedent created as the USTR attempts to challenge measures that are covered by the General Agreement, namely in Article 18(B), . . . [Thereby] undermining the well-established machinery of the GATT" (statement to the GATT Special Council Session, 21 June 1989).

For its part the United States responded in a conciliatory fashion. Deputy USTR Rufus Yerxa repeated earlier statements by USTR Hills that the United States was prepared to use the GATT as a forum for super 301 discussions and to use the GATT dispute settlement mechanism to resolve the US complaint against Brazil (William Dullforce, "Unfair Traders Refuse Meetings," *Financial Times*, 23 June 1989, 24).

In October 1989 the United States formally requested GATT consultations with Brazil over its super 301 complaint. USTR reported that Brazil had offered to reduce its list of banned items and expand its de facto quotas in the course of several formal and informal discussions. However, Brazil's alleged slowness in reducing the number of import bans led USTR to request formal GATT dispute settlement proceedings in January 1990.[11]

It is not surprising that not much was accomplished in the US-Brazil consultations of late 1989 and early 1990. In late 1989, Brazil was in the throes of its first political campaign for direct election of the president since the military takeover in 1964, and the lame-duck Sarney administration was unwilling or unable to make binding commitments.

In December 1989 a hitherto largely unknown provincial politician, Fernando Collor de Mello, was elected president. In contrast to his opponents, who generally endorsed the traditional state-led development model, Collor "talked of opening his country to the outside world and unshackling the economy" ("A Survey of Brazil," *The Economist*, 7 December 1991, 17). In a surprise victory, Collor defeated his leftist opponent, Luis Inácio Lula da Silva, by a fairly narrow margin of 35 million votes to 32 million.

Upon taking office on 15 March 1990, Collor immediately announced a sweeping market-oriented reform. It included elimination of import bans and the Law of Similars and reduction in barriers to foreign direct investment.[12]

By July 1990, Brazil had eliminated its quantitative import restrictions except for the informatics "market reserve" program. The liberalization

---

11. Described in USTR, "Section 301 Table of Cases," 6 June 1991.

12. For a description of the reforms, see the GATT's *Trade Policy Review of Brazil* (1993a, chapter 4).

abolished the foreign exchange allocation system, which "lay at the core of Brazil's commercial policy and its approach to the management of its balance of payments" (GATT 1993a, 88–89). Tariffs became the primary mechanism of protection, and the simple nominal average fell from 35 percent in 1989 to 14 percent in 1993, with the maximum rate dropping from 85 percent to 35 percent.

On 21 May 1990 USTR Hills announced that she had terminated the investigation. Hills said the case was ended because President Collor's "bold trade liberalization initiative" had resolved US complaints (Office of the United States Trade Representative, press release no. 90-35, 21 May 1990).

Brazil continued to liberalize after the super 301 threat was lifted. In September 1990 the government announced that it would amend the Informatics Law to eliminate import controls and the market reserve policy by October 1992.

In July 1991, Ambassador Ricupero announced to the GATT Council that Brazil would abandon future recourse to quantitative restrictions under Article 18(B) (*International Trade Reporter,* 17 July 1991, 1064–65). The announcement was greeted with widespread applause in international trade and financial policy circles. The US representative to the GATT's BOP Committee called it "a historic moment," Inter-American Development Bank president Enrique Iglesias said that the move "had received the support of the international financial community," and US Treasury Undersecretary David Mulford used similar words (*Gazeta Mercantil,* 15 July 1991, 2).

The Modest Role of Super 301

What explains the initially cautious and later bold reforms in Brazil's trade policy since 1988? In our view, super 301 played at best a modestly useful role in bringing about these changes; it certainly did not have a decisive or even a major impact on the decision. The very depth, breadth, and ongoing nature of the liberalization suggests that it was not carried out by a reluctant government responding only to the super 301 gun to its head. Similarly, Hudec (1993, 584) describes the reform as "far beyond what any GATT complaint could have produced."

In our view, it is not possible to single out one decisive factor. Rather, it was the gradual coming together of both internal and external pressures that finally brought about the changes.

External pressures were certainly important. In our view, pressure from Brazil's external creditors, including the US Treasury, were much more significant than super 301 per se. Brazil was increasingly eager to improve its bruised relations with its creditors and to regain access to international capital markets. Trade liberalization was part of the broader reform prescribed by Brazil's lenders. Fritsch and Franco (1991a, 11) describe the reforms as undertaken in part "to improve the climate of Brazil–United States relations to pave the way to a reopening of debt negotiations following a long moratorium."

Internal pressures were also very important. Fritsch and Franco (1991a, 9) also note that foreign pressures reinforced "the slow move of the opinion of local elites toward deregulation—especially in the sphere of trade and industrial policy. . . ." The shift in scholarly and business attitudes away from the import-substitution model appears to reflect a growing recognition of its heavy economic costs.

This change in attitudes is most clearly illustrated by growing dissatisfaction with the informatics "market reserve" program. Many scholars came to chafe under the difficulties in obtaining state-of-the-art personal computers because imports were banned or under quotas. Brazilian scholars on the international conference circuit often returned home loaded with computer hardware purchased at one-half or less of the cost in Brazil. At least a few of these scholars went on to influential advisory positions where they advocated reform.

Business users of computers also grew increasingly critical of the market reserve program because it raised their production costs and consigned them to using outdated technology. Cline (1987, 60) estimates that the annual cost of the program to Brazilian informatics users was over $500 million in 1985. Not included in this estimate is the "potentially more serious impact of retarding technical change generally in the economy" (Cline 1987, 63).

The Sarney administration reacted to these foreign and domestic pressures with a cautious movement toward liberalization. By contrast, Collor seized on the public's disaffection with the economic state of affairs and turned it into a mandate for very significant reform. He played very astutely on the public's distaste for political corruption and railed against the bureaucratic "maharajahs" who got rich by controlling large parts of the economy. Collor's election was thus another very important factor in Brazil's liberalization. Election of a less reform-minded, or even a protectionist, president could have led to a very different outcome.

Super 301 was simply an add-on to all of these forces for change. Few private Brazilian observers believe that it had more than a modest positive impact, and several government officials say that it was irrelevant.

It is important to emphasize, however, that super 301 was adroitly used in this case. US willingness to use the GATT for discussions with Brazil lowered the atmospherics and kept the case out of the political limelight in Brazil during the elections. US diplomacy thereby managed to avoid handing a nationalistic cause to those presidential candidates who supported the old import-substitution regime.

Brazil's renunciation of future use of Article 18(B) set a precedent supporting the graduation concept for the more advanced developing countries. Although Brazilian diplomats continue to insist that they endorse the special and differential principle for less advanced developing countries, the fact that the leading proponent of special and differential itself has been graduated is a potent message to others.

The United States also made modest progress in the GATT in guarding against Article 18(B) abuse. The Uruguay Round's "Understanding on the Balance of Payments Provisions of the General Agreement on Tariffs and Trade 1994" commits members to publicly announce timetables for the removal of import restrictions for balance of payments purposes. Members also commit to give preference to "price-based measures" (e.g., tariffs) over QRs. Perhaps more important than the vapid language of the understanding, the Brazil super 301 case puts members on notice that the United States might challenge the abuse of Article 18(B) and use the GATT's dispute settlement procedures to do so. This is a clear message that the rules of the game have changed.

A number of Brazilian observers are concerned about the weak Brazilian consensus for a more liberal trade policy (Abreu 1993, 9; Fritsch and Franco 1991a, 20–23). Continued public support depends greatly on the success of the overall reform program in restoring adequate growth. If that effort fails, public and elite opinions could swing quickly back toward the old protectionist model.

If super 301 contributed to Brazil's reform, it was because it added quiet impetus to other, more powerful external pressures and to a significant domestic political shift. A more confrontational use of super 301 during the elections would probably have delayed the reform effort by inciting a nationalistic backlash. The case thus underscores the importance of allowing the president wide discretion over the timing, content, and conduct of trade negotiations.

Insurance and Investment in India

Substantial liberalization has taken place in India during the last few years, but in the spring of 1989, when USTR Hills and staff were surveying the world for super 301 candidates, India was a relatively closed economy with high trade barriers and heavy regulation. Among the many trade barriers cited in the National Trade Estimate Report in 1989 were tight restrictions on foreign investment and a virtual ban on the import of most types of insurance. The restrictions on insurance and foreign investment were designated by Hills as priority practices in May 1989 and investigations were initiated for each complaint in June.

India is the only country of the three named under the super 301 procedures that failed to reach any compromise with US negotiators. In April 1990, USTR Hills redesignated as priority practices Indian barriers to insurance and foreign investment and, in June, issued a formal determination that India's policies with respect to these sectors were unreasonable and injured US trade interests. She declined, however, to take retaliatory action at that time "given the ongoing negotiations on services and investment in the Uruguay Round of global trade talks" (USTR, press release, 14 June 1990). No other countries or practices were named in 1990, and Hills proclaimed that completion of the Uruguay Round would be the administration's top trade priority that year. Hills also indicated she would review India's practices following the conclusion of the Uruguay Round, but the round did not end as scheduled in December 1990 and no further action was taken against India.

India is not especially dependent on the US market, nor is trade as important to its economy generally as it is in other countries against which section 301 has been effective. Also, given India's colonial past and its leadership in the Nonaligned Movement, it would have been politically difficult for Indian officials to be seen as caving in to unilateral US pressure, especially when the internal constituency for liberalization in India was so underdeveloped. Thus expectations among US negotiators as to the likelihood of positive outcomes in the Indian cases must have been low. Indeed, USTR does not appear to have tried very hard to engage India in meaningful negotiations.

The Case for Super 301 Designation of India

In June 1989 testimony before the House Ways and Means Subcommittee on Trade, Willard Workman of the US Chamber of Commerce noted that

> India maintains a wide range of government restrictions on imports and foreign investment, such as mandatory technology transfer, tariffs among the world's highest and a virtual ban . . . on the importation of any consumer or domestically producible goods. (US House Ways and Means Committee 1989, 60)

During the comment period earlier in the spring, the Chamber had recommended that India be named a super 301 priority country, arguing that it clearly fit the criteria of having numerous and pervasive trade barriers. The Chamber argued that the removal of those barriers—along with the removal of barriers to the Japanese, South Korean, and Brazilian markets— had the greatest potential for increasing US exports, given India's relatively large and well-educated middle class (estimated at some 80 million people), larger than that in most European countries.

USTR Hills, at the same hearing, stated that the administration wanted to "use super 301 to support and complement our Uruguay Round initiatives" and had chosen the practices it had because they were "emblematic of *broader* areas of concern to the global trading system" (emphasis in original). Having selected government procurement and technical barriers to trade in Japan, and quantitative restrictions in Brazil, the administration chose to focus in India on two of the new areas under negotiation in the Uruguay Round, services and investment. The 1989 National Trade Estimate Report asserted that Indian policies "severely restrict potential US investment and impose unacceptable conditions" on foreign firms that do choose to invest in India. The barriers specifically cited were restrictions on entry, screening requirements, and, for those that do get in, equity participation, local content, and export performance requirements. With respect to insurance, the report noted that the government monopoly in that sector restricted foreign firms to a few narrow lines, such as reinsurance and marine cargo insurance.

When asked what India planned to do in response to the super 301 complaints, Commerce Minister Dinesh Singh replied succinctly, "Nothing" (*Financial Times*, 8 June 1989). He noted that the ban on foreign participation in the insurance sector had been in place since the industry was nationalized in the 1950s and that it barred private Indian companies as well as foreigners. Singh noted also that many other developing countries restricted foreign investment and that such restrictions were fully compatible with GATT rules at that time. Finally, Singh argued that it was illogical to ask India to negotiate the same issues in two forums, noting that if India made concessions in the super 301 context, it would have less leverage in the multilateral negotiations (*Financial Times*, 8 June 1989).

Many observers thought the designations were simply "punishment for India's failure to toe the American line in the GATT" (*Financial Times*, 12 June 1989, 19). Others, in trying to explain why a country that was only the 24th largest US export market and whose bilateral surplus with the United States was well under $1 billion would be chosen, concluded that it must have been a "last minute political decision taken so as to avoid appearing to victimize Japan by singling it out." And many of these same observers further reasoned that India "might not have too much to fear from the US demands" (*Financial Times*, 19 June 1989).

Political Economy of US-India Trade

An import-substitution development strategy reduces trade to a relatively small role in the economy. India's trade dependence is far less than that of Korea or Taiwan and is just over half that of Brazil, another country pursuing import substitution until recently. Measured by the share of exports of goods and services in gross domestic product, India's trade dependence in 1990 was only 6.6 percent, while Brazil's was 11 percent, Korea's 40 percent, and Taiwan's over 50 percent.[13] The proportion of India's total merchandise exports going to the United States in 1989 was 20 percent, higher than that of Argentina or most European countries (including intra-EC trade), but lower than the 30 percent that was the

13. IMF, *International Financial Statistics,* and Central Bank of the Republic of China, *Financial Statistics.*

average in successful section 301 cases. But the share of India's GDP accounted for by exports to the United States was much lower than the average in successful cases, 0.6 percent versus 7.5 percent.

Pressures for freer trade began percolating in India in the 1970s. In 1984, Prime Minister Rajiv Gandhi, citing India's need for increased investment and foreign technology, slowly began to liberalize trade barriers and restrictions on foreign direct investment. Nevertheless, in analyzing India's position in the Uruguay Round in the late 1980s, Indian economist Ashok V. Desai (1989a, 92) "could find no powerful domestic popular forces for a change in trade policy." Desai noted that "most of the daily press" is owned by Indian industrialists and "supports protection" (Desai 1989a, 91). Even consumers, Desai argued, do not typically challenge the government position that India has a balance of payments problem that requires import restrictions. According to Desai, many of the large industrial enterprises engaged in exporting were also engaged in import-substitution activities and took no strong position on trade policy. Their silence made it difficult for the government to push for liberalization. Radical changes in policy are also discouraged by the diffusion of political power in India's democratic system, which Desai compares to "a supertanker which requires many miles and hours to change course. . ." (1989b, 33).

When the super 301 designations were announced, even sympathetic Indian businessmen expressed concern that it would set back the tentative moves toward reform since, as one said, "No one likes to do anything under pressure" (*Financial Times,* 19 June 1989). Business groups, the government (including both the bureaucracy and the ruling party), and opposition parties protested the US designation. According to the Congressional Research Service, the US effort to liberalize the Indian economy won only "backhanded support from a few economic thinkers and press commentators" (Ahearn, Cronin, and Storrs 1990, 38). Thus Indian opposition to concessions in the super 301 negotiations was nearly unanimous.

In the United States, the limited US involvement in either exporting to India or investing there meant that there were few American firms with a *tangible* stake in opening up India. The Chamber of Commerce might *anticipate* large sales in the future, but expectations are often a less important motivating factor in spurring political activity than a threat to existing interests (Destler and Odell 1987, chapter 3). Some large US companies with investments in India, including Citicorp and PepsiCo, publicly opposed retaliation against India over its foreign investment restrictions, saying that it had proved to be a good place to do business.[14] While India could not injure the US economy with counterretaliation against its exports (less than 1 percent of US exports went to India in 1989), it

---

14. See, for example, *International Trade Reporter,* 9 August, 1989, 1036 and 13 June 1990, 838; and *Financial Times,* 25 May 1990, 4).

could, if it chose, retaliate against the US investors that were potential hostages of the Indian government.

In sum, Indian interests were solidly behind their government in opposing the American demands. American interests, on the other hand, were divided, with firms already in India opposing the US position for fear they would suffer the consequences. As John Odell (1993) has shown, this distribution of domestic political interests in two countries is the least likely to produce an outcome favorable to the country issuing the retaliatory threat.

The Role of GATT

India previously had been the subject of only one other section 301 investigation (case no. 301-59), as a result of which the United States expanded the Indian market for imported almonds. In that case, however, the United States also brought two GATT cases, one alleging that India's quotas violated Article XI and the other protesting they were illegal under the Import Licensing Code. Perhaps anticipating a negative outcome, India agreed to lower and bind its tariffs and to expand its quota before the panel completed its deliberations.

But US negotiators could not appeal to GATT in the super 301 cases since investment and services were not then covered by GATT rules, a point that Indian diplomats emphasized repeatedly. Moreover, Indian officials threatened to lodge a complaint in the GATT if the United States retaliated against Indian exports in violation of US GATT obligations (*International Trade Reporter*, 9 August 1989, 1036). If USTR could not find a GATT-legal form of retaliation and raised bound tariffs on Indian exports, the United States almost certainly would have been found guilty by a dispute settlement panel of violating its GATT obligations.

If found guilty, the US negotiators would have faced the unpalatable choice of either withdrawing the retaliation against India or ignoring the panel decision, with potentially serious consequences for the Uruguay Round and GATT's institutional viability. The announcement of retaliation at the mid-June deadline could also have disrupted the multilateral negotiations, coming as it would have barely a month before the 23 July deadline for agreeing on a framework for finalizing the round by December (*Financial Times*, 12 June 1990). Thus in addition to India's lower economic vulnerability to trade retaliation, relative to other countries against which section 301 had proved effective, domestic and international political circumstances undermined the credibility of the US threat to retaliate.

Assessing the Outcome

India and Brazil were designated by USTR in order to cushion the super 301 blow to Japan and because of their trade policies and negotiating positions in the Uruguay Round. Faced with the unpromising circumstances in India, US negotiators apparently did not expect a positive response from India and did not push very hard to get even minor concessions. The section 301 investigations were initiated in June, but two months later Indian officials said no one from USTR had even approached them about beginning negotiations. Indian officials also said they did not regard retaliation as very likely, since the decision would be discretionary under section 301 because the barriers to foreign services and investment did not violate any trade agreement.

Nevertheless, there are indications that the cases had some effect on India. In August 1989 the Indian ambassador to the United States, Karan Singh, stated that India would not negotiate under threat of retaliation but might consider easing some limits on foreign investment. In September India for the first time accepted the principle of negotiating trade-related intellectual property issues in the GATT, "an extremely significant move" according to GATT sources (*International Trade Reporter*, 20 September 1989, 1423).[15] The new Indian government that was elected in the fall of 1989 proposed the next spring to retain the 40 percent limit on foreign equity but streamline other licensing requirements.

But no acceptable agreement was reached, and Hills redesignated the two Indian sectors as super 301 priorities at the end of April 1990. When the deadline for completing the section 301 investigations arrived in mid-June, Hills determined that the Indian practices were unreasonable and a burden on US commerce, but, as allowed by the statute, she also determined that taking retaliatory action against India's barriers was not in the US interest at that time. She promised to review India's practices with regard to insurance and foreign investment the following January, after the expected completion of the Uruguay Round. The round was not completed as scheduled, but Hills chose to take no action against India.

In the summer of 1991, long after the super 301 threat had passed, the Indian government elected the previous fall adopted an economic reform program that substantially liberalized the restrictions on foreign investment. According to a report of the Indian Ministry of Trade released in April 1993, the value of foreign investment proposals approved by the Indian government had increased eightfold from August 1991 to December 1992 compared with August 1990 to December 1991, from 5.3 billion rupees to 43 billion rupees. Also, in late 1993 a government-appointed commission recommended liberalization of the insurance market, including privatization of the two state-owned firms and new entry by both domestic and foreign firms.

---

15. India had previously insisted that the negotiation of intellectual property issues be confined to existing international organizations or conventions such as the World Intellectual Property Organization (WIPO). The United States rejected this demand because WIPO has no enforcement mechanism.

The decision in June 1990 not to retaliate was probably driven by a desire not to disrupt the Uruguay Round negotiations, then scheduled to conclude in 1990. Though wise under the circumstances, the failure to retaliate also had a cost to the extent it undermined the credibility of US threats in the future.

Some success was ultimately achieved in this case, but it cannot be attributed in any significant degree to US pressure. As in Brazil, significant trade liberalization occurred only after a government was elected that was committed to economic reforms because it believed them to be in the interests of the country, not simply because foreigners demanded it.

7

Super 301: Korea and Taiwan

Although super 301 was aimed primarily at Japan, it was not Congress's only target. As described in chapter 6, Congress was also increasingly frustrated by the behavior of newly industrializing economies (NIEs) whose export-led development strategies targeted the relatively open US market while they protected home markets. South Korea and Taiwan were the most visible examples in the mid-1980s because of the size of their bilateral surpluses with the United States.

The Reagan administration tackled the issue of special and differential treatment for the NIEs in January 1988, when it announced that a year hence, South Korea and Taiwan (along with Singapore and Hong Kong) would be "graduated" from preferential tariff treatment under the Generalized System of Preferences (GSP). Later that year, the American Meat Institute filed a section 301 complaint against Korean restrictions on beef imports and the administration "broke new legal ground" in the General Agreement on Tariffs and Trade (GATT) by directly challenging Korea's balance of payments justification for its beef quotas (Hudec 1993, 242–43). In spring 1989, the Bush administration added to the pressure on the NIEs to give up special differential treatment under the GATT by citing Brazil's long-standing and extensive array of quantitative restrictions on imports as a super 301 priority (chapter 6). South Korea and Taiwan escaped because they had negotiated preemptive concessions to avoid designation.

The concessions offered by South Korea and Taiwan to avoid designation as priority countries are frequently cited as evidence of super 301's effectiveness. In a formal bilateral agreement with the United States, South

171

Korea promised to liberalize restrictions on foreign investment, eliminate "special laws" promoting import substitution in certain sectors, and improve the transparency of its customs procedures, labeling and testing requirements, and other technical standards. Taiwan did not conclude a formal agreement with US negotiators; rather it presented an "action plan" for reducing its bilateral surplus with the United States that US Trade Representative Carla Hills said would be sufficient to avoid a super 301 designation if it were fully implemented. Despite the conventional wisdom, however, both the value of the original concessions and the degree to which they have been meaningfully implemented are open to question.

Super 301 Designation as Leverage

As discussed in chapter 2, once priority designations were made under super 301, the procedures—chiefly negotiating deadlines and criteria for retaliation—were identical to those for a regular section 301 case. The super 301 provisions might have provided additional negotiating leverage in two ways: by inducing concessions from countries that wanted to avoid designation and by making the retaliatory threat more credible because of high expectations and additional political pressure on USTR from Congress and the private sector in super 301 cases. Japan had no incentive to negotiate prior to being designated in 1989 because the intense pressure from Congress virtually ensured that it would be named. South Korea and Taiwan, however, were anxious to avoid being on the list, and both apparently felt there was a high enough probability of being named that they were willing to offer concessions to avoid it.

South Korea, in particular, had reason to think it would be on the super 301 list. When the US Trade Representative's office solicited comments from the private sector as to what practices and countries should be designated under super 301, South Korea topped the list with 22 complaints, most in the agricultural sector. Japan was a relatively distant second with 16, followed by India with 10, Taiwan with 9, and Brazil with 7. In addition to the narrow, sector-specific complaints, the US Chamber of Commerce recommended naming Korea, India, Brazil, and Japan as priority foreign countries (PFCs), while the AFL-CIO wanted USTR to designate Korea, Taiwan, and Germany, along with Japan as PFCs. Based on 1986 data, those four countries, plus Hong Kong and Italy, also would have qualified as "excessive trade surplus countries" under the original Gephardt amendment provisions (Bello and Holmer 1990, 76). Thus, Korea and Taiwan must have been high on the list of potential super 301 candidates. And given the Bush administration's desire to avoid isolating Japan by naming it alone, it seems probable that one or both countries would have been on the list had they not made preemptive offers.

Forces for Market Opening in South Korea and Taiwan

Although the specifics differed in important ways, both Korea and Taiwan had developed rapidly in the 1960s and 1970s following an export-led growth strategy. The role of trade policy in this strategy was not as protectionist as in the import-substitution countries, such as Brazil and India, but it was mercantilist, promoting exports while limiting imports to the minimum necessary to meet industrial and consumer needs. In the 1980s, both countries came under increasing pressures—both internal and external—to liberalize their economies. Many policymakers in both countries had come to believe that some liberalization was necessary for continued growth. Then, in the mid-1980s, their bilateral surpluses with the United States exploded (table 7.1a and b), spurring US negotiators to push for even broader and faster liberalization.

In South Korea, economic reforms began in the early 1980s in response to the excesses of the heavy-industry promotion of the 1970s, which contributed to inflationary pressures and balance of payments problems (SaKong 1993, chapter 4; Cho 1994, chapter 3). In Taiwan, financial scandals triggered reforms in the mid-1980s. Though both governments had their own reasons for pursuing economic liberalization, significant obstacles remained, and trade liberalization tended to proceed gradually and in fits and starts.

Both Korea and Taiwan had suffered for decades under Japanese colonial domination prior to World War II, and Korea in particular emerged from that experience leery of foreign investment and dependence on other countries for key goods. Security concerns have been cited as an important reason for Korea's decision to undertake the heavy and chemical industry development drive in the 1970s (Haggard 1990, 130–31; Cho 1994, 150). Prior to the 20th century, Korea had kept itself largely isolated from the rest of the world, thus earning the name the "Hermit Kingdom." Some Korean observers argue that

> Korea has had no liberal trade tradition. Indeed, Korea's inward-looking history and tradition [have] acted as a powerful psychological counterweight to both internal and external pressures for market opening. (Kim and Chung 1989, 150)

Nevertheless, macroeconomic and structural imbalances arising from the heavy-industry effort of the 1970s forced the South Korean government to adopt economic reforms. According to former Finance Minister Il SaKong, the decision to further open their markets to imports "was based on the belief that to increase international competitiveness, import liberalization was inevitable," but, he concluded, "it is important to have the right sequence for market openings because of the differing speeds at which asset and product markets can adjust" (SaKong 1993, 88 and 93). Thus, as one observer described it (Petri 1987, 21), flexibility and pragmatism are "essential features of Korea's governing style. . . . [L]iberalization

Table 7.1a　US trade with Taiwan, 1981–93

Year	US imports from Taiwan (millions of dollars)	US exports to Taiwan (millions of dollars)	Bilateral trade balance (millions of dollars)	Taiwanese imports from the US as a percent of total imports	Taiwanese exports to the US as a percent of total exports
1981	8,049	4,033	−4,016	22.5	36.1
1982	8,892	4,006	−4,886	24.2	39.4
1983	11,611	4,291	−7,320	22.9	45.1
1984	15,429	4,765	−10,664	23.0	48.8
1985	15,480	4,274	−11,206	23.6	48.1
1986	19,757	5,115	−14,642	22.5	47.7
1987	24,604	7,096	−17,508	21.9	44.1
1988	24,865	11,882	−12,983	26.2	38.7
1989	25,481	10,983	−14,498	23.0	36.3
1990	22,651	11,138	−11,513	23.0	32.4
1991	23,020	12,684	−10,336	22.5	29.3
1992	24,593	14,509	−10,084	21.4	30.5
1993	25,096	15,336	−9,760	21.1	29.8

Table 7.1b　US trade with Korea, 1981–93

Year	US imports from Korea (millions of dollars)	US exports to Korea (millions of dollars)	Bilateral trade balance (millions of dollars)	Korean imports from the US as a percent of total imports	Korean exports to the US as a percent of total exports
1981	5,141	4,998	−143	23.1	26.8
1982	5,667	5,286	−381	24.6	28.8
1983	7,475	5,732	−1,743	24.0	33.8
1984	9,857	5,887	−3,970	22.5	36.0
1985	9,980	5,728	−4,252	21.0	35.6
1986	12,805	5,862	−6,943	20.7	40.1
1987	16,964	7,646	−9,318	21.4	38.9
1988	20,160	10,637	−9,523	24.5	35.4
1989	19,803	13,082	−6,721	25.1	32.4
1990	18,437	13,961	−4,476	24.3	29.9
1991	16,983	14,876	−2,107	23.5	25.5
1992	16,649	13,839	−2,810	17.0	22.3
1993	17,089	14,073	−3,016	n.a.	n.a.

n.a. = not available

Sources: US Department of Commerce, "Survey of Current Business," various issues; on Taiwan, Council for Economic Planning and Development, *Taiwan Statistical Data Book;* Republic of China; IMF, *Direction of Trade Statistics* yearbooks, various issues.

is being tried as an experiment, and will be pursued in a form that yields the most positive economic results."

Korea's top economic policymakers tend to be technocrats, often trained in US universities (SaKong 1993, 170). These technocrats were cautious with regard to trade liberalization, but the bureaucrats further down the hierarchy, many of whom were close to the industries they regulated, were often hostile. Moreover, that hostility in some cases impeded the implementation of decisions made at the top. In a meeting with EU External Economic Relations Commissioner Sir Leon Brittan in late 1993, recently elected President Kim Young Sam reportedly said he supported trade liberalization because "it's good for Korea" but then pointed to the cabinet members who had accompanied him and said, "The problem is that *they* do not believe that" (*Wall Street Journal,* 30 March 1994, A1).

As political liberalization proceeded in the late 1980s, economic decision making became less insulated from political pressures, and economic reforms became more difficult to sustain. One Korean observer (Young 1989, 142) warned in 1987 that

> Korea is delicately poised between favorable economic conditions and unfavorable political conditions [because of democratization] for import liberalization. Many developments could easily tilt the balance away from import liberalization. For instance, anything that endangers high growth or current account surpluses will be detrimental to the program.

Indeed, just as Young foresaw, support for trade liberalization declined as economic conditions deteriorated in late 1989 and 1990.

Because of its smaller size, Taiwan was forced to be somewhat more open to both imports and foreign investment than South Korea. In addition, the vulnerability arising from Taiwan's uncertain political status in the world after mainland China's reentry into diplomatic circles meant that "international economic ties had a crucial political function, serving as a surrogate for formal political relationships" (Haggard 1990, 146). This gave Taiwan an important incentive to avoid or quickly resolve disputes with the United States.

Taiwan's economic strategy also stressed macroeconomic stability much more heavily than did South Korea's policymakers, and imports were viewed by many government economists as a useful discipline on inflation. Nevertheless, engineers rather than economists dominate the Industrial Development Bureau (IDB) of the Ministry of Economic Affairs, which has primary responsibility for trade, foreign investment policy, and industrial policy. The Council for Economic Planning and Development, which comprises several cabinet members and whose staff is more heavily weighted toward economists, is supposed to set overall policy. But one student of Taiwan's economic policy has argued that IDB's key "role in industrial policy formation . . . helps to explain why, rhetoric apart, Taiwan has moved only gradually to liberalize imports in sectors it wishes to encourage" (Wade 1990, 203–04).

In addition to these internal motivations, a second major source of pressure for reform in these countries came from the United States. While applauding the liberalization that was occurring, US policymakers viewed the pace as insufficient and pushed hard for both faster and broader market opening, especially after 1985. Because both South Korea and Taiwan pegged to the US dollar, the value of their currencies followed the dollar down in 1986 and 1987, and their exports gained significant price competitiveness vis-à-vis Japan and other countries whose currencies appreciated in that period. Both exports and the size of their bilateral surpluses with the United States increased rapidly in this period. US policymakers responded by urging these countries to unpeg from the dollar and to allow their currencies to appreciate. Congress added to this pressure in the 1988 Omnibus Trade and Competitiveness Act, requiring the Treasury Department to identify countries that "manipulate" their currencies "for purposes of preventing effective balance of payments adjustments or gaining unfair competitive advantage in international trade" and to open bilateral negotiations with such countries that also have significant trade surpluses, both globally and with the United States (Destler and Henning 1989, 107–16).

Simultaneously, US negotiators stepped up pressure on South Korea and Taiwan to liberalize. From September 1985 through the end of 1988, South Korea was the subject of five section 301 investigations, more than any other country in that period. Two were initiated by USTR, on insurance and intellectual property, while three others were brought by private industry, on cigarettes, wine, and beef. The president cited Taiwan twice for violating bilateral agreements (one on customs valuation and the other on beer, wine, and tobacco products) and threatened retaliation if compliance was not forthcoming within a short period (see case nos. 301-56 and 301-57 in the appendix). Although there were fewer formal section 301 actions against Taiwan than against South Korea, some US observers argue that US trade negotiators are tougher with Taiwan than with any other trading partner but that the pressure is less public. Taiwan was under constant bilateral pressure during this period to liberalize in a number of areas, agriculture in particular.[1]

Both Korea and Taiwan were highly dependent on the US market and thus vulnerable to US pressure on trade issues. In 1983–87, Taiwan sold nearly half its exports in the United States and Korea over a third. And, although the United States accounted for more than 20 percent of imports in both Korea and Taiwan, the two together bought less than 10 percent of US exports. Neither could credibly threaten to counterretaliate. Finally,

---

1. One example is the turkey parts dispute. In early 1988, street protests by farmers, radical students, and opposition party members forced the government to reimpose restrictions on imports of agricultural items, including turkeys and parts. Even though the trade was only worth about $2 million to US exporters, US negotiators threatened not only to retaliate, but to gradually escalate the value of the retaliation if the barriers were not removed (*Far Eastern Economic Review,* 15 September 1988, 62–64). This differs strikingly from most other cases where US negotiators were careful to link the value of retaliation closely to the value of US exports believed to be lost due to a barrier.

Taiwan was even more vulnerable than these numbers suggest since it is not a member of the General Agreement on Tariffs and Trade and thus had no defense whatsoever against US trade actions. Both countries also depend on the United States for security guarantees.

As might be expected from the analysis in chapter 4, section 301 was used relatively effectively against Korea and Taiwan. All five cases against Taiwan since 1975 have achieved positive though limited results, as have five of seven cases against Korea.

With both countries, however, there have been problems with implementation. Just as the success of GATT in lowering tariffs is said to have exposed the shoals of nontariff barriers, US pressure seems to have driven Korean and Taiwanese trade policy to increase their reliance on less transparent forms of protection. Nonagricultural tariffs and quantitative restraints on some products have been reduced or eliminated, but administrative discretion of various sorts has been used to dilute some of the effects. Examples include certain state monopolies, nontariff taxes, technical standards, and import licensing. Liberalization of investment controls in Korea and of services in both countries has been very slow because these sectors are heavily regulated domestically.

Thus US beer, wine, and tobacco product exporters won the right in a 1986 agreement to bypass the Taiwan state monopoly and deal directly with importers and retailers, but US producers complain that high commodity taxes and lax treatment of untaxed contraband products continue to restrict their sales, especially of cigarettes and wine. Also, in 1990, despite an earlier commitment to abide by the GATT Customs Valuation Code (which calls for basing duty calculations on the invoice price), Taiwan reverted to administratively determined values for US automobile exports. In Korea, foreign access to the insurance market was negotiated repeatedly during the 1980s but still required two different section 301 cases more or less finally to resolve. In 1989, Korea was placed on the special 301 priority watch list for failing to implement intellectual property rights laws that it had passed as part of a 1986 agreement resolving another 301 case. And the US-Korean dispute over beef flared again in 1993, and the earlier agreement had to be renegotiated and clarified.

The Agreement with Korea

Korea had ample reason to believe that it would be named a priority foreign country under super 301. In addition to the five formal section 301 investigations conducted by USTR from 1985 through 1988, five other petitions had been filed and withdrawn, three complaining about the lack of adequate enforcement of Korea's pharmaceutical patent laws and two seeking improved access for US films. In January 1989 the Reagan administration terminated GSP eligibility for Korea, along with Taiwan, Singapore, and Hong Kong, citing their competitiveness in world markets. A month later, Korea was named as a priority country, along with the European Community, under the telecommunications provisions of the 1988 Trade Act.

Given this steady drumbeat of US pressure, as well as the size of Korea's $10 billion trade surplus with the United States (it was the fifth largest in 1988, after Japan, Taiwan, Germany, and Canada, in that order), Korean officials understandably viewed designation as a super 301 priority as a virtual certainty. That does not explain, however, why the Koreans preferred to negotiate preemptively. A former trade negotiator, Kim Chulsu, offered four reasons: (1) fear that designation would trigger an outbreak of anti-Americanism in Korea; (2) concern that it would provide ammunition to obstructionists who opposed Korea's already announced plans for liberalization; (3) commercial uncertainty resulting from the mere possibility of retaliation; and (4) "[a genuine belief] that the branding of Korea as an 'unfair trader' would be unfair" (Kim 1990, 254). Another high-level Korean official said that, from the government's perspective, the best possible outcome for South Korea was to not be designated and the worst was for Japan not to be named while South Korea was named. Concerns about being labeled a "second Japan" provided additional incentive for South Korea to negotiate preemptively.

In March and April, Korea launched a major push to avoid designation, sending top government officials and "buying missions" to defuse the pressure. Then Chief Trade Negotiator Kim Chulsu, Trade and Industry Minister Han Seung-Soo, and Deputy Prime Minister and head of the Economic Planning Board Cho Soon all traveled to the United States carrying warnings of a backlash. Minister Han also raised the national security linkage, arguing that designation, which he claimed would have symbolic significance whether or not it resulted in retaliation, would " 'strengthen the hand of protectionists in our country' and would be tantamount to giving certain economic matters greater priority then security issues. 'It would not be wise to destabilize [Korea's] democratization program' " (*Journal of Commerce,* 20 April 1989).

On 18 May 1989, US and Korean negotiators signed a three-part agreement that was intended to modestly liberalize agriculture, lift performance requirements and other restrictions on investment, and phase out Korea's "localization" laws, which permitted ministries to restrict imports in particular sectors as part of their development plans. The third part of the agreement also sought to make Korea's regulation of imports more transparent (table 7.2).

Trade Minister Han had announced at the end of January, several months before the super 301 process began, that Korea would soon adopt a liberalization schedule for 540 agricultural and fishery products. During the negotiations in March and April, despite the fact that agricultural and food products dominated the list of complaints registered with USTR by the private sector, Korean negotiators insisted that they could go no further on agricultural liberalization than they had in Han's announcement. That plan would phase out the licensing requirements on agricultural products over a number of years but would leave in place extremely high tariffs. US negotiators also wanted reductions in tariffs and relief from onerous phytosanitary and other regulations that inhibited American exports. Throughout, however, the Korean negotiators remained adamant, and in the end the two sides agreed to disagree on agriculture.

Although the United States insisted it was inadequate, Korean officials would commit only to accelerate the "liberalization" of some products by six months, lower the tariffs on seven products of particular interest to the United States (almonds, pistachios, avocados, raisins, cherries, alfalfa products, and wood particle board), abolish the orange juice mixing requirement by 1 September, eliminate the whiskey quota by 1 January 1990, and resolve a long-standing dispute over fresh cherry fumigation standards.[2] The duty reductions, however, left tariffs of 35 to 40 percent on five of the seven items, including cherries.

In addition to complaints that the remaining tariffs were still highly restrictive, several agricultural exporter groups complained in 1990 that phytosanitary standards and lengthy customs procedures had become more of a burden since the modest nominal concessions offered in the super 301 agreement of the previous year. The Northwest Cherry Growers group also complained that Korea had not "properly implemented" the agreement on fumigation procedures. Also during the year following the agreement, US grapefruit exports were damaged by allegations by Korean consumer groups that American grapefruit had been treated with Alar, though US growers claimed that Alar was not used on any citrus product. Finally, in 1994, USTR solicited comments from interested parties that might show that Korea's commitments in the 1989 agreement had been impaired by regulatory barriers or customs requirements (*Federal Register*, 9 June 1994, 29863).

The parts of the agreement dealing with investment and localization issues sought to improve the predictability and transparency of Korean trade regulation and liberalize restrictions on foreign direct investment. In addition to promising to simplify and take steps toward harmonizing technical standards and regulations affecting imports, Korea also agreed to repeal a number of "special laws allowing a variety of measures intended to promote "localization" of production in particular sectors, including pharmaceuticals and technology. Korea also agreed to eliminate performance requirements as a condition of entry and to prohibit export performance requirements; some limited performance requirements connected to operation were allowed. It also agreed to replace the case-by-case approval process with a notification process in liberalized sectors

---

2. Cherry imports had been nominally liberalized in 1985, but the fumigation standards had effectively kept foreign cherries out of the market.

and committed to specific liberalization schedules for advertising, travel services, and pharmaceuticals.

In the spring and summer of 1990, Korean government officials responded to deteriorating economic conditions, including inflation and a rapidly declining trade surplus, by promoting an "austerity campaign." Although officials claimed that the campaign was aimed at reducing consumption of luxury goods generally, imported consumer products seemed to be especially hard-hit. In addition, in December 1990 US negotiators complained that Korea had helped to derail the Uruguay Round negotiations by supporting the European Community and Japan in their refusal to give ground on agricultural liberalization. On 29 December 1990, an exasperated USTR Carla Hills threatened to retaliate against Korean trade: "If we do not get a change in policy, we will certainly withdraw concessions that would otherwise be available to the Koreans (*International Trade Reporter*, 2 January 1991, 4). The austerity campaign subsided in the first half of 1991 allegedly in response to US pressure, but in September 1991 the campaign against conspicuous consumption was renewed, though officials again denied any discrimination against imports (*Journal of Commerce*, 26 September 1991, 3A).

In January 1992, Presidents George Bush and Roh Tae-woo launched a bilateral effort to resolve trade problems by attacking "generic" barriers rather than through sector-by-sector negotiations as in the past. The first progress report on the Presidents' Economic Initiative (PEI) was issued in October 1992, with one source concluding that

> The most significant element of the report appears to be the promise of substantial improvements in the transparency of Korean standards and customs procedures. . . . Apart from the changes in standards and customs procedures, the most important element of the report is the recommendation for gradual easing of Korean restrictions on foreign investment. (*Inside U.S. Trade*, 2 October 1992, S-1)

The report thus focused on two of the areas supposedly addressed in the super 301 agreements: the transparency of Korean technical standards and regulations affecting imports, and continuing restrictions on investment (Korea's commitments and follow-through are summarized in table 7.2).

In particular, standards and testing and labeling requirements for food products and pharmaceuticals, two sectors specifically mentioned in the 1989 agreement, were targeted for reform. In the investment area, although an Economic Planning Board document (1989, 10) had promised that by the end of 1992, "Korea's foreign investment system will be fully liberalized," Deputy USTR Nancy Adams used the infamous "peeling an onion" metaphor to describe efforts to liberalize investment in Korea and noted that there had been less progress in that area than in others (*Journal of Commerce*, 7 June 1993, 4A). In addition to seeking further liberalization of restricted sectors, the Presidents' Economic Initiative sought to simplify the information requirements for investment and to address problems on the availability of finance and foreign exchange for foreign investors.

This initiative was followed by the Clinton administration's Dialogue for Economic Cooperation (DEC) with South Korea, which, like Bush's PEI, was intended to improve the business climate in South Korea. Just a month before the two countries released their joint report on the DEC process in June 1994, however, the Meat Industry Trade Policy Council urged USTR to initiate a section 301 investigation into South Korean practices inhibiting meat imports. For example, in March, South Korea decided without warning to reclassify certain types of sausage so that they had a shelf life of only 30 days, less than the time required to process, ship, and distribute the product (*International Trade Reporter,* 15 June 1994, 958).

With regard to foreign investment, the problems are even greater. In early 1994, a Hong Kong–based consulting firm released the results of a survey of 95 corporate managers and bankers on business conditions in several East Asian countries, including China, Hong Kong, Indonesia, Japan, Malaysia, Philippines, Singapore, South Korea, Taiwan, and Thailand. The survey concluded that South Korea "was the most protectionist nation in Asia" and "discriminated more than any other nation against foreign investment" (*Financial Times,* 23 June 1994, special section). The 1994 National Trade Estimate Report also noted that South Korea had the reputation of being "a particularly difficult market in which to invest."

Taiwan's Promises

The United States and Taiwan did not reach a formal agreement as a result of the super 301 process. Rather, Taiwan offered a "detailed action plan" for improving economic relations with the United States. The plan promised to reduce the bilateral trade deficit by 10 percent per year (as called for in the original Gephardt amendment to what became the 1988 omnibus trade bill) by reducing tariffs and import licensing requirements, continuing to send "Buy American" missions to the United States, diversifying the markets for its exports to reduce "dependency" on the US market, stimulating domestic demand, and improving intellectual property protection. Based on the expectation that the plan would be fully implemented, USTR Hills opted not to designate Taiwan as a super 301 priority country (Taiwan's commitments and follow through are summarized in table 7.3).

As in Korea, Taiwanese officials offered very little agricultural liberalization, promising only to reduce average tariffs from 26 to 20 percent. They did not offer to liberalize licensing requirements or nontariff barriers restricting imports of agricultural products and promised only to "review the proposal that we liberalize importation to our country of agricultural

Table 7.2   Assessment of the super 301 agreements with Korea

Commitment	Assessment
Border closure, standards and testing requirements, and customs procedures	
Agreed to terminate border closure measures affecting primarily pharmaceuticals, effective 1 July 1990. Made other promises to improve transparency and reduce arbitrariness in customs procedures: "The Korean Government will ensure that its customs regulations, procedures and appeals process are transparent and apply in a uniform and expeditious manner."	According to the 1994 National Trade Estimates (NTE) Report, "US industry continues to report cases where Korean customs and quarantine clearance procedures are excessively slow and arbitrary. Chocolate products, cosmetics, electronic goods, electrical appliances, and other consumer goods considered 'luxury goods' have taken three to six weeks to clear port although they are not subject to any restrictions under Korean law." USTR also expressed concern about tariff reclassifications, often without warning, affecting products liberalized under previous bilateral agreements. In March 1994, for example, Korea suddenly reclassified certain sausage imports, which had been liberalized in 1991, subjecting them to a shelf requirement of 30 days, which was less time than it took to process, ship, and distribute the product (*International Trade Reporter*, 15 June 1994, 958).
Also promised to make labeling and testing requirements more transparent and uniform, in particular with regard to food products, cosmetics, pharmaceuticals, and electrical products.	According to the 1994 NTE report, "Many standards and regulations still have no scientific basis, deviate substantially from international practices in both substance and implementation, and serve mainly to keep imported products out of the market." The report also specifically mentioned problems with food and other agricultural products and medical equipment.

Investment

Agreed to eliminate performance requirements in liberalized sectors and to continue to reduce the number of restricted sectors "on an expeditious basis."

According to the 1993 NTE Report, "82 percent of the sectors in Korea's standard industrial classification system were open to foreign equity investment *in principle*," up only 3 percentage points since 1989.

Promised to approve or disapprove investment applications within 60 days (unless the application was incomplete, technical data was required, or the investor was seeking tax exemptions), and to convert the approval system to a notification system for liberalized sectors.

The government of Kim Young Sam announced new economic reforms in 1993, including a promise to "seek to operate its foreign direct investment (FDI) regime under a *true* notification system" (emphasis added; cited in Graham 1993, 4). But E. M. Graham (1993, 6) notes that foreign "business leaders have learned to be skeptical about reform of FDI policy in Korea. The present system of notification, itself introduced but a short time ago as a reform measure, is more intrusive in practice than on paper and, indeed, arguably acts as a de facto screening mechanism."

Agreed to remove travel agencies, advertising, and pharmaceuticals from the negative list, and specifically promised that foreign firms would receive equal treatment with the Korean Broadcasting Organization (KOBACO).

According to the 1993 NTE Report, "In those service sectors where foreign investment is allowed, cumbersome and arbitrary regulations continue to limit the activities of foreign firms competing with established domestic firms. *Television advertising* and cable tv services also face burdensome screening requirements" (emphasis added).

Table 7.3 Assessment of the super 301 commitments by Taiwan

Commitment	Assessment
Pledged to reduce its bilateral surplus with the United States by 10 percent annually through 1992, for a cumulative 30 percent reduction from the 1988 level. The plan for doing so included measures to increase domestic demand and efforts to diversify Taiwanese export markets, thus decreasing dependence on the US market.	After a sharp reduction in the bilateral imbalance in 1988, in part due to Taiwanese purchases of gold, Taiwan's surplus with the US increased in 1989 before declining sharply, by 20 percent in 1990 and 10 percent in 1991. Averaged with the more than 10 percent rise in the 1989 surplus, Taiwan's surplus with the US declined by about 6.5 percent per year in 1989–91; excluding 1989, however, Taiwan did achieve the cumulative 30 percent reduction by 1992 (table 7.1).
To increase imports from the US, Taiwan pledged to reduce tariffs from an average 12.57 percent in 1988 to 7.00 percent in 1992. The reductions were primarily on manufactured products, the average tariff on which was scheduled to be halved to 5 percent; on agricultural products, Taiwan agreed to lower tariff by much less, with a final average rate of 20 percent. Taiwan also promised to simplify its import licensing procedures and to continue buying missions to the US.	According to the 1993 NTE report, Taiwan fell just short of the 1991 average duty rate target of 8.1 percent, with average ad valorem duties of 8.9 percent; the report also noted that further reductions would be postponed pending completion of Taiwan's negotiations with GATT members on accession. According to the report, the average tariff on agricultural products was near its 1991 target of 21.3 percent (247). There appears to have been little change in the number of products covered by Taiwan's licensing system or in the complaints regarding licensing requirements and delays. Taiwan computerized its customs clearance system for air cargo only in November 1992 and will not do the same for ocean-borne cargo until 1994 (248).
Agreed to gradually liberalize its services markets, including allowing US shipping companies to engage in the trucking business, giving more flexibility to branches of foreign banks, and considering allowing US insurance companies to establish joint ventures and subsidiaries.	According to the 1994 NTE report, as of the end of 1993, Taiwan still discriminated against foreign banks in the areas addressed in the 1989 action plan, still did not allow US insurance companies to establish subsidiaries, though they were allowed to invest in local insurance companies (with restrictions), and legislation to allow US shipping companies to enter the trucking business did not pass the lower house of the legislature in 1993.
Promised to "adopt effective measures to strengthen protection of intellectual property rights."	After being on various watch lists since 1989, Taiwan was named a priority country under the super 301 provisions in April 1992.

products." As with Korea, however, complaints about Taiwan's restrictions on agricultural and food imports had dominated the complaints received by USTR prior to the super 301 designations. In manufacturing, Taiwan pledged to lower the average nominal duty rate to 5 percent by 1992, a target very nearly achieved according to the 1993 National Trade Estimate Report. But Taiwan's commitments on intellectual property rights were not satisfactorily implemented from the perspective of US industry and trade officials. Taiwan was named as a priority country under special 301 in spring 1992 and barely avoided further action in 1993 because of alleged lack of enforcement of the intellectual property laws passed under previous US pressure.

Taiwan did achieve its targets of reducing the bilateral trade imbalance by 30 percent from its 1988 level by 1992, but the rate of improvement slowed significantly thereafter. This adjustment in Taiwan's trade position was also much less than in Korea (figure 7.1), even though the New Taiwan dollar appreciated more than the won did against the dollar. By the end of 1992, South Korea's surplus with the United States had declined by 70 percent, as compared with 40 percent for Taiwan. The New Taiwan dollar appreciated nearly 40 percent from 1985 to 1992, while the Korean won appreciated 23 percent before beginning to depreciate again in 1990, ending up in 1992 only 10 percent lower than in 1985. The decline in Taiwan's bilateral surplus with the United States was so close to the promised 30 percent figure as to raise suspicions that it was as much due to government management as to policy reforms.

Conclusions

The trade concessions Korea and Taiwan offered to preempt designation as priority foreign countries are frequently cited as evidence of super 301's effectiveness and of the need to renew it. The evidence, however, does not support this conclusion. This raises the question of why the substantial leverage that US negotiators apparently had vis-à-vis South Korea and Taiwan in the late 1980s did not produce more significant results.

Other than the pledge to cut tariffs, Taiwan's other concessions were mostly vague promises to consider further liberalization. Korea's concessions were impressive on paper and have been largely carried out—on paper. The actual liberalizing effect is much less impressive. Increasing labor costs and an appreciating currency in 1987–89 (from 823 won/dollar to 671 won/dollar) contributed to elimination of Korea's trade and current account surpluses in 1990 and to significant deficits in 1991. Three years of double-digit growth ended in 1989, and growth slowed to its lowest level in a decade in 1992. The deterioration in the trade balance was due as much to decreased competitiveness of Korean exports (because of

Figure 7.1 Korean and Taiwanese surpluses with the United States, 1985–92
(quarterly data, seasonally adjusted)

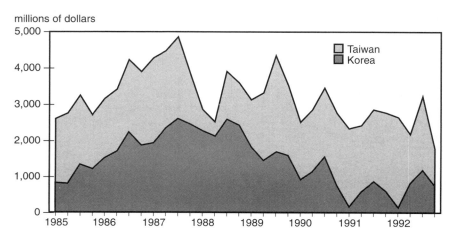

millions of dollars

increasing wages and value of the won) as to increased imports. Foreign goods provided an easier target, however; in 1990 an "antiluxury" campaign, nominally intended to reduce consumption and increase saving, seemed instead to be aimed primarily at reducing consumption of imported goods. In other areas, administrative red tape continued to restrict trade and investment, even though many formal policies, rules, and regulations were eliminated as promised.

US negotiators did get a political victory from Korea and Taiwan at a crucial time. The concessions from Korea and Taiwan, announced in April 1989, reduced the domestic political backlash from the USTR's choice of a relatively narrow list of designated priorities (Ahearn, Cronin, and Storrs 1990). But little actual market opening was gained as a result of these agreements.

South Korea is now beginning to realize that it can no longer compete on the basis of cheap wages and that it needs foreign investment and technology if it is to stay competitive internationally. Since the election of President Kim Young Sam in 1993, South Korea does appear to be genuinely interested in liberalization, especially of its foreign investment restrictions (see, e.g., *Financial Times*, 23 June 1994, special section; *Wall Street Journal*, 25 February 1994, A9; and 30 March 1994, A1). Thus, a central policy lesson from this chapter is the same as was drawn in chapter 6: countries engage in substantial trade liberalization only when it is perceived to be in the country's own interest.

8

Brazil: Intellectual Property Protection for Pharmaceuticals

The United States initiated a section 301 action in 1987 in response to the complaints of the Pharmaceutical Manufacturers Association (PMA) that Brazil's failure to provide patent protection encouraged piracy that cost the US R&D-based pharmaceutical industry millions of dollars annually in lost sales. The case was part of a broader US effort to encourage stronger international protection of intellectual property rights (IPR). The US strategy included both pressure for a multilateral agreement on intellectual property rights in the Uruguay Round and threats of section 301 and other sanctions to force countries with the most costly lack of IPR to take immediate unilateral steps to strengthen protection in areas of interest to US exporters and investors (USTR, "Administration Statement on the Protection of US Intellectual Property Rights Abroad," 7 April 1986).

Brazil was a leading opponent of the American IPR agenda in the Uruguay Round and initially refused to take part in bilateral negotiations under the threat of section 301. The United States responded in 1988 with retaliation against Brazilian exports worth $39 million. Brazil, in turn, responded with a GATT complaint against illegal US retaliation. In 1990 US sanctions were removed, and Brazil withdrew its GATT complaint after the new, reform-minded president, Fernando Collor de Mello, agreed to introduce IPR legislation. Brazil's subsequent failure to enact acceptable patent protection led USTR to designate it a priority foreign country in April 1993 and to renew the threat of section 301 sanctions. After further negotiations, in February 1994 USTR withdrew its second threat when the Brazilian government again promised new legislation by June.

This case thus has been pending for over seven years, and even now the outcome is unclear because even if the legislation passes it will take several years to determine if it is being effectively implemented and enforced. This pattern of repeated US threats and unfulfilled foreign promises over long periods is quite common in intellectual property negotiations (table 8.1). It is also evident in many of the cases involving services described in the appendix. IPR disputes are especially difficult to resolve because they often involve a sharp conflict of interests between the United States and the target country. However, similar difficulties in other areas are likely as the United States seeks to reduce regulatory and structural impediments to trade and investment in a number of countries in the aftermath of the Uruguay Round. It seems to take a very long time to effectively address deeply rooted structural or regulatory differences among nations.

This case points to the limitations of section 301 as a lever in addressing objectionable practices that have strong political support in the target country. Even though the Brazilian government repeatedly promised to change its IPR laws, it was unable or unwilling to deliver because of widespread opposition in its local generic industry, parts of the government, and the legislature. This case therefore stands in contrast to the US-Japan and US-European negotiations on market access for financial services, which also involved regulatory issues but where there were effective constituencies for change in the target countries (see chapter 11).

US retaliation against Brazil may have given impetus to the then-stagnant IPR negotiations in the Uruguay Round. But the sanctions were clearly illegal, and other GATT members widely condemned them. Repeated US refusals to establish a GATT panel to hear Brazil's complaint significantly undermined US credibility as an advocate of reform of the dispute settlement process.

Recent US Strategy

What Are Intellectual Property Rights?

Intellectual property rights give investors the ability to receive economic benefits from producing ideas, technology, research and development, and other creative works such as books, computer software, art, and films. Without these rights—embodied in patents, trademarks, and copyrights—it is often difficult for owners of intellectual property to prevent others from copying or using their ideas and products. Government enforcement of IPR is therefore often necessary to encourage those who can produce intellectual property to spend time and money to do so. The fundamental and often-debated policy issue is the right balance between society's interest in promoting innovation, which is spurred by strong IPR protection, and the social benefits of rapid diffusion of new ideas, technology, and products, which IPR protection can impede.

Table 8.1 Results of regular and special 301 intellectual property rights (IPR) cases

Case	Date initiated	Date resolved[a]	Duration (months)	Results
Brazil, Informatics including copyright protection and import barriers for software (301-49)	September 1985	June 1988	33	In late 1987, Brazil passed a copyright law for software. There have been continuing US complaints about its enforcement. In September 1990 Brazil announced that the market reserve policy for informatics, including software, would end by October 1992.
Korea, IPR including pharmaceuticals (301-52)	November 1985	ongoing	101	In July 1986 an agreement was announced that would "dramatically improve" IPR. There have been repeated US complaints about enforcement, and Korea has been placed on the priority watch list continuously since 1992.
Brazil, Pharmaceuticals (301-61 and 301-91)	June 1987	ongoing	84	Retaliation was imposed in October 1988 and lifted in June 1990 pending promised legislative changes; retaliation was threatened again in 1993 and the threat lifted in February 1994 pending promised legislative changes by June 1994.
Argentina, Pharmaceuticals (301-68)	August 1988	ongoing	69	Complaint was withdrawn in September 1989 pending promised legislative changes, which had not occured by June 1994.
Thailand, Copyright (301-82)	November 1990	ongoing	42	Retaliation was imposed and GSP benefits cut; designated a priority country from 1991–93; downgraded to priority watch list in 1994.
Thailand, Pharmaceuticals (301-84)	January 1991	ongoing	40	Retaliation was imposed and GSP benefits cut.
India, IPR (301-85)	May 1991	ongoing	36	Retaliation was imposed and GSP benefits cut; designated a priority country from 1991–93; downgraded to priority watch list in 1994.
China, IPR (301-86)	May 1991	ongoing	36	An agreement was signed in January 1992, but in June 1994 USTR designated China a priority country under special 301.
Taiwan, IPR (301-89)	May 1992	April 1994	24	Agreement was reached in June 1992, but Taiwan was placed on the priority watch list in April 1993 due to "serious enforcement problems"; it was downgraded to the watch list in April 1994 to monitor compliance.

a. Date resolved is based on the authors' judgment that there is reasonable evidence that an agreement is being effectively implemented. These resolution dates may occur either before or after a 301 case is formally terminated.

Society encourages and benefits from individual creativity by granting owners the right of an adequate financial return on commercially valuable intellectual property. But society also benefits from the diffusion of intellectual property to the largest possible number of users. By enforcing certain property rights, society grants the owner of intellectual property temporary and limited power to set prices. The granting of exclusive marketing rights necessarily restricts the use of intellectual property to those willing to pay a price generally above the owner's cost of production or to those willing to risk being punished for theft.

Countries have adopted different IPR regimes to reach what they judge to be the right balance between encouraging the creation of intellectual property and promoting its diffusion. There is a continuum of national policy regimes that generally reflect a country's level of economic development and comparative advantage in innovative and artistic products. The more advanced industrial countries, with substantial capacity to produce intellectual property, tend to favor strong property rights.[1] The very poorest countries tend to favor weak or poorly enforced regimes that allow their citizens inexpensive access to the benefits of innovation. Somewhere in between are the middle-income developing countries, which produce products using pirated intellectual property but also are beginning to create their own.[2] These middle countries are torn between the competing interests of entrenched "pirate" industries and their emerging inventors and artists, who would benefit from a stronger IPR regime.

These different national perspectives on the costs and benefits of intellectual property rights create a clash of economic interests between countries that export intellectual property and those that import it. Governments in exporting countries face pressure from domestic constituencies to secure a strong *international* IPR regime to maximize the export profits of their intellectual property owners. Similarly, governments in importing countries face strong domestic pressures to give their consumers and producers cheap access to imported intellectual property by limiting property rights.

This conflict of economic interests between countries that import and export intellectual property gave rise to much debate during the Uruguay Round over the appropriate international IPR regime. What is the optimum term for a patent or copyright? Is the optimal domain for IPR the

---

1. However, the United States has frequently criticized two of the most technologically advanced countries, Germany and Japan, for their inadequate copyright protection for computer software. The United States also criticized Canada for its limited protection for pharmaceuticals until Canada changed its laws in 1993.

2. The PMA notes that it is only a relatively small number of developing countries that lack some process or product patent protection for pharmaceuticals. There are, however, problems of inadequate enforcement of IPR in a large number of both developed and developing countries.

entire world or just the major countries that produce and use the intellectual property?[3] The 1993 Uruguay Round agreement on intellectual property rights represents the current international consensus on the appropriate balance between the interests of exporting and importing nations.

The United States is probably the world's leading exporter of goods and services embodying intellectual property.[4] Maskus (1993, 16) calculates that US exports of such goods amounted to nearly $60 billion in 1989, compared with similar Japanese exports of about $50 billion. Another measure of US competitiveness in these goods and services is net receipts from foreigners of royalties and license fees for technology, patents, and trademarks. In 1988 the United States had net revenue from foreign sources of nearly $9 billion for these forms of intellectual property, compared with nearly a half-billion dollar outflow for Japan (Maskus 1993, 17).

Countries that do not produce much intellectual property but have the ability to use or copy it have tended to resist US proposals to strengthen IPR. The resisters, which tend to be relatively poor countries, believe that weak protection allows them relatively inexpensive access to intellectual property. Some countries justify their unwillingness to pay on the grounds that (1) it is equitable since they are poor and the foreign owners tend to be rich, (2) granting stronger IPR will not yield economic benefits commensurate with the higher prices they would pay, and (3) the failure of a small number of poor developing countries to pay for intellectual property does not appreciably diminish its creation.[5]

Owners of intellectual property understandably take a different view. They argue that (1) theft is theft, and national poverty is no excuse—the lack of adequate IPR is equivalent to the expropriation of foreign investment that occurred in some developing countries in the 1950s and 1960s; (2) some foreign firms will not invest or sell in countries that have weak IPR protection, and thus these countries deny themselves the foreign capital, technology, and managerial expertise that would promote economic development; and (3) the very high costs and great uncertainty involved in the development of some types of intellectual property, such as in pharmaceuticals, means that producers will tend to underinvest in these activities unless they have essentially global protection. Indeed, they argue that innovators will tend to underinvest in precisely the medicines, technologies, or products that most benefit poor countries because IPR protection is so weak in these countries.[6]

---

3. See Deardorff's (1990) lucid discussion of these issues, as well as the more detailed analysis in Siebeck (1990).

4. We say "probably" because there are no generally available comparative measures of trade in IP-intensive goods and services.

5. See Deardorff (1990) and Subramanian (1990) for fuller discussion.

6. See Gadbaw and Richards (1988, chapter 3) and Diwan and Rodrik (1991) for fuller discussion.

The arguments for and against stronger IPR protection in poor countries boil down to the question of whether the benefits (greater access to intellectual property and associated investment and expertise) outweigh the costs (higher prices for the goods and services). The theoretical and limited empirical literature suggests that in a wide range of conditions the world welfare–maximizing international IPR regime does *not* include all the developing countries, especially the poorest. Based on our survey of the literature, we believe that these issues of developing countries' and world welfare are unresolved.[7]

US Multilateral IPR Initiatives

American interest in strengthening international protection of intellectual property stems from the fact that the United States is a major producer and exporter of intellectual property. A related rationale was the desire of some US trade officials to mobilize a new American export constituency to support the broader effort at multilateral liberalization in what eventually became the Uruguay Round. In turn, US efforts to promote a new trade round were intended to stave off protectionist pressures in the United States and abroad on the famous bicycle theory that unless trade liberalization moves forward, the trading system will topple under new protectionism.[8]

US efforts to strengthen GATT rules on IPR date back to the Tokyo Round in 1974–79 (Bradley 1987). In the final stages of the Tokyo Round and immediately afterward, the United States and the European Community unsuccessfully sought a GATT agreement to discourage trade in counterfeit trademarked goods. At the highly contentious November 1982 GATT ministerial meeting, the United States sought to establish a work program on new issues—services, intellectual property, and investment— that would eventually lead to a new round. The US proposals on the new issues met with widespread skepticism and some hostility, particularly from the developing countries, led by Brazil and India.

Desultory discussions on intellectual property followed over the next four years. Brazil and India continued to oppose including IPR in the GATT and used a series of procedural maneuvers to thwart US efforts to get multilateral consensus for putting IPR on the agenda for the next

---

7. For general surveys, see Mansfield (1994) and Siebeck (1990). See Subramanian (1991), Helpman (1993), and Deardorff (1992) for theoretical analyses and Maskus (1990) for an empirical simulation. The level of development and innovative capacity required for developing countries to benefit from stronger IPR is an unresolved empirical issue. There is a fairly strong consensus among economists that the very poorest developing countries do not benefit from stronger IP protection (Deardorff 1990).

8. On the role of US exporters of intellectual property and services in supporting the Uruguay Round, see Barfield (1989, 310). On the role of US export interests in resisting protectionism, see Destler and Odell (1987).

round.[9] Finally, at the September 1986 GATT meeting in Punte del Este that launched the round, the United States secured a statement in the Ministerial Declaration that the participants would "aim to develop a multilateral framework of principles, rules and disciplines dealing with international trade in counterfeit goods. . . ." Even after the round was under way, Brazil and India continued to lead resistance to IPR negotiations until about April 1989 (Hudec 1993, 184).

Unilateral US Efforts

In the early 1980s Congress and the business community encouraged the president to seek stronger intellectual property protection abroad by arming USTR for the first time with a number of retaliatory weapons. Policymakers saw these unilateral initiatives as complementing US efforts to put IPR on the GATT agenda because they demonstrated that the United States would act aggressively on its own if target countries refused to negotiate in a multilateral forum.

The 1983 Caribbean Basin Economic Recovery Act gave the president discretion to consider whether participating countries provided adequate IPR as a condition for receiving US tariff preferences (Davis 1991, 513). The Trade and Tariff Act of 1984 amended the criteria for access to the Generalized System of Preferences (GSP) to give the president discretion to deny GSP to countries that had inadequate IPR (Mesevage 1991, 423–25).

The 1984 Trade Act also amended section 301 to give the president legal authority for the first time to retaliate in cases where target countries failed to provide "adequate and effective protection of intellectual property rights." In addition, the 1984 Trade Act gave USTR authority to initiate section 301 cases without waiting for private petitions. As part of the Reagan administration's Trade Policy Action Plan, in September 1985 USTR initiated the first section 301 investigation involving intellectual property rights. The case (301-49) involved Brazil's informatics policy, which, among other things, failed to provide adequate copyright protection for computer software.[10] A second USTR-initiated IPR case (301-52) was launched against Korea in November 1985. In April 1986 USTR Clayton Yeutter announced a strategy on IPR that included both multilateral negotiations in the GATT and bilateral discussions backed by the vigorous use of section 301 and other trade levers (USTR, "Administration State-

---

9. A number of developing countries argued that IPR should not be included in the GATT's agenda but rather should be negotiated in the World International Property Organization (WIPO). The United States rejected WIPO because it had no enforcement mechanism. See Sell (1989) for a discussion of how US trade policy was influenced by Brazil's and India's positions in WIPO negotiations during the early 1980s.

10. See Odell and Dibble (1988) for an excellent case study of the US-Brazil informatics dispute.

Box 8.1 Special 301 for intellectual property

The United States is among the world's largest exporters of intellectual property–intensive goods and services. US producers have complained since the early 1980s that they have lost sales worth many billions of dollars because of foreign theft of their intellectual property.

The special 301 provisions of the 1988 Trade Act give the president authority to retaliate against foreign countries that violate US intellectual property rights (IPR).

Special 301 requires the US Trade Representative to identify, within 30 days of issuing the National Trade Estimates Report, "those countries that deny adequate and effective protection of intellectual property rights, or deny fair and equitable market access to United States persons that rely on intellectual property rights." USTR is further directed to identify "priority foreign countries" that (1) commit the most onerous or egregious acts, (2) have the greatest adverse impact on the United States, and (3) are not engaged in good-faith negotiations or are not making significant progress in bilateral or multilateral negotiations.

USTR must decide whether to initiate section 301 investigations of the priority foreign countries within 30 days of designating them. Investigations are not required if they would be detrimental to US economic interests. The investigations must be completed within 6 to 9 months (compared with 12 to 18 months for regular 301). USTR has wide discretion to retaliate against the priority countries if they fail to meet US demands.

The first special 301 report was issued in May 1989 (USTR, "Fact Sheet: Special 301 on Intellectual Property," 25 May 1989). USTR Carla Hills pointed to progress in a number of countries and observed that although several countries might have been identified as priority foreign countries, they were all engaged in good-faith negotiations, either bilaterally or in the Uruguay Round. USTR did not designate any priority countries but instead established a priority watch list and a regular watch list. Brazil, China, India, Korea, Mexico, Saudi Arabia, Taiwan, and Thailand were included in the priority watch list and 17 other countries were placed on the regular watch list. It was not until 1991 that USTR identified any priority foreign countries under special 301. In April 1994 USTR Mickey Kantor created a fourth category called special mention for countries that have made progress in improving IPR protection but needed to do more (USTR, "Fact Sheet: Special 301 on Intellectual Property," 30 April 1994).

This box draws heavily on the intellectual property of Judith Bello and Alan Holmer (1990).

ment on the Protection of Intellectual Property Rights Abroad," 7 April 1986).

The "special 301" provisions of the Omnibus Trade and Competitiveness Act of 1988 gave further impetus to the unilateral pursuit of intellectual property protection (box 8.1). Special 301 establishes criteria for USTR to identify "priority foreign countries" that deny adequate and effective

IPR. It sets an abbreviated deadline of just six to nine months for investigations.

Although special 301 was intended to pressure USTR to move expeditiously against alleged violators, it also allows the president and USTR considerable discretion in wielding retaliatory threats. USTR need not identify priority countries if they are engaged in good-faith negotiations or are making progress in bilateral or multilateral negotiations. Retaliation is no more "mandatory" under special 301 than it is under the regular and super 301 provisions of the 1988 Trade Act (see chapter 2).

USTR Carla Hills used her full discretionary authority when she issued her first special 301 decisions on 25 May 1989 (USTR, "Fact Sheet: Special 301 on Intellectual Property," 25 May 1989). She announced that, because of significant progress in various negotiations, she had decided not to designate any priority foreign countries, although several were eligible. Instead, she established both a priority watch list and a regular watch list, identifying countries whose lack of adequate and effective IPR deserved special scrutiny. USTR again declined to identify priority countries in 1990, and it was not until 1991 that any priority countries (China, India, and Thailand) were designated.

USTR also has been cautious in retaliating against alleged IPR violators. In early 1988 the United States was on the brink of retaliating against Brazil in the informatics case when settlement was reached at the last minute. However, it was not until October 1988 that the United States first retaliated, this time also against Brazil but in a separate IPR case involving pharmaceuticals. In 1989 the United States retaliated against Thailand's lack of acceptable IPR by withdrawing GSP benefits. India lost $80 million in GSP benefits in 1992 due to its failure to provide adequate intellectual property protection for pharmaceuticals.

USTR's cautious but purposeful approach to designating priority countries and actually retaliating was constructive and well-advised. The two Brazil IPR cases demonstrated US commitment to use retaliation if necessary. By 1989–90, some progress was being made on IPR in the Uruguay Round. In April 1990, USTR announced that the administration's top trade priority was successful completion of the Uruguay Round by the end of the year (USTR, "Fact Sheet: Trade Liberalization Priorities," 27 April 1990). The decision not to designate new super or special 301 priority countries was intended to avoid disrupting the delicate multilateral negotiations, which then seemed poised for successful conclusion. The United States thus showed that it was prepared to act unilaterally but preferred to act multilaterally if progress in GATT was evident. Similarly, the three new special 301 cases against China, India, and Thailand in early 1991, after it was evident that conclusion of the round was not imminent, demonstrated to home and foreign audiences USTR's unwavering commitment to IPR.

USTR's caution was also wise because it is often very difficult and time-consuming to reach agreements on adequate and effective IPR protection, as the Brazil pharmaceuticals case most vividly illustrates. Special 301's six- to nine-month timetable for obtaining acceptable agreements seems excessively optimistic (table 8.1). However, USTR's broad discretionary authority has allowed US negotiators some latitude to reduce the risk of counterproductive threats and actual retaliation and thereby to achieve some successes, both in the Uruguay Round and bilaterally.[11]

The Case against Brazil

The Pharmaceutical Manufacturers Association alleged that Brazil's denial of product and process protection for pharmaceuticals was an unreasonable practice under the terms of the 1984 Trade Act's revisions to section 301.[12] The PMA said that its members had lost sales of at least $160 million between 1979 and 1986, a figure that could exceed $280 million between 1987 and 2000.

The PMA's members had a substantial commercial presence in Brazil. In 1985, 18 US-controlled affiliates held 37.5 percent of the total pharmaceutical market, with annual sales of $600 million. Their investment in Brazil totaled $700 million, generating employment for 18,000 people. Exports by PMA members to Brazil were $50 million in 1985.

The PMA argued that the absence of patent protection limited its members' ability to recoup research and development expenditures for existing products and reduced the resources available for R&D for new products. PMA estimated spending for each new patented product at more than $100 million and seven to ten years in research and development. Brazilian competitors that infringed US patents did not incur these R&D costs and therefore could sell their products at significantly lower prices than the US patent holders, both in the Brazilian market and in other countries with inadequate IPR.

Brazil's Code of Industrial Property excludes product and process patent protection for pharmaceuticals. The US government and industry had repeatedly complained about the absence of patent protection

---

11. See Davis (1991) for an argument that special 301 does not formally allow USTR as much discretion as has been exercised and a proposal to amend the law to give USTR more discretion. See annual USTR fact sheets on special 301 for a listing of IPR agreements and activities since the mid-1980s. PMA and industry officials, for example, cite the 1992 agreement with China, the 1993 agreement with Hungary, and the 1993 NAFTA agreement with Mexico as substantial successes for their industry. Industry officials also cite Korea, Taiwan, Chile, Canada, Bulgaria, and Indonesia as countries where significant progress in IPR protection for pharmaceuticals has occurred as a result of negotiations with the United States.

12. The PMA's petition was filed on 11 June 1987 by the law firm of Covington and Burling and is on file in the USTR's public reading room under docket no. 301-61.

between 1984 and 1986, but to no avail. In the spring of 1987, the PMA threatened to file a 301 petition but was persuaded to postpone it in hopes of a quiet, negotiated settlement. Some US diplomats were said to be concerned about a backlash in Brazil against high-visibility US pressure for IPR reform (*International Trade Reporter*, 13 May 1987, 641–42). The previous informatics case, which was announced on Brazil's independence day, had provoked a strong populist reaction in Brazil that may have impeded resolution of that dispute.

In June, however, Brazilian Ambassador Marcilio Moreira informed Assistant USTR Jon Rosenbaum that his government would not change its patent law. Moreira asserted that Brazil was in compliance with the terms of the World Intellectual Property Organization (WIPO) and offered to debate the issue in WIPO. Shortly thereafter, PMA filed its petition, and on 23 July USTR Clayton Yeutter initiated an investigation.

The timing of the investigation was not particularly auspicious. US-Brazil economic relations were already tense because of US demands that Brazil liberalize its Informatics Market Reserve policy, which restricted imports of computers and software. US insistence on better IPR protection was seen in some Brazilian quarters as yet another American challenge to Brazil's long-standing import-substitution policies to promote industrial development and as punishment for Brazil's leadership in opposing parts of the US agenda for the Uruguay Round. The Brazilians were in no mood to negotiate, and the bilateral discussions that followed were not fruitful.

One year later, in July 1988, President Reagan decided that Brazil's failure to provide patent protection for pharmaceuticals was actionable under section 301. The president announced a retaliatory "hit list" of $200 million in Brazilian exports. PMA president Gerald Mossinghoff applauded that action, noting that it would "reinforce the usefulness of the 301 process and the progress made by the administration in improving intellectual property rights in Asia and Latin America, as well as its efforts to add intellectual property protection in the General Agreement on Tariffs and Trade" (*International Trade Reporter*, 27 July 1987, 1057). Brazilian President Jose Sarney condemned the US action as "a violation of basic principle of international law and GATT rules." During a visit to Brazil in early August, Secretary of State George Shultz proposed bilateral technical discussions to resolve the issue, and Ambassador Moreira announced that "now the dialogue has begun" (*International Trade Reporter*, 17 August 1987, 1163).

The new dialogue notwithstanding, on 20 October 1988 President Reagan imposed 100 percent tariffs on $39 million worth of Brazilian exports.[13] The products targeted included $27 million in paper products, $11.9 million in nonbenzenoid drugs, and $100,000 in consumer electron-

13. The president's decision may have been motivated by the approach of the statutory 12-month deadline, but he had authority to defer retaliation.

ics, reportedly to preempt emerging Brazilian exports in this sector (*Journal of Commerce,* 21 October 1988, 1A).

The US announcement of retaliation may have provoked a counterproductive reaction in Brazil. President Sarney reportedly rescinded an order to Brazil's patent and trademark office to draft amendments to protect pharmaceutical processes but not products.[14] And the Brazilian Congress inserted provisions (later removed) in the draft constitution to prohibit even process patents. Brazil also filed a GATT complaint on this indisputably illegal retaliation and received vociferous support from other GATT members.

In the midst of the pharmaceuticals dispute, in May 1989 USTR designated Brazil as a super 301 priority foreign country for its quantitative import restrictions (see chapter 6). Brazil denounced the US action and again refused to negotiate. The Bush administration lowered its rhetoric in the summer and fall of 1989 to avoid giving political ammunition to left-wing and nationalist candidates in Brazil's presidential and congressional campaigns. Ambassador Paulo Tarso Flecha de Lima, secretary general of the Foreign Affairs Ministry, praised the Bush administration's commitment to improved trade relations and announced the resumption of regular meetings. He warned, however, that political conditions in Brazil were not ripe for a resolution of the pharmaceuticals dispute (*International Trade Reporter,* 4 October 1989, 1283–85).

In March 1990, Brazil's new president, Fernando Collor de Mello, took office and announced a sweeping economic reform that included elimination of the quantitative import restrictions targeted in the super 301 case. In May, USTR Carla Hills announced the termination of the super 301 investigation in response to President Collor's "bold trade liberalization initiative."

Hills visited Brazil in early June and pressed hard for patent protection for pharmaceuticals (*International Trade Reporter,* 13 June 1990, 855–57). Alluding to Brazil's growing interest in acquiring state-of-the-art technology and encouraging foreign investment, she pointedly noted that Brazil's access to them depended on the strength of its intellectual property rights. Minister of Science and Technology Jose Goldemberg reportedly promised improved IPR for pharmaceuticals as soon as it was politically feasible. The head of the Association of Brazilian Exporters, Marcus Pratini de Moraes, announced that he would support improved IPR if the United States would remove its sanctions, end its export subsidies for processed oilseed products, and provide better access for Brazilian exports of orange juice and steel.

In late June 1990, the Brazilian government said it would propose legislation offering patent protection for pharmaceutical products and

---

14. A patent on the process used to manufacture a drug is less protective than a patent on the product because producers can circumvent a process patent through small changes in the way a drug is made.

processes (*International Trade Reporter*, 4 July 1990, 996–97). Immediately thereafter, Hills announced the end of US retaliation in the pharmaceuticals dispute.

Nearly a year later, in May 1991, President Collor sent his proposed IPR reforms to Congress. They included a 20-year term for product and process protection for pharmaceuticals. The president requested that the legislation be considered under a fast-track procedure within 45 days, but Congress sidetracked it.

The proposed legislation attracted strong opposition from powerful legislators and the domestic pharmaceutical industry, represented by the Brazilian Association of Fine Chemicals (ABIFINA), which warned of a "violent increase in the price of medicines" and the devastation of domestic firms (*International Trade Reporter*, 17 April 1991, 585). The association introduced its own legislation to defer patent protection for 9 to 13 years and offered patent terms that fell far short of US proposals.

The president and Congress exchanged counterproposals for patent legislation four times over the next two years. By April 1993 the new Clinton administration was sufficiently frustrated to designate Brazil a priority foreign country under special 301 and to launch an investigation a month later (USTR, press release, "USTR Announces Further Actions Under the Special 301 Provisions of the 1974 Trade Act," 28 May 1993). Senator Max Baucus (D-MT) observed, "We have been very patient, but after years of waiting it seems clear that no adequate law will come without American pressure" (*International Trade Reporter*, 2 June 1993, 888). Foreign Minister Fernando Henrique Cardoso, however, warned that the Brazilian Senate might respond to US pressure by weakening the proposed IPR protection (*International Trade Reporter*, 12 May 1993, 775–76).

At the end of the six-month statutory deadline for special 301 investigations, USTR Mickey Kantor announced in November that he would defer a decision on retaliation for three months, until 28 February 1994, based on Brazilian promises that the patent legislation would move forward.

US and Brazilian negotiators met several times in the ensuing three months. Brazilian diplomats and exporters were anxious to avoid a repetition of US sanctions and were especially concerned about a loss of GSP benefits. The Brazilian Congress, however, rejected US threats. The president of the Senate, Humberto Lucena, observed that "no one votes on this kind of matter under international pressure" and warned that the Senate might water down the proposed legislation (*International Trade Reporter* 2 February 1994, 289). Brazilian diplomats also warned that Brazil would boycott the signing of the Uruguay Round agreements in April and would not attend the Western Hemisphere economic summit in December if sanctions were imposed.

Just days before the ultimate special 301 deadline, USTR announced on 24 February 1994 that it had reached an agreement for IPR reforms and a timetable to pass the patent protection law by 15 June and a copyright law by 1 January 1995. The agreement reportedly goes beyond the Uruguay Round intellectual property agreement by including some protection for products in the developmental pipeline but not yet marketed. USTR Mickey Kantor applauded Brazil for "demonstrating its leadership role through the early implementation of the Uruguay Round intellectual property provisions" (USTR, press release, "USTR Kantor Announces Termination of Special 301 Investigation of Brazilian Intellectual Property Rights Regime," 25 February 1994). He called the Brazilian commitment to improved IPR a contribution "toward the advancement of hemispheric economic integration." PMA President Mossinghoff also praised the agreement but noted that legislation still had to be passed and implemented.

The 15 June deadline passed, but the promised legislation did not. In July 1994, when this book went to press, a PMA official was cautiously optimistic that the legislation would eventually pass but noted that the upcoming Brazilian presidential election created uncertainty about its timing and content.

Lessons and Assessment

Lessons

It is too early to judge the outcome of the US-Brazil pharmaceuticals dispute. Assuming satisfactory legislation is passed, a key issue for future assessment is whether the law is effectively enforced. As discussed below, there is a pandemic problem of inadequate enforcement even in those countries that have accepted the need for stronger intellectual property protection.

USTR has had a number of successes in negotiating IPR agreements—the agreement with Mexico is widely cited as highly successful and a model for future deals. But in a number of other cases—for example, Argentina, Thailand, India, Taiwan, and China—it has been difficult to secure meaningful and well-enforced IPR protection. The Brazil pharmaceuticals case is perhaps an extreme example of the problems encountered, but it also illustrates these problems quite well.

Perhaps the clearest lesson from this case is that, even with highly credible US threats of retaliation, it is exceedingly time-consuming and difficult to achieve effective IPR protection in developing countries in which powerful groups oppose it. The Brazil pharmaceuticals case has been one of the longest-running IPR disputes thus far—seven years to date. None of the IPR cases has been satisfactorily resolved within the special 301 deadline of six to nine months, and most are still ongoing (table 8.1). The use of no less than three graduated special 301 watch lists testifies that it often takes considerable time to convince target countries to strengthen IPR.

The difficulty in achieving stronger IPR protection in some countries is inherent in the sharp conflict of economic interests between those who benefit from strong intellectual property rights and those who are hurt. Many countries that do not produce much intellectual property believe that they benefit, sometimes substantially, from piracy. In many cases, as in the local Brazilian pharmaceutical industry, those producer interests that benefit from weak IPR are politically powerful and can delay change for a very long time. Consumers of imported goods and services have some interest in lowering import barriers. But consumers of pirated intellectual property have little interest in stronger property rights unless there are significant differences in the quality of pirated versus protected goods and services or unless stronger IPR protection generates significant access to new products or valuable innovation. The political imagery of large multinational firms exercising monopoly power over domestic consumers and locally owned firms makes it easy for politicians to resist change, particularly in the case of pharmaceuticals, where access to low-cost medicines for poor people is at issue.

Foreign owners of intellectual property have strong financial incentives to seek stronger protection in large and growing developing-world markets. There is much debate over the value of sales and profits lost due to piracy. The PMA recently updated its estimates of its members' annual sales losses, putting the figure in 1993 at $500 million in Brazil (PMA, press release, "PMA Welcomes Announcement of Brazilian Patent Legislation," 25 February 1994). The US International Trade Commission (1988, 4-3) estimated that all US owners lost sales valued at nearly $24 billion in 1986.

There are good reasons to believe that sales figures significantly overestimate the true economic losses (Maskus 1993, 19–20).[15] But there are also credible estimates that the losses are quite large. Maskus and Eby Konan (1994), for example, estimate that the lack of IPR for pharmaceuticals in Mexico, Argentina, Brazil, and India costs international drug companies between $167 million and $1.5 billion in lost profits annually. Given the high costs and great regulatory and scientific uncertainties involved in developing new medicines, improved IPR in these countries might have a significant impact on the profits of PMA's members.[16]

---

15. Most economists consider forgone profits a better measure of economic losses. However, a number of officials in IP-based industries, particularly pharmaceuticals, have argued that, due to the time and cost required to build a reputation and name recognition, the lack of an early, significant market presence can have negative implications for long-run profits even after a firm eventually enters the market.

16. See Nogues (1990) on how the US regulatory environment and the high costs of R&D encourage the pharmaceuticals industry to take an aggressive approach to IPR in developing countries.

The owners of intellectual property are well-organized and devote considerable resources to their cause. The PMA, for example, consists of the largest American pharmaceutical manufacturers, and it conducts a sophisticated lobbying campaign aimed at the US Congress and the administration. In the Brazil dispute, the PMA was unified in its approach and relentless in its pressure on the US government. PMA enjoyed strong political support in Congress and with top USTR officials because it was an important and valued member of the industry coalition supporting the Uruguay Round.[17] It also lobbied long and hard in Brazil.

Despite a unified stance by the US government and industry and a demonstrated willingness to retaliate, it still took seven years to reach a point in which the case seemed likely to be resolved. US threats may have played some constructive role in concluding the dispute, but their contribution has been at best modest. Thus far, retaliatory threats have yielded two promises but no results.

As in the super 301 case involving Brazil, we believe that gradual changes in domestic economic and political conditions in Brazil were more important factors in explaining the shift in Brazilian policy. As described in chapter 6, by the late 1980s many in government and industry, as well as the Brazilian public at large, had grown increasingly skeptical about the efficacy of Brazil's import-substitution policies, which its weak IPR regime had undergirded. President Collor's election was a reflection of the voters' new willingness to switch to trade and investment liberalization to promote industrial development and growth.

After several years of stagnating living standards and lingering foreign debt problems, Brazil was increasingly eager to repair its badly frayed economic relations with the United States. Improved bilateral relations would open the door to expanded trade and investment and to debt relief. The Bush administration was happy to encourage the Collor government's market-oriented reforms and to win Brazil's cooperation, as a leader among developing countries, in bringing the Uruguay Round to a conclusion by the end of 1990.

Economic reformers in Collor's government and in parts of the private sector were particularly eager to encourage foreign direct investment (FDI) for its own sake and to acquire the world-class technology that Brazil lacked, in part because of its closed market and restrictive foreign investment policies. The US government and industry advocates of improved IPR had long argued that a strong IPR regime was an important inducement to FDI and technology transfer. The US government also had repeatedly linked bilateral agreements on technology transfer to resolution of the pharmaceuticals dispute.[18]

---

17. The pharmaceuticals industry is also a fairly significant financial contributor to members of Congress (Makinson 1990, 1166).

18. *International Trade Reporter* 8, 17 April 1991, p. 586. There are also reports that in February 1994 the US Treasury tried to put pressure on Brazil to reform its patent laws as a condition

Fritsch and Franco (1991b, 81) argue that Brazil's willingness to strengthen intellectual property protection "depends on the potential rate of innovation of its firms. . . . [T]his protection will only occur when technological capability increases to a point beyond which the absence of intellectual property rights would inhibit R&D expenditures and innovative effort." They explain that Brazil was eventually willing to grant better copyright protection for computer software in the course of the informatics dispute because "many domestic firms were already developing marketable products." By contrast, the long-standing failure to resolve the pharmaceuticals dispute is ascribed to the perceived lack of benefits for Brazil.

The benefit-cost calculus in Brazil for IPR in pharmaceuticals may be changing in ways that bode well for future patent protection. In 1992, the 10 largest foreign and domestic pharmaceutical manufacturers in Brazil announced a $1 billion investment for research and new production facilities for Brazil over the next decade. They pointedly made these expenditures conditional on passage of a satisfactory patent law (*Journal of Commerce*, 27 April 1992, 4A). Although Brazilian R&D activity in pharmaceuticals and biotechnology is still very low, it is rising, and local inventors are calling for changes in the patent law. One prominent example is Luiz de Castro, a high official in Brazil's Ministry of Science and Technology. de Castro had to seek a foreign patent for a biotechnology process using Brazil nuts that he developed because current Brazilian law does not allow such patents. de Castro observed that "the absence of an adequate law today is really counter-productive . . . even [international] scientific cooperation has been difficult because of the lack of an adequate law" (*Washington Post*, 5 May 1993, F3).

Even the Brazilian Office of Patents and Trademarks (INDI), which US firms have long criticized for its resistance to strong IPR, may be changing its attitude. The reform-minded head of the agency, IPR lawyer Jose Roberto Gusmao, has pushed for changes to make INPI's decision-making process transparent and timely and to better enforce existing property rights. He observed that "if Brazil is interested in foreign investors, it must guarantee a favorable environment, which includes clear rules and information on criteria about individual cases. We must create more favorable conditions, if we are to receive foreign investments and foreign companies" (*International Trade Reporter 11,* 1 June 1994, 864).

Such views have not yet overcome the widespread perception that IPR offers few benefits and excessive costs to the developing world, and this perception probably best explains the difficulties in reaching IPR agreements with Brazil and many other developing countries, section 301 threats notwithstanding. Unless US retaliation is relatively large, the costs of defiance may be less than the costs of complying with US demands.

---

for debt relief. If true, Treasury's pressure was of limited utility since at the time Brazil had $30 billion in reserves and negotiated a debt restructuring with the commercial banks in the absence of an IMF standby loan agreement.

For the same reason, even when formal agreements are concluded, many target countries have been reluctant to vigorously enforce their new intellectual property commitments. USTR acknowledges the enforcement problem, and in 1993 General Counsel Ira Shapiro reported that "special 301 will be focused more in the future on the issue of obtaining effective enforcement of existing laws."[19] As discussed in chapter 12, we recommend that USTR be given increased resources to monitor compliance with existing agreements because this capacity is important to getting satisfactory results.

However, the experience with the Brazil pharmaceuticals case and others listed in table 8.1 suggests that USTR monitoring per se will not solve the enforcement problem if countries believe that the costs of effective IPR exceed the benefits. There are various carrots and sticks USTR might use to affect a country's cost-benefit calculation.

One obvious way to raise the costs to target countries of failing to have adequate and well-enforced IPR is to threaten retaliation more frequently and in larger amounts. But if retaliatory threats fail, more frequent and larger use of sanctions will also impose higher costs on US consumers and users of imports. We think that USTR's cautious use of threats and sanctions in general has been wise and reasonably effective and do not recommend that they be wielded more aggressively.

As described in chapters 3 and 13, the conclusion of the Uruguay Round dramatically changes the calculus of retaliatory threats. We argue there that, in general, the expanded coverage of GATT/WTO trade rules and the strengthened dispute settlement mechanism will greatly reduce the need for retaliatory threats and will increase their effectiveness when they are used in conjunction with the new mechanism. However, the WTO's phase-in periods and its special provisions for disputes involving intellectual property will significantly reduce the efficacy of special 301 for the initial five to ten years after the Uruguay Round agreements go into effect.

Recognizing that it takes time to design and implement effective IPR and that the gains from intellectual property protection increase with a country's level of development, the WTO agreement provides a five- to ten-year phase-in period for developing countries to implement the agreement. The WTO's dispute settlement mechanism (DSM) cannot be used to challenge developing countries' lack of IPR during this phase-in period.

Moreover, the fast-track, fully automated procedures of the new mechanism do not apply to nonviolation nullification and impairment IPR cases for the first five years of the agreement. Thus, it will be impossible to obtain WTO authority to retaliate in nonviolation disputes for the first five years. This provision will mainly affect IPR disputes involving the

---

19. Statement before the Senate Finance Committee, Subcommittee on International Trade, hearing on Special 301 and the Fight Against Trade Privacy, 103 Cong., 19 April 1993, 71.

advanced industrial countries, since developing countries already are exempt from any challenge for five to ten years.

The US IPR community, the pharmaceuticals industry in particular, is dissatisfied with the long phase-in periods for developing countries. Harvey Bale, PMA's senior vice president, has suggested that the WTO agreements "would effectively remove special 301 as a US trade policy tool."[20] We believe that this assessment is correct for developing-country targets for the next five to ten years. However, even when the WTO's dispute settlement mechanism is not available, the United States still has some economic levers available.

Probably the most readily available threat is denial of GSP tariff benefits, which are not bound under the WTO and can be unilaterally restricted. GSP already has been restricted in IPR cases involving India and Thailand, albeit to limited effect. The Uruguay Round tariff cuts and the "graduation" process for GSP beneficiaries as they become more developed limit the efficacy of this threat. Other possible threats include denial of bilateral aid and technology transfer and pressure on multilateral lending agencies to deny loans to recalcitrant countries. GSP, aid, and loans are given for a variety of humanitarian and geopolitical purposes outside the realm of IPR. These same levers are being proposed as tools to enforce stronger human and worker rights and environmental protection. We expect that it will be difficult to develop the political and interagency consensus in the United States necessary to use these sanctions credibly for IPR protection and therefore believe they will be of limited effectiveness. Moreover, since these threats are most effective against the very poorest countries, the potential gains to US owners of intellectual property are likely to be fairly small.

In the future, we expect that the more potent levers to encourage improved intellectual property laws and enforcement will be "carrots" that raise the benefits or reduce the costs of effective IPR for developing countries. Until recently, US intellectual property owners and the US government have viewed stronger protection and enforcement as a right not requiring the reciprocal exchange of trade concessions. In the future, however, one of the more significant inducements to stronger IPR may be admission to regional trade agreements. Mexico agreed to far-reaching changes in its IPR regime in preparation for the NAFTA negotiations. Consequently, the PMA lauded NAFTA for representing "the highest intellectual property standards and enforcement in any international agreement."[21] It is widely expected that the NAFTA's IPR provisions will serve as a model for future free trade agreements (FTA) that the United

---

20. Senate Finance Committee, Subcommittee on International Trade, hearing on Special 301 and the Fight Against Trade Privacy, 103 Cong., 19 April 1993, 48.

21. Senate Finance Committee, Subcommittee on International Trade, hearing on Special 301 and the Fight Against Trade Privacy, 103 Cong., 19 April 1993, 40.

States may negotiate with countries in the Western Hemisphere or in the Asia Pacific. Although the United States will have great bargaining leverage, IPR negotiations in a regional FTA will be more reciprocal than a special 301 negotiation. US trading partners must be convinced that the overall package of benefits offered by the United States will outweigh the potential costs of an IPR agreement.

Effective enforcement of intellectual property rights is costly.[22] For developing countries that perceive few, if any, economic benefits from a strong IPR regime, it may be helpful for the United States to provide technical and financial assistance in establishing effective enforcement mechanisms, as called for in Article 67 of the WTO's intellectual property agreement. Assistance could be through bilateral aid programs or under the auspices of multilateral donor institutions through their existing programs to improve overall economic governance and the legal framework for doing business.

Officials in a number of intellectual property-based industries believe that a profound change is occurring in developing-country attitudes toward improved intellectual property protection. A growing number of hitherto skeptical poor countries are coming to accept stronger IPR as part of a broader developmental strategy to encourage domestic R&D and investment and to attract foreign investment. The US government and the private sector make this developmental argument frequently and forcefully, for example, in negotiating bilateral investment and technology transfer treaties and in discussions between private investors and developing-country policymakers.

Many observers attribute this change in developing-country attitudes both to US pressure and to global market forces, which are encouraging countries to establish an environment hospitable to domestic and foreign investors. In several of our other case studies, we found that US external pressure for policy reform is most effective if it complements the activities of a reform-minded constituency in the target country. Building a domestic consensus in favor of policy reform can be time-consuming and difficult, particularly in the case of IPR, where there are often sharply competing domestic interests. US threats can help if they are deftly used, preferably in conjunction with promises of benefits such as technology transfer and investment. Conversely, heavy-handed US pressure can provoke a counterproductive reaction in the target country if public threats are issued at the wrong time—for instance, during an election campaign.

On balance, we believe that USTR's discretionary use of special 301 has been deft and reasonably effective in achieving improved IPR. It is

---

22. Even rich countries find enforcement difficult. A recent story about an "epidemic" of piracy in the United Kingdom suggests that lost sales amount to $1.5 billion annually, with most of the pirated goods produced locally rather than imported. The United Kingdom's IPR laws are enforced by 1,500 local trading standards departments that complain of overstretched resources (*Financial Times*, 16 May 1994, 7).

understandable that some in Congress and the private sector are frustrated with the slow pace of change and with often ineffective enforcement. It would be a mistake, however, for Congress to reduce presidential discretion in the use of special 301 in the hope that this would somehow speed up reform. Patient educational efforts to convince developing countries that stronger IPR is in their economic interest coupled with "carrots" such as aid, trade, technology transfer, and investment are likely to be the most effective inducements to change.

Assessment: Impact on the Multilateral Trading System

It is not easy to assess what impact this case had on advancing US goals for intellectual property rights in the Uruguay Round. Developing countries recognized the US timing and choice of Brazil for unilateral initiatives as a tactic to advance the then-stagnant Uruguay Round intellectual property negotiations by demonstrating that in the absence of such an agreement the United States was prepared to move unilaterally and aggressively against a leading opponent of its IPR agenda. As we suggest in chapter 3, at the very least it seems plausible that aggressive unilateralism encouraged developing countries to negotiate on intellectual property in the round as a way of establishing rules to restrain US unilateralism. Certainly by 1989 Brazil had become noticeably more accommodating in the GATT's IPR negotiations. In any event, the United States and its European and Japanese allies succeeded in obtaining a far-reaching IPR agreement in the WTO that will eventually bind developing countries to quite significant minimum standards of protection. Hudec (1993, 190) observes that "getting this far was a major constitutional event for GATT." Achieving effective intellectual property protection will take five to ten years under the WTO agreement, but the seven-year history of the Brazil pharmaceuticals case suggests that it would also take considerable time using special 301.

We are unable to judge whether US success in getting a stronger IPR regime in the WTO will on balance improve world economic welfare. American and other countries' intellectual property owners will certainly benefit. But in contrast to the clear gains from liberalization of barriers to trade in goods and services and to foreign investment, it is not clear the stronger IPR protection is in the interests of the poorest developing countries. The global welfare effects are at best ambiguous.

It is quite likely that the pharmaceuticals case severely damaged US credibility as the *demandeur* of reform of the GATT dispute settlement mechanism. There is no doubt that the retaliation against Brazil was GATT-illegal because it raised tariffs that had been bound in previous negotiations. When Brazil sought to bring a GATT complaint against the retaliation, the United States repeatedly blocked formation of a panel to settle the dispute. This lawless behavior evoked what a GATT spokesman described as "the most massive support we have seen in a panel dispute," with the great majority of the GATT membership that voiced opinions endorsing Brazil's request and condemning the United States (*International Trade Reporter*, 15 February 1989, 194). At a special GATT Council meeting in February 1989 held to discuss US aggressive unilateralism, the case was cited as an example of the dangers that US behavior posed for the trading system.[23] The Brazilian representative pointedly noted the hypocrisy of the United States blocking the panel when it was the leading advocate of reforming the dispute settlement mechanism to prevent just such behavior by other countries (GATT, Minutes of Meeting, C/M/228, 16 March 1988, 18).

In the face of overwhelming foreign opprobrium, the United States eventually agreed to set up the panel, whose activities were then suspended by mutual consent to allow the United States and Brazil to negotiate. In 1990 Brazil withdrew its GATT complaint after the United States lifted its sanctions.

GATT legal scholar Robert Hudec (1993, 283–84) cites the case as an example of a "negative outcome" for the dispute settlement system. The United States imposed GATT-illegal retaliation and used it to extract concessions from Brazil, thus making a mockery of the dispute settlement process.

To repair the damage done to its credibility as a leading proponent of GATT reform will require that the United States scrupulously abide by the new WTO dispute settlement mechanism and use special 301 only in ways consistent with WTO's rules and procedures.[24]

---

23. GATT Council, "Discussion on Unilateral Measures," Document C/163, 16 March 1989. The United States was at the time also blocking an adverse panel finding in the EC complaint involving section 337 of the 1930 Tariff Act and an EC request for a ruling on US retaliation against the Community's ban on hormone-fed beef.

24. For example, the United States must extend the special 301 deadline to conform to the 12- to 18-month timetable for WTO dispute settlement and raise bound tariffs in retaliation only with WTO authorization.

9

European Union: Oilseeds

CHARLES ICELAND

In a 1987 study, Dale Hathaway noted that "continual bickering over GATT rules for agriculture has eroded the credibility of the entire GATT dispute settlement process. Unless credibility can be restored, this erosion of confidence will spread to other areas until no meaningful trade rules remain." He presciently observed that the success or failure of the Uruguay Round of trade negotiations might hinge on the outcome of its agricultural negotiations (Hathaway 1987, 3).

The oilseeds dispute between the United States and the European Union (and its predecessor European Community) showed how weak the GATT dispute settlement process was and how eroded general confidence in the global trading system had become. The oilseeds agreement that was eventually reached became the keystone of a larger agricultural agreement between the United States and the European Union (the Blair House agreement), which in turn unlocked the Uruguay Round agreement.

During the course of the case, two GATT dispute settlement panels sustained the United States' claim that the EC oilseeds subsidies nullified and impaired the zero tariff bindings that the original European Economic Community (EEC) had offered during the Dillon Round of GATT negotiations (1960–61). Despite these rulings, the European Community refused to roll back its subsidies. Following a US threat under section 301 to impose high tariffs on $1 billion worth of EC exports to the United States, the two sides reached an agreement in December 1992.

In early 1993, France threatened to veto the broader Blair House agreement, including the oilseeds deal, if changes were not made. David Buchan and Quentin Peel wrote in November 1993 that the French

Charles Iceland was formerly a research assistant at the Institute for International Economics.

... regard GATT as a pistol held to the nation's head and see images of their past collective life passing nostalgically in front of them: Van Gogh's golden wheat fields, which would lie forever fallow because of the Blair House cuts in subsidized cereal exports; or arty Truffaut films, which would be pushed out of French cinemas by Hollywood blockbusters given their freer rein under GATT. (*Financial Times,* 29 November 1993, 15)

In the end, the United States relented and agreed to some modifications of Blair House. Previously, the United States had categorically rejected such modifications and had signaled in various ways that it might de-emphasize the Community in its international trade strategy. The conventional wisdom is that negotiators accepted a less than satisfactory oilseeds agreement in the interest of securing a deal on agriculture that would allow completion of the Uruguay Round.[1]

Evolution of US-EU Agricultural Trade Conflict

In the early postwar era the principal objective of US agricultural trade policy was to ensure that imports did not undermine domestic support programs. The quotas and other measures used to protect agriculture were in violation of US GATT obligations, so in 1955 the Eisenhower administration was granted a formal waiver. One observer wrote:

[T]he opportunity to include agriculture with the other industries covered by the various GATT agreements was lost. The American action confirmed the view that agricultural policy was a matter for domestic decision, not international agreement. (Butler 1983, 106–07)

In 1962, however, the focus of US agricultural trade policy began to shift. On 14 January the EEC Council of Ministers approved the final regulations establishing the Common Agricultural Policy (CAP). The United States had supported formation of the EEC to strengthen the Western alliance in its confrontation with the Soviet Union but objected to the highly protectionist effects of the CAP and the impact on US exports. The EEC, on the other hand, regarded the CAP as the glue needed to keep the Community together.[2]

On 11 October President Kennedy signed the Trade Expansion Act of 1962, which in section 252 dealt with "foreign import restrictions." Section 252 was the predecessor to section 301 of the Trade Act of 1974 and was aimed primarily at barriers to US agricultural exports. It explicitly

---

1. *Inside U.S. Trade,* 10 September 1993, 16. The views of US farm groups on this issue were expressed by the American Farm Bureau Federation in a 14 September 1993 letter to President Clinton.

2. Talbott (1978) discusses how CAP affected the EEC.

mentioned "variable import fees" as a practice to which the president was authorized to respond (see chapter 2). The following year, President Kennedy used this authority to retaliate against the EEC variable levy on poultry in what came to be known as the chicken war.[3]

During the Dillon Round of GATT negotiations (1960–61), the EEC offered what then appeared to be a relatively minor set of market-access concessions, but these later proved to be a gaping hole in the CAP wall of protection. Oilseeds and starch- and protein-rich grain substitutes were not subject to variable levies because these products were regarded as either insignificant or producible only at noncompetitive high cost.[4] The EEC offered in the Dillon Round to bind the tariff on these products at zero, meaning it could not raise the tariff without providing compensation to affected suppliers.

The combination of rising CAP support prices for grain, dairy, and meat products and zero duties on oilseeds and other products such as tapioca (manioc), corn gluten feed, and citrus pellets seriously distorted relative prices among feed grains and grain substitutes. This distorted supply and demand, which allowed the substitutes to push grain out of EC feeding troughs and "exacerbated the surpluses on the grain market, which were already raising serious financial and trade-policy problems. . ." (Hartmann 1991, 59; see also Hathaway 1990, 54–55).

Robert Hudec (1988) argues that as the CAP evolved, the United States drew three "lines in the sand" and used GATT rules to back them up:

- The first line was drawn during the chicken war, which Hudec argues was a failed attempt to limit the levels of the EEC's variable levies.

- The second line was US "insistence upon preserving GATT bindings and other GATT disciplines on products not covered by variable levy regimes. . . ."—for example, the zero tariff bindings on nongrain animal feeds and GATT disciplines on subsidies for processed products such as canned fruits and vegetables (Hudec 1988, 40).

---

3. US negotiators first tried to convince the EEC to change the variable levy to either a bound ad valorem tariff or a tariff-rate quota, but never challenged the GATT-legality of the variable levy. In retaliating, the US charged that a variable levy upset the balance of concessions previously negotiated and cited its rights to compensation under Article XXVIII of the GATT. This provision allows countries to negotiate changes in bound tariffs or to raise them unilaterally if no agreement can be reached with principal suppliers. If the latter, Article XXVIII also allows countries affected by the tariff change to seek compensation or to do "compensatory withdrawal" of concessions previously made (raise their own tariffs) to restore the balance of concessions. See Talbott (1978) for a detailed analysis of the chicken war.

4. CAP prices for grains and other products had not yet risen to the unreasonable levels they would eventually attain. Thus oilseeds and other substitutes did not yet pose much of a threat.

- The third line of containment involved defending third-country markets against subsidized EC exports.

Although section 252's focus on agriculture was removed when it was replaced by section 301 in 1974, its role in defending these lines in the sand is clear from the early pattern of cases investigated. Exactly half of the first 16 cases investigated under section 301 between 1975 and 1979 involved disputes over the CAP. Three cases defended the second line in the sand, challenging EC measures to protect processed products or to undermine the zero duty on feedgrain substitutes (see cases 301-4, 301-7, and 301-8 in the appendix). Three more challenged EC export subsidies in third markets (cases 301-5, 301-6, and 301-16 in the appendix). Case 301-3 questioned the Community's use of supplementary levies on top of the normal variable levy on egg products, and case 301-11 disputed EC tariff preferences on citrus imports from Mediterranean countries and North Africa.

Agricultural trade disputes with the European Community and other suppliers intensified in the early 1980s when export demand began to falter as a result of slower world economic growth (Hathaway 1987, 16). Rather than curtail production, many countries exported their excess supply (massive stock accumulations), often with the aid of large export subsidies. US agricultural exports plunged.

US agriculture could not blame all its misfortunes in the early 1980s on EC agricultural policies, however. Other major problems for US agricultural exports included (1) the strength of the dollar, which peaked in 1985 at a level 50 percent higher than its 1980 value; (2) worldwide recession in 1982–83; (3) severe debt problems (and lack of foreign exchange to pay for imports) in Eastern Europe and among developing countries; (4) the US embargo on grain sales to the USSR in 1980 and its continuing impact on US sales in that market; (5) the negative effects of the United States' own farm price support programs, which keep US prices high; and (6) increased subsidies in Brazil and Argentina, which led to increased competition from those suppliers (Madison 1983, 115). Nor could the United States claim to have a clean record itself on government intervention in agricultural markets. For example, in 1982, President Reagan imposed very restrictive import quotas on sugar, blaming collapsing world prices in part on EC export subsidies.[5]

Notwithstanding these other problems, growing EC support for agriculture in the early 1980s constituted a legitimate US grievance. According to one observer, "European production has grown while internal consumption is barely rising, generating an increasing surplus volume for export. . . . Ted Halow's comment that 'European farmers are producing

---

5. Hathaway (1987, 41) notes that the European Community went from being a net sugar importer in 1967 to being the world's largest exporter in the mid-1980s as a result of the CAP.

not for consumers but for intervention' is difficult to refute" (Butler 1983, 114).

Increasing Tensions in the 1970s

High EC export subsidies, import levies, and support prices put increasing strain on US-EC relations in the 1970s. According to Hillman, agricultural protection was costing EC consumers as much as $20 billion annually by the early 1980s. He also noted the impact of EC variable levies on US agricultural exports, pointing out that between 1974 and 1982 exports not subject to the levy rose 84 percent, while those subject to the levy rose only 6 percent (Hillman 1983, 76). Wayne Sharp, counselor for agricultural affairs at the US Mission to the European Community, stated in late 1982 that the United States wanted

> . . . to challenge EC export subsidies and persuade the EC, preferably by reason, but also by threat or even retaliation should that prove necessary, to respect our trading rights both within the EC market and in trade with third countries. . . . I can assure you that our agricultural concerns will not be put aside in order to improve our relations. Agriculture is indeed a fundamental part of our relationship with the Community. (quoted in Hillman 1983, 75)

US negotiators had tried to address the subsidy problem during the Tokyo Round of multilateral trade negotiations concluded in 1979. The US agricultural sector wasted no time in testing the just-approved Subsidies Code, filing three section 301 complaints in 1981 challenging EC export subsidies on sugar, poultry, and pasta (cases 301-22, 301-23, and 301-25). US negotiators also brought a complaint under the code in October 1981 on EC subsidies for wheat flour exports, the subject of a section 301 case since 1975 (case 301-6). It became clear that the Subsidies Code would not provide a solution to US-EC agricultural disputes when the dispute settlement panel appointed in the wheat flour case could not operationally define the key "equitable share" standard that was supposed to determine when export subsidies violated the code (Hudec 1993, 490–92).

Nor was section 301 very effective in disciplining EC agricultural policies. In many of these cases the European Community agreed under pressure from the GATT and the United States to abolish the offending practice, only to replace it with another, equally protective practice. In 1978, for example, the European Community abolished a minimum import price system for tomato concentrates, case 301-4, but soon after adopted subsidies to EC processors to offset the cost of using higher-priced protected inputs. This pattern of only minimal or even illusory concessions was repeated again and again in US-EC trade disputes (see cases 301-3, 301-5, 301-7, 301-8, and 301-26 in the appendix).

The United States responded more aggressively in 1982, when it imposed quotas on imports of sugar. Secretary of Agriculture Richard

Lyng directly linked the quotas to EC sugar export subsidies, case 301-22, saying the United States "was forced" to impose them in response to the European Community's "very irresponsible" actions (*U.S. Export Weekly*, 22 March 1983, 976; also case 301-22 in the appendix).[6] The case did not bring about EC export subsidy reform, however. Then in February 1983 the United States "retaliated" against EC wheat flour export subsidies (case 301-6) by granting a subsidy to US exporters large enough to capture the entire Egyptian market for one year (previously about 25 percent of EC wheat flour exports). In a March 1983 speech, USDA Secretary John Block said that actions like the Egyptian sale illustrate the seriousness of US intentions (*U.S. Export Weekly*, 22 March 1983, 977; also case 301-6 in the appendix).

With these issues still unresolved in 1985, the United States established the Export Enhancement Program of ongoing export subsidies to combat the European Community's export subsidy program (Hudec 1993, 492; US Senate, Committee on Agriculture 1987, 198–99; case 301-6 in the appendix). Aggressive US actions again failed to curb EC subsidies but may have influenced the Community's decision to put its export subsidies on the table in the Uruguay Round.

Aggressive Unilateralism and the CAP

In 1985 the United States turned up the heat still higher. In July 1985, two months prior to President Reagan's announcement of the Trade Policy Action Plan for combating foreign unfair trade barriers, the United States announced retaliation against EC tariff preferences on citrus products granted to certain Mediterranean countries (case 301-11). A GATT panel had ruled that these preferences nullified and impaired US benefits under the GATT, but the European Community had blocked adoption of the report. The retaliation, withdrawal of tariff concessions on EC pasta imports, served a dual purpose because the United States also had challenged EC pasta export subsidies in case 301-25. A Subsidies Code panel had ruled, 3 to 1, that the EC subsidies violated the code, but the code committee was sharply divided on the issue, and the ruling was never adopted (Hudec 1993, 493–95). The Community responded by counterretaliating against US exports of lemons and walnuts. This is one of only two section 301 cases in which US retaliation has prompted binding counterretaliation.[7]

---

6. Destler and Odell (1987, 14) argue that the real motivation was to buy votes in Louisiana for President Reagan's economic plan.

7. The Canadian beer case, 301-80, is the other. In the European Community enlargement case, 301-54, retaliatory and counterretaliatory measures were imposed at levels deliberately chosen to have no actual trade effect.

The citrus case was finally resolved in August 1986. The United States received tariff concessions on the citrus products in question, both sides lifted their retaliatory duties, and the United States and European Community also exchanged tariff concessions on additional products. The two sides also agreed to resolve the pasta dispute within one year. The pasta agreement, signed in September 1987, was expected to result in half of the Community's exports of pasta to the United States being subsidy-free.

In September 1985, as part of the action plan, President Reagan directed USTR to recommend retaliation in another EC canned fruit case, 301-26, the third of four on these products, unless an agreement was reached by December. The complaint that EC production subsidies impaired EC tariff bindings had been supported by a GATT panel report, but the European Community blocked its adoption. In December 1985 an agreement was reached to lower the EC subsidies in question.

The canned fruit saga illustrates the difficulties US negotiators faced in battling the CAP. Two earlier cases (301-4 and 301-7) had challenged border measures imposed to protect fruit and vegetable processors. Those measures were removed following negative GATT rulings, but the European Community replaced them with the subsidy scheme challenged in case 301-26. Three years later, however, USTR charged that the 1985 agreement was not being implemented satisfactorily. Finally, in May 1989, USTR initiated an investigation into whether the European Community had violated the agreement and announced simultaneously that a hearing would be held in 30 days to determine whether EC practices were actionable under section 301. The announcement also included a hit list of products for possible retaliation. On 30 June USTR Carla Hills announced that a tentative agreement had been reached with the European Community to reduce canned fruit subsidies and that any action would be postponed to 1 October, pending finalization of the agreement.

In March 1986 the United States again threatened the European Community with retaliation unless it rescinded new trade restrictions on agricultural imports that were being instituted as a result of Spain and Portugal's accession to the community (301-54). The European Community threatened counterretaliation. Subsequent negotiations failed to yield results, the United States again threatened retaliation, and in January 1987 the European Community made agricultural and industrial concessions valued at $400 million per year for four years. US agricultural exporters, however, felt that this compensation fell far short of their losses.

Two other cases touched on the sensitive area of health and safety standards and their use as protectionist devices. Both involved EC regulations affecting imports of meat. In 1988 the European Community banned the sale of beef from cattle treated with growth hormones, claiming that it was responding to consumer concern. The United States argued that the ban was not based on scientific evidence and that it represented an illegal trade barrier masquerading as a health measure. Threats of retaliation, counterretaliation, and counter-counterretaliation were exchanged. When the European Community implemented the ban in January 1989, the United States retaliated with 100 percent tariffs on $100 million in imports from the European Community. Steps were taken to prevent the trade war from escalating, and the European Community offered some minor exceptions to the ban (for pet food and beef that could be certified as hormone-free). The European Community delayed implementing its counterretaliatory measures, avoiding further escalation, but the basic issue remains unresolved.

In the second case, the European Community declared most US pork and beef slaughterhouses ineligible to export to the European Community under the Community's Third Country Meat Directive. US negotiators challenged the directive, arguing that it violated the national treatment principle of the GATT because domestically produced meat that did not cross internal borders within the European Community did not have to meet the same standards. Before the GATT panel could rule, the two sides reached an agreement in which the Community "relisted" some US plants as eligible to export under the meat directive. But the European Community later revoked the eligibility, and the case had to be reopened. In October 1992 a second agreement was concluded based on the findings and recommendations made by a joint US-EC veterinary group. The group studied differences between US and EC inspection requirements and identified areas where US regulations and standards could be considered "equivalent" to those under the Third Country Meat Directive. It is too early to safely judge whether this agreement will really resolve the problem.

Overall, US negotiators seem not to have achieved much success case by case in 301 challenges to the CAP. What success they have had occurred largely after the shift to more aggressive tactics in 1985.[8] USTR retaliated in the linked pasta and citrus cases and identified retaliation targets and set short deadlines for action in the enlargement and canned fruit cases. Viewed cumulatively, the 301 cases challenging the CAP may have had more impact than is apparent from a case-by-case assessment. For example, the GATT complaints against minimum import prices, licensing schemes, and feed-mixing requirements have constrained the European Community to use on-budget subsidies rather than off-budget border measures. The decision to counter EC export subsidies with the Export Enhancement Program (EEP) also increased CAP costs, increasing internal pressures to bring the CAP budget under control. In May 1992 the European Community finally adopted a major CAP reform package, which then set the parameters for the EC stance in the Uruguay Round over

---

8. Prior to adopting a more aggressive 301 strategy in 1985, USTR could boast of only one success in nine EC CAP cases. Since then, the record is a much improved five of nine.

the next 18 months (US Department of Agriculture, Economic Research Service 1992, 55).

Oilseeds Case

By the early 1980s, half of US agricultural exports to the European Community entered duty-free as a result of those long-ago tariff bindings in the Dillon Round (Butler 1983). Closing the open flanks of EC agricultural trade policy in order to substitute EC products for imports was deemed necessary to help counter increasing farm budgets and growing commodity surpluses (Hartmann 1991, 58–59; Ames 1990, 288 and 292; Hathaway 1987, 30–31 and 33).

In the late 1970s, the European Community launched an oilseeds subsidy scheme. Payments were made to oilseeds processors to compensate them for using EC oilseeds, the prices of which were well above world prices (Hathaway 1987, 32–33). Data in table 9.1 demonstrate the impact this subsidy program had on production and trade flows: EC oilseeds production increased from roughly 1 million metric tons in the late 1970s to well over 12 million metric tons in the early 1990s. The ratio of net imports to total EC consumption fell from 93 to 45 percent over this period (and the European Community share of the EC market conversely increased from 8 to 55 percent).

An early attempt to obstruct oilseeds imports was an EC requirement that importers and domestic producers of vegetable proteins (which included soybeans and soybean meal) pay a deposit that would be returned only if the importer or producer bought 50 kilos of surplus nonfat dry milk for each 1,000 kilos of soybean meal. Imports made up 85 percent of the vegetable proteins targeted by the regulation. The European Community terminated the mixing requirement in October 1976, about six months after the US soybean industry filed a section 301 complaint and after USTR had filed a GATT complaint (see case 301-8 in the appendix; Hudec 1993, 466–67; Hartmann 1991, 60).

The European Community also proposed two other measures that limited imports of oilseeds products. One was the payment of a premium for the use of grain in livestock feed (Hartmann 1991, 60). The second was a stiff tax on all vegetable oils in the European Community.

> The [oils] tax would have two desirable effects from the point of view of EC policymakers. It would skew prices in favor of animal fats, especially butter, and help reduce dairy surpluses. And it would provide large revenues to finance expansion of local oilseed production to displace imports of seeds, meal, and oil, and reduce the costs of grain surpluses. (Hartmann 1991, 60)

The vegetable oils tax was vigorously opposed by oilseeds and oilseeds product exporters to the European Community, and the United States

Table 9.1 EC oilseeds production, imports, and net import penetration, 1964–91[a] (millions of metric tons)

	Oilseeds[b]			Soybeans		
	Production	Net imports	Net import penetration	Production	Net imports	Net import penetration
1964–65	0.5	3.2	0.87	0.0	3.1	0.99
1965–66	0.5	3.7	0.88	0.0	3.5	1.00
1966–67	0.5	3.9	0.89	0.0	3.7	1.00
1967–68	0.6	3.9	0.87	0.0	3.6	1.00
1968–69	0.7	4.2	0.85	0.0	4.0	0.99
1969–70	0.8	5.7	0.89	0.0	5.7	1.00
1970–71	0.9	6.2	0.89	0.0	5.8	1.00
1971–72	1.1	7.0	0.87	0.0	6.5	0.99
1972–73	1.2	7.5	0.87	0.0	7.0	1.00
1973–74	1.1	9.5	0.89	0.0	9.1	1.00
1974–75	1.3	8.2	0.87	0.0	8.1	1.00
1975–76	1.1	9.5	0.90	0.0	9.1	0.99
1976–77	1.1	9.7	0.90	0.0	9.1	1.00
1977–78	1.0	12.0	0.93	0.0	11.0	1.00
1978–79	1.3	13.3	0.90	0.0	11.8	0.99
1979–80	1.4	14.7	0.93	0.0	12.6	1.00
1980–81	2.3	11.5	0.81	0.0	10.0	0.97
1981–82	2.5	13.1	0.85	0.0	12.1	1.00
1982–83	3.4	12.4	0.80	0.0	11.7	1.00
1983–84	3.5	10.3	0.74	0.1	9.4	0.98
1984–85	4.7	10.6	0.70	0.1	9.8	1.00
1985–86	5.7	10.7	0.65	0.3	10.0	0.96
1987	11.9	13.4	0.54	1.8	13.2	0.90
1988	10.8	11.6	0.51	1.7	10.9	0.85
1989	10.4	14.2	0.57	2.0	13.0	0.87
1990	12.0	12.6	0.51	2.2	12.0	0.85
1991	12.6	10.4	0.45	1.8	10.0	0.85

a. Data through 1986 are for EC-10 and since 1987 are for EC-12.
b. Oilseeds comprise rapeseed, soybeans, and sunflower seed.

Source: US Department of Agriculture, Economic Research Service.

threatened to retaliate if it was adopted. The European Community finally dropped the idea in 1987 (see also Hathaway 1987, 3–34).

Section 301 Complaint

On 16 December 1987 the American Soybean Association (ASA) filed a section 301 petition alleging that subsidies provided to EC oilseeds processors encouraged purchase of EC oilseeds, to the detriment of imported oilseeds. ASA claimed that as a result, "the US soybean industry has suffered a decline of 35 percent in the volume of exports of soybeans and soybean meal to the EEC since their peak at 15 million metric tons, worth $3.5 billion, in 1982, to 10 MMT, worth about $2.0 billion, in 1986"

Table 9.2 US exports of soybeans to the European Community, 1980–90 (millions of dollars)

Year	Value
1980	3,139
1981	3,421
1982	3,611
1983	2,894
1984	2,368
1985	1,639
1986	1,962
1987	2,053
1988	2,006
1989	1,639
1990	1,433

Source: US Department of Agriculture, Foreign Agricultural Service.

(table 9.2; ASA Section 301 petition, 2–3; 53 *Federal Register*, 14 January 1988, 984).

On 5 January 1988, USTR initiated an investigation and requested consultations with the European Community (53 *Federal Register*, 14 January 1988, 984). The United States requested the establishment of a GATT dispute settlement panel after extensive consultations failed to resolve the dispute (USTR Fact Sheet, 5 November 1992). After the European Community had delayed appointment of panel members for almost a year, USTR Hills told the Senate Finance Committee in April 1989 that the United States would have to "take very strong action on July 5 that comports with the 301 mandate, if the European Community continues to refuse to permit a panel to be appointed" (*International Trade Reporter*, 26 April 1989, 515). In May the two sides announced that the European Community would agree to proceed immediately with GATT dispute settlement procedures, and panel members were announced on 1 June (*International Trade Reporter*, 24 May 1989, 649; Hudec 1993, 559).

In its report of 14 December 1989 the GATT panel found that

> ... the Community Regulations providing for payments to seed processors conditional on the purchase of oilseeds originating in the Community are inconsistent with Article III:4 of the General Agreement, according to which imported products shall be given treatment no less favorable than that accorded to like domestic products. ...

It also found that

> ... benefits accruing to the United States under Article II of the General Agreement in respect of the zero tariff bindings for oilseeds in the Community Schedule of Concessions were impaired as a result of the introduction of production subsidy schemes which operate to protect Community producers of oilseeds completely from the movement of prices of imports and thereby prevent the tariff concessions

from having any impact on the competitive relationship between domestic and imported oilseeds."

The panel recommended that the Community take steps to bring its policies in line with its GATT obligations.

Following release of the report, the European Community indicated it would accept the GATT panel conclusions and adapt the Community regulations in the context of the Uruguay Round, which was then scheduled to conclude in December 1990. Compliance measures would be in place for the crop year beginning in 1991. The panel report was adopted by the GATT Council on 25 January 1990.

By mid-1991, however, the Uruguay Round had still not ended, and the European Community had failed to take ameliorative action. It advised that it would implement the panel's recommendations in a new oilseeds regime to be adopted by 31 October 1991, and that the reforms would apply to all oilseeds harvested during 1992 and thereafter (USTR Fact Sheet, 5 November 1992).

The United States was not satisfied with the reforms announced by the European Community that fall and asked that the GATT panel reconvene to determine whether these reforms would be consistent with the panel's findings (USTR Fact Sheet, 5 November 1992).

On 16 March 1992 the panel found that the new oilseeds regime proposed by the European Community was no longer discriminatory. However, it also found that the new support system "effectively offsets the general movement of import prices and renders the level of Community production substantially insensitive to the general movement of world market prices, and thereby continues to impair the benefits the United States could reasonably expect to accrue to it under the tariff concessions in question." The GATT panel (1992, 23 and 27–28) recommended that the European Community "act expeditiously to eliminate the impairment of the tariff concessions, either by modifying its new support system for oilseeds or by renegotiating its tariff concessions for oilseeds under Article XXVIII." EC agriculture ministers unanimously rejected the GATT panel report on 31 March. UK Farm Minister John Gummer emphasized that "we already changed our system of subsidies to the oilseed sector to meet the GATT demands" (*International Trade Reporter*, 1 April 1992, 589).

On 30 April Deputy USTR Rufus Yerxa announced the US intention to raise tariffs affecting $1 billion of imports from the European Community. This action came after the European Community indicated that it was not then prepared to make the required changes to its oilseeds subsidy regime (USTR, press release, 30 April 1992). On 12 June, USTR published a list of products worth $2 billion that would be pared down to $1 billion and then subjected to punitive duties (57 *Federal Register*, 12 June 1992, 25087; USTR, press release, 9 July 1992).

A week later the Community offered to open talks on compensation under Article XXVIII of the GATT, and the United States accepted. The talks had to be completed by mid-September. One trade journal observed that the offer reflected the European Community's intention of maintaining its current system of oilseeds subsidies but also represented "a major switch in the Community's longstanding rejection of US allegations that by encouraging domestic production, EC subsidies to oilseeds producers are responsible for the reduction in US exports" (*International Trade Reporter*, 10 June 1992, 1000; 24 June 1992, 1082). The two parties met four times over the summer, but according to USTR, "the EC failed to tender or accept any offer that would comply with its GATT obligations or compensate the United States for the continuing impairment" (USTR, press release, 5 November 1992; also see statement of Rufus Yerxa to GATT Council, 29 September 1992).

At a 29 September GATT Council meeting the European Community asked for a working party to review the Article XXVIII negotiations but the United States dismissed this proposal, calling it a stall tactic, and instead requested binding arbitration to determine the amount of damages. The European Community rejected this proposal. US Ambassador Yerxa stated at the meeting that the "central issue" preventing resolution of the dispute was the difference in estimated damages: $2 billion (United States) versus $400 million (European Community).

> [T]he EC offer of $400 million globally would, if taken in subsidy reform . . . reduce EC oilseed production by less than 2 million tons. But they haven't even offered this in the form of subsidy reform. Rather, they have chosen to offer us piecemeal concessions on various products, the total value of which is just over half of the EC's own damage figure. Moreover, they have adopted a 'divide and conquer' policy, attempting to buy off exporting countries one at a time with a few tons of beef, a few turkey parts, or a few bushels of corn. (Statement of US Ambassador Rufus Yerxa to the GATT Council, 29 September 1992)

On 4 November, with no further progress, Yerxa asked the GATT Council to authorize the United States to suspend concessions worth $1 billion. But the European Community blocked the request, which would have required a consensus of all GATT members (Statement of US Ambassador Rufus Yerxa, 4 November 1992; USTR press release, 5 November 1992). The following day the United States announced that it would impose 200 percent duties on $300 million worth of white wine, rapeseed oil, and wheat gluten imported from the European Community beginning 5 December 1992. Increased tariffs on additional goods would be assessed at a later time, if warranted (USTR, press release, 5 November 1992).

Oilseeds Agreement

On 20 November the two sides reached an agreement on oilseeds. The agreement permitted continued subsidization of oilseed production but put a limit on the amount of land eligible under the subsidy program.[9] The US Department of Agriculture estimate the agreement might limit EC oilseeds production to 8.5 to 9.7 million tons, but in a 30 November letter to USTR, the American Soybean Association claimed it would allow 10.5 to 12.5 million tons (*Inside U.S. Trade, Special Report,* 11 December 1992, S-1). EC oilseeds production totaled 12.6 million metric tons in 1991 (table 9.1).

Farm groups, including the American Farm Bureau Federation, the American Soybean Association, and the National Oilseed Processors Association, expressed disappointment with the agreement. ASA stated that "US soybean farmers will continue to suffer the loss of a $2 billion market in the EC, and will receive no compensation for this loss . . . . [B]eyond these major shortcomings, though, the agreement has the potential of gradually slowing and possibly reversing current trade-distorting trends in EC oilseed production" (ASA release, 20 November 1992; NOPA release, 25 November 1992).

The larger importance of the oilseeds agreement is its role in the negotiation of the wider Blair House agreement struck that day on agricultural export subsidies and internal supports, which had impeded completion of the Uruguay Round negotiations.[10] Blair House also resolved a number of long-standing bilateral issues, including restrictions on imports of corn

---

9. The oilseeds agreement was summarized by USDA (1993, 46, table 13.1) thus:

■ Establishes an area-based payment trigger for oilseeds producers. The EC-12 base is set at 5.128 million hectares from 1995–96.

■ Base area is reduced by arable crop set-aside rate or 10 percent, whichever is greater.

■ Oilseeds area receiving compensation must not exceed the base area minus the required set-aside (area trigger).

■ Oilseeds payments will be cut by 1 percent for every 1 percent overshoot of area trigger.

■ Cuts in payments will be carried over through following marketing years and will accumulate until compensated area falls below the trigger.

■ A limit is placed on production of oilseeds for industrial uses on set-aside land of 1 million tons annually expressed in soybean meal equivalents.

■ Growers of confectionery sunflower seeds will not receive oilseeds payments.

■ If the European Community expands, the base area will be increased by no more than the average oilseed area in the new countries in the three years preceding their accession.

■ The Community grants tariff rate quota of 500,000 tons of corn into Portugal as compensation to the United States.

■ The Community will incorporate oilseeds pact into its schedule of commitments for Uruguay Round.

■ The United States agreed to forgo any further compensation claim for impairment of the binding.

■ If the United States or the Community feel agreement has been breached, they agree to binding GATT arbitration.

10. USDA (1993, 45) describes the Blair House deal.

gluten feed and malted barley sprouts and continued access for US feed-grains to the Spanish market under the US-EC enlargement agreement.

France Threatens a Veto

Elections in the United States and France in November 1992 and March 1993, respectively, ushered in new administrations that had promised tougher action on international trade issues in their campaigns. During the US election campaign, for example, Bill Clinton declared that "the United States can no longer afford to turn the other cheek when our competitors close their markets to our goods, steal our intellectual property, dump and subsidize their products, violate trade agreements, and target our industries. . . ."[11]

During the parliamentary elections campaign in France, both the ruling Socialists and opposition conservatives took a hard line on trade and called for renegotiation of the US-EC agreement. The *Journal of Commerce* wrote that "the common thread is the feeling that France's powerful farm lobby represents not only important votes, but also a way of life close to the hearts of a good part of the French population." The French government had expressed unhappiness with the accord after it was concluded in November, but indicated that it would judge the farm accord as one piece of a global GATT accord. But in late January, French negotiators were once again claiming that "the zero binding should be taken back" (*Journal of Commerce*, 25 January 1993, 3A).

In early February the French government announced that it would subsidize rapeseed– and sunflower seed–based diesel fuels. "French Agricultural Minister Jean-Pierre Soisson made it clear that one of the main objectives of the new program is to help France's struggling farmers avoid production limits and set-aside obligations imposed by the reform of the European Community's common agricultural policy" (*International Trade Reporter*, 17 February 1993, 271). Later that month, with the campaign heating up, the French prime minister notified the EC president that if a vote were held on the pact during a March meeting of EC foreign ministers, France would use its veto power (*Journal of Commerce*, 5 March 1993, 3A; see also *Journal of Commerce*, 12 March 1993, 3A).

In late February, US oilseeds producers advised Kantor not to reopen the oilseeds agreement, even though it was "far from fair," because obtaining a better agreement was unlikely. But they did advise Kantor that the United States should retaliate against EC exports, if the European Community failed to ratify the deal before the 1993 planting season began (*Inside U.S. Trade*, 5 March 1993, 6).

---

11. Clinton-Gore campaign release, "Manufacturing for the 21st Century: Turning Ideas into Jobs," 8 September 1992, 8.

In late March the French center right won a sweeping victory in the legislative elections. The new French government expressed opposition to the oilseeds deal and stated its desire to reopen the US-EC farm trade agreement in early April (*Financial Times*, 6 April 1993, 16). During the campaign the center right had even criticized the Socialists' decision to agree to CAP reform in May 1992 (*Journal of Commerce*, 30 March 1993, 5A).

With a new French government demanding changes in the oilseeds and Blair House agreements and a new US administration promising to correct alleged lax trade policies of the Reagan and Bush years, the stage was set for confrontation between the United States and France. The French hard line also heightened tensions within the European Community, most notably between France and Britain. The Germans and the British both wanted a softer French position, which would facilitate the signing of a Uruguay Round deal. Germany had traditionally been among the most protectionist EC members with respect to its agricultural sector. But rising CAP costs combined with the costs of reunification, convinced the German government that agricultural supports had to be reduced. Nevertheless, the Germans were reluctant to put too much overt pressure on France and chose instead to play the role of mediator (*Financial Times*, 29 November 1993, 15).

The Oilseeds Deal Is Ratified

In early May the United States and the European Commission stepped up the pressure on France to accept the oilseeds agreement. US Agriculture Secretary Mike Espy said it was "time-urgent" for the European Community to implement the oilseeds agreement, or else US suppliers would push for the $1 billion in sanctions to be imposed. And EC farm commissioner Steichen warned France that it could be outvoted if it continued its opposition: "This is not a question of unanimity. It will be settled by a qualified majority" of member states (*Financial Times*, 5 May 1993, 6).

On 10 May French Foreign Minister Alain Juppe signaled that France could accept the oilseeds deal if EC partners agreed to pay more for land set aside to curb production. This would require renegotiation of the 1992 CAP reforms. France, however, remained firmly opposed to the Blair House agreement, arguing that its requirements were not compatible with the May 1992 CAP reforms (*Financial Times*, 6 April 1993, 16; 7 April 1993, 5; *Journal of Commerce*, 6 April 1993, 5A).[12] Especially objectionable to the French were the parts of the accord that called for a 21 percent cut in subsidized EC farm exports and continuation of nearly unhindered US

---

12. It was reported that senior EC agriculture officials had already concluded that EC undertakings within the GATT/Blair House agreement were compatible with the May 1992 reforms.

exports of corn gluten feed" (International Monetary Fund, *Morning Press*, 11 May 1993; *Inside U.S. Trade*, 11 June 1993, 4–5).

On 8 June EC foreign ministers finally approved the oilseeds deal after France obtained concessions for French farmers from other member states. The foreign ministers also adopted two "clarifying declarations" at France's insistence. "One stated that the EC Council and the EC Commission view the oilseeds agreement as independent from the agriculture issues being dealt with in the Uruguay Round, as well as from other farm issues dealt with in the Blair House accord, such as the accord on US corn gluten feed exports to the EC. . . . [The] second declaration calls for the EC Commission to rapidly propose on an equitable basis a manner in which the EC might split up among member states the 5.128 million hectares established in the accord as the ceiling on subsidized oilseeds acreage in the Community." According to one source, France might seek a larger share of the acreage for French farmers. In addition, the Commission was asked to issue a report on production of oilseeds for nonfood uses by the end of 1996 (*Inside U.S. Trade*, 11 June 1993, 4).

Agriculture and the End of the Uruguay Round

France continued threatening to unravel the Uruguay Round package of deals unless greater US concessions in the Blair House agreement were forthcoming. On 19 July 1993 France called for a special meeting of EC foreign and farm ministers in September to discuss reopening Blair House (*Financial Times*, 20 July 1993, 4). And on 6 September France formally requested modification of the Blair House agreement, including the restraints on subsidized exports and the bilateral deal allowing continued US corn gluten exports (*Financial Times*, 7 September 1993, 1).

The most readily available and credible negotiating leverage the United States had to use against the French demands was the threat to reopen the oilseeds deal and with it the prospect of 301 retaliation. On 27 August a senior US trade official warned that "the EC must recognize that Blair House was, itself, a painful compromise and that many US farm groups would like even deeper cuts in EC subsidies. Reopening this issue poses the serious risk of unraveling the Uruguay Round and reviving the oilseeds dispute. We feel certain that the EC will live up to its agreements" (USTR, press release, 27 August 1993).

On 14 September, 19 US farm groups sent a letter to President Clinton warning him not to allow France and Germany to reopen Blair House:

> The US-EC accord reached last November at the Blair House was acceptable to our organizations only because it was viewed as helping to end six years of tension and stalemate over agricultural trade issues in the GATT talks, and averted a major trade conflict over the European Community's illegal oilseed subsidies.

> The Blair House accord fell short of our minimum objectives in a number of key areas, including export subsidies, the "peace clause," and, most notably, the oilseed dispute. If the Blair House agreement is reopened or modified in any way, we would insist on substantial improvements in these and other areas.
>
> There must be no misunderstanding or confusion on this point: If the Blair House deal is weakened in any respect, our support for the Uruguay Round will be lost.
>
> Reopening Blair House as the French have proposed would shift the status of the negotiations back to early November when the US threat of retaliation over oilseeds was real and imminent. Should this effort to undercut the Blair House agreement continue, we urge you to be prepared to pursue this option. (American Farm Bureau Federation letter to President Clinton, 14 September 1993).

In a similar letter a few days later, Senator Robert Dole (R-KS) and other farm-state senators urged President Clinton to stand firm and not renegotiate the Blair House accord (Office of Senator Dole, press release, 17 September 1993; *Inside U.S. Trade*, 24 September 1993, 2).

Pressure to avoid a reopening of Blair House also came from members of the 14-member Cairns Group of agricultural exporting nations, who warned that any attempt to do so would result in a mass walk-out from the global trade talks.[13]

The pressure on the French government was intensifying from all directions. On 15 September French farmers attempted to blockade Paris in demonstrations (*Journal of Commerce*, 15 September 1993, 18A). On 19 September British Prime Minister John Major warned that French opposition to the Blair House agreement was wrong and dangerous. A senior aide to the prime minister said the UK was determined to stop the French from wrecking the Uruguay Round. Britain was reportedly drawing up a list of EC issues on which life could be made "difficult" for France. It was also reported that "officials said Mr. Major had been assured that the Cairns Group of 14 agricultural exporting nations would impose penal tariffs on French products if Paris was thought to be imperiling the round" (*Financial Times*, 20 September 1993, 1).

At a so-called EC Jumbo Council meeting held on 20 September, France and Germany circulated a paper that identified France's five chief difficulties with Blair House.[14] Consensus was reached at the meeting that the EC Commission should test whether the United States would agree to accept

---

13. *Journal of Commerce*, 17 September 1993, 3A. It was reported that the Australian minister for trade had written Leon Brittan, Rene Steichen, and Mickey Kantor "stressing that the dispute over Blair House is not solely a European or trans-Atlantic issue, but something of grave concern to all farm-exporting nations."

14. *Financial Times*, 21 September 1993, 1. The French demands included (1) extension of the so-called peace clause preventing unilateral sanctions by either side; (2) flexibility to make the cuts on subsidized food exports at any point during the six-year life of the agreement; (3) ensuring that EC food mountains are exempt from export curbs; (4) strengthening of existing provisions to prevent surges in cheap US cereal substitutes; and (5) guarantees that the European Community will get a full share of any growth in world food markets.

"amplification" of Blair House to accommodate the French. At the same time, UK Foreign Secretary Douglas Hurd cautioned, "I cannot conceive how the EC will continue with the normal transaction of business if it were seen as causing the collapse of the Uruguay Round." And Germany warned of "catastrophic dangers" to its economy if the Uruguay Round deadline were not met. EC Trade Commissioner Sir Leon Brittan warned of the danger of the United States extracting new concessions in other areas of the GATT talks if a farm trade compromise were to take place (*Financial Times*, 21 September 1993, 1).

In response to the EC announcement that Sir Leon would raise French concerns with Mickey Kantor in his upcoming visit to Washington, USTR Kantor stated that "we will not reopen the Blair House agreement, either directly or indirectly" (USTR, press release, 21 September 1993). Kantor characterized French dissatisfaction with Blair House as "an internal EC matter" in which the United States would not involve itself. He also issued a not-so-subtle threat, saying that the United States had been "too Eurocentric in our policies" and that US policy in the future would focus more on Asia (*Financial Times*, 23 September 1993, 14). This threat would be repeated even more explicitly in the coming weeks.

Kantor faced pressure not to reopen Blair House because of the negative repercussions this would have on the Uruguay Round and NAFTA (*Inside U.S. Trade, Special Report*, 24 September 1993, 1–6). Congressional Democrats and Republicans agreed that a Uruguay Round deal was doomed, if the United States budged on Blair House (*New York Times*, 27 September 1993, D1). It was also reported that "with the [NAFTA] in trouble in Congress it is no time to be seen buckling under EC pressure" (*Financial Times*, 28 September 1993, 7).

Meanwhile, France began softening its anti-American rhetoric, with one French official saying "a realization had set in among French officials that anti-American rhetoric was only hardening the US position and could backfire" (*Journal of Commerce*, 30 September 1993, 1A). In early October, French Foreign Minister Alain Juppe warned a Gaullist audience of the dangers of protectionism (*Financial Times*, 4 October 1993, 3). German Chancellor Helmut Kohl, addressing the French Senate, also made a strong plea against protectionism, saying it would be a fatal error for Europe to close its markets.

The French now proposed an "interim" Uruguay Round agreement that would leave out difficult issues such as agriculture and audiovisual goods. Both of these issues stimulated fears in France that its culture and heritage would come under siege if imports were allowed greater access. This was not regarded as a viable option, even among EC trade negotiators (*Financial Times*, 22 October 1993, 5). Peter Sutherland, director general of the GATT, was said to be "astonished" by the French proposal.

Meanwhile, in a column appearing in the *Financial Times* in October, Kantor further developed the threat that European protectionism would cause the United States to turn away from the newly dubbed European Union and toward Latin America and Asia:

> ... With APEC and NAFTA, the US is taking advantage of the two fastest growing areas in the world. ... Meanwhile, as most world economies are moving toward greater openness, European protectionist impulses are growing. ... The most recent example is France's insistence on renegotiating the Blair House Accord, which would reduce agricultural subsidies tied to production. The French position, which threatens the entire Uruguay Round, is opposed by nearly every country. ... The US will have an active role in Europe for as long as we can see. Our desire in Europe is to have greater access for US goods, not to see US business focus on other parts of the globe. If Europe blocks efforts to expand trade, it will be hurting itself most. US trade will continue to expand with Asia and Latin America, and Europe will be left out. ...."[15]

In November, the US House of Representatives approved the NAFTA agreement; two days later President Clinton went to Seattle to meet with leaders of the Asia Pacific Economic Cooperation (APEC) countries. The Cairns Group also issued a warning at this time that a substantial market access package was essential if it was to accept the Blair House accord. Australian Trade Minister Peter Cook stated that if French-counseled EU pressure led to a weakening of Blair House, "the chances of acceptance would be zero." Cairns Group members reportedly regarded the accord as "a lamentable dilution of the earlier draft GATT agreement on farm trade reform" (*Financial Times*, 19 October 1993, 5).

As the pressures on France increased, Prime Minister Balladur conceded in a television interview that GATT was "a trap for his government," offering it only a choice between an international or a domestic crisis (*Financial Times*, 19 October 1993, 5). In mid-November it was reported that the French government was trying to soothe farmers' anxiety over a possible GATT deal by increasing aid to them. Government and farm union officials denied it was a payoff to scale down Blair House demands, saying it was for adjustment to CAP reforms.

At the same time, US negotiators wanted very much to conclude the Uruguay Round negotiations by the December deadline, which also marked the expiration of the president's negotiating authority. Senior administration officials had already dropped their categorical rejection of EU demands to "clarify" the Blair House agreement, and the administration had reportedly begun an internal assessment of changes it could make to Blair House that would have the least detrimental effect on US agriculture (*Inside U.S. Trade*, 26 November 1993, 1 and 16–17).

Following "high-level" warnings from Britain and Germany that a Uruguay Round stalemate could "risk splitting the EU," Prime Minister

---

15. *Financial Times*, 13 October 1993, 11; also *New York Times*, 24 November 1993, A17, and 25 November 1993, A8, for discussion that includes European reactions and subsequent US attempts to mend fences with Europe.

Balladur indicated that France was ready to reach a compromise on the agricultural dispute (*Washington Post*, 30 November 1993, 1), as long as "French national interests are protected" (*Financial Times*, 1 December 1993, 1). On 2 December the *Financial Times* (2 December 1993, 4) reported that German Chancellor Helmut Kohl, speaking after the latest Franco-German summit meeting in Bonn, "warned that a deal was necessary, not only to guarantee the future of free world trade, but also for the future cohesion of the European Union."

On 30 November, 19 US farm groups again warned President Clinton to maintain the Blair House agreement or risk losing their support for GATT. The American Soybean Association and the National Sunflower Association did not sign the letter, however, since US vegetable oil exports would be helped if the United States agreed to French demands to make the cuts in subsidized exports more gradual (*Inside U.S. Trade*, 3 December 1993, 11–12).[16]

On 3 December it was reported that the two sides had agreed on the outlines of a deal on farm trade (*Journal of Commerce*, 3 December 1993, 1). The United States would allow a more gradual timetable for the cutting of subsidized farm exports, to assist the Union in reducing its grain mountain of about 25 million tons by exporting up to an additional 8 million tons of grain a year. "France, Europe's largest farm exporter, will be the main beneficiary of the switch." The peace clause, which exempts certain agricultural policies from GATT challenges, would also be extended.[17] In return, the European Union would allow the United States greater market access for certain agricultural products and trim tariffs on a number of manufactured goods (*Financial Times*, 6 December 1993, 1 and 3).

After initially balking at the compromise, France on 8 December pronounced itself satisfied with the farm deal though Juppe stated that France's approval was still contingent on an internal EU agreement that no additional concessions would be extracted from EU farmers. In exchange for renegotiating Blair House, the Union had agreed to deeper overall tariff cuts than the United States (EU cuts would average 50 percent, while US cuts would average 43 percent). But since details of the cuts

---

16. The original agreement called for basing subsidized export reductions on their average level in 1986–90. Because subsidies increased sharply in both the European Community and the United States in that period, this formula would have required sharp cuts in subsidized exports. The final agreement changed the base period to 1991–92, which avoided the sharp initial cuts. This more than doubled the allowable level of US exports during the first six years after Uruguay Round implementation (*Inside U.S. Trade*, 10 December 1993, S-13; Uruguay Round GATT Agreement, Report of the Agricultural Technical Advisory Committee on Oilseeds and Products, Part 1, Comments on A11 Oilseeds and Products Except Peanuts and Peanut Products, 3).

17. US Department of Agriculture, Economic Research Service (1993, 48) summarizes the "peace clause."

were not made public, it was, according to the *Wall Street Journal* (8 December 1993, A3), "hard to judge whether the US gained deeper concessions from the EC than it would have without an agricultural deal."

Evaluation and Conclusions

In the end, the European Union, and France in particular, got most of what it wanted from the GATT negotiations on agriculture: effective nullification of the zero tariff bindings previously granted to oilseeds, in exchange for a liberalization of the Common Agricultural Policy that had already been undertaken in 1992.[18] If the predictions of EU policymakers prove accurate, the Union's own CAP reforms will reduce the level of subsidized exports enough to make the Blair House provisions redundant (*Financial Times*, 10 December 1993, 2).

The US oilseeds industry found the final Uruguay Round agreement "only barely acceptable." In particular, it argued that

> . . . very little benefit will accrue to the US oilseed industry from the internal support reductions required by the Uruguay Round. The enormous oilseed production subsidies of the European Union will not be required to be reduced as a result of the Uruguay Round agreement because they are classified as production neutral. The effect of the Uruguay Round agreement is to make GATT-legal the EU oilseed subsidies that were accepted under the Blair House agreement.[19]

Although an agreement was reached, this section 301 case is judged a failure from the US perspective:

- The United States accepted a deal that provided for only a modest rollback in the amount of land eligible for oilseeds subsidy payments with no guaranteed limit on overall production.

- US and other oilseeds exporters were not compensated for past losses.

- The US oilseeds sector appears to have accepted the agreement only because it did not believe a better deal was possible.

Moreover, this dispute could well undermine US private-sector faith in using section 301 to combat unfair trade practices. The US oilseeds indus-

---

18. Hartmann (1991, 58) summarizes the European Uruguay Round position.

19. Uruguay Round GATT Agreement, Report of the Agricultural Technical Advisory Committee on Oilseeds and Products, 1–4. ATAC argued that the European Union's oilseeds subsidy regime was not production-neutral, because the Union requires farmers to actually plant oilseeds in order to receive per-hectare income supports. ATAC also pointed out that no commitment had been received by the European Union to eliminate individual member state payments to producers to induce them to plant industrial-use oilseeds on set-aside land. France and Italy had reportedly been making such payments since the Blair House agreement.

try did everything right, had plenty of congressional support and two GATT panels to back it up, but wound up with precious little.

Why was the oilseeds case outcome so different from that of the enlargement case, wherein US threats induced the European Community to pay compensation?

- First, deterring new protectionist measures is generally easier than compelling reform of established ones.[20]

- Second, the retaliatory threat in the enlargement case appears to have been much more credible than that in the oilseeds case. When the European Community refused to discuss compensation in the enlargement case, President Reagan dispensed with the normal section 301 procedures, immediately releasing a list of products that would be retaliated against just a few months hence if no agreement was reached. The oilseeds case, by contrast, dragged on for years.

- Third, the European Union succeeded in tying the outcome of the oilseeds case very closely to the outcome of the Uruguay Round. This greatly raised the potential cost of retaliation to the United States and forced it to compromise.

But why did the United States then agree to "amplify" the Blair House deal when it appeared to have extensive support from within the European Union and from other Cairns Group members as well?

- Though Germany and the United Kingdom pushed the French very hard (especially with last-minute German arm-twisting) to secure French acquiescence, Germany was not prepared to isolate France completely.

- The French threat to torpedo the round was at least plausible. French politicians and pundits convinced many in France that the country was economically and culturally under siege. Prolonged recession in Europe (12 percent unemployment in France) made it easier to prey on people's fears.

- Finally, the Clinton administration placed a high priority on concluding the round by the 15 December deadline because it feared the price that Congress might extract for extending its negotiating authority.

What are the lessons of the oilseeds case? First, USTR should, in general, avoid cases where the barrier in question is entrenched, the probability of counterretaliation is high, and the potential costs of retaliation and

---

20. See Schelling (1960, chapter 2). Paarlberg (1986, 159) makes a similar point regarding GATT's effectiveness in combating agricultural protectionism.

counterretaliation are also high. USTR balked at retaliating against $1 billion of EC exports, lowering the figure to $300 million in November 1992. That may have increased the credibility of the threat and contributed to conclusion of Blair House. But it also underscored the incredibility of the earlier threat.

Second, as has been argued in several of the cases studied in this book, having allies in the target country or region who favor reform is usually critical to success. The United States got as much on agriculture as it did in the Uruguay Round because of the 1992 CAP reform, which was strongly supported by Britain and Germany.[21] But once the obstacles to CAP reform were worked out internally, it proved impossible for US negotiators to reopen the deal and move the European Community any further.[22] Thus while the United States had allies in Britain and Germany, with respect to forcing France to accept the CAP reforms, these allies could go no further than that. The internal negotiations in the European Community on oilseeds also illustrate the role that side payments can play in facilitating an agreement.

Finally, the oilseeds and other agricultural disputes with the European Union reinforce the conclusion elsewhere in the book that a trade agreement that lacks a domestic constituency and the political will to abide by it is a scrap of paper that will not achieve much (see chapters 6 through 8). The European Union has consistently finessed the intent of the last agricultural trade agreement. This bodes poorly for the new "peace clause." As long as there is an EU commitment to protect and promote its agricultural sectors, trade conflict will persist.

---

21. Weiss (1989) discusses Germany's shift from agricultural protectionism.

22. Paarlberg (1986, 160–61) argues that

> changes in existing CAP mechanisms are hard enough for the council to adopt even without the complication of international negotiations. Within the council, farm policy decisions must be laboriously "log rolled" into tight and carefully balanced packages. These packages cannot easily be taken apart or subjected to piecemeal change. All the more so in the context of a formal negotiation with foreign trade competitors. In such a context, internal advocates of change can be further weakened by the appearance that they are advocating capitulation to a foreign power.

10

Japan: Beef and Citrus

AMELIA PORGES

This was the best negotiation we ever had with Japan. The reason was that everyone got something out of it. What did we get? An end to the quotas. What did they get? Time for a phaseout and some breathing room. And the world got a step forward in liberalization. Everybody came out a winner.

—Michael B. Smith, Deputy USTR[1]

To succeed, negotiators must find their way with imperfect information through a dim landscape of threats and promises to arrive at a deal that is acceptable to all parties. They do so as part of a bargaining and political process that takes place at two levels: between the negotiators, and between each negotiator and the domestic interests he or she represents. This chapter considers the successful negotiation between the United States and Japan on liberalizing the Japanese import quotas for beef, oranges, and orange juice. Between the summers of 1987 and 1988, the negotiators found a cooperative and stable solution to a long-standing source of bilateral conflict and achieved acceptance of this solution by domestic interests in both countries.

Amelia Porges was formerly senior legal officer, Division of Legal Affairs, General Agreement on Tariffs and Trade; previously associate general counsel, Office of the United States Trade Representative, and visiting fellow, Institute for International Economics. This account does not discuss details of negotiations except to the extent that such details are already public. The facts in this article are limited to information on the public record, including the extensive accounts in the Japanese press. The analysis is the author's and does not necessarily reflect the views of the GATT Secretariat or USTR.

1. Interview, 20 March 1989.

Table 10.1 US exports to Japan of beef and citrus, 1985–93
(millions of dollars except where noted)

Year	Beef, chilled or frozen	Fresh oranges and tangerines	Orange juice	Total beef and citrus	Total US agricultural exports to Japan	US share of beef and citrus markets (percentages)
1985	351	73	3	427	5,409	7.9
1986	471	68	2	542	5,106	10.6
1987	550	80	3	632	5,723	11.0
1988	829	73	10	913	7,640	11.9
1989	1,003	83	19	1,105	8,162	13.5
1990	950	89	18	1,057	8,058	13.1
1991	879	85	21	985	7,729	12.7
1992	1,114	93	31	1,238	8,437	14.7
1993	1,229	91	19	1,338	8,739	15.3

Source: USDA, *Foreign Agricultural Trade of the United States;* table from Caplan (1993).

All of the beef and citrus quotas concerned have now been removed; increased imports (table 10.1) and declining consumer food prices in Japan have been the beneficial result.

That Japan in the end yielded to the US demand to repeal beef and citrus quotas is all the more striking considering the previous track record of the United States on this issue. Twice before, in 1979 and 1984, the United States had demanded that these quota restrictions be removed, but both times Japan held out to the end to retain them. Rather than face a breakdown of negotiations, the United States made a last-minute retreat. Indeed, the US side's first major problem in 1987–88 was to convince the Japanese side that this time the demand for quota elimination was serious and would not be withdrawn.

This chapter considers what made it possible to reach this agreement between negotiators and sell it to domestic interests on both sides. Between 1984 and 1988, US-Japan relations saw many changes, including the new and more aggressive use of section 301, upheavals in the Japanese domestic political scene, and the brokering of trade deals by ruling-party politicians. The international context changed as well, with the start of the Uruguay Round and its agenda for agricultural trade negotiations. Like other recent studies, the analysis here concludes that bilateral pressure and domestic politics are both essential to explaining the results of trade negotiations. This case also offers examples of creative interaction between the domestic and international levels, as well as "aggressive multilateralism" (utilization of the GATT) to achieve very specific goals in a bilateral negotiation.

The Issue

Years of contention preceded the US-Japan trade negotiations discussed here. In 1962, under pressure from its trading partners, Japan had disinvoked Article XII, the GATT provision permitting developed countries to restrict imports for balance of payments purposes. Since that time, Japan had gradually eliminated almost all of its quantitative import restrictions, but a few quotas remained, including those on beef, fresh oranges, and orange juice.

Approximately 80 percent of the quota amount for fresh, frozen, and chilled beef was allocated to the Livestock Industry Promotion Corporation (LIPC), the state trading organization responsible for supporting domestic beef prices; the rest was traded through 36 traditional designated beef importers. Fresh, chilled, and frozen beef was subject to a 25 percent tariff, which was not subject to a GATT concession and could legally be raised at any time.

As for citrus, the orange and orange juice quotas were allocated to only a few importers. Oranges and orange juice were subject to tariffs of 40 percent in the winter season and 20 percent otherwise. Also, Japanese bottlers of orange juice (imported as 5-to-1 concentrate) were required to blend concentrate with the juice of domestic mikan oranges. Importation and sale of single-strength orange juice was effectively prohibited.[2]

First Round: 1977–78 Negotiations

Talks first focused on the beef and citrus issue in 1977–78, late in the Tokyo Round, and the issue stayed on the agenda, off and on, for the decade that followed. The Carter administration, as part of a general push to open the Japanese market, strove to eliminate agricultural import quotas and to increase access for quota items. From the beginning, the claim was made that the import quotas violated GATT rules and that the United States might bring the case to the GATT. After a series of talks in the winter of 1977–78, agreement was reached in January 1978 to increase yearly LIPC imports of "high-quality beef" to 10,000 tons on a global basis, to increase fresh orange imports to 45,000 tons, and to increase the citrus juice quota to 4,000 tons. In spring 1978 the US side again pushed to eliminate the citrus quota in the context of the Tokyo Round and backed away. The United States then progressively hardened its position, due to a split among Japanese citrus importers, pressure from Florida citrus

---

2. The mixing requirement was carried out through issuance of administrative guidance in the form of a *tsutatsu* (circular) from the director general of the Ministry of Agriculture, Forestry and Fisheries (MAFF) Agricultural Production Bureau to the organizations of users of imported juice concentrate.

interests, Japanese government action to tighten administration of the beef quota, and the need to sell the Tokyo Round to Congress.

Finally, in December 1978, US trade negotiator Robert Strauss withdrew the demand to end the quota on citrus, and Agriculture Minister Ichiro Nakagawa agreed to gradual expansion of high-quality beef purchases to 30,800 tons, of the fresh orange quota to 82,000 tons, and of the orange and grapefruit juice quotas to 6,500 tons and 6,000 tons, respectively. Of the fresh orange quota, 45,000 tons was targeted for "seasonal citrus" in the months of June, July and August, off-season months for Japanese and California producers in which Florida oranges would be on the market. Similarly, the concept of "high-quality beef" (carefully defined as grain-fed beef of a type that at the time was produced only in the United States) provided a limited market opening, made politically feasible for Japan because it avoided competition with domestic dairy beef.[3]

Second Round

Preparation for the second (1984) round began in 1980, as the US side raised beef and citrus on the bilateral agenda and began work on its position for the time after the 1979 agreement would expire. In 1982–83 the United States again demanded elimination of the quotas on beef and citrus and also pursued talks on tariffs and quotas on other agricultural products.

An attempt was made to reach agreement before the Reagan-Nakasone summit of May 1983; afterward, the United States requested consultations under GATT Article XXIII:1 (a prerequisite to GATT dispute settlement proceedings) on a group of 13 other agricultural items under quota, and these consultations were held in July 1983. During the winter of 1983–84 the US side moderated its demands and proposed a schedule for "eventual" elimination of the quota regime, including quota increases for the global beef quota, high-quality beef, and oranges. Nevertheless, the 1978 agreement expired on 31 March 1984 with no new agreement in place.[4]

In April 1984 talks between USTR William Brock and Agriculture Minister Yamamura initially reached an impasse over the size of the beef quota increase. Brock instructed his staff to prepare to take the beef and citrus case to GATT dispute settlement. The following morning, Yamamura

---

3. This paragraph is based on the account in Sato and Curran (1982). In the world market for beef, Japan, Korea, Australia, New Zealand, the United States and Canada, which are all free of the highly contagious foot-and-mouth disease (FMD), export freely to each other and ban imports of fresh, chilled, and frozen beef from the FMD area (countries not free of FMD). Australia and the United States, the two major non-FMD exporters, have been rivals in opening the Japanese beef market.

4. On the 1983–84 talks, see Reich, Endo, and Timmer (1986).

agreed to a larger increase in the beef quota; the National Cattlemen's Association, fearful of a GATT challenge to US restrictions on meat imports, agreed to settle; and the two negotiators shook hands on a deal.

Months later, the detailed agreement emerged: a timetable for expansion of quotas during the period to 31 March 1988, expanding the yearly global beef quota to 177,000 tons (including 58,400 tons of high-quality beef and 4,000 tons in the hotel quota), the orange quota to 126,000 tons, and the orange juice quota to 8,500 tons. Grapefruit juice would be liberalized by 1 April 1986. The 1984 agreement also provided for a "new measure," the "Simultaneous-Buy-Sell" system (SBS), to facilitate contact between foreign beef suppliers and Japanese buyers. SBS, intended to facilitate access for higher-value beef, would apply to 10 percent of LIPC-controlled imports, making it possible for meatpackers abroad to negotiate directly with end users in Japan concerning cut specifications and price. Also in 1988, a separate agreement was reached on the 13 smaller items, providing quota expansion and a two-year moratorium on GATT dispute proceedings.

Third Round

As the late-1987 date for reopening of beef and citrus negotiations approached, the negotiators again began to take their positions. From then until the talks ended in summer 1988, events took place that altered each side's "win set" (the limits of what it would accept in an agreement) as well as its perceived cost of failing to reach agreement. These changes were brought about by domestic political developments, by intervention from the other side, and by other events external to both Japan and the United States.

A year before, in September 1986, the Uruguay Round had been launched with agricultural trade reform as its central theme. The Uruguay Round context raised the stakes in the beef and citrus talks for both sides. Brock's successor, Clayton Yeutter, was an agricultural policy expert and former USDA official who maintained his own family farm. Yeutter had been a major player in launching the round and had tabled the ambitious initial United States proposal: complete phase-out of all subsidies and import barriers on agricultural products, except for straight income support or other payments decoupled from marketing or production. For the first time, the United States had offered to eliminate agricultural trade restrictions under section 22 of the Agricultural Adjustment Act and the 1979 Meat Import Act. Japan, the world's major food importer, had proposed retention of import barriers for sensitive products, stressing the need for food security (Franklin 1988, 70–73).

Japanese Agricultural Politics in Mutation

In 1987 Japanese agricultural policy was itself at a turning point. Due to the rising yen and a fall in dollar-based world prices, agricultural imports in 1986 had risen 9 percent in volume over 1985, and import prices had dropped by 28 percent,[5] except for quota products. The price difference between domestic and foreign food had given rise to criticism by mass media and the public, as well as increasing pressure on food processors to lower their cost of raw materials or move offshore. Agriculture also found itself at war with industrial exporters: on the one hand, industry saw agriculture as attracting trade friction, and on the other, agriculture saw itself as being used to appease foreign governments for an industrial trade surplus that was not agriculture's fault.

Agricultural policy in Japan had been made by the classic triangle of legislature, bureaucracy, and interest groups: the agriculture "clan" (*zoku*) of Liberal Democratic Party (LDP) Dietmen; the Ministry of Agriculture, Forestry, and Fisheries (MAFF); and organized farm groups, principally the Zenkoku Nogyo Kumiai Rengokai (Nokyo) and its political wing, Zenkoku Nogyo Dantai Chuo Rengokai (Zenchu).

As for the first leg of the triangle, prime-ministerial intervention in MAFF policy had traditionally been rare and normally was eclipsed by the influence of Diet groups (Muramatsu 1987, 212). In 1988 there were over 200 agriculture groups in the Diet, of which the principal ones active on beef and citrus were the Livestock Industry Promotion Corporation (260 members, chaired by Sadanori Yamanaka) and the Tree Fruit Agriculture Promotion Caucus (200 members, chaired by Tokutaro Higaki) *(Nihon Nogyo Shimbun* 1987). Yamanaka, the LDP's tax expert, headed the LDP Tax Policy Investigation Committee and was a key player in Prime Minister Noboru Takeshita's plans to enact a value-added tax (Yamaguchi 1987b).

Agriculture politics had been based on the two staples of rice and subsidies. The key occasion for demonstration of political zeal was the yearly setting of the price at which MAFF's Food Agency would buy rice from producers, under the wartime laws that put rice production and sales under government control. After MAFF had calculated a price based on the cost of production, groups of Dietmen (dubbed the "Viet Cong") would mobilize, obtain an increase in the level, then disappear. The difference between the producer price and the lower, regulated consumer resale price was made up by a subsidy from the national budget (see Hemmi 1982; George 1986). When rice surpluses in the late 1960s forced cutbacks in the system, rice policy became more complex and led to the rise of a

---

5. Agricultural White Paper for fiscal 1986, reported in *Nihon Keizai Shimbun*, 3 April 1987 (evening ed.), 1.

new group of agriculture politicians, the "comprehensive farm policy faction" (*sōgō nōseiha*).

The *sōgō nōseiha* politicians pushed for a farm policy balancing the interests of producers, processors, distribution, and consumers for all crops. By the mid-1970s they became the mainstream in the LDP agriculture *zoku*, and their leaders, Ichiro Nakagawa and Michio Watanabe, were recognized with the post of agriculture minister. Minister Nakagawa took the initiative in settling the 1978–79 beef and citrus talks. Minister Watanabe's action in 1979 to force through quality differentials in the rice price effectively split the rice lobby and would provide the opening wedge for the ministry and the *sōgō nōseiha* to take the guiding role in setting policy.[6] In the 1980s Watanabe's generation had moved up, to be succeeded by a younger group known as the "Gang of Eight." The Gang of Eight shared the *sōgō nōseiha*'s orientation toward comprehensive farm policy, their expertise in working the system, and their affinity for a right-wing stance favoring a strong defense and the alliance with the United States; they were described as combining

> ... the combat capability to push all-out for farmer demands, spearheading the regiment of the LDP agriculture *zoku*, and the adjustment capability to persuade the party and agricultural interest groups with a certain line when they have reached their limits.[7]

Beef and citrus were important substitute crops for rice and were valued as a means to advance structural change in agriculture. Every political party, from the LDP to the Japan Communist Party, was on record as opposing liberalization of beef and citrus.

As for the second leg of the triangle, in the mid-1980s MAFF was pushed by demographic and economic changes to reevaluate postwar farm policy. While occupation-era land reforms had democratized landholding, they had also kept farm size down, inhibited capital inflow by banning corporate farming, and kept productivity growth in agriculture well below that in industry. MAFF figures showed that only 20 percent of farm households were run by a full-time farmer and projected that in 1995, the number of such households would drop to 600,000, 43 percent of the farming population would be over 65, and absent basic change, the lack of successors for retiring farmers would inevitably lead to rural depopulation. In November 1986, MAFF published a major report, *Nijūisseiki e mukete no Nōsei no Kihon Hōkō* (Basic Direction of Agricultural Policy toward the

---

6. This discussion synthesizes Hemmi (1982, 238–42) and Kankai (1987, 112–16).

7. *Nihon Keizai Shimbunsha* (1983, 107) lists the Gang of Eight as Tokutaro Higaki, Tsutomu Hata, Koichi Kato, Hyosuke Niwa, Takami Eto, Takashi Sato, Eiichi Nakao, and Taiichiro Okawara. Nakao, Eto, and Sato were members of Ichiro Nakagawa's Seirankai group in the late 1970s. Watanabe remained close, and was chairman of the LDP's Policy Affairs Research Council (its central policymaking organ) in 1987–88.

21st Century). The report set basic changes in agricultural policy: more cost-consciousness, increased competition in distribution, and reforms in price support formulas and land laws to increase farm size and provide incentives for increased productivity. The 1986 report (MAFF 1987a, 14; 1986, 69) also proposed that

> . . . the existing Japanese agricultural trade system should be reviewed considering the position of each pertinent product in Japanese agriculture, in order to improve market access toward enabling international market prices to be reflected in domestic ones by using such measures as ad valorem tariffs.

The Japanese side in the 1987–88 beef and citrus negotiations was led at the working level by Director General Hidero Maki of the MAFF Economics Bureau and his staff, working with the Ministry of Foreign Affairs on the one hand and the producer bureaus for livestock and horticultural crops on the other.[8]

The same changes meant challenge as well for the third major actor in farm policy, Nokyo. Nokyo is based on village-level cooperatives, to which virtually every Japanese farmer belongs and which are a major vehicle for administering agricultural policy at the farmer level. Zennoh, Nokyo's trading arm, purchases rice as an agent for the food control system, markets farm produce, and has a major share of sales to farmers of feedgrains, fertilizer, pesticides, fuel, and farm needs. Zennoh is Japan's major importer of US feedgrains. Zenkyoren, Nokyo's insurance arm, is the largest Japanese insurance company, and Nokyo's savings scheme, Norin Chukin, is one of the world's 10 largest banks (Yamaguchi 1987a). Nokyo's business interests fed the war chest of its political arm, Zenchu.

Nokyo had used its clout to obtain subsidies for production and rural development and import protection. The complexity of the programs and their importance to rural areas in turn provided brokerage opportunities to *zoku* Dietmen. Budget constraints had forced subsidy reform to some extent, but the more limited the budget, the more important political sponsorship becomes. MAFF entered into the equation through the statutory discretion given to MAFF in running subsidy programs; discretion put the MAFF minister in nominal charge of subsidy allocation and gave the bureaucracy bargaining chips in dealing with Nokyo and the Diet.

By the late 1980s, Nokyo was on the defensive. After MAFF and the LDP had agreed to reduce the producer rice price in 1986, Nokyo had pressured both into keeping the price unchanged, at some cost to its

---

8. Maki was elevated during the negotiations to the newly created position of vice minister for international affairs. See Maki (1987). The producer bureaus were represented by directors general Takashi Yoshikuni (citrus) and Akio Kyoya (livestock); Kyoya became the administrative vice minister of MAFF in fiscal 1993. The Ministry of International Trade and Industry (MITI) was also peripherally involved in its role in administering import quotas. On Japanese representation see Yabunaka (1993).

relationship with each. Criticized heavily in the media, Nokyo was unable to stop the rice price from being cut in 1987 for the first time in 31 years. Management problems in its businesses led to financial losses, a further loss of credibility, and a shrinkage in Zenchu's war chest. Zennoh's monopoly position in distributing farm inputs led to questions about whether the benefits of yen appreciation were being passed through to the farmer. Nokyo's bottom-up decision-making structure handicapped it in reaching a unified position on issues that split its membership, such as quality differentials in the rice price; and in the new and more complicated world of structural reform, it was even more difficult for Zenchu to be a player. Moreover, MAFF's goal of promoting a more efficient (full-time) farming sector meant MAFF's and Nokyo's interests would conflict, given the increasing dominance of part-time farmers in Nokyo's membership.

The beef and citrus issue of 1988 brought two members of the Gang of Eight to the forefront, Tsutomu Hata and Koichi Kato. Both are second-generation Dietmen and were 20 years younger than the LDP leadership at the time. Hata was agriculture minister in 1985–86 and chaired the LDP's key policymaking body in agriculture, the Comprehensive Agricultural Policy Investigation Committee (*Sōgō nōsei chōsakai*). The central LDP group on the import issue was the Subcommittee on Agricultural Products Liberalization (*Nōsanbutsu jiyuka taisaku shoiinkai*). An open-membership group first established during the 1978 beef and citrus negotiations, it has played a key role in every agricultural trade negotiation since then. In 1987–88 its chairman was Kato, and its immediate past chairman was Hata. Hata had been one of Takeshita's core supporters in gaining control of the former Tanaka faction, and then the prime ministership. His central role in settling the US-Japan talks on plywood in 1985 and cigarette imports in 1986 had impressed policymakers with his sense for handling foreign issues. While serving as agriculture minister in 1985–86, he had stated he was willing to "challenge taboos" to introduce market principles into the rice distribution system and had said that high raw materials costs would simply drive the food processing industry offshore (Kankai 1987, 117–19; Miyashita 1987). Kato, a former diplomat who had made his initial reputation in defense policy, was the de facto number two of the Miyazawa faction. He agreed with Hata that farm policy should be less centered on protecting rice producers at all cost and more oriented toward increasing competitiveness (Kankai 1987, 122–23).

Beef and citrus also involved the prime minister in both his foreign and domestic policy roles. Yasuhiro Nakasone, the prime minister through early November 1987, was foreign policy incarnate: the host of the 1986 Tokyo summit, he used his "Ron-Yasu" relationship with President Ronald Reagan as a domestic political asset. Bypassing the bureaucracy, he built his own personal staff. He targeted urban white-collar voters to compete with the Socialist Party: the Nakasone-sponsored Maekawa

Report of April 1986 called for a reorientation of the Japanese economy toward domestic demand, urging that farm policy foster full-time farmers, make greater use of market principles, and improve market access for imports under quota. Nakasone's victory in the July 1986 elections showed that the Maekawa Report and his image as an international leader added up to a winning political formula. Follow-up recommendations to the Maekawa Report in 1987 urged that agricultural policy shift focus to include not just producers but consumers and the food industry as well. Policy should seek stable food supplies at more acceptable prices that would be lowered by reducing the spread between domestic and overseas prices, enhancing Japanese agricultural productivity, and handling import policies appropriately (Keizai Shingikai [1987, para. 2.3.5.2] and *Nihon Keizai Shimbun*, 22 April 1987).[9] The Economic Planning Agency released a backup survey showing that food cost twice as much in Japan as in the United States, and half again as much as in Germany (*Nihon Keizai Shimbun*, 24 April 1987).

Forced out of office in October 1987, Nakasone picked his successor, Noboru Takeshita, inheritor of the Tanaka faction with a reputation as a superlative domestic power broker and master of pork-barrel politics but no track record as a world leader. In Takeshita's first six months he launched himself on a program of diplomacy and summits with foreign leaders, building toward the G-7 summit of June 1988 in Toronto (Imai 1988, 20–23; Iguchi 1988). The political importance of foreign relations, and especially of managing the relationship with the United States, made the Foreign Ministry a natural ally for Takeshita in his push to fill Nakasone's shoes.

The business community, under pressure from the rising yen, actively pushed for agricultural liberalization. In early 1988, Nikkeiren, the Japan Federation of Employers' Associations, urged that the cost of living be reduced through agricultural liberalization as an alternative to wage increases (*Japan Agrinfo News*, March 1988, 6). Keidanren, the chief big-business organization, issued reports on the food industry emphasizing that agricultural protectionism would cost jobs and tax revenues by forcing the food-processing industry to go offshore (Keidanren 1988).

United States Digs In

As negotiations opened in 1987, USTR Yeutter committed himself publicly on many occasions to end the beef and citrus quotas when the 1984 agreement expired. Brock and Strauss before him had also publicly com-

---

9. On Nakasone and the "new middle mass" see Calder (1988, 115–16, 125–26). The Maekawa Report directly influenced the MAFF "21st Century" report referred to above.

mitted themselves to quota elimination, but both eventually accepted continued quotas.

But now there were important differences from earlier years: the US beef industry's interest in exports had intensified and so had its political activity; USTR Yeutter had succeeded in getting the Uruguay Round launched with a theme of agricultural trade reform; and the United States and Japan were engaged in a GATT dispute concerning Japanese agricultural import quotas that would greatly affect the outcome of the negotiations.

Moreover, the US beef industry was faced with long-term demand stagnation in the health-conscious American market. To keep growing, the American industry needed export markets. The industry had brought two section 301 cases on barriers to access to the European Community; it had pushed negotiations on access to the Korean market, which would result in a 1988 GATT case against the Korean beef import embargo; and now most of all, the beef industry targeted Japan, which was already the market for 80 percent of US beef exports.

The quota system prevented lower dollar prices from stimulating imports, which was bad enough. Beyond that, however, LIPC absorbed the maximum share of quota economic rent through its control of over 80 percent of imports under quota in combination with its practice of buying frozen boxed beef by public tender.

Moreover, because LIPC's mission was to stabilize the domestic beef price and the price could not exceed a fixed ceiling, LIPC could not pursue the classic quota-holder strategy of maximizing profits by selling a limited quantity of higher-value goods. Instead, LIPC maximized profits by buying the lowest-cost product, frozen Australian grass-fed beef. The US industry estimated that freeing the market could cause Japanese prices to drop by 40 percent and US exports to increase to 1.6 million tons by the year 2000 (*Inside U.S. Trade*, 5 June 1987, 8). The Meat Industry Trade Policy Council, a coalition of beef and pork producers and packers and the American Farm Bureau Federation,[10] endorsed opening of the Japanese beef market in July 1987 and again in December 1987. MITPC had strong support in Congress, led by Senator Max Baucus of Montana.

The industry was represented in Japan by the US Meat Export Federation (USMEF), a nonprofit organization funded half by voluntary industry contributions and half by the US Department of Agriculture (USDA). USMEF represented over 90 member organizations, including the 37,000-member National Cattlemen's Association and over 50 packing houses. By 1988 the organization had 11 years of on-the-ground experience dealing with LIPC and MAFF through its Tokyo office. Philip Seng, its Japanese-

---

10. MITPC includes the American Farm Bureau Federation, the American Meat Institute, the National Cattlemen's Association, the National Pork Producers Council, and the US Meat Export Federation.

speaking representative, had accumulated a web of contacts in the Japanese meat world and in the press. He educated the US industry to push for elimination of both the quota and LIPC's role in importing beef and developed a list of demands to improve quota administration and to expand the SBS system in the near term.

The US orange producers were split. Under the quota regime, quota allotments had been dominated by politically connected Kazuo Fujii and other importers with ties to the West Coast marketing cooperative, Sunkist Foods.[11] As the yen rose, so had profits for the exporters and importers of oranges. Throughout the 1987–88 negotiations, Sunkist and allied West Coast producers, backed by most of the California congressional delegation, actively lobbied the administration, arguing that the quota was not very restrictive and that priority should be given not to quota elimination but to a cut in the 40 percent ad valorem seasonal tariff on oranges. Fujii also visited Washington to lobby Congress and the administration in favor of continued quotas (Smith interview, 20 March 1989).

Under the quota, the main effect of the tariff was to take a wedge from the markup on imported oranges and transfer it to the Japanese treasury; a tariff cut would make quota trade even more profitable. But this position was not supported by all concerned with the orange trade. The California Department of Agriculture and some smaller California producers supported quota elimination, as did Nisseikyo, the orange importers' organization not allied with Fujii.

Florida, led by the growers' cooperative Florida Citrus Mutual, pushed for quota elimination for fresh oranges and orange juice and interim access for single-strength orange juice. Florida had seen results from earlier elimination of the quotas on fresh grapefruit and grapefruit juice. As long as any tonnage quotas were in place, higher-value California dessert oranges would out-compete Florida juice oranges. Japanese import rules in 1988 did not permit any imports of single-strength juice, a Florida specialty. In juice, because of the low-price competition from Brazil in frozen concentrate, Florida's strategy was to compete in consumer-ready, high-quality products; Florida saw Japan as a juice market potentially one-third the size of the US market. Florida pushed for a tariff cut on grapefruit (where Florida had over 90 percent of the Japanese market), but not oranges or juice.[12]

The executive branch was strikingly unified on the beef and citrus issue, in contrast to the situation on some other Japan trade issues of the 1980s.

---

11. See Kusano (1983) at 38–42 (on importer groups), 55–58 (on the Fujii-Sunkist relationship), 76–81 (on Fujii's political connection to Watanabe and the effect on import quota licensing decisions), and 197–200 (on the Fujii-Sunkist connection and its effect on entry by new importers connected with Florida).

12. Interview, Bobby McKown, Florida Citrus Mutual, 3 March 1988. Opening the Japanese market would also reduce Brazilian competition in the US juice market. Texas leaned toward the Florida position but was out of the market because of citrus canker.

The pro-market ideology of the Reagan administration made it difficult to favor continuation of the beef and citrus quotas. Yeutter's position was guided by his firm convictions and by the need to convince Congress in the context of the 1988 trade bill that he could negotiate more effectively without legislation that would reduce the administration's discretion. The chief negotiator was his deputy, Michael Smith, a veteran diplomat who began his trade policy career in the US-Japan textile wars of the early 1970s. Smith had been the chief negotiator with Japan and for multilateral negotiations from 1980 through 1988, including the 1984 beef and citrus negotiations. Smith made a point of meeting with Hata and Kato each of the many times he visited Tokyo in the spring of 1988. Smith's guide, strategist, and coordinator on industry positions was Ellen Terpstra of the USTR agricultural office, who worked closely with USDA trade and industry experts and State Department officials.

The other key development came from the discussions on the 13 agricultural product groups other than beef and citrus, which had been the subject of a two-year cease-fire agreed in 1984. As the end of the cease-fire approached, talks were held on improvements in access, amid skeptical comments on whether quota elimination would benefit US producers.[13]

In July 1986 the United States brought a formal complaint under GATT Article XXIII:2 on 12 of these 13 items, and in October the GATT Council established a dispute settlement panel on the 12, which became known as the GATT 12.[14] Resort to GATT was perceived as shifting the argument from rent seeking to principle, a move facilitated by Yeutter's pro-market orientation and by the small direct stakes, only $300 million per year in imports. MAFF for its part vowed to use the case to demonstrate the GATT legality of the quota regime.[15] The timing of the case offered a way to litigate beef and citrus by proxy. The panel of experts considered written submissions and three rounds of oral arguments from April through October 1987. From early 1987 onward the US side refused to open talks with Japan on beef and citrus unless Japan would agree to quota elimination and name a date.

---

13. *Nihon Keizai Shimbun*, "Nosan 13-hinmoku kyogi: Nichibei no honne o saguru" (The 13 agricultural items: in search of the real motivation of Japan and the United States), 6 December 1985, 5.

14. The GATT 12 were (1) prepared and preserved milk and cream; (2) processed cheese; (3) dried legumes (peas and beans); (4) starch and inulin; (5) peanuts; (6) prepared and preserved beef; (7) nonsucrose sugars and syrups; (8) fruit purees and pastes; (9) fruit pulp and canned pineapple; (10) noncitrus fruit and vegetable juices; (11) tomato juice, ketchup and sauce; and (12) other sugar- and dairy-based food preparations (the miscellaneous import quota). Each of these product groups may include various distinct subquotas and tariff lines. The remaining item discussed before, provisionally preserved oranges and tangerines, was dealt with as part of the fresh orange quota from 1986 onward.

15. *Nihon Nogyo Shimbun*, "12-hinmoku no yunyu seigen: Gatto ni ihan senu," 17 March 1987.

The GATT 12 Report

The first turning point in the negotiation came on 30 October 1987, when the dispute settlement panel on the GATT 12 case delivered its decision to the parties. The Japanese side had argued that the import quotas were justifiable under Article XI:2(c)(i), an exception for enforcement of domestic supply-control schemes originally included in the GATT to accommodate US agricultural quotas. The panel found that for 10 of the 12 product groups, GATT rules did not permit the import restrictions that were in place; moreover, the GATT rules on import quotas applied to state-traded items such as beef. Since the Japanese government was not reducing beef production but promoting it, the panel found that the quota on prepared and processed beef was GATT-illegal. The panel also rejected the argument that the special characteristics of agriculture, including other countries' agricultural import restraints, ought to justify Japan's own quotas.

A GATT panel decision advises the contracting parties to the GATT acting jointly (described for this purpose as "the Contracting Parties") as to the recommendations or rulings that they should make in a case under GATT Article XXIII:2. When the panel report is adopted, either by the Contracting Parties or by the GATT Council acting on their behalf, the government concerned must follow the recommendations or face the possibility that discriminatory retaliation will be authorized against its exports.

Negotiated settlement of a case is an option at any time and in practice has precluded almost all recourse to authorized retaliation under GATT. The objective of dispute settlement is to open markets through policy change by a foreign government, but such change can only come about through negotiation. Thus the 1979 "Framework Decision" on dispute settlement (GATT 1979, para. 4) recognizes that

> [t]he aim of the CONTRACTING PARTIES has always been to secure a positive solution to a dispute. In the absence of a mutually agreed solution, the first objective of the CONTRACTING PARTIES is usually to secure the withdrawal of the measures concerned if these are found to be inconsistent with the General Agreement. The provision of compensation should be resorted to only if the immediate withdrawal of the measure is impracticable and as a temporary measure pending the withdrawal of the measures which are inconsistent with the General Agreement.

The GATT 12 panel decision reinforced US negotiators, who demanded immediate quota elimination and substantial compensation for any continuation of quotas pending phaseout (Smith interview, 8 August 1994).

The decision had a political impact in Japan disproportionate to the trade volume immediately at stake. The 12 items had survived successive rounds of quota elimination, after all, because each product involved was internationally uncompetitive and had intense regional support. While

Zenchu president Mitsugu Horiuchi initially stated that it would be hard for Japan to reject the GATT panel decision, he soon had to yield to grass-roots pressure (*Nihon Keizai Shimbun*, 18 April 1988, 4), threatening to retaliate against US exports of feedgrains to Japan.[16] Four LDP product caucuses held a press conference for foreign reporters on 17 November at which Yamanaka criticized the United States for keeping its own agricultural import quotas in place while attacking Japan's. He revealed that the four caucuses had collected signatures from 90 percent of all LDP Dietmen on a petition opposing import quota elimination of the 12 categories (*Journal of Commerce,* 18 November 1987). Zenchu had collected 25 million signatures in an anti-import liberalization drive since April and was pushing on toward 30 million.

Japanese efforts to settle the case after 30 October were rejected by the US side, despite a letter appealing to "Ron" Reagan from "Yasu" as one of Nakasone's last acts in office.[17] On 6 November, Takeshita took office. In his first major policy address, on 27 November 1987, he urged the importance of improved market access, liberalization of capital and financial markets, restructuring the economy, and "all the other changes that are needed," stating that

> . . . there may be times when we will have to ask the people to forbear and endure. Japan is one of the countries that has benefited the most from free trade, and I hope that the people will understand that these reforms are needed to reconcile Japan's economy with the rest of the world's economies. (*Investor's Daily,* 30 November 1987, 31 [Reuter])

At the GATT's annual session in early December, the Japanese delegation exercised its prerogative and blocked adoption of the panel report.[18] However, Takeshita was due to meet with President Reagan in January, and a successful summit was crucial for his success as a prime minister (*Mainichi Shimbun,* 18 November 1987). The criticism of blockage in Geneva convinced LDP political figures that a substantive solution was necessary. While in Hokkaido farmers shredded an effigy of Reagan and burned a Ford pickup truck, in Tokyo the LDP leadership persuaded LDP agricultural Dietmen, using the Subcommittee on Agricultural Products Liberalization, that Japan could not hold out against world opinion. The

---

16. *Nihon Keizai Shimbun,* 12 November 1987, 3 (on Horiuchi threat to divert Zennoh grain purchases from the United States to Argentina). The threat never was carried out. Japanese government import statistics for feedgrains imports for 1985–88 show a steady rise in imports of corn from the United States and a steady decline in imports from Argentina. From October 1987 to September 1988, Japanese imports of US corn rose 19 percent year-over-year and Argentine corn fell 53 percent.

17. See Yomiuri, Nikkei, *Japan Times,* 18 November and Nikkei, Sankei, Mainichi, 20 November 1987 (evening eds.).

18. *Washington Times,* 3 December 1987, C5; 4 December 1987, D3 (Reuter). On presession discussions in Japan, see *Nihon Keizai Shimbun,* 27 November 1987, 5.

package involved keeping the two most politically sensitive quotas, on dairy products (Hokkaido) and starch (starch potatoes from Kyushu and Hokkaido); the remaining eight would be liberalized, with details of substitute measures and compensatory subsidies to be worked out later. At an LDP-Cabinet summit on 6 January, the LDP leadership agreed to quota elimination for the eight (*Japan Times*, 7 January 1988). By the time of the 13 January Takeshita visit to Washington, Takeshita and MOFA Minister Uno were able to state about the GATT 12 issue that Japan would "deal with it appropriately."

On returning from Washington, Takeshita briefed his agriculture minister, Takashi Sato, and told him to take appropriate measures. On 27 January, Maki briefed the subcommittee on MAFF's package: acceptance of the report, quota elimination for eight items but not starch or dairy, and domestic and border measures to increase competitiveness of the eight. On 29 January the subcommittee gave its approval, and on 1 February, the date that Sato announced the decision, MAFF established a project team to study measures for liberalization of agricultural products (*Japan Agrinfo Newsletter*, March 1988, 4).

The panel report was adopted on 2 February in Geneva. In Tokyo, MAFF officials floated compensation and adjustment proposals to be discussed later with the United States (*Journal of Commerce*, 3 February 1988, 5A). On 3 February, Yeutter announced that if the Japanese government did not agree to quota elimination and fix the date by 31 March, the United States would take the beef and citrus issue to the GATT (*Journal of Commerce*, 4 February 1988, 5A).

Opening Phase

The first phase of bargaining on beef and citrus lasted through the expiration of the 1984 deal on 31 March 1988. The US side continued to demand that agreement by Japan to quota elimination and a "date certain" be preconditions for any talks, and compensation for any continuation of quotas beyond 1 April. The position did not change even after two visits to Washington by Maki in mid-February and mid-March to discuss Japan's response to the panel report. Meanwhile, in Tokyo the machinery was creaking into motion: the press reported precautionary feasibility studies by MAFF on beef and citrus quota elimination in mid-February (*Asahi Shimbun*, 17 February 1988; *Mainichi Shimbun*, 10 February 1988). It also reported liberalization leaks from high-level bureaucratic sources. Editorials started to appear in the press favoring liberalization (*Journal of Commerce*, 26 February 1988, 5A). On 8 March Michio Watanabe, chairman of the LDP's Policy Affairs Research Committee, was reported as suggesting that Japan could refuse to liberalize, but if the United States retaliated, others would follow (*Mainichi Shimbun*, 9 March 1988). In early March a delegation of LDP hardliners, led by Dietman (and Gang of Eight member) Takami Eto, was sent to Washington for exposure to the prevailing winds there.[19] Later, LDP Secretary General Shintaro Abe was said to have stated that Japan would lose a GATT case on beef and then have to liberalize (*Sankei Shimbun*, 25 March 1988, 2). Coverage on the 1988 US omnibus trade bill noted that the legislation would authorize retaliation in the event of a GATT violation.

But it was still too early for the Diet to be publicly convinced that the US side was serious. Japanese politicians repeatedly cited US agricultural import restrictions and referred to the California-Florida split on citrus; California and its powerful congressional delegation actively supported tariff cuts and did not support quota elimination. Memories were still fresh of the last-minute settlement in 1984. Yamanaka had just succeeded in protecting his starch-potato constituency from quota elimination, and Takeshita needed him on tax reform.[20] The agriculture committees of both houses of the Diet passed antiliberalization resolutions. At a press conference on 22 March, USTR Yeutter and Agriculture Secretary Lyng reiterated their readiness to go to the GATT if there were no solution by the end of the month, leaving possible resort to section 301 open. The Diet beef and citrus caucuses issued antiliberalization statements urging a vigorous GATT defense (*Yomiuri Shimbun*, 23 March 1988, 1).

In late March the LDP leadership decided to send MAFF Minister Sato to Washington. Sato was preceded by a delegation from Zenchu and producer organizations, which held a press conference announcing support for Zenchu from the National Farmers Union and four other US family farm organizations. Yeutter issued a strong response reaffirming his position, emphasizing that most US farm organizations wanted quota elimination (*Japan Agrinfo News*, April 1988, 5).

Minister Sato's visit was a last-ditch attempt to see if a settlement was possible on Japanese terms; a report from him directly would be valuable in persuading LDP hardliners (*Asahi Shimbun*, 5 April 1988, 2). At this point, the press was already urging that he negotiate a date for quota elimination.[21] Sato was accompanied by Maki and a ministry delegation as well as Hata and three other Dietmen, who kept in touch with Kato and the LDP leadership during the talks. During Sato's visit, the Senate Finance Committee sent a letter to Yeutter on beef, stating that "It is time to let the Japanese know that their beef quotas must go."

---

19. Diet delegations sent for exposure to Washington are a recurring theme in US-Japan agricultural talks, recurring because this tactic has successfully moved negotiations forward. Kusano (1983, 95) states that in 1978, after a trip to Washington, Eto and Eiichi Nakao (both members of the agricultural policy Gang of Eight) "changed their position 180 degrees." See also discussion of LDP mission with Eto in June 1983, in *Nihon Keizai Shimbunsha* (1983, 109–10).

20. See Yamaguchi (1987a) on Yamanaka's tax policy role.

21. *Nihon Keizai Shimbun*, 29 March 1988.

Negotiations ended in a room on Capitol Hill during the evening of 31 March, between Yeutter's meetings with the trade bill conference committee. Yeutter instructed the USTR Geneva office to immediately request a GATT Council meeting to seek establishment of a GATT panel on beef and citrus; at the meeting, Japan blocked panel establishment until the next regular GATT Council meeting, scheduled for 4 May.

Second Phase: The Variable Levy

The next phase took place between 1 April and 4 May. Between Sato's return and Takeshita's departure for Europe 28 April, the prime minister and the LDP leadership succeeded in brokering a deal for beef and citrus quota elimination and engineering acceptance of it by the LDP agriculture *zoku*. During the preceding months, Takeshita had reacted to US sanctions on Japanese construction companies by personally intervening in the construction issue, sending his close ally Ichiro Ozawa to settle the issue with Smith immediately before Sato's visit. He had distanced himself personally from the agriculture issue, delegating resolution of the issue to Hata and chief cabinet secretary Keizo Obuchi. But from April onward, the Prime Minister's Office became more and more involved in the beef and citrus issue, pushing for a bilateral settlement involving quota elimination. GATT was a factor; so was Takeshita's talk with Reagan at the January summit, in which he had promised to consider the consumer viewpoint in dealing with the beef and citrus issue. Takeshita did not want a reputation as a leader unable to deliver. On 5 April the government announced that liberalization of the beef and citrus quotas would be desirable (*Asahi Shimbun*, 5 April 1988, 2; *Nihon Keizai Shimbun*, 7 April 1988, 2).

By early April, most of the LDP wanted to let the issue be settled in the GATT. A bilateral settlement would be the responsibility of the party, but if GATT were to rule that the quotas were illegal, Dietmen could plead *force majeure* and let the ministries take responsibility for losing the case. Moreover, GATT was the voice not of the United States alone but of the world trading system, and a GATT case would put off any decision. However, during April five factors came together to persuade the ruling party to accept a bilateral solution.

First, MAFF and Foreign Ministry bureaucrats campaigned to persuade LDP Dietmen that bilateral negotiations were better than going to GATT, and that a positive policy for the future would make farmers more secure than endless foot-dragging on liberalization. They told them that GATT would condemn the beef quota for sure, perhaps even in the summer of 1988; afterwards, Japan would lose control. US demands for compensation would become less flexible, more legalistic, and harder to reject, and it would be difficult to negotiate substitute forms of protection (*Asahi Shim-*

bun 9 April 1988, 3; *Nihon Keizai Shimbun* 17 April 1988, 2). Even citrus was not secure. The quota on oranges would fall unless Japan could prove that oranges and mikan were "like products."[22] As for orange juice, the MAFF practice of requiring bottlers to mix imported concentrate with domestic mikan juice violated the national treatment provisions of GATT, which explicitly prohibit such mixing requirements.[23]

Second, prominent members of the agriculture *zoku* led by Hata and Kato argued the need to face up to quota elimination and make a positive policy for adjustment. Kato and Hata contended that the Americans were likely to be more flexible in bilateral negotiations than in a multilateral GATT context. From the timing standpoint, for farm-district Dietmen it was best to settle beef and citrus well before the rice price decision in July, and if quota elimination were inevitable, it would be best if the decision were as far as possible behind them by the summer 1989 upper-house election. Hata also worked on Zenchu, to try to soften their rejection of liberalization (*Asahi Shimbun*, 7 April 1988, 2). Maki was sent to Washington again in the second week of April, and Smith traveled to Tokyo for technical talks on 21–23 April.

Third, on 10 April the LDP won a by-election by a wide margin in a citrus district in Saga where the government's 5 April liberalization statement had been a point of some controversy. Fourth, with the election over, and reassured about the farm vote, the LDP could talk freely about quota elimination. Takeshita and Abe both spoke out on 10 April in favor of a bilateral solution (*Asahi Shimbun*, 11 April 1988, 1 and 3).

Fifth and most important was evolution of a post–quota elimination deal, worked out among the ministries and the LDP. Oranges would be liberalized in five years and beef in three. Because the regular tariff of 25 percent on beef was not subject to a GATT concession, it could be raised, so the proposal was to impose a new variable levy tied to the domestic stabilization price. With the consent of the Ministry of Finance, the levy receipts would be reserved for adjustment: a deficiency payment scheme for calf prices and subsidies for increasing beef producers' efficiency. The money would show tangible evidence of zeal and would discharge MAFF's legal mandate to stabilize beef prices.

A few years before, Japan had replaced the import quota on pork with a variable levy tied to a price stabilization scheme. A certain rough justice was seen in a variable levy, since the European Community had one too, and the United States had its own means of agricultural protection.

---

22. Since tangerines, the product closest to mikan, were not subject to quota, the Japanese side would have had a difficult time (in light of the legal analysis in the GATT 12 case) showing that import quotas on oranges were necessary to the effectiveness of the domestic production restrictions on mikan.

23. See analysis in *Nihon Keizai Shimbun,* 10 May 1988, 5. The GATT analysis in articles such as this one is remarkably detailed and technically accurate.

Because orange tariffs were subject to a GATT tariff concession and could not be freely raised, post–quota elimination citrus measures would focus on subsidies and low-interest loans for conversion to other crops.

The catch was that a variable levy was the last thing the US side could agree to. The symbolic freight of the European Community's variable levy in US agricultural trade relations was such that any agreement by Yeutter to a new Japanese variable levy would have weakened his credibility with the US agricultural community and Congress, and with it the ambitious position he had pushed in the Uruguay Round (Smith interview, 8 August 1994). When Minister Sato came to Washington on 27 April with Maki and Hata to propose replacement of the beef quota with a variable levy, Yeutter and Smith refused even to discuss it. Negotiations ended 3 May. The United States went forward with its GATT case; on 4 May the GATT Council established dispute settlement panels for the US dispute against Japan (beef and citrus) and for a separate Australian dispute against Japan (beef alone). Procedural maneuvering on the new panels continued through May and early June in Geneva.

Third Phase

Recriminations for the rupture began even before the delegation left Washington. The Japanese press, predicting a GATT loss and speculating about trade retaliation, blamed the slip-up on MAFF and the Foreign Ministry for advising that the United States would consent to a variable levy (*Asahi Shimbun,* 5 May 1988, 2 and 4). Minister Sato had gone to Washington twice and had not yet succeeded in getting a negotiation going with Yeutter. Takeshita's ability to deliver was under question, and Hata and Kato had lost face as well. But there was no going back. Zenchu, which had simply opposed liberalization, was put in the position of opposing the breakoff of talks and the resort to GATT (*Asahi Shimbun,* 5 May 1988, 3). From here on, quota elimination was taken for granted; the rest was a debate over the conditions under which it would take place.

What Yeutter had rejected was the variable levy; the US negotiators had signaled that they would accept a tariff increase but had pushed for the tariff on beef to be bound at some level. MAFF gave up on a variable levy and began to evolve a plan for raising the beef tariff, establishing a fund with the receipts, and reorganizing LIPC as an organization to administer deficiency payments (*Mainichi Shimbun,* 12 May 1988). The Prime Minister's Office, the LDP leadership, and the Foreign Ministry pushed for a fixed tariff of 50 to 60 percent, but MAFF and the *zoku* still wanted a surcharge that could be earmarked for adjustment measures.

From this point forward, the Prime Minister's Office and the Foreign Ministry pushed with increasing intensity for a settlement clearing away the beef and citrus issue before the Toronto summit in June. The summit would be the first meeting between Takeshita and the collective economic leadership of the world, and the agenda was to focus on trade, the Uruguay Round midterm review, and agriculture. Takeshita was under pressure to equal Nakasone's foreign affairs performance. A continuing impasse on beef and citrus, or another breakdown in talks, would be an unacceptable cloud on the summit. The specific deadline that emerged for a settlement was 20 June, the date of Takeshita's scheduled meeting with Reagan in Toronto (*Nihon Nogyo Shimbun*, 20 May 1988, 1 [Hata-Abe agreement on timing]).

After Smith, visiting Tokyo on 19 May, rejected a variation on the surcharge proposal, Takeshita intervened through Obuchi's deputy, Ichiro Ozawa, who had been Takeshita's personal emissary to settle the US-Japan construction issue with Smith in March (*Nihon Keizai Shimbun*, 21 May 1988). Smith met with Ozawa and convinced him that the surcharge would not be accepted. Two days later, Obuchi announced that the government would abandon the surcharge idea and that the issue would be resolved soon under guidance from the prime minister (*Nihon Keizai Shimbun*, 23 May 1988). During May as well, USMEF's Tokyo representative, Philip Seng, met with traditional meat import quota holders, persuading them that ending the quota would make it possible for them to prosper by producing beef in the United States for the Japanese market. The importers' backing for liberalization undercut a key source of support for the beef quota (Seng interview, 22 August 1994).

Resistance from the *zoku* was still strong. Yamanaka threatened to resign his tax policy chairmanship; he and Higaki asked Takeshita to have the negotiations handled entirely by Minister Sato and the Hata-Kato-Hori triad. The tariff equivalent of the beef regime had been discussed in the negotiations; while the LIPC markup was equivalent to a 95 percent tariff, the US side had argued that taking into account the quota restriction, the equivalent tariff impact was at the 300 percent level (*Nihon Keizai Shimbun*, 26 May 1988). On 25 May USTR accepted a section 301 petition that had been filed on 6 May by the Florida citrus industry backed by the state's congressional delegation.[24]

Maki was sent to Washington again for talks on 31 May through 5 June. The US side was reported as rejecting Maki's first proposal of a variable tariff and counterproposing that Japan solve its problems with emergency safeguards measures to be applied in the event of an import surge (*Yomiuri Shimbun*, 20 June 1988 evening ed., 3). By the end of the talks, the two sides were considerably closer. The US side had moved back from a two-year deadline for beef to three years, with a declining tariff increase in the three years after quota elimination, and the safeguards measures. For

---

24. For Florida, the 301 petition called attention to that state's priority, quota elimination, in the face of the competing objective of tariff reduction backed by the large and politically influential California and Arizona delegations.

oranges, the United States proposed three years to quota elimination and a tariff cut to 20 percent year round (*Asahi Shimbun*, 14 June 1988, 3).

Final Phase

The week before the summit, Smith and an interagency delegation traveled to Tokyo for the final stage 14–20 June. Yeutter had stated in advance that he would not go to Tokyo unless Smith judged that agreement was within reach. Using this tension, Smith pushed hard during the first four days of working-level talks, as the two sides moved closer.

The last week was also the finish line for the LDP agriculture *zoku*. But by mid-June they faced not just beef and citrus but other, higher-stakes issues for farmers. The yearly struggle over the rice price was coming up in July. Up for decision was not just a proposed reduction in the nominal price but also the permanent policy change proposed by the 1986 MAFF report, which would reorient price policy toward full-time farmers. These changes would affect practically every farmer in Japan, not just the minority who produced beef or mikan oranges. And there was an even larger issue issue in the offing: Takeshita's highest priority, tax reform. The *zoku* Dietmen had to choose. The party leadership, MAFF and the Prime Minister's Office consulted intensively with them, mediated by Hata and Kato. According to Smith, the turning point came on 18 June. Smith demanded that his agriculture experts and Philip Seng of USMEF give him an exact tariff equivalent for quota restrictions on beef combined with the LIPC markup. He then gave the Japanese side the number—376 percent ad valorem—and proposed that the tariff on beef be raised from 25 percent to the high level of 70 percent ad valorem in the first year after quota elimination. The 70 percent would decline by 10 percentage points per year in the subsequent two years and would remain at 50 percent. The ultimate tariff level would be left to negotiation in the Uruguay Round. After making its own calculation of tariff equivalents, the Japanese side agreed to the proposal (Smith interview, 20 March 1989; Kupfer 1989).

Yeutter arrived late on 18 June and led the final negotiations the following day, in which the two sides reached fundamental agreement. Remaining details and the text were settled in negotiations that night. The two last and most difficult issues were the tariff cut on oranges and the form and wording of the emergency measures on beef. The negotiations ended with a final session into the early hours of 20 June, before initialing of the ad referendum text in the morning (Yabunaka 1993). Minister Sato reported the results to the Kato subcommittee the same day and received approval conditional on a good financial package of producer adjustment measures. MITI, the other economic ministries, and industrial exporters were reported to have breathed a sigh of relief (*Yomiuri Shimbun*, 21 June 1988).

The agreement gave neither side everything that it wanted. The United States did not get immediate quota elimination but received instead a phase-out of two years for the orange juice blending requirement, three years for the fresh and frozen beef and fresh orange quotas, and four years for orange juice. The 1988 agreement also provided separate access for imports of single-strength juice and orange juice mixtures and guaranteed newcomers part of the quota increase in oranges and juice. The United States had demanded tariff cuts on citrus and other products as compensation for the delay in quota elimination; the tariff cuts were limited to grapefruit, lemons, nuts, and frozen peaches and pears, and did not include the tariff on fresh oranges.[25] The US beef exporters achieved their objective of eliminating LIPC from the pricing, purchase, and sales of imported beef, and limiting its functions to price stabilization for domestic beef and dairy products. In 1988–91 the beef quota was to increase by 60,000 tons per year, to almost double the 214,000 tons imported in fiscal 1987; SBS was expanded to cover 60 percent of LIPC imports in fiscal 1990.[26]

The quota was eliminated on 1 April 1991 and replaced by an increase in the tariff from 25 percent to 70 percent ad valorem in fiscal 1991, declining to 60 percent in fiscal 1992 and 50 percent on 1 April 1993; the tariff after 1 April 1994 would be subject to negotiation in the Uruguay Round. A similar compromise took place on safeguards after quota elimination, with agreement that Japan could impose a 25 percent emergency tariff surcharge during the period from 1 April 1991 to 31 March 1994 if beef imports exceeded 120 percent of the previous year and/or take import relief action under GATT Article XIX. Neither the surcharge nor any action under Article XIX was taken in this period.

Later in the week of 20 June, Japanese Agriculture Minister Sato and a negotiating team flew to Australia and quickly negotiated a bilateral agreement on liberalization of the Japanese beef market. The text of the Japan-Australia agreement signed 24 June was almost identical to the beef portions of the text initialed with the United States, but included special provisions for chilled beef (a market Australia had developed).

---

25. For text, see *International Legal Materials* 27:1539 (1988). The text is structured as an exchange of notes, covering an annex and an attachment. The note from Japan states the intention of the Japanese government to implement the measures in the annex and the attachment, and provides for annual consultations. The US letter acknowledges receipt of the Japanese letter and notes withdrawal of the GATT and section 301 actions. The core obligations appear in the annex and further details in the attachment. The English text uses the phrase "import allocation system" (translated as *yunyu wariate seido*) rather than the word *quota*.

26. Early in 1988, the Livestock Industry Promotion Deliberation Council estimated annual rates of increase of 4 to 5 percent for beef demand and 2.2 percent for domestic supply, leaving a supply shortage of 320,000 to 400,000 metric tons per year by fiscal 1995 (*Nihon Keizai Shimbun*, 6 February 1988, 5). Fiscal 1987 beef imports included an extra 37,000 tons allocated late in the fiscal year in order to meet demand and prevent domestic beef prices from rising.

Final Beef-Citrus Text

The final text of the US-Japan beef and citrus settlement was signed in Washington on 5 July 1988. On that date, the United States withdrew its GATT complaint on beef and citrus, and the Florida citrus industry withdrew its section 301 petition. The GATT 12 settlement was signed on 2 August, providing for quota elimination on 8 of the 12 items plus some value-added dairy products; expansion of the peanut quota; renegotiation of tariffs on other items; and improvements for trade in feedgrains.

On 19 June, the last night of negotiations, Hata stressed the need to turn immediately to adjustment measures to reassure farmers about the future. The following day, Minister Sato announced that he would work with producer organizations on measures to strengthen beef and mikan producers (*Nihon Keizai Shimbun,* 20 June 1988, 3; *Japan Agrinfo Newsletter,* July 1988, 3). In the fall of 1988 the Diet approved a supplemental budget of ¥104.4 billion for fiscal 1988 for adjustment measures, of which ¥68.3 billion were for citrus production adjustments. The Diet also enacted a calf price deficiency payment scheme, for implementation from fiscal 1990, based on income from the beef tariffs.[27]

Since 1988

The 1988 agreement began immediately to affect beef trade because of the changes in import procedures. The 36 traditionally authorized importers were joined by tens of new importers, including Daiei and other supermarket chains and major meat processors. On 1 April 1991 the quota was eliminated, and the buffer it had provided against exchange rate changes disappeared. Beef imports rose from the fiscal 1987 quota level of 177,000 tons to 462,000 tons in fiscal 1993: in dollars, beef imports from the world rose almost 70 percent from $1.2 billion in 1988 to almost $2 billion in 1992 (*Nihon Keizai Shimbun,* 13 June 1993, 8; Tahara 1993, 2–3; Caplan 1993, 84). Japan did not impose the emergency tariff surcharge or take import relief action under GATT. Imports of beef now exceed domestic production.

The increase in beef imports has disproportionately affected domestic producers of dairy beef and other lower-quality beef. LIPC data show that between Japan's 1988 fiscal year and fiscal 1992, wholesale prices dropped by 45 percent for the lowest grade of dairy beef and rose by 8

27. USDA/FAS GEDES Voluntary Report, March 1989 (unclassified). Initial government-LDP agreement had been on a total of ¥106 billion for mikan (a subsidy for conversion of mikan land averaging ¥3,000,000 per hectare [$9,064 per acre]), and through Yamanaka's efforts the commitment was made to earmark the entire amount of the post–quota elimination beef tariff receipts for beef to beef subsidies. *Nihon Keizai Shimbun,* 26 August 1988, 5; *Mainichi Shimbun,* 26 August 1988, 9.

percent for the highest grade of highly marbled *wagyu* beef. Prices of typical high-quality cuts of beef have fallen by 25 to 50 percent. Even though the dairy industry has been protected by import quota, most support payments under the feeder calf price stabilization program have gone to dairy calf producers as the price of dairy calves has collapsed. Since low-priced beef is competing with pork and chicken, prices of all three have fallen and are not expected to rise (*Japan Agrinfo Newsletter*, February 1994, 3). *Wagyu* beef production has grown in volume, and market share has remained approximately at the pre-1988 level. And *wagyu* producers have now built a small and growing export trade in super-premium beef.

On 6 August 1993 MAFF officials summoned representatives of 41 importers to seek "understanding and cooperation in making sure there is 'orderly demand in the market.'" Seven declined to appear, and Daiei announced it would ignore MAFF's request (*Nikkei Weekly*, 16 August 1993; *International Herald Tribune*, 13 August 1993; *Financial Times*, 22 August 1993).

US orange producers were split on the settlement as they had been during the negotiations. Florida interests announced their satisfaction, withdrawing their section 301 petition; Sunkist president Russell Hanlin told the Japanese press that by cutting the tariff on grapefruit and not oranges, the settlement favored Florida (*Nihon Keizai Shimbun*, 2 July 1988). MAFF carried out a 20 percent mikan capacity reduction in 1988–90. As the elimination of the fresh orange quota in 1991 coincided with a frost in California and greatly increased export prices, imports fell, but the following year imports more than doubled and the domestic wholesale price fell by half. Imports of concentrated orange juice by bottlers rose 57 percent in the year after the juice quota was eliminated in April 1992 and have grown even more since; the price of imported juice is now half that of domestic mikan juice, although single-strength juice remains a premium product with a small market share. MAFF has announced further production adjustments (*Nihon Keizai Shimbun*, 10 September 1992, 25 and 17 July 1993; *Japan Agrinfo Newsletter*, September 1993).

The most striking immediate testimony to the effect of import quota elimination was the increase in Japanese investment in food production and packing abroad. Rising costs in Japan, including yen appreciation and raw material costs, had already been pushing Japanese food processing companies offshore. Japanese trading companies, meat packers, and traditional beef importers clearly saw opportunities to leverage their existing position in the Japanese beef market by acquiring offshore sources for Japanese-style beef. By 1992, Japanese firms owned wholly or jointly at least 9 large cattle ranches, 9 feedlots, and 21 meatpackers, representing 15 to 20 percent of US beef exports to Japan. Japanese firms have invested in Florida citrus and California rice.[28] In Australia, Japanese ownership of packers rose from 4 percent to 15 percent in 1988, and Japanese firms bought eight feedlots worth A$189 million; Japanese investors reportedly own one-third of Australia's feedlot capacity (*Christian Science Monitor*, 13 March 1989, 3; Coyle and Dyck 1989, 29). Yet it would be wrong to jump to the conclusion that Japanese captive imports reduce net benefits of the market opening to the United States. The compensation represented by the opportunity to participate in this trade may have substantially aided acceptance of quota elimination by powerful traditional importers that otherwise stood to lose.

Conclusions

Agreement opened the market. There is no question that the 1988 beef and citrus agreement opened the market. Exports, and in particular exports from the United States, have risen substantially since quota elimination. And the size of this market opening is notable within the universe of trade negotiating episodes: while the authors of this book estimate that the total increase in value of US exports in all successful cases amounted to between $4 billion and $5 billion yearly, the increase in value of US exports of beef, oranges, and orange juice to Japan since 1987 amounts to nearly 20 percent of that amount. Dollar estimates of this market opening also should take into account that the beef and citrus agreement was an important milestone in achieving the Uruguay Round goal of tariffication without exceptions, which will open many other markets in Japan and elsewhere.

Negotiations on border measures are more successful. The beef and citrus case confirms the observation elsewhere in this volume that success in negotiations comes more easily when the issues concern border measures rather than internal market measures or state trading. Compared to a simple demand for quota elimination or tariff reduction, a demand for specific regulatory changes requires much more attention to detail and more follow-up. The US push to widen participation in the import trade through expansion of SBS paid off in August 1993, when the supermarket chains were able to resist government urgings that they decelerate imports. Yet this push was backed by USMEF's on-the-ground experience and ability to follow up in Tokyo, motivated by the prospect of very substantial short-term gains. Orange juice exporters that had less prospect of immediate gain and had invested less met initial disappointment in dealing with the complexities of the hotel juice quota.

---

28. On beef, see Bolling (1992, 7). Soon after the 1988 settlement, Sumitomo Shoji, Japan's largest importer of grapefruit, announced it had bought a 25 percent share of Florida's largest citrus orchard, with the intention of importing Florida oranges (*Journal of Commerce*, 20 July 1988, A1; Kobayashi 1988, 308–09). On investment in rice land by Mitsubishi Trading Company, see *The Economist*, 4 March 1989.

The agreement supports the multilateral trading system. The quotas ended; this result furthered trade on a nondiscriminatory basis (see box 10.1). Furthermore, the tactics used by first the US side and then both sides in developing the agreement relied on and were supported by the norms embodied in the GATT; even in the last phase, where the parties negotiated a bilateral settlement, both parties looked to the predicted outcome of a GATT case and the likelihood of retaliation legitimized by GATT. The multilateral source of the pressure helped soften the agricultural hardliners in Japan.

The focus on GATT in the beef and citrus negotiations flowed from the result in the GATT 12 dispute on agricultural quotas. This dispute had offered an opportunity for the United States to use GATT dispute settlement as an alternative to accepting an inadequate Japanese compromise offer. The choice of GATT reflected the US appetite for confrontation and litigation, the value it placed on third-party dispute settlement, and US substantive interest in furthering GATT case law on agricultural import quotas. The United States had met with a string of disappointments on agricultural isues in the GATT in the early 1980s, but the GATT 12 panel decision showed how effective it could be to use the GATT as a forum. And as it happened, the GATT rules involved were useful in addressing the problems faced by US exporters. Yet the particular decision on beef and citrus, and its timing, were not inevitable consequences of the GATT 12 panel decision or its timing. The literature on bilateral bargaining throws light on this.

Putnam's model of international bargaining[29] looks at the negotiation between delegation chiefs and at the separate negotiation between each chief and the domestic interests that determine the "win set" options, or range of acceptable results for that side. Having separated the two levels, it then becomes possible to look at interactions between them. As Putnam notes, the distribution of outcomes in the negotiation between delegation chiefs (or governments) is related to the size of the win set for the domestic interests on each side: the less flexibility a negotiator has, and the more restrictive his or her instructions, the better leverage he or she may have. Putnam's contribution is to point to the tactical possibilities for negotiators to alter their own and the other side's win-sets by tying their own hands, by side payments to their own side, or by pressure, side payments or persuasion aimed at foreign domestic interests (as opposed to the other government). It is the tactical maneuvering by both sides that is of greatest interest here and that is most useful to understand.

In June 1987 a prediction that Japan would agree to elimination of the beef and citrus quotas would have been met with disbelief. The prevailing view was that import controls had unbeatable support in the political

---

29. Putnam (1988), reprinted as annex to Evans, Jacobson, and Putnam (1993); see also Schoppa (1993) and Odell (1993).

Box 10.1 A discriminatory market opening?

Some critics of US trade negotiating tactics have cited the beef and citrus negotiations as an example of "American pressure put on Japan to open her beef market . . . aimed at getting Japan to increase her imports of American beef by increasing the quota for the United States, rather than getting Japan to liberalize her import regime, the most likely consequence of which would be Australia out-competing both Japan and the United States" (Bhagwati and Irwin 1987). Similarly, before 1988 Japanese interests argued in support of continued beef quotas that US exporters of premium grain-fed beef could not compete with lower-priced Australian suppliers in a free market, and some US analysts have argued that the United States would have been better off leaving the quota system in place (Alston, Carter, and Jarvis 1989). This box discusses whether the results support the push for quota elimination rather than managed trade—and whether the 1988 agreement was unfairly biased in favor of US interests.

Events since 1988 have borne out Yeutter's insistence on quota elimination. Although import figures have not risen each year—due to inventory over-hangs, crop failures, and the Japanese recession—imports have well exceeded the level that would have been politically tolerable under the quota system. Loosening of administrative restrictions on importing has brought participation by new players such as supermarket chains, which have political power to resist new import restrictions. In a larger perspective, if Japan had not liberalized its market, there would be no hope of liberalization in other high-potential East Asian markets such as Korea; had the United States accepted Japan's quotas, the Uruguay Round agricultural settlement could have been quite different.

Who benefited from market opening? Figures 10.1a-c show that since Japan's fiscal 1988, the Australian and US shares of imports of beef have been stable at 52 to 53 percent and 42 to 43 percent, respectively. The overall beef import market has increased to 250 percent of the fiscal 1987 beef quota. USDA analysts (Dyck, Webb, and Spinelli 1993) find that with the growth in exports of beef, a value-added product, US exports to Japan of feedgrains have begun to decline, but that increased feed use in the United States largely compensates for the lost feedstuff exports. In search of opportunities at the high end of the market, since 1988 US packers have invested in the technology for chilled beef (a premium market segment dominated by Australia), and Australian producers have established feedlots to compete with US grain-fed beef. Imports of chilled beef for household use have steadily expanded and accounted for 53 percent of beef imports in 1993. The quota system is gone. The results have been greater diversification of the market and greater competition, in a system in which the winner will be determined by the marketplace.

In the fresh orange market, US exporters have retained an import share above 90 percent in all years since 1988 and will benefit in addition from tariff cuts agreed in the Uruguay Round. The greatest surprise has been in sales of frozen orange juice concentrate, where in 1985 the US share of imports had dropped to 9 percent. Caplan (1993) states that since 1987, US orange juice exports to Japan increased 8.5 times in volume and more than 9 times in value, from $3.3 million to $30.9 million, and US import share rose to 37 to 38 percent in 1991 and 1992. Factors behind the US comeback include Florida's recovery from a series of freezes in the 1980s and use by Florida packers of low-cost Brazilian concentrate in blends for export. However, Brazil, producer of 60 percent of the world's orange juice, remains dominant in the Japanese market for bulk concentrate. Florida sales of fresh, not-from-concentrate juice have not grown as anticipated, due to Japanese insistence on high-temperature pasteurization.

Figure 10.1a Japan: beef imports of categories under import quota restrictions, 1979–93

thousands of metric tons

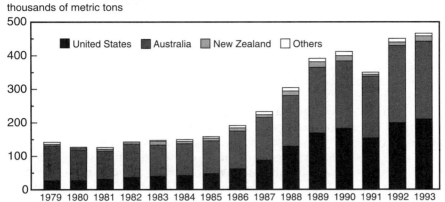

Japanese fiscal year

Figure 10.1b Japan: orange juice imports, 1979–93

millions of liters

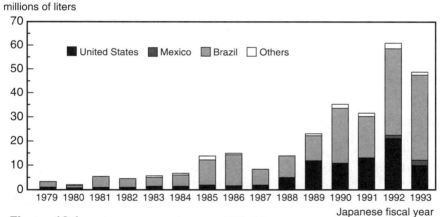

Japanese fiscal year

Figure 10.1c Japan: orange imports, 1979–93

thousands of metric tons

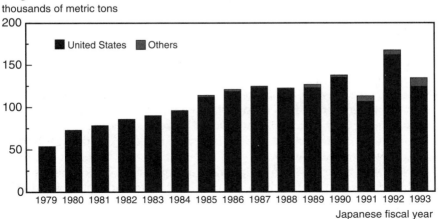

Japanese fiscal year

and economic system of Japan, that Japan's hands were tied, in Putnam's phrase, leaving little flexiblity. In fact, Japanese agricultural policy was already undergoing fundamental rethinking, pushed by unavoidable demographic changes; MAFF had even independently proposed tariffication. Decentralization measures instituted since the 1970s had located industrial plants in rural Diet districts, increasing the proportion of part-time farmers, reducing rural Japan's dependence on farming, and increasing its dependence on industrial exports.

But farm policy was based on rice policy, and beef and citrus, as substitute crops, were seen as a way out of the rice problem. While the LDP targeted the urban vote, it still needed the rural vote, in a system where rural areas were greatly overrepresented in the Diet. In Putnam's terms, import protection was a side payment to agriculture and importers by the LDP. Changes internal to Japan were untying the hands of Japanese negotiators, but support for quotas was so strong that the changes described here would not have happened in the absence of external pressure.

A focus on the interaction between the governments concerned would point to the use of threats: generalized congressional pressure on Japan, the specific threat of the section 301 petition filed by Florida Citrus Mutual, and the implicit threat of multilateral retaliation involved in resort to GATT. Yet, even though congressional pressure on Japan during the period was intense, unlike other issues where Congress took direct action (such as the December 1987 Brooks-Murkowski sanctions on Japanese construction), congressional pressure on beef and citrus was confined to expressions of support for administration negotiators. The 1988 trade bill's provision on beef and citrus was a sense-of-Congress resolution urging a market-opening agreement. The Florida petition on section 301 came relatively late and appears to have been targeted primarily at reinforcing Florida's push for quota elimination, against political opposition from California orange producers; there was no section 301 petition on beef.

The Use of GATT

The use of GATT norms increased the cost of defiance by depriving the Japanese measures of legitimacy and increasing the likelihood of retaliation, not only by the United States but also by other parties. Had Japan ultimately refused to comply with a panel report, the United States or any other party to the dispute would have had the right to ask for authorization of retaliation against Japanese trade. Even though Japan might have been able to block such an authorization, a request of this nature would have singled out Japan as a target and would have led to a public confrontation in which Japan would have had nothing to gain and much to lose.

"Aggressive multilateralism" (appeals to GATT norms) made it more difficult for the United States to back down. It also reduced the political cost of compliance, by reinforcing the tie between trade liberalization on beef and citrus and Japan's dependence on participation in the GATT system. The GATT disputes procedure channeled US-Japan conflict into an argument over the application of legal rules, not a contest of force in which someone would have to take responsibility for making concessions. The GATT panel report on the "12 items" was a reasoned decision by neutral panelists, accepted by the Japanese side, on general principles and with multilateral support. The panel decision was a sort of *force majeure* making quota elimination inevitable: the press persistently speculated that if Japan fought a case on beef and citrus and lost, then quotas would have to go in two years anyway. Finally, the GATT context provided a legal means to implement the final result, through a tariff-based solution within the most-favored nation (MFN) framework of the GATT.

The use of GATT also increased the cohesion of the US side. The negotiations took place during the passage of the 1988 trade bill, which treated violations of US rights with maximum severity. Legislators who were supporting a more rights-oriented trade policy could not at the same time support foreign quotas that appeared to be in violation of GATT norms; conversely, the administration had to vigorously attack such policies if it was to avoid statutory changes in the trade bill that would have required mandatory retaliation in section 301 cases. Years later, Smith recalled the remarkable unity within the administration on beef and citrus, in contrast to the divisions seen in some other US-Japan negotiations of that period. The Uruguay Round context of the talks also meant that the United States, too, was negotiating its domestic agricultural policies and had proposed to give up its own agricultural import restrictions. Support from beef producers was important for Yeutter's overall objectives in the round. All of these factors supported aggressive multilateralism by a United States that had learned to care about its GATT rights.

Strategy and Tactics

Both sides engaged to some degree in a strategy of tying their own hands and attempting to seize advantage by removing their own flexibility to give the other side what it wanted. Actions of this type included Japanese explanations of the unmovable opposition of the Diet and the electorate to quota elimination; the United States' frequent use of Congress as the "bad cop" in trade negotiations; and in this case, the consistent refusal of Yeutter and Lyng to discuss any renewal of the 1984 agreement that did not include a firm date for quota elimination. GATT also served as a source of precommitment. Early on, US negotiators used the "12 items" case as a proxy for beef and citrus, and later stages of the negotiations were regularly punctuated with threats to go to the GATT.

Both sides also engaged in tactics aimed at altering the win set of domestic interests on the other side: direct persuasion of domestic interests, public diplomacy, public threats for political effect, changing the level of a negotiation, tactics described in Schoppa's (1993) study of the Structural Impediments Initiative (SII) talks as "participation expansion" among elites and the public, and "alternative specification."

Japanese domestic farm policy, and even routine agricultural trade policy, was a classic example of a policy made in normal times entirely by a small group of actors in a "subgovernment" consisting of MAFF, Nokyo, and *zoku* Dietmen; even in the 1979 and 1984 beef and citrus negotiations the prime minister was not personally involved. However, once an agricultural issue became raised on the bilateral trade agenda, the players within the Japanese government would change (bringing in trade negotiators from the MAFF Economics Bureau and the Foreign Ministry).

Even more, once any issue is placed on the agenda of the first summit attended by a new prime minister, his personal prestige becomes engaged. The deadline for resolution of the beef and citrus negotiations was the June 1988 Toronto summit, planned around the theme of agricultural trade policy. Moreover, keeping in mind the memory of the semiconductor retaliation, business groups, too, kept an eye on the beef and citrus talks, since the low level of Japanese agricultural exports meant that any retaliation would inevitably affect Japanese industrial exports.

US interests also used public diplomacy to widen public involvement in the beef and citrus issue, similar to actions reported by Schoppa in the SII talks. USMEF spent $7 million promoting imported beef in 1987, including a press campaign asking why consumer food prices had not fallen as the yen rose. Yeutter and Lyng hammered on the same theme in press conferences. During a visit to Japan in April 1987, Lyng used supermarket visits to call attention to the high cost of food in Japan (*Asahi Shimbun,* 21 April 1987, 9). Supermarket chains ran sales of beef at "liberalization prices."

Threats, arguments, trial balloons, leaks, and position statements by politicians were exhaustively reported in the magnifying mirror of the Japanese press. The press also picked up the arguments of antiprotection groups on the high price of beef and the failure of importers to pass through the benefits of yen revaluation. The result showed in opinion polls on agricultural quota elimination, which appeared in the Japanese press in spring 1988: consistently, and more strongly in urban areas, although most voters did not favor liberalization of rice, a solid majority favored liberalization of beef and citrus. In a 1988 survey of Tokyo consumers by Shufuren (the Japan Housewives Association), the percentage favoring liberalization of rice imports even exceeded that of those opposed.[30]

---

30. *Mainichi Shimbun,* 21 May 1988, translated in *Japan Agrinfo Newsletter,* July 1988. The survey reportedly found 39.5 percent of consumers surveyed favored quota elimination (or quota elimination under certain conditions); 28.5 percent were opposed. The figures are a

Schoppa also points to "alternative specification" (restructuring the possible solution for an issue, or altering the way in which ideas emerge from the "policy primeval soup"). This too was a key factor in the beef and citrus outcome. In previous episodes, the United States had pushed for phase-out of the quotas by a date certain, with no replacement form of protection other than perhaps adjustment subsidies. In 1988 the policy context of the Uruguay Round led to the alternative of tariffication—after the proposal for a variable levy proved to be outside any acceptable outcome for Yeutter. The proceeds of the tariff then became available for side payments for calf price supports to ease adjustment.

Attempts by Japanese interests to alter the US side's win set included lobbying in Washington by Zenchu and others, and Zenchu's threat to retaliate by switching its purchases of feedgrains to non-US suppliers. Yet Yeutter and Lyng were able to resist the pressure. Although Sunkist valued a tariff cut more than quota elimination, and was able to mobilize significant congressional support for its position, the USMEF had convinced the cattle industry that quota elimination was the only way to substantially expand exports of high-value US feedlot beef; the Florida citrus industry saw quota elimination as the only way it would be competitive in Japan; and the US cattle, feed, and ancillary industries are many times larger than Florida and California citrus combined. More generally, on agricultural issues producer groups are always mobilized and already have views on what they want; consumer groups can be mobilized but only if they can be reached with the message. For this reason, US persuasion of Japanese consumers worked, and Japanese persuasion of US farm groups did not (Andrew Moravcsik, personal communication).

Postscript

Compensation to those affected by quota elimination lowered the immediate political costs of the 1988 agreement, but these political costs have been substantial. Both Yamanaka and Higaki lost their Diet seats in the two years after 1988.

In a major policy statement in June 1992, MAFF announced a reorientation of postwar farm policy to respond to the aging of the farm work force. Farm laws would be revised to make corporate farming possible and increase farm size, and rice distribution would be further deregulated (*Japan Agrinfo Newsletter,* July 1992, 2; *Mainichi Shimbun,* 14 May 1992, evening ed., 1). The precise dimensions of these changes will be clear only when they have been enacted into law.

The end of the story for beef and citrus came with the conclusion of the Uruguay Round. In the end, Japan yielded to the multilateral consensus on

---

big shift from 1982, when only 7.5 percent favored quota elimination and 51.5 percent were opposed.

tariffication without exception and agreed to transform its prohibition on rice imports into a tariff quota system permitting access for foreign rice. Japanese negotiators obtained "special treatment" (delayed tariffication) for rice as part of a package deal that involved additional tariff cuts on other products, including beef and citrus. The tariff on beef will be bound at 50 percent ad valorem as of entry into force for Japan of the World Trade Organization agreement. Under a US-Japan bilateral agreement, the applied MFN tariff will decline to a final rate of 38.5 percent ad valorem by 2000; if quarterly beef imports increase more than 17 percent on a year-over-year basis, the tariff may snap back to the bound rate. The fresh orange tariff will also decline, to a bound rate of 16 percent, and orange juice tariffs will be cut as well. Tariffication without exception, and binding of duties, will also apply to all remaining agricultural import quotas in Japan. The Japanese government has announced that it will move quickly to provide adjustment measures to ease the transition for Japanese farmers.

11

Japan and the European Community: Financial Services

The US objection to even limited reciprocity has been the risk that reciprocity will be used and that retaliation would follow. The impact could be devastating to confidence in world financial markets and established patterns of monetary and capital flows.[1]

—David C. Mulford, former Under Secretary of the US Treasury

Judge not, that ye be not judged.   —Matthew 7:1

The United States has long sought to ensure access to foreign markets for US financial firms. Until the late 1980s, however, the United States deliberately eschewed making demands for reciprocity backed by retaliatory threats to open foreign financial markets. US policy is changing, and there is considerable political pressure to seek some form of reciprocity and to use threats of retaliation to open foreign markets.

This chapter assesses the evolution of US policy through two case studies of recent US efforts to secure or maintain access to Japanese and European financial markets. The lesson we draw from these two incidents is a cautionary one. Reciprocity is a dangerous, two-edged sword: it creates precedents that can later be used against the United States. US policymakers effectively used reciprocity to open up the Japanese government bond market. But the United States was made profoundly uncomfortable by the European Community's calls for reciprocity in exchange for access to the newly liberalized European financial market. Our advice to US policymakers is: do unto other economic superpowers as you would

---

1. Testimony before the Task Force on the International Competitiveness of US Financial Institutions, House Committee on Banking, Finance and Urban Affairs, 28 February 1990.

have them do unto you. In the final section, we discuss alternative bargaining approaches to secure financial market access that would be preferable to unilateral demands backed by threats of retaliation.

US Policy on Access to Financial Markets

Until fairly recently, the US approach to financial market access has been to provide, and to seek from foreign governments, unconditional national treatment (see box 11.1 for a glossary of market-access terms). The US Treasury defines national treatment as granting foreign firms equality of competitive opportunity with domestic firms in similar circumstances (US Department of the Treasury 1986). The Federal Reserve Board considers that equality of competitive opportunities "exists if US companies are allowed to compete on essentially equal terms with domestic institutions in the host country, even if some specific regulations or requirements applied to US companies differ from those applicable to domestic companies" (US Federal Reserve System Board of Governors 1989).[2]

As is illustrated in what follows, national treatment is a somewhat ambiguous concept, and that ambiguity can be a source of international tension. But at the broadest level, national treatment means that governments should treat foreign firms at least as well as domestic firms and that any discriminatory treatment should not impede foreign firms' ability to compete in the host-country market.

Traditionally, the United States has provided *unconditional* national treatment to foreign firms. Of course, the United States also exhorts other countries to grant national treatment to US firms. But the United States has not, until recently, required foreign governments to reciprocate with national treatment for American firms as the quid pro quo for access to the US market.

There have been two main rationales for the US policy of unconditional national treatment. First, the Federal Reserve and, until recently, the Treasury have emphasized that the United States benefits from having foreign competition and investment and that open US financial markets serve as a model for other countries. The benefits of free trade in financial services are, like the benefits of free trade in goods, lower prices and greater

---

2. A distinction is sometimes made between de facto and de jure national treatment. The distinction highlights the fact that even if foreign and domestic firms operate in an identical legal and regulatory framework (de jure national treatment), foreign firms may suffer a disproportionate adverse impact that could constitute de facto denial of equality of competitive opportunities. US government authorities tend to use the phrase "equality of competitive opportunity" synonymously with de facto national treatment. In what follows, all references to national treatment are to the de facto version, unless otherwise specified. We use national treatment to refer both to entry and operation in a host-country market. In practice, national treatment does not necessarily include the right of establishment.

product diversity for consumers. Moreover, the United States is more credible in calling on other countries to liberalize because it can cite its own openness and the benefits of such a policy.

The second rationale for unconditional national treatment is less explicit than the first but is often voiced in private by Treasury and Fed officials. These officials are nervous about reciprocity in any form because they fear it might lead to conflicts, in turn disrupting global financial markets and injuring US firms. Former Treasury Under Secretary Mulford's 1990 statement at the beginning of this chapter is a rare public expression of this aversion to reciprocity. It is worth exploring in some detail the US regulatory authorities' concerns about reciprocity because they go to the heart of the debate about whether "tough" trade policy works and, equally important, whether it is worth the risks.

The Treasury, which is the lead US agency on financial market access, has been under considerable pressure over the last 10 years to secure better access for US firms in foreign financial markets. This pressure comes from both Congress and the private sector. It reflects their concern that foreign firms benefit from access to open US financial markets, but American firms do not receive equality of competitive opportunity in some foreign markets. Over time, the Treasury has shifted its position on unconditional national treatment toward acceptance of reciprocal national treatment.

The US policy of unconditional national treatment is enshrined in the International Banking Act (IBA) of 1978. The IBA was itself a response to congressional and private-sector complaints that the absence of a comprehensive US regulatory framework governing foreign banks gave them a competitive advantage over US firms. The IBA sought to establish a regulatory environment in which US and foreign firms would enjoy equality of competitive opportunities in the US market. In general, the act provides foreign firms with national treatment and, in some cases, with better-than-national treatment by grandfathering certain pre-1978 activities.[3]

Reflecting congressional concern over US firms' access to foreign markets, the IBA also required a Treasury assessment of whether US financial firms receive national treatment abroad. Congress has requested periodic updates of these national treatment studies to pressure the Treasury to act vigorously to secure competitive opportunities for US firms. The first such study was issued in 1979 and was updated in 1984 and 1986 at the request of Senator Jake Garn (R-UT), then-chairman of the Senate Banking Committee.[4] In his letter to Treasury Secretary James Baker requesting

---

3. See Houpt (1986) for discussion of the evolution of US international banking laws.

4. The fourth national treatment study, issued in December 1990, was required by the Omnibus Trade and Competitiveness Act of 1988, which mandates updates at least every four years.

the 1986 study, Senator Garn expressed concern "over the continuing slowness of progress by some of our trading partners toward treatment of our institutions with the same fairness that we treat theirs." Senator Garn reminded Secretary Baker that in 1983 the senator had introduced legislation that would require US regulators to use reciprocity as a criterion in considering foreign banks' applications to establish US branches (US Treasury 1986, 230–31).

The US Treasury at that time strongly opposed any notion of reciprocity. In his response to Senator Garn's letter, before the 1986 study was even begun, Secretary Baker reminded the senator that "the Treasury continues to believe that a policy of national treatment, seeking equality of competitive opportunity, is preferable to a policy based on reciprocity" (letter from Secretary Baker to Senator Garn, printed in US Treasury 1986, 232).

In responding to "reciprocity" proposals, the Treasury has often interpreted the term in its strictest sense as mirror-image reciprocity.[5] Mirror-image reciprocity would require US authorities to grant to foreign banks only those rights that their home countries allow to US firms. The Treasury argued that this approach would be an administrative nightmare, unworkable in practice. Roughly 60 foreign countries have banks in the United States. Under mirror-image reciprocity, the US government might face the difficult task of administering up to 60 different regulatory regimes for foreign banks.

A second Treasury objection to mirror-image reciprocity was that it could hurt US firms. The Treasury has been uncomfortably conscious of the fact that foreign governments could emulate US demands for reciprocity, to the detriment of American firms. In its 1986 national treatment study, the Treasury presciently warned that US firms would be particularly vulnerable to demands for mirror-image reciprocity from countries with universal banking systems, under which banks are allowed to conduct securities activities (US Treasury 1986, 19). Germany, France, and to a lesser extent the United Kingdom permit universal banking. By contrast, the Glass-Steagall Act in the United States and Article 65 of the Securities and Exchange Law in Japan generally prohibit both foreign and domestic banks from owning securities operations. Under the national treatment principle, US banks are allowed to engage in securities business in Germany and the United Kingdom, and German and British banks cannot own securities affiliates in the United States.[6] Under the principle of mir-

---

5. See, for example, Treasury Secretary Donald Regan's testimony before the Senate Banking Committee on Senator Garn's bill, where he acknowledges that the bill does not seek mirror-image reciprocity and then proceeds to critique mirror-image reciprocity (excerpted in US Treasury 1986, 18).

6. However, 17 foreign banks' securities operations in the United States were grandfathered by the International Banking Act—an example of better-than-national treatment. Under pressure from the European and US governments, Japan has allowed foreign banks to establish securities affiliates in Japan—another instance of better-than-national treatment.

Box 11.1 Market access terminology: A reader's guide

The very ambiguity of the concept of reciprocity can itself be a source of international conflict. To help clarify the discussion, we offer the following definitions of some frequently used terms. Seen from the perspective of a country that has relatively few barriers to foreign firms, the terms are listed in ascending order of the level of demands they make for openness in foreign markets.

Unconditional National Treatment: A policy that treats foreign firms at least as well domestic firms, in fact as well as in law. Any discriminatory treatment should not impede foreign firms' ability to compete on essentially equal terms with domestic firms. Example: the US International Banking Act of 1978 enshrined the principle in US law.

Reciprocal (Conditional) National Treatment: A policy that conditions the offer of national treatment to foreign firms on the provision of national treatment by their home governments. Examples: the Schumer amendment to the US Omnibus Trade and Competitiveness Act of 1988 and the EC's Second Banking Directive of 1989 (see, however, "effective market access," below), and the Fair Trade in Financial Services bills of the 1990s.

Effective Market Access: An ambiguous term introduced by the European Community in its Second Banking Directive. In one context in the directive, it seems to be synonymous with reciprocal national treatment. In a second context, it appears to imply a more demanding type of reciprocity, perhaps mirror-image reciprocity (see below).

Better-than-National Treatment: A policy that provides foreign firms with better competitive opportunities than domestic firms. Examples: provisions of the US International Banking Act of 1978 and current Japanese government policies, respectively, that allow some foreign banks under certain conditions to conduct securities business in the United States and Japan, although domestic firms are not allowed to do so.

Mirror-Image Reciprocity: Viewed from a US perspective, a policy that would give foreign firms only those rights that their home countries allow US firms. Examples: the original draft of the Second Banking Directive was interpreted by some as demanding that US financial authorities allow EC firms the same rights in the US market that US firms receive in the Community, and the original House version of the Schumer bill contained a similar demand for "equal access." The final versions of the Second Banking Directive and the Schumer amendment reverted to reciprocal national treatment.

ror-image reciprocity, US banks operating in universal banking countries could be prohibited from conducting securities operations there.

Other financial market regulators, particularly the Fed, also are concerned that reciprocity could lead to retaliation and thence to global financial market instability. Indeed, their counterparts in central banks and finance ministries in the other major banking centers share US officials' concerns. The regulators' overriding objective is to maintain the safety and soundness of the financial system. Financial authorities worry that US demands for some form of reciprocity could lead to US retaliation and foreign counterretaliation. They warn that such financial conflicts could impede financial flows, damage firms under the US authorities' supervision, and, in the worst case, precipitate a financial market crisis. They are also concerned that conflicts over reciprocity could undermine their cooperative efforts in other areas, such as exchange rate management and bank supervision.

The US financial authorities' aversion to reciprocity was reinforced in the late 1980s and early 1990s by the growing importance of foreign purchases of US government debt in financing the budget deficit. They worry that, at a minimum, restraints on foreign participation in US financial markets, particularly US government debt markets, would reduce demand, raise interest rates, and thus make it more expensive to finance the deficit.

Many regulators thus prefer unconditional national treatment over reciprocity because it preserves the benefits of open financial markets at home and reduces the risks of international conflicts that could hurt US firms and destabilize global markets. In the view of many financial regulators, the potential costs of market disruption or closure through retaliation outweigh the potential gains in market access from the successful use of reciprocity.

The Treasury has, however, responded to congressional and private-sector pressures to secure equality of competitive opportunities for US firms operating abroad. Until the early 1990s, the Treasury sought international acceptance of unconditional national treatment through both multilateral and bilateral negotiations. US efforts in multilateral forums focused largely on the Organization for Economic Cooperation and Development and on the GATT services negotiations in the Uruguay Round. In the OECD, the United States exhorted its trading partners to adhere to national treatment (OECD, "Declaration on International Investment and Multinational Enterprises," Paris, 2 June 1976). In the Uruguay Round negotiations, the United States initially urged that unconditional national treatment be a guiding principle for liberalization of financial services, but by 1991 Treasury shifted to a reciprocal or conditional national treatment approach.

The United States also has actively sought national treatment from its trading partners in bilateral negotiations. The national treatment principle is often embodied in the Treaties of Friendship, Commerce, and Navigation and the Bilateral Investment Treaties that the United States has signed with many of its trading partners. Moreover, as the national treatment studies document, the Treasury has held extensive bilateral discussions to encourage further liberalization in countries where US firms have complained of inequality of competitive opportunity.

Critics of unconditional national treatment complain that the pace of foreign liberalization has been too slow and that US firms still face significant problems of market access. The leading targets of US firms' complaints have been Japan and several developing countries, including China, Korea, Taiwan, Brazil, and Mexico until the 1993 NAFTA.[7] Proponents of legislation requiring conditional national treatment claim it would give the Treasury a more effective lever to pry open foreign markets.

In recent years, the Congress has repeatedly sought to pass legislation mandating financial market reciprocity. In addition to Senator Garn's 1983 proposal, in 1987 and 1988 the Senate passed two reciprocity bills that subsequently failed to pass the House of Representatives.[8] There was considerable debate over financial market reciprocity in the drafting of the Omnibus Trade and Competitiveness Act of 1988. In the end, the 1988 act contained only one provision on financial market reciprocity: the Primary Dealers Act, better known as the Schumer amendment, after its author, Congressman Charles Schumer (D-NY).

The Schumer amendment, which is discussed at length in the next section, is an important step in the evolution of US financial market access policy for several reasons. First, the Schumer amendment stands out as the first and thus far the only US legislation that mandates financial market reciprocity. Second, it set a precedent in defining reciprocity as reciprocal national treatment, meaning that foreign firms would receive national treatment in the US market only if their home countries offered equality of competitive opportunities to US firms. This precedent was adopted by the European Community in its Second Banking Directive and by the Senate Banking Committee in its various Fair Trade in Financial Services bills introduced between 1990 and 1994. Third, the reciprocity provision was carefully crafted to put pressure on Japan, reflecting Congress's view that market access in Japan should be a high priority.

The Schumer Amendment

Since the early 1980s, Japan has been the primary target of US efforts to promote financial market liberalization and market access for foreign firms. The two countries have held ongoing and extensive negotiations on these issues, but many US observers characterize progress as frustratingly slow. The languid pace of Japanese liberalization, together with the rapid growth of Japanese firms' operations in US financial markets, has stimulated considerable pressure from Congress and the private sector for reciprocity.

US efforts to encourage Japanese financial liberalization began in 1983 with the creation of a US Treasury and Japanese Finance Ministry working

---

7. See US Department of the Treasury (1986, 234–35) for the results of a survey of US banks' complaints that was conducted by the Bankers' Association for Foreign Trade. See also the 1990 national treatment study.

8. See Title XV of Senate bill 1409 in 1987 and sections 909 and 910 of the Proxmire Financial Modernization Act of 1988.

group on yen-dollar exchange rate issues. These yen-dollar talks addressed three issues: internationalization of the yen, market access for foreign financial firms, and liberalization and deregulation of Japanese financial markets to allow interest rates to be market-determined.[9] In what follows, we summarize the results of the market-access discussions.

In the 1983–84 yen-dollar negotiations, the Japanese affirmed their commitment to provide foreign firms with equal competitive opportunities. The Japanese addressed long-standing foreign complaints about the lack of transparency in the regulatory and policy process by acknowledging that greater transparency was "a central element in facilitating both the access of non-Japanese financial institutions to and their operations in Japanese capital markets" (Japanese Ministry of Finance–US Department of the Treasury Working Group 1984, 22). To improve transparency the Japanese issued written guidelines, eliminated swap limits on the conversion of foreign currency into yen, liberalized rules on overseas yen lending, and clarified brokerage requirements in the bill discount market.

The Japanese also responded to several specific US complaints about market access. For example, they allowed three US banks to acquire securities branches during the course of the negotiations (Frankel 1984, 46). Foreign firms also complained that, despite changes in the Tokyo Stock Exchange's constitution to permit foreign membership, the lack of available seats effectively excluded foreign members. The Ministry of Finance explained that the Tokyo Stock Exchange was an autonomous organization outside its control but agreed to ask the exchange to study ways to facilitate foreign membership and to assist foreign firms' efforts to join. In May 1984, the ministry agreed to a new policy permitting foreign banks to engage in the increasingly lucrative management of trust funds.

The final market-access issue covered in the 1983–84 yen-dollar talks was the problem of foreign participation in the Japanese government bond market, an issue that the Schumer amendment subsequently addressed in 1987–88. Until 1984 foreign firms had been denied access to the underwriting syndicate for 10-year bonds, the most important and heavily traded government debt instruments. In April 1984 several foreign firms were admitted to the syndicate and together received a share of less than 1 percent of the issue (US Federal Reserve System Board of Governors 1989, 22).

The problem of foreign participation in the Japanese government bond market took on symbolic importance because, like barriers to membership in the Tokyo Stock Exchange, it was a clear denial of national treatment. The US Treasury continued to press the issue in subsequent yen-dollar discussions. Treasury urged that foreign firms be allocated larger shares

---

9. For a description of the early discussions, see Japanese Ministry of Finance–US Department of the Treasury Working Group (1984) and Frankel (1984).

within the syndicate and that an auction system be created to allow Japanese and foreign firms to compete in the important 10-year bond market.

Notwithstanding the Treasury's urgings, progress on market access in the government bond market was slow. This modest progress was particularly galling to some members of Congress because several Japanese-owned firms already were primary dealers in the US government securities market and still others were applying for primary dealer status.[10] The applications of Nomura Securities and Daiwa Securities to the Fed prompted 38 congressmen, headed by Charles Schumer, to send a letter on 30 October 1985 to Gerald Corrigan, president of the Federal Reserve Bank of New York, complaining about the continued market-access problems that US securities firms faced in Japan. The congressmen urged Corrigan to deny primary dealer status to Nomura and Daiwa "until United States–based securities firms are accorded full reciprocal treatment in the Japanese securities markets." Corrigan responded by noting that Congress had rejected reciprocity in the International Banking Act of 1978. He pointed out that the Federal Reserve was instead guided by the principle of national treatment, and he emphasized that the Fed was "strongly encouraging other countries to open their doors as we open ours" (Gerald Corrigan, 27 December 1985 letter to Congressman Schumer).

Congressman Schumer continued to press Corrigan on the issue of reciprocity in 1986. He warned that "where the benefits of a policy of national treatment are so lopsided in favor of the firms of one of our trading partners, that policy cannot last very long" (24 July 1986 letter to Gerald Corrigan).

In December 1986, the Federal Reserve Bank of New York announced the addition of five new primary dealers, including Nomura and Daiwa. The New York Fed also approved two foreign acquisitions of existing primary dealers, one of which (Aubrey Lanston) was purchased by a subsidiary of the Industrial Bank of Japan.

The New York Fed also released a letter from Corrigan to Congressman Schumer explaining the Fed's decision. The letter addressed an issue of mounting concern to the US financial and policy communities: the large US dependence on foreign financing for the federal budget deficit. Corrigan emphasized the benefits of foreign participation in the US government debt markets "at a time when the enormous burden of our cumulative fiscal deficits makes this especially important" (11 December 1986 letter to Congressman Schumer).

Corrigan reported further liberalization in Japan, including Finance Ministry support for a larger allocation of underwriting shares for foreign

---

10. Primary dealers are firms authorized to trade government securities directly with the Federal Reserve Bank of New York and that serve as market makers.

firms in the government bond market. The letter reaffirmed the US commitment to national treatment. But Corrigan also pointedly noted the Fed's "expectations that naming Japanese-owned firms as primary dealers must be viewed as a catalyst for further significant actions such as these with respect to the Japanese market in the period ahead." He also issued a clear warning of an adverse Fed reaction if Japanese efforts to improve market access should falter. "Absent that flow of [market-opening] actions, we would see little scope for further action on our part and might well have to rethink actions already taken" (11 December 1986 letter to Congressman Schumer, p. 3).

In concluding his letter to Congressman Schumer, however, Corrigan emphasized the Fed's priority of maintaining the soundness and safety of global financial markets. He pointed to the emergence of a single, around-the-clock global market in London, New York, and Tokyo and the need for convergence in the regulatory and supervisory regimes in these financial centers. He closed by observing that "while achieving more open access to foreign financial markets is important, we must not lose sight of longer run issues raised by the globalization of our financial markets" (11 December 1986 letter to Congressman Schumer, p. 4).[11]

In March 1987, Congressman Schumer introduced his amendment to H.R. 3, the House of Representatives' version of the 1988 trade bill. The Schumer amendment prohibited the Federal Reserve from designating, or continuing a prior designation of, foreign firms as primary dealers in US government securities if their home governments denied US firms "equal access" in their government securities markets. "Equal access" roughly meant mirror-image reciprocity because it required that foreign governments allow US firms "to act in a capacity that is substantially equivalent to that in which the United States permits primary dealers to act."[12]

In April 1987, shortly after introducing his reciprocity bill, Congressman Schumer traveled to Japan with a delegation that included Jake Garn (R-UT), who was the senior Republican on the Senate Banking Committee, and several influential members of the House Banking and Budget Committees. The delegation met with Prime Minister Yasuhiro Nakasone, Finance Minister Kiichi Miyazawa, and top executives of Japanese banks and securities firms to strongly urge further and faster opening of Japanese financial markets. Their objectives included expanded foreign membership in the Tokyo Stock Exchange and greater participation in the government bond market. Schumer earned the sobriquet "Hurricane Schumer" in the Japanese press for the vigor of his advocacy.

---

11. At that time, US and British financial authorities were exhorting Japan to join them in an agreement on minimum capital levels for banks. Corrigan may have worried that market-access negotiations might complicate discussions on capital requirements.

12. Omnibus Trade and Competitiveness Act of 1988, Conference Report to Accompany H.R. 3, Report 100-576, 20 April 1988, 854.

The visiting congressmen supported US firms' request that 10-year government bonds be issued by auction rather than through fixed allocations in the syndicate. In a 24 April 1987 letter about the trip to House Banking Committee Chairman Fernand St. Germain, Schumer reported that "the top executives of the four largest securities firms in Japan indicated a willingness to participate in an open auction system, but so far the proposal has met stiff opposition from the Finance Ministry, particularly within the Banking Bureau, which is reluctant to relinquish the banking syndicate's dominant position in this field."

The use of foreign pressure (called *gaiatsu* in Japanese) to strengthen the position of Japanese government officials and domestic firms that seek liberalization is a well-known tactic (see chapters 5 and 10). In the case of the 10-year bond market, the supporters of liberalization appear to have been the large Japanese securities houses. Within the 10-year bond syndicate, banks were allocated a fixed share of 76 percent, and securities firms received 24 percent of new issues. The smaller securities firms were allocated a disproportionately large share of the market. The big Japanese securities firms were reportedly eager to expand their restricted share of the market and therefore found US pressure for an auction helpful. The Finance Ministry's Banking Bureau, which regulates the banks, the banks themselves, and smaller securities firms are said to have opposed the auction system. The big securities firms, the Finance Ministry's Securities Bureau, and some officials within the International Finance Bureau and the Government Debt Division supported the proposed change.

Congressman Schumer argued that his proposed legislation would give leverage to Japanese supporters of market opening:

> There are people on the Japanese scene who wish to open up Japanese players, but they cannot, and the bottom line reason that I think legislation works better in fact than talking—if the legislation is narrowly and carefully drawn, as I believe the [Schumer] proposal in the House is—is that it changes the playing field.
>
> In fact what we are doing is giving those forces in Japan that want to open up a weapon. They go to the Ministry of Finance and they say . . . look, if you do not do it, we have certain problems that we did not have before.[13]

The congressional delegation's visit, the Schumer amendment per se, and more generally the House of Representatives' passage of a trade bill replete with tough reciprocity provisions such as the Gephardt amendment appears to have shaken the Japanese financial community. High-level executives from Nomura and Daiwa, which were targets of the original Schumer bill, publicly called for a switch to a government bond auction and expanded membership for foreigners on the Tokyo Stock Exchange ("Schumer, Gephardt Amendments Alarm Japanese Business

---

13. US Senate, Committee on the Budget, Hearings on United States' Access to the Japanese Financial Markets, 6 May 1987, 99–100.

Community," *Japan Economic Journal*, 9 May 1987, 1).[14] In April and May 1987, the Ministry of Finance announced the introduction of a limited auction for 20 percent of the 10-year bond issue, and the stock exchange announced plans to expand its membership and consider additional foreign applications.

On 27 May and 4 June 1987, Makoto Utsumi, director general of the Finance Ministry's International Finance Bureau, wrote to Schumer, informing him of these and other actions to increase foreign firms' access to Japanese financial markets.[15] Schumer claimed credit for the introduction of the auction, saying it was "a direct result of pressure brought by the Schumer amendment, according to Finance Ministry officials" (Office of Congressman Charles Schumer, press release, "Status of Action on Japanese Financial Market Issues," 9 June 1987).

In May 1987, Senate Banking Committee Chairman Donald Riegle (D-MI) introduced the Senate's counterpart to the Schumer amendment. The bill differed from Mr. Schumer's in one critically important respect: it substituted reciprocal national treatment for mirror-image reciprocity (or, "equal access") as the standard against which to judge foreign applications for primary dealer status. This reciprocal national treatment standard eventually became law in the Omnibus Trade and Competitiveness Act of 1988.

The Treasury and Federal Reserve strongly opposed the Schumer amendment. In March 1987, when it was introduced in the House Banking Committee, Treasury officials reportedly told the committee's chairman, Fernand St. Germain, that the president considered the amendment so unacceptable that he might veto the entire trade bill.

While publicly opposing the Schumer amendment, Treasury used the threat of legislation to press Japan for further liberalization. In April 1987, before the congressional delegation arrived in Japan, the Ministry of Finance announced modest increases in the share of foreign firms in the bond syndicate. In July, Treasury Assistant Secretary David Mulford, who was in charge of the yen-dollar negotiations, emphatically warned Japan that Treasury faced growing political pressure to abandon the US policy of unconditional national treatment for Japanese financial firms in the United States. He complained that Japanese firms with international financial operations should be strongly promoting openness in Japan but in fact were not. Mulford pointedly cited the slow pace of liberalization in the government bond market: "The share of issues underwritten by

---

14. The Gephardt amendment, subsequently abandoned, threatened import barriers against countries, particularly Japan, that maintained large trade surpluses vis-à-vis the United States (see chapter 2 for more details).

15. Utsumi's letter of 4 June also announced that Ministry of Finance had invited four US banks' securities affiliates to apply for securities licenses in Japan, a privilege denied Japanese banks and an example of better-than-national treatment.

all foreign firms was recently increased from 0.9 percent to 2.2 percent. When no such restriction exists in our government bond market, this kind of penny ante response to a major issue of access and fairness is the kind of action which is undermining Japan's credibility" (Remarks before The Japan Society, printed in *Treasury News*, 16 July 1987).

Federal Reserve Bank of New York President Gerald Corrigan also opposed the Schumer amendment. He told the Senate Budget Committee that Japan was making progress on financial market access and therefore:

> ... I am opposed to legislative efforts along the lines of the so-called "primary dealer" amendment that was incorporated into the trade bill passed by the House or as recently proposed by Senators Proxmire and Riegle. As I see it, such legislation could have the effect of stalling rather than accelerating discussions and negotiations, while possibly producing unintended adverse side effects—both in terms of general attitudes toward market liberalization and attitudes regarding capital inflows to the U.S. It would be one thing to consider a legislative approach in an environment in which progress and good faith negotiations were not taking place. However, this is not the current situation. (Statement before the Senate Committee on the Budget, 6 May 1987, 9)

US financial firms with operations in Japan were noticeably reluctant to publicly support the Schumer amendment. In Schumer's private meetings with US banking and securities executives in Japan in March 1987, they reportedly were reticent to talk about their market-access problems until one executive from a US bank broke the ice, and a deluge of complaints followed. In the Senate Budget Committee's hearings on US access to Japanese financial markets, Chairman Lawton Chiles (D-FL) reported that several US firms declined to testify because they feared Japanese retaliation. Corrigan replied that he could not judge whether US firms' fears had any basis in fact but noted that, on market-access problems, US firms "sure as hell are not shy about talking about them to me" (Senate Committee on the Budget, 6 May 1987, 64).

In our interviews with US financial executives, we found none who acknowledged supporting the Schumer amendment. Many members of the US financial community were privately vociferous in their complaints about market access in Japan, although most also acknowledged significant cumulative progress since the mid-1980s. It may be that US financial firms with substantial operations in Japan welcomed the pressure Schumer's bill placed on the Japanese but avoided public support for fear of retaliation by Finance Ministry officials, who like all regulators, have innumerable ways of making life unpleasant for firms they oversee. The large US financial firms, moreover, also share some of the regulators' distaste for reciprocity legislation and disliked the precedent the US legislation set. Several of them, notably the international banks, know that they could be targets for retaliation, particularly in Europe, where universal banking is the norm. It could be that US firms preferred a form of brinkmanship, where the threat of legislation brought improvements in market access, but the legislation was not passed.

Faced with strong opposition from Treasury and the Federal Reserve and at best tepid public support from the US financial community, the House and Senate readily agreed to a compromise in April 1988 that substituted reciprocal national treatment for mirror-image reciprocity. The final version of the Primary Dealers Act of 1988 illustratively lists seven types of discriminatory barriers facing US firms in Japan. However, it requires the Federal Reserve to seek reciprocal national treatment for US firms abroad in only one specific area: the underwriting and distribution of government debt instruments. The Fed is enjoined from designating, or continuing to designate, foreign firms as primary dealers if their home countries do not accord US firms equality of competitive opportunities.

The act grandfathers firms that had acquired, or informed the Fed of their intention to acquire, a primary dealer before 31 July 1987. It also exempts firms from Israel and Canada because of their free trade agreements with the United States. The act went into effect 12 months after passage of the 1988 Trade Act.

Congressional staff report that there was no disagreement on the adoption of a reciprocal national treatment standard in place of the mirror-image reciprocity ("equal access") criterion in the House bill. The staff felt that Schumer readily understood the dangers and drawbacks of mirror-image reciprocity. They speculated that he initially adopted it to get Japanese attention and as a tactical negotiating position with Congress and the administration. Adoption of reciprocal national treatment, instead of mirror-image reciprocity, may have helped reduce if not eliminate the Treasury's and Fed's opposition and made a presidential veto less likely.

The grandfathering of existing operations is fairly standard legislative procedure. It is also consistent with the precedent of the International Banking Act of 1978, which grandfathered certain operations of foreign firms. The cutoff date for grandfathering existing firms, however, was a matter for negotiation. The 31 July 1987 cutoff date was a compromise, apparently intended to leave the big Japanese securities firms, particularly Daiwa and Nomura, vulnerable to US retaliation while grandfathering the operations of a number of Japanese banks, including the Industrial Bank of Japan's recent acquisition of the primary dealer Aubrey Lanston. It is not clear whether the date was chosen to put maximum pressure on Japanese-owned primary dealers to support liberalization of the government bond market. Certainly, it put pressure on the big-four securities houses, which were already in favor of a bond auction. But selection of an earlier cutoff could have also pressured one or more powerful Japanese banks that were large Japanese government bond dealers and that opposed the auction system.

The decision to have the act go into effect one year after passage of the Omnibus Trade and Competitiveness Act of 1988 was also a compromise.

It was felt that the one-year grace period gave the Japanese reasonable time to improve the competitive opportunities of foreign firms. The president signed the trade act, which contained the Schumer amendment, on 23 August 1988. The Primary Dealers Act, therefore, went into effect 23 August 1989.

In September 1988, two weeks after passage of the 1988 Trade Act, the Japanese Ministry of Finance announced a further opening of the government bond market. As of 1 April 1989, 40 percent (up from the previous 20 percent) of the 10-year bond issue would be auctioned by competitive bidding. Foreign firms' share of the 60 percent of the issue still allocated by the syndicate would rise to almost 8 percent (from 2.5 percent) effective 1 October 1988. In addition, foreign firms would be allowed to be co-managers of the issue, and Salomon Brothers subsequently became the first foreign co-lead manager ("Japan Unveils New Measures to Widen Foreign Role in Government Bond Market," *Wall Street Journal*, 7 September 1988).

These new market-opening initiatives were applauded by Federal Reserve Bank of New York President Corrigan and Treasury Assistant Secretary Mulford. US financial executives at Merrill Lynch and Salomon Brothers also welcomed them. And Schumer was triumphant:

> Our campaign to open up Japanese financial markets without resorting to protectionism is succeeding in a big way. This is a major triumph for a tough but fair approach to trade policy, and hopefully the next president will see the success we have had in this area and use it as a model for trade policy as a whole. (*Wall Street Journal*, 7 September 1988)

In early 1989, in preparation for its ruling under the Schumer amendment, the Federal Reserve undertook a study of Japanese and other government bond markets to determine if US firms were denied equality of competitive opportunities (US Federal Reserve System Board of Governors 1989). The Fed's report is notable because it provides the first serious conceptual framework for evaluating whether foreign firms enjoy de facto national treatment. Moreover, the Fed was very conscious that it was setting a significant precedent for subsequent assessments of national treatment, not just by US authorities, but also by foreign authorities, particularly the European Community.

The Fed's report focused on de facto national treatment because de jure discrimination against foreign firms is relatively easy to identify. The report defined four criteria for determining whether foreign firms are especially competitively disadvantaged by laws, regulations, policies, or practices that are not explicitly discriminatory.

The first criterion asks whether "foreign firms suffer a significantly disproportionate impact from a particular law, regulation, or practice, or is the adverse impact widely shared by domestic firms as well?" The report suggested that circumstantial, but not conclusive, evidence of denial of equal competitive opportunities "would exist if foreign firms were largely absent from a significant market. . . ."

The second criterion is whether a suspect rule, law, or practice can be explained "in terms of clear and compelling economic goals." Rules without a reasonable economic justification would be judged less favorably than those with a compelling rationale. The Fed was careful to emphasize that "equal competitive opportunities do not require a near duplication abroad of the familiar conditions prevailing in home markets." Thus, for example, the existence of a government bond syndicate rather than an auction system is not necessarily evidence of denial of national treatment if there is an economic efficiency rationale for the syndicate. Possibly anticipating European criticism of US laws such as the Glass-Steagall and McFadden Acts, the Fed also strongly emphasized its belief that "national authorities must preserve the right to determine the structure of their own financial markets" if they can be justified in reasonable economic terms.

The third criterion is whether foreign firms face market-access problems similar to the normal difficulties new or small entrants face in any market. Such inherent market-access problems are not a denial of national treatment.

The final criterion is whether foreign firms can express their views to host-country authorities. This criterion attempts to get at the alleged lack of policy transparency in Japan. The Fed's criterion goes beyond simple transparency, however, and asks further whether the host country's financial authorities are responsive to legitimate foreign complaints about denial of competitive opportunities. The report argues that if the authorities are taking or planning actions that will remove impediments to foreign firms, this is evidence of "an environment of equal competitive opportunities."

The Fed applied these criteria to the government bond markets of Japan and the United Kingdom, the two countries immediately affected by the Schumer amendment.[16] It found that neither Japan nor the United Kingdom denied foreign firms equality of competitive opportunities.

The Fed, however, did not give Japan an unequivocal clean bill of health. The report acknowledged that there had been substantial progress in opening the government debt market, particularly in the important 10-year bond market. But it also pointed to continuing concerns of foreign firms about market access. The report therefore recommended that Fed officials continue to use every opportunity to urge Japan to liberalize.

On 21 August 1989 the Federal Reserve Board voted 5 to 1 to allow Japanese firms subject to the Schumer amendment to continue as primary dealers. The dissenting vote came from Governor Martha Seger, who was skeptical of whether much progress had been made in opening the

---

16. The report also surveyed the government bond markets of the Federal Republic of Germany and Switzerland because of possible future applications for primary dealer status from firms from these countries.

government bond market. Moreover, other board members made it clear that their decision was not irrevocable and that continuing progress was required (*Wall Street Journal*, 22 August 1989, A2).

Congressman Schumer was mildly critical of the report. He acknowledged that the Fed's decision was correct because of Japan's efforts to open the market. But he worried that the Fed, by taking such a positive tone, might have lost leverage with the Japanese. He felt "the Fed should have said the Japanese are on the right road, but aren't all the way there yet" (*Wall Street Journal*, 22 August 1989, A2).

The US financial community's reaction was grudgingly favorable to the report. During its preparation, the Fed had consulted extensively with US financial firms. None of these firms urged the Fed to deny primary dealer status to Japanese firms, although several voiced continuing concern about the pace and extent of Japan's liberalization.

Did the threat of the Schumer amendment play an important role in opening the Japanese government bond market? Those we interviewed in government and the financial community were virtually unanimous in saying that it did.

Why was the Schumer amendment effective? Explanations varied. Many observers pointed to fairly strong pressures from within Japan to liberalize the market. As noted earlier, the large securities houses were particularly eager to increase their market shares. They reportedly found US demands for an auction to be helpful in supporting their own position. Of course, the fact that the four largest Japanese securities firms also were vulnerable to US retaliation sharpened their interest in liberalization.

Primary dealer status was viewed as an important objective for the large Japanese securities firms. The US government debt market is by far the largest in the world, and US securities are traded globally. Being a primary dealer is not a particularly lucrative business, but this status is important for firms that aspire to be major players in global government debt markets. The Fed denies that primary dealers enjoy any special relationship with it. However, primary dealer status does confer prestige, and certain large investors will do business only with primary dealers. Moreover, primary dealers are the firms closest to the market and may receive some informational advantages from this proximity.

Many of the largest banks strenuously opposed opening the market because they feared a loss of market share. However, several fairly large and medium-sized banks saw the auction system as a way of improving their position. Finance Ministry officials reported that these divisions within the Japanese banking community helped neutralize the opposition of the big banks.

Conditions in the Japanese government bond market may have also facilitated the willingness to move to an auction system. Japanese interest rates fell substantially between 1983 and the first quarter of 1987, when they stabilized. At the same time, the volume of new issues of 10-year bonds was declining. Both factors contributed to a strong bond market, and this in turn may have muted Japanese banks' and securities firms' opposition to new foreign entrants.

Within the Japanese government, there were conflicting views on the merits of opening the market further. The Ministry of Finance's Banking Bureau opposed liberalization because it could weaken the dominant position in the market of the banks it regulated. The ministry's Securities Bureau supported liberalization to enhance the position of the securities firms it regulated. Others in the Finance Ministry are reported to have been influenced by US arguments that greater competition in the market would lower the costs of issuing government debt. Still others in the ministry supported this liberalization as part of a larger process of enhancing Tokyo's status as a global financial center. The prime minister's office and the Foreign Ministry reportedly were eager to avoid yet another conflict with the United States, particularly in 1989, when the Japanese government was expecting significant trade tension due to the new super 301 retaliatory provisions of the 1988 Trade Act (see chapter 2).

The Schumer amendment was intelligently designed to place heavy pressure on the Japanese government and securities firms. The key ingredients in that pressure were the mandatory nature of retaliation and the presence of a one-year deadline.

The threat of retaliation was credible because the Federal Reserve had limited discretion. Of course, the Fed had to use its own judgment in determining whether US firms had equality of competitive opportunities in the Japanese market. And the Fed itself was on record as strongly opposing reciprocity and the Schumer amendment. But the Fed's decision also was under intense public scrutiny and the Congress's watchful eye. The fact that the Fed is an independent agency that zealously guards its autonomy added to the credibility that its decision would be made on strictly economic criteria. To allow more Japanese firms primary dealer status, the Federal Reserve therefore had to find strong evidence that Japan was making substantial efforts to open the market. The Japanese government was faced with a clear choice: liberalize substantially or face certain retaliation.

When it appeared likely that the Schumer amendment would be enacted, the Japanese reportedly asked US financial authorities how much they had to liberalize to avert retaliation. Adding to the pressure on Japan, the US authorities refused to give any quantitative guidance and instead urged the greatest possible use of an auction system. The Japanese government's response, immediately after the 1988 trade bill was passed, was to announce quite substantial improvements in foreign firms' access to the market. In addition, there are unsubstantiated reports that the Japanese verbally promised increases in the proportion of future 10-year bond issues that would be auctioned beyond the 40 percent announced in September.[17]

---

17. These reports are indirectly substantiated by the fact that the Ministry of Finance subsequently opened 60 percent of the issue to auction effective October 1990 ("Japan May Widen

The Japanese government bond market, the world's second largest, is a potentially important one for foreign firms. New issues in Japan in 1989 were about half the size of the US market and roughly five times larger than in Germany (Industrial Bank of Japan 1990, table 1). Just as Japanese firms seeking to be global players want access to the US market, foreign firms want access to the Japanese market. The market has not been viewed as an especially profitable one. Indeed, the auction system is likely to sharpen competition and reduce profit margins. But several US firms believe their experience in US government debt markets and their creativity in introducing new products will help them to make money in the Japanese market. In fact, several US firms, notably Salomon Brothers and Goldman Sachs, have become large and reportedly profitable players in Japan.[18] But as US financial authorities frequently point out, their goal in seeking market access is not to guarantee profits for US firms. Rather, the US objective is to promote efficient markets and to ensure equal opportunities for US firms to compete for profits.

In sum, we believe that the Schumer amendment contributed to opening the Japanese government bond market. It appears that the single most important complementary factor was the existence of a coalition of Japanese firms and policymakers who desired to liberalize the market for their own reasons. The Schumer amendment's threat of retaliation bolstered their arguments for liberalization and may have helped swing the political balance in their favor. The consensus among those interviewed is that it at least speeded up liberalization that would have occurred eventually.

Besides helping to open this one market, the Schumer amendment may also have encouraged Japanese liberalization in other markets. The Japanese government may have moved faster with liberalization in other financial markets to avoid provoking Congress into passing other legislation such as the numerous Fair Trade in Financial Services bills of 1990–94.

As discussed below, the Schumer amendment also set an important precedent that could hurt US firms in the future. The Federal Reserve was clearly conscious of creating dangerous precedents and sought to minimize the potential damage by carefully defining rational criteria for determining whether foreign firms were receiving national treatment. In its report on the Schumer amendment, the Fed took pains to emphasize that equality of competitive opportunities did not require the host country to allow foreign firms the same rights and privileges they enjoyed in their home countries. The Fed's concern about adverse precedents was

Foreign Access to Bond Auctions," *Financial Times*, 9 January 1990).

18. In interviews with Japanese firms, the authors found that US firms purchased roughly 16 percent of the 10-year bonds auctioned between April 1990 and February 1991, with Salomon Brothers alone taking 30 percent in some auctions. In 1993 foreign firms' share of some auctions reached nearly 60 percent.

sharpened by the fact that the European Community had recently pressed for reciprocity in return for access to EC financial markets. The Fed report (US Federal Reserve Bank Board of Governors 1989, 9) reminded its readers that US firms were vulnerable to reciprocity demands:

> The Federal Reserve has argued—most recently in discussions with Europeans on the reciprocity provisions in the European Community's financial services directives—that the inability of European banks to conduct securities activities in the United States within the bank or to branch freely throughout the country, as they can in their home countries, does not constitute a violation of the principle of national treatment, since domestic US firms are similarly constrained.

The Second Banking Directive

> There has been much speculation about the motives of the Commission in devising this powerful "unconventional" weapon and where it will be directed. It is my observation that reciprocity is a missile aimed at Tokyo but will land in New York and explode on Capitol Hill.[19]
> —*John G. Heimann, vice chairman of Merrill Lynch Capital Markets*

The 1989 Second Banking Directive was a key component in the European Community's effort to create a single Community-wide financial market. It provides firms with a single banking license that allows them to operate anywhere in the Community under their home-country's financial rules (Key 1989b). Given universal banking in some member countries, this combination of a European license and home-country rules creates significant competitive pressure for regulatory convergence toward a universal banking system where firms can conduct both commercial and investment banking activities.

The European Commission's first draft of the Second Banking Directive was issued in February 1988. The most controversial part of the directive was its Article 7, on reciprocity. The article was vaguely worded and sought undefined "reciprocal treatment" from foreign countries in return for continued access to the newly liberalized EC financial market. It imposed a mandatory Commission review of all applications by third-country firms to establish EC subsidiaries.[20] Applications could be suspended indefinitely if the Commission determined that the Community did not receive reciprocity from the foreign country.

It was not clear in the initial draft whether existing foreign-owned subsidiaries' rights to the single banking license were grandfathered. In

---

19. "US Perspectives of 1992," speech to the Euromoney International Financial Markets Conference, Frankfurt, 20 October 1988.

20. The directive applies only to foreign subsidiaries that are incorporated in the European Community and therefore are viewed as EC firms. It does not apply to foreign branches, which are not EC firms.

fact, subsequent remarks by External Affairs Commissioner Willy De Clercq suggested that existing firms were *not* grandfathered.

Several large US banks were concerned by the draft directive's reciprocity provisions. The very vagueness of Article 7 stirred fears among American firms with operations in Europe that they might be denied a single banking license if any single EC member country claimed a denial of reciprocal treatment in the US market. US firms were particularly concerned that the Commission might insist on mirror-image reciprocity. In that case, the Commission might challenge the Glass-Steagall Act's separation of commercial and investment banking or barriers to interstate banking imposed by the McFadden Act and some state laws. The large money center banks opposed Glass-Steagall and McFadden restrictions, but they worried that their European operations could be jeopardized by a US-EC conflict over reciprocity. The possibility that their existing subsidiaries would not be grandfathered was a major concern, since several US firms, notably Citicorp and American Express, had extensive European operations.[21] Finally, the fact that the decision-making process would be vested in the Commission raised fears about arbitrary or biased decisions made by EC bureaucrats not subject to close political control.

The reciprocity provisions also sparked strong opposition from several member countries, notably the United Kingdom and Germany. The UK Treasury and Bank of England, the German Bundesbank, and these countries' finance and economics ministries had several objections to the reciprocity provisions. The financial authorities in both countries are generally leery of protectionist policies. Like their counterparts at the US Treasury and Federal Reserve, their primary objective is to maintain the safety and soundness of domestic and global financial markets. They worried that injudicious EC demands for reciprocity might spark a trade war that would damage firms under their supervision and disrupt international financial flows. London and Frankfurt are Europe's largest financial markets and would bear the largest burden of any potential conflict or market disruption.

Perhaps at least as important as these concerns, the UK and German financial authorities strenuously objected to the Commission's usurpation of their regulatory power to admit foreign firms' subsidiaries to their home markets. In 1988 the United Kingdom was host to 50 percent ($39 billion) of all US bank subsidiaries' assets in the European Community, and Germany was second with nearly 22 percent.[22] London is the world's second largest financial market and is host to more foreign than British

---

21. In 1989, US banks operated 204 subsidiaries with assets of $104 billion in the Community (US Department of the Treasury 1990, 153).

22. Testimony by Manuel H. Johnson, vice chairman of the Board of Governors of the Federal Reserve System, before the House Committee on Banking, Subcommittee on Financial Institutions Supervision, 26 September 1989, table 1.

financial firms. It owes its preeminent position to the UK regulatory environment, which promotes competition and welcomes foreign firms. The German financial authorities aspire to make Frankfurt a leading global financial center on a par with London, Tokyo, and New York. They are undertaking a major liberalization of their own markets to promote greater competition and make Frankfurt more attractive to domestic and foreign firms.

The UK and German governments therefore had misgivings about allowing EC bureaucrats almost unlimited authority to determine whether foreign firms could establish subsidiaries in London and Frankfurt. At the very least, reciprocity demands aimed at other major financial powers such as Japan and the United States could make London and Frankfurt less attractive to foreign firms. In the worst case, UK and German firms might suffer retaliation from third countries. Moreover, the UK and German financial authorities had nothing to gain from EC-administered reciprocity, since both countries already had their own discretionary reciprocity provisions.[23]

The strongest private-sector opposition to the directive's reciprocity provisions came from the UK banking community, including both British and foreign-owned banks. Their unanimous opposition stemmed from the belief that they individually and collectively benefited from London's position as one of the world's most open financial markets. Acting through the British Bankers' Association, they strongly supported the UK government's position on reciprocity and also made their views known directly to the Commission. The German banking community appears to have been somewhat more ambivalent. EC officials say some of the most vociferous complaints they received about market access in the United States came from German banks. Some German bankers therefore may have experienced a touch of *schadenfreude* at the extreme discomfort the directive's reciprocity provisions gave US financial authorities. Publicly, however, the German banking community supported its government's position against reciprocity. Interestingly, German government officials say that the most strenuous opposition to reciprocity came from large manufacturing firms, which believed they would be targets of US retaliation. These officials say they did nothing to discourage such fears because they found the manufacturers' opposition helpful in bolstering their case against reciprocity.

The US government was closely monitoring the entire EC 1992 process, including the Second Banking Directive. It was well aware of US firms' apprehensions, and of course the Federal Reserve and Treasury objected to reciprocity on general principles. However, perhaps because the directive's reciprocity provisions were so vague, the US government did not

---

23. See Part X of the UK Financial Services Act of 1986, Article 91 of the UK Banking Act of 1987, and Article 53 of the Banking Law of the Federal Republic of Germany.

voice strong public objections until six months after the draft directive was issued.

A series of statements by EC officials in the spring and summer of 1988 helped incite a strong American response. In April 1988, Lord Cockfield, the EC commissioner for financial institutions, visited the United States and gave a speech on the Community's 1992 program at the Institute for International Economics. The speech itself was upbeat and unthreatening. In the question and answer period, however, several US bankers questioned Lord Cockfield about what the directive's reciprocity provisions really meant. Lord Cockfield told them that US firms would face market-access problems in Europe unless the United States removed Glass-Steagall restrictions on EC banks in the US market.[24] Lord Cockfield's remarks thus confirmed the worst fears of US bankers and the interpretations of reciprocity they had been hearing from lower-level EC officials in Brussels. Given Lord Cockfield's stature as a commissioner and one of the most influential architects of Europe 1992, his remarks were taken very seriously.

US concerns were further heightened by several speeches given in July 1988 by Willy De Clercq, the commissioner for external relations and trade. His references to reciprocity were vague and undefined. He did, however, explicitly deny that existing US subsidiaries would be grand-fathered.[25] Moreover, he suggested that it was fair to ask the United States for reciprocity since the EC financial market was more open than the US market and EC firms were constrained by US restrictions on interstate banking (*Financial Times*, 14 July 1988, 2).

In sum, in the space of four months, two key EC commissioners had suggested that the Community might challenge the Glass-Steagall and McFadden restrictions on EC firms. Moreover, it appeared that existing European subsidiaries of US banks were at risk of being denied EC banking licenses if the United States and the Community got into a fight over reciprocity. By the summer of 1988, US fears of a protectionist Fortress Europe were at a fever pitch.

The US government's response came swiftly on the heels of De Clercq's statements. In late July the Treasury asked the Institute for International Economics to host a meeting at which Acting Treasury Secretary Peter McPherson would give the first official US government response to Europe

---

24. There is no extant transcript of the question and answer period, and this account is based on the recollection of US bankers and government officials who were present. For a description of Lord Cockfield's statements, see Thomas L. Farmer's remarks at the Bankers' Association for Foreign Trade annual meeting, 30 April–4 May 1989, 1–2.

25. Many US and European government officials and bankers, however, believe that US subsidiaries established in the Community before the directive became effective are grand-fathered under Article 58 of the Treaty of Rome, which requires that foreign subsidiaries be treated as EC firms.

1992. Treasury billed the speech as a response to Lord Cockfield, but the fact that Treasury arranged the speech on very short notice soon after De Clercq's statements suggests it was also a response to De Clercq. Officials at the US Trade Representative's office reportedly urged their Treasury colleagues to respond forcefully to head off what they feared was the first in a series of protectionist policies emanating out of the Europe 1992 initiative.

In his 4 August speech, Secretary McPherson applauded the Community's efforts to achieve the single market.[26] He went on to object to the reciprocity provisions in the Second Banking Directive as approximating mirror-image reciprocity. He indirectly rebuffed Cockfield's and De Clercq's challenges to US banking law by asserting that "the danger of this approach is that legitimate differences in national regulatory regimes could be used to justify discrimination against foreign firms." McPherson also issued a gentle warning:

> If barriers against foreign owned firms are raised in the context of completing the internal market . . . the EC will undermine support in the United States—and elsewhere—for multilateral efforts toward a more open international financial and trading system. Indeed, the intensification of protectionism in Europe would certainly evoke a response from the US government.

McPherson's speech was given in the dog days of August when most European policymakers are on vacation, but it nevertheless caught their attention immediately. EC officials say the message came through as clear and credible: the United States would retaliate against EC restrictions on US firms. The US response to Europe 1992 provoked a spirited discussion within the Community on how to respond to US charges that the newly unified Europe was turning protectionist. No one, of course, would acknowledge any protectionist motives, and the EC heads of government were on record at their June 1988 Hanover Summit as saying "the internal market should not close in on itself."

There was, however, considerable debate over whether the Community could use the leverage of its huge open market to encourage liberalization in third countries. Some commissioners reportedly argued for an aggressive use of reciprocity, citing the US example of section 301 in the 1974 Trade Act. Others opposed reciprocity because it was contrary to free market principles and likely to provoke US retaliation.

In October 1988 the Commission issued a clarifying statement on reciprocity entitled "1992 Europe—World Partner."[27] The statement, in fact,

---

26. "The European Community's Internal Market Program: An American Perspective," Institute for International Economics, Washington, 4 August 1988.

27. EC Office of Press and Public Affairs, "1992 Europe—World Partner," *European Community News* No. 28/88, 20 October 1988.

did not clarify completely what the Commission meant by reciprocity. It said what reciprocity was not: it was not protectionism, and it was not mirror-image reciprocity. But the statement confirmed the Commission's intention to seek some sort of guarantees of market access for EC firms in third countries in exchange for access to the European market. On the more positive side, the statement did clarify that existing subsidiaries would be grandfathered.

In November 1988 the EC Council of Ministers met and reportedly rejected the Second Banking Directive's reciprocity provisions as too protectionist. The council is said to have instructed the Commission to redraft Article 7 to provide for more liberal foreign access to the Community.

Some EC observers say it would have been difficult for the two commissioners most closely associated with reciprocity, Cockfield and De Clercq, to accept a significant watering down of Article 7. Virtually everyone we interviewed felt that the fortuitous advent of a new Commission in January 1989 was a decisive event in the revision of the Second Banking Directive. The key figure in the redrafting of Article 7 was Commissioner for Financial Institutions Sir Leon Brittan. Those who know Brittan invariably describe him as a pragmatic free trader. He is also said to be a supporter of the Atlantic alliance and was therefore eager to avoid a US-EC dispute over reciprocity. He found like-minded views in Frans Andriessen, the new external relations commissioner, and Martin Bangemann, the new commissioner for the internal market.

Throughout 1988, the US financial community monitored the EC discussion of the Second Banking Directive. It made its opposition to reciprocity known to the Commission and member governments mainly through quiet diplomacy. Demarches were made by individual US firms and jointly through the American Chambers of Commerce in London and Brussels and through the Washington-based Bankers' Association for Foreign Trade (BAFT).

In March 1989 the US financial community decided to go public with their objections to the directive's reciprocity provisions. The BAFT issued an unambiguously titled report, *Reciprocity: A Step in the Wrong Direction* (March 1989), which stressed the benefits of open markets and the dangers of reciprocity. It argued that national treatment was the best principle for regulating foreign firms. The BAFT report also pointed out that EC banks received national, and sometimes better-than-national, treatment in the United States. Buried in the report was a brief warning of US retaliation: "If it were invoked against the US, [Article 7] could possibly provoke retaliation against EC banking organizations in the U.S." (p. 26). An appendix listed the nine EC banks (seven German and two French) whose securities operations were grandfathered under the International Banking Act of 1978. The report did not explicitly mention that these nine firms enjoying better-than-national treatment would be the most obvious candidates for US retaliation. Some US bankers and Treasury officials privately, and later publicly, affirmed that these EC firms were targets.[28]

The BAFT report had been circulated privately to US and EC officials for some time before it was released publicly. The release may have been intended to influence the European debate on the revisions to Article 7 that were then under way in the Commission. The report was sent to Sir Leon Brittan, other top EC and national officials, and leaders in the European banking sector.

In April 1989 Sir Leon introduced revisions to the directive's reciprocity provisions that went a long way toward alleviating the critics' concerns. In announcing the revisions, Brittan gave strong assurances that the Community had no protectionist intentions:

> The proposed changes to the directive send a clear message to our trading partners: that we welcome the establishment of their banks in the Community. We will seek only to hit back if there is in effect national discrimination against us. Where our partners have banking laws which are effectively nondiscriminatory, but less liberal, these will be a matter for negotiation. We are fully entitled to argue that our most liberal banking market is an example that the rest of the world should follow.[29]

The proposed revisions offered a form of reciprocity that was substantially more liberal than the original, vague version might have been. The new proposal eliminated the mandatory suspension of applications for banking licenses while the Commission investigated whether EC firms received reciprocal treatment. Instead, the member states were required to inform the Commission of any market-access problems their firms experienced abroad. In addition, the Commission was required to undertake a study of EC firms' market-access difficulties and issue a report to the EC Council six months before the directive went into effect.

The revised directive defined two criteria to govern when the Commission could seek to improve market access for EC firms in third countries. The first criterion was whether EC firms abroad received "effective market access comparable to that granted by the Community." If this criterion was not met, the Commission could submit proposals to the EC Council for negotiations with the third country in question, but there was no explicit provision for retaliation.

---

28. Treasury Under Secretary Mulford warned, "If US firms are discriminated against in the EC, there would likely be consequences for EC national institutions. An obvious first step might be to scrutinize the 'better-than-national treatment' privileges which many European financial institutions currently enjoy in the United States" (Testimony before the House Committee on Banking, Subcommittee on Financial Institutions Supervision, 28 September 1989, 4).

29. EC Office of Press and Public Affairs, "EC Commission Clarifies Reciprocity Provisions in Proposed Second Banking Directive," *European Community News* No. 10/89, 13 April 1989, 1–2.

The second criterion was whether EC firms in third countries received "national treatment offering the same competitive opportunities as are available to domestic credit institutions and the conditions of effective market access are not fulfilled." If this national treatment standard was not met, the Commission could require an EC member state to suspend its decision on granting a license application. The Commission could also decide in this case to initiate negotiations on its own authority with the third country. The suspension of license applications would not apply to foreign firms already established in the Community—their rights were explicitly grandfathered. The suspension of applications could not continue for more than three months unless the EC Council of Ministers decided by qualified majority vote to extend it.

On 1 May 1989 Sir Leon Brittan gave a speech before the Bankers' Association for Foreign Trade's annual meeting in Phoenix that further clarified what the proposed revisions meant:

> We would only act to limit or suspend new authorizations and acquisitions by a parent bank from a third country in cases where the Community's banks do not enjoy "national treatment" and the same competitive opportunities as that third country's own banks and where the condition of effective market access has not been secured. "National treatment" simply means non-discrimination between domestic and foreign banks. Of course, it must work in practice and not be a mere legal formality. That is why we use the word "effective market access." But any country providing genuine national treatment to Community banks would be under no threat. (p. 10–11)

Sir Leon assured his audience that there would be no EC sanctions against US banks because of Glass-Steagall or other restrictions on EC banks, so long as they were genuinely nondiscriminatory. He pointed to the economic benefits for the Community and its trading partners of internal EC market liberalization. He said the Community hoped to persuade the United States to follow its example and liberalize Glass-Steagall and interstate banking restrictions, for the benefit of both US and EC firms. But he emphasized: "We are not using threats to get you to open your markets, only persuasion" (p. 12).

As a prelude to final approval of the directive, the EC Council of Ministers discussed the revisions and adopted a "common position" accepting them on 24 July 1989. The council formally approved the revised Second Banking Directive in December 1989.[30] In announcing the final adoption of the Second Banking Directive, Sir Leon Brittan and Pierre Bérégovoy, the French finance minister and president of the Council of Ministers, issued a joint statement:

---

30. Second Council Directive of 15 December 1989 on the coordination of laws, regulations, and administrative provisions relating to the taking up and pursuit of the business of credit institutions and amending Directive 77/780/EEC, 89/646/EEC, *Official Journal of the European Communities* No. L386/1–13.

> The Banking Directive sets an example of how the European Community
> approaches relations with third countries across the financial services sector. The
> reciprocity provisions will ensure freer access for Community credit institutions
> into third country markets and provide an example of openness for other countries
> to follow.[31]

The US reaction to the revised directive was generally quite favorable. In his remarks before the Bankers' Association for Foreign Trade's annual meeting in April 1989, the association's general counsel praised Brittan's efforts to revise the directive and called the new proposals "welcome news" and "very much in the right direction." Privately, US bankers said they preferred no reciprocity provisions at all, but they were able to live with the new provisions. Large US financial firms, most of which have EC subsidiaries, do not expect problems with the new reciprocity provisions, since their current subsidiaries are grandfathered and can branch freely. Representatives of several US banks that actively opposed reciprocity said the final result was much better than they expected. A staff member of one of the largest US firms said he thought his firm had achieved 85 to 90 percent of its objectives.

The US government's response to the revisions was somewhat mixed. An interagency task force on the EC internal market program said the revisions in the directive were "from the perspective of non-EC banks . . . a very positive and welcome evolution in the reciprocity provision"(US Government Task Force on the EC Internal Market 1990, 7). The US Treasury was less gratified by the final version. Treasury Under Secretary Mulford reportedly urged Sir Leon to abandon reciprocity entirely when they met in Washington in the spring of 1989. Brittan reportedly rebuffed this request and described the new version as intellectually and politically defensible. Sir Leon is said to have received assurances that Treasury would not actively oppose the new reciprocity measures. In the fall of 1989, after the EC Council had accepted the revisions but before it had given final approval, Mulford publicly expressed Treasury's continuing reservations (Testimony before the House Committee on Banking, Finance, and Urban Affairs, Subcommittee on Financial Institutions Supervision, 28 September 1989, 3):

> We still see dangers in the EC concept of reciprocity. Once this "club in the closet"
> is on the books, there will be a temptation to use it especially given the EC's
> desire to promote changes in the US financial system. If actually used—or rather,
> misused—this would run the risk of provoking a retaliation action from US
> authorities.

Role of Retaliation in the Banking Case

What role did US threats of retaliation play in encouraging the Community to modify its initial position on reciprocity? As in the case of the Schumer

---

31. EC Office of Press and Public Affairs, "European Community Adopts 1992 Banking Directives," *European Community News* No. 46/89, 18 December 1989.

amendment, the decisive factor in the revision of the Second Banking Directive was the existence of a powerful internal EC coalition that strongly opposed the reciprocity provisions. To understand the importance of this antireciprocity coalition, it is necessary to delve into the history of the original reciprocity provisions.

EC officials involved in drafting the original directive and others who followed it closely say that the reciprocity provisions were the focal point of an ongoing struggle for power between the Commission and the financial authorities in the United Kingdom and Germany. The reciprocity provisions were inserted at the last minute by Commission staff, reportedly by staff in the offices of Lord Cockfield and Commission President Jacques Delors. One Commission staff member described the original Article 7 as being "scribbled on the corner of a desk shortly before the directive was shown to the commissioners for the first time." The reciprocity provisions were not subject to the normal scrutiny of, and discussion with, the member states' permanent representatives in Brussels and their financial authorities.

Commission staff say there was no advance discussion of reciprocity during the normal drafting process because their attention was focused entirely on the internal market liberalization effort, and no one even considered the external implications. At the last possible minute, some staff recognized a gaping procedural hole in the directive. The Commission was supposed to be setting policy for the 12 member states, but the power to admit third-country banks to the Community was still vested in the national financial authorities. Commission staff believed that power to control entry should be reserved for the Commission. With the single banking license, a foreign bank once admitted to one member state could branch freely throughout the Community. As one Commission staff member put it, "We wanted a procedure whereby the Bank of England could be prevented from making decisions for the Twelve."

The initial reciprocity provision gave the Commission almost unlimited veto power over new entrants and possibly over old entrants as well, given the uncertainty about grandfathering. Commission staff freely acknowledged that they had not thought carefully about what they meant by reciprocity, hence their use of the undefined term "reciprocal treatment." They knew the language of Article 7 was crude and fully expected it to be rewritten.

Commission staff did not expect the uproar of criticism that ensued from some member states and the US banking community. Financial authorities from several member states, including some potentially sympathetic to reciprocity, were outraged that they had not been consulted.

The UK and German financial authorities led the counterattack on reciprocity. They objected to Article 7 on the grounds that it was potentially protectionist. They also argued that the concept of reciprocity was so vague that its use risked provoking endless disputes both within the

Community and with trading partners. They also worried that it would set unfortunate precedents on reciprocity for other directives in the areas of investment services and insurance. Privately, government officials from the United Kingdom and Germany told us that their overriding concern was to prevent EC bureaucrats from making decisions about whether foreign banks could enter their home markets. They were particularly concerned about the enormous discretionary authority that would be vested in the Commission under the draft directive and the potential for its abuse, given the lack of adequate political control by the Council of Ministers. Financial officials from the Netherlands and Luxembourg reportedly shared some of the British and German reservations but were not as strongly opposed.

Commission staff say they were also greatly surprised by the strong response from the US government and private sector. They were virtually unanimous in saying that, at the time of drafting, it never occurred to them that the United States would be a target of the reciprocity provision. Rather, their main targets were Japan and perhaps eventually some of the more advanced developing countries such as Taiwan and Korea.[32]

Another rationale of the Commission was to position the Community in the financial services negotiations in the Uruguay Round. The staff felt that the existence of a reciprocity clause would give the Community greater leverage in the GATT negotiations. Several staff members closely involved in drafting the initial Article 7 acknowledged that they had not thought carefully about how reciprocity could give the Community bargaining power. It was described as a "weapon in the pocket." Without Article 7, they believed foreign firms would have free access to the Community's financial markets, and therefore the Community would have difficulty in extracting any reciprocal concessions.

If the reciprocity provisions of the directive were viewed by the European participants as an internal power struggle, how did Article 7 become a near *casus belli* between the United States and the Community? It is useful to recall the atmosphere of US-EC trade relations in 1988 because they contributed to serious antagonism and suspicion on both sides.

In early 1988, when the draft directive was first introduced, the US Congress was drafting the Omnibus Trade and Competitiveness Act. The Community strongly objected to several provisions in the bill, which it viewed as highly protectionist, and vociferously criticized the unilateral threats of retaliation embodied in the section 301, special 301, and super 301 provisions. The Community also strongly opposed the general notion of reciprocity that Congress then was considering in areas such as telecommunications and financial services.

---

32. It is not clear how much leverage the original reciprocity provisions would have provided vis-à-vis developing countries, since few of these countries have substantial banking activities in the Community.

The United States, on the other hand, had strong concerns about the direction of EC trade policy. There was ongoing US criticism of European agriculture policy and Airbus subsidies for damaging US exports. There were also growing fears that the Community would seek to alleviate some of the inevitable adjustment costs of internal market liberalization by raising its external trade barriers. The phrase "Fortress Europe" summed up US fears of incipient EC protectionism.

The Second Banking Directive brought these US concerns about Euro-protectionism into sharp focus. The directive was one of the first pieces of internal market legislation that had significant implications for the Community's trading partners. US officials viewed the directive's original reciprocity provisions as a potential harbinger of a more general protectionist thrust in EC trade policy. Several US officials told us that the government decided to respond forcefully to the Second Banking Directive, not only because of its own perceived flaws, but because it would set important precedents for future EC policy, particularly in investment services and insurance.

It is against this backdrop of US-EC tensions that the inflammatory Cockfield and De Clercq statements on reciprocity must be viewed. All of the EC officials we interviewed strongly denied that the directive's reciprocity provisions were in any way a Community response to the 1988 trade bill then wending its way through Congress or to US rhetoric on reciprocity. But in the heat of US-EC trade tensions, the directive provided certain commissioners and staff with a useful debating point to needle the United States, which they perceived as demanding free trade while passing protectionist legislation.

It is particularly ironic that the task of needling the United States fell to Commissioners Cockfield and De Clercq, both widely viewed as pragmatic free traders. Both men also have reputations as staunch supporters of European unification. Several Commission staff members suggested that Cockfield and De Clercq were irritated by what they viewed as hypocritical US complaints about European protectionism. It was suggested to us that Cockfield and De Clercq were simply responding in kind to US provocations when they attacked the Glass-Steagall and McFadden Acts and demanded reciprocity. In any event, Commission staff insisted that Cockfield and De Clercq were not presenting a Community consensus on reciprocity, since in fact that policy had not yet been decided within the Community.

Many of the Europeans we interviewed said that US complaints about Article 7 forced the Community for the first time to grapple with the far larger issue of how the EC's internal market liberalization program would affect its external trade relations. We were told repeatedly that the Commission had given virtually no serious thought to this question until the controversy arose over the Second Banking Directive. Indeed, there are only fleeting references to external economic relations in key EC documents on the 1992 program such as the Commission's white paper on completing the internal market.[33] This near-total preoccupation with the internal dimensions of Europe 1992 is understandable, given the enormous task the Commission faced in completing the internal market. In retrospect, however, several of our European discussants suggested that the Commission should have produced a white paper on external relations to accompany the white paper on the internal market.

The internal European debate on reciprocity involved a number of complex issues and a variety of players operating with different motives. On one level, it was a fight between free traders and protectionists. The British and German governments and the British banking community— the pragmatic free traders—wanted to reap the benefits of open markets. The strongest support for reciprocity came from France, Belgium, Italy, Spain, and Greece, where bankers and government officials worried about their firms' ability to compete with German and British banks in the newly liberalized market. They supported reciprocity because it would give some protection against competition from non-Community, and particularly Japanese, firms.

The European debate on reciprocity, however, was not simply or even primarily about free trade versus protectionism. Within some governments, the Commission, and the European Parliament, reciprocity was also an issue of "fairness"—as it was in the US debate on the 1988 trade bill. The Community had made great efforts to liberalize its internal market in the face of serious economic and political obstacles. In particular, the Community had created the world's largest and most open financial market. Many Europeans, even some putative free traders, asked: Is it not fair that outsiders should pay an admission fee for entry to our huge and lucrative market? And is it not fair to make the price of admission improved market access for EC firms in third countries?

The debate over reciprocity was largely a struggle for power between the Commission and the British and German financial authorities. However, to a lesser extent, it also involved a power struggle between the Commission and the European Parliament. Currently, the Parliament plays primarily an advisory role to the Commission, which must listen and respond to the Parliament's views on proposed legislation. On average, the Commission accepts about three-quarters of the Parliament's proposed amendments, so the Parliament is increasingly a force to be reckoned with (Colchester and Buchan 1990, 15). The Parliament looks for opportunities to influence the Commission's decisions as a way to affirm its own authority.

---

33. The only reference to external trade relations in the white paper alludes vaguely to reciprocity: "Moreover the commercial identity of the Community must be consolidated so that our trading partners will not be given the benefit of a wider market without themselves making similar concessions" (Commission of the European Communities 1985, 8).

The reciprocity debate was described to us by one member of Parliament as a useful vehicle for pressing the Commission to acknowledge the Parliament's authority. There was broad public support for reciprocity through Europe, largely on grounds of fairness. The Parliament strongly supported inclusion of the original reciprocity provision and, in fact, suggested that it be strengthened to cover foreign bank branches.

In sum, there was quite broad and reasonably strong support for reciprocity within Community institutions. How then was the compromise eventually reached that significantly liberalized Article 7?

Many European observers point to Treasury Secretary Peter McPherson's August 1988 speech as an important turning point in the European debate. McPherson's gentle threat of retaliation caught the attention of the entire Commission and of high-level policymakers in the European member states. The speech was the heaviest shot in a long barrage of criticism of the Community for what foreigners viewed as incipient European protectionism, and it forced the Commission and the member states to come to grips with foreign fears of European protectionism. The Commission's hastily written and ambiguous October 1988 explanatory memorandum, "1992 Europe—World Partner," failed to convince the United States completely of the Commission's benign intentions. British and German central bankers and Finance Ministry officials reportedly lobbied their colleagues in the other member states to agree to liberalizing revisions in Article 7. The Council of Ministers intervened in November 1988 and ordered the reciprocity provisions changed to demonstrate that the Community had no protectionist intentions.

When Sir Leon Brittan arrived in January 1989, he had a clear political mandate to revise the directive. His closest allies are said to have been Frans Andriessen, commissioner for external affairs, and Martin Bangemann, commissioner for internal market affairs. Brittan displayed considerable diplomatic skill in building a consensus among his more skeptical Commission colleagues. Brittan argued that the stakes were very high and noted that he was deeply worried by what he viewed as rising protectionist pressures in the United States. The Commission should avoid giving the United States what one staff member described as a "pretext" for becoming more protectionist on the grounds that it was only responding to Europe. The Commission needed to send a clear signal to the world that the Community was open—that there was no Fortress Europe. After some debate, the Commission reached a consensus on the broad outlines of a revision.

The directive then went back to the staff for redrafting. The vagueness in the original draft allowed the staff considerable scope to liberalize the reciprocity provisions as they were "clarifying" them. In place of the undefined term "reciprocal treatment," the drafters substituted the better understood concept of national treatment.[34] Where no language existed in

---

34. However, there is still considerable ambiguity surrounding the term "effective market access." The term is used in two contexts in the directive, one implying that it refers to de

the original on grandfathering, the drafters inserted a clear grandfathering clause. It is reported that much of the liberalizing language came from UK and German financial authorities through their permanent representatives in Brussels.

Commission staff say that the decision to adopt a reciprocal national treatment standard was their own. They were well-aware of the Schumer amendment but say it was not a model for their own efforts. Several did, however, agree with our suggestion that it would be difficult for the United States to object to reciprocal national treatment in the directive, since it was already embodied in the Schumer amendment. Commission staff members were also eager to point out that the Schumer amendment mandates retaliation, whereas retaliation in the Second Banking Directive is discretionary, limited initially to three months' duration and subject to political control by the Council of Ministers. They did acknowledge, however, that the Schumer amendment is limited to one (albeit very large) market, while the directive covers all European banking markets.

In the end, Brittan had relatively little trouble convincing the EC Council of Ministers to accept his proposed revisions. The council had previously reached a consensus in favor of liberalization. It looked to the Commission to devise specific proposals on how to achieve this goal. The Commission used its considerable power as a broker of ideas and drafter of legislation to provide the technical solution to the council's political problem of assuring the world that Europe was not protectionist.

Dealing with the European Parliament was more difficult because that body was not in favor of liberalizing the reciprocity provisions. Brittan met with Parliament to explain the Commission's proposal. He firmly rejected the Parliament's suggestions for strengthening reciprocity but paid homage to the need to consult the Parliament by agreeing to share draft reports on the treatment of EC banks in third countries.

Conclusions and Policy Recommendations

Fairness and reciprocity often are in the eyes of the beholder. The United States effectively used demands for reciprocal national treatment and threats of retaliation to open the Japanese government bond market. But the European Community's demands for "reciprocal treatment" in exchange for access to the newly liberalized European financial market evoked a swift US counterthreat. These two episodes provide useful insights into how policies seeking reciprocity and using retaliatory threats are implemented. They offer lessons on how to wield the retaliation weapon most effectively, and equally important, what sort of reciprocity is an appropriate goal.

---

facto national treatment and a second, "effective market access comparable to that granted by the Community," implying something approximating mirror-image reciprocity.

We draw two key policy conclusions from these case studies. First, the United States should avoid setting precedents that it cannot live by. With the Schumer amendment, the United States moved away from unconditional national treatment and toward the precedent of reciprocal national treatment enforced by mandatory retaliatory threats under tight deadlines. Yet US officials objected when the European Community adopted reciprocal national treatment, backed by a far milder threat than is contained in the Schumer amendment. Moreover, recent US Treasury demands for additional access to the Japanese financial market look increasingly like demands for mirror-image reciprocity rather than national treatment.[35] Yet the United States unhesitantly threatened retaliation when the initial Banking Directive draft suggested that the European Community might seek mirror-image reciprocity and take action against US firms.[36]

A second lesson is that threats can be effective under certain conditions, but the benefits must be weighed against the costs, especially when threats must be carried out. Retaliation in the financial sector entails greater risks than in the goods sector because of its tendencies toward volatility and instability and because of the linkages between finance and other sectors. Therefore, such retaliatory threats should be exercised with great caution. The first rule of financial market access policy should be to forswear the use of retaliatory threats if the national treatment standard is met.

What Role for Reciprocity?

These two cases illustrate that neither reciprocal national treatment nor mirror-image reciprocity is a useful principle for resolving the most significant financial market access problems likely to arise among the economic superpowers in the foreseeable future. In what follows, we describe the limitations of each principle.

---

35. See, for example, the US Treasury (1990) for US complaints about Japanese interest rate controls and the slow pace of approval for new products, neither of which involves a clear-cut violation of national treatment.

36. Several US Treasury officials who have read this study and given extremely valuable comments believe that these characterizations are unfair because the administration and the Fed were consistent in their opposition to both the Schumer amendment and the initial reciprocity provisions of the draft Second Banking Directive. However, the president signed the 1988 Trade Act, and it became the law of the land. Moreover, as described below, the Treasury (but not the Fed) now supports the current Fair Trade in Financial Services bill, which seeks reciprocal national treatment, albeit with no time deadlines and greater discretionary retaliatory authority for the Treasury. Treasury officials also strongly object to the characterization of their seeking something approaching mirror-image reciprocity from Japan. When asked to define what they seek from Japan, they describe their objective as "effective market access," which they define (as do some EC officials) as going beyond de facto national treatment.

Mirror-image reciprocity simply is not an appropriate principle for resolving financial market access problems. Demands for mirror-image reciprocity assume there are no legitimate reasons for countries to maintain different financial market regulatory regimes. The Federal Reserve is absolutely correct in asserting that, as long as they provide national treatment, governments have every right to determine their own financial market regulatory regimes if they can be justified in reasonable economic terms. Insistence on mirror-image reciprocity is a prescription for endless international conflicts.

Reciprocity is a two-edged sword. Unless a country has absolutely no regulations that can possibly be construed as barriers to foreign access, demanding mirror-image reciprocity is likely to establish unfortunate precedents that will be regretted later. US financial markets are currently more open than Japan's but are less open than the European Union's markets since 1992. It is not in the US interest to insist on mirror-image reciprocity vis-à-vis Japan unless America is prepared to accept EU demands for mirror-image reciprocity.

There appears to be a growing international consensus that reciprocal national treatment is an acceptable standard for financial market access. In 1988 the world's leading financial power first set the precedent of reciprocal national treatment through the Schumer amendment. The European Community quickly adopted the same principle in its Second Banking Directive of 1989. Every year since 1990, the Senate Banking Committee has introduced the Fair Trade in Financial Services Act, which would grant the Treasury discretionary authority to retaliate against countries that do not provide reciprocal national treatment. The bill was sponsored by the Senate Banking Committee's chairman, Donald Riegle, and its ranking Republican, Jake Garn. It also enjoys strong support in the House, where Charles Schumer, an influential member of the Banking Committee, and Richard Gephardt, the House majority leader, have praised it.

Unfortunately, reciprocal national treatment, while more intellectually defensible than mirror-image reciprocity, is not a panacea for financial market access problems.[37] Reciprocal national treatment is largely irrelevant to market-access problems between the three economic superpowers because the European Union and Japan already generally provide national treatment.[38] There are certainly significant violations of national treatment in many developing countries and in the emerging market economies of Eastern Europe. However, reciprocal national treatment will not be terribly effective in opening these markets; because these countries have few

---

37. We have benefited greatly from Sydney Key's (1992) incisive analysis of the limits of national treatment.

38. Nowhere in the Treasury's 1990 national treatment study does the Treasury accuse Japan of denying de facto national treatment, although as the Fed has argued, a significant lack of transparency could violate the national treatment principle.

financial firms operating abroad, they are not currently very vulnerable to threats to restrict their access to US financial markets.[39] In sum, the benefits of reciprocal national treatment will be small—at best, improved access to a few narrow product markets in a handful of industrial countries and to the relatively small markets in a few less developed countries or in Eastern European as their firms begin to go abroad.

In the foreseeable future, the leading sources of financial market access problems between the economic superpowers are likely to involve differences in national regulatory regimes that are nondiscriminatory between foreign and domestic firms. Examples include the slow pace at which Japan approves the introduction of new financial products (in which US firms often have a competitive advantage) or the Glass-Steagall Act, which disadvantages European universal banks in US markets. National treatment—whether reciprocal or unconditional—does not address such nondiscriminatory obstacles. In the final pages of this chapter, we propose an alternative approach to negotiating improved market access that would address these obstacles.

What Role for Retaliation?

In both cases studied here, the threat of US retaliation played a significant role in helping to secure or maintain access to important foreign financial markets. In neither case, however, was the threat of retaliation decisive. Rather, in both cases the existence of a powerful domestic coalition of private firms and public officials who favored open markets was the crucial factor. Without the strong support of this domestic constituency, it is doubtful that US pressure would have had much constructive impact.

The threat of US retaliation helped those in Europe and Japan who favored open markets in two ways. First, it was an action-forcing event that focused the attention of high-level policymakers who ultimately had to give their approval for policy change, and thus it moved decision making forward. Second, the US threat mobilized the support of those EC and Japanese firms that US retaliation would have injured. Their support for open markets was very important in influencing high-level policymakers to make the ultimate decision.

In both of these conflicts, the threat of US retaliation was considered highly credible by all the participants. Under the Schumer amendment, retaliation was mandatory absent compelling evidence of market-opening progress. In the case of the Second Banking Directive, most participants believed that Congress would surely require retaliation, possibly under

---

39. Korea is an exception, since Korean financial firms are increasingly establishing operations in the United States and the European Union.

the new section 301 provisions of the 1988 Trade Act.[40] Many of the US, European, and Japanese policy officials interviewed believed that the conflicts could not be allowed to devolve into outright trade warfare. Several bankers and government officials cited the analogy of nuclear deterrence: the consequences of retaliation were so unacceptable that all parties had no real option but to reach a negotiated settlement.

Based on our interviews, we believe that the European Community would have eventually liberalized its reciprocity provisions and Japan would have opened its government bond market. It simply took time to build the internal consensus that it was in their interest to have open markets. US pressure accelerated these decisions, but that pressure could not have succeeded in the absence of an internal constituency. The clear implication for future disputes is that US negotiators and US firms should form tacit coalitions with those who favor open markets in the target country.

Another factor that contributed importantly to the resolution of these two conflicts was the existence of an international network of financial market regulators and supervisors who share basic attitudes and goals and cooperate regularly. It is trite but also true to say that we live in an interdependent world in which national financial markets are increasingly linked and are becoming ever more global. Events in one big national market are quickly transmitted abroad, for better or worse. Central bankers and finance ministry officials in the major industrial countries share the common goal of preserving the soundness and safety of national and global financial markets. The top financial regulators meet regularly in Basel at the Bank for International Settlements (BIS) to ensure effective international cooperation in this area. Their staffs are in constant contact with their counterparts abroad, sharing information and cooperating on prudential and regulatory issues on an ongoing basis.

This network of formal and informal contacts among bank regulators and other financial authorities played an important role in both disputes. In the conflict over the Second Banking Directive, German and UK financial authorities were influential in urging their counterparts in the other EC member states to accept revisions in Article 7. The German Bundesbank, in particular, is believed to have played a key role in encouraging the French

---

40. Congress, in fact, did not take a direct role in the dispute over the Second Banking Directive. Members of the House and Senate Banking Committees were monitoring the dispute but did not play the very active role that they did in the case of market access in Japan. Several US bankers said they were not eager for Congress to become involved because they feared it would provoke more involvement by the European Parliament, which strongly supported reciprocity. The credibility of congressionally required retaliation may have been strengthened quite late in the process by a visit to Europe in March 1989 by a Senate Finance Committee delegation headed by its chairman, Lloyd Bentsen. The delegation met with a number of leading European policy officials and business leaders and reportedly made clear on at least one occasion that the Congress would insist on retaliation if US firms were hurt by the Banking Directive (US Senate Finance Committee 1989a).

Finance Ministry—whose minister, Pierre Bérégovoy, was president of the EC Council of Ministers—to accept a more liberal approach to reciprocity. The Federal Reserve's and US Treasury's strong objections to reciprocity were clearly communicated to their European counterparts at BIS, OECD, and G-7 ministerial meetings as well. In the redrafting of Article 7, substantial technical input came from British and German financial authorities and reportedly also from former Bank of England staff in the private banking community.

Long-standing ties between US and Japanese financial authorities also contributed to the resolution of the dispute over access to the Japanese government bond market. The ongoing yen-dollar talks provided an important regular forum for discussion of possible solutions. Moreover, the yen-dollar talks provided Treasury staff with substantial expertise on Japanese financial markets on which they drew to argue convincingly that an auction system would both benefit Japan and address US complaints about market access.

The financial authorities involved in both of these cases had two strong reasons to seek a peaceful solution to the conflicts. First, as described earlier, they all have a strong aversion to reciprocity because it can lead to conflicts that could undermine the integrity of the financial system. Second, they oppose anything like mirror-image reciprocity because it challenges their authority to regulate for prudential reasons. The Japanese Finance Ministry and the US Treasury may or may not agree with the separation of commercial and investment banking required by their national laws. But they do not want foreign governments seeking reciprocity to challenge their authority to regulate. Our policy conclusion is that in future market-access disputes, decision-making authority should remain firmly vested in the Treasury, which should have maximum discretion in the use of retaliatory threats.

There is a strong belief in Congress, parts of the private financial sector, and even among some frustrated Treasury officials that retaliatory threats should be used more vigorously to force open foreign financial markets. For example, the Fair Trade in Financial Services bill grants the Treasury discretionary authority to retaliate against countries that do not provide reciprocal national treatment to US firms. After some internal debate, the Treasury initially opposed the bill, as did most large US financial firms. Treasury Under Secretary Mulford's statement of February 1990 criticizing reciprocity, cited at the beginning of this chapter, was the Treasury's initial position on the bill. In April 1991, however, the Treasury reversed its position and withdrew its opposition.[41] The Treasury, USTR, and the

---

41. Testimony by Barry S. Newman before the House Committee on Banking, Housing and Urban Affairs, Subcommittee on Economic Stabilization, 24 April 1991 and testimony by Lawrence H. Summers before the House Committee on Banking, Subcommittee on Financial Institutions Supervision, 1 February 1994.

Council of Economic Advisers all support the concept of reciprocal national treatment as laid out in the Fair Trade in Financial Services legislation of 1993 and 1994. The Federal Reserve, however, continues to oppose it (testimony of Fed Governor John P. LaWare before the House Committee on Banking, Subcommittee on International Development, Finance, Trade, and Monetary Policy, 9 November 1993).

Despite the apparent success of retaliatory threats in the two cases studied here, we believe threats should be used only as a last resort against economic superpowers such as Japan and the European Union. We share the financial authorities' concern that, if push ever really came to shove, a financial conflict between any of the leading economic powers could have potentially devastating effects on global financial markets. As far as the large financial centers are concerned, the potential costs of market disruption or closure will generally far outweigh the potential gains from retaliatory threats.

The main danger of retaliatory threats is that the threat would fail and the United States would feel compelled to retaliate. Retaliation against other economic superpowers could impose significant costs on the United States. At a minimum, these costs would include a loss of investment by firms from the target country (most likely Japan) and other foreign firms, which would worry that they would be the next targets. Indeed, Vice Minister of Finance Makoto Utsumi warned of such a Japanese response if the Fair Trade in Financial Services bill became law.[42]

The first rule in financial market access policy should be to forswear the use of threats when the national treatment principle is met. This rule is essential to prevent the inappropriate use of threats that could lead to international conflicts between the superpowers and, ultimately, market closure. To their credit, most versions of the Fair Trade in Financial Services bill contain a provision intended to reassure the European Union that, because it offers national treatment, it is not a target for US retaliatory threats (*Financial Times* 29 May 1990, 2; Senate Banking Committee 1990). However, the Union objected that some early versions of the bill contained an implicit threat because they do not grandfather the rights of existing EU firms in the United States to expand into new activities, a right explicitly guaranteed in the Second Banking Directive at the strong urging of the United States. Without this grandfathering, some US policymakers worry that the bill might provoke the Union into reconsidering the grandfathering of existing US subsidiaries in the Second Banking Directive.[43]

---

42. Some in the press interpreted Utsumi's remarks as a threat that "Tokyo would respond by curbing credit to the United States, creating a 'very, very harmful' situation" (see, e.g, Clyde H. Farnsworth, "Japan's Stern Warning on Trade Sanctions," *New York Times*, 29 January 1991, D18). In fact, the Reuter transcript of the 28 January 1991 Mulford-Utsumi news conference suggests that Utsumi warned that the bill would send a discouraging signal to Japanese firms that "might be very, very harmful *for both of us*" [emphasis added].

43. See, for example, the statements of Eugene McAllister (State Department), Bruce Wilson (USTR), and John LaWare (Federal Reserve) before the House Committee on Banking,

This does not mean that the economic superpowers should abjure the use of retaliatory threats against each other. Rather, threats should be used judiciously and only if good-faith negotiations fail. Threats may be justified, for example, to deter major violations of international agreements or generally accepted international principles governing market access. Thus, we believe the United States was justified in threatening retaliation over the Second Banking Directive because its original reciprocity provisions could have violated the national treatment principle. Similarly, the Schumer amendment served a useful role in enforcing the national treatment principle in one egregious case of discrimination.

Alternative Approaches to Market Access

In relations among the major industrial countries, there are better alternatives to demands for reciprocity backed up by retaliatory threats in order to open foreign financial markets. Our preference is for true, *reciprocal* negotiations—be they bilateral, multilateral, or "minilateral" among a small group of like-minded countries. The great advantage of reciprocal negotiations is that they can lead to mutually beneficial liberalization while reducing the risk of costly conflicts.

There are several models for negotiations leading to improved market access for all parties. The Canada–United States Free Trade Agreement (FTA) and the North American Free Trade Agreement (NAFTA) are examples of successful bilateral negotiations in which all parties came away satisfied that they had improved access to the other's financial markets (Schott and Smith 1988, 142–45). The ongoing multilateral negotiation on financial services in the Uruguay Round is a moderately promising but so far disappointing vehicle for achieving liberalization among a large number of countries at differing stages of development. The OECD has held periodic discussions to develop voluntary Codes of Liberalization based on the national treatment principle.

These approaches to market access have important strengths and weaknesses. One strength of the Canada-US FTA, NAFTA, and the Uruguay Round negotiations is that they involve liberalization in both goods and services, including financial services. As a result, parties that might not highly value an agreement on financial services alone may nevertheless be induced to open financial markets as part of a broader package of liberalization involving other products of greater interest. A special merit of the Uruguay Round and OECD approaches is that they seek to strengthen adherence to the national treatment principle, which is a necessary but not sufficient condition for improved market access.[44]

Subcommittee on Economic Stabilization, 24 April 1991. Recent versions of the Fair Trade in Financial Services Act do provide for grandfathering of existing operations.

44. Treasury officials involved in the US-Canada negotiations point out that the negotiators could not agree on how the national treatment principle should be applied so they struck a series of ad hoc deals that in several instances provided for better-than-national treatment

The main weakness of the Canada-US FTA, the OECD codes, and probably of the Uruguay Round is that they do not deal with nondiscriminatory obstacles to market access such as Japan's Article 65 or the Glass-Steagall Act. As discussed earlier, it is just such different but nondiscriminatory regulatory environments that are likely to give rise to conflicts among the major industrial countries.

Our preferred approach to these nondiscriminatory regulatory obstacles is "minilateral" negotiations. The model we have in mind is very similar to the negotiations on capital adequacy requirements among the Group of 10 industrial countries under the auspices of the BIS's (Basel) Committee on Banking Supervision.[45] As might be expected of negotiations involving complex and sensitive issues of different national regulatory regimes and international banking competitiveness, the Basel Committee negotiations were slow and difficult. Agreement was reached first between the authorities of the two leading financial markets—the United Kingdom and the United States—and later broadened to include Japan, Germany, the European Community, and others.

The key ingredients to such an approach to improved market access would be:

- participation by the financial authorities of the leading financial powers—the United States, European Union, and Japan—with admission open to any other countries willing to join;

- a political mandate to propose changes in national regulatory systems that would improve market access, subject to legitimate prudential concerns about maintaining safety and soundness in the system, consumer protection, and competition;

- patience.

It will not be easy to negotiate changes in national regulatory systems. Few governments will appreciate foreign pressure to change what they view as strictly domestic policies. The OECD and the Uruguay Round negotiations rely on the national treatment principle precisely because it allows for differences in national regulations as long as they are nondiscriminatory. What we are proposing goes well beyond national treatment. To reduce nondiscriminatory regulatory obstacles to foreign market access may require either very substantial changes in some countries' regulations to allow for international harmonization and/or a willingness to allow

---

for US firms in Canada.

45. It is also known as the Basel Committee or the Cooke Committee after its long-standing chairman, Peter Cooke of the Bank of England. For a description of the committee's negotiations leading to the 1988 Capital Agreement, see Peter Cooke (1989).

foreign firms to operate in the host country under their home country's rules.[46]

It will undoubtedly take considerable time to develop consensus first among regulatory authorities and eventually among politicians on which national regulations can be changed to improve market access while satisfying legitimate concerns about safety and soundness, consumer protection, and antitrust issues. US policymakers have grown exceedingly frustrated at the slow pace of Japan's market-opening efforts under the yen-dollar negotiations. Europeans, flush with their successful market liberalization in the Europe 1992 process, are impatient with both Japanese and US plodding. It would be a serious mistake, however, if this impatience were translated into unilaterally imposed deadlines for action backed by threats of retaliation. The "gun to the head" approach to securing improved financial market access, which the United States has employed with Japan and the EC has tried with the United States, is simply inappropriate for countries that bear primary responsibility for the safety and soundness of the entire global financial system.

Reciprocal negotiations on market access may be difficult and slow. But they are preferable to the alternative—the risk of endless conflicts that could close rather than open markets and could, in the worst case, precipitate a financial crisis. In conducting economic relations among the major financial powers, policymakers would do well to follow a simple rule: do unto others as you would have them do unto you.

---

46. For a valuable analysis of what rules—home country, host country, or harmonized rules—could govern trade in financial services, see Sydney J. Key and Hal S. Scott (1991).

III

Conclusions and Recommendations

12

Super 301: A Two-Edged Sword

If one is to engage in public diplomacy, it had better be diplomatic.[1]

—Carla Hills

Speak softly and carry a big stick.[2]

—Theodore Roosevelt

In this chapter we assess the results of the super 301 cases, including the "noncases" involving Korea and Taiwan. We conclude that the 1988 super 301 legislation was reasonably effective in achieving congressional objectives but was actually no more likely to produce results than regular section 301, as implemented since September 1985. Moreover, super 301 is unnecessarily inflammatory and adds little or no additional negotiating leverage. Super 301 is also undesirable to the extent it forces the president to trade off competing national interests simply because the timing of the deadline for priority designations is bad. For these reasons, we do not support proposals to statutorily lock in President Clinton's executive order renewing super 301, much less other proposals floated in Congress for a "super duper" 301, along the lines of the various Gephardt proposals.[3] President Clinton's super 301 is a kinder, gentler version of the original, but it is still unnecessary and potentially counterproductive.

---

1. Remarks to the Institute for International Economics, 24 June 1992.

2. Speech at the Minnesota State Fair, 2 September 1901.

3. See chapter 2 for a discussion of some of the versions of the Gephardt amendment, as well as other proposals for "super duper" 301s.

When skillfully and consistently employed, regular 301 can be an effective tool for negotiating clearly defined trade barriers. Here we propose safeguards for ensuring that 301 remains an effective negotiating tool, that the neglect of international economic policy that occurred in the first half of the 1980s is not repeated, and that trade agreements are vigorously enforced. The evidence from the broad survey of section 301 cases in chapter 4 and the detailed case studies in part II, however, suggests that ill-defined structural barriers are not amenable to negotiation under a 301-type process, regardless of the procedural form. Proposals for addressing those trade problems are discussed in chapter 13.

The Results in 1989–90

The original super 301's only "super" feature was that it forced the US Trade Representative to designate priority countries and practices by a definite date each year, a process widely perceived as labeling targeted countries unfair traders. To the extent that countries wanted to avoid this label, the original super 301 could increase USTR's leverage in negotiations with those countries. A second source of potential leverage was the weight of congressional expectations, which might have made USTR's retaliatory threats more credible. Beyond these two differences in potential bargaining power—one legal, one political—super and regular 301 are procedurally identical (table 2.3 in chapter 2).

There is not much evidence, however, that these potential sources of leverage were particularly helpful when super 301 was implemented in 1989–90. Contrary to conventional wisdom, the threat of super 301 designation did not garner significant concessions from South Korea or Taiwan (chapter 7). Neither government offered meaningful concessions on agriculture, which was the subject of the majority of private-sector complaints submitted to USTR during the designation process. South Korea's major concessions on paper were in the areas of investment and other administrative barriers raised by customs procedures and technical standards setting. But effective implementation was lacking, and disputes in these areas remained at the center of bilateral negotiations five years later.

In Taiwan's case there was no formal agreement. USTR simply noted that the government of Taiwan had put forward an "action plan" for reducing the bilateral surplus by 30 percent over three years—the Gephardt target—and for improving economic relations with the United States and therefore did not designate it. The surplus reduction target was met, in large part because of the sharp appreciation of the New Taiwan dollar. By contrast, over the same period, South Korea's global surplus was eliminated and its surplus with the United States reduced by nearly 80 percent (even though its currency appreciated by much less). Taiwan's only firm commitment for liberalizing its treatment of imports was a promise to reduce the average tariff on industrial products (from 10 to 5 percent) and on agricultural products (from 26 to about 20 percent). This continued the process begun in the early 1980s of cutting selected tariffs in the face of American demands.

Nor does the weight of congressional expectations appear to have conveyed much additional leverage. India refused to negotiate its barriers to insurance and foreign investment bilaterally and declined to make concessions, yet it suffered no consequences. Nor can the results in Brazil be attributed in any significant degree to the super 301 threat. President Fernando Collor de Mello was elected in December 1989 on a platform advocating broad economic reforms, and shortly after taking office in March 1990 he announced a sweeping reform program, including the elimination of most quantitative import barriers. (These cases are discussed in chapter 6.)

That leaves the three cases targeting Japan, but the pressure on Japan in trade negotiations is always intense. Proponents of super 301 claimed that past trade negotiations had not resulted in increased US exports and that a more aggressive approach was needed. But it is not true that past bilateral agreements had no impact on US exports, nor is it clear that the results under super 301 were significantly better. Agreements were reached in all nine previous section 301 negotiations with Japan, and in six of those nine we concluded that the agreements had contributed to increases in US exports sufficiently significant to be termed successes.[4] The original semiconductor agreement, which expired in 1991, also resulted in large increases in US exports, though not the 20 percent market demanded by US negotiators. We thus do not classify it as a success (see the discussion in chapter 3).

Agreements were also reached in all three super 301 cases targeting Japan, but the results in two have been the subject of ongoing disputes. The satellite case appears to have eliminated discriminatory Japanese practices, and the results to date have not been challenged by US negotiators or exporters. But the outcome in the supercomputer case is less clear; it appears to be a "results-oriented" outcome with the Japanese government unilaterally deciding what the result should be. Cray, for one, disagreed with the apparent initial assigned US share of one-third of public supercomputer procurements (it won three of the nine procurements made in 1991–92), and USTR opened a review of Japan's compliance with the agreement in 1993. The dispute died down after six of fifteen procurements in fiscal 1993 went to US suppliers, but it could well recur.

The third case involved Japanese barriers to imports of wood products. In August 1994, the American Forest Products Association responded

---

4. Gold and Nanto (1991) also found that US exports to Japan between 1985 and 1990 in sectors subject to market-access agreements had increased faster than either total US exports to Japan or to the world.

to a USTR solicitation of public comments on practices that should be considered for designation as priorities under the renewed super 301 at the end of September. The AFPA submission does not explicitly call on USTR to redesignate Japan but urges US negotiators to make monitoring of the 1990 agreement a "priority area" in which US and Japanese negotiators agree on "benchmarks to ensure its successful implementation" (the AFPA comments are on file in the USTR office).

AFPA's demands go far beyond mere implementation of the 1990 agreement, however, and its submission to USTR does not contain compelling evidence that Japan has violated either the letter or the spirit of the 1990 agreement. First, several of the barriers contained in the complaint were not dealt with in the earlier agreement. Second, the industry is not satisfied with the level of tariff reductions on wood products achieved in the Uruguay Round, but Japan fulfilled its commitment in the super 301 agreement to negotiate average tariff reductions of about a third. Finally, the industry cites the lack of change in the composition of US exports of wood and wood products as evidence of Japan's failure to live up to its commitments. But to the extent that tariff escalation is the major barrier to value-added exports—and that has consistently been the focus of US industry efforts to liberalize the Japanese market—one would not yet expect to see much impact in the trade figures. The negotiated tariff cuts will not even begin until Japan ratifies the Uruguay Round agreement and then will be phased in over five years.

Thus, judging the outcomes rather generously, we conclude that four of the six formal super 301 investigations resulted in market opening of varying degrees, slightly below the 76 percent success rate achieved from 1985 through 1988 (see chapter 3). A harsher judge, however, might exclude Brazil from the list of successes because the super 301 case had little or no influence on President Collor's election and the subsequent economic policy shift; this exclusion would lower the success ratio to three of five (60 percent). If Japan's compliance with the supercomputer agreement is ultimately judged to be unsatisfactory, the overall results would tally below the average for section 301 cases resolved since 1985.

The failure of super 301 to achieve more than it did highlights the limitations of bilateral trade negotiations based on unilateral demands generally and of the super 301 process specifically. First, the negotiations with Brazil, Korea, and Taiwan all suggest that even relatively vulnerable countries engage in substantial and widespread liberalization only when their policymakers believe it is in their interest to do so. Fear of US retaliation may squeeze out marginal concessions or promises that are held out with one hand and taken back with the other. But Brazil's new president liberalized trade barriers as part of an overall economic reform; the super 301 case may have accelerated the pace of liberalization, but it did not cause it. Korea and Taiwan were not ready to accelerate their gradual liberalization programs, as the United States wanted, and largely avoided doing so. India's reformist prime minister, P. V. Narasimha Rao, did not take office until well after termination of the super 301 cases and has pursued substantial liberalization of investment rules with no additional US pressure.

With regard to super 301 specifically, the process again foundered on the rocks of political reality. First, in trying to minimize the collateral damage to other trade and foreign policy interests, USTR Hills felt compelled to designate priority practices in other countries besides Japan. She was fortunate in the Brazil case because of the election of Collor but was forced to swallow India's intransigence in the interest of preserving momentum in the Uruguay Round and in order to avoid the humiliation of a likely negative finding of the General Agreement on Tariffs and Trade (GATT) panel had she retaliated against Indian exports. Although India may have been deserving based on the statutory criteria of numerous and pervasive trade barriers, the failure to retaliate—though justified under the circumstances—carried a cost in terms of future negotiating credibility.

Also, the political pressures and high expectations associated with the first round of super 301 designations probably contributed to USTR's apparent willingness to accept agreements for agreement's sake with Korea and Taiwan. The timing of those deals allowed USTR to tout how effectively it was using super 301 and to deflect some of the congressional criticism engendered by its not naming Japan a priority foreign country generally for the number and pervasiveness of its trade barriers. Thus, USTR accepted commitments from Korea in areas that by their nature involved a great deal of bureaucratic involvement and discretion, but apparently did not provide for the sort of monitoring and follow-up that would have been necessary to ensure meaningful implementation. Taiwan simply did not have to promise very much to get off the hook. Ultimately, it is naive to expect that broader political and economic concerns will not factor into trade policy decision making. And it would be folly to try to legislate them out of the process.

Super 301 Is Unnecessary and Undesirable

Super 301 is not necessary for an effective US trade policy because it adds very little negotiating leverage to that which already exists under regular section 301. The limited *potential* leverage that it provides was of limited practical utility in 1989–90 because of political realities that cannot—and should not—be eliminated through procedural manipulation. Super 301 is undesirable because the potentially significant—and unnecessary— costs outweigh the limited benefits.

In October 1991, USTR initiated against China perhaps the largest section 301 case ever undertaken. This case, described in more detail in box 12.1,

Box 12.1 Regular versus super 301: the China case

On 10 October 1991, the United States initiated a regular section 301 case to address what the administration described as "China's web of barriers to imports" (President Bush's letter to Senator Max Baucus, 19 July 1991, 8). Several influential senators characterized the China case as "the largest . . . ever undertaken" (Letter from Max Baucus and other senators to President Bush, 30 July 1992, 1). In August 1992, the United States published a hit list of $3.9 billion of Chinese exports for possible retaliation, and China threatened counterretaliation against $4 billion of US exports. On 10 October 1992, the deadline for US retaliatory action, the two sides concluded an agreement. Deputy USTR Michael Moskow estimated that, if fully implemented, the agreement might increase US exports by billions of dollars annually (*Journal of Commerce*, 13 October 1992, 3A).

US trade officials had begun meeting with Chinese negotiators in June 1991 to discuss market-access issues. In July, responding to a letter from Max Baucus and several other senators urging action, President Bush promised to initiate section 301 proceedings if consultations with the Chinese in August failed to yield substantial market-opening commitments (Letter from President Bush to Senator Baucus, 19 July 1991, 3 and 10).

Thus, Congress and administration officials strongly supported the case, both believing that China's pervasive market-access barriers had to be addressed, especially since Chinese protectionism appeared to increase after 1988 (Letter from President Bush to Max Baucus, 19 July 1991, 9). Also of concern to US officials was the ballooning bilateral trade deficit, from $6 billion in 1989 to nearly $13 billion in 1991. By 1993, the bilateral deficit with China had nearly doubled again, to $23 billion, second in size only to the deficit with Japan.[1] The president charged that China's protectionist policies "undoubtedly contributed to a 17 percent decline in US sales to China in 1990" (Letter from President Bush to Max Baucus, 19 July 1991, 9)

During the negotiations, USTR focused on barriers that affected major US export interests and that appeared to be inconsistent with GATT principles,

illustrates how the much-maligned regular 301 can be a powerful crowbar for opening foreign markets. The USTR investigation in case no. 301-88 addressed a broad array of Chinese trade barriers, and it was "super" in magnitude. The United States threatened retaliation against $3.9 billion of Chinese exports. Although super 301 had expired a year earlier, the USTR announcement of the investigation certainly looked as though China had been targeted based on super 301-like criteria: the number, pervasiveness, and adverse impact of its trade barriers on US exports. The case was resolved precisely on the deadline for US retaliation, with China agreeing to very substantial liberalization involving the elimination of up to 80 percent of its nontariff barriers over four years.

Several features of this case support our conclusions regarding when section 301 is most likely to produce results and illustrate how regular 301 can achieve substantial market opening as well as super 301 could. First, Congress and the administration were united in support of the including various quantitative restrictions, technical barriers to trade, and the lack of transparency in China's regulation of international trade. US negotiators also sought liberalization of China's high tariffs and import-substitution policies (USTR, Fact Sheet, 10 October 1991; USTR, press release, 21 August 1992). The agreement included specific Chinese commitments to substantially reduce all these barriers. A subministerial working group was established to monitor compliance (USTR, press release, 10 October 1992).

Avoiding section 301 retaliation was not China's only incentive for reaching agreement with the United States. US negotiators made it clear that China's prospects for gaining membership in GATT would be slim unless it met US demands. It was also suggested that the market-access talks had "a very direct relationship with continuing MFN status for China" (*Inside U.S. Trade*, 25 September 1992, 16–17; Max Baucus statement, *Financial Times*, 11 October 1991, 4). When the agreement was signed, the United States then stated that it would "support China's accession to the GATT."

In sum, this case closely resembles the kind of action that Congress intended under super 301 (see the case summary in the appendix for further details). It addressed a broad array of trade-restricting practices in a high priority country, and it resulted in liberalization that could have a large impact on US exports. While unusual leverage was available to negotiators in this case, it nevertheless illustrates how USTR, having identified priorities, can use regular 301 to negotiate the removal of significant trade barriers, credibly threatening to retaliate if necessary.

—Charles Iceland

---

[1]These official statistics from the US Department of Commerce overstate to some degree the size of the bilateral deficit because of the difficulties in measuring reexports in both directions through Hong Kong. Lardy (1994, chapter 4) attempts to adjust the figures to take these problems into account; his estimates show a similar pattern but at a somewhat lower level, with the US bilateral deficit increasing from $4 billion in 1989 to $9.5 billion in 1991 and $14 billion in 1992.

case, which increased US negotiators' credibility when they threatened retaliation.

Second, China was relatively dependent on the US market, with about one-third of its exports being sold in the United States. This is the average level of export dependence correlated with success in other 301 cases (see chapter 4). In addition, China's desire to rejoin the GATT, which requires US approval, provided additional leverage, as did the annual most-favored nation (MFN) renewal process.

Third, China's highly restrictive trade regime offered many clearly visible and measurable targets, including numerous high tariffs and quotas on products of interest to the United States. Moreover, USTR chose to focus on barriers "that appear to be inconsistent with the multilateral rules and trade liberalization principles that would apply if China were a member of the GATT" (USTR, Fact Sheet, 10 October 1991). Inclusion of GATT issues gave US negotiators more credibility and leverage with their Chinese counterparts because they could plausibly claim that they were not seeking to extract unilateral advantages for the United States. The United States could thus portray itself as the law-enforcing cop rather than as a corrupt, bribe-taking bully. This issue of GATT conformity also may have made it easier for China to offer concessions, which China could reckon as part of the unavoidable price of its accession.[5]

Fourth, as in the super 301 cases against Japan, USTR has assiduously monitored China's implementation of the agreement. In 1993, when it appeared that China was backsliding on its commitments, USTR again set a deadline for retaliation if China did not fulfill its promises. China acceded to US demands.

Finally, the regular 301 process gave USTR the latitude to try informal persuasion first and then to move to a formal 301 investigation only when deemed necessary and appropriate. Control over timing allowed USTR to put maximum pressure on China without endangering negotiations in other, noneconomic areas, such as human rights. USTR initiation also sent an important signal that the administration gave the case high priority.

These elements—US unity and commitment, a vulnerable target, the transparency of the barriers negotiated, GATT consistency, diligent monitoring and enforcement, and careful timing—are important to the success of most 301 cases. When the president and Congress agree on trade priorities, when the president has the flexibility to determine the timing and content of negotiations, and when the United States is seeking to uphold international trade norms, regular 301 can be an effective policy instrument. And, as in the China case, the president can direct USTR to designate any country or any practice as a priority for negotiation at any time. The China case also demonstrates that, using regular 301, USTR can credibly threaten to retaliate and can achieve significant market-opening results.[6]

The marginal benefits of super 301 must be weighed against the potential costs. First, some foreign governments simply will not respond to highly publicized threats under super 301. Certainly, the Indian government easily resisted the super 301 threat and in fact won domestic and

---

5. We do not wish to push the GATT conformity theme too far. Some Chinese concessions on intellectual property were not made available to other countries on an MFN basis. US negotiators say the Chinese insisted on these discriminatory provisions.

6. Several readers have quite reasonably questioned whether it is valid to attribute success in this case to section 301, given the unusual leverage provided by threats to deny China MFN status under the Jackson-Vanik (section 402) provisions of the 1974 Trade Act and by threats to impede China's accession to the GATT. Clearly, MFN renewal and China's GATT accession provided implicit leverage, and in fact US negotiators explicity invoked GATT accession. Nevertheless, the 301 case precipitated the agreement with China, and US and other exporters were able to benefit sooner than if they had had to wait for China to liberalize on its own or as part of GATT accession. Thus we view it as legitimate to count this case as a success for section 301.

international praise for standing up to US bullying. The European Community avoided super 301 designation entirely by threatening to counter-retaliate and by warning of dire consequences for the Uruguay Round negotiations.[7] Both the European Community and China can credibly threaten counterretaliation against the United States because they have counterretaliated in past trade disputes (see chapter 4).[8] And the day may be drawing nearer when Japan will finally say "no."[9]

If some US trading partners, particularly the larger ones, refuse to negotiate, the United States must either retaliate or lose credibility. Either outcome carries potentially large economic and political costs. While systemic and structural barriers are a legitimate problem for US exporters in some cases, forcing the president to address them by designating countries as unfair traders is simply not an effective solution. The new Clinton super 301 assiduously avoids labeling a country as an unfair trader. However, the popular perception both in the United States and in target countries, particularly Japan, is quite likely to be the same as before. Thus, even the kinder, gentler Clinton super 301 runs an unnecessary risk of failure.

A second potential cost of the super 301 process stems from the annual deadline for setting priorities. It is a truism that the president is the final arbiter who must weigh sometimes conflicting economic, foreign policy, and security goals and decide what is in the national interest. The super 301 deadline can put the president in the undesirable position of having to decide whether to designate a priority unfair trading country or practice precisely when he is negotiating with that country on other US priorities. One can easily imagine a super 301 deadline falling in the midst of delicate negotiations with China on arms proliferation, with Japan on aid to the

---

7. The deputy head of the EC mission to the United States, Corrado Pirzio-Biroli, warned: "It is hard to see how the USTR could succeed in implementing the 1988 trade act vis-à-vis the EC without prompting the most serious trade war since the 1930s" (Bhagwati and Patrick 1990, 262).

8. In 1983, China temporarily stopped buying US wheat in retaliation for the Reagan administration's unilateral imposition of quotas on its textile and apparel exports after negotiations to renew a bilateral agreement under the Multi-Fiber Arrangement broke down. A compromise was worked out soon thereafter (Destler and Odell 1987, 16). In 1991, while seated next to a Boeing representative, Prime Minister Li Peng publicly threatened counterretaliation against Boeing if the United States did not renew China's MFN status. Similar threats were levied against US grain and aircraft exporters during a 1993 debate on MFN.

In 1985, the European Community raised tariffs on US lemons and walnuts in response to US retaliation against subsidized EC pasta exports (section 301 case no. 11, EC tariff preferences for citrus, and no. 25, pasta export subsidies). In 1993, the Community imposed $15 million in sanctions in counterretaliation for a US ban on EC bids for $20 million in US government contracts during a dispute over government procurement.

9. During trade negotiations with the Clinton administration, Japan has steadfastly refused to accept quantitative targets for measuring progress under trade agreements. After the breakdown of the US-Japan framework negotiations in February 1994, a director general at MITI, Yoshihiro Sakamoto, reportedly warned that Japan might counterretaliate against any GATT-illegal US retaliation. (*Financial Times*, 1 March 1994, 4).

former Soviet Union, with both Japan and South Korea on sanctions against North Korea, or with the Europeans on joint military intervention in some political hot spot. The super 301 deadline may force the president to make unnecessary and costly trade-offs among US interests when, if he had greater discretion on timing, he could achieve more by pursuing US goals one at a time.

A third potential cost of reviving super 301 is erosion of US leadership and credibility in multilateral and regional trade negotiations. Super 301 is universally reviled by US trading partners, who associate it with the worst excesses of US aggressive unilateralism: that is, the labeling of countries as unfair traders and of specific practices as unreasonable when there is no violation of international rules or agreements. Having agreed in the Uruguay Round to rules in the new areas—services, intellectual property rights, and investment—and significant reform of the GATT dispute settlement process (in part to restrain US unilateralism), many countries will bitterly resent renewed use of super 301, or any section 301 action that violates US GATT obligations.

Why should America's trading partners accept US leadership in negotiating further reciprocal liberalization in the World Trade Organization (WTO) or in regional forums in the Western Hemisphere and Pacific Basin if US negotiators continue to make demands for unilateral liberalization backed by the threat of super 301? Many Asian countries, in addition to Japan, are particularly hostile to super 301 because they see themselves as potential targets. Diplomats from these countries say privately that continued use of super 301 would undermine the Asia Pacific Economic Cooperation (APEC) forum and make it difficult to launch negotiations for freer trade and investment in the region.

In any negotiation—including the back and forth between the executive and legislative branches over US trade policy—there can be a tension between flexibility and credibility. Presidents want to retain maximum flexibility to conduct policy as they see fit. But a majority in Congress will not always share the president's priorities, may not agree with the means chosen to pursue them, or may not believe his assurances that he will try "to do better." Therefore, Congress often seeks to circumscribe executive-branch discretion, as it has done over the years in repeatedly amending section 301. And in international trade negotiations, the less discretion a negotiator has as to whether to retaliate, the more credible a threat to do so is likely to be. But imperfect information between negotiating partners, miscalculation, or simple obstinacy may prevent agreement, and since retaliation can be quite costly, some flexibility is often needed. Achieving the appropriate balance between flexibility and credibility in negotiations is always difficult. Below we suggest two amendments that would modestly restrict USTR's discretion in section 301 cases. These changes, we believe, would achieve many of the benefits of super 301 without the costs.

Alternatives to Super 301

Congress created the original super 301 because many members felt that the executive branch had not consistently and aggressively attacked unfair trade practices abroad, especially alleged systemic and structural barriers in Japan. The super 301 requirement that the USTR designate priority countries and practices each year was intended to keep the administration's feet to the fire. Super 301 proponents assumed that any reasonable priority-setting exercise would naturally end up with Japan at the top of the list. The other amendments to 301, which apply to *all* section 301 cases, were intended to strengthen USTR in negotiations, ironically, by tying negotiators' hands—that is, by setting clear deadlines and by making retaliation mandatory in some cases. Another reason for making retaliation mandatory in cases involving violations of trade agreements was the perception among many in Congress that the terms of some past trade agreements had not been met.

Congress and industry had good reason to be frustrated with the way section 301 was used in the early 1980s. Cases dragged on for years, and little was achieved in the way of rule enforcement, much less market opening. Although few observers criticize President Clinton or USTR Kantor for lack of aggressiveness in attacking foreign trade barriers, they will not be in office forever, and it is not unreasonable for Congress to seek some insurance that the neglect of the early 1980s will not recur. We make two recommendations for guarding against such neglect. First, we suggest that the House Ways and Means and Senate Finance Committees be permitted to petition USTR to initiate section 301 investigations. Second, we recommend adoption of a modified version of Senator Max Baucus's proposed Trade Agreement Compliance Act (TACA), last introduced in the Senate in 1993. Recommendations for dealing with broader structural trade disputes, such as the "Japan problem," are addressed in chapter 13.

Setting Trade Priorities

The proposal to allow the House Ways and Means Committee and the Senate Finance Committee to petition USTR to open 301 investigations dates back at least to the debate over the 1988 Omnibus Trade and Competitiveness Act, when it was considered and rejected. It has periodically been revived; for example, Senator Max Baucus proposed such a measure in super 301 renewal legislation introduced in 1993.[10]

---

10. An untitled bill introduced by Senator Baucus in the first session of the 103rd Congress. A 1994 version to extend super 301 authority (S. 1858), introduced on 22 February, omits this provision.

Under this proposal, if members of either committee believed that the executive branch was neglecting foreign trade barriers, they could submit a petition. This would be one means of ensuring that the president maintains a constructive dialogue with Congress on trade priorities. This proposal does not unduly limit the president's discretion or allow Congress to initiate section 301 actions; it only permits Congress to petition the executive branch to do so. USTR can reject any congressional petition that it deems to be without merit. Moreover, the proposal allows the president to maintain considerable discretion over the timing of investigations. The USTR could negotiate with the congressional trade committees on the timing of petition submissions or whether USTR would initiate the investigation on its own.

Critics argue that Congress long ago distanced itself from direct involvement on sector-specific trade matters because its members wanted to be insulated from special interest group pressures. They fear that this proposal just opens a Pandora's box in which USTR would be bombarded with congressional petitions seeking relief on behalf of a variety of private interests. But there are at least two important reasons for believing that will not happen.

First, past behavior under similar circumstances does not suggest that Congress would abuse such authority. The House Ways and Means Committee and the Senate Finance Committee have for years had the power to order the International Trade Commission (ITC) to initiate escape-clause investigations (section 201 of the Trade Act of 1974).[11] This authority has been invoked only four times, all in the late 1970s. In three of the four cases, private petitioners had brought earlier cases in which the ITC had found injury and had recommended import relief that the president then rejected. The congressionally initiated cases also ended in ITC recommendations for relief, and in each case the president this time provided modest import relief: orderly marketing agreements for footwear and three years of increased tariffs for high-carbon ferrochromium and bolts, nuts, and large screws of iron or steel (the legislation allows for up to five years, with a possible three-year extension). In the fourth case, involving sugar, the ITC again found that the industry was injured by imports and recommended reduced quotas, but the president rejected the recommendation and provided no relief.

Second, USTR can still reject any petition or, if that is politically impossible, set the terms of the investigation. USTR has in fact resisted quite strong congressional or industry pressure to use section 301 for protectionist purposes. In 1982, for example, more than 100 members of the House and 43 senators signed letters to USTR William Brock urging him to accept

---

11. Either of the committees or the president can order the ITC—an independent agency—to initiate investigations. The USTR, however, is a part of the executive branch and cannot be ordered by simple congressional committee resolution to do something.

and vigorously pursue a section 301 petition soon to be filed by the Footwear Industries of America (FIA). The FIA claimed that a variety of trade barriers to footwear imports in a number of countries were diverting exports to the US market and injuring the domestic industry. Escape-clause (section 201) protection for the industry had expired in June 1981, and President Reagan had rejected ITC's recommendation to extend it. Although the FIA also argued that trade barriers in a number of countries inhibited its members' ability to export, that was not a focus of the petition filed with USTR. Despite the political pressure, USTR significantly pared the list of both countries and practices that it would investigate—limiting the investigation to alleged denial of market access for US exporters in Korea, Taiwan, Brazil, and Japan—and, in so doing, shifted the focus from imports of footwear to exports and market access abroad.

Thus, the record suggests neither a blithe willingness on the part of these committees to abuse authority of this type nor an unwillingness on the part of USTR to stand up to congressional pressure if necessary. Nor will members of the two trade committees, who represent a wide range of sectoral and regional interests, always agree on every case that comes before them, providing further discipline on the number of cases forwarded. More generally, as I. M. Destler (1992, 203 and 210) concluded in his analysis of American trade politics, despite the unusual pressures on the system in the 1980s,

> the system held. Congress pressed its priorities—its predisposition toward tough-ness—but Congress refrained from reclaiming, directly, the primary trade power granted by the Constitution. . . . [In the 1988 Trade Act] and subsequently, legisla-tors have given renewed evidence of their preference to delegate product-specific trade responsibility.

Enforcing Trade Agreements

Our second set of proposals aim to strengthen the monitoring and enforce-ment of existing trade agreements. Many trade negotiators argue that USTR and the relevant agencies already adequately monitor agreements and that USTR already has the authority to retaliate for noncompliance. While largely true—especially in recent years when monitoring and dis-pute settlement mechanisms have become more important in bilateral trade agreements—the past record is spotty, and some industries have had legitimate complaints about the quality of US agreements and their enforcement. Essentially, our proposals are an insurance policy against future neglect.

The Trade Agreement Compliance Act (TACA) proposed by Senator Baucus would allow any interested party, as defined in the statute and implementing regulations, to petition USTR to investigate whether trading partners are abiding by existing bilateral agreements. (GATT agreements are explicitly excluded from this procedure.) USTR would have 90 days to issue a determination. If USTR determined that an agreement was being violated, it would be required to retaliate under section 301(a) (mandatory action) unless it invoked one of several waivers (see chapter 2). As drafted by Baucus, TACA states that nothing in the act should ''be construed to require actions inconsistent with the international obligations of the United States, including obligations under the General Agreement on Tariffs and Trade.'' Thus, this language does not require but would permit GATT-illegal retaliation.

As discussed in more detail in chapter 13, the new dispute settlement rules under the World Trade Organization do place some constraints on US unilateral action. Both to make US trade policy more effective and to avoid undermining the international trade regime, we recommend that the language in TACA should be modified to preclude the possibility of US retaliation in cases involving GATT commitments unless a GATT panel has ruled on the matter, finding that the foreign trade barrier was a violation of one of the agreements under the WTO. If the bilateral agreement in question involves issues not covered by the GATT or any other multilateral agreement under the WTO and USTR determines that a violation has occurred, USTR would have to devise a form of retaliation that does not violate US obligations (see chapter 13).

Finally, we recommend that the institutional structure for monitoring and dispute settlement in the 1990 super 301 wood products agreement should be emulated wherever appropriate and feasible (see chapter 5). Since additional monitoring requirements would impose greater staff and other resource burdens on USTR and its sister agencies, Congress may have to put its money where its mouth is and come up with additional funds for these purposes. If foreign trading partners know that the United States is scrutinizing current agreements, they are more likely to abide by them. This should help to reduce the risk of recurrent disputes.

Summary

The detailed analysis of the super 301 cases in chapters 5 through 7 leads to the conclusion that this crowbar was not as strong as its proponents thought. In its most significant successes, it appears to have deterred Japan from targeting the satellite industry for development and helped reduce a number of Japanese barriers to wood products imports. But the outcome in the case targeting Japanese public procurement of supercomputers has been the subject of repeated dispute, and the role of super 301 in encouraging Brazilian liberalization of its quantitative import restrictions was modest at best. The market-opening commitments from Taiwan were quite limited, while negotiators failed to get any concessions at all in the two Indian cases. The market-opening promises South Korea made to avoid super 301 designation were more significant but went largely unfulfilled.

Overall, super 301 appears to have been no more successful in market opening than regular 301 had been in the late 1980s. Generously counting the supercomputer and Brazil import licensing cases and the Taiwan "noncase" as successes, the super 301 success rate is 62.5 percent (five of eight). That is actually slightly below the 76 percent success rate (16 of 21) for regular 301 cases resolved during 1985–88.

The success rate since 1988 has dropped back to a level just below 50 percent. But not too much should be made of this finding. First, the success rate excluding cases seeking improved intellectual property protection is still a respectable 60 percent. As described in chapter 4, the less transparent the barrier and the less well-defined the rules, the less likely is section 301 to result in meaningful market opening. Chapter 8 also describes in detail the difficulties in negotiating, monitoring, and enforcing agreements intended to improve protection of intellectual property.

Second, there is nothing in the results of these cases to suggest that renewing or "putting teeth into" super 301 would improve the record. To the contrary, three of these cases were initiated by USTR, and four were special 301 cases—meaning USTR had been required to designate negotiating priorities and had been subject to even stricter negotiating deadlines than in regular section 301 cases. Four of these cases resulted in retaliation—withdrawal of Generalized System of Preferences benefits because of the lack of intellectual property protection in three—and in the two other cases, USTR published retaliation hit lists. In other words, there was a great deal of aggressive unilateralism in these cases, but to no avail.

In concluding, it is important to emphasize that neither regular 301, the original and Clinton super 301s, nor a quantitative Gephardt-like approach is a solution to all of America's market-access problems, including those with Japan. It is very difficult and time-consuming to attack structural barriers to trade. In most such cases, section 301 and Gephardt-type approaches are likely to be ineffective and may be counterproductive. Proposals for alternative policy approaches to this class of trade problems are offered in the following chapter.

13

Toward Aggressive Multilateralism

In Dodge City and in the territory on West, there's just one way to handle the killers and the spoilers, and that's with a US marshal and the smell of gunsmoke.

—voice-over to the 1950s radio show "Gunsmoke"

In the film *Rashomon*, Akira Kurosawa tells the story of an alleged murder from four irreconcilably different perspectives. Viewers see the movie from varied perspectives as well: as a metaphor for the subjectivity or unknowability of truth, as a study of class conflict, or—Kurosawa's own interpretation—as a simple illustration that people habitually lie to put themselves in the best possible light. Writing this book was like watching *Rashomon*. After years of research and hundreds of interviews with participants, it was still hard to describe objectively what really happened in the cases we examined. It was even more difficult to add up all the evidence and assess what it means.

We have benefited greatly from talking to many participants and close observers of the cases we studied. Virtually all of them were sincerely eager to help us learn the truth. What was striking was how differently people viewed the same event. Some of those perspectives are understandable: a Japanese negotiator will naturally view section 301 in a different light than a US negotiator. Other differences in perspective were harder to understand. We would ask people, "What was the decisive factor in the outcome of this case?" and get dramatically different interpretations, even from people in the same country operating out of the same government agency, and at the same time. Undoubtedly, some of these differences in interpretation were merely self-serving. But for the most part we

329

believe that they were honest differences in perspective: where you stand determines what you see.

These differences in interpretation or perspective make it hard to answer fundamental questions such as "what role did US retaliatory threats play in the outcome of this case?" or "in the absence of a US threat, would liberalization have occurred eventually anyway?" We tried to gather as many viewpoints and as much evidence as possible, and in the end we made judgments—subjectively. We also have tried to give as much detail as we reasonably could, both in our case studies and in our empirical work, to allow readers to make their own judgments. We had two conscious biases. In assessing the efficacy of US threats in opening foreign markets, we tended to give the benefit of the doubt to the evidence that threats were effective. Thus, if there was reasonable evidence that US threats were somewhat helpful in at least partly achieving US market-opening objectives, we scored that case a success. In contrast, in assessing the impact of US aggressive unilateralism on the global trading system, we gave the benefit of the doubt to the evidence that retaliatory threats have undermined, rather than strengthened, the General Agreement on Tariffs and Trade (GATT).

In this chapter we first summarize our findings and then draw policy recommendations and conclusions. The discussion is organized around three key questions. First, was section 301 market-opening or market-closing, and second, what were the broader consequences of an aggressive policy for the international trading system? Our conclusion is that on balance section 301 has been reasonably successful since 1985 in achieving the US goal of opening foreign markets and that aggressive unilateralism made a modestly positive contribution in moving the global trading system toward significant reforms.

The third question is, how if at all can an aggressive unilateral strategy continue to serve the national interest in light of the reforms adopted in the Uruguay Round? These reforms have profoundly changed the political and economic calculus of aggressive unilateralism. US failure to adjust to these changes could reduce the efficacy of future retaliatory threats, hence increasing the probability that retaliation will be imposed, and could also risk the loss of gains achieved in the Uruguay Round. In other words, now that the US marshal has brought law and order to Dodge City, it is important that the United States act as a law-abiding member of the community of nations instead of continuing to dispense "frontier justice," acting unilaterally in trade disputes as judge, jury, and executioner.[1]

We divide this discussion of the future of aggressive unilateralism into two further questions. What role should reciprocity play in US trade policy? And what role should retaliation play? With exports becoming a

---

1. The metaphor of aggressive unilateralism as "frontier justice" is from J. David Richardson (1983, 280–81).

more important source of US growth, more than ever the US national interest is served by defending the market-opening principles of national treatment and nondiscrimination. If the United States is to maintain its leadership of the international trading system, it must play by the same fair trade rules it demands of others. Domestically, US negotiators' political credibility hinges on their ability and willingness to vigorously enforce US rights under trade agreements. In chapter 12 we offered some suggestions for ensuring that the will to enforce agreements does not flag. Here we offer recommendations on how to use retaliatory threats most effectively to achieve the twin US goals of opening foreign markets and strengthening the global trading system. We propose that the United States pursue a strategy of aggressive multilateralism within the new World Trade Organization and a strategy of creative minilateralism outside the WTO.

Section 301, Market Opening, and the GATT

Careful analysis of 72 cases investigated between 1975 and 1992 leads us to conclude that section 301 was reasonably successful in opening foreign markets, especially after 1985. The analysis challenges the assumptions of 301's critics, concluding that 301 neither triggered major trade wars nor resulted in significant trade diversion. Nor did US aggressive unilateralism in the late 1980s and early 1990s cause the collapse of the Uruguay Round or prevent significant multilateral liberalization and reform of GATT rules. To the contrary, American arm-twisting provided an important incentive for its trading partners to negotiate rules that strengthened the international trading system and discouraged US unilateralism.

In about half of the 72 cases we studied, at least modest market opening was achieved. This compares with a success rate of just 17 percent for US foreign policy sanctions over a similar period (1973–90) (Hufbauer, Schott, and Elliott 1990). The contrast is even more striking in recent years. From September 1985, when President Reagan announced the Trade Policy Action Plan that launched aggressive unilateralism, through 1992, 60 percent of section 301 cases resolved were at least modest successes. This compares with just one out of three section 301 cases that achieved some improved market access prior to that. Dividing the sample of cases roughly into periods marked by the passage of trade bills in 1974, 1979, 1984, and 1988, section 301 had its greatest success in 1985–88, when 76 percent of all cases resolved were at least partially successful.

Still suspicious of the administration's commitment to section 301, however, Congress tried in the 1988 Omnibus Trade and Competitiveness Act to codify the more aggressive strategy employed since 1985. The 1988 amendments tightened negotiating deadlines, made retaliation in certain cases mandatory (unless waivers were invoked), and of course added the super 301 process requiring USTR to designate priority countries and practices. But the success rate for the six cases investigated under super 301 in 1989–90 is actually slightly lower, 67 percent, than the 76 percent success rate achieved the previous four years. Moreover, the success rate for all cases resolved after approval of the 1988 act dropped to around 50 percent.

The reasons for the recent decline in 301's effectiveness are not entirely clear, but these results do suggest that the way in which section 301 is used is far more important in determining outcomes than the specific language of the statute. And if the results from using super 301 are no better than those for regular 301 skillfully used, there is no justification for renewing super 301, especially given the hostility it generates among the United States' trading partners (see the discussion in chapter 12).

The number of section 301 petitions filed and investigations initiated by USTR has also dropped in recent years. In 1992 and 1993, there were only three new section 301 cases: one filed by a private petitioner that USTR closed when it determined there was no discernible impact on US exports (case no. 301-90 regarding Indonesian pencil slats) and two special 301 investigations (301-89 against Taiwan and 301-91 against Brazil). This pace compares to four per year in 1990 and 1991 and an average of six investigations opened annually in 1985–89. The emphasis on intellectual property rights (IPR) cases is also notable: half of the 12 cases initiated since 1989 have involved IPR issues.

The surge in intellectual property cases in recent years provides a partial explanation for the declining effectiveness of section 301. If the IPR cases are excluded from the sample of cases resolved since 1988, the success rate is a respectable 60 percent (12 of 20). The IPR cases are particularly difficult to resolve because they tend to become politicized and because there is typically little internal support for increased protection of intellectual property (see chapter 8). These cases thus support the finding that having allies in the target country that favor market opening helps US negotiators. The cases also highlight the importance of being able to clearly identify and define the barrier to be negotiated. Improving intellectual property protection in developing countries often requires extensive systemic changes that are impossible to achieve in a short time without substantial domestic political support.

The pace of 301 petition filings and investigations initiated by USTR may pick up again as interested parties begin to test the new dispute settlement procedures of the WTO. If so, policymakers should keep in mind the lessons from chapter 4 as to how and when section 301 is most likely to produce positive results. As noted above, two of the most important factors contributing to positive outcomes are domestic political support for reform in the target country and the transparency of the barrier targeted. US pressure is far more likely to overcome readily identified, specific barriers—such as tariffs and quotas—than broader, less easily defined or more subjective barriers, such as government procurement or administrative and regulatory impediments to trade. Also, the more dependent a trading partner is on the US market, the more likely it is to comply with US demands for market opening.

The statistical analysis described in chapter 4 also supports the conclusion that the change in practice and rhetoric of US trade policy after 1985 contributed to a higher probability of success in section 301 cases. Figure 1.3 in chapter 1 shows the dramatic increase in the use of public threats and retaliation after 1985. The analysis does not, however, support a conclusion that highly publicized retaliatory threats, as we have defined them, were a significant factor in the improved results.[2]

One unexpected result was the finding that initiation of an investigation by USTR was not a statistically significant factor in determining outcomes. We expected that the credibility of retaliatory threats would be greater if USTR initiated a case because its reputation would be on the line. While this may be true, the results are clouded by USTR's use of self-initiation to push liberalization in new areas. Five of the six USTR-initiated cases that ended in failure targeted nontraditional areas: intellectual property protection, services, and restrictions on foreign investment. Still, USTR's success rate in cases it initiated in these areas (three of nine), was better than when an IPR or services case was brought by a private petitioner, where just one of nine cases was successful. In other types of cases, USTR-initiated investigations resulted in positive outcomes 10 of 11 times. (The one failure was USTR's bid to remove the European Union's ban on beef from cattle treated with hormones.)

One other result is worth emphasizing. Although the sample of cases is too small to draw definitive conclusions, it is interesting that the improved record with respect to the European Union is accounted for *primarily* by USTR-initiated cases. Three of four cases USTR initiated against the Union were successful versus only one of six others initiated after 1985. It may be that the Union's cumbersome decision-making process, involving consultation with 12 member governments, requires high-visibility events such as USTR initiation to persuade EU policymakers to take a dispute seriously.

In sum, our case studies and empirical work lead us to conclude that section 301 as implemented since 1985 has been reasonably successful in opening foreign markets. We attribute the improved success since 1985 to greater US commitment to opening foreign markets and to improved implementation of the law. The timing of the improvement, as well as the empirical analysis, leads to the conclusion that the change in how effectively and aggressively the law was used, rather than the 1988 Trade

---

2. We define public threats as USTR initiation of an investigation, the announcement by the president or USTR of a determination that an unfair practice exists, or publication of a retaliation "hit list."

Act's purported improvements in the law, explains the greater efficacy of section 301. The decline in the success rate since 1989 suggests there may also have been unique factors in the political and economic environment that contributed to 301's effectiveness in the late 1980s that may not be replicable in the future, an issue to which we will return.

It should also be emphasized that trade gains from use of section 301 are relatively small, though not negligible. It is very difficult to quantify how much US exports may have increased because of section 301. The total value of US exports in *all* the successful cases after markets were opened was about $4 billion. The Japanese tobacco and beef cases alone have increased US exports by nearly $2 billion, and the semiconductor case (though not classified as a success; see chapter 3 and the appendix) adds another $1 billion or so. But the increase in US exports in all the other cases combined probably adds up to no more than a few hundred million dollars. With total US exports in 1993 of $465 billion, this suggests section 301 might have increased US exports by around 1 percent annually. This compares with a potential increase in US exports from the Uruguay Round tariff liberalization of 8 to 10 percent after the cuts are fully implemented (Schott 1994).

Given its relatively modest impact on US exports, it would be a Pyrrhic victory if section 301 and other US trade threats undermined the global trading system that has contributed so importantly to global welfare since 1947. Far more difficult than assessing section 301's utility as a market-opening tool is analyzing whether, on balance, aggressive unilateralism moved the multilateral trade regime forward or set it back. There are two major obstacles to answering this question.

First, any judgment must rest on a highly subjective evaluation of the counterfactual: what would have happened in the absence of aggressive unilateralism? Would US political support for the GATT have been fatally weakened if the president had not used section 301 to deflect protectionist pressures and to build an export-oriented coalition to support the Uruguay Round? Was it fear of the world's most powerful nation acting as self-appointed judge, jury, and enforcer of trade rules that impelled other countries to agree to US demands for GATT reform? Or did the round come to a successful conclusion despite US threats and bullying?

To reiterate the results summarized above, aggressive unilateralism was generally market-opening rather than market-closing. Contrary to the fears of many, the more aggressive use of section 301 did not result in frequent retaliation by the United States, and it provoked counterretaliation in only three cases. It is an obvious point, but one often obscured in the heated rhetoric over section 301, that forcing trading partners to open their markets usually benefits both the United States and the target country. And if the liberalization is on a most-favored nation basis, it will be consistent with GATT rules, it will benefit exporters from third countries, and in most cases it will improve global welfare.[3] We found very little evidence in the 72 cases we studied that US demands had resulted in significant trade diversion. Only two agreements were explicitly discriminatory, both involving retroactive protection only for US patents, and in those cases US negotiators say they acquiesced in, but did not demand, more favorable treatment.

Overall, the pattern of retaliations and the rarity of explicitly discriminatory trade deals both suggest that US negotiators were aware of the potential effects of their actions on the international trading system and consciously sought to minimize negative consequences. US trade negotiators had to walk a fine line in the late 1980s, being aggressive enough to keep Congress and the business community mollified but not so aggressive as to cause US trading partners to walk away from the negotiating table in the Uruguay Round. Congress did not grab back the reins of trade policy in the late 1980s, and the Uruguay Round was eventually brought to a successful end. We conclude that aggressive unilateralism contributed positively to both outcomes.

A second difficulty in assessing the systemic impact of aggressive unilateralism is that the ultimate answer depends on how well the trading system operates in the future. No one can answer that question sensibly until the new system has been in operation for several years. The system's success will depend on the willingness of the economic superpowers to uphold and enforce its rules and principles—something that was sadly lacking in the 1980s. In the final section of this chapter we offer recommendations on what the United States could do to make the system work effectively.

From Aggressive Unilateralism to Aggressive Multilateralism

As long as the Uruguay Round was ongoing, US negotiators could plausibly, if not always convincingly, argue that the weaknesses and inadequacies of the GATT left no alternative to an aggressive unilateral policy. But with many of the reforms they demanded now incorporated in the WTO, including much stronger dispute settlement rules, such claims will be less credible, and US disobedience will be less justifiable. Other unusual features of the trade policy environment in the 1980s also mean that aggressive unilateralism is likely to be a less effective and more dangerous strategy than it has been in the past.

---

3. Intellectual property protection is one area where reforms may not improve global welfare in all cases; see chapter 8 and the sources cited therein.

Like the GATT success with tariff reduction—one result of which was to reveal hidden nontariff barriers in many countries—section 301 may be a victim of its own success. The combined result of bilateral agreements negotiated under section 301 and the Uruguay Round will be to eliminate or substantially reduce many of the most egregious trade barriers around the world. What is left are the less well-defined, often structural, behind-the-border barriers, which are less amenable to a process like section 301. In such cases, unilateral demands backed by retaliatory threats often politicize issues and may delay liberalization by creating resentment among constituencies that would otherwise be sympathetic.

In addition, as pointed out to us by a Korean official who commented on a draft of the study, the more systemic the barrier, the greater will be the number of groups that must cooperate in eliminating it and the less will be the control that the central government has over the policy. In his words,

> Broad-based changes in the mental attitudes of low-level bureaucrats, consumers, and the society at large are needed as part of an effective solution to structural problems. Institutional changes that are not accompanied by a corresponding change in mentality are meaningless. (Private communication, 13 August 1993)

This same official also offered an explanation for why super 301 might be less effective than regular 301 and argued further that it would be even less effective in the future. Though not referring explicitly to the South Korean experience in 1989–90, the official noted that the ill will the process engendered might make it harder for a target government to faithfully implement an agreement negotiated under a super 301 threat than otherwise. This observer also noted that super 301 would never regain its initial shock value. Moreover, he argued, being designated a priority country may not have the stigma that it previously had in some countries because the United States was perceived in 1989 as "making scapegoats of the smaller US trading partners like Korea, Brazil, India, and Taiwan while acting cowardly with bigger and stronger trading partners such as the EC." Finally, the fact that India suffered no consequences from its defiance "diminishes the credibility of retaliation" under super 301, according to this official.

Another reason a 301 of any type may be ineffective in the future—at least as long as policymakers can avoid a recurrence of severely misaligned currencies and other macroeconomic imbalances—is that key US trading partners were unusually dependent on the US market in the mid-1980s when 301 had its greatest success. As shown in tables 7.1a and b, the share of South Korea's and Taiwan's exports sold in the United States increased in the mid-1980s but has since dropped. A similar pattern can be observed for Japanese exports. South Korea and Taiwan in particular have consciously tried to diversify their export markets to reduce dependence on the United States, and their US exports as a share of their total exports were lower in 1992 than in 1982.

In general, US trading partners' resentment toward aggressive unilateral tactics is likely to be greater and their willingness to compromise less now that the Uruguay Round is concluded. Fears that escalating disputes might cause the collapse of the round also served as a useful discipline for negotiators on both sides of bilateral trade disputes. In the absence of broad multilateral negotiations, negotiators may feel less constrained, and there may be a greater chance of disputes getting out of hand, with less market opening and more market closing than over the past decade. Many countries also had to overcome serious doubts about making dispute settlement a more legalized and less diplomatic process, but they did so in the expectation that the new rules would constrain US actions as well as their own.

Section 301 and some of the other tools of aggressive unilateralism will continue to be necessary components of American trade policy. Both to protect their credibility with Congress and to guard the credibility of the new WTO, US negotiators must carefully monitor and vigorously enforce trade agreements, using 301 where necessary. The United States should continue to be aggressive in defending its rights under the WTO, but it should press its claims multilaterally rather than unilaterally. In addition, if US compliance with dispute settlement rulings against it remains as poor as in the past, other countries will have little incentive to comply with those rules, and the entire system could unravel. In what follows, we suggest ways in which the United States can demonstrate constructive leadership for a more open trading system, while also protecting US global economic interests.

What Role Should Reciprocity Play in US Trade Policy?

At least from the establishment of the GATT in 1947 until the late 1970s, the guiding concepts of US trade policy have been national treatment, nondiscrimination, and "reciprocity at the margin" in bilateral and multilateral negotiations to reduce impediments to trade. National treatment means that the United States expects its trading partners to give US exports the same treatment with respect to internal rules and regulations as they do domestically produced goods and to give American firms operating in their territory the same competitive opportunities that their domestic firms enjoy.[4] Nondiscrimination means that, with some important exceptions, the United States extends the benefits of trade liberalization negotiated with one country to all of its other trading partners. Reciprocity at

---

4. For purposes of exposition, we take national treatment to include the right of establishment, which is not always the case in practice. See chapter 11 for an extended discussion of national treatment.

the margin means that the United States expects, in negotiations to reduce trade impediments, that the overall value of concessions it offers to trading partners in all sectors will be roughly commensurate with the overall value of the concessions that it receives in return (Cline 1982).

By the early 1980s there arose a growing political challenge to the traditional postwar concepts of reciprocity. Despite seven postwar rounds of multilateral trade negotiations, the American market was seen by many in Congress and US industry as still far more open than most foreign markets. Although tariffs and other border restrictions had been reduced, there was still a thicket of nontariff barriers, such as subsidies and administrative guidance, that impeded US exports. Many developing countries were criticized as free riders who benefited from most-favored nation (MFN) status but had no reciprocal obligation to lower their trade barriers. The rising US trade deficit in the 1980s, and particularly the seemingly intractable nature of the bilateral deficit with Japan, reinforced concerns that US firms faced significant barriers abroad. Many in US trade policy circles believed that the current system was manifestly unfair and that it was time to employ a stronger concept of reciprocity that gave US firms the same access to foreign markets that foreign firms enjoyed in the United States—often on a sector-specific basis. As described in chapter 2, there was mounting interest in a results-oriented trade policy that measured success, not in terms of improved international rules or ineffectual bilateral agreements, but rather in terms of increased sales.[5]

National Treatment and Mirror-Image Reciprocity

One consequence of American reliance on market forces is the fact that a number of US markets are substantially more open and less regulated than those abroad. Telecommunications, airlines, and retail sales are perhaps the most prominent examples. Many American firms are understandably frustrated that foreign firms have better access to the US market than American firms enjoy in some heavily regulated foreign markets. Periodically, there are calls for something approximating mirror-image reciprocity, where foreign firms would be denied full access to the US market unless US firms receive equivalent access abroad.

The 1989 US-EC dispute over the Second Banking Directive is a useful warning about the pitfalls of mirror-image reciprocity (see chapter 11). Some in the Community insisted that it was unfair that US financial services firms should have full access to the universal banking system and enlarged financial market in Europe when European firms had less commercial opportunity in the American market. The United States resisted EC demands for mirror-image reciprocity and insisted that US firms continue to receive national treatment—to be treated at least as

---

5. US officials are fond of using the phrase, "when we hear the cash register ring," to describe what they mean by results.

well as European firms in the European market. European attempts to discriminate against American firms would almost certainly have led to US retaliation, possibly followed by EC counterretaliation. The case points to the dangers of one country trying to impose its regulatory regime on another. Rightly or wrongly, US-based financial service providers are more heavily regulated than are European-based firms. Regardless of the historical reasons or efficiency implications of this difference in regulatory environments, European threats of retaliation to force the United States to deregulate were met with US outrage and threats of counterretaliation.

The lesson from the Second Banking Directive dispute is that, whatever its flaws, reciprocal national treatment is a reasonable principle to guide future negotiations aimed at liberalizing regulatory barriers. Unilateral demands for mirror-image reciprocity backed by threats of market closure are not appropriate for addressing disputes arising from differences over important social priorities or different assessments of risk. Moreover, it is a principle that the United States may not be able to live with itself. It is no longer the case that *all* US markets are less regulated or more open than their foreign counterparts. The financial services sector is a prime example. Another area is pesticide regulation, where US standards are often stricter than those of other countries. Encouraging countries to liberalize is one thing; telling them that their economies should look just like ours is a prescription for conflict.

A second area in which US views of reciprocity have changed is with respect to unconditional MFN. Until 1985, when President Reagan signed the US-Israel Free Trade Agreement (FTA), the United States had shunned the trend toward regional arrangements that was occurring throughout much of the rest of the world. Since then, the United States has entered into the Canada-US FTA, which was later expanded to include Mexico. Chile is next on the list, and the United States is also considering regional negotiations to further liberalize trade in the Western Hemisphere and perhaps the Asia Pacific.

Typically, in regional arrangements, the tariff concessions that each prospective member offers are available only to other members of the FTA or customs union. MFN status in these arrangements, then, is conditional on membership. The rationale for conditional MFN in some cases is to avoid free riders. In other words, regional arrangements based on conditional MFN may allow like-minded countries to move further and faster in liberalizing than would be possible if all GATT members were included in the negotiation. Conditional MFN may also serve as an incentive to reluctant countries that are not party to the negotiations to consider liberalization they would otherwise avoid, and thus regional liberalization may become the basis for broader multilateral negotiations.

The danger, of course, is that spreading regional arrangements and increased use of conditional MFN could undermine the core nondiscrimination principle supporting the multilateral trading system. An unfortunate gap in the recent Uruguay Round agreement was the failure to strengthen GATT Article XXIV on monitoring and oversight of regional arrangements. Article XXIV places disciplines on regional arrangements, and the mechanisms for ensuring that GATT's standards are met need to be substantially improved.

Results-Oriented Approaches

An extreme version of a results-oriented negotiating approach is a "voluntary" import expansion (VIE) scheme that defines achieving a specific market share as the standard for success. The demand for VIEs is driven by the perception that the Japanese market is protected by informal barriers and collusive business practices that are not amenable to traditional "rules-oriented" trade negotiations.

Bergsten and Noland (1993) and Tyson (1992) argue that VIEs may be the only viable option in some cases and that they can enhance competition and lead to freer trade when properly implemented. Bergsten and Noland (1993, 194–95) offer four warnings on the use of VIEs:

- VIEs are subject to capture by producer interests in the importing or exporting country, which are likely to try to manipulate them to restrict competition—for example, by excluding third-country exporters.

- Any quantitative targets set are arbitrary, and therefore the negotiated outcome could be inferior to what would prevail if the underlying barrier to exports could be removed. For example, a VIE in the Japanese cigarette market would have been unlikely to permit the huge increase in US exports that occurred when Japanese barriers were dismantled.

- VIEs increase the risks of retaliation, possibly even trade wars, if arbitrarily set targets are not met for reasons over which the target country government has limited control.

- VIEs can create dangerous precedents that could come back to haunt the *demandeur*. For example, the United States might find itself excluded from VIEs negotiated by other countries, or it might even become the target of demands for VIEs.

Despite these caveats, Bergsten and Noland follow Tyson (1992, 263–66) in believing that there are limited circumstances under which VIEs can be competition-enhancing.[6] They offer these criteria for deciding whether VIEs will enhance world economic welfare: there is strong evidence of barriers to market access, even if a specific, tangible barrier cannot be identified; foreign firms and products are demonstrably competitive; the

---

6. See Greaney (1993) for a theoretical analysis of cases where VIEs are not competition-enhancing.

best option—that is, removing the market-access barrier—is not available (for example, improved antitrust enforcement); the products in question are intermediate, not consumer, goods; and VIEs are implemented on an MFN basis (C. Fred Bergsten, "Japan's Trade Access Limitations Require Unorthodox Responses," *Financial Times*, 15 October 1993).

The ongoing impasse in the US-Japan framework talks over the Clinton administration's demand for quantitative targets or indicators in trade agreements suggests this will not prove a fruitful approach.[7] The head of the American negotiating team, Deputy USTR Charlene Barshefsky, described US goals in 15 October 1993 testimony before the House Committee on Foreign Affairs:

> This negotiation is results-oriented—process and procedural change is not enough unless it leads to concrete change in the marketplace. We will be using objective indicators, both quantitative and qualitative, to measure these results; as the Framework specifies, tangible progress towards market access and sales must be made.

The Japanese had been burned by the experience in the semiconductor case, which resulted in the first-ever retaliatory sanctions by the United States against Japan, and they vowed never again to accept quantitative targets or indicators that might trigger US retaliation. The framework negotiations collapsed over this issue on 11 February 1994 at a meeting between President Clinton and Prime Minister Morihiro Hosokawa. Negotiations remained stalled on most issues as of August 1994, despite substantial US retreat from its initial demands for "quantitative targets" to demands for "objective" indicators. The Clinton administration erred in elevating a pragmatic policy tool—one that should have limited applicability if properly used—to a position of principle at the center of the negotiation. Japanese politicians and diplomats waged a skillful public relations campaign against their US counterparts, arguing that US efforts to set quantitative targets would be antithetical to Prime Minister Hosokawa's efforts to deregulate markets and get the bureaucracy out of the business of managing trade. Despite the shared interest in opening the Japanese market, many foreign governments and GATT Director General Peter Sutherland criticized what they called the US attempt to manage trade.

Many of the Japanese barriers that so frustrate US trade negotiators derive from structural differences in the two economies and differences in their domestic regulatory regimes. For example, some observers point to differences in competition policies (e.g., government aid to industries,

---

7. President Clinton and Prime Minister Kiichi Miyazawa signed the framework agreement on 10 July 1993, calling it a new approach to resolving US-Japan trade disputes, including the use of "objective criteria, either qualitative or quantitative or both" to assess progress in achieving market opening (USTR, press release, "United States–Japan Framework for a New Economic Partnership," 10 July 1993, 9).

antitrust, and antidumping policies) as potentially important structural impediments to freer trade and investment.[8] Such differences are not necessarily unfair—they often reflect different social preferences—but they can lead to trade disputes. The answer in most cases is not to manage trade, which reinforces the Japanese bureaucracy's predilection for regulating the economy, but to find creative ways to manage the conflict.

It is simply not true that traditional rules-oriented negotiations fail to work with Japan. The Market-Oriented Sector-Specific (MOSS) talks (box 5.2), which attempted to address domestic regulatory or structural impediments, are criticized for being long and arduous, but they did produce tangible results. The Congressional Research Service surveyed the results of past US-Japan trade negotiations, including the MOSS talks, and concluded that US exports of manufactured goods to Japan in negotiated sectors doubled over 1985–92, nearly twice as large an increase as for total US exports to Japan or the world (cited in Elwell and Reifman 1994, 14). Our analysis of past section 301 cases also shows that trade agreements with Japan often do result in actual market opening. We did not accept achievement of an agreement as sufficient for calling a case a success and still found that 75 percent of cases targeting Japan resulted in some liberalization.

As described in chapter 4, however, 301-type negotiations work best when there is a well-defined, visible barrier. For the less visible, often informal barriers that sometimes make the Japanese market difficult to penetrate, other negotiating approaches are more appropriate.

Although the Structural Impediments Initiative (SII) talks were much criticized and rejected by many as ineffective, getting at deeply seated regulatory obstacles and fundamental differences in economic structure is bound to be time-consuming and difficult. Such efforts require a profound understanding of the reasons for the differences, how they may impede trade, and how they can be changed without undermining legitimate economic objectives or social preferences.[9] The understanding of Japanese financial and wood products markets that was gained in the yen-dollar talks and MOSS negotiations, respectively, contributed importantly to the success of the Schumer amendment–inspired US-Japan negotiations on opening the government bond market and the super 301 wood products agreement.

If some structural and regulatory differences are indeed important obstacles to trade, then long-term negotiations aimed at international

---

8. See Graham and Richardson (forthcoming) and Bergsten and Noland (1993, chapter 1).

9. For example, the United States sets aside some of its government procurement expenditures exclusively for small and minority-owned US businesses as part of a social policy aimed at encouraging the development of these businesses. Other countries, however, complain that these set-asides restrict their commercial opportunities (see, e.g., the Canadian Department of Foreign Affairs and International Trade 1994 *Register of US Barriers to Trade* and the European Commission's 1994 *Report on United States Barriers to Trade and Investment*).

convergence are the most promising option. Bergsten and Noland (1993, 210–18) propose Structural Convergence Talks (SCT) between the United States and Japan on issues such as competition policy, product liability law, and foreign investment regulations. Bergsten and Graham (1994) propose multilateral or regional negotiations on a code to liberalize foreign investment. There are relatively few good models for these sorts of negotiations. Some observers believe that the European Union's concept of "mutual recognition" of different national regulations that are determined to be functionally equivalent is a promising approach. But it is important to recognize that it took many years of difficult negotiations among EU countries to make national policies sufficiently compatible so that they could be recognized as equivalent.[10] There should be no illusion: there are no quick fixes to structural and regulatory impediments.

What Role Should Retaliation Play in US Trade Policy?

The establishment of the WTO in 1995 has substantially changed the political and economic calculus of retaliation for the United States and its trading partners. For issues falling within the WTO's broad purview, the credibility and political weight of retaliatory threats is enhanced. Resort to WTO-approved retaliation should be infrequent because credible threats will rarely have to be carried out. Conversely, the new dispute settlement procedures make the United States a more likely target of retaliation if it refuses to play by the new rules it so forcefully sought. Moreover, if the United States continues to use trade threats in ways that violate GATT norms or procedures, the cost in terms of the integrity of the multilateral system would be much greater than in the past, when the United States could more plausibly argue that the rules were inadequate.

With the completion of the Uruguay Round, American policy goals should continue to be the strengthening of the global trading system, now embodied in the WTO, and improved access for US goods, services, and investment in foreign markets. However, in the new international economic order, the role of US retaliatory threats will have to change if they are to be effective (box 13.1). The increased success rate for section 301 since 1985 is not a good predictor of how effective it will be after 1995, when the WTO comes into existence. Consequently, we offer recommendations on how trade threats can be used to achieve US objectives in this

---

10. See Sydney Key (1989a) on the need for convergence as a prerequisite for mutual recognition. On the potential pitfalls of harmonization, see Martin Wolf (1994), and see Jagdish Bhagwati (1994) on the danger that efforts to promote international harmonization of labor and environmental standards could lead to protectionism. For the alternative view that such harmonization would reduce US standards to a lowest common denominator, see Wallach (1993) and Ralph Nader, "WTO Means Rule by Unaccountable Tribunals," *Wall Street Journal*, 17 August 1994, A12.

Box 13.1 The impact of the Uruguay Round on the effectiveness of US retaliatory threats

US threats are strengthened if . . .

- disputes involve issues covered by the WTO and the United States wins its case using the new dispute settlement process.

US threats are weakened if . . .

- disputes involve issues covered by the WTO and the United States fails to follow dispute settlement procedures by (1) issuing a section 301 determination before the dispute settlement process is complete; (2) retaliating after losing a case; (3) using threats or pressure to force countries to withdraw their complaints or otherwise acquiesce to US demands; or (4) failing to comply with a ruling if it is a losing defendant;

- disputes involve issues not covered by the WTO and the United States retaliates by withdrawing WTO-covered concessions (e.g., bound tariffs).

The effectiveness of US threats is unchanged if . . .

- disputes involve issues not covered by the WTO or nonmembers and the United States does not withdraw WTO-covered concessions.

---

new environment. Our recommendations fall into two categories: those involving issues the WTO covers and those involving problems not currently within the WTO's purview.

As described in chapter 3, the new dispute settlement mechanism is a radical change from the old. For most cases, the process will move from establishment of a panel to a final decision within 12 to 18 months. With some exceptions, the entire process, including approval for retaliation, is fully automatic and can be stopped only by the unanimous consent of the members.[11]

Thus, the new dispute settlement mechanism to a very large degree resolves US complaints that the process was slow, easily blocked, and lacked the credible threat of retaliation. It was US pressure, via aggressive unilateralism, that convinced the other GATT members to address these US concerns. Ironically, some members of the US business and policy communities now complain that the new dispute settlement mechanism reduces US ability to wield unilateral trade threats and makes it easier for other countries to challenge US trade practices and to obtain WTO authority to retaliate if the United States fails to abide by the dispute settlement process.

---

11. The exceptions are for disputes involving nonviolation nullification and impairment under Articles XXIII:1(b) and (c) and for the first five to ten years of the intellectual property agreement.

Both of these complaints are reasonably accurate. But limits on US unilateralism are the price of American success in getting its trading partners to adopt a stronger dispute settlement mechanism and new or improved rules in agriculture, services, intellectual property rights, and investment. The United States used a combination of sweet reason and aggressive unilateralism to convince other nations that it was in their interest to accede, albeit only partially, to US goals. The implicit quid pro quo was US agreement to significantly restrain, but not eliminate, its unilateral use of retaliatory threats. However, the United States can and should aggressively seek enforcement of the WTO's trade rules. This aggressiveness will now have to be channeled through the WTO's dispute settlement process. Henceforth, the United States will have to pursue a strategy of aggressive *multilateralism.*

Bello and Holmer (1992) describe the new dispute settlement process as "the internationalization of section 301." In a fairly wide range of circumstances, the new dispute settlement procedures significantly strengthen the efficacy of US trade threats. For cases and countries covered by the WTO, the dispute settlement process will generate a decision within regular 301's 18-month timetable.[12] If the United States wins such cases, it is virtually assured of receiving WTO authority to retaliate if the losing country fails to remove the offending practice or to offer adequate compensation.[13] Retaliatory threats under this system are more credible and carry more political weight because they are no longer unilateral acts of frontier justice, but rather carry the approval of the entire international trading community.

We anticipate that the incidence of retaliation under this process will be quite low for two reasons. First, the more credible the threat, the less likely it will have to be implemented. Second, the multilateral and judicial nature of the process gives political cover to governments in the losing countries to make the required changes in their trade practices. The target country will no longer appear to be acquiescing to unilateral demands. Rather, politicians can explain to their citizens that they are simply bringing national practices into conformity with international law. Thus, target country governments should find it politically easier to comply.

Some US critics, however, object that "the threat of unilateral action to protect US interests has been repealed without changing a word of US

---

12. The dispute settlement process may not always be able to reach a decision within the six- to nine-month special 301 timetable for intellectual property cases or the seven- to eight-month period for certain subsidies cases.

13. As noted previously, the new dispute settlement process is automatic from establishment of panels to authorization to retaliate unless the WTO Council decides unanimously to block the process. The new dispute settlement mechanism expresses members' strong preference for removal of the offending practice over either compensation or retaliation. Disputes over the appropriate amount of compensation or retaliation are subject to binding arbitration on an expeditious timetable.

law."[14] The statement that the United States will be more constrained in wielding unilateral threats under the WTO is largely true but somewhat misleading. The United States retains the ability to issue unilateral threats and carry them out. The WTO simply raises the price that the United States may have to pay if it acts unilaterally in certain types of cases. If the United States decides to violate WTO procedures by acting unilaterally, it faces a greater risk of foreign counterretaliation—at least by some members, notably the European Union, China when it joins, and Canada—and erosion of its leadership.

Potential US violations of the new dispute settlement procedures would include:

- issuing section 301 determinations before the dispute settlement process is complete;

- retaliating in areas covered by WTO rules without WTO approval;

- using threats or arm-twisting to force a plaintiff to withdraw a complaint or otherwise acquiesce to US demands;

- failing to comply with a dispute settlement ruling if it loses a case.

The first two violations are straightforward. The new dispute settlement process enjoins members from unilaterally convicting others of alleged transgressions of WTO rules and from retaliating without (virtually automatic) multilateral WTO approval. The price of internationalizing section 301 is a US commitment to act multilaterally. Section 301 already requires USTR to use existing dispute settlement mechanisms where appropriate, though the vagueness of many GATT rules gives USTR considerable discretion in determining whether a particular case involves a potential GATT violation and thus whether it must invoke those procedures. The 301 statute as amended by the 1988 Trade Act also allows the president to waive "mandatory" retaliation in GATT cases that the United States loses.

The last two types of potential violation could be more problematic because the United States has a lamentable record of pressuring other countries and failing to comply with GATT panel rulings, as described in chapter 3. If the United States persists in these types of violations, there will be further erosion in America's already weakened leadership. If US failure to abide by the dispute settlement process is frequent, it could fatally weaken the WTO and forfeit all the economic gains that the United States worked so hard to achieve in the Uruguay Round.

Hudec (1993, 364) warns that if the United States continues its *unjustified* disobedience to WTO norms and rules:

---

14. From a memo by the Economic Strategy Institute, sent by ESI President Clyde Prestowitz to House Majority Leader Richard Gephardt (*Inside U.S. Trade,* 17 December 1993, 5).

> ... the dispute settlement reforms would likely produce the worst of all worlds. They will assert the authority of GATT law more forcefully, but if the major GATT countries are not ready to change their behavior, these stronger demands will only produce more visible and dramatic legal failures. And if that were to happen, the credibility of GATT legal obligations would almost certainly plunge.

Another class of cases in which US attempts to use unilateral threats will carry a heavier cost than in the past are those areas covered in the Uruguay Round that have limited exemptions from legal challenges using the new dispute settlement mechanism. For example, in the Blair House agreement, which was subsequently incorporated into the Uruguay Round package, the United States committed itself not to challenge certain agricultural subsidies and other measures. And in the agreement on intellectual property rights, the United States agreed not to apply the new dispute settlement procedures to nonviolation nullification and impairment cases for an initial five-year period and to allow a phase-in period for developing countries that exempts them from legal challenges for five to ten years. In these cases, if the United States unilaterally threatens retaliation, it will further undermine its credibility. Moreover, if the United States actually retaliates by withdrawing WTO-covered concessions, it will almost certainly face automatically authorized counterretaliation if the target country requests it.

A third class of cases where the cost of retaliatory threats has increased involves issues not now covered by the WTO, such as competition policy, worker rights, and most environmental issues. In disputes over these issues, if the United States were to retaliate by withdrawing WTO-covered concessions, its actions would be illegal, and it would face an increased risk of WTO-approved counterretaliation. For issues not covered by the WTO or involving countries that are not members, the United States retains the right to unilateral action as long as it does not withdraw WTO-covered concessions. This obviously limits the types of threats the United States can wield. Permissible types of pressure would include removal of preferential tariffs for developing countries, denial of admission to US-centered free trade agreements such as NAFTA, denial of debt rescheduling under the Brady Plan, or reductions in bilateral aid. Clearly, developing countries are the most vulnerable to these types of economic pressure.

Another complaint heard in some US business and policy circles is that the new dispute settlement mechanism makes American trade practices easier to challenge and more subject to foreign retaliation. Alan Wolff, a leading trade lawyer and former top official at USTR, says of the new dispute settlement process:

> We thought of ourselves as plaintiffs. We wanted to place foreign practices in cross hairs of a rifle sight and make sure we couldn't miss. All too often we'll be the ones in the cross hairs. (*Wall Street Journal,* 24 November 1993, 2)

Similarly, Bello and Holmer (1992, 799) call the new procedures "a boon for plaintiffs [and] conversely a bane for defendants." Yet the United States pressed for the "fully automated conveyer-belt" approach to dispute settlement, and it must now accept that what is good for the goose is also good for the gander. But, again, this does not mean that the United States *must* remove its objectionable practices. It simply means that the United States must bear the now-higher cost of international opprobrium and the risk of foreign retaliation if it fails to conform to the rules. We expect there will be few cases where the US government determines that there is a compelling US national interest in violating the new dispute settlement rules. Otherwise, the outlook is bleak for the future of the new WTO.

Making Retaliatory Threats More Effective

For issues covered by the WTO, the United States should pursue a strategy of aggressive multilateralism that aims to enforce existing WTO agreements and to improve the functioning of the new trading system. There are three key elements in this strategy.

First, the United States should vigorously use and rigorously abide by WTO dispute settlement procedures. USTR should be aggressive in challenging alleged violations of WTO rules. By the same token, it is essential that the United States scrupulously abide by WTO procedures for using the dispute settlement process and comply fully and as quickly as possible in cases where it is a losing defendant.[15] Failure to do so will seriously undermine the WTO reforms.

Second, to be constructively aggressive and win legal challenges in the WTO, the United States needs to considerably strengthen its own capacity to conduct legal and economic analysis. The problem is not the quality of existing staff, who are often extremely competent and hard-working. Rather, there are simply not enough of them. A fairly small increase in expenditure on analytic staff at the trade agencies can yield huge policy payoffs. The United States needs to devote considerable staff resources to develop a long-term strategy for using the dispute settlement process to enforce the current trade rules and to clarify ambiguities, especially in the new areas of services, intellectual property rights, and investment.

Third, the United States should also support the strengthening of legal and economic analytic capacity in the WTO. The secretariat will play an absolutely crucial role in advising and assisting dispute settlement panel members. The quality and timeliness of dispute settlement decisions will

---

15. Part of the source of US delays in rectifying GATT violations has been congressional lassitude in passing corrective legislation on issues that are often low on the list of national priorities. This sort of lagged response is inherent in the US system of government, but it is still important for the president to use his powers of persuasion, and to expend political capital if necessary, to get Congress to pass the needed legislation expeditiously.

depend importantly on the quality and quantity of secretariat staff available for dispute settlement proceedings. In addition, we strongly endorse Hudec's (1994) call for a professionalization of the dispute panels and particularly of the appellate body. The quality of decisions rendered is absolutely fundamental to the effectiveness of the new trade regime, and it is thus an area to which the United States should devote considerable attention.

Creative Minilateralism

For issues and countries outside the WTO, we recommend a US strategy of creative minilateralism. The goal of US policy should be to use creative diplomacy to enlarge the WTO's coverage of issues and countries. To do so may require the use of trade threats, but they should be used only after a sustained effort at good-faith negotiations has unequivocally failed. Hence, patience is required. Agreements among groups of like-minded countries could then provide the conceptual basis and demonstration effect for extension to the WTO via multilateral negotiations. The most productive context for minilateral negotiations might be regional free trade negotiations in the Western Hemisphere or Asia Pacific, or talks among the three economic superpowers on structural and regulatory harmonization or convergence.

The strategy of creative minilateralism includes the following tactics. First, the United States should pursue Structural Convergence Talks on structural or regulatory impediments with Japan, the European Union, and other interested parties. Regular 301 and perhaps the threat of antitrust actions provide all the retaliatory leverage the United States needs. Super 301 is unnecessary and potentially counterproductive, as discussed in chapter 12. The keys to success in removing structural and regulatory impediments are profound understanding of the causes and consequences of these barriers and an influential constituency for change in the target countries. Both of these take time to develop, and so, again, patience is required.

Second, the US government needs a much stronger analytic capacity to assess the nature of structural and regulatory obstacles and the best options for correcting them. We recommend establishing an independent Trade Assessment Commission (TAC) along the lines of the Australian Industry Commission (see chapter 5).[16] It would provide estimates of the costs and benefits of the entire range of US and foreign policies and practices that impede trade and investment and recommend ways to remove them while still achieving their legitimate economic, social, or

16. See Gary Banks (1990) for descriptions of the Industry Commission and the evolution of the idea of an independent analytic agency from the Long (1989) and Leutweiler (1985) reports.

political objectives.[17] US leadership in establishing such an agency would give significant impetus to other countries to establish their own analytic capacities, if only as a defensive measure to respond to US "aggressive empiricism." The costs of such an agency would be quite small, and it would provide a powerful lever for US negotiators.

Third, many of our case studies strongly suggest that US pressure for improvement in market access is most effective when there is a politically effective constituency in the target country that also favors liberalization. The Brazil super 301 case, the US-EC dispute over the Second Banking Directive, and the US-Japan Schumer amendment negotiations illustrate how external pressure can be a constructive adjunct to internal support for policy change. Conversely, the Korea super 301 negotiations, the Brazil IPR cases, and the US-EC oilseeds case illustrate how difficult it is to achieve reform when there is little or no effective political support for change in the target country.

We therefore recommend that the United States aggressively publicize how other countries' trade impediments impose significant costs on their domestic firms and consumers. The United States told Japanese consumers about the rather shocking differentials between some US and Japanese prices during the SII talks, and US firms are publicizing the costs to Japanese consumers of barriers to wood products imports. We suggest a much more aggressive and sustained transparency effort, using analytic and empirical input from our proposed Trade Assessment Commission. Success in these types of negotiations is more likely if the United States is "pushing on an open door" and has the support of influential groups in the protected market.

Finally, the United States should provide technical assistance to developing countries that agree to structural and regulatory harmonization. In many cases, poor countries lack the technical and administrative expertise to design and implement efficient regulatory regimes or to enforce intellectual property rights and competition policy. The United States, either acting through the US Agency for International Development or in conjunction with other countries and the international lending institutions, should offer to finance consultants and training programs for its poorer trading partners.

In sum, the dual strategies of aggressive multilateralism and creative minilateralism are intended to ensure that the United States and the world reap the benefits of the Uruguay Round and that the process of trade liberalization continues. The 1980s were a time of conflict and change in the global trading system. Under the circumstances, USTR generally wielded the section 301 crowbar deftly and constructively, employing an aggressive unilateral strategy to induce support abroad for strengthening

---

17. See Richardson (1993) for an analysis of the costs of self-imposed US obstacles to its own exports for a model of the type of calculations we have in mind.

of the multilateral trade system and, in the interim, to bolster support at home for liberal trade policies.

While no negotiated agreement is ever regarded as perfect by any party to it, the new international trade rules and strengthened dispute settlement process, if faithfully implemented, go a considerable way toward meeting US demands. The United States should aggressively encourage the agreement's faithful implementation. Section 301 can be a useful tool in this cause, especially when the violation can be clearly identified and defined. Section 301 may also be useful in encouraging additional liberalization in areas not covered by the WTO rules, though usually only if it complements domestic pressure from a local constituency in the country that also favors reform. But in terms of a general strategy, the Clinton administration now must choose: Will it be the sheriff, aggressively enforcing multilateral rules from within the system? Or will it become a vigilante, turning its back on the system and using force to pursue its unilateral demands?

APPENDIX

Section 301 Table and Case Summaries

Summary table: assessments of section 301 cases

Case no.	Target country/ region	Period of case[a]	Type of product	Actual value of US exports to the target[b]	GATT panel established?	GATT panel ruled?	Negotiating objective achieved?	Degree of trade liberalization resulting from 301[c]
1	Guatemala	7-1-75/ 6-29-76	Services (shipping)	Negl. (based on data in USTR files)	n.a.	n.a.	**Nominally**	Some, but ultimately by Federal Maritime Commission under other authority.
2	Canada	7-17-75/ 3-14-76	Agricultural (eggs)	$15 million (1976–78 average)	Working party advisory opinion	Mixed, adopted	**Largely**. Canada approximately doubled quota for US egg exports	Net effect of case unclear; data suggest possible diversion of Canadian eggs from US market.
3	EC	8-7-75/ 7-21-80	Agricultural (egg albumin)	Less than $5 million (1977–81 average)	No	No	**Partially**. EC removed supplementary levies but increased import levy.	**Modest** based on data.
4	EC	9-22-75/ 1-5-79	Agriculture-related (canned fruits and vegetables)	About $25 million (based on data in USTR files)	Yes	Mixed, adopted	**Nominally**. Soon after EC dropped MIPs, it instituted direct subsidies to offset cost to processors of protected fruits.	**None**
5	EC	11-13-75/ 6-19-80	Agricultural (malt)	Less than $5 million	No	No	**Not at all**	**None**. Based on data showing increasing EC exports to Japan 1977–82; see also case 301-6.

continued next page

Summary table: assessments of section 301 cases (continued)

Case no.	Target country/region	Period of case[a]	Type of product	Actual value of US exports to the target[b]	GATT panel established?	GATT panel ruled?	Negotiating objective achieved?	Degree of trade liberalization resulting from 301[c]
6	EC	12-1-75/ 1-83[d]	Agricultural (wheat flour)	$180 million (average US exports to the world, 1978–82)	Yes	Unable to reach conclusion on most issues, did not find code violation; US blocked adoption.	**Not at all.** However, petitioner received some relief. US eventually imposed retaliatory export subsidies, in 1983 on a wheat flour sale to Egypt; subsidies later formalized in EEP.	**Negative.** EEP has further distorted world markets, though it may have contributed to EC willingness to put export subsidies on table in Uruguay Round.
7	EC	3-30-76/ 6-18-80	Agriculture-related (canned fruit)	About $20 million (1979–81 average)	No	No	**Nominally.** EC converted variable levy to a fixed duty, but retained calculation method for sugar content; also direct subsidies added in 1978.	None
8	EC	3-30-76/ 1-5-79	Agricultural (soybeans and soy meal)	About $3 billion (1979–80)	Yes	Mixed, adopted	**Nominally.** Mixing requirement lifted but subsidies to soybean processors continued to reduce US market share.	None
9	Taiwan	3-15-76/ 12-1-77	Manufactured (home appliances)	About $30 million (1977–79)	n.a.	n.a.	**Largely.** Increase in tariffs reversed, some reduced further, though all remained at high levels.	Modest

10	EC, Japan	10-6-76/1-30-78	Manufactured (steel)				President found that there was not sufficient justification to claim the EC/Japanese understanding on steel created an unfair burden for the US.	**Significant** in principle, since resolution led to mutual concessions.
11	EC	11-12-76/8-10-86	Agricultural (citrus)	$10–$20 million (industry estimated average annual loss from EC preferences from 1970–84 at $48 million)	Yes	Nonviolation N&I of US benefits; blocked by the EC		**Partially.** Preferences maintained, but two sides exchanged concessions on a number of products.
12	Japan	2-14-77/3-3-78	Manufactured (thrown silk)	About $5 million (1979–81)	Yes	Not disclosed	**Largely.** Share of market preserved for US manufacturer.	**None.** Restricted market reallocated, not opened; data support conclusion that US gain was at the expense of other exporters.
13	Japan	8-4-77/12-85	Manufactured (leather)	About $100 million (1987–90) ($250 million was the anticipated value of the combined retaliation/compensation package in this case and no. 36)	Yes	Against Japan; adopted	**Partially.** Japan provided compensation rather than liberalize its leather market. Value of compensation unclear, however, since products—e.g., glass, paper, and auto parts subsequently reappeared on negotiating agenda.	**Modest.** Japan converted quotas to tariff rate quotas and lowered other tariffs.

continued next page

Summary table: assessments of section 301 cases (continued)

Case no.	Target country/ region	Period of case[a]	Type of product	Actual value of US exports to the target[b]	GATT panel established?	GATT panel ruled?	Negotiating objective achieved?	Degree of trade liberalization resulting from 301[c]
14	USSR	11-10-77/ 7-12-79[e]	Services (marine insurance)	Negl. (less than $10 million expected, even if full liberalization achieved)	n.a.	n.a.	**Nominally.** Disrupted by Afghan invasion.	None
15	Canada	8-29-78/ 10-30-84[d]	Services (broadcasting)	About $20 million (1974, based on data in USTR files)	n.a.	n.a.	**Not at all.** US enacted mirror legislation.	Negative
16	EC	11-2-78/ 8-1-80	Agricultural (wheat)	About $6 billion (average US exports to the world, 1978–82); petitioner estimated displaced exports of $500 million	No	No	**Nominally.** Agreement to monitor wheat trade and to consult had no substantive impact on problem.	None
17	Japan	3-14-79/ 1-6-81	Agriculture-related (cigars)	Negl. (industry anticipated $5 million with liberalization)	Yes	No. Agreement reached before announced.	**Nominally.** Only modest increases in exports until after 1985 cigarette case, which addressed many of the same issues (see case 50).	Very little if any
18	Argentina	5-25-79/ 7-25-80[e]	Services (marine insurance)	Negl. (industry anticipated less than $10 million even if full liberalization achieved, data in USTR files)	n.a.	n.a.	**Nominally.** An agreement to negotiate sometime in the future with no commitment to change anything.	None

	Country	Date	Sector (product)	Trade affected				Result
19	Japan	10-22-79/ 1-6-81	Agriculture-related (pipe tobacco)	Negl. (about $1 million anticipated after liberalization)	Yes	No	**Nominally** (see case 17).	**Very little if any**
20	Korea	11-5-79/ 12-29-80	Services (insurance)	$3 million ($10 million in additional premiums anticipated by industry; based on data in USTR files)	n.a.	n.a.	**Nominally.** Two of three issues supposedly resolved, including the commercially most significant (according to the industry), recurred in 1985 case (see case 51).	**None.** Agreement provided larger share of restricted (marine insurance) market to US firm but did not liberalize the market.
21	Switzerland	12-6-79/ 12-11-80	Manufactured (eyeglass frames)				US, not Swiss, regulations changed; brought US standards more in line with international standards.	
22	EC	8-20-81/ 6-28-82[e]	Agricultural (sugar)	$2 billion (US imports, 1980–81)	No	No	**No**	**Negative** if 301 case contributed to decision to impose import quotas.
23	EC	9-17-81/ 12-84[e]	Agricultural (poultry)	About $250 million (US exports to the world, 1978–80)	Conciliation under the	Subsidies Code	**Nominally**	**None** if subsidies only restrained; **negative** if three parties worked out a market-sharing arrangement.
24	Argentina	10-9-81/ 11-16-82[d]	Manufactured (leather)	$100 million to $150 million (US imports of Argentine hides, data in USTR files)	n.a.	n.a.	**No.** US revoked concessions extended in bilateral agreement Argentina failed to implement.	**Negative.** US retaliation resulted in higher tariffs on leather.
25	EC	10-16-81/ 9-15-87	Agriculture-related (pasta)	About $30 million (US imports from Italy, 1981–86)	Yes	Divided panel against EC, never adopted	**Partially.** Subsidies reduced, not eliminated.	**Modest**

continued next page

Summary table: assessments of section 301 cases (continued)

Case no.	Target country/ region	Period of case[a]	Type of product	Actual value of US exports to the target[b]	GATT panel established?	GATT panel ruled?	Negotiating objective achieved?	Degree of trade liberalization resulting from 301[c]
26	EC	10-23-81/ 12-85	Agriculture-related (canned fruit and raisins)	About $50 million (1980–81)	Yes	Against EC, except on raisins; EC blocked adoption	**Nominally.** Differing interpretations of commitments led to recurrence of frictions.	None
27/ 31, 33	Various European countries	1-12-82/ 11-16-82	Manufactured (specialty steel)				President directed USTR to request that the USITC initiate an escape clause investigation.	
32	Canada	6-3-82/ 9-23-82	Manufactured (subway cars)				Case terminated because same allegations were being investigated as a CVD case.	
34	Canada	9-13-82/ 12-82[e]	Manufactured (front-end loaders)	About $50 million (1982, based on data in USTR files)	No	No	**No.** Case apparently not pursued.	None
35	Brazil	10-25-82/ 1985[e]	Manufactured (footwear)	Negl.	No	No	**Partially.** Little help for US industry, which was seeking import relief not export opportunities.	Modest
36	Japan (see case 301-13 above)	10-25-82/ 12-85	Manufactured (footwear)	$45 million (see case no. 301-13)	—	—	**Partially**	Modest (see case 13)
37	Korea	10-25-82/ 1985[e]	Manufactured (footwear)	Negl.	No	No	**Partially.** Little help for US industry, which was seeking import relief not export opportunities.	Modest

38	Taiwan	10-25-82/ 12-19-83	Manufactured (footwear)				No basis for allegations of unfair trade barriers found in investigation.	
39	Korea	3-16-83/ 12-15-83	Manufactured (steel wire rope)	Less than $30 million (US imports; data in USTR files)	No	No	Unknown. Petition withdrawn, no determination made.	
40	Brazil	4-16-83/ 1985[e]	Agricultural (soybean oil and meal)	About $200 million (Brazil's exports to the world, 1986–87)	No	No	Partially	Modest
41	Portugal	4-16-83/ 1985[e]	Agricultural (soybean oil and meal)	Negl.	No	No	No. Superseded in 1986 by EC enlargement dispute.	None
42	Spain	4-16-83/ 1985[e]	Agricultural (soybean oil and meal)	About $100 million (USTR estimate of losses; 1990 NTE Report)	No	No	No. Superseded in 1986 by EC enlargement dispute.	None
43	Taiwan	9-29-83/ 3-22-84	Agricultural (rice)	About $60 million (Taiwan's exports to the world, 1980–83)	n.a.	n.a.	Partially. Subsidies reduced but not eliminated.	Modest
44	Argentina	9-21-83/ 5-25-89[e]	Services (air couriers)	About $5 million (1982, based on data in USTR files)	n.a.	n.a.	Partially. Fees modified, not eliminated.	Modest
45	Taiwan	12-19-83/ 4-26-84	Manufactured (motion picture films)	About $9 million (1980–82 average, based on USTR files)	n.a.	n.a.	Partially. A portion of quota restored and commitment from Taiwan to eliminate quota.	Though IP problems remain (see case 89), case appears to have contributed to elimination of film quota within a few years.
46	EC	5-25-84/ 7-17-85	Services (satellite launching)				President determined that no unfair practice existed.	

continued next page

Summary table: assessments of section 301 cases (continued)

Case no.	Target country/ region	Period of case[a]	Type of product	Actual value of US exports to the target[b]	GATT panel established?	GATT panel ruled?	Negotiating objective achieved?	Degree of trade liberalization resulting from 301[c]
47	EC	8-17-84/ 1984[e]	Manufactured (fertilizer)	Small?	No	No	**No.** Case apparently not pursued.	**None**
48	Japan	6-14-85/ 6-4-91	Manufactured (semiconductors)	About $800 million (1987–90 average, up from about $250 million in 1985–86; $165 million in retaliation)	No	No	**Nominally.** Neither govt. nor petitioner regarded market share gains as sufficient to lift sanctions imposed; moreover, gains did not occur until late in agreement period, when additional sanctions were threatened.	**Negative** because retaliation imposed. But US market share did increase finally and the gains by 1990–91 probably exceeded the value of the sanctions.
49[g]	Brazil	9-16-85/ 10-6-89	IP/manufactured (informatics)	About $100 million (value of planned retaliation)	n.a.	n.a.	**Partially**	**Modest**
50[g]	Japan	9-16-85/ 10-6-86[e]	Agriculture-related (cigarettes)	About $1 billion (up from less than $100 million prior to 1986)	No	No	**Largely**	**Significant**
51[g]	Korea	9-16-85/ 8-14-86	Services (insurance)	Perhaps $20 million[h]	n.a.	n.a.	**Yes.** Gained entry and expanded business opportunities for additional US firms.	Agreement specified entry for two US firms initially; additional foreign firms later permitted entry but still have less than 10 percent of market.

	Country	Dates	Sector	Estimated loss			Outcome	Success
52[g]	Korea	11-4-85/ 8-14-86	IP (general)	About $150 million (industry's estimate of losses; in USTR files)	n.a.	n.a.	**Nominally.** Protection laws passed, not enforced until additional pressure of special 301 process in 1989.	**None** until later. Retroactive protection initially provided only to US parties.
53	Argentina	4-4-86/ 12-88[e]	Agricultural (soybean oil and meal)	About $200 million (Argentina's exports to world, 1986–87; industry estimated loss as $160 million)	No	No	**Partially.** Export taxes reduced, but not eliminated.	**Modest**
54[g]	EC	3-31-86/ 1-30-87	Agricultural (corn, sorghum, oilseeds)	$400 million (based on value of compensation)	No	No	**Largely.** EC agreed to compensation, but not in perpetuity as desired by US.	**Modest.** Need to twice negotiate extensions has exacerbated tensions between US and EC over agriculture.
55	Canada	4-1-86/ 6-1-90	Natural resource (fish)	Less than $9 million (industry estimate of loss)	Yes	Against Canada; adopted	**Partially.** Industry did not get what it wanted, reportedly mirror-image legislation in the US.	**Modest**
56[g]	Taiwan	8-1-86/ 10-1-86	Manufactured (customs valuation)	Perhaps $200 million[i]	n.a.	n.a.	**Partially**	**Modest**
57[g]	Taiwan	10-27-86/ 12-5-86	Agriculture-related, manufactured (beer, wine, tobacco)	$100 million (1987–89)	n.a.	n.a.	**Partially**	**Modest**
58[g]	Canada	12-30-86/ 1-8-87	Natural resource (softwood lumber)				Section 301 used in this case for administrative purposes only until Canadians could implement export tax.	

continued next page

Summary table: assessments of section 301 cases (continued)

Case no.	Target country/ region	Period of case[a]	Type of product	Actual value of US exports to the target[b]	GATT panel established?	GATT panel ruled?	Negotiating objective achieved?	Degree of trade liberalization resulting from 301[c]
59	India	1-6-87/ 6-8-88	Agricultural (almonds)	$15 million (1989)	Yes	No. Agreement reached before report completed.	**Partially.** Quota expanded but not eliminated.	**Modest.** Data suggest possible trade diversion.
60	EC	7-14-87/ 12-88[e]	Agriculture-related (meatpacking)	About $30 million (based on data in USTR files)	Yes	No. Agreement reached before report completed.	**Nominally.** Temporary, administrative access provided to US meatpackers but no change in regulation; case recurs in 1990 (see case 83).	**None**
61	Brazil	6-11-87/ 6-27-90	IP (pharmaceuticals)	Greater than $40 million (based on level of retaliation)	n.a.	n.a.	**Nominally.** Retaliation lifted when Collor promised to submit patent legislation to Congress, but it had not passed as of mid-1994.	**Negative** during period of retaliation.
62[g]	EC	11-25-87/ 1-1-89[d]	Agriculture (beef)	About $100 million (based on amount of retaliation)	No	No	**Not at all**	**Negative.** Retaliation imposed.
63	EC	12-16-87/ 1-31-90	Agriculture (soybeans)	About $2 billion (down from $3 billion in late 1970s/ early 1980s)	Yes	Against EC, adopted	**Nominally**	Only resolved as part of Uruguay Round.
64	Korea	1-22-88/ 5-31-88	Agriculture-related (cigarettes)	About $100 million (up from less than $10 million).	No	No	**Partially**	**Modest.** Continuing political campaign against imported cigarettes.

65	Korea	2-16-88/ 4-26-90	Agriculture (beef)	$180 million in 1991–93 (up from less than $10 million).	Yes	Against Korea, adopted	**Partially**	**Significant** if full liberalization is carried out.
66	Japan	5-6-88/ 7-5-88	Agriculture (citrus)	About $100 million	Yes	No. Agreement reached before reported completed.	**Largely.** Quotas eventually eliminated.	301 case may have contributed modestly to resolution of dispute, which was being negotiated long before petition was filed.
67	Korea	4-27-88/ 1-18-89	Agriculture-related (wine)	Less than $10 million	No	No	**Partially**	**Modest**
68	Argentina	8-10-88/ 9-23-89	IP (pharma-ceuticals)	Industry estimated loss as $80 million in 1987	n.a.	n.a.	**Nominally.** Since promised legislation not passed.	**None** to date.
69[9]	Japan	11-21-88/ 7-31-91[e]	Services (construction)	$200 million (1990, USTR fact sheet)	n.a.	n.a.	**Partially.** List of eligible projects expanded, not eliminated.	A few US firms appear to have been largely coopted.
70	EC	11-14-88/ 2-26-90	Manufactured (fabricated copper)	About $6 million (US imports, 1988–89)	Yes	No. Agreement reached before reported completed.	**Largely.** Export restrictions removed.	**Modest**
71[9]	EC	5-8-89/ 10-1-89	Agriculture-related (canned fruit)	Less than $5 million	No	No	**Partially.** Negotiations on implementation continuing.	**Modest**
72	Thailand	4-10-89/ 11-23-90	Agriculture-related (cigarettes)	About $170 million anticipated by industry if ban lifted (based on data in USTR files)	Yes	Against Thailand, adopted	**Nominally.** Import ban lifted, but remaining tariffs prohibitive.	**None**

continued next page

Summary table: assessments of section 301 cases (continued)

Case no.	Target country/region	Period of case[a]	Type of product	Actual value of US exports to the target[b]	GATT panel established?	GATT panel ruled?	Negotiating objective achieved?	Degree of trade liberalization resulting from 301[c]
73[g]	Brazil	6-16-89/ 5-21-90	Manufactured (import licensing)	Perhaps $100 million[i]	US requested panel but not established before case resolved	No	**Largely.** Import licensing system eliminated.	**Significant** if implemented, though very little due to US pressure as compared with Collor election and shift in policy.
74[g]	Japan	6-16-89/ 6-15-90[e]	Manufactured (satellites)	About $50 million (1980–90 average)	n.a.	n.a.	**Largely**	**Modest** if implemented.
75[g]	Japan	6-16-89/ 6-15-90[e]	Manufactured (supercomputers)	About $30 million	n.a.	n.a.	**Partially.** Disputes over implementation.	**Modest** if implemented.
76[g]	Japan	6-16-89/ 6-15-90[e]	Manufactured (wood products)	About $700 million (US exports of lumber and other wood products)	No	No	**Partially.** Tariffs not reduced as much as desired.	**Significant** if implemented fully following Uruguay Round.
77[g]	India	6-16-89/ 6-14-90	Investment	US stock of FDI in 1990 was $500 million	n.a.	n.a.	**Not at all**	**None**
78[g]	India	6-16-89/ 6-14-90	Services (insurance)	Gross insurance premiums in 1986 valued at $2.6 billion (1989 NTE Report)	n.a.	n.a.	**Not at all**	**None**
79	Norway	7-11-89/ 4-26-90	Manufactured (highway toll machines)	Less than $10 million (based on data in USTR files)	No	No	**Nominally.** Some compensation received.	**None**

80	Canada	5-15-90/ 8-5-93	Manufactured (beer)	About $30 million, 1989–90 ($80 million planned for retaliation)	Yes	Against Canada, adopted	Nominally. Problems with implementation of agreement by provinces.	Little so far
81[g]	EC	11-15-90/ 12-21-90	Agricultural (corn, sorghum, oilseeds)	$400 million	No	No	Partially. Only a one-year extension achieved (extended for another year at end of 1991).	Modest
82	Thailand	11-15-90/ 12-20-91	IP (books, records, and movies)	Greater than $100 million (based on industry estimates of losses due to piracy).	n.a.	n.a.	Nominally. USTR terminated case based on promises from Thailand to revise its copyright law and enforce it vigorously.	Not to date. Thailand was renamed as a priority country in April 1992 and 1993.
83	EC	11-28-90/ 10-93	Agriculture-related (meatpacking)	About $30 million (based on data in USTR files)	No	No	Nominally at least. Agreement reached in fall 1992.	Too early to judge results.
84	Thailand	1-30-91/ 10-92[a]	IP (pharmaceuticals)	About $20 million (industry estimate of losses)	n.a.	n.a.	Nominally (see case 82).	None to date.
85[g]	India	5-26-91/ 2-26-92	IP (general)	Greater than $200 million for pharmaceuticals and $150 million for copyright violations (based on industry estimate of losses)	n.a.	n.a.	Nominally and not at all. Compromise reached on copyright and film quota, but India renamed as priority country in April 1992 because of its refusal to extend patent protection to pharmaceuticals, also problems in implementing copyright commitments.	GSP eligibility withdrawn for about $60 million in Indian exports to US.

continued next page

Summary table: assessments of section 301 cases (continued)

Case no.	Target country/ region	Period of case[a]	Type of product	Actual value of US exports to the target[b]	GATT panel established?	GATT panel ruled?	Negotiating objective achieved?	Degree of trade liberalization resulting from 301[c]
86[g]	China	5-26-91/ 1-17-92	IP (general)	Greater than $400 million (estimate by USTR; $300 million in planned retaliation)	n.a.	n.a.	**Nominally**. Agreement reached but IP laws not enforced.	**None** to date.
87[g]	Canada		Natural resource-based (softwood lumber)					Similar to case 58; same issue.
88[g]	China	10-10-91/ 10-92	General (QRs, licensing, technical barriers, and lack of transparency in import regulations)	About $2 billion, based on USTR retaliation threat	n.a.	n.a.	**Nominally** at least. Too early to fully assess results.	**Significant** if fully implemented.
89[g]	Taiwan	4-29-92/ 6-5-92	IP (copyright)	$370 million (USTR estimate)	n.a.	n.a.	**Nominally** given problems with implementation in 1993.	**None** to date.
90	Indonesia	8-18-92/ 12-31-92	Pencil slats				USTR found no evidence of injury to US industry, so even if practice existed, it was not restricting or burdening US trade.	

| 91[9] | Brazil | 5-28-93/ 2-25-94 | IP | No estimate | n.a. | n.a. | **Nominally** or better depending on passage of IP bill by Brazilian Congress and subsequent enforcement. |

negl. = negligible

n.a. = not applicable

IP = intellectual property

a. The first date is when the petition was filed; the end date is either when the case was terminated, suspended, or otherwise concluded.

b. Unless otherwise indicated, the figures represent the value of US exports to the target country after the case was concluded. The trade gain (in successful cases) or loss (in failures) would typically be a much lower figure and, in cases involving homogeneous products, the *net* gain or loss might be close to zero. The overstatement of actual loss is even greater in the cases involving export subsidies that affect third markets; in those cases, the smaller of US or the target's exports to the world are provided, even though it is likely that US exports compete with subsidized exports from other countries in only some of the US markets. The export figures provided are intended only to give a general idea—an order of magnitude—of the potential stakes involved and of the importance of trade in the sector to the US economy; in other words, these data are meant only to distinguish "big" cases from "small" ones.

c. Negative if retaliation was imposed with no other resolution, none if there was no resolution or if other measures were substituted for the targeted practice or policy, modest if the practice was modified but not eliminated, and significant if the practice was eliminated or if there is a credible commitment to phase it out.

d. Retaliation imposed with no other resolution.

e. Case suspended or otherwise dormant.

f. The United States initially asked that the council rule without further deliberation since a similar quota on raw leather had previously been ruled GATT-illegal (see case 301-13). The United States withdrew its request after several delegations objected and asked that a panel be appointed, but a bilateral solution was achieved before the panel could be established.

g. USTR initiated.

h. Estimate based on $10 million in premiums expected from the first insurance agreement, increased by average growth of total gross insurance premiums in Korea. See petition in case 301-20 and Yoon Je Cho, "Some Policy Lessons from the Opening of the Korean Insurance Market," *The World Bank Economic Review* 2, no. 2 (May 1988): 241–54.

i. A simplified estimate of the costs of revocation of GSP eligibility is used as a proxy for the value of the retaliatory threat in this case. Taiwan had $11 billion in GSP-eligible exports to the United States in 1986. Assuming the same proportion of Taiwan's eligible exports enter duty-free as the average for all GSP recipients (around 40 percent), and using the average tariff rate of 5 percent for all US imports, the cost to Taiwan of losing GSP eligibility might be roughly $200 million (data from USITC Annual Report, 1987).

j. The value of US exports to Brazil increased 9.3 percent in the four quarters after elimination of the quantitative restrictions, as compared with the previous four quarters. The two percentage points by which this figure is higher than the annual average for 1987–89 is attributed to the liberalization (data from IMF, *Direction of Trade Statistics*).

Case Summaries

Unless otherwise noted, the source is either the public case files of the US Trade Representative or, primarily for summaries of GATT actions, Hudec (1993). Unless noted, the source for data in the tables is the UN Trade Database.

Case 301-1

Complaint. On 1 July 1975 Delta Steamship Lines, Inc., filed a petition alleging that Guatemalan Government Decree No. 41-71, issued in 1971, was discriminatory and an unreasonable burden on US commerce. The decree required that goods imported duty-free under Guatemala's industrial development laws be carried on Guatemalan carriers and imposed a penalty of 50 percent of total freight charges for violations of the decree. There were a number of exemptions from the decree if Guatemalan carriers could not handle the cargo in a timely manner, and the decree authorized Guatemalan carriers to contract with foreign carriers if necessary "to provide transport services in an effective manner. . . ." Simultaneously, Delta filed a petition with the Federal Maritime Commission (FMC) seeking relief under section 19 of the Merchant Marine Act of 1920, which provides broad authority "to make rules and regulations affecting shipping in the foreign trade of the United States" in response to foreign government or private actions having an impact on US shipping.

Delta argued in its petition that the decree discouraged US exporters from placing any shipments to Guatemala with Delta because of uncertainties as to which cargoes might be subject to the decree. Delta had met over the previous two years with "Guatemala National Flag Lines" and government officials in Guatemala to try to work out "an equitable agreement" that would allow Delta " 'equal access' to cargoes moving in the United States/Guatemala trade."

In hearings before the interagency Trade Policy Staff Committee in September 1975, Flota Mercante Gran Centroamericana S.A. (Flomerca) testified that Delta was not excluded from carriage of US-Guatemalan trade for two reasons: first, it had never been refused a waiver to carry reserved cargoes, and second, reserve cargoes accounted for only 15 percent of total trade between New Orleans and Guatemala. Flomerca claimed that in 1974 Delta had carried 37 percent of the total trade between those destinations and had earned $300,000 in freight revenues since January 1974 on exonerated cargoes. The FMC, however, found that US carriers had been virtually excluded from the US-Guatemalan trade because most US exports to Guatemala were in the exonerated categories and because of the unpredictability of application of the decree.

GATT role. Not applicable.

Outcome. On 4 December 1975 the FMC notified the State Department of its finding that Decree No. 41-71 "created conditions unfavorable to the foreign trade of the United States" and requested that it seek a diplomatic solution to the dispute; the FMC advised the State Department that "absent such resolution by February 14, 1976, the Commission would have no recourse but to promulgate a final regulation that would impose countervailing fees on Guatemalan carriers and associated carriers transporting goods from the United States which are to be imported duty-free into Guatemala." At the request of the State Department, the FMC postponed implementation of the regulation following an earthquake in Guatemala. In April 1976 Delta requested that its section 301 petition be withdrawn, saying it had reached an agreement with Flomerca. USTR terminated the investigation on 29 June 1976.

In August, however, the FMC again prepared to issue the proposed rule but again postponed it based on assurances from "the Guatemalan flag lines of a satisfactory resolution of the problem." Then, in April 1977, according to Delta, Guatemala again began imposing penalties on US exporters using American carriers; in June, the FMC issued the proposed rule for countervailing fees and asked for comments. On 14 December 1977 the FMC issued the final rule to become effective 13 January 1978. Effective 18 January 1978 the FMC suspended implementation of the regulation based on a Guatemalan commitment to provide waivers for all exonerated cargoes carried by US shipping lines from 13 January until 20 February 1978 when a new, purportedly nondiscriminatory law replacing Decree No. 41-71 would go into effect.

Assessment. The petitioner apparently believed that the Federal Maritime Commission had more leverage using section 19 of the Merchant Marine Act of 1920 than USTR did using section 301 of the 1974 Trade Act and decided to press its case through the FMC. Even the April 1976 agreement with Flomerca that prompted Delta to withdraw its 301 petition followed an explicit retaliatory threat by the FMC (the proposed rule to impose countervailing fees on Guatelemalan shipping lines). Although possibly overstating the lack of leverage, this case is considered a failure for section 301.

Case 301-2

Complaint. In July 1975 the United Egg Producers (UEP) and the American Farm Bureau Federation (AFBF) separately filed petitions claiming that a licensing system recently adopted by Canada for imports of US shell eggs and processed egg products was an unfair trade practice. The Canadian quotas restricted US egg exports to 0.36 percent of the Canadian market, approximately 54,000 cases compared with 195,000 cases shipped to Canada by US shell egg producers in 1974 (an unusually good year; see table A.1). Both the UEP and AFBF recommended that the United States impose quotas on imports of Canadian eggs at the same level as the Canadian quotas.

The UEP seemed equally concerned with the imports of Canadian eggs into the US market as with its access to the Canadian market. In 1974 the UEP had charged that the Canadian Egg Marketing Agency (CEMA) was dumping eggs in the United States as a means of getting rid of its surplus stocks. Citing a price response of 7 percent for every 1 percent change in supply, UEP claimed that Canadian marketing practices in 1974 cost US egg producers $46 million and that the continuation of similar export practices in 1975 could cost them that much or more.

GATT role. The United States filed a complaint in September 1975 and asked for a working party advisory opinion while continuing to pursue bilateral negotiations. (It did not request establishment of a dispute settlement panel because it would "give unwarranted suggestion that negotiations had already failed.") The working party found that Canada was in compliance with Article XI requirements that import quotas be accompanied by restrictions on domestic production, but it could not determine whether the base period for calculating the quota was appropriate. It recommended bilateral settlement of this issue using a different base period because of the annual fluctuations in egg trade. Finally, the working party could not decide whether the quotas nullified or impaired the tariff binding. The working party report was adopted by the GATT Council in February 1976 (Hudec 1993, 461–62).

Outcome. In its termination announcement, USTR said that in its negotiations with Canada, it had sought "removal of the *restrictive effect* of the

Table A.1   United States and Canada: trade in eggs, 1970–79

	US exports to Canada			US imports from Canada		
Year	Millions of dollars	As share of total	As share of total Canadian imports	Millions of dollars	As share of total	As share of total Canadian exports
1970	6.5	48.5	83.3	3.9	38.2	84.8
1971	5.0	37.3	80.1	2.0	50.0	83.3
1972	6.1	35.9	90.2	1.3	76.5	56.5
1973	7.4	35.2	87.4	5.4	80.6	72.0
1974	10.0	34.6	93.5	5.3	89.8	64.6
1975	7.6	48.7	53.3	2.4	77.4	27.3
1976	15.6	42.3	79.4	0.9	40.9	12.5
1977	14.9	25.3	85.3	3.5	57.4	32.4
1978	15.4	24.8	68.1	2.7	57.4	22.7
1979	18.5	28.5	56.4	1.4	30.4	14.3

Source: Canadian data and US export data are from SITC Rev. 2 trade statistics; US import data are from US Department of Commerce Schedule A trade statistics.

quota on US exports of eggs. . ." (emphasis added). Canada agreed to nearly double the quota for US eggs to 100,000 cases and to "deal with problems which might arise in the future involving Canadian exports of shell eggs to the United States and other markets." USTR terminated the investigation on 14 March 1976.

Assessment.   The doubling of the shell egg quota, an outcome in accordance with the GATT working party recommendation for settling the dispute, and the increase in US exports (table A.1) indicate that US objectives were largely achieved. The data on US imports, however, show a 40 percent decline in imports from Canada and a decline in total imports of nearly a third. Combined with the petitioners' statements regarding Canadian dumping of eggs in the US market, these data raise questions about possible trade diversion. Nevertheless, this case appears on balance to have been a modestly liberalizing outcome and generally consistent with GATT rules, an assessment supported by at least one official involved. (The 1989 National Trade Estimate Report noted that Canada had agreed to liberalize the egg quota during negotiation of the Canada–United States Free Trade Agreement, increasing it from 0.675 percent of the prior year's production to 1.647 percent [p. 27].)

Case 301-3

Complaint.   Seymour Foods, Inc. filed a petition on 7 August 1975 complaining that a recent increase in the European Community's import levy on albumin (dried egg whites) and frequent changes in the supplemental levy on as little as three days' notice, "impairs this complainant's ability to contract for the future delivery of egg albumin to [EC] customers and places in jeopardy those contracts for delivery now in effect." The petitioner noted that the latest increase in the regular levy represented 10 percent of the value of the imported product.

GATT role.   The United States, which has never raised a legal challenge to the variable levy, did not take this case to GATT.

Outcome.   USTR conducted informal consultations with the European Community and monitored egg albumin exports to the Community. According to the termination notice published in the *Federal Register*, "The European Community ceased imposition of the supplementary levies in September of 1976 but has increased import charges steadily since that date." However, since the volume and value of US egg albumin exports to the European Community both had increased despite the increasing import levies, USTR determined that action under section 301 was "no longer necessary" and, with the petitioner's agreement, terminated the case in July 1980.

Table A.2 US exports of albumin and derivatives to the European Community, 1974–90

Year	Millions of dollars	As share of total US exports	As share of total EC imports
1974	2.0	49.6	10.2
1975	1.7	50.6	11.2
1976	1.8	50.2	9.5
1977	3.6	42.7	14.0
1978	3.3	31.4	13.5
1979	2.2	25.1	8.6
1980	6.1	33.6	18.8
1981	5.7	21.4	20.5
1982	2.9	15.0	13.4
1983	0.9	5.7	4.4
1984	0.7	6.4	2.5
1985	0.4	2.7	1.2
1986	0.4	1.7	1.1
1987	1.8	7.1	3.8
1988	1.1	5.0	2.3
1989	2.1	14.7	3.9
1990	2.3	12.7	3.3

Assessment. With the elimination of the supplementary levy, US negotiating objectives were partially achieved. Contrary to USTR's finding, however, after an initial increase, the value of US exports declined in both 1978 and 1979 before increasing sharply (and temporarily) in 1980–81 (table A.2). Still, since average US exports to the Community were higher than they had been before elimination of the supplementary levy, this is regarded as a modestly liberalizing outcome. This assessment is supported by one official involved in the case.

Case 301-4

Complaint. On 22 September 1975 the National Canners Association (NCA) filed a petition claiming that recently implemented European Community import restrictions were unfair trade practices. The regulations, to be phased in over two years, established a minimum import price (MIP) system for tomato concentrates and an import licensing system for certain canned fruits and vegetables and included provisions for the complete suspension of imports of canned and other processed fruits, vegetables, and juices. The MIP and suspension provisions could be applied to products regardless of whether they were covered by the licensing system, with no showing of injury or threat of injury, and without advance notice. NCA claimed that the regulations would also lead to trade diversion, reducing US sales in third markets and possibly sales in the US market as well (as occurred, in particular in the canned peach market, in the late 1980s).

According to 1974 data provided in the petition, US producers exported less than $1 million of tomato concentrates to the European Community, but the value of the products subject to the licensing provisions was $6 million (canned tomatoes and juice, canned peaches, pears, green beans, wax beans, and peas) and of the products potentially subject to the suspension provisions another $20 million (canned apricots, cherries, fruit cocktail, pineapple, orange and grapefruit juices, asparagus). Total US exports of these products to all destinations were valued at just over $100 million in 1974.

GATT role. The US complaint to GATT "followed [a] strategy of claiming violation of all remotely applicable GATT texts, regardless of consistency between claims" (Hudec 1993, 462). According to Hudec, the MIP requirement raised the issue of whether GATT permission to restrict imports of price-supported primary products could be stretched to include processed products made from them; the licensing system "appeared to an early-warning device for import surges, as well as a warning to importers of those products to act with restraint. The complaint appeared to be driven by the threat of restrictions rather than the burden of the procedure itself."

A dispute settlement panel was appointed, and its report was adopted on 18 October 1978. The panel found that the MIP requirement was not in compliance with Article XI because the European Community surplus disposal program for fresh tomatoes "was not sufficiently mandatory to be considered a governmental restriction of domestic production or marketing, nor a measure which operated to remove a temporary surplus. . . ." However, the panel ruled that tomato concentrates did meet the article's test of being a "perishable" product (a finding cast in doubt by a later ruling in the GATT-12 case against Japan; see chapter 10).

On the licenses and security deposits, the panel found that automatic licensing was not a quantitative restriction under the meaning of Article XI and that the expense to the importer associated with the security deposits was a "fee or charge" covered by Article VIII. But, the panel found, the "administrative burden/uncertainty of the license procedure was not *onerous* enough to violate Article VIII" (emphasis in original). The panel further ruled that, since it was in violation of Article XI, the MIP constituted prima facie nullification and impairment, but that the license/security deposit system did not since it was not onerous enough to constitute a violation (Hudec 1993, 462–65).

Outcome. In mid-1978, before adoption of the GATT panel report, the European Community abolished the MIP system for tomato concentrates for what it said were internal reasons. At about the same time, however, the Community adopted a system of subsidies to processors to offset the cost of using higher-priced, protected inputs (see case 301-26 on this issue). Following adoption of the GATT report, USTR determined that action under section 301 was no longer required and terminated the case effective 5 January 1979.

On 30 January 1979 the Canners League of California filed countervailing duty petitions against nine European Community member countries claiming the league had been injured by European Community subsidies on canned tomatoes and tomato concentrates. Although the Department of Commerce found that the products were being subsidized, the US International Trade Commission did not find that the industry had been injured as a result (Destler 1992, appendix B).

Assessment.   By classifying tomato concentrates as a perishable product within the meaning of Article XI, the GATT panel skirted the issue of whether processed products made from agricultural products subject to domestic management programs could also be legitimately subject to import restrictions under Article XI. Thus, no precedent was established. And, although the MIP system was abolished, this achievement was a hollow one since the Community replaced border measures with subsidies paid to processors to offset the higher cost of domestic inputs.

Case 301-5

Complaint.   On 13 November 1975 the Great Western Malting Co. filed a petition claiming that EC subsidization of malt exports to Japan and other countries was an unfair trade practice. The petitioner claimed it lost "virtually its entire Japanese market" as a result of sharply increased European Community export subsidies. Moreover, Great Western claimed that European Community exporters had been able to book shipments of sufficient quantity in June/July 1975 (when the subsidy rates were the highest) "to cover Europe's export capability to Japan and other countries until June 1976."

GATT role.   USTR said it used this case "to illustrate the type of subsidy problem which the United States sought to eliminate in the Multilateral Trade Negotiations," but it did not file a complaint under the GATT dispute settlement procedures. Chile had filed a complaint regarding EC barley malt export subsidies in 1977 but did not pursue it. After conclusion of the Tokyo Round, Chile requested consultations with the Community under the Subsidies Code on two other occasions, in 1980 and 1981.

Outcome.   After USTR "brought the problem . . . to the attention of the European Community Commission," the Community in 1976 reduced the amount of subsidy on malt exports. Then, claiming that the Tokyo

Table A.3 US and EC malt exports to Japan, 1974–83

| Year | United States | | European Community | |
	Millions of dollars	As share of total US exports	Millions of dollars	As share of total EC exports
1974	2.3	23.7	33.7	11.4
1975	3.0	40.0	42.3	11.6
1976	2.6	38.2	35.0	10.3
1977	1.8	25.7	26.9	7.5
1978	2.3	31.9	38.9	9.7
1979	0.7	11.1	40.4	9.5
1980	2.4	26.1	49.3	10.1
1981	0.5	6.3	46.0	8.7
1982	1.5	8.2	53.2	9.6
1983	3.0	32.3	49.9	9.3

Round Subsidies Code had addressed the issues raised in the petition, USTR determined that action under section 301 was no longer required, advised the petitioner that "should European Community export practices again result in significant problems, the issue will be raised with the EC," and terminated the case effective 19 June 1980.

In October 1992 the USDA announced a new package of Export Enhancement Program (EEP) subsidies for barley malt, with one official noting, "The EC's high subsidies on barley malt, which are two to three times greater than those awarded under the EEP, have allowed the European Community to dominate world malt trade...." (*International Trade Reporter*, 14 October 1992, 1757).

Assessment. The Subsidies Code did not resolve the problem of agricultural export subsidies, and average US exports declined by $1 million in 1977–79 compared with 1974–76, while EC exports to Japan returned to previous levels after a temporary decline in 1977 (table A.3). That very little appears to have been achieved in this case is also apparent from Chile's continuing problems with the European Community on this issue.

Case 301-6

Complaint. In December 1975 the Millers' National Federation filed a petition alleging that EC subsidies on exports of wheat flour of up to $50 per ton adversely affected US exports to third markets and violated GATT Article XVI. After bilateral consultations between the United States and the European Community failed to resolve the dispute, the United States tried to resolve it in the context of the Tokyo Round negotiations on subsidies. When those negotiations failed to address the specific problems in this case, President Jimmy Carter determined on 31 July 1980 that the EC subsidies were inconsistent with the GATT and directed the USTR to pursue dispute settlement procedures.

GATT role. A dispute settlement panel was established in December 1981 to consider the US claims that EC export subsidies for wheat flour violated the recently negotiated Subsidies Code because they resulted in the Community having a "more than equitable share of world trade," caused market displacement, and resulted in price undercutting. According to Hudec (1993, 491), "The GATT complaint was viewed as an important first test of the new Subsidies Code dispute settlement procedure."

Despite an increase in EC world market share from 28 percent in the three years prior to authorization of export subsidies (in 1962) to 73 percent in the late 1970s, and a decline in US market share from 28 percent to 11 percent over the same period (US figures), the GATT panel was unable to define operationally the Subsidies Code's "equitable share" standard. Thus, the panel was unable to reach a conclusion as to whether subsidies had allowed the European Community to capture more than an equitable share; it did not find market displacement as defined in the Subsidies Code; and it was unable to come to a conclusion about price undercutting based on the information available to it. Arguing that the proof of "more than equitable share" was clear, the United States tried to have the Subsidies Code Committee rule on its complaint but was blocked by the European Community and others. The United States in turn blocked adoption of the panel report. As of the end of 1989, the panel report remained on the GATT Council's list of unfinished business (Hudec 1993, 490–92).

Outcome. Frustrated over the delays in the dispute settlement process, in January 1983, a month before the panel released its report, the United States "retaliated" by granting a subsidy to US wheat flour exporters large enough to capture the entire Egyptian market for one year (previously about 25 percent of EC exports of wheat flour). At a May meeting of the Subsidies Committee, the European Community demanded compensation from the United States for the Egyptian wheat flour sale and a commitment from the United States that such sales would not be repeated; when the United States refused, the Community requested that a panel be established to consider the matter. US delegates welcomed the request, saying they expected to be vindicated (*U.S. Export Weekly*, 24 May 1983, 287).

In a June council meeting, the European Community reported that it had unilaterally reduced its wheat flour exports from 4.1 million metric tons in 1981–82 to 2.6 million metric tons in 1982–83 in response to panel urgings to limit exports. The European Community also pledged to limit its 1983–84 world market share of wheat and wheat flour sales to 14 percent but then threatened to reconsider the pledge when the United

States refused to limit its exports to the Community of corn gluten feed (Paarlberg 1986, 162). In 1985, with no further resolution of the issue, the administration established the Export Enhancement Program (EEP) of export subsidies to combat the EC export subsidy program.

Assessment. Although the petitioner received some relief from the injury caused by EC subsidies as a result of the EEP, world markets were further distorted, and USTR did not achieve its objective of reducing subsidies. Hudec (1990b, 127–28), cites this case as an example of "general legal breakdown" in the GATT, and although he notes that the US subsidy for the Egyptian shipment was "pretty clearly in violation of Subsidy Code rules," he concludes that the US retaliation was "justified." He argues further that "even though retaliatory subsidies turned out not to be a very effective form of pressure, the European Community did put its CAP export subsidies on the table in the Uruguay Round. Thus, the US retaliation may have helped open the door to possible legal reforms that may in turn bring these subsidy practices back into the GATT legal discipline" (Hudec 1990b, 128).

The US General Accounting Office concluded in a study of the EEP that "EEP, combined with the dollar's decline and lower loan rates, has increased the financial cost of the EC's Common Agricultural Policy, particularly through increased subsidy payments, and has contributed to realizing agreement to include agricultural subsidies in the round of multilateral trade negotiations under the General Agreement on Tariffs and Trade (US Senate, Committee on Agriculture, Nutrition, and Forestry 1987, 198–99).

Case 301-7

Complaint. On 30 March 1976 the National Canners Association (NCA), which later changed its name to the National Food Processors Association, filed a petition alleging that the variable levy imposed on the calculated added sugar content of canned fruit was a violation of EC tariff bindings on canned fruit, unjustifiable and unreasonable, and a burden and restriction on US commerce. (The NCA had previously filed a similar petition under section 252 of the Trade Expansion Act of 1962.) The NCA claimed that because the levy was determined on a quarterly basis (prior to 1971 the calculation had been done even more frequently), based on the difference between the world price for sugar and the EC "gate" price, it created uncertainty and delays for EC importers of canned fruit, who could buy the domestic product free from the additional charges, delays, and uncertainty as to final price. Despite EC claims that the levy was intended to protect the domestic sugar industry, the NCA alleged that "the levy in fact is intended to provide further protection to the EC fruit canning industry, which is already protected by a bound, fixed tariff [of 25 percent]

... as well as [a] ... discriminatory system of import licenses ... and provisions for suspension of imports" (see case 301-4).

GATT role.   The United States and the European Community consulted on this issue during the Tokyo Round, but the United States did not take the case to GATT.

Outcome.   In the context of the Tokyo Round agreement, the European Community agreed on 11 July 1979 to convert the variable levy on added sugar to a fixed 2 percent duty. The month before, the National Food Processors Association (successor to the NCA) had written USTR requesting renewal of its earlier complaint (suspended when the United States decided to pursue the issue in the MTN), arguing that, even with conversion of the variable levy to a fixed duty, the method used to calculate the added sugar volume in each shipment of canned fruit would still cause uncertainty and delays in the importation of canned fruit and thus was an unfair trade practice. In June 1980, USTR, after consulting with the petitioner, determined that this issue should be pursued outside the context of section 301 and terminated the case.

Assessment.   Although the United States nominally received a concession when the European Community agreed to convert the variable levy to a fixed duty, no actual liberalization was achieved since the Community retained the disruptive calculation method and substituted direct subsidies for the import levy (see also cases 301-4 and 301-26).

Case 301-8

Complaint.   On 30 March 1976 the National Soybean Processors Association and the American Soybean Association filed a complaint alleging that a recent decision by the European Community to impose a deposit requirement on imports and domestic production of vegetable proteins, including soybeans and soybean meal, was a "protectionist device having the effect of a tariff," which violated the EC zero tariff binding on soybeans and meal. The deposit would be returned only if the importer or producer bought 50 kilos of surplus nonfat dry milk (NFD) for each 1,000 kilos of soybean meal. The intent of the regulation, in force for only six months, appears to have been to reduce the "milk mountain" by forcing producers and importers of vegetable proteins to mix NFD with their animal feeds.

GATT role.   A dispute settlement panel was established in September 1976, and the United States requested that the panel continue deliberations and issue a ruling on the practices even after the European Community terminated the mixing requirement in October. According to Hudec (1993, 466), "The United States was concerned to protect the integrity of tariff bindings on these protein feeds, which having been kept outside the CAP variable levy system, had become an extremely important export." The panel ruled that the regulation violated some parts of Article III because it was an "internal" quantitative restriction the effect of which was to "protect" domestic milk production, and because the application of the regulation to imported corn gluten but not to domestically produced corn gluten violated the national treatment provisions in Article III:4. The panel further ruled that the regulations did not violate Articles I (MFN) and II (tariff bindings) and did not rule on the nullification and impairment claim. The report was adopted in March 1978 (Hudec 1993, 466–67).

Outcome. The European Community had characterized the program as temporary, and it removed only 0.4 million tons from a 15 million-ton import market before it was terminated in October 1976. USTR terminated the investigation in January 1979.

Assessment. Although the particular practice in question was eliminated in a relatively short time and with negligible injury to US exporters in the short run, the European Community continued to directly subsidize the oilseeds sector, and the United States was not able to establish a precedent that EC practices affecting animal feed imports violated its zero tariff binding on those products. Finally, in 1989, a GATT panel ruled that the EC oilseeds program nullified or impaired US benefits from the tariff binding (see case 301-63). (An industry official commenting on this case supported this assessment.)

Case 301-9

Complaint. Charles C. Rehfeldt, executive vice president of Lai Fu Trading Co. in Taiwan, filed a complaint on 15 March 1976 claiming that recent increases in import duties on certain consumer electronics and other household appliances to "confiscatory" levels "nullifies, impairs, discriminates and burdens U.S. commerce in their market." Rehfeldt, though not recommending in his petition that Taiwan's eligibility be revoked, also claimed that the new tariff levels were contrary to criteria for eligibility under the Generalized System of Preferences (GSP) encompassing "the extent to which [eligible countries] have assured the United States that they will provide the United States with equitable and reasonable access to their markets." The revised tariff schedule defined certain imports as "luxury items" and included increases in the duty on color televisions from 45 to 60 percent, with similar increases for air conditioners, refrigerators, and audio and stereo equipment.

The petitioner claimed that the tariff increases were the result of pressure from the Taiwan Electrical Appliance Manufacturers Association. Taiwan claimed that the increased duties were a temporary measure, initially implemented in March 1975 for one year and extended in March 1976 for an additional year, to deal with balance of payments pressures resulting from the global recession and that the increases would be rescinded as soon as the government determined that the balance of payments crisis was over. The Taiwanese also argued that any attempt to link the increased duties to GSP eligibility was illegitimate because the increases had been declared several months before President Gerald Ford had issued the proclamation granting GSP.

GATT role.   Not applicable since Taiwan is not a GATT member.

Outcome.   USTR appears to have accepted the Taiwanese argument that the tariff increases were necessary to deal with a balance of payments crisis. However, "[w]hen it was determined that the ROC was maintaining duty surcharges on imports of certain home appliances long after the balance of payments rationale had disappeared, the United States opened extensive bilateral consultations with representatives of the ROC seeking removal of those surcharges." USTR terminated the case effective 1 December 1977 after Taiwan agreed to lower the tariffs at least to their levels prior to 1975, and in some cases even lower.

Assessment.   US negotiators not only achieved a reversal of the increased tariffs, the tariffs on some items were lowered still more. Trade data also show US exports of consumer electronics increasing nearly 40 percent (from low levels) after the tariffs were lowered (table A.4). According to an official involved, however, relief was too late to save Rehfeldt, who had already gone out of business.

Case 301-10

Complaint.   On 6 October 1976 the American Iron and Steel Institute (AISI) filed a petition claiming that a recent agreement between the European Community and Japan to limit Japanese steel exports to the Community would result in diversion of up to 1.5 million net tons or more of Japanese steel to the US market in 1976. AISI requested that the USTR seek both to eliminate the burden and to obtain compensation for injury already sustained as a result of the agreement.

GATT role.   Although AISI claimed that the agreement violated Article XIII providing for nondiscriminatory administration of quantitative restrictions, the United States did not take the case to the GATT.

Outcome.   In response to an overwhelming number of antidumping petitions filed by the steel industry during 1977, President Jimmy Carter ordered Under Secretary of the Treasury Anthony Solomon to devise

Table A.4 US exports to Taiwan of household appliances, 1972–80 (millions of dollars)

Year	Television receivers	Audio equipment	Heating/cooling machinery and equipment	Home electrical equipment and appliances	Home refrigerators and freezers	Air conditioning machines and parts
1972	10.2	0.7	n.a.	n.a.	n.a.	n.a.
1973	15.7	2.2	18.3	1.2	n.a.	n.a.
1974	21.9	2.2	33.4	4.0	n.a.	n.a.
1975	15.3	2.9	35.8	2.9	n.a.	n.a.
1976	23.0	3.9	26.4	3.4	n.a.	n.a.
1977	20.0	5.0	20.0	4.3	n.a.	n.a.
1978	29.2	3.3	n.a.	n.a.	4.0	9.2
1979	24.4	4.3	n.a.	n.a.	4.8	14.1
1980	26.7	2.0	n.a.	n.a.	6.4	12.5

n.a. = not available

Source: US Department of Commerce, Schedule B export data.

an alternative relief plan for the steel industry. On 3 January 1978 the administration announced it would implement Solomon's relief plan, which involved setting "trigger prices" for imported steel and putting sales below that level on an antidumping investigation "fast track." On 18 January 1978 the president determined that, based on the evidence compiled in the investigation, there was "not sufficient justification to claim that the EC/Japanese understanding created any unfair burden on the United States," and on 30 January 1978 USTR announced that further action on the petition was being "discontinued."

Case 301-11

Complaint.   In November 1976 the Florida Citrus Commission and the California-Arizona Citrus League, Texas Citrus Mutual, and Texas Citrus Exchange filed petitions, subsequently consolidated, alleging that EC tariff preferences on citrus fruits and juices granted to certain Mediterranean countries reduced their exports to the European Community and were a violation of GATT Article I, providing for most-favored nation treatment. After getting tariff concessions only on grapefruit in the Tokyo Round, US negotiators initiated consultations with the Community under GATT auspices.

GATT role.   When consultations failed to resolve the dispute, the European Community agreed in November 1982 to establishment of a dispute settlement panel, but disagreement over composition and terms of reference delayed its first meeting for almost a year. The panel finally submitted its report in December 1984, agreeing with the US position that the EC preferences were legal under the "special and differential treatment" provisions for developing countries, but that the preferences on lemons and oranges "nullified and impaired" US benefits under the GATT. The panel recommended a lowering of EC tariffs on lemons and oranges as the best solution (Hudec 1993, 502–05).

Outcome.   After the European Community twice blocked adoption of the GATT panel report, the United States responded by withdrawing tariff concessions on pasta imports from the Community, worth about $36 million, effective 1 November 1985 (delayed from July 6; see case 301-25). The California-Arizona Citrus League had submitted an estimate to USTR that US citrus growers were losing about $48 million in exports of fresh oranges and lemons to the Community as a result of the preference scheme. The Community counterretaliated by raising tariffs on US exports of lemons and walnuts, one of only two cases in which binding counterretaliation was imposed (see also cases 301-54 and 301-80). The GAO notes that the effects of both retaliations were moderated by stockpiling, by the

United States of pasta and by the European Community of walnuts (GAO 1987, 38).

The citrus dispute was finally resolved in August 1986, with the two parties agreeing to rescind all duty increases. The United States received tariff preferences on citrus; the European Community also agreed to reduce tariffs on almonds and peanuts, while the United States reduced its tariffs on a number of food products of interest to EC exporters. The two parties also agreed to settle the pasta dispute within one year.

Assessment. Hudec (1990b, 121, note 10) regards the citrus and pasta cases as examples of "general legal breakdown" in which US retaliation may have been justified. Though the industry regarded the agreement as a "step backwards" because it legitimated the European preferences, the case is judged as at least a partial success. Even though the EC preferences remained, it resulted in an exchange of additional concessions along with the lifting of the retaliatory tariffs (table A.5). In addition, the industry believes the case was helpful to its interests by enhancing the credibility of US threats, which it believes provided impetus to the negotiations with Japan over access to its citrus market (GAO 1987, 37–38).

Case 301-12

Complaint. George F. Fisher, Inc. filed a petition on 14 February 1977, claiming that agreements negotiated by Japan with Brazil, China, Korea, and Italy had resulted in US exporters being unable to complete shipments under existing contracts and in a total halt to new orders for US-produced thrown silk yarns. In addition, imports from other sources had occasionally been licensed, but, so the petitioner claimed, no US shipments had been allowed since mid-1976. The petitioner imports raw silk, contracts with mills (primarily in Pennsylvania, which filed a brief in support of the petition) to process it into yarn, and then sells it to domestic weaving mills and exporters. Petitioner said its exporting customers reported that MITI had ordered Japanese foreign exchange banks not to open new letters of credit for thrown silk after 26 February 1976 and that, because of unspecified administrative procedures issued by MITI, payments made on already open accounts would not be honored. (The petitioner said it had tried unsuccessfully to obtain copies of the MITI regulations.) The means of enforcement for the restrictions was later changed to a "prior permission" licensing system.

In July and August 1977, USTR, which said it had been "holding discussions" on the problem with Japan since mid-1976 (before the petition was filed), solicited public comments and held public hearings on proposed action against Japan in the forms of either quotas or increased tariffs on imports of certain silk, and pig and hog leather items (the leather items evidently added on the basis of public comments received).

Table A.5 Selected US citrus and nut exports to the European Community, 1975–90 (millions of dollars)

| Year | US exports "nullified and impaired" | | Grapefruits | Additional products for which US received compensation | | |
	Oranges	Lemons		FCOJ	Peanuts	Almonds
1975	25.4	13.8				
1976	20.0	12.5				
1977	16.8	13.4				
1978	11.3	9.9				
1979	9.9	8.6				
1980	22.2	13.6	34.1	17.1		
1981	10.8	12.1	31.3	22.6		
1982	1.9	2.4	32.0	14.7		
1983	9.8	5.3	38.7	16.1	103.0	116.5
1984	0.5	1.1	20.9	14.6	126.5	148.6
1985	5.9	3.4	24.0	7.3	124.6	183.5
1986	3.9	1.3	38.5	8.6	133.4	195.1
1987	7.2	1.1	48.8	12.5	138.1	259.0
1988	1.9	0.9	64.2	19.2	98.7	327.8
1989	1.6	0.7	62.9	19.9	121.0	246.2
1990	2.8	0.5	46.4	23.6	122.2	314.0

FCOJ = frozen concentrated orange juice

Source: US Department of Commerce, Schedule B export data.

Table A.6   US silk yarn and thread exports to Japan, 1975–81

Year	Millions of dollars	Share of total Japanese imports
1975	3.0	2.4
1976	2.8	2.2
1977	1.0	1.4
1978	2.8	2.3
1979	6.8	5.5
1980	4.1	4.2
1981	5.1	6.0

GATT role.   The United States complained that the restrictions on thrown silk imports, which were intended to support the domestic silk industry by using a state trading monopoly to "stabilize" prices for raw silk imports, were discriminatory and thus violated Articles I, XI, XIII, and XV (governing exchange arrangements). It requested and the council authorized formation of a dispute settlement panel in July 1977 "in case further consultations failed. . . ." Membership was announced in November, and the panel delivered its ruling privately to the concerned parties. When the United States and Japan reported that they had reached a settlement of the dispute, the panel rewrote its report to merely describe the facts and the nature of the settlement (Hudec 1993, 469–70). The panel report allegedly found in favor of the United States, but its legal ruling has never been disclosed (private interview).

Outcome.   The *Federal Register* notice announcing termination of the case in March 1978, states merely that "Japan has agreed to make adjustments satisfactory to the United States." Hudec (1993, 470) cites US sources as saying "Japan opened a country-specific quota for the U.S. supplier."

Assessment.   Given the Japanese refusal to dismantle its restrictions on silk imports, USTR negotiators could do no more than try to restore US access. The data suggest, however, that negotiators not only restored previous market share levels but enlarged them. The US gain thus may have been at the expense of other suppliers, though US exports remained a small proportion of the total (table A.6). (One participant in the episode recalled South Korea threatening to retaliate if Japan reduced its share of the market.)

Cases 301-13, 36

Complaint.   The Tanners Council of America (TCA) filed a petition in August 1977 claiming that Japanese quotas and excessively high tariffs on leather were a violation of GATT. The quotas were imposed in 1949 for balance of payments reasons, but Japan gave up its GATT balance of payments exemption in 1963. The TCA estimated that the quotas limited total Japanese leather imports to $8.7 million in 1976, of which the United States exported $2.5 million. Yet the Japanese imported $290 million in hides and skins (of which the United States sold $118 million), leading to an estimate of domestic Japanese production of leather of $600 million (not counting production from domestic hides). The TCA claimed that, in addition to lost exports to the Japanese market, Japanese protection of its industry also injured the American tanning industry by raising the price of hides and by allowing Japanese tanners to undersell US tanners in third markets. In October 1982 the Footwear Industries of America filed a petition alleging that it also was denied access to the Japanese market for leather footwear as a result of quotas and administrative practices in Japan.

Japan maintained the quotas to protect its Dowa minority, which had been historically discriminated against and for whom the tanning and footwear industries were important sources of employment. Hudec (1993, 472–73) says maintenance of the quotas reflected a "desire to avoid a difficult social problem (rather than economic losses per se). . . ." Thus, the Japanese claimed that, while they had been gradually enlarging the quotas over time and would continue to do so, they could not eliminate them entirely.

GATT role. President Carter declined to challenge Japan's high tariffs on leather and footwear since they were legally bound under the GATT, but he directed the USTR to pursue bilateral negotiations and GATT dispute settlement on the quotas, which it claimed violated Articles XI, X (on transparency), and XIII (on nondiscrimination in administration). A Japanese position paper explaining the problems of the Dowa expressed regret that the United States had chosen to take the case to GATT and, pointing out that other developed countries had maintained "residual" import restrictions in sensitive sectors, argued that to pursue such cases through GATT, since they are likely to result in affirmative rulings for the plaintiff and recommendations to eliminate the restrictions in a timely manner, could result in "increasing cases of open disregard of such recommendations. If retaliatory measures are taken one after another, we fear that there would occur grave frictions in trade" (brief in USTR section 301 files).

On 26 February 1979, before the GATT panel could issue a ruling, the United States and Japan reported that they had reached a settlement. Adoption of the panel report so stating was delayed, however, while other suppliers examined the settlement; after six months of "technical discussions," during which Hudec (1993, 472–73) speculates the agreement may have been modified to reduce adverse impact on other suppliers, it was adopted on 6 November 1979. Shortly after, Canada and India filed separate GATT complaints, and each country reportedly came to agreements with Japan to increase its leather quota in each of the next three years.

Although US leather exports nearly doubled under the settlement, from $5.3 million in 1979 to $9.8 million in 1982, bilateral consultations resulted in no mutually acceptable resolution after it expired at the end of March 1982 and the United States refiled its GATT complaint in November. The GATT panel released its report in March 1984, ruling that social problems per se could not justify quotas, which were in violation of Article XI; the panel could not rule on a possible Article XIX (safeguards) defense since Japan had not invoked it. The panel also suggested that the GATT Council consider allowing extra time for compliance because of Japan's social problem; several delegations expressed "disappointment" with this recommendation when the report was adopted by the GATT Council in May (Hudec 1993, 508–09).

In March 1985 the United States filed a GATT complaint against the quotas on leather footwear and requested that the Council rule immediately since the same quota as applied to raw leather had already been ruled illegal. Several delegations opposed the request for an immediate ruling, and a panel was established in July. Before the panel could meet, a settlement was reached as a result of bilateral consultations (Hudec 1993, 526).

Outcome. The United States had scheduled hearings on appropriate retaliatory measures for 27 February 1979 but canceled them when Japan agreed to a three-year deal to expand some of the quotas on 23 February. However, when US exports of leather actually declined in the first year following the agreement, President Carter directed the USTR to renew consultations with Japan on implementing the agreement and to report to him within six months.

Bilateral negotiations failed to produce a new agreement when the three-year deal expired in March 1982, the Footwear Industries Association filed a 301 petition in October, and the United States refiled its GATT complaint in November. After the GATT ruling in 1984, Japan removed some quotas and proposed withdrawing its tariff bindings on leather and converting the quotas to (quite high) GATT-legal tariffs. The United States rejected the proposal, however, and, on 7 September 1985 President Reagan directed the USTR to recommend appropriate retaliatory measures unless these cases were resolved by 1 December. This was one of several moves under section 301 made as part of the president's Trade Policy Action Plan (see also cases 301-26, 301-49, 301-50, and 301-51). On 21 December 1985 USTR Clayton Yeutter announced that an agreement had been reached. Japan still refused to fully liberalize the leather and footwear quotas. But it agreed to provide $236 million in compensation through reduced tariffs on $2.3 billion in US exports to Japan, including paper, engines and auto parts, and telecommunications equipment, and acquiesced in US tariff increases on $24 million in imports of leather and leather goods from Japan, effective 31 March 1986.

On 1 April 1986 Japan expanded the quotas and eventually replaced the remaining quotas with tariff-rate quotas. Japan then raised the issue of the GATT legality of the US retaliation once the illegal quotas had been removed but did not pursue the matter. Hudec (1990) concludes GATT would have authorized retaliation in both the leather and footwear cases had it been asked to do so.

Assessment. While industry and USTR objectives of eliminating the quotas were not achieved, Japan did liberalize the restrictions on leather and footwear imports somewhat, and the US retaliatory tariffs on US imports of those products from Japan provided some minor relief. Leather manufacturers appear to have gained more from the process than footwear producers. Trade data show only a one-time increase in US leather foot-wear exports to Japan from an average of $26 million in 1985–86 to just over $40 million since. Leather exports, however, increased more steadily, from around $20 million in 1985–86 to $160 million in 1990, and the ratio of hides to leather in US exports to Japan declined from about 15 to 1 to 3 to 1 (Gold and Nanto 1991, 15 and 39).

Potentially more important from a national economic perspective was the liberalization of the Japanese market in other areas as compensation for maintaining the other quotas. It remains unclear, however, how mean-ingful the concessions were since many of the products listed as benefiting from lower tariffs have been the subject of subsequent market access negotiations (for example, paper, glass, and auto parts; note that the paper agreement arising from the January 1992 Bush trip to Tokyo emphasized private sector behavior, not government barriers, and that no mention of tariffs was made). Also, during a July 1986 Senate Finance Committee hearing, Senator Charles E. Grassley (R-IA) said that Japan had stalled in lowering tariffs on aluminum ingots as promised in the compensation agreement (US Senate, Finance Committee 1986, 10). These problems apparently necessitated a separate negotiation and agreement in October 1986, which more than doubled US exports, but mostly of unwrought and waste and scrap aluminum (Congressional Research Service 1991, 11–12). Despite continuing problems in these sectors, we nonetheless judge this case to be a partial success for US negotiators.

Case 301-14

Complaint. In November 1977 the American Institute of Marine Under-writers (AIMU) filed a petition alleging that the Soviet Union unreason-ably required that marine insurance on virtually all trade (both exports and imports) between the United States and Soviet Union be placed with the Soviet state insurance monopoly. AIMU estimated in its petition that this restriction cost American insurers up to $7.5 million in premiums in 1976 (assuming they insured all trade between the two countries). According to other data provided by the petitioners, AIMU insured about 12 percent of bilateral trade between the United States and the Soviet Union in 1975 and 1977 (1976 figures are distorted by a single, unusually large, sale of heavy equipment), which would generate an estimated $70,000 to $80,000 in premiums.

AIMU originally contacted administration departments, including the US Department of Commerce, regarding cargo insurance in trade with the Soviet Union after signing of the US-USSR grain agreement. Then Secretary of Commerce Frederick Dent wrote AIMU's president in March 1973 that the matter would be taken up in forthcoming US-USSR maritime talks scheduled for April. A 1977 Commerce Department letter to AIMU following a second round of US-USSR marine cargo insurance talks in February reported that the Soviets, while indicating a willingness to give more insurance to US underwriters, "resisted any formalization of a sharing principle. . ."; the letter indicated that the US negotiators' position was that US insurers should receive an equal share of marine cargo insurance.

GATT role.   Not applicable.

Outcome.   On 9 June 1978 President Carter determined that the Soviet practice was unreasonable and a burden and restriction on US commerce, and he directed USTR to establish an interagency committee to make recommendations on possible further actions and means of achieving the elimination of those practices. After further consultations, an agreement was signed on 5 April 1979 "whereby each party would have a substantial share of the marine cargo insurance" arising from US-Soviet bilateral trade. The parties also agreed to an annual review of the distribution of marine cargo insurance in bilateral trade between the two countries. The case was suspended effective 12 July 1979, pending the first year's review. On 24 July 1980 USTR announced that the review had been impossible because of the disruption in US-USSR relations after the Soviet invasion of Afghanistan; the suspension continued "until such time as a thorough review and assessment can be conducted."

Assessment.   Although an agreement was reached, it appears to have never been implemented as a result of the disruption of relations after the Afghanistan invasion. AIMU indicated in letters to USTR in August and September 1981 that its members had insured only 1.2 percent of bilateral trade with the USSR in 1979, and since March 1980 had insured cargoes valued at only $850,000. Commerce figures for 1980 show US-Soviet bilateral trade of $2 billion, despite the grain embargo and other sanctions. Two-thirds of the companies reporting to AIMU also reported no opportunities to offer quotes on shipments that they might have turned down. Also, the president of AIMU told GAO (1982, 28) that he did not expect the Soviet Union to honor the agreement because it specified no penalties for noncompliance and no dispute settlement mechanism.

Case 301-15

Complaint.   An August 1978 petition filed by several US television licensees on the Canadian border alleged that Canada discriminated against US broadcasters by denying tax deductions for Canadian tax purposes for advertisements placed with US broadcasters. The new tax policy was perceived as less "unfair" than the previous policy of "commercial deletion" (simply substituting Canadian commercials for American ones during US-origin programming), but petitioners claimed that the restriction still deprived them of "substantial" advertising revenues, and was unreasonable and discriminatory. (Bart Fisher, who served as legal counsel for the US broadcasters in their 301 petition, argues that the threat of a 301 filing had been "a primary motivating factor in securing removal of the . . . commercial deletion policy" [Fisher and Steinhardt 1982, 644]).

The petitioners argued that the Canadian practice was unreasonable because it allowed Canadian viewers to continue to enjoy US programming without paying anything for it (in the form of advertising costs). Moreover, they argued that the Canadian cable industry had become profitable by appropriating US signals, for which it did not have to pay. Thus the only form of compensation for the US broadcasters was through advertising fees. The petitioners also argued that the Canadian practice, because it was discriminatory, violated the spirit of the GATT, in particular the provisions for national treatment. The petitioners claimed that the Canadian regulation reduced their revenues from Canadian advertising from $19 million in 1975 to $9 million in 1977. The 1987 National Trade Estimate Report (p. 57) estimated that the Canadian policy cost US broadcasters $10 million to $20 million in revenues. (A similar restriction on advertising for the Canadian market in US magazines and newspapers was estimated to cost US publishers $100 million to $150 million in lost advertising revenues annually [p. 58].)

GATT role.   Not applicable.

Outcome.   On 31 July 1980 President Carter determined that the Canadian practice was unreasonable and a burden on US commerce, and since negotiations had produced no other solution he recommended legislation to mirror the Canadian practice. The legislation was finally enacted in the Trade and Tariff Act of 1984. In a 1982 written statement submitted to the Subcommittee on Trade of the House Ways and Means Committee, representatives of the petitioners estimated that the revenue lost to Canadian broadcasters as a result of the mirror legislation would be no more than $5 million and probably closer to $2 million (US House of Representatives, Committee on Ways and Means 1982, 242). The statement also noted that the "prospect of [mirror legislation] has been proven insufficient to move the Canadians" in the two years since it had originally been proposed by President Carter, and the petitioners called on Congress to authorize stronger action.

Assessment.   No change in the Canadian policy was achieved; in fact, the outcome was a further restriction of trade due to the US retaliation.

Case 301-16

Complaint.   On 2 November 1978 Great Plains Wheat, Inc. (GPW), a wheat marketing and promotion organization supported by state wheat commissions in nine states, filed a petition that EC export subsidies for wheat were unfair and discriminatory and had had the effect of "substantially" reducing US wheat exports in third markets. GPW estimated that the subsidies would displace 3.3 million metric tons of US exports at a cost of $495 million (including the price-depressing effects of the subsidies), with an additional $390 million lost as a result of lower prices for remaining US exports. The petitioner concluded that, while supportive of US efforts to negotiate a meaningful subsidies code in the Tokyo Round, "no immediate relief can be expected through the traditional GATT procedures," or from measures likely to be agreed to in the negotiations. Thus, the petitioner called for immediate retaliation under section 301.

GATT role.   The United States consulted with the European Community in July 1979 "to ensure that the EC undertook its subsidy practices in a manner consistent with Article XVI:3 during the 1979/80 marketing year." US and EC representatives met again, in June 1980, after the Tokyo Round agreements and codes went into effect.

Outcome.   During the second round of consultations, the two parties agreed they "would monitor developments in world wheat trade, exchange information, and meet to discuss future problems that may arise in world trade in wheat." The case was terminated 1 August 1980. At that time, USTR said that if new problems arose that could not be dealt with through bilateral consultations, "the petitioner would be free to submit a new petition." Just a week before termination, the chairman of US Wheat Associates had written USTR expressing concern about recently announced export authorizations that were 75 percent higher than the previous year, and about a recent sale to China for which the subsidy was $119.90 per ton, "the highest subsidy level recorded during 1979/80."

Assessment. The accord that was reached between the United States and the European Community was essentially an agreement to disagree and did nothing to resolve the problem of agricultural export subsidies.

Case 301-17, 19

Complaint. On 14 March 1979 the Cigar Association of America filed a petition alleging that practices of the Japan Tobacco and Salt Public Corporation (JTS) that raised prices to "exorbitant" levels, restricted distribution, and limited advertising of imported cigars were unreasonable and burdened or restricted US commerce. The petitioner estimated that elimination of the restrictive practices and a 55 percent reduction in the retail price of US cigars sold in Japan would increase US exports to around $5 million per year. On 22 October 1979 the Associated Tobacco Manufacturers filed a petition alleging similar practices caused losses of US exports of pipe tobacco of $1.3 million. Both associations also expressed concern over planned legislation in Japan that would establish ad valorem tariffs on these products of 60 percent and 110 percent, respectively, "where none had existed before." Japan countered that it was merely breaking out the tariff portion of the total payment previously made in a lump sum to JTS.

GATT role. The United States requested a GATT dispute settlement panel, claiming that the JTS practices violated Article III (national treatment) and Article XVII, which requires state trading enterprises to make purchases and sales "solely in accordance with commercial considerations. . ." (Hudec 1993, 481). As part of a preliminary agreement reached with the Japanese in December 1980, USTR agreed to ask the panel to delay further action until the spring, at which time, if the agreement had been implemented, it would request termination of the GATT review. Thus, the panel report merely reported the settlement and did not make a ruling (Hudec 1993, 481–82).

Outcome. The United States and Japan formally reported an agreement to GATT on 4 March 1981 and implementation on 4 May 1981. Under the accord, Japan agreed to lower the tariff on cigars from 60 to 35 percent ad valorem and on pipe tobacco from 110 to 60 percent ad valorem, to increase the number of retail outlets for foreign tobacco products from 14,000 to 20,000 (still less than 10 percent of the total number of 250,000) and to allow advertising in Japanese language media for the first time (USTR, Semiannual Report to Congress on Section 301, July–December 1980, 7–8). However, according to Ryan (1990, 327), the Japanese simultaneously raised the excise tax on all tobacco products so that the retail price of foreign tobacco products was higher than before the tariff reduction. Moreover, negotiations on the continued restrictions on distribution and

Table A.7 US exports of cigars and other manufactured tobacco to Japan, 1978–90

Year	Millions of dollars	Share of total US exports	Share of total Japanese imports
1978	0.5	3.2	12.9
1979	0.5	0.9	8.4
1980	0.4	1.2	9.4
1981	0.8	2.0	20.0
1982	0.6	0.9	13.6
1983	0.8	1.3	24.7
1984	0.6	0.9	18.9
1985	0.5	0.6	19.6
1986	0.6	0.3	20.9
1987	1.2	0.5	37.6
1988	1.0	0.4	25.0
1989	0.5	0.2	8.5
1990	1.1	0.4	6.8

advertising continued up to USTR's initiation of another investigation in September 1985 (see case 301-50).

Assessment.   Although an agreement was reached, the evidence from Ryan (1990) and the data in table A.7 suggest that the Japan tobacco monopoly continued to restrict the import of tobacco products until after the abolition of the monopoly in 1985 and the signing of a second bilateral agreement with the United States in 1986 (see case 301-50). The data in the table also suggest the possibility of some trade diversion following the 1981 agreement, but the numbers are so small as to be insignificant.

Case 301-18

Complaint.   The American Institute of Marine Underwriters filed a petition on 25 May 1979, alleging that the Argentine government "severely restricts and hinders competition in the marine market so that virtually all insurance on exports and imports must be placed with Argentine companies." The petitioner claimed the Argentine practices had cost it between $2.5 million and $6 million per year (depending on whether the assumed premium rate was 0.3 percent or 0.5 percent of the cargo value), for a cumulative loss in 1974–77 of $12 million to $20 million.

GATT role.   Not applicable.

Outcome.   On 25 July 1980 USTR indefinitely suspended the investigation because the government of Argentina had agreed to participate in multilateral negotiations, "one of the objectives of which would be to work toward an agreement to apply the principle of national treatment in the insurance sector." Argentina conditioned its participation on the willingness of a "significant" number of less developed countries to participate in such negotiations.

Assessment. This appears to have been another case in which the two parties agreed to disagree. According to a GAO report on foreign barriers to US insurance exports, USTR negotiators in this case did not feel they had much leverage to force Argentine concessions, nor did they harbor hopes for obtaining negotiated concessions given the absence of international rules governing services trade (GAO 1982, 30).

When the meeting launching the Uruguay Round was finally held in September 1986, "the foes of [including services on the agenda] were reduced to a core Group of 10 led by India and Brazil and also including Argentina, Cuba, Egypt, Nicaragua, Nigeria, Peru, Tanzania, and Yugoslavia. . . . To appease the Group of 10, the decision to include services was separated from the rest of the ministerial declaration and attributed to trade ministers and not to the contracting parties" (Aronson and Cowhey 1988, 42).

Argentina finally implemented allowing exporters and importers to choose any insurance carrier, including foreigners, in May 1994. The total market is estimated to be worth $300 million (*Journal of Commerce*, 19 May 1994).

Case 301-19

See case 301-17.

Cases 301-20, 51

Complaint. In November 1979 American Home Assurance Co. (AHA)—a subsidiary of AIG and the only foreign insurance firm licensed to write any form of local insurance in Korea—filed a petition alleging that Korea had not fulfilled an April 1977 agreement to reduce the discriminatory treatment of AHA. AHA claimed the discriminatory treatment violated the national treatment provisions of the US-Korea Treaty of Friendship, Commerce, and Navigation.

After bilateral consultations with Korea, USTR in November 1980 solicited comments on, *inter alia*, proposals for retaliation. Among the retaliatory options considered by the interagency committee were denying entry into US ports to ships owned by companies related to Korean insurance firms; imposing a substantial port entry fee on such vessels; barring Korean construction companies related to Korean insurance firms from bidding on US government contracts; and increasing duties on imports of products manufactured by affiliates of Korean insurance firms. Apparently the committee was leaning toward the latter option when Korea promised to allow more open competition in its insurance market. The petition was then withdrawn, and USTR terminated the investigation in late December 1980 (GAO 1982, 30–31).

In an exchange of letters in January 1981, Korea promised to grant AHA a full license to write marine insurance by 1 June 1981; to allow AHA to sell fire insurance to individuals and businesses not covered by the compulsory fire pool and to phase out the "noncompulsory" fire insurance pool, which would give AHA increased access to the market; and to revise the retrocession sharing system in the reinsurance market.

GATT role.   Not applicable.

Outcome.   In September 1985 USTR initiated an investigation (301-51) into continuing Korean restrictions on and alleged discrimination against foreign insurance providers. In this case, USTR cited Korea's refusal to allow foreign firms to underwrite life insurance. American Life Insurance Co. (ALICO), another affiliate of AIG, complained that Korea had refused it a license to underwrite life insurance. In addition, AHA charged that Korea had not effectively implemented the 1980–81 agreement, for example, by ignoring practices of Korean banks that prevented de facto access to the fire insurance market, despite the de jure phasing out of the noncompulsory pool (see also GAO 1987, 30–31).

According to an October 1985 memo to the file, USTR officials informed representatives of Korea's non-life insurance and life insurance associations that US industry wanted de facto national treatment for non-life insurance by 1986 and for life insurance by 1987–88 at the latest. A USTR official also stressed the political aspect: "Korea simply had to allow flexibility, at pain of losing significant portions of the U.S. merchandise export market." The investigation was terminated 14 August 1986, after Korea agreed to license qualified US firms to underwrite both life and non-life insurance. Korea also agreed that its insurance authorities would review all applications in a "timely manner." The agreement was amended and clarified on two subsequent occasions, in September 1987 and January 1988.

Assessment.   The first case is judged to be a failure since two of the three issues negotiated—access to the compulsory fire pool and the reinsurance market—recurred in the 1985 case. The second case appears to be a partial success: Though foreign firms still hold a small share of the market, more firms have been licensed and have been allowed to expand their businesses in Korea. It appears, however, that Korea discriminated against non-US foreign firms, at least initially.

Case 301-21

Complaint. On 6 December 1979 Universal Optical Co. filed a petition alleging that Swiss customs practices intended to determine the gold content of eyeglass frames shipped as samples destroyed their appearance and thus "effectively preclude[d its] ability to obtain orders from Swiss customers." Petitioner noted that similar samples could be imported into the United States without damage and reexported without payment of duty. They asked USTR to pursue the complaint with the Swiss government in order to "secure reciprocal treatment" for samples sent to that country for the purpose of taking orders.

GATT role. No GATT violations were alleged by the petitioner.

Outcome. During the investigation, USTR found that the Swiss standard for marking of gold content (much more precise than that of the US) was "consistent with that of many countries" (USTR, Semiannual Report to Congress, July–December 1980, 9). The United States amended its law setting marking and content requirements for gold items to bring those requirements "more into conformity with international practice." The petitioner withdrew its petition and USTR terminated the case on 11 December 1980.

Assessment. 301 "leverage," to the extent there was any, was directed at petitioner's own government, not the Swiss government. There do not appear to have been negotiations with the Swiss government, thus no "negotiating objectives" to achieve.

Case 301-22

Complaint. On 20 August 1981 the Great Western Sugar Company filed a petition alleging that EC subsidies on exports of sugar violated the GATT Subsidies Code and were an unreasonable burden on US commerce. The petitioner estimated that depressed prices caused by the subsidies would cost US sugar producers $2.2 billion in lost revenues (based on an assumed price effect of 15.66 cents per pound; the New York landed price of Caribbean sugar actually dropped from 35.67 cents per pound in the first quarter of 1981 to 12.31 cents per pound in the fourth quarter). The petitioner estimated that the price effects for corn and other sweeteners would result in losses for those industries of between $0.8 billion and $1.6 billion depending on the price assumption.

GATT role. In 1978 Australia and Brazil had separately filed GATT complaints claiming that the EC subsidies violated the Subsidy Code. Hudec suggests that the EC's refusal to join the International Sugar Agreement "may have been the true objective of the complaints. . . ." A dispute settlement panel ruled in October 1979 that the European Community subsidy had a depressing effect on prices, which constituted "serious prejudice," and that the ineffectiveness of measures to control domestic production constituted "threat of prejudice." But the panel could not agree whether the subsidies violated the "equitable share" standard. The Community accepted the overall finding of no violation, but not specific findings with respect to price effects and prejudice. In 1981 the EC replaced government funding of export subsidies with producer contributions, which it claimed were not subsidies subject to Article XVI (Hudec 1993, 473–76).

At the urging of petitioner, the United States filed a GATT complaint in April 1982 claiming that the new EC export rebate system still violated GATT provisions governing subsidies on several counts. A day after the United States filed its complaint, another complaint was filed by major sugar exporters (Argentina, Australia, Brazil, Colombia, Cuba, Dominican Republic, India, Nicaragua, Peru, and the Philippines). Consultations were held among the various parties, but no dispute settlement panels were requested and no rulings made (Hudec 1993, 499–500).

Outcome. The 1981 farm bill restored price supports for sugar and urged the administration to meet the price targets without federal expenditures. On 22 December 1981 President Reagan raised the duty on sugar from its statutory minimum to the maximum and imposed additional fees under section 22 of the Agricultural Adjustment Act of 1933. In May 1982, as a result of collapsing world sugar prices, the president imposed quotas on imports of sugar, which had to be progressively tightened over the next several years in order to meet the target prices in the farm bill in the face of weak world prices. In a March 1983 speech, Secretary of Agriculture Richard E. Lyng blamed the imposition of the quotas on EC export subsidies, saying the United States "was forced" to impose the quotas in response to the Community's "'very irresponsible' actions" (*U.S. Export Weekly,* 22 March 1983, 976).

In June 1982 the president determined that the EC practices were inconsistent with the GATT and a burden on US commerce; he ordered the USTR to continue bilateral consultations with the Community and to support multilateral efforts in the GATT and the International Sugar Agreement (ISA). On 29 July 1987 the petitioner filed a request to reactivate the case. USTR refused, saying export subsidies were being addressed in the Uruguay Round.

Assessment. The 301 case appears to have had no impact on EC export subsidies but resulted in a highly favorable outcome for petitioners, with US imports of sugar dropping sharply. To the extent that the 301 case contributed to the decision to impose highly restrictive import quotas, the impact on US welfare and the international trading system would have to be judged as negative.

Case 301-23

Complaint. On 17 September 1981 the National Broiler Council and 11 other representatives of the US poultry industry filed a petition claiming that EC export subsidies violated the GATT Subsidies Code, displaced US sales in third-country markets and were unreasonable and unjustifiable. The petitioners alleged that EC subsidies had displaced US exports and allowed EC exporters to capture more than "an equitable share" of the Middle Eastern market in particular. According to testimony by the National Broiler Council, US market share had dropped from 90 percent in the 1960s to less than 1 percent in the 1980s (US Senate Committee on Agriculture 1987, 238–39). The petitioners also expressed concern that "expansion of the geographic scope . . . and product coverage" of the subsidies posed a threat to US exports in other markets as well (USTR, Semiannual Report to Congress, July–December 1985, 14). A concerned member of the EC Parliament had earlier written the Commission to inquire whether there was a possibility that recent sales to traditional US markets in East Asia might spark "another chicken war" (document on file at the Commission's Washington office).

The petitioners alleged that EC subsidies to the poultry industry had increased from $3.5 million in 1967 to over $100 million in 1980, with a subsidy for whole chicken exports in January 1980 of $300 per metric ton. They argued that these subsidies had contributed to a decline in the US share of the non-EC whole chicken market from 40 percent before initiation of the subsidies to around 10 percent in 1974–76, though they admitted market share had recovered to 25 to 30 percent in the late 1970s.

GATT role. In February 1982 the United States filed a complaint with the GATT claiming that the EC subsidies violated the Subsidies Code (by resulting in a more than "equitable share") and nullified and impaired US benefits. In consultations, the European Community claimed that its subsidized prices were being driven down by Brazilian subsidized prices. In September 1983 the United States filed a similar GATT complaint charging Brazil with violating the Subsidies Code. It then requested that conciliation procedures under the code be initiated on both complaints simultaneously (Hudec 1993, 495 and 513–14).

Outcome. In July 1982 the president determined that the EC practices were inconsistent with the GATT and its codes and directed USTR to complete its examination of the effects of Brazil's subsidies, to seek a resolution "in the most effective manner, including, as appropriate, the pursuit of dispute settlement procedures," and to report to him on the

Table A.8 US, EC, and Brazilian shares of world poultry exports, 1970–89 (percentages except where noted)

Year	Millions of dollars	US share	EC share	Brazilian share
1970	260.4	15.0	82.7	negl.
1971	280.8	13.1	84.0	negl.
1972	337.3	12.5	85.2	negl.
1973	501.5	12.7	84.6	negl.
1974	518.1	14.0	81.7	negl.
1975	593.9	15.2	79.9	0.6
1976	742.2	23.3	69.1	2.6
1977	895.7	20.0	69.4	3.5
1978	992.9	20.8	66.2	4.7
1979	1,255.9	20.8	64.6	6.5
1980	1,786.5	21.7	56.0	11.7
1981	2,133.4	21.9	50.4	16.7
1982	1,681.8	17.2	53.8	16.8
1983	1,476.0	17.5	56.5	16.5
1984	1,459.7	17.3	53.1	18.2
1985	1,418.1	15.8	54.0	17.4
1986	1,804.9	16.2	57.2	12.8
1987	2,181.3	17.6	56.1	10.4
1988	2,227.0	19.5	62.4	9.6
1989	2,230.9	22.2	69.5	n.a.

negl. = negligible or zero
n.a. = not available

status of the case in September 1982. The president noted that the case would not be resolved within the time frame "contemplated" under section 301 but that "it is essential that the United States, before further pursuing its international rights in this matter, has developed and thoroughly examined all information relevant to the nature and extent of subsidized poultry exports on the world market." The trilateral consultations conducted under auspices of the Subsidies Code were suspended in December 1984, reportedly after the three parties "agreed on a program of mutual restraint with regard to export subsidies" (Hudec 1993, 495). According to USTR's July–December 1985 semiannual report to Congress on section 301 (p. 15), Brazil had "changed its subsidy programs, substantially reducing subsidies on poultry exports" since the conciliation process began. There was no mention of reductions in EC subsidies. In fact, the data in table A.8 suggest that the European Community, not the United States, gained from the reduction in Brazil's market share.

Moreover, according to testimony by the National Broiler Council in 1987, "Almost six years after the case was originally filed, it is no closer to reaching a resolution. U.S. exports to the Middle East remain at relatively low levels, although the Export Enhancement Program has helped to regain a small share of this market" (US Senate, Committee on Agriculture,

Nutrition, and Forestry 1987, 238–39). The Broiler Council claimed that US negotiators were reluctant to retaliate in the early and mid-1980s because of Brazil's large foreign debt and that "knowing this, Brazil refuses to rule out the subsidization of its poultry exports . . . [and], with this knowledge, the EC will continue to have an excuse to maintain its export subsidies as long as it claims it is merely competing against Brazil. U.S. exporters will continue to be caught in the middle of an export subsidy war."

Assessment.   The United States claimed it was not interested in a market-sharing arrangement to resolve the dispute (*U.S. Export Weekly*, 28 June 1983, 469), but some of the Europeans suspected that was exactly what US negotiators were seeking: a free hand in Southeast Asia while the EC and Brazil split the Middle Eastern market (*U.S. Export Weekly*, 22 May 1984, 977). Based on the statements of the National Broiler Council, it appears that US negotiators were seeking to stem the losses while the petitioners wanted some rollback of those losses in the Middle East. If that is the case, the outcome might be considered a negotiating "success" but a failure from the petitioners' perspective, since trade data suggest that the declining US market share was stopped but not reversed (table A.8).

Case 301-24

Complaint.   In response to a 1979 section 301 petition from the Tanners Council of America alleging injury as a result of an Argentine ban on exports of cattle hides, the United States and Argentina negotiated an agreement under which Argentina agreed to convert its ban to an export tax of 20 percent, which would then be phased out over two years. In return, the United States agreed to grant concessions on imports of Argentine corned beef and cheese and to eliminate the 5 percent ad valorem tariff on cattle hide leather.

On 9 October 1981 the Tanners Council of America (TCA) filed a second petition alleging breach of the trade agreement. The TCA claimed Argentina had failed to completely phase out the export tax and, in addition, had imposed a minimum export price on hides that raised the effective tax. The TCA also claimed that Argentina's practices injured the US leather industry in its domestic market and placed it at a disadvantage in third markets because of higher raw material prices. Petitioner estimated the damage to the US industry as being in the "hundreds of millions of dollars" over the previous decade.

GATT role.   The alleged violations involved a bilateral trade agreement, and no GATT issues were raised by the petitioner.

Outcome.   On 20 October 1981 President Reagan proclaimed a suspension of the tariff on bovine leather imports and raised the applicable duty to 1 percent ad valorem. After bilateral consultations failed to produce a mutually acceptable agreement, the president, in October 1982, announced termination of the agreement and restored the US duty on bovine leather imports to its preagreement level of 5 percent ad valorem. No determination was made under section 301; the agreement was terminated using authority in section 125 of the Trade Act of 1974.

Assessment. Although an agreement was reached to end the hide embargo, Argentina in the end did not fully implement it. Retaliation may have provided some relief to US leather producers, but it did not achieve the objective of ending the hide embargo. In 1990 the US industry filed a countervailing duty case claiming that the hide embargo constituted an illegal subsidy, and for the first time the Department of Commerce ruled that an export restriction could constitute an actionable subsidy (see also cases 301-40/42 and 301-53). Duties have been imposed on a case-by-case basis since October 1990.

Case 301-25

Complaint. In October 1981 the National Pasta Association (NPA) filed a petition charging that EC export subsidies on pasta violated the Subsidies Code and resulted in increased exports to the US market. Data provided by the petitioner showed that Italian pasta exports to the United States increased more than 2.5 times between 1975 and 1980. Still, the Italy-America Chamber of Commerce, Pasta Products Committee, submitted a statement opposing the pasta petition and claiming that the NPA had not filed a subsidy complaint under the countervailing duty law because it could not have proved injury.

GATT role. The EC refused to consult bilaterally, and the United States requested formation of a dispute panel under the Subsidies Code to review the complaint. In 1983 the panel ruled 3 to 1 that the subsidies were in violation of the GATT code. The panel delivered its report to the Subsidies Code Committee in May 1984, but the committee was split on the legal issue and deferred action on the report (Hudec 1993, 493–95).

Outcome. In the summer of 1985, President Reagan issued a determination in case 301-11, regarding EC tariff preferences on certain citrus products. He found that the EC practice in that case was unreasonable and discriminatory, and he ordered retaliation in the form of higher tariffs on EC pasta exports (to 40 percent ad valorem on pasta not containing egg and 25 percent ad valorem on pasta containing egg). The European Community counterretaliated (see case description above). As part of the agreement resolving the citrus dispute, signed in August 1986, the two parties agreed to rescind all duty increases and to settle the pasta dispute within a year.

In June 1987, 20 US senators, led by John Heinz (R-PA), sent a letter to USTR Yeutter urging him to negotiate the elimination of pasta export subsidies and stating further that failure to achieve a satisfactory agree-ment would "cast doubt on the Administration's ability to administer Section 301 . . . and will increase congressional resolve to amend" it (*International Trade Reporter*, 1 July 1987, 844). The United States and European Community finally signed an agreement on 15 September 1987, under which the Community promised to eliminate subsidies on half its pasta exports and reduce subsidies on the other half by 27.5 percent.

Assessment.   Given the reductions in export subsidies, this case is judged as at least a partial success for US negotiators.

Cases 301-26, 71

Complaint.   In October 1981 the California Cling Peach Advisory Board, along with several other organizations, filed a 301 petition alleging that EC processing subsidies for canned peaches, canned pears, and raisins violated GATT Article XVI. The subsidy program for canned peaches (and for tomato concentrate, canned tomatoes, and juice) had been estab-lished in May 1978, just after the European Community had abolished a minimum import price system found illegal by the GATT (see case 301-4). Canned pears were added in 1979–80, and raisins in 1981. Petitioners claimed that the subsidies threatened US exports not only to the European Community, but to third countries as well.

GATT role.   US negotiators requested appointment of a dispute settle-ment panel in March 1982. The panel's report, issued in July 1984, found that the subsidies to canned peach and pear producers nullified or impaired benefits expected by the United States as a result of earlier EC tariff concessions. But the panel did not find nullification or impairment with respect to raisins (see Hudec 1993, 496–98). The European Commu-nity blocked the GATT Council from adopting the finding.

Outcome.   In September 1985, as part of his initiative to counter domestic protectionist pressures by demonstrating his resolve to attack unfair national trade estimates, the president directed USTR to recommend retal-iation in this case unless an agreement was reached in December. An agreement was reached to lower EC subsidies in December 1985. In August 1988 the United States informed the European Community that recently announced subsidy levels were not consistent with the 1985 agreement, and in May 1989 USTR initiated an investigation into EC compliance with the 1985 agreement. Hearings on a list of items for

Table A.9 US prepared fruit exports to the European Community, 1973–90 (millions of dollars)

Year	Canned fruit[a]	Raisins
1973	28.4	9.6
1974	21.3	16.3
1975	21.0	12.1
1976	15.9	14.1
1977	18.5	15.9
1978	27.9	13.0
1979	15.1	24.7
1980	27.4	41.3
1981	19.6	24.1
1982	11.8	18.3
1983	7.1	16.5
1984	3.5	23.4
1985	1.5	25.4
1986	2.1	42.8
1987	3.0	56.6
1988	5.7	64.1
1989	7.4	61.2
1990	9.1	73.6

a. Includes fruit cocktail and canned pears, peaches, cherries, and pineapples.

Source: US Department of Commerce, Schedule B export data.

possible retaliation were held in early June. In late June the European Community agreed to lower subsidies, and the two sides clarified their interpretation of the agreement.

Assessment. Case 301-26 must be considered a failure since the European Community did not fully comply with its provisions and US canned fruit exports continued to decline (table A.9). The second case, 301-71, is considered a partial success since it appears to have resolved the issue, more or less.

Cases 301-27/31, 301-33

Complaint. On 12 January 1982 the Tool and Stainless Steel Industry Committee et al. filed petitions claiming that domestic subsidies to the specialty steel industries in Austria, France, Italy, Sweden, and the United Kingdom violated the GATT Subsidies Code and that imports from those countries injured the US industry. In July they added a complaint against Belgium.

GATT role. Consultations were held under the Subsidies Code, but no dispute settlement panel was established.

Outcome. On 16 November 1982 the president directed USTR to request that the US International Trade Commission (ITC) initiate an "escape clause" investigation under section 201 of the Trade Act of 1974. In May 1983 the ITC found injury from imports; in July, President Reagan granted relief through a combination of tariff and quotas. The European Community demanded compensation and, when no agreement could be reached on the appropriate level of compensation, retaliated against US exports of chemicals, plastics, and selected other products worth $160 million annually (Hufbauer, Berliner, and Elliott 1986, 196).

Assessment. The petitioner reportedly regarded the section 301 process as helpful in building the political support that led to Reagan's decision to provide import relief (GAO 1987, 34). If 301 helped the petitioner get protection that would not be justified on its own merits, that would be considered a negative outcome.

Case 301-32

Complaint. The AFL-CIO et al. filed a petition on 3 June 1982, alleging that Canadian export credit financing for subway cars destined for the United States violated the Subsidies Code and burdened US commerce. The Budd Co. was the only US bidder on the project for the New York Metropolitan Transportation Authority (MTA); it petitioned the Treasury Department for a matching credit subsidy from the Export-Import Bank, filed a motion with the US district court in New York seeking an injunction to prevent completion of the contract until the Treasury Department had made its decision, and also filed a countervailing duty petition with the Commerce Department (*U.S. Export Weekly*, 29 June 1982, 462).

On July 13 Treasury Secretary Donald Regan announced that the Treasury would not authorize the Eximbank to match the Canadian financing offer. Although the department conceded that the financing offer clearly exceeded OECD limits on permissible export credits for sales to developed countries, Regan said it had concluded that the financing was not determinative in New York's decision to award the contract to the Canadian bidder (Bombardier). Commerce announced on 15 July that it was initiating a countervailing duty investigation, while USTR announced four days later that, despite the Commerce action, it would also initiate an investigation on the basis of Budd's 301 petition (*U.S. Export Weekly*, 20 July 1982, 552).

GATT role. Consultations were held under the Subsidies Code. In requesting the consultations, USTR William Brock said the administration was concerned that the case, if unchallenged, might set a precedent for subsidization of other bids by other governments. An unnamed trade official said, "We want to make our position on this issue very clear, as well as our willingness to take action if need be. This situation merely brings into focus the general subsidized export financing problem with which we are confronted" (*U.S. Export Weekly*, 29 June 1982, 462).

Outcome. Although an investigation was initiated in July, it was terminated in September because the same allegations were the subject of a countervailing duty investigation filed by the Budd Co. On 9 February 1983 the Commerce Department determined that the Canadian railcar exports were subsidized by up to $110, 565 per railcar (*International Trade Reporter*, 8 February 1983, 732–33). Before the ITC could render its final injury determination, however, Budd withdrew its petition, saying its point had been made and that it did not want New York to have to pay countervailing duties; the three unions that had joined Budd in its complaint concurred with the request. Budd reportedly withdrew its petition in return for a promise from the MTA not to buy foreign-made cars during the next three years; representatives of the unions involved in the case (the United Auto Workers and the United Steel Workers of America, as well as the AFL-CIO) "expressed satisfaction with the outcome, and particularly with MTA's 'Buy American' promise." MTA Chairman Richard Ravitch welcomed Budd's decision and said he looked forward to "working together with Budd for the production of the MTA commuter rail cars . . . and to doing business with Budd in the future." (*U.S. Export Weekly*, 22 February 1983, 801)

Case 301-34

Complaint. On 13 September 1982 J. I. Case Co. filed a petition alleging that a Canadian practice of granting duty and sales tax remissions on front-end wheel loaders and parts thereof imported by companies that also produced in Canada was inconsistent with GATT and the Subsidies Code, and was unreasonable and a burden on US commerce. The petitioner claimed that the subsidy amounted to over $20,000 per machine and adversely affected its competitive position in Canada, as well as other export markets. Counsel for Caterpillar Tractor Co. and Clark Equipment Co., two of the three companies that Case cited as benefiting from the duty remissions (International Harvester being the third), filed a brief with USTR asking that the petition be rejected. They argued that the Canadian remission scheme was not an illegal subsidy, did not violate any GATT provision, and was not a burden on US commerce.

GATT role. The United States consulted with Canada but did not pursue formal dispute settlement procedures.

Outcome. As late as the end of 1985, the case was still being reviewed by the interagency 301 committee according to USTR's semiannual report to Congress (July–December 1985, 10).

Assessment. USTR does not appear to have put much emphasis on the case, perhaps concluding that the petitioner did not have a strong case or that it did not want to pursue a case on which the domestic industry was split. Canada's duty remission schemes were addressed in the context of the free trade agreement, and the number of remission orders reportedly has declined (USTR National Trade Estimates Report, 34; interview).

Case 301-35, 37, 38

(for case 301–36, see entry for 301-13)

Complaint. On 25 October 1982 the Footwear Industries of America, Inc., along with the AFL-CIO-affiliated Amalgamated Clothing and Textile Workers and the United Food & Commercial Workers International, filed a petition alleging that restrictive import practices employed by a number of countries resulted in lost US exports and diversion of exports to the US market. The petition was supported by letters from the US House of Representatives (signed by 110 members from both parties) and the US Senate (signed by 43 senators from both parties) urging USTR to accept the petition and pursue it vigorously.

USTR rejected the petitioners' complaints with regard to the European Community, France, Italy, the United Kingdom, and Spain, and where petitioner complaints involved bound tariff levels. USTR also declined to investigate the charge that the alleged practices resulted in diversion to the US market. Eventually, USTR initiated investigations into the practices of Brazil, Korea, Taiwan, and Japan that deny market access to US exporters; the Japanese investigation was combined with a previously opened investigation into Japan's leather quotas (see case 301-13). The petitioners tried again in August 1983 to get USTR to investigate the diversion issue, but the appeal was rejected.

In January 1984 the footwear association filed a section 201 escape clause petition, but the ITC found that, despite increasing imports, industry profits were high and concluded there was no injury. In the Trade and Tariff Act, passed in October 1984, Congress modified section 201 to say that "the presence or absence of any factor which the Commission is required to evaluate" should not be "dispositive." The Senate Finance Committee requested in November that the ITC reopen the footwear case. Since the first investigation had been completed, imports had increased further and profits had begun to decline. In July 1985 the ITC found injury and recommended relief in the form of auctioned quotas; the president rejected import relief.

GATT role. The United States consulted with each of the countries on various occasions in 1983 and reportedly threatened to take Korea to GATT (Ryan 1990, 311), but no dispute settlement panel was appointed (except in the Japanese case, see case 301-13 above). With respect to the case against Brazil, USTR concluded that a GATT case had little chance of being successful—because Brazil had a valid balance of payments defense, because other practices complained of were not discriminatory, and because evidence of nullification and impairment was lacking.

Outcome. On 19 December 1983 the president determined that no unfair practices existed with respect to Taiwan, but he directed USTR to pursue offers from the Taiwan Footwear Manufacturers Association to assist US footwear producers in marketing and promoting their product in Taiwan and to pursue with the government indications that proposals for further tariff reductions on certain types of footwear would be "received sympathetically" (temporary tariff reductions on some types of footwear had been extended through mid-1984, and legislation was pending to make them permanent).

In November 1984 Brazil agreed to lift a 100 percent surcharge, to lift a ban on the issuance of import licenses, and to reduce tariffs on a number of footwear categories, at least temporarily. The Brazilian government provided confirmation in June 1985 that these measures were being fully implemented. South Korea had made nonrubber footwear imports eligible for automatically approved licenses in July 1983, and in 1984 it instituted a phased reduction in tariffs on certain categories of footwear from 40 percent to 20 percent.

Assessment. The centrality of the diversion argument in the complaint, as well as the subsequent filing of a section 201 petition, indicate that the industry was concerned primarily with imports in the US market. USTR shifted the focus of the investigation from the import to the export side and apparently was able to negotiate liberalizing agreements with Brazil and Korea, though they were unlikely to benefit the US industry. Section 301 is written broadly enough that trade practices that increase the level of exports to the US market could be actionable under its provisions. This case, as well as the various steel petitions (case numbers 10, 27-31, 33, and 39), suggest a reluctance on the part of USTR to use section 301 against imports. Only in the EC pasta case did USTR use section 301 to attack imports resulting from an unfair trade practice, though USTR has used section 301 to ensure US producers' access to imported inputs (Argentine hides, 301-24; Canadian fish, 301-55; and EC copper and zinc scrap, 301-70). Some observers claim this hesitation undermines the effectiveness of section 301 as a trade remedy.

Case 301-39

Complaint. On 16 March 1983 the Committee of Domestic Steel Wire Rope and Specialty Cable Manufacturers filed a petition claiming that

Korean subsidies to its domestic steel wire rope industry violated the Subsidies Code. USTR rejected additional allegations regarding export subsidies, trademark infringement, and trade diversion as a result of restraints on exports to Japan. The petitioner had filed a dumping complaint with the ITC and Commerce Department the previous fall and, in November, the ITC made a preliminary finding of injury "by reason of imports of steel wire rope from Korea which are allegedly sold at less than fair value." However, the Department of Commerce, in September 1983, issued a final ruling of no sales at less than fair value.

GATT role. The United States requested consultations under the Subsidies Code.

Outcome. On 29 November 1983 the petitioner withdrew the petition but in a letter to USTR expressed satisfaction that USTR was undertaking "full scale investigations" into several of the issues it had raised. However, General Counsel Jeanne Archibald responded that, while USTR was seeking information on possible Korean subsidies, it was not a formal investigation. The case was terminated 15 December 1983. The association filed another dumping case against Korea in spring 1992.

Assessment. It appears that USTR concluded that the petitioner did not have a valid complaint (perhaps because of the Commerce ruling in September) and pressured the complainant to withdraw its petition.

Cases 301-40, 41, 42

Complaint. On 16 April 1983 the National Soybean Processors Association (NSPA) filed a petition alleging that certain practices by the governments of Argentina, Brazil, Canada, Malaysia, Portugal, and Spain burdened and restricted US commerce. USTR decided not to pursue the allegations against Canada because its government indicated that the crushing subsidy provided by the province of Alberta for rapeseed would be terminated at the end of June or to pursue those against Argentina and Malaysia because some practices were not sufficiently supported in the petition and others (the imposition of differential export taxes) were not considered export subsidies. (The USTR's position on differential export taxes apparently derived from the Commerce Department's refusal to consider export restrictions as actionable subsidies; see 301-24 and 301-53.) USTR decided to investigate allegations that Brazil and Spain grant subsidies on the production and export of soybean oil and meal that are inconsistent with GATT Article XVI and that Portugal and Spain maintain "unjustifiable" quantitative restraints on the import of soybean meal and oil, respectively.

Given the relatively small roles played by Spain and especially Portugal in world soybean oil and meal markets, some sources suggested that the US complaint might be motivated by the fact that "both Spain and Portugal are negotiating to join the EC, which would put their soybean trade in another category altogether" (*International Trade Reporter,* 13 December 1983, 445). In Brazil's case, a 1990 US Department of Agriculture report on oilseed policies in various countries concluded that, while Brazil's differential tax system was "responsible for Brazil's becoming the largest exporter of soybean meal in the world," overall Brazil's policies toward the oilseed sector had negatively affected Brazil's competitiveness and lowered the overall level of exports (of soybeans and products) (Bickerton and Glauber 1990, 61–62).

GATT role.   The United States held consultations under the regular GATT provisions and under the Subsidies Code but did not request appointment of a dispute settlement panel.

Outcome.   During consultations in Geneva in November and December 1983, all three countries defended their practices as being consistent with the GATT. On 13 February 1984 President Reagan determined that continuation of the GATT dispute settlement procedures was the most appropriate action. US industry representatives expressed fears that Brazil's suspension the previous fall of most subsidies would be revoked if the pressure was removed. But representatives of US firms operating in Brazil claimed in July that "all the subsidies have disappeared . . . [because] the government can no longer afford [them] . . . they're not really needed . . . [and] there's been pressure from Europe and the U.S." (*International Trade Reporter,* 4 July 1984, 21).

In a 16 August 1984 memorandum to USTR, the NSPA expressed concern about the absence of progress in the complaints against Spain and Portugal, noting that neither had responded fully to USTR requests for information. In a July 1986 statement to the Senate Finance Committee, John G. Reed testified on behalf of the NSPA that there had been "significant progress" in some areas, but that he was "hard-pressed to attribute these gains in any major degree to the section 301 investigations" (US Senate, Finance Committee 1986, 82–83). Reed said that Portugal had phased out its state trading monopoly and that Spain had ended one substantial export subsidy, but he attributed both moves to the countries' accession to the European Community.

Assessment.   There was no resolution in the cases against Portugal and Spain. Portugal imposed quotas on soybean and soybean oil imports as part of its accession agreement, but those quotas have been maintained at nonbinding levels as a result of the agreement negotiated to resolve the EC enlargement case (301-54). The Spanish case also appears to have been superseded in 1986 by the enlargement dispute; however, while the enlargement agreement provided for continued access to the Spanish market for corn and sorghum, it does not appear to have resolved the oilseed problem. In 1990 the National Oilseed Processors Association (NOPA) urged that Spain's policies with regard to soybean oil be cited as a priority practice under super 301; the USTR report on national trade estimates for that year estimated that Spain's policies (a tax on domestic consumption and subsequent subsidized export of surpluses) cost US producers up to $100 million in lost sales to Spain and third markets.

Brazil apparently did reduce subsidies to the oilseed sector, and trade data show its world market share declining from an average of 36 percent in the early 1980s to 31 percent in the period 1986–88. The 1987 USTR Foreign Trade Report (p. 37), however, noted that bilateral consultations in December 1985 about differential export taxes "did not achieve a satisfactory result." NOPA also recommended to USTR in spring 1989 that Brazil's differential export taxes on oilseeds and products be designated as a priority practice under super 301. Nevertheless, this case is considered a partial success since the differential was reduced.

Case 301-43

Complaint. On 13 July 1983 the Rice Millers Association (RMA) filed a petition alleging that Taiwan's rice export subsidies had depressed world prices, caused a decline in US rice exports, and increased the burden on the US rice program. The RMA withdrew its petition in August to allow time for a negotiated solution, but when none could be reached, the RMA refiled its petition on 29 September 1983. The petitioner estimated that the damage to the US rice industry as a result of subsidized exports of Taiwanese rice would be $300 million annually; including the impact on downstream industries and the US taxpayer, the RMA estimated the total injury as $400 million and forwarded a list of items for possible retaliation of that amount.

GATT role. Not applicable because Taiwan is not a GATT member.

Outcome. Although no explicit retaliatory threat was ever made, Taiwan apparently feared that it might lose its GSP eligibility if it did not address US concerns on this issue (GAO 1987, 37). On 1 March 1984 Taiwan agreed that it would not release rice from Provincial Food Bureau stocks in excess of 1.375 million metric tons (MMT) during 1984–88 and that annual sales would decline from 0.375 MMT in 1984 to 0.2 MMT in 1988. Moreover, Taiwan pledged that the rice would be offered for sale only to countries with an annual per capita income below $795 (as reported by the World Bank). The petitioner agreed to withdraw its petition on 9 March, and USTR terminated the case on 22 March. The petitioner's letter withdraw-

Table A.10 US and Taiwanese exports of rice to the world, 1980–88 (millions of dollars)

Year	US	Taiwan
1980	1,289	60
1981	1,527	27
1982	997	63
1983	926	94
1984	845	42
1985	665	6
1986	625	20
1987	576	33
1988	805	23

Sources: Taiwan data from *Taiwan Statistical Data Book*, 1989; US data from *Statistical Abstract of the United States.*

ing its petition congratulated USTR for its "excellent work in achieving a negotiated resolution of this dispute." Trade data show Taiwan's exports of rice dropping from an annual average of $60 million in 1980–83 to only $20 million a year in 1985–88 (table A.10).

Assessment. US negotiating and petitioner objectives appear to have been largely achieved in this case, at least temporarily. The 1989 National Trade Estimate Report (p. 165) noted that Taiwan's exports in 1988 were 0.1 million metric tons, about half the agreed level. Still, in both 1989 and 1990, the Rice Millers Association submitted public comments to USTR requesting that Taiwan (along with Japan, South Korea, Nigeria, and the European Community) be cited under super 301 for its trade practices regarding rice, including dumping subsidized rice on world markets, as well as prohibiting imports. No mention of this issue is made in USTR reports after 1989.

Case 301-44

Complaint. In September 1983 the Air Courier Conference of America (stimulated by DHL) filed a petition complaining that Argentina discriminated against foreign air courier services by mandating that international delivery of time-sensitive documents be handled by the Argentine postal service. The petitioner further alleged that other restrictions placed on international couriers had the effect of artificially increasing the price of those services and improving the competitive position of Argentine couriers, the Argentine postal service, and the US postal service. The petitioner also claimed that Argentina's policies were the first attempt by a "commercially advanced nation" to restrict international courier services and might set a dangerous precedent. The petitioner said that prior to adoption of the resolution, American couriers had earned about $5 million in revenues from transportation of packages originating in Argentina and bound for other destinations.

GATT role.   Not applicable since the issue involved trade in services.

Outcome.   In October 1984 USTR held hearings on proposed recommendations for retaliation. On 16 November 1984 the president determined that Argentina's policies were unreasonable and a restriction on US commerce; he directed USTR to hold another round of consultations as requested by Argentina and, if no resolution was achieved, to submit a proposal for appropriate action under section 301 within 30 days. Before the deadline, Argentina terminated its ban on certain US services but replaced it with heavy discriminatory taxes. In late 1988 Argentina reduced the taxes and improved transparency of its regulations.

In February 1989 congressional testimony, USTR Hills said that an interagency analysis had suggested that "unless we get a correction of this type of abusive conduct [harassment of DHL at airports in Argentina] . . . that we consider eliminating Express Mail by our Postal Service to Argentina. . . . And in this particular instance, we have reached out for a non-trade-related retaliation so that we are not violating our GATT undertakings. . . ." (US House of Representatives, Committee on Ways and Means 1989, 76).

Negotiations continued, and an agreement was finally reached on 25 May 1989. Each party pledged to treat the other's air couriers in a nondiscriminatory manner and to provide national treatment for all foreign air courier service providers. The agreement also stressed the importance of transparency in regulation of air courier services. Finally, the United States recognized the right of the Argentine postal monopoly to impose a nominal fee on international courier items in Argentina, but the two agreed that the fee should be "related" to domestic and internal postal charges and should not be greater than international charges for equivalent courier services.

Assessment.   Although the agreement says that the Argentine fees should not be greater than international charges for similar services elsewhere, the 1993 National Trade Estimate Report noted that Argentina's postal monopoly charges a fee on outbound shipments "well in excess" of any other country, with only six others charging any fee at all. The report notes that Argentina eliminated a fee on inbound shipments in 1991 but that progress stalled in 1992. The 1994 National Trade Estimate Report notes that Argentina has been liberalizing services, and this particular is not mentioned; thus, this case is interpreted as at least a partial success for US negotiators.

Case 301-45

Complaint. On 19 December 1983 the Motion Picture Export Association of America (MPEAA) filed a petition alleging that a reduction in the number of distribution licenses granted by Taiwan made it uneconomical to operate there, and that this action was "unjustifiable and unreasonable" and burdened US commerce. The petitioner claimed that the action would effectively block its members from a market that had been worth between $8 million and $9 million in annual revenues from film rentals in 1980–82.

Taiwan argued that its reduction in the import quota granted to MPEAA, from 85 films to 50, was reasonable because the proportion of "reinspected" films (films that had been previously imported and screened) had increased; this was cited as proof that MPEAA's production had decreased and that it was able to fill its quota only by importing old films. Taiwan also argued that total exports of US films had not been affected because the 35 films taken away from MPEAA members had been reallocated for the importation of other American films.

GATT role. Not applicable since Taiwan is not a GATT member.

Outcome. The petition was withdrawn on 17 April 1984 and the case terminated after Taiwan agreed to create a special quota category of 15 films that would be admitted after the base quota had been filled and as long as none of them were reissues. Effective 1 July 1986 Taiwan eliminated the quota, including limits on reissued films. The number of copies of a film that could be imported and the number of theaters in which they could be shown remained limited (USTR 1987, 304).

Assessment. It is not clear that the petitioner gained much from the phasing out of the quota since the Taiwanese government allegedly tolerated "video parlors" that showed pirated movie videos, which reduced business at regular movie theaters. This was an issue in the 1992 designation of Taiwan under the special 301 provisions included in the Trade Act of 1988. Nevertheless, US negotiators and the petitioner appear to have partially achieved their objectives, an assessment supported by at least one participant in the case.

Case 301-46

Complaint. On 25 May 1984 Transpace Carriers, Inc. filed a petition alleging that the member states of the European Space Agency (ESA) subsidized the commercial satellite launch services of the French firm Arianespace. The alleged subsidies included a two-tier pricing system, with higher prices charged for member-state launches than for export launches, provision of administrative and other support by the French space agency at below cost, and subsidized insurance rates for missions.

GATT role. Not applicable.

Outcome. Because of heavy government involvement in the evolution of the launch services industry everywhere, the president determined that the practices of the member states of the ESA were not unreasonable or a burden or restriction on US commerce. The investigation revealed that some allegations could not be supported by evidence on the record and that others involved practices that "were not sufficiently different from U.S. practice in this field to be considered unreasonable under Section 301." However, the president noted that "because of my decision to commercialize expendable launch services in the United States, and our policies with respect to manned launch services [the shuttle], it may become appropriate for the United States to approach other interested nations to reach an international understanding on guidelines for commercial satellite launch services at some point in the future."

Case 301-47

Complaint. On 17 August 1984 the Fertilizer Institute filed a petition alleging that the EC standard for water solubility of triple superphosphate had no agronomic justification, was discriminatory, had the effect of creating an unnecessary obstacle to international trade, and thus was inconsistent with the GATT Agreement on Technical Barriers to Trade (the standards code). The petitioner claimed that the standard favored North African suppliers, especially Morocco, had caused a decline in US exports, and suppressed US export prices (by forcing US exporters to offer discounts).

GATT role. The two parties consulted at least once under the GATT standards code.

Outcome. No resolution was ever reported.

Assessment. Nothing was achieved in this case because USTR apparently did not pursue it; the reason is not clear.

Case 301-48

Complaint. In 1985 the US semiconductor industry and US government accused the Japanese industry of engaging in unfair trading practices: selling semiconductors at "less than fair value" in the United States and in third markets (i.e., dumping semiconductors) and restricting foreign access in the Japanese home market. In June 1985 the Semiconductor Industry Association (SIA) filed a 301 petition complaining about the lack of market access in Japan. Shortly thereafter, Micron Technology filed a petition with the Department of Commerce alleging that Japanese producers were dumping 64K DRAM (dynamic random-access memory) chips; in September Intel, Advanced Micro Devices, and National Semiconductor followed with a petition alleging dumping of EPROM (erasable, programmable, read-only memory) chips; and, finally, in an unprecedented action, the Department of Commerce initiated a dumping investigation on DRAMs of 256K and above.

In August 1986 the US and Japanese governments reached an agreement intended to resolve the section 301 and dumping investigations. In exchange for suspension of the dumping cases on EPROMs and DRAMs 256K and above, the Japanese firms agreed to provide information on their costs; the Department of Commerce then calculated "fair market values" (FMV) for each Japanese firm's sales. Sales into the US market below the FMV price would be presumed to be dumped and would be subject to duties. The agreement also provided for monitoring of Japanese sales to third countries to ensure that dumping in those markets did not make the United States a "high-price island" and thereby encourage US semiconductor users to move production offshore. In exchange for suspension of the section 301 action, the Japanese indicated in a secret side letter that foreign market share in Japan should reach 20 percent by the end of the five-year agreement (up from about 10 percent) (Tyson 1992, 106–110).

GATT role. US negotiators did not choose to take this case before a GATT panel. Japan filed a GATT complaint charging that the US retaliation violated Articles I and II (see below) but did not request that a panel be established to consider the claim (Hudec 1993, 546–47).

In order to enforce the dumping provisions of the agreement, MITI provided "administrative guidance" to firms producing in Japan regarding the level of output and exports, thus removing the incentive to compete on price. The agreement thus appears to have facilitated the formation of a MITI-led cartel among Japanese producers (Tyson 1992, 113–118). As Kenneth Flamm (1991, 23) has noted:

> The irony of the 1986 agreement was that, after a decade of complaints by American producers over the role of MITI in issuing 'administrative guidance' to Japanese industry, U.S. trade policy helped create a regime that considerably reinforced MITI's power and influence over the Japanese semiconductor industry and encouraged Japanese producers to limit competition with each other.

The European Community lodged a complaint charging that Japanese monitoring of exports and administrative guidance constituted an illegal restriction of exports, thus raising prices in third markets that had not complained of dumping. The European Community also claimed that the market-access portion of the agreement favored US exporters, thus violating the Article I most-favored nation (MFN) obligation. The panel did find that Japanese practices discouraging exports were an illegal restriction of trade but did not find evidence that the agreement had resulted in discrimination in favor of US suppliers. Japan changed its monitoring system for semiconductor exports to bring its policy in line with the recommendations of the panel (Hudec 1993, 541–42).

Outcome.   In April 1987 President Reagan determined that Japan was not abiding by the agreement and imposed retaliatory tariffs on $300 million worth of Japanese exports. Of this total, $164 million was in retaliation for the lack of progress toward the 20 percent foreign market share, and $136 million was for continued dumping in third-country markets. The dumping sanctions were eliminated in June and November 1987, but the market access retaliation remained in place. There followed a running three and a half year "press release war," in which the two governments, industry spokesmen in both countries, and the US Congress issued statements on the alleged lack of progress in achieving the 20 percent market share target. The US industry and members of Congress repeatedly urged that Japan be named under super 301 in 1989 and 1990 for failure to comply with the market access agreement, but USTR declined.

In June 1991 the United States and Japan extended the semiconductor agreement for five years (with a review in 1994). The agreement states that "the government of Japan recognizes that the US semiconductor industry expects that the foreign market share will grow to more than 20 percent by the end of 1992 and considers that this can be realized." The US government agreed to lift its retaliation on $164 million of Japanese goods. The 20 market share was reached briefly in the fourth quarter of 1992, surging from a 15.5 percent share in the first three quarters of the year, then dipped below that level again until spiking back up at the end of 1993, when the United States again threatened retaliation (*Journal of Commerce*, 13 March 1993, 1A; *Financial Times*, 23 March 1994, 4).

Assessment.   Although the foreign market share for semiconductors in Japan increased by about 50 percent in the latter half of the 1980s (from around 10 percent to 14 or 15 percent), this case is judged to be a failure since the increase was not deemed sufficient enough by either the petitioner or USTR to lift the sanctions until a new agreement was negotiated in 1991.

Though the GATT panel did not find that the market-access agreement violated MFN obligations, it is a difficult issue to evaluate because non-US foreign suppliers were such a small part of the Japanese market when the case began. According to the World Semiconductor Trade Statistics data base, the total foreign market share in Japan in 1986 was 8.6 percent, of which only 0.6 percent was held by non-US suppliers (table A.11). By 1991, the US share of the Japanese market had increased almost 50 percent to 12.6 percent while the non-US foreign share had more than doubled to 1.45 percent (worth more than $300 million). Also, Tyson (1992, 111 and 123) claims that the increased prices for DRAMs resulting from the dumping provisions of the agreement stimulated investment in Korea, Taiwan, and elsewhere, thus contributing to a more competitive global market (see also Bergsten and Noland 1993, 127–40).

Data from the SIA (measured on a slightly different basis than the data in table A.11) show the US market share increasing by another 33 percent after the signing of the second agreement, reaching 16.7 percent in the first half of 1994. Over that period, other foreign sales more than doubled to 4 percent in 1993–94. The value of the non-US foreign market share reached $1 billion in 1993 (data provided by USTR).

Case 301-49

Complaint. On 16 September 1985 USTR initiated an investigation into Brazil's informatics policies, including restrictions on imports and foreign investment, and lack of copyright protection for computer software. This case and cases 301-50 (Japanese tobacco) and 301-51 (Korean insurance) were initiated on the same day as part of the president's "trade policy action plan," announced 23 September as part of an effort to defuse protectionist pressures in Congress. This was the first time USTR used its authority to initiate a case.

GATT role. Although this case involved market-access issues, investment and intellectual property issues were also prominent. Deputy General Counsel Judith Hippler Bello explained USTR's policy on such "mixed" cases to a congressional committee in 1986, noting that USTR sometimes did not take these cases before GATT "because the cases involved significant issues outside the GATT that we did not want to handle separately from the GATT issues" (US House of Representatives, Committee on Agriculture 1986, 16).

Outcome. In October 1986 President Reagan determined that Brazil's policies were unreasonable and a burden on US commerce. He directed USTR to continue negotiations and, if no resolution was achieved by the end of December, to notify the GATT of USTR's intentions to suspend tariff concessions on imports from Brazil as compensation for Brazil's restrictions on the informatics industry. On 30 December the president suspended the import restriction part of the case in response to a Brazilian commitment to make its administrative policies more transparent, not to extend them to new areas, and to allow the "market reserve policy" to

Table A.11 Sales of semiconductor devices in Japan, 1986–87 and 1990–91

Year	Value of Japanese market (millions of dollars)	Sales of US firms		Sales of European firms		Sales of rest of world[a]	
		Millions of dollars	Percent of total	Millions of dollars	Percent of total	Millions of dollars	Percent of total
1986	11,852	950	8.02	65	0.55	8	0.07
1987	14,667	1,238	8.44	56	0.38	19	0.13
1990	20,257	2,388	11.79	152	0.75	118	0.58
1991	22,496	2,833	12.59	167	0.74	159	0.71

a. Mostly Asian companies, other than Japanese.

Source: Dataquest, Inc.

expire as scheduled in 1992. On 30 June 1987 the president suspended the intellectual property portion of the investigation in response to passage by Brazil's lower house of legislation providing copyright protection for software. In testimony just after the president's announcement, the Computer and Business Equipment Manufacturers Association (CBEMA) and the American Electronics Association (AEA) expressed varying degrees of support for the decision. CBEMA lauded the announcement because, while "it acknowledges that progress has been made, it also acknowledges that much remains to be done" (US House of Representatives, Committee on Energy and Commerce 1987, 62). The AEA said the president's decision was "appropriate at this stage" but expressed concern as to the credibility of Brazil's commitment to end the market reserve policy in 1992 (US House of Representatives, Committee on Energy and Commerce, 1987, 74).

In the fall of 1987, the Brazilian government rejected a licensing agreement between a US software company and six Brazilian informatics companies for an operating system. In November President Reagan announced his intention of retaliating against $105 million in Brazilian exports, equivalent to the estimated loss in US exports of software, and banning the importation of Brazilian informatics products covered under Brazil's market reserve policy. The president noted that Brazil did not at that time export the latter type of products to the US, but that "this action will prevent the Brazilian informatics industry from entering the U.S. market as long as it imposes a market reserve on computer software" (*Department of State Bulletin*, January 1988, 60–61). (Deputy USTR Michael B. Smith had testified in the July hearings before Congress that US firms in the computer sector as a whole had probably lost sales of as much as $350 million to $450 million annually as a result of Brazil's restrictions.) The administration argued that the Brazilian decision established a precedent that "effectively bans U.S. companies from the Brazilian software market." That would leave only the market for mainframe and "similar" computers open to foreigners.

In December 1987 Brazil passed a law that would, *inter alia*, increase access to the Brazilian software market, and in February 1988 the president decided to postpone retaliation while reviewing implementation of the law. In June 1988 the USTR announced that it did not intend to pursue retaliation at that time. In September 1989 Brazil lifted restrictions on remittances from sales of foreign software and indicated its willingness to "work constructively" with the United States on investment issues. The investigation was terminated on 6 October 1989.

Brazil's lower house passed legislation in July 1991 expanding the opportunities for foreign investment but leaving substantial administrative discretion in the hands of the National Informatics Council to approve investments and tax breaks on those investments. The legislation also included a provision authorizing the suspension of all imports from any country that takes actions contrary to international convention, a provision apparently aimed at US trade sanctions (*International Trade Reporter*, 31 July 1991, 1151).

In July 1992 the Ministry of the Economy in Brazil announced that tariffs on computer parts would be sharply reduced or eliminated, while tariffs on fully assembled computers and equipment would also be reduced but by much less. For example, while the tariffs on chips and microprocessors, previously in the 30 to 50 percent range, were eliminated, the tariff on assembled computers was reduced in the initial phase to only 45 percent, from 50 percent, falling to 35 percent a year in July 1993. Some foreign industry executives interpreted the move as signaling continued support for the domestic Brazilian industry even after the end of market reserve (*International Trade Reporter*, 5 August 1992, 1343). The market reserve policy was allowed to expire at the end of 1992 as promised, but during 1993 a tax on remittances of fees or royalties for software was reimposed (USTR National Trade Estimate Report 1994, 24).

Assessment. Though problems remain, the market reserve policy expired as promised in 1992, and the case resulted in some increased transparency in the regulation of the computer sector, some liberalization of Brazil's investment policy, and improved copyright protection for software. While not a complete success, this case would appear to have resulted in at least partial achievement of US goals.

Case 301-50

Complaint. On 16 September 1985 USTR initiated an investigation of Japanese practices discouraging US cigarette exports, including high tariffs, a ban on foreign investment in tobacco manufacturing in Japan, and restrictions on distribution (see also cases 301-17 and 301-19). The USTR announcement also noted that other barriers, including the government monopoly on the importation and sale of tobacco products, had recently been modified and liberalized but found that the other barriers remained. An economic analysis prepared for Philip Morris and attached to the brief filed by the US Cigarette Export Association (USCEA) estimated that the application of a high ad valorem excise tax to imported cigarettes after the 18.8 percent import duties had been applied raised the "actual incidence of cigarette protection" to 41.2 percent and that the effective rate of protection, since the tobacco monopoly was able to import tobacco duty-free, was over 100 percent.

Japan Tobacco Inc. (JTI), the successor to the Japan Tobacco and Salt Public Corporation, in a reply brief claimed that the tobacco market in Japan had been "thoroughly liberalized" and that the allegations in the USCEA brief "relate[d] to past practices that, to the extent they existed in fact, have already been eliminated through the Japanese government's reform measures." JTI claimed that, though its stock was held by the

Table A.12   US exports of cigarettes to Japan, 1978–90

Year	Millions of dollars	Share of total US exports	Share of total Japanese imports
1978	39.2	5.2	93.1
1979	40.1	4.4	82.2
1980	44.9	4.2	82.3
1981	73.9	6.0	100.0
1982	67.3	5.4	94.8
1983	80.4	7.1	90.1
1984	95.4	8.5	92.1
1985	95.4	8.1	89.1
1986	128.0	9.8	69.6
1987	494.0	24.1	96.5
1988	609.0	22.9	81.1
1989	877.7	25.9	93.0
1990	1,313.8	27.6	100.0

government, it was not a monopoly (up to one-third of its stock was to be sold to the public), that pricing and distribution had been liberalized, the tariff reduced, and that a program to put JTI on essentially the same basis as importers in the payment of excise taxes would be phased in over the next three years. USCEA retorted that despite de jure liberalization, the Japanese tobacco market remained de facto closed. Ryan (1990) claims that by May 1985, "all GATT-violating trade practices had been eliminated and the only outstanding issues were the tariffs and US investment."

GATT role.   The United States alleged that the Japanese practices violated the national treatment provisions of the US-Japan Treaty of Friendship, Commerce, and Navigation. It did not take the case to GATT, perhaps because the major issue, as Ryan argues, was a GATT-legal tariff. There may also have been a concern that Japan would use an Article XX defense, which allows exceptions to GATT obligations for protecting health and safety (as was later, unsuccessfully, attempted by Thailand; see case 301-72).

Outcome.   In October 1986, just before the deadline for concluding the investigation, USTR Clayton Yeutter announced that an agreement had been reached under which Japan agreed to reduce its tariff on cigarettes to zero, accelerate the phase-out of the discriminatory deferral for JTI in excise tax payment, make the price approval process more transparent and automatic, and address discriminatory distribution practices. The investigation was suspended, to be terminated when Japan fully implemented the agreement.

Assessment.   Although significant liberalization occurred and US exports exploded—from less than $100 million before 1986 to more than $1 billion in 1990 (table A.12)—some administrative barriers apparently remain. The 1989 National Trade Estimate Report (p. 97) notes that "Although Japan has implemented its commitments [under the agreement] inefficiencies in Japan's local tobacco tax reporting and collection systems continue to inhibit the distribution of" US cigarettes. The report says further that Japan Tobacco, Inc. involvement in retail licensing and the placement of vending machines has also affected US sales.

Case 301-51

See the entry for case 301-20.

Case 301-52

Complaint. On 4 November 1985 USTR initiated an investigation into Korean intellectual property policies, which denied patent protection for pharmaceutical and agricultural chemical products, and copyright protection for software and audio recordings, and permitted Korean firms to register trademarks similar to or even identical to foreign trademarks "not well known" in Korea. In addition, USTR alleged a lack of effective enforcement of laws on the books to protect copyrights for literary works. The International Intellectual Property Alliance (IIPA) estimated losses from insufficient copyright protection for records and tapes, motion pictures, books, and software in Korea at $146 million, nearly half of it on books. The National Agricultural Chemicals Association estimated its losses in Korea from piracy at $6 million to $12 million, with potential significant growth in those losses over time.

GATT role. Not applicable.

Outcome. On 21 July 1986 the two countries reached an agreement under which Korea agreed to enact by 1 July 1987 comprehensive copyright laws, including protection for computer software; to accede to various international conventions governing intellectual property by October 1987; to amend its patent law to protect pharmaceutical and agricultural chemical products; and to remove performance requirements for trademarked goods. USTR terminated the investigation in August 1986. However, in October 1987 and April 1988, Bristol Myers and Squibb Corporation filed and withdrew a number of complaints regarding Korea's enforcement of its patent protection laws. In June 1988 USTR established an interagency task force to study Korean intellectual property policies and practices, and warned Korea that it would reopen the 301 investigation if progress was not made.

In March 1989 Jack Valenti, testifying for the IIPA, told a congressional committee that Korea had "failed to enforce meaningfully its new copyright law;" Joseph Bainton of the International Anti-Counterfeiting Coalition added that, while US pressure had "spurred" Korea to strengthen its copyright and patent laws, "Unfortunately, the . . . laws have had little domestic support and, thus, it appears implementation and enforcement may be difficult (US House of Representatives, Committee on Energy and Commerce 1989, 78 and 92). In spring 1989, Korea was placed on the priority watch list under the special 301 provisions of the 1988 Trade Act.

Korea responded by cracking down on patent and copyright violations and in November 1989 was moved to a secondary watch list. In early 1992, however, the IIPA urged USTR to return Korea to the priority list because of backsliding, in particular on software protection. The IIPA claimed that its members' losses due to piracy had increased from $100 million in 1990 to $183 million in 1991, with most of that loss coming from illegal copying of software ($123 million, up from $25 million in 1990). Korea remained on the priority watch list through the spring of 1994.

Assessment. Ryan (1990, 395) concludes that the United States "did not achieve its objectives with regard to bureaucratic implementation of the policy reforms" it thought had been agreed to in 1986. Ryan, USTR, and the industry all agree that Korean enforcement improved and piracy was substantially reduced after Korea was placed on the priority watch list in spring 1989 (Ryan 1990, 392–93; USTR National Trade Estimate Report 1991, 144–45). Based on Korea's return to the priority watch list in 1992, however, those gains appear to have been temporary.

Another problem with the agreement in this case is that it discriminated in favor of US exporters. Although, US negotiators did not ask for it, only prospective protection is available to all countries; Korea insisted that retroactive patent protection be addressed through "administrative guidance" by the bureaucracy, rather than in the legislation. Thus, American pharmaceutical and other chemical products patented between 1980 and 1 July 1987, but never sold in either the US or Korean markets, could be produced and marketed in Korea only with the permission of the US patent holder (Ryan 1990, 389–91). After four years of negotiation, including threats from the European Community to revoke Korea's preferential trading rights in the Community, a similar agreement was signed between the European Community and Korea in September 1991 (*Journal of Commerce*, 30 January 1992, 3A).

Case 301-53

Complaint. The National Soybean Processors Association (NSPA) filed a petition in December 1985 alleging that differential taxes imposed on soybeans, and soybean oil and meal, constituted an export subsidy in violation of GATT provisions. NSPA withdrew the petition at the request of USTR, which informed NSPA that these issues were being negotiated with Argentina by the World Bank, which was seeking replacement of the export taxes with a less distortionary land tax as a condition for a restructuring loan. Argentina would agree only to reduce the level of the taxes, however. On 4 April 1986 NSPA refiled its petition and the USTR opened an investigation (US Senate, Finance Committee 1986, 87–88).

In February 1986 the export taxes on oilseeds and oilseed products were 28.5 percent and 16.5 percent, respectively (US International Trade Commission 1987, 5–14). NSPA claimed that the tax differential distorted Argentina's export mix, encouraging exports of processed soybean products, and thus depressing world prices for soybean oil and meal and reducing US exports of those products. An economic analysis prepared for the petitioner estimated that the losses to the industry included $161 million in exports and $76 million in lost profits. While a USDA study found that Argentina's differential export taxes did tend to skew its exports toward processed products, it concluded that the producer subsidy equivalent (PSE) of Argentina's policies toward the sector as a whole was negative, to the tune of 15 percent of total product value (Bickerton and Glauber 1990, 63).

GATT role.   None.

Outcome.   Argentina reportedly reduced the taxes on soybeans, and oil and meal, respectively, to 15 percent and 3 percent in 1987 (USITC 1987, 5–14). Then, on 14 May 1987, the president suspended the investigation following a decision by Argentina to eliminate the taxes on exports of both soybeans and products within 180 days. Instead, in February 1988, Argentina reduced the differential by 3 percent, but then, in July, established a tax rebate on oil and meal exports. Consultations were revived in August 1988, and in December Argentina suspended the tax rebate scheme. According to one source, Argentina eventually reduced the export tax on products to zero but left the tax on oilseeds at 6 percent, thus retaining a differential, albeit reduced. But, as noted in the 1990 USDA study (p. 65), "the key issue raised by the NSPA remains unresolved." The report went on to say that "Argentina's financial difficulties and small tax base discourage any government initiative to eliminate export taxes." In 1990 submissions to USTR for purposes of choosing super 301 priority practices, the National Oilseeds Producers Association listed Argentina's differential export taxes on oilseeds and products.

Assessment.   US negotiating objectives appear to have been partially achieved, since the export taxes and the differential were reduced though not eliminated.

Case 301-54

The following is based on Odell and Matzinger-Tchakerian (1988), as well as USTR public files.

Complaint. When Spain and Portugal acceded to the European Community in March 1986, trade barriers against third country agricultural imports rose to EC levels under the Common Agricultural Policy (CAP). The accession agreement provided that Spanish tariffs on feedgrains would rise from 20 to 100 percent. In addition, as a transitional measure, 15 percent of Portugal's grain import market would be reserved for EC members, and quotas would be placed on soybean and soybean oil imports. The United States objected that the quantitative restraints were illegal under the GATT and that it would suffer export losses of up to $1 billion annually. The United States demanded that the quotas be rescinded and asked the European Community to delay implementation of the accession agreement until compensation for US losses in both markets could be negotiated. The European Community rejected the proposed delay but offered to negotiate under GATT Article XXIV. The United States refused on the grounds that GATT negotiations would take too long.

GATT role. None.

Outcome. On 31 March 1986 the United States threatened retaliation by 1 May (for the Portuguese quotas) and 1 July (for the application of the variable levy to Spanish agricultural imports) unless the new trade restrictions were rescinded. The value of trade affected by retaliation was set at $1 billion, with the heaviest losses to be imposed on France (white wine, brandy, and cheese); other products, originating in Germany, Italy, the United Kingdom, and the Netherlands, were targeted. The retaliatory targets were listed in advance and carefully selected to injure EC groups that were politically well-organized. On 9 April the European Community threatened counterretaliation and targeted politically effective US groups such as producers of corn gluten feed, wheat, and rice. Shortly thereafter, the United States offered to engage in "mininegotiations," limited to US agricultural losses under Article XXIV:6. The European Community rejected the offer, insisting on "global" negotiations to include the overall impact on both US agricultural and industrial exports.

To avoid precipitating a full-blown trade war while discussions were under way, President Reagan imposed nonbinding quotas in retaliation for the Portuguese quotas on US soybeans and soybean oil. EC Commissioner Willy De Clercq and USTR Clayton Yeutter then agreed to a temporary truce on 2 July 1986 with respect to the impact of Spanish accession on US exports. The Community agreed to increase its feedgrain imports for six months, and the United States agreed to suspend its retaliatory tariffs until 31 December. With the deadline looming, USTR threatened to impose prohibitive duties on $400 million worth of EC agricultural exports, with the duties to be levied after 30 January 1987 unless an agreement was reached. The case was settled on 29 January. The European Community made agricultural and industrial concessions valued at $400 million per year for four years, with the agreement to be reviewed in mid-1990. During the interim, both the Portuguese quotas and US retaliatory quotas were adjusted as necessary to avoid restrictive effect.

When the Uruguay Round was not completed as scheduled at the end of 1990 and the Community balked at continuing the compensation, USTR initiated a new section 301 investigation (301-81) on 19 November 1990 and announced it would notify GATT by 1 December of its intention to withdraw concessions on 31 December if no agreement extending compensation was reached with the Community. Simultaneous with this announcement, USTR also released the list of items on which it proposed to raise tariffs if necessary. On 5 December USTR announced that it had notified GATT on 30 November of its intention to retaliate against $400 million of EC exports of cheese, liquor, and other products. On 28 December USTR announced that an agreement had been reached with the European Community to continue compensation and that it was terminating its investigation. On 8 July 1991 USTR announced that it was terminating the nonbinding quotas in response to a 7 March letter from the EC Commission stating that the Portuguese quotas (nonbinding) on oilseeds and vegetable articles had been lifted.

Assessment. This case is viewed as a partial success, since the United States received compensation, for the first time ever, in a dispute over EC enlargement. However, many US feedgrain exporters felt the compensation fell far short of their losses. Odell (1993) reports that a number of EC participants acknowledged that US retaliatory threats were decisive in forcing an agreement. He presents considerable evidence to support his hypothesis that the credibility of the US threat was due in large part to a coalition of US feed grain exporters that strongly supported the threat.

Case 301-55

Complaint. On 1 April 1986 a group of 10 fish processors with operations in Washington state or southeastern Alaska filed a complaint alleging that a Canadian prohibition on the export of unprocessed herring and salmon unfairly disadvantaged US processors by denying them access to raw materials. The petitioners estimated that the net injury, in terms of value added, as a result of forgone US exports of salmon and herring averaged $9 million per year in 1981–85.

GATT role. The United States requested establishment of a dispute settlement panel in February 1987 to review its claim that the Canadian export restrictions were inconsistent with GATT Article XI. In March 1988 the GATT Council adopted the panel ruling, agreed with the United States that the restrictions were not justified under either Article XI:2(b) or XX(g) (conservation) because no restrictions had been placed on domestic production. Canada responded that it would eliminate the restriction and replace it with a landing requirement for conservation purposes, effective 1 January, 1989 (Hudec 1993, 542–44).

Outcome.   Canada did not eliminate the export prohibition, and on 28 March 1989 USTR determined that Canada denied US rights under GATT and solicited comments on a proposed retaliation "hit list." The day before the scheduled hearings on the hit list (26 April 1989), Canada repealed the export ban and substituted requirements that all Pacific roe herring and salmon caught in Canadian waters be landed in British Columbia prior to export for conservation reasons. The United States claimed that the new landing requirements were also inconsistent with GATT and, moreover, violated the just-negotiated bilateral free trade agreement (FTA). In May the two countries agreed to submit the dispute to an FTA dispute settlement panel, which found in favor of the United States in October. The FTA panel ruled that a landing requirement applicable to 100 percent of a catch was "too broad" to be justified as a conservation measure.

On 23 February 1990 the United States and Canada reached an interim agreement allowing the United States to deliver 20 percent in 1990 and 25 percent in 1991–93 of salmon and roe herring directly to the United States, while the remainder would be subject to Canadian landing require-ments. (The FTA panel suggested that 10 percent to 20 percent be exempted from the landing requirements.) In addition, sampling by Cana-dian inspectors could be done on board specially equipped "tender ves-sels." Also, Canada could require that roe herring not be exported to third countries unless it had been processed to the same degree as required in Canada. Canada reserved the right to establish a cost-recovery system in the future, but the United States asserted that any such charges "cannot be so high as to impose a trade barrier. We would regard charges like that to be a violation of this arrangement, and we would react accordingly" (see also, *International Trade Reporter,* 28 February 1990, 287). The case was terminated effective 1 June 1990.

Assessment.   US objectives appear to have been at least partially achieved, since, according to sources, the 20 percent level would provide about all the fish that US processors in the area could handle. The outcome was also supportive of the international system since it implemented the findings of two different dispute settlement panels (recall that the FTA panel had recommended an exemption from landing requirements of only 10 to 20 percent).

Case 301-56

Complaint.   On 1 August 1986, without benefit of an investigation, Presi-dent Reagan determined that Taiwan's use of a duty-paying system based on administratively determined import values was in violation of a bilateral agreement under which Taiwan had agreed to abide by the provisions of the GATT Customs Valuation Code; this code requires use of the transaction value for imports. The 1985 National Trade Estimate Report (p. 200) had cited this practice, noting that Taiwan applied a 5 percent "uplift" to the price of all imports before calculating the applicable duty and used "artificial duty-paying schedules" for selected products (for example, apples and cosmetics). The president directed USTR to propose an appropriate method of retaliation. Some in Congress called for revocation of Taiwan's GSP eligibility for its alleged violation of commitments in this case, as well as another case involving US exports of beer, wine, and tobacco products (see case 301-57 below).

GATT role.   Not applicable since Taiwan is not a GATT member.

Outcome.   In an exchange of letters on 11 August, Taiwan agreed to abolish the system by 1 October; the case was terminated after USTR confirmed Taiwan had done so. In a 1991 review of US–Taiwan trade relations, however, a US trade negotiator said Taiwan's valuation of auto imports for customs purposes had been discussed: "We think there are potential problems in the way they're valuing imports and assessing duties. . . . Car manufacturers think they're higher than they should be" (*International Trade Reporter,* 20 March 1991, 437). The 1991 USTR report (p. 207) noted that Taiwan had recently begun refusing to accept auto exporters' declared invoice values for customs purposes, instead substituting an arbitrary valuation that "could render these transactions unprofitable." Differential commodity taxes are also applied to some (particularly larger) auto imports.

Assessment.   The customs valuation system was changed as promised by Taiwan. Although there have been some problems in recent years in the auto sector, this case still appears to be a partial success.

Case 301-57

Complaint.   In October 1985 Taiwan promised to change certain practices with regard to the importation of beer, wine, and tobacco products within six to twelve months. In July 1986 congressional testimony, USTR Clayton Yeutter cited this agreement as one reached "without the filing of a section 301 case" (US Senate, Finance Committee 1986, 35). In October 1986, however, and without benefit of an investigation, President Reagan determined that Taiwan had not honored the agreement and that the practices in question were unfair. He directed the USTR to propose appropriate retaliatory actions. (Florsheim Shoe Co. submitted a lengthy brief

US beer, wine, and cigarette exports to Taiwan, 1985–92 (thousands of dollars)

Year	Beer	Wine	Cigarettes
1985	129	162	negl.
1986	880	266	4,355
1987	513	3,724	118,767
1988	2,522	1,111	119,152
1989	3,784	1,159	55,545
1990	6,812	2,236	107,602
1991	6,594	1,519	75,408
1992	6,810	1,855	60,342

negl. = negligible
Source: US Department of Commerce.

opposing retaliation against nonrubber shoes, one of the items on the "hit list.")

GATT role. Not applicable because Taiwan is not a GATT member.

Outcome. On 5 December 1986 Taiwan agreed to lift the import ban on beer, cease requiring that the retail price of imported beer, wine, and tobacco products be marked up at a higher rate than domestic products, and allow imported products to be sold at all retail outlets where domestic products are sold. Implementing regulations in some cases, however, violated the agreement and had the effect of keeping US products out during the Chinese new year celebration. These problems were purportedly resolved in negotiations in May 1987 (USTR National Trade Estimates Report 1987, 306). Wine exporters also complained that the remaining monopoly taxes were so high as to keep their product out.

Assessment. US objectives appear to have been largely achieved in this case with respect to cigarettes; however, after US exports of tobacco and products increased fourfold from 1986 to 1988, they dropped slightly in 1989 reportedly because of smuggling, especially of Japanese cigarettes, which are formally banned as part of Taiwan's effort to reduce its trade deficit with Japan. For reasons that are unclear, the Taiwanese government reportedly has done little to combat the smuggling (*Far Eastern Economic Review*, 29 March 1990, 64).

US wine exports to Taiwan increased sharply in 1987, from $0.27 million to nearly $4 million, but then dropped back to just over $1 million in 1988 and 1989 (table A.13). In both 1989 and 1990, the Wine Institute and the Association of American Vintners filed comments with USTR requesting that Taiwan's discriminatory treatment of wine imports be named as a priority practice under super 301. In 1990 the California Wine Institute also submitted public comments, claiming that the 1986 agreement had been only partially implemented and that, though the market had been liberalized somewhat, US products still could not compete as a result of remaining high tariffs and administrative barriers.

Case 301-58

Section 301 was used for administrative purposes to impose a 15 percent tax on imports of Canadian softwood lumber only until Canada could impose an export tax as agreed in settlement of a countervailing duty case.

Case 301-59

Complaint. On 6 January 1987 the California Almond Growers Exchange filed a petition alleging that India's quantitative restrictions, high tariffs, and import license requirements for almonds (shelled and unshelled) were inconsistent with the GATT and caused a burden on US commerce. The petitioner estimated that these practices raised the landed Bombay price of US almonds by 330 percent and had resulted in average annual lost sales of $2.5 million over the previous five years; the petitioner also claimed that, under free market conditions, Indian demand over the next five to ten years might be worth $34 million. Six years of bilateral consultations after India increased the restrictiveness of the quotas and licensing requirements in 1981 had failed to resolve the dispute.

GATT role. In June 1987 the United States filed two complaints in the GATT, one against India's quotas and one against the import licensing procedures (under the licensing code) (Hudec 1993, 548–49). Disagreement over the terms of reference delayed establishment until November 1987. After several months of additional delay in appointing panel members, Senator Pete Wilson (R-CA) ratcheted up the pressure, sending a letter to the Indian ambassador saying, "Unless immediate cooperation is forthcoming, I will demand that the U.S. withdraw from the dispute process altogether and regaliate against Indian imports, specifically, Indian cashews" (*International Trade Reporter*, 8 March 1988, 324). Panel members were finally agreed upon 20 April, but an agreement was reached before either panel could make a ruling.

Outcome. In May 1988 India agreed to increase the quota to $20 million for three years and to abolish it if its trade balance improved to a certain level; it also agreed to reduce and bind its almond duty. USTR terminated the case on 8 June 1988.

Year	Millions of dollars	Share of total US exports	Share of total Indian imports
1980	3.1	0.9	n.a.
1981	4.5	1.9	n.a.
1982	6.9	3.8	n.a.
1983	3.6	2.1	30.8
1984	3.5	1.4	31.8
1985	6.7	2.1	82.4
1986	2.3	0.8	32.1
1987	3.9	1.1	46.4
1988	11.6	2.5	78.9
1989	14.9	3.7	72.5
1990	15.9	3.4	58.0
1991	11.9	3.3	61.6
1992	12.5	3.3	28.0
1993	19.0	4.4	n.a.

n.a. = not available

Assessment.   US objectives in this cases were partially achieved since some liberalization did occur (table A.14). By 1992 India reportedly had decided to grant open general licenses for the import of almonds, which was the original objective of the petition. Although the data suggest there may have been some trade diversion, one source said privately that the other major suppliers have family ties in India, that they are typically able to ship all they want because there is often no foreign exchange effect, and that the shipments do not always show up in the trade statistics.

Case 301-60, 83

Complaint.   On 14 July 1987 the American Meat Institute, the American Meat Export Federation, the American Farm Bureau Federation, the National Pork Producers Council, and the National Cattlemen's Association jointly filed a petition claiming that the European Community's Third Country Meat Directive was an unjustifiable and discriminatory trade barrier to US exports of beef, pork, and lamb. The petitioners claimed that the directive subjected meat imports from the United States to regulatory requirements that "are not observed within the EEC member countries, are not fully enforced or observed [with respect to shipments] across national boundaries in the EEC, [and] are not based on or justified by any scientific analysis. . . ."

GATT role.   The United States claimed that the directive violated Article III:4 on national treatment because the health requirements applied to imports but not to domestic products. EC health standards for slaughterhouses applied only to meat crossing intra-EC national borders, but only about 20 to 30 percent of EC meat crosses national borders. A panel was established in December 1987, but it was not composed before a settlement was reached. The European Community had blocked US requests for a panel at the October and November Council meetings (Hudec 1993, 551–52).

Outcome.   In April 1988 the European Community published a list of US slaughterhouses found to qualify under the directive, including all or most of those involved in exporting. However, on 30 October 1990 the European Community confirmed a decision made pursuant to the directive to "delist" all US pork plants previously declared eligible to export to the Community, effective midnight 31 October. Similar action against beef plants became effective 1 January 1991. The United States held consultations with the European Community on 19–20 November and, according to the USTR, both sides "demonstrated a willingness to continue efforts to reach a mutually satisfactory resolution of the matter."

On 28 November 1990 the National Pork Producers Council and American Meat Institute (AMI) filed a second petition. It claimed that the directive cost the US industry $30 million in exports and $12 million to $15 million in additional expenditures to comply with the directive. Including price effects from oversupply in the US market, the petitioners estimated total losses of around $110 million (AMI press release, 13 October 1992). The investigation was initiated on 10 January 1991; in May USTR Hills announced that the United States would not take the issue before another GATT panel, pending the outcome of the bilateral talks. (*International Trade Reporter*, 15 April 1992, 675).

In the summer and fall 1991, the European Community "relisted" 4 of 25 plants previously involved in exporting to the Community; another 10 were expected to become eligible under a compromise worked out between US and EC negotiators that certified that the US slaughterhouses met "minimum standards of hygiene" (*International Trade Reporter*, 25 September 1992, 1394).

In April 1992 US negotiators announced that EC negotiators had accepted the principle of "equivalency" of standards as the basis for an agreement (*International Trade Reporter*, 15 April 1992, 675). In October, over the protests of the industry, USTR announced that they had an agreement "in principle" and terminated the 301 investigation "in anticipation of" a final agreement being signed by the end of the year (*International Trade Reporter*, 21 October 1992, 1806). On 13 November 1992 USTR announced that an agreement had been signed based on the findings and recommendations made by a joint US/EC veterinary group that studied differences between US and EC inspection requirements (USTR press release, 13 November 1992). The group had identified 60 differences in US and European meat inspection requirements, had resolved many, and had made suggestions for resolving the others. The agreement included a schedule for resolving the outstanding issues and also "interim require-ments for determining the eligibility" of US meat processors to supply the European Community, which were expected to facilitate EC approval of additional US plants. The US Meat Export Federation said the agree-ment would enable the United States to continue progress in reestablishing trade with the Community and that it expected "16 meat processing plants to be added to the EC 's approved list by the end of the year, bringing to 48 the total of U.S. plants approved for exports to the EC " (*International Trade Reporter*, 4 November 1992).

Assessment. In the first case, 301-60, negotiators were able to obtain only a temporary respite, and the regulation was not altered; since there was a recurrence of the dispute within a few years, the achievement of an agreement in that case cannot be considered more than a nominal success. It is too early to confidently judge the outcome in case 301-83.

Case 301-61

See chapter 8.

Case 301-62

Complaint. In December 1985, responding to consumer concerns about the effects on children, the European Community banned the sale of beef from cattle treated with growth hormones. The EC Commission admitted that its ban of all five legal hormones was a response to "political pressure rather than scientific evidence." A special scientific working committee commissioned by the Community to examine the safety of hormone use in animals declared the three natural hormones—estrogen, progesterone, and testosterone—"not harmful" and claimed there were insufficient data to draw final conclusions about the synthetic hormones—zeranol and trenbolone.

In November 1987 President Reagan declared he would impose retalia-tory duties on a variety of EC exports if the European Community imple-mented its Animal Hormone Directive, scheduled to go into effect 1 January 1988. The United States argued that the ban was an illegal trade barrier, disguised as a health and safety standard for which there was no scientific support. The European Community responded that, whether or not scientifically based, the ban passed GATT muster because it treated domestically produced and imported beef in the same manner, thus meet-ing GATT requirements for nondiscrimination.

The European Community delayed implementation for a year, but as the new deadline approached the United States reiterated its threat to retaliate, and the Community threatened to counterretaliate against US exports of honey, canned sweet corn, nuts, and dried fruit. The United States then threatened to escalate the dispute and block all US imports of EC beef, valued at $450 million (four times US sales to the Community), under the reciprocal meat inspection provisions of the 1988 Trade Act.

GATT role. The United States maintains that the ban represents an "illegal trade barrier masquerading as a health measure" and has tried to refer the case to a "technical expert group" under the GATT standards code. The European Community has blocked this attempt, arguing that the code does not cover production methods. Meanwhile, the Community offered to submit the dispute to a GATT dispute settlement panel and appealed to the GATT to rule against the US retaliation as illegal (Hudec 1993, 545). There was widespread condemnation of US retaliatory measures at a GATT Council meeting in February 1989. Many countries backed the contention of Tran Van Thinh, head of the EC delegation, that unilateral US trade actions, based on section 301 of its trade act, were endangering the multilateral trading system.

Outcome. On 1 January 1989 the European Community implemented its hormone ban, and the United States responded with retaliatory tariffs on $100 million of EC products, the estimated value of US beef exports affected by the ban. These products included boneless beef, processed pork hams and shoulders, prepared or preserved tomatoes, soluble or instant coffee extracts, some fermented beverages with less than 7 percent alcoholic content, some fruit juices, and packaged pet food. The European Community decided to delay implementation of counterretaliatory measures, despite Italian pressure to hit back; Italian tomato producers were particularly hard hit by the US retaliation.

In the ensuing months, steps were taken to prevent the trade war from escalating. The European Community exempted pet food, and some US producers offered to ship hormone-free beef (which would only affect 15 percent of beef exports, since the other 85 percent was in the form of offal, which would have been virtually impossible to certify as hormone-free). The US government reduced the level of retaliation to reflect the increased exports of pet food containing beef and hormone-free beef exports.

By March 1990 USTR was receiving complaints from US importers about the retaliatory measures. On 13 November 1990 the EC Court of Justice threw out European pharmaceutical industry complaints calling for the nullification of the directive, stating that "damage done by hormones could neither be proved nor disproved" and that "the ban was necessary to ensure that different rules in member states did not set up barriers that restricted trade and distorted competition."

Assessment. While further escalation was avoided, the basic issue remains unresolved. This case must be judged a failure, since US retaliation failed either to change EC policy or to induce EC compensation.

Case 301-63

See chapter 9.

Case 301-64

Complaint. On 22 January 1988 the US Cigarette Export Association (CEA) filed a petition alleging that practices of the Korean Monopoly Corporation were unreasonable, discriminatory, and a burden on US commerce. The CEA claimed that the monopoly fixed the retail price of imported cigarettes at prohibitive levels through a combination of import duties and excise taxes; used administrative procedures to restrict the import and distribution of foreign brands; and prevented foreign investment, including joint ventures, in the tobacco sector. The petitioner estimated that the barriers cost its members $520 million in exports annually. The 1985 National Trade Estimate Report (p. 135) estimates the total value of the Korean market for cigarettes as $1.8 billion.

GATT role. None.

Outcome. On 27 May 1988 USTR announced that the two parties had concluded an agreement to provide "nondiscriminatory and open access to the Korean cigarette market" as of 1 July. The government found afterward, however, that the agreement was not fully ratifiable. Opposition leader Kim Dae Jung reportedly encouraged his party members to support domestic tobacco farmers and shun foreign cigarettes. According to the *Far Eastern Economic Review* (29 March 1990, 64), "Many South Koreans still view smoking foreign cigarettes as a treacherous indulgence. . . . The anti-foreign cigarette campaign has helped limit foreign producers' market share to 4.5 percent, half the share Washington predicted in 1988." By the beginning of 1992, the foreign share was still only 4 percent (*Financial Times*, 31 January 1992, 17).

Foreign cigarette producers also complain that a provision making the allocation of municipal revenues proportional to the number of South Korean cigarettes sold in the area gives an incentive to local governments to encourage the consumption of domestic cigarettes. "The justification for the system is that taxes on South Korean cigarettes form a substantial part of government revenues" (*Financial Times*, 31 January 1992, 17) According to one source, this case was a "perhaps unfortunate choice that fell right into the laps of the anti-U.S. propagandists, who charged that the 'imperialist' United States was trying to 'force' Koreans to buy products officially labeled as harmful to the health of its own people. Cigarettes eventually were liberalized, only to fall victim to a major campaign by the press, the YMCA, and by 'consumer' groups (actually anti-

Table A.15 US exports of cigarettes to Korea, 1985–93

Year	Millions of dollars	Share of total US exports	Share of total Korean imports
1985	2.1	0.2	609.8
1986	5.6	0.4	702.0
1987	6.1	0.3	155.8
1988	56.4	2.1	145.3
1989	106.8	3.2	85.6
1990	100.5	2.1	96.6
1991	89.9	2.1	75.1
1992	84.6	2.0	76.2
1993	96.6	2.5	n.a.

n.a. = not available

foreign lobbyists) who labeled smokers of foreign cigarettes as unpatriotic" (*International Trade Reporter*, 29 August 1990, 1346).

Assessment. Although the concessions made by Korea appear on paper to have been substantial, USTR's achievement of its negotiating objectives must be viewed as only partial at this point. This conclusion would appear to be supported by USTR's own admission in its 1991 National Trade Estimate Report (p. 149) that it had had problems getting Korea even to discuss implementation problems because of the anti-import bias that had developed in Korea in 1990.

It is also not clear how much credit section 301 should get for delivering the outcome in this case. According to some sources, the deal came about because the tobacco industry hired former Reagan White House aide Michael Deaver to lobby South Korea. Deaver reportedly promised to help South Korea fight a textile quota bill then being considered in Congress. The Koreans reached agreement with USTR in May 1988, and Reagan vetoed the textile bill later that year (*National Journal*, 1 January 1994, 22; *The New Yorker*, 13 September 1993, 85). Although Reagan probably would have vetoed the textile legislation in any case, South Korean concerns may have been serious enough to provide additional leverage. Whatever the reason, US exports of cigarettes to Korea increased from barely $10 million in 1986–87 to more than $100 million in 1989 (table A.15), and the case is treated as a partial success.

Case 301-65

Complaint. The American Meat Association filed a complaint in February 1988 alleging that Korea's restrictive licensing requirements on meat imports violated Article XI of GATT and nullified and impaired tariff concessions by Korea. Although the licensing system had been instituted in 1967, with beef on the restricted list from the beginning, Korea had generally licensed shipments based on a six-month quota. On 21 May 1985, however, Korea had changed the regulations to require a license for each individual shipment and had simultaneously stopped approving licenses. It had allowed only one shipment of imported beef for domestic consumption since then (49 tons for the annual meeting of the International Monetary Fund held in Seoul).

A small amount of exports of high quality beef for use on Korean airlines and ships continued, but no more shipments for domestic consumption had been made. Most US exports of beef to Korea were high-quality cuts, primarily to the Korea Hotel Supply Center, and did not compete with domestically produced beef; but Korea apparently decided to halt high-quality beef imports as well, primarily for political reasons. In order to try to deflect the 301 investigation and avoid a GATT panel, Korea offered to resume beef imports beginning in May 1988. In July it established an import quota of 14,500 metric tons for the remainder of 1988 and a 1989 quota of 50,000 metric tons. In its comments on the 301 petition filed with USTR, Korea also argued that complete liberalization could harm US interests in two ways. On the one hand, Australian and New Zealand were more price-competitive and were likely to capture more of the market if it were liberalized on an MFN basis. And, on the other, reduction in the number of cattle raised domestically in Korea would concomitantly reduce US grain exports to Korea.

GATT role. The United States had initiated GATT dispute settlement procedures and held bilateral consultations with Korea even before the section 301 petition was filed. In March it requested formation of a dispute settlement panel; Australia, the largest supplier of beef to Korea (including lower-priced cuts), filed a similar complaint a few days later, "in part to ensure that the US complaint was not settled at Australia's expense" (Hudec 1993, 198). A joint panel was authorized in May 1988. On 24 May 1989 the GATT panel issued a ruling that the Korean beef import restrictions violated Article XI, were not justified for balance of payments purposes, and should be phased out.

Korea refused to allow adoption of the report at GATT meetings in June or July. On 25 August 1989 USTR solicited comments on a proposed determination that Korea's policies were a violation of US rights under the GATT and on what action would be appropriate. Effective 28 September 1989 USTR made the determination as proposed and announced that the appropriate action would be the suspension of tariff concessions on products of interest to Korea. However, USTR also determined that it was "necessary and desirable" to delay retaliation to allow additional time for GATT proceedings. USTR further announced that a list of possible items for retaliation would be published in the *Federal Register* in mid-November if substantial progress toward resolving the dispute had not been made by that time. On 8 November 1989 Korea allowed the GATT panel report to be adopted and opened consultations with the United States on implementation of the panel's recommendations (Hudec 1993, 554–56).

Outcome. Although Korea's restoration of a quota for beef imports in mid-1988 resulted in US exports of beef to Korea of $25.6 million in the last half of 1988 and $41.1 million in the first half of 1989, the United States continued to pursue the GATT case and, after its ruling, to press Korea to eliminate the quotas as recommended. The United States and Korea initialed an agreement on 21 March 1990, formalized by an exchange of letters on April 26–27, under which Korea agreed to fully liberalize its beef market by July 1997. During the transition period, Korea made specific commitments to raise its beef quotas in each of the next three years, reaching 66,000 metric tons in 1992, and then to design the "remaining transitional regime" so as to increase imports further. USTR terminated the investigation effective 26 April 1990.

In March 1993 the US Meat Export Federation complained that the Korean government was gradually cutting the amount of imported beef available for sale in the Korean market, thereby raising imported beef prices and decreasing its competitiveness (*Journal of Commerce*, 19 March 1993, 7A). In April the United States expressed disappointment when Korea announced that it would raise the quota to only 99,000 metric tons. Korea imported about 130,000 metric tons in 1992, well above the 66,000 metric-ton quota. US industry worried that the lower-than-expected quota would be used as a limiting factor. Talks broke up without agreement, and no further meetings were scheduled (*Journal of Commerce*, 29 April 1993, 9A).

On 29 June USTR Kantor announced that the United States and Korea had reached an agreement under which Korea would increase the quota to 99,000 metric tons in 1993, 106,000 in 1994, and 113,000 in 1995. Korea would also allow increasing quantities of beef to be sold directly to Korean retailers and distributors. Ten percent of the 1993 quota would be sold in this fashion; in 1994 this figure would rise to 20 percent and in 1995 to 30 percent (*International Trade Reporter*, 7 July 1993, 1129–30). On 21 July Korea told the GATT Council that it hoped to eliminate remaining restrictions by June 1995 (*International Trade Reporter*, 28 July 1998, 1238).

Assessment. Given implementation problems and the need to renegotiate in 1993, this case is judged to be a partial achievement of US goals (table A.16).

Case 301-66

See chapter 10.

Case 301-67

Complaint. On 27 April 1988 the Wine Institute and Association of American Vintners filed a petition complaining that Korean tariffs and

Table A.16 US exports of beef to Korea, 1985–93

Year	Millions of dollars	Share of total US exports	Share of total Korean imports
1985	5.6	1.2	75.7
1986	1.9	0.3	1,087.6
1987	1.5	0.2	389.9
1988	25.1	2.3	58.5
1989	78.8	5.7	36.2
1990	115.5	7.5	38.1
1991	176.6	10.3	38.8
1992	211.5	10.5	44.3
1993	151.1	7.8	n.a.

n.a. = not available

quotas on table wine imports, along with a distribution system that contributed to price escalation on imports, made imported wine uncompetitive with domestic products; that there was an absolute ban on certain
types of wine imports; and that certification, labeling, and other administrative regulations "impeded access" to the Korean wine market. The
petitioners estimated their losses over the past five years as $45 million
(c.i.f. import value) with potential losses over the next five years of $61 million.

GATT role. None.

Outcome. On 18 January 1989 the United States and Korea reached an
agreement intended to provide nondiscriminatory treatment for wine
imports. Under the agreement, Korea pledged to reduce the tariff on wine
from 100 to 35 percent effective 1 July 1989 and to 30 percent six months
later. Additional reductions would be made through 1993. The quotas for
certain types of wine were doubled, and Korea promised to eliminate
them effective 1 January 1990 and to eliminate quotas on other types of
wine a year later. The agreement also purportedly "clarified" the administrative requirements regarding labeling and testing, and liberalized the
distribution system. The investigation was terminated 18 January 1989.

Assessment. Though the liberalization Korea promised was significant,
there have reportedly been problems with implementation, though the
1991 USTR National Trade Estimate Report does say that Korea reduced
the tariff on wine to 35 percent in July 1989 as promised. The limited
trade data available do not show much of an increase in US exports,
certainly not to the levels the petitioners anticipated (table A.17). Nevertheless, the case is judged a partial success.

Case 301-68

Complaint. In August 1988 the Pharmaceutical Manufacturers Association (PMA) filed a petition alleging that Argentina denied product patent

Table A.17 US exports of wine to Korea, 1985–93

Year	Millions of dollars	Share of total US exports	Share of total Korean imports
1985	0.04	0.12	8.14
1986	0.03	0.07	3.23
1987	0.39	0.60	53.15
1988	0.30	0.33	7.38
1989	0.26	0.28	8.50
1990	0.15	0.12	3.00
1991	0.34	0.24	9.80
1992	0.43	0.26	7.60
1993	0.96	0.58	n.a.

n.a. = not available

protection for pharmaceuticals and discriminated against US firms in its product registration practices. Portions of the petition estimating injury as a result of Argentina's practices contain confidential data and were not made public.

GATT role.   Not applicable.

Outcome.   In August 1989 USTR solicited public comments on whether Argentina's policies were actionable and what if any action would be appropriate. On 23 September 1989, just prior to a Washington visit by Argentine President Carlos Menem, the PMA withdrew its petition based on its understanding that the Argentine government had given "reasonable assurances that it [would] address constructively the issue of patent protection for pharmaceutical products." According to USTR's 1990 report to Congress on section 301 developments (p. 17), "As of December 1990, Argentina had undertaken efforts to simplify its drug registration procedures and revise them to improve transparency."

The report also stated that the government of Argentina was "formulating its strategy to pursue patent protection for pharmaceuticals." In July 1992 it appeared that the strategy was to use pharmaceutical patent protection as leverage in the Uruguay Round and not to pass patent legislation, introduced in the Argentine Congress in September 1992, until the multilateral negotiations were completed. One Argentine legislator said, "If trade barriers in general were lowered, we would be more inclined to reform our patent law. Important points for us are on traditional Argentine exports like leather and beef" (*International Trade Reporter*, 8 July 1992, 1183). In 1993 Argentine legislators linked patent protection to reductions in agricultural subsidies by the United States and the European Union (*Journal of Commerce*, 19 May 1993, 4A).

Assessment.   The timing suggests that the administration pressured the PMA to withdraw its petition in order to avoid a confrontation just before

President Menem's visit to Washington. Although Argentina has improved the transparency of its regulatory process, it still had not passed legislation to provide patent protection as of mid-1994. Thus any "success" in achieving an agreement appears to have been nominal.

Case 301-69

Complaint. On 21 November 1988, as required by the 1988 Trade Act, USTR initiated an investigation into possible unfair trade practices in Japan's construction industry with a view to opening the Japanese market to US engineering, architectural, and construction services exports. Original US negotiations with Japan had focused on opening particular, large, publicly funded projects to foreign bidding. In a March 1988 agreement, Japan had agreed to a list of 14 "major projects" that would be open to foreign bidding. The section 301 investigation focused both on ensuring implementation of the Major Projects Arrangements, by making bidding procedures more open and transparent, and on expanding the list of projects open to foreign bidding.

In March 1989 testimony before the Section 301 Committee, the International Engineering & Construction Industries Council (IECIC) complained that, while Japanese contractors had increased their contract volume in the United States from $50 million in 1982 to $2.2 billion in 1987, US design and construction firms had been "virtually unable to penetrate the Japanese market, despite significant efforts to do so." The IECIC specified achievement of two goals as being necessary for US firms to be able to compete on "an equal basis" with Japanese firms in Japan: an open and transparent bidding system on all public projects; and rigorous enforcement of laws against collusive bidding (called *dango* in Japan) and restrictive subcontractor arrangements.

GATT role. Not applicable.

Outcome. On 21 November 1989 USTR determined that Japanese practices with respect to procurement in the public sector were unreasonable and a burden on US commerce, but it further determined that retaliatory action was not appropriate at that time, pending implementation of certain commitments made by Japan to improve access for US firms. USTR Hills also announced her intention of continuing negotiations on outstanding issues and of conducting a full review of the Major Projects Arrangements (originally signed in May 1988) in May 1990.

On 28 April 1991 USTR announced that negotiations had not yet resulted in a satisfactory implementation of measures to address the practices found to be unreasonable and solicited comments on a retaliatory proposal to bar Japanese firms from entering into contracts with certain federal agencies for the construction, alteration, or repair of any public buildings or public works in the United States. The deadline for comments was 31 May 1991.

On 1 June 1991 the two countries announced they had reached an agreement that would more than double the number of projects available to American companies in Japan, including 11 Japanese suggestions and six American requests. In addition, the agreement included new guidelines to improve the transparency of the bidding process, a dispute settlement mechanism to handle disagreements over contract awards, and a commitment from Japan to toughen enforcement of its anti-*dango* laws (*International Trade Reporter*, 5 June 1991, 846; *JEI Report*, 7 June 1991, 1).

A fact sheet accompanying the announcement of the agreement showed that American firms had less than $200 million of a $165 billion public sector construction market and less than $300 million of the total public and private construction market in 1990 (worth $550 billion); Japanese firms had $3.3 billion in contracts in the $435 billion US construction market but less than $100 million of the $110 billion public construction market (80 percent of which is state and local).

US and Japanese negotiators were unable to agree during follow-up discussions on a US demand for 35 more projects to be added to the list of projects subject to special bidding procedures. On 29 October the Japanese Construction Ministry announced revisions to the bidding system intended to make it more transparent and to bring in factors other than price, including technological capability and safety precautions (*International Trade Reporter*, November 1992, 1899). In March 1993 former Construction Minister and LDP "kingpin" Shin Kanemaru was indicted for evading taxes on millions of dollars in cash and gold he had stashed away. Press reports revealed the pervasiveness of bid rigging on construction contracts in Kanemaru's home district. Japan's largest daily newspaper, the *Yomiuri Shimbun*, called for "drastic" reform of the public works bidding system, though also arguing against negotiating under the threat of sanctions (*Washington Post*, 9 May 1993, H1). Prime Minister Kiichi Miyazawa suffered a no-confidence vote in the Diet in early June, in part because of his failure to strongly back political reforms intended to reduce corruption in Japanese politics (*International Trade Reporter*, 7 July 1993, 1109; *Japan Economic Institute Report*, 21 January 1994).

On 30 April 1993 USTR Kantor identified Japan in the report to Congress required by Title VII of the 1988 Trade Act as discriminating against U.S. companies in procurement of construction, architectural, and engineering services (*International Trade Reporter*, 23 June 1993, 1017). One source noted that "after all the grandly trumpeted agreements, US companies have achieved only a 0.07 per cent share of the Japanese public sector construction and design market and 0.003 per cent share of the private sector market" (*Financial Times*, 19 October 1993, 5).

On 30 June USTR formally cited Japan for discriminating against US firms in bidding for construction contracts, but it delayed consideration of retaliation until 1 November. USTR summarized US goals as getting Japan "to fulfill four principles in opening up its construction market: an open and competitive bidding system, application of such a system in all big projects above a certain level, greater enforcement of anti-monopoly laws, and the enhancement of annual data collection to assess progress made." Thus, the Clinton administration changed the negotiating strategy significantly, departing from the Reagan/Bush strategy of not frontally challenging the designated bidder system and settling for a sort of setaside program instead.

On 26 October Japan announced an action plan under which it would "(1) adopt an open and competitive bidding system to replace the closed designated bidder system; (2) apply the reforms to all government and quasi-government construction projects above a specified threshold; (3) evaluate the corporate structure and global technical capabilities of foreign firms; (4) take steps to prevent *dango* or bribery, including banning firms from bidding on public works contracts; (5) strictly apply its Anti-Monopoly Law and; (6) establish objective, transparent and published standards for bidding and contracting procedures." The action plan would be further developed and finalized by January 1994. USTR expected the details would include "an impartial complaint mechanism covering all public works procurements; elimination of requirements to form joint ventures; open, transparent, competitive and non-discriminatory tendering and contract procedures; and establishment of a system to monitor foreign access to Japan's public works market." Kantor said he would recommend to the president postponement of sanctions until 20 January 1994. "We expect Japan to announce a detailed plan of reforms which addresses our well-known concerns prior to that time, making the imposition of sanctions unnecessary." (USTR statement, 26 October 1993).

In January Japan's cabinet approved a plan that would go into effect 1 April. "U.S. officials said that they had begun a preliminary review of the construction plan and that it appeared to address most major U.S. concerns." (*Wall Street Journal*, 18 January 1994, A9).

Assessment. The outcome in the 301 case appears to represent a partial achievement of US objectives: the list of projects open to US bidding was increased, but not eliminated as the United States wanted. Actual US export gains, however, seem to have been limited. According to one report, the number of US firms licensed to participate in Japanese public works increased from three to thirty since the Major Projects Arrangement was signed. But the same report also notes that the value of contracts won by US firms dropped 36 percent in 1992 from the previous year's level (*Wall Street Journal*, 10 June 1993, 1). Other critics of the agreement argued that it served as much "as a fence as an open door" because US firms had no opportunity to bid on projects not on the list. This allegation contradicts the Japanese argument that the list of set-aside projects should be kept limited and temporary because it was intended only to give US firms the experience needed to bid on any project.

Nevertheless, and despite the decision to cite Japan under Title VII in June 1993, this case is classified as a partial success because the subsequent agreement expanded US demands rather than simply seeking to enforce the previous agreement.

Case 301-70

Complaint.   On 14 November 1988 the Copper and Brass Fabricators Council, Inc. filed a petition claiming that restrictions imposed by Brazil, the European Community, and the United Kingdom (separately) on exports of copper scrap, copper alloy scrap, and zinc scrap tended to depress the price of scrap in those markets, raise it in other markets, and thus provided an unfair advantage to brass fabricators in those countries. The petitioner later withdrew the petition with regard to Brazil, and USTR initiated an investigation with regard to the allegations against the European Community on 29 December 1988. No separate investigation of the UK case was opened because USTR determined that it did not have restrictions separate from those of the European Community.

GATT role.   The United States claimed that the EC restrictions violated Article XI's general prohibition against export restrictions and were not justified by the short-supply exception. A dispute settlement panel was established in July 1989, and the first meeting of the panel was held in November. On 18 January 1990 the United States reported that a settlement had been reached and requested that the proceeding be terminated (Hudec 1993, 578–79).

Outcome.   In return for the United States terminating the GATT panel process, the European Community confirmed in a letter to USTR that the quotas on exports of copper and zinc scrap had expired on 31 December 1989 and that a review of market conditions indicated they did not need to be revived in 1990. The EC letter also stated that "the EC Commission does not expect fundamental changes in the situation in the market for copper scrap and waste in the foreseeable future which would necessitate or justify the reintroduction of export restrictions on copper scrap . . . or the imposition of a system of licensing which would have a restrictive effect on international trade." Based on the exchange of letters, petitioner withdrew its petition on 26 February 1990, and USTR terminated the case.

Assessment.   US objectives appear to have been largely achieved in this case.

Case 301-71

See case 301-26.

Case 301-72

Complaint. On 10 April 1989 the US Cigarette Export Association (CEA) filed a petition alleging that Thailand and the Thailand Tobacco Monopoly (TTM) maintained an effective ban on imports of cigarettes and prohibited foreign investment in cigarette manufacture. The petitioner also alleged that restrictions on advertising were intended to put foreign cigarettes at a competitive disadvantage. The petitioner estimated that with liberalization of the Thai cigarette market it could capture 25 percent, which would be worth $166 million of exports.

GATT role. Thailand initially blocked a US effort to have a dispute settlement panel appointed in February 1990, but one was authorized by the GATT Council in April. On 21 September 1990 the panel ruled that Thailand's import restrictions on cigarettes violated GATT Article XI and were not justified under Article XX (exceptions to protect health and safety), but it rejected the US allegation that Thailand's excise tax violated the national treatment requirements of Article III.

Outcome. With the panel's report and recommendation due to be discussed at the next GATT meeting on 7 November 1990, the United States, on 15 October asked for public comments on a proposed determination that Thailand's policies violated US rights under GATT, and on what would constitute appropriate action. According to press reports in Bangkok, USTR had planned to publish a proposed retaliatory "hit list" but postponed it when Thailand indicated a willingness to lift the restrictions on cigarette imports and asked the United States to resume bilateral negotiations. The list reportedly included $350 million in Thai exports to the United States, including tuna, jewelry, coffee, rubber, sugar, and tobacco (*International Trade Reporter*, 17 October 1990, 1581). On 23 November 1990 USTR made its determination as proposed, but based on the Thai government announcement that it would no longer ban the importation of cigarettes and would provide nondiscriminatory national treatment for foreign cigarettes, USTR terminated the investigation.

Assessment. Thailand eliminated the practices that had effectively prevented cigarette imports, but GATT-legal tariffs and taxes kept US exports low. By summer 1991 US cigarette brands were still only available in duty-free shops in Thailand because the combination of a (nondiscriminatory) 55 percent excise tax on top of a 30 percent import duty priced them out of the market. According to a US embassy official, the excise tax and import duty were GATT-consistent and thus difficult to challenge (*Journal of Commerce*, 9 July 1991, 4A).

Cases 301-73, 74, 75, 76, 77, 78

See chapters 5–7.

Case 301-79

Complaint. AMTECH Corporation filed a petition on 11 July 1989, complaining that the government of Norway had engaged in unfair and discriminatory practices with respect to the public procurement of an electronic highway tollgate system for Oslo. Specifically, AMTECH charged that a decision by the Ministry of Transport to reverse the decision of the Oslo Toll Road Authority to award the contract to petitioner violated the national treatment provisions of the GATT and the GATT government procurement code. AMTECH further stated that, after the 301 petition was filed, the Oslo authority announced that it intended to award the contract to AMTECH as originally planned but that the Minister of Transport transferred the authority for granting the contract to another entity and added six new criteria for evaluating bids. (Norway is reported to have feared that the US Navy's decision to buy Norwegian-made air-to-sea missiles might be rescinded if Norway did not reconsider the toll-system contract [*Financial Times*, 11 October 1989].) Petitioner estimated that the value of US goods and technology affected by the contract was about $4.5 million, but it noted that the actual injury could be far higher because of the effect on its ability to get future contracts in other markets.

GATT role. Consultations were held under the GATT procurement code, and the issue was discussed in the Committee on Government Procurement.

Outcome. In an exchange of letters, Norway agreed to provide compensation to AMTECH for the losses it suffered in making a bid and preparing to ship the equipment after initially being informed it had won the contract. Norway also made it clear that AMTECH'S technology met the specifications of the project and was "found to be proven, reliable, competitive . . . and commercially available." Norway also promised to carry out future procurements in accordance with the provisions of the procurement code. In announcing the agreement, USTR Hills said, "This case illustrates the importance of the [GATT] government procurement code. . . . The United States is determined not only to pursue our existing rights under the agreement, but also to ensure a successful resolution to the current negotiations in the code to expand the opportunities available to U.S.

suppliers" (*International Trade Reporter*, 2 May 1990, 630). The case was terminated 26 April 1990.

Assessment.   Although Norway did not reverse its procurement decision with respect to the Oslo toll system, it did appear to address petitioner's concern about its international reputation and the potential for receiving other contracts. However, a year after terminating the 301 investigation, the USTR named Norway under Title VII of the 1988 Trade Act as a country apparently in violation of its procurement code obligations, this time with respect to a toll system for the city of Trondheim. The United States also filed a complaint under the Government Procurement Code of the GATT (*Journal of Commerce*, 25 September 1991, 2A). In May 1992 the panel ruled that Norway's procurement policy in this case violated the procurement code, and Norway promised to bring its policies in compliance (*Journal of Commerce*, 14 May 1992, 1A).

Case 301-80

Complaint.   On 15 May 1990 G. Heileman Brewing Co., Inc. filed a petition alleging that Canadian provincial markups and restrictions on distribution of beer discriminated against imports and violated both the GATT and Canada–United States Free Trade Agreement (FTA). On 14 September 1990 The Stroh Brewery Co. filed a petition making similar allegations, which USTR combined with the earlier complaint.

In January 1991 three major Canadian brewers—Labatt, Molson, and Pacific Western—filed dumping complaints against Heileman, Stroh, and Pabst Brewing Co. In September Revenue Canada issued a final determination finding a weighted average dumping margin of 30 percent; the Canadian International Trade Tribunal (ITT) issued its final ruling that British Columbia brewers had been injured as a result in October (*International Trade Reporter*, 11 September 1991, 1315; 4 December 1991, 1773). During consideration of the complaint, the Canadian Bureau of Competition Policy opposed imposition of full antidumping duties, citing estimates that the tariff-equivalent of the various nontariff barriers protecting British Columbia brewers was 50 percent. In August 1992 a binational panel, appointed under the dispute settlement procedures of the Canada–US FTA, sent the decision back to the Canadian ITT, ruling that the tribunal had incorrectly included the cost to Canadian brewers of switching packing from bottles to cans in its injury calculation (US beer is packaged primarily in cans, while Canadian beer is usually packaged in bottles) (*Inside U.S. Trade*, 4 September 1992, 10).

GATT role.   At the end of the Tokyo Round, Canada had "transmitted a nonbinding statement of provincial intentions to eliminate discriminatory sales restrictions and to limit or eliminate excess mark-ups [on liquor].

The EC (and others) considered these changes had not occurred" (Hudec 1993, 155). The European Community brought a complaint in 1985 claiming that these practices of Canadian provincial liquor boards were inconsistent with the GATT. Though declining to rule on whether the provincial sales restrictions violated provisions on state trading enterprises per se (Article XVII), or on whether either the sales restrictions or markups violated national treatment provisions, the panel did rule that markups on bound items could not exceed markups on domestic products unless cost-justified and that the sales restrictions, though not import restrictions per se, violated Article XI. The panel report was adopted in March 1988.

Canada also pledged during the FTA negotiations with the United States to "end all restrictions" on the sale of imports, to freeze the markup on beer, and to eliminate the markup on spirits immediately and on wine in seven to ten years. In December 1988 Canada agreed to extend generally the liberalization agreed to in the FTA. At a June 1990 meeting, the United States claimed that most of the GATT-inconsistent practices were still in place and requested Article XXIII (nullification and impairment) consultations. At GATT Council meetings in October and November 1990, the United States asked Canada to provide a plan and timetable for implementing the recommendations of the 1988 GATT panel report. Canada refused and in December the United States requested that a dispute settlement panel be authorized to consider whether US benefits were being nullified or impaired by Canadian practices.

In October 1991 the GATT panel ruled against Canada on many, though not all, of the practices complained about by the United States. It further ruled that Canada's "failure to make serious, persistent and convincing efforts" to comply with the 1988 GATT panel report was a violation of Canada's obligations and constituted prima facie nullification or impairment of US benefits. The panel recommended that Canada report to the GATT Council in March 1992 on the measures it was taking to address the panel's findings. In February 1992 another GATT panel ruled that some US national and state practices that resulted in different tax treatment of domestic and imported beer violated GATT provisions.

Outcome. On 27 December 1991 USTR issued its determination that the Canadian practices violated GATT and announced that retaliatory duties would be imposed no later than 10 April 1992 if Canada had not eliminated the illegal practices. On 31 March 1992 Canada submitted a response to the GATT panel report that explained its plan to phase out discriminatory provincial provisions by 31 March 1995. But the United States rejected the proposal as insufficient and reiterated its demand that increased access be granted to US brewers by the coming summer.

On 13 April US Customs informed importers that they would be liable retroactively for duties if retaliation was imposed in the future. The next day Deputy USTR Julius L. Katz announced that the United States would delay retaliation while negotiations continued. The delay was reportedly due to intervention from the White House following a phone call from Prime Minister Brian Mulroney (*Journal of Commerce*, 15 April 1992, 1A). The Liquor Control Board in Ontario announced that, while it would continue to sell US beer from its inventories, it would order no more until the dispute had been resolved (*International Trade Reporter*, 22 April 1992, 717). On 24 April the two sides announced that an agreement had been reached under which Canadian provincial authorities would end the discriminatory pricing provisions applied to imports by 1 July 1992 and which split the difference on when provincial restrictions on the distribution of imported beer would be lifted, setting September 1993 as the deadline (Canada had wanted the deadline to be March 1994, and the United States had insisted on March 1993) (*Journal of Commerce*, 27 April 1992, 1A).

At the end of April, however, Ontario announced a doubling of its tax on nonrefillable cans of beer, wine, and spirits for environmental reasons. Although the tax applies equally to domestic and imported products in cans, most US beer is packed in cans while 80 percent of domestic beer in Ontario is sold in bottles (*Journal of Commerce*, 26 May 1992, 1A). At a June 19 GATT Council meeting, the United States protested the can tax (and also accepted the panel report on Canada's complaint about US practices that discriminated against Canada's beer exports) (*International Trade Reporter*, 24 June 1992, 1083). Also in June, Ontario released its new rules for beer imports, including the increase in the can tax, which the United States claimed, contrary to the agreement of April, would actually have the effect of raising the price of US beer relative to Canadian beer (*Journal of Commerce*, 29 June 1992, 1A). In July the United States filed a GATT complaint with the Anti-Dumping Committee regarding Canada's antidumping duties on US beer exports, and Canada agreed to the appointment of a panel (*Journal of Commerce*, 10 July 1992, 1A).

On 14 July 1992 the United States, citing actions by Ontario and Quebec, requested GATT Council authorization to retaliate against $80 million in Canadian exports, claiming that Canada had yet to comply with the GATT panel ruling on beer. The Canadian delegate, noting he did not think authorization was warranted, warned that if the United States retaliated without GATT authorization Canada would "reserve the right to retaliate in kind" (*Journal of Commerce*, 15 July 1992, 3A). On 24 July, in an attempt to contain the dispute, the United States imposed a 50 percent duty on beer imported only from Ontario. Canada responded by imposing a 50 percent duty on US beer exported to Ontario but singled out Heileman and Stroh, the original petitioners. The gesture was largely symbolic since Ontario had suspended orders of US beer in April pending resolution of the dispute (*Journal of Commerce*, 27 July 1992, 1A).

On 5 August 1993 the United States and Canada signed a memorandum of understanding (MOU) intended to resolve the dispute. It was reported that following a meeting between President Clinton and Canadian Prime Minister Kim Campbell "U.S. negotiators dropped their opposition to Ontario's environmental levy, and began work to conclude the deal on the basis of a mid-June offer by Ontario to cut its minimum price, lower service charges, and open access for U.S. beers in the (Ontario brewers' retail) outlets." It was reported that Stroh "strongly supports" the settlement, but Heileman said it did little to break down the major barriers to US beer sales. Anheuser-Busch said it would oppose a deal that failed to eliminate the environmental levy (*Inside U.S. Trade*, 6 August 1993, 1, 18–19).

Serious problems arose only a few months into the agreement. Deputy USTR Rufus Yerxa warned Canada in November 1993 that Quebec's decision to establish a minimum price for beer would be "justifiable grounds" for terminating the MOU. In December, Heileman, Stroh, and Anheuser-Busch asked the United States to block imports of Canadian beer in response to continued foul play by all but one Canadian province (Alberta) (*Journal of Commerce*, 7 January 1994, 3A). In February 1994 USTR Kantor once again threatened to terminate the MOU and revive the sanctions against Canadian beer exports (the sanctions had been lifted following the signing of the MOU in August 1993). Quebec's minimum price for beer was reportedly the main point of contention in consultations taking place between the two countries (*Inside U.S. Trade*, 4 February 1994, 4–5).

In early March the United States was reported to be on the verge of terminating the agreement. Adding to the dispute over Quebec's minimum pricing policy was the recent decision by Quebec to deny Stroh permission to arrange for its own warehousing (*Journal of Commerce*, 8 March 1994, 1). In April, however, Quebec granted a warehousing license to Stroh, allowing it to market its beer by the summer. US and Canadian negotiators agreed to attach an annex to the MOU codifying the warehousing deal, and USTR decided not to terminate the MOU even though the two sides could not agree on how to deal with the minimum price provisions in British Columbia and Quebec. Negotiators agreed to continue discussions on that issue (*Inside U.S. Trade*, 15 April 1994, 1; 6 May 1994, 3).

Assessment. Given the continuing disagreements over implementation, this case is judged to have resulted in only nominal agreement.

Case 301-81

See case 301-54.

Case 301-82

Complaint. In November 1990 the International Intellectual Property Alliance (IIPA), the Motion Picture Export Association of America, Inc.

(MPEAA), and the Recording Industry Association of America (RIAA) filed a petition alleging that the government of Thailand inadequately enforced copyright laws. The petitioners estimated the losses as a result of piracy as between $70 million and $100 million annually. On 26 April 1991 USTR named Thailand as a "priority country" under the special 301 provisions of the 1988 Trade Act for its failure to adequately protect copyrights and pharmaceutical patents (see case 301-84, below).

GATT role.   Not applicable.

Outcome.   In June, Thailand adopted a new trademark law intended to reduce counterfeiting. A few days before the investigation deadline in December, USTR Hills determined that Thailand's failure to protect intellectual property was "unreasonable" and a burden on US commerce, but she decided to delay retaliation and terminated the investigation as a result of "recent action and commitments by the Thai government to improve and strengthen copyright laws and enforcement." USTR cited increased numbers of police raids on illegal copying establishments and stepped-up prosecution of alleged pirates. However, USTR Hills said she would monitor follow-through on the promises made and review her decision in April, imposing retaliation at that time if necessary. Thai elections were scheduled for March, and the US government reportedly did not want to disrupt that process (*Journal of Commerce,* 12 December 1991, 10A; 19 December 1991, 3A).

Assessment.   Thailand was renamed a priority foreign country in both 1992 and 1993. In April 1993 it was reported that Thailand was cracking down on vendors of pirate video tapes in order to avert US sanctions (*Journal of Commerce,* 7 April 1993, 5A). A major sticking point in negotiations was reportedly the failure of Thai courts to punish copyright pirates. The IIPA reportedly threatened to petition for Thailand's complete removal from the GSP program by June 1 due to its "abject failure" to stop copyright piracy (*Inside U.S. Trade,* 9 April 1993, 6).

On 30 April 1993 Thailand was named a priority foreign country (PFC). On 6 May the two countries announced they had reached an agreement laying out measures that Thailand would take by 31 July. Thailand would introduce legislation to amend its copyright law and establish a special court for IPR violations (*Inside U.S. Trade,* 7 May 1993, 21). In 1994 Thailand was not redesignated as a PFC but was put on the priority watch list. The 1994 National Trade Estimates Report criticized Thailand's copyright laws and regulations as inadequate but praised increased enforcement activities in 1993 and the Thais' stated intention to bring their copyright regime in conformity with international standards.

Given the persistent problems in getting agreements implemented, this case must be considered no better than a nominal success.

Case 301-83

See entry for case 301-60.

Case 301-84

In January 1991 the Pharmaceutical Manufacturers Association (PMA) filed a petition complaining that the government of Thailand did not provide adequate patent protection for pharmaceutical products. The petitioner estimated that overall lost sales in Thailand by "US-based" PMA members were between $16 million and $24 million annually. On 26 April 1991 USTR named Thailand as a priority foreign country under the special 301 provisions of the 1988 Trade Act for its lack of protection of pharmaceutical patent rights.

In January 1989 the United States had announced that, effective 1 July, it was revoking duty-free status under the Generalized System of Preferences for a number of Thai exports because of inadequate patent and copyright protection for pharmaceuticals and computer software, respectively. In announcing the decision, outgoing USTR Clayton Yeutter stated that in his view, Thailand should be named a priority country under the provisions of the trade act that spring if there were not "significant changes" in Thailand's policies before then. No countries were named as special 301 priority countries in either 1989 or 1990. However, Thailand was placed on the priority watch list released by USTR Hills in 1989.

GATT role. Not applicable.

Outcome. On 27 February 1992 the Thai legislative assembly passed a bill providing patent coverage for pharmaceuticals, food and drinks, biotechnology, and agricultural machinery. Thai officials said the legislation was designed to comply with the draft GATT-negotiated intellectual property accord in the interest of strengthening international rules and reducing US pressure. Critics claimed the law conceded too much to the United States and should have included a four-year grace period before extending patent coverage to pharmaceuticals. They argued that the concessions would encourage the United States to press for more unilaterally instead of going through the GATT (*Journal of Commerce*, 4 March 1992, 3A).

On 15 March 1992 USTR Hills announced her determination that Thailand's "acts, policies and practices related to patent protection are unreasonable and burden or restrict U.S. commerce," but she deferred action until 11 October, when a new Thai government was expected to be in place following March elections. Hills said the amendments to Thailand's patent law passed by the legislative assembly in February were inadequate because they did not provide pipeline protection and because of authority granted to a newly created Thai Pharmaceutical Board relating to compulsory licensing and monitoring of pricing of pharmaceuticals. The PMA released a statement the same day praising Hills's decision and expressing its deep dissatisfaction with the amendments to Thailand's patent law; PMA President Gerald Mossinghoff called the amendments unacceptable.

On 9 October 1992 the determination against Thailand was reiterated, but action was again postponed because of political instability, which had necessitated a second round of elections in September, with a new government installed only on 1 October. Hills said she had instructed USTR negotiators to meet with the new government and warned that "if negotiations are not successful, I am prepared to take action under our trade laws, including withdrawal of GSP benefits" (USTR, press release, 9 October 1992).

Thailand was redesignated as a priority foreign country under special 301 in both 1992 and 1993. In April 1993 it was reported that US negotiators seemed satisfied with a proposed safety monitoring procedure that would prevent pirated pharmaceuticals from being produced and sold in Thailand. (*Inside U.S. Trade*, 9 April 1993, 6). On 6 May USTR Kantor and Thailand's Minister of Commerce, Uthai Pimchaichon, reached an understanding on steps Thailand would take to protect intellectual property. Thailand would have until 31 July to demonstrate that adequate legislative and enforcement measures were being taken (*International Trade Reporter*, 12 May 1993, 794). In 1994 Thailand was moved to the priority watch list. The USTR fact sheet on special 301 focused primarily on inadequate copyright protection in explaining the placement of Thailand on the priority list.

Assessment.   Given the persistent problems in getting agreements implemented, this case must be considered no better than a nominal success.

Case 301-85

Complaint.   On 26 April 1991 USTR named India as a priority country under the special 301 for inadequate patent protection for some products and the complete lack of protection for other classes of products, particularly pharmaceuticals. USTR also cited India's inadequate enforcement of copyrights and restricted market access for motion pictures. On 26 May USTR initiated an investigation into these practices.

GATT role.   Not applicable.

Outcome.   On 26 February 1992 USTR Hills announced that India's refusal to extend patent protection to pharmaceuticals was "unreasonable and burdens or restricts U.S. commerce," but she delayed taking action against India saying, "We will continue to urge changes in India's position in bilateral negotiations and in the Uruguay Round and will assess whether trade action is appropriate." Hills praised India's efforts in strengthening its trademark an copyright laws, and its decision to eliminate its import quota on motion pictures and to otherwise liberalize its motion picture and video market.

On 29 April, however, Hills again designated India as a priority country under the special 301 provisions for its refusal to extend patent protection to pharmaceuticals, and she suspended GSP eligibility for imports of pharmaceutical products from India, worth about $60 million in 1991 (*International Trade Reporter*, 15 July 1992, 1223). An official of the Indian Communist Party accused the United States of "intellectual hooliganism," and some members of parliament called on the government to retaliate against the US action by cancelling joint exercises with the US Navy scheduled for the summer (*Journal of Commerce*, 1 May 1992, 5A). India reportedly wanted to keep discussions on intellectual property protection at the multilateral level, while the United States wanted to pursue negotiations bilaterally as well as multilaterally.

Assessment. Given that India was designated as a priority country in both 1993 and 1994 because of its refusal to extend patent protection to pharmaceuticals, this case must be judged a failure.

Case 301-86

Complaint. USTR named the People's Republic of China a priority country under special 301 for its complete lack of patent protection for pharmaceuticals and agrichemicals, and lack of copyright protection for US works. USTR claimed that "piracy of all forms of intellectual property is widespread in China, accounting for significant losses to U.S. industries." On 26 May, as mandated by the special 301 provision, USTR initiated an investigation into the practices.

GATT role. Not applicable.

Outcome. On 26 November 1991 the USTR announced that US and Chinese negotiators had been unable to reach agreement by the deadline but that the investigation was being extended because of the complexity of the issues involved. The following week, USTR published in the *Federal Register* a proposed determination that China's practices were unreasonable and burdened or restricted US commerce and proposed a retaliation "hit list" of products accounting for approximately $1.5 billion in Chinese exports to the United States. USTR noted that "to the extent possible, items on the list have been selected with a focus on the Chinese government-run and -owned state sector. Major items on the list include women's or girls' silk blouses, rubber and plastic footwear, leather luggage, and radio and tape players."

On 16 December USTR announced that it would decide what action to take against China no later than 16 January 1992 if no agreement was reached by that time. Public hearings on the proposed retaliation list covering about $1 billion in Chinese exports were held 6–7 January with the intent of paring the list to about $300 million. On 7 January China threatened to impose counterretaliatory tariffs on 25 percent of its imports from the United States, including aircraft, cotton, corn, steel, and chemicals, if the United States went ahead with its planned retaliation (*Journal of Commerce*, 8 January 1992, 1A).

At the deadline, US and Chinese negotiators announced they had reached an agreement satisfactory to both sides. While China agreed to accede to the Berne and Geneva conventions, thus strengthening and codifying its copyright protection for all countries, and agreed to extend copyright protection for software on an MFN basis, it refused to extend patent protection to any country other than the United States. The memorandum of understanding (MOU) also apparently provided copyright protection only for US works during the interim period until China's accession to the Berne and Geneva conventions became effective. The case was terminated 16 January 1992.

China's legislature approved accession to the Berne and Geneva conventions at the end of June; the accession should become effective by 15 October as pledged in the MOU (*International Trade Reporter*, 8 July 1992, 1177).

In July the European Community negotiated an agreement with China extending patent protection to its firms, and in August the Japanese did the same (*Journal of Commerce*, 1 September 1992, 3A). The legislature approved the revised patent law on 4 September, to become effective 1 January 1993. The director of the Chinese Patent Office said the revised law "basically accords to relevant international standards" though conceding it met only "the lowest level required by international standards." A Western analyst characterized the revisions as fulfilling "for the most part" commitments in the MOU with the United States. Two areas covered in the MOU were not included the legislative revisions but were expected to be covered in implementing regulations due to be written by the January 1993 effective date: conditions for compulsory licensing; and retroactive protection for US patents for products not marketed in China between 1986 and 1993 (*International Trade Reporter*, 16 September 1992, 1609).

Assessment. US industry, though pleased with the Chinese agreement, has not been satisfied with the implementation. Also, the agreement was discriminatory in parts and thus was not supportive of the international trading system, though the European Community and Japan have subsequently negotiated separate agreements of their own.

In January 1994 Treasury Secretary Bentsen and USTR Kantor accused China of failing to comply with the MOU. Kantor "emphasized that the U.S. is particularly upset that 26 factories in China are producing pirated compact discs. The CDs are being exported to other markets, including Canada, which is 'really hurting us,' he said." According to an industry source, the main problem is that China's copyright law does not make piracy a criminal offense (*Inside U.S. Trade,* 28 January 1994, 16).

At the end of April, USTR decided to delay for 60 days a decision identifying China (along with Argentina and India) as a priority country under special 301. The decision was driven by a desire not to complicate the president's upcoming decision on whether to renew China's MFN status given the lack of progress on human rights in that country (*Journal of Commerce,* 22 April 1994, 1A). At the end of June, however, Kantor designated China a priority country, charging that lax enforcement of IPR laws was costing US firms $480 million annually (*International Trade Reporter* 6 July 1994, 1066).

Again, despite progress in terms of getting better nominal legal protection for intellectual property, the agreement failed in spurring meaningful enforcement, and the case must be judged a failure.

Case 301-87

Section 301 again was used for administrative purposes to "withhold or extend liquidation of entries of imports of softwood lumber products originating in certain provinces and territories of Canada," pending completion of the countervailing duty investigation the Commerce Department initiated. The action followed Canada's decision to unilaterally terminate the memorandum of understanding that had resolved a US countervailing duty case against Canada in 1986 (see case 301-58).

Case 301-88

Complaint. On 10 October 1991 USTR initiated an investigation into a number of Chinese practices affecting US exports, including quantitative restrictions (QRs), import licensing requirements, technical barriers to trade, and lack of transparency of laws and regulations pertaining to restrictions on imports. USTR emphasized that the barriers selected were significant and appeared to violate multilateral rules and principles that would apply if China were a member of GATT. USTR also said it would continue to consult with China over reductions in very high tariffs on some products. The investigation was in response to China's failure to make firm commitments to "take substantial measures to remove trade barriers" in negotiations held in August.

GATT role. Not applicable.

Outcome. Although some progress reportedly was made in the negotiations on the transparency of Chinese trade regulations, the Chinese refused to discuss specific timetables for phasing out their QRs and other trade restrictions, arguing they were necessary as infant industry protection. On 21 August 1992 USTR released a list of $3.9 billion worth of Chinese exports that might be subjected to retaliatory tariffs, with footwear, silk apparel, leather goods, minerals, industrial hardware, and electronics products leading the list. Hearings were scheduled for 23–25 September (*Inside U.S. Trade*, 28 August 1992, 1).

On 9 September 1992, a few days after President Bush announced his decision to sell advanced jet fighters to Taiwan (reversing a decade-old policy banning such sales), China threatened to counterretaliate against $4 billion worth of US exports if the United States carried through on its threat in the 301 case. Chinese officials said their hit list would include aircraft, computers, chemicals, wood products, and cotton (*Journal of Commerce*, 10 September 1992, 1A). The following day, an unidentified "official in charge of agriculture" directly linked Chinese imports of American wheat to Bush's decision to sell F-16s to Taiwan (*Journal of Commerce*, 15 September 1992, 3A). In response, Senator Robert Dole (R-KS) warned that any move by China affecting US wheat exports would undermine support in the US Senate for the president's veto of legislation withdrawing or placing conditions on China's MFN status (*Inside U.S. Trade*, 25 September 1992, 16).

At the deadline, USTR announced agreement on a sweeping package of liberalization measures by China, including publication of all "laws, regulations, policies, and guidance" regarding trade; elimination of most quantitative restrictions within two years and on some products, including telecommunications equipment, by the end of 1992; immediate elimination of the import substitution policy prohibiting imports of products made in China; reductions in some tariffs; and agreement to resolve problems involving phytosanitary and other technical standards. USTR negotiator Michael Moskow predicted the agreement would mean "hundreds of millions of dollars" in additional US exports annually in the short run, increasing to billions of dollars in increased exports once the agreement was fully implemented (USTR, press release and fact sheet, 10 October 1992; *Journal of Commerce*, 13 October 1992, 3A). In addition to terminating the investigation immediately, the United States also promised to "staunchly support China's achievement of contracting party status to the GATT...."

On 12 March 1993 a senior US trade official said the administration was concerned with "possible non-implementation or even backsliding" on market access pledges (*International Trade Reporter*, 17 March 1993, 476). On 25 October Deputy US Trade Representative Charlene Barshefsky set a deadline of 31 December for Chinese compliance with the memorandum of understanding. Issues of concern included publication of trade regulations, standardization of agricultural testing, and liberalization of quota and licensing restrictions. Barshefsky did not specify what action would be taken if the deadline were not met. Barshefsky's statement followed a 20 October charge by USTR Kantor that the Chinese were failing to live up to the terms of the MOU (*International Trade Reporter*, 27 October 1993, 1795–96).

On 1 January 1994 China dismantled quotas and import licenses on 283 products and reduced tariffs on 234 products. At the same time, however, China raised import controls on various other products using quotas and compulsory bidding. Some of these products had already been protected by unpublished quotas. International bidding procedures would be required for a list of 171 products to ensure that domestic Chinese products could successfully compete with imports. (*International Trade Reporter*, 5 January 1994, 4).

Assessment.   Though the agreement on paper suggests quite substantial liberalization by China, implementation problems suggest that an assessment in 1994 would be premature.

Case 301-89

Complaint.   On 29 April 1992 USTR Hills announced that Taiwan (along with India and Thailand) had been designated as a priority country under special 301 because of its inadequate copyright protection for computer software, sound recordings, and video games. USTR estimates that piracy of these items cost US producers $370 million in 1991 (*Journal of Commerce*, 1 May 1992, 5A). Earlier in April, a US delegation visited Taiwan to discuss its intellectual property policies. Although Taiwan had promised to crack down on the movie pirates and to amend its export regulations to require proof of a valid copyright for computer and software shipments, the United States rejected the offer as inadequate (*International Trade Reporter*, 15 April 1992, 668).

Within hours of being designated, Taiwan raided several of the establishments showing illegal copies of US movies. Within a few days, Taiwan's legislature began to review legislation to toughen intellectual property laws, and government officials reportedly were looking for ways to acclerate the process (*International Trade Reporter*, 6 May 1992, 799). As negotiations continued into late May, the executive director of the American Chamber of Commerce in Taiwan, Winchell Craig, noted that anti-American sentiment was on the rise in Taiwan and cautioned that it might affect other American firms trying to land contracts under Taiwan's infrastructure expansion and improvement program. He said the ultimate cost might be $300 billion (*Journal of Commerce*, 27 May 1992, 5A).

GATT role.   Not applicable.

Outcome. On 5 June 1992 USTR announced that it had reached an agreement with Taiwan. It terminated the investigation and revoked Taiwan's designation as a priority country. During follow-up discussions on implementation in August, however, US negotiators expressed concern that Taiwan was not "adequately controlling exports of pirated computer software programs and compact disc recordings" and that it had refused to provide a timetable for the implementation of commitments to provide patent protection for pharmaceuticals and agriculture chemicals "in the pipeline" (*Inside U.S. Trade*, 4 September 1992, 7).

In March 1993 US officials indicated that Taiwan's failure to implement the bilateral copyright agreement meant it was failing to meet the terms of the June 1992 MOU. According to reports, the threat of sanctions under special 301 "was implicitly conveyed." At issue was the Taiwanese legislature's refusal to approve the agreement unless eight key provisions were removed. But according to the International Intellectual Property Alliance, removing these provisions would "gut major and critical elements" of the agreement; the provisions addressed parallel imports, protection of preexisting works, and protection for sound recordings. Taiwan's recent announcement of measures to protect pharmaceuticals and agricutural chemicals and improve its export monitoring system was welcomed by US officials, but they stressed that significant problems remained (*Inside U.S. Trade*, 19 March 1993, 4).

On 22 April Taiwan's parliament passed into law the eight provisions and revised local copyright laws to bring them in accord with the agreement. But lawmakers also registered a statement of protest, saying that "out of concern for the damage threatened U.S. 301 retaliatory trade sanctions would have on our domestic industry, we had no choice but to pass these bills. . . . Regarding the U.S.'s unreasonable actions, the legislature believes it has seriously harmed the traditional friendship of the two nations, and this legislature expresses extreme regret about it." The president approved the revisions to the copyright law on 26 April, with regulations to go into effect 28 April (*International Trade Reporter*, 28 April 1993, 701–02).

On 30 April USTR Kantor named Taiwan to the special 301 priority watch list, a step below the priority country designation. Kantor, however, singled Taiwan out for an immediate action plan: "If USTR determines that [Taiwan] does not meet U.S. requirements by July 31, it will reclassify it and decide on further action. According to USTR, Taiwan has committed to implementing improvements by 1 July in its export licensing system for computer software and compact discs. Other areas of concern are cable TV systems, copyright piracy by cable TV stations, video game piracy, and trademark enforcement." Taiwan was reportedly stepping up its intellectual property rights enforcement. On 10 May, 100,000 pirated videos and laser discs were destroyed; statistics released by the Taiwanese government showed a marked increase in the number of illegal videos being seized; and courts were reportedly getting tougher on intellectual property rights violators (*International Trade Reporter*, 12 May 1993, 794).

On 28 December 1993 the Taiwanese legislature passed what were deemed as the most extensive amendments to the country's patent law since its inception in 1949. The amendments bring the law in line with the Trade Related Intellectual Property (TRIPs) provisions of the GATT, adopt the Paris Convention priority system for applying for patents, and establish a patent office and audit board. However, the amendments failed to grant very clear restrictions on parallel imports, which the United States desired. A prominent Taiwanese patent lawyer noted that TRIPs did not address parallel imports (*International Trade Reporter*, 12 January 1994, 50).

Assessment. The proof of the pudding will be in the eating: Will the new laws be enforced by authorities? In 1994 USTR moved Taiwan from the priority watch list to the watch list. There are reports, however, that the increase in piracy and counterfeiting in China is partly due to Taiwanese businessmen moving their operations to the mainland following the Taiwanese government crackdown (*International Trade Reporter*, 11 May 1994, 749; *Wall Street Journal*, 23 March 1994, A14).

Case 301-90

Complaint. On 18 August 1992 P&M Cedar Products, Inc. (P&M) and Hudson ICS filed a petition charging that various Indonesian government practices affecting the export of pencil slats—differential taxes on log and wood product exports, underpricing of government timber stocks, and failure to enforce the terms of timber concession contracts—constituted illegal export subsidies that restricted US exports in third markets.

GATT role. None.

Outcome. On 31 December 1992 USTR terminated the investigation, determining that the Indonesian practices, even if a GATT violation as alleged, had not adversely affected US exports and thus were not actionable under section 301.

Assessment. This case is not judged as a negotiating success or failure since there were no significant unfair practices to be negotiated. It might be deemed a success for global welfare, since public comments in the case opposing action against Indonesia alleged that P&M had had "a virtual monopoly on the world pencil slat market until the recent advent of Jelutong [a tropical timber grown in Indonesia] as a low-cost substitute for cedar." Sources also noted that P&M had "allied itself with the Rainforest Action Network, a conservation group, in boycotts of Jelutong pencils

and in an attempt to restrict the sale of Jelutong products in California''
(*Inside U.S. Trade*, 29 January 1993, 17).

Case 301-91

See chapter 8.

References

Abreu, Marcelo de Paiva. 1993. "Brazil-US Economic Relations and the Enterprise for the Americas Initiative." Washington: Inter-American Development Bank, WP-TWH-31 (March).

Advisory Committee for Trade Policy and Negotiations. 1989. "Analysis of the US-Japan Trade Problem." Washington (February).

Agricultural Technical Advisory Committee on Oilseeds and Products. 1994. *Uruguay Round GATT Agreement, Report of the Agricultural Technical Advisory Committee on Oilseeds and Products, Part I: Comments on All Oilseeds and Products Except Peanuts and Peanut Products.* Submitted to the US Congress (14 January).

Ahearn, Raymond J., Richard Cronin, and Larry Storrs. 1990. *Super 301 Action Against Japan, Brazil and India: Rationale, Reaction and Future Implications.* CRS Report 90-25F. Washington: Congressional Research Service, Library of Congress (26 January).

Ahearn, Raymond J., and Albert Reifman. 1986. "US Trade Policy: Congress Sends a Message!" In R. E. Baldwin and J. D. Richardson, *Current US Trade Policy: Analysis, Agenda and Administration.* National Bureau of Economic Research Conference Report. Cambridge, MA: NBER.

Alston, Julian M., Colin A. Carter, and Lovell Jarvis. 1989. "It May Not Benefit Americans." *Choices,* fourth quarter: 26.

Ames, Glenn C. W. 1990. "US-EC Agricultural Policies and GATT Negotiations." *Agribusiness* 6, no. 4: 283–95.

Anderson, Kym, and Yujiro Hayami, eds. 1986. *The Political Economy of Agricultural Protection: East Asia in International Perspective.* Sydney, London, and Boston: Allen and Unwin.

Anderson, Kym, and Rod Tyers. 1987. "Japan's Agricultural Policy in International Perspective." *Journal of Japanese and International Economies* 1: 31.

Anjaria, S. J. 1987. "Balance of Payments and Related Issues in the Uruguay Round of Trade Negotiations." *World Bank Economic Review* 1, no. 4: 669–88.

Archibald, Jeanne S. 1984. "Section 301 of the Trade Act of 1974." In *Manual for the Practice of International Trade Law.* Washington: Federal Bar Association.

Aronson, Jonathan David, and Peter F. Cowhey. 1988. *When Countries Talk: International Trade in Telecommunications Services.* Cambridge, MA: Ballinger Publishing Company.

Australian Bureau of Agricultural and Resource Economics (ABARE), ed. 1987. *Japanese beef policies: Implications for trade, prices and market shares.* Occasional Paper 102. Canberra: Australian Government Publishing Service.

Australian Bureau of Agricultural and Resource Economics (ABARE), ed. 1988. *Japanese agricultural policies: A time of change.* Policy Monograph No. 3. Canberra: Australian Government Publishing Service.

Balassa, Bela. 1977. *Policy Reform in Developing Countries.* Oxford: Pergamon Press.

Balassa, Bela. 1989. *New Directions in the World Economy.* London: Macmillan.

Balassa, Bela, and Marcus Noland. 1988. *Japan in the World Economy.* Washington: Institute for International Economics.

Balassa, Bela, Gerardo M. Bueno, Pedro-Pablo Kuczynski, Mario Henrique Simonsen. 1986. *Toward Renewed Economic Growth in Latin America.* Washington: Institute for International Economics.

Banks, Gary. 1990. "Transparency, Surveillance and the GATT System." Unpublished paper. Canberra: Australian Industry Commission (May).

Barfield, Claude. 1989. "Services, Intellectual Property and the Major Issues of the Uruguay Round." *Georgia Journal of International and Comparative Law* 19, no. 2: 307–12.

Bayard, Thomas O., and Kimberly Ann Elliott. 1992. " 'Aggressive Unilateralism' and Section 301: Market Opening or Market Closing?" *World Economy* 15, no. 6 (November).

Bello, Judith H., and Alan Holmer. 1989. "Special 301: Its Requirements, Implementation and Significance." *Fordham International Law Journal* 13: 259–75.

Bello, Judith H., and Alan F. Holmer. 1990. "The Heart of the 1988 Trade Act: A Legislative History of the Amendments to Section 301." In Jagdish Bhagwati and Hugh T. Patrick, *Aggressive Unilateralism: America's 301 Trade Policy and the World Trading System.* Ann Arbor: University of Michigan Press.

Bello, Judith H., and Alan F. Holmer. 1992. "GATT Dispute Settlement Agreement: Internationalization or Elimination of Section 301?" *The International Lawyer* 26 (Fall): 795–802.

Bergsten, C. Fred. 1983. "Comment." *Industrial Change and Public Policy.* Kansas City: Federal Reserve Bank of Kansas City.

Bergsten, C. Fred. 1988. *America in the World Economy.* Washington: Institute for International Economics.

Bergsten, C. Fred, and William R. Cline. 1987. *The United States–Japan Economic Problem.* Washington: Institute for International Economics.

Bergsten, C. Fred, and Marcus Noland. 1993. *Reconcilable Differences? United States–Japan Economic Conflict.* Washington: Institute for International Economics.

Bergsten, C. Fred, and Edward M. Graham. 1994. *The Globalization of Industry.* Washington: Institute for International Economics. Forthcoming.

Bhagwati, Jagdish. 1978. *Anatomy and Consequences of Exchange Control.* Cambridge, MA: Ballinger Publishing Co.

Bhagwati, Jagdish. 1990. "Aggressive Unilateralism: An Overview." In Bhagwati and Patrick, *Aggressive Unilateralism: America's 301 Trade Policy and the World Trading System.* Ann Arbor: University of Michigan Press.

Bhagwati, Jagdish. 1993. "The Diminished Giant Syndrome." *Foreign Affairs* 72, no. 2 (Spring): 22–26.

Bhagwati, Jagdish. 1994. "Fair Trade, Reciprocity and Harmonization: The New Challenge to the Theory and Policy of Free Trade." In A. V. Deardoff and R. M. Stern, *Analytical and Negotiating Issues in the Global Trading System.* Ann Arbor: University of Michigan Press.

Bhagwati, Jagdish, and Douglas A. Irwin. 1987. "The Return of the Reciprocitarians: US Trade Policy Today." *The World Economy* 10 (June): 109–30.

Bhagwati, Jagdish, and Hugh Patrick, eds. 1990. *Aggressive Unilateralism: America's 301 Trade Policy and the World Trading System.* Ann Arbor: University of Michigan Press.

Bickerton, Thomas W., and Joseph W. Glauber. 1990. *World Oilseed Markets—Government Intervention and Multilateral Policy Reform.* Washington: US Department of Agriculture.

Bolling, H. Christine. 1992. *The Japanese Presence in US Agribusiness.* Washington: US Department of Agriculture, Economic Research Service.

Borden, William. 1984. *The Pacific Alliance: United States Foreign Policy and Japanese Trade Recovery, 1947–1955.* Madison: University of Wisconsin Press.

Bradley, Jane. 1987. "Intellectual Property Rights Investment and Trade in Services in the Uruguay Round: Laying the Foundations." *Stanford Journal of International Law* 23 (Spring): 57–98.

Bradley, Jane. 1989. "The Section 301 Process Under the New Trade Law." *East Asian Executive Reports* (February). Based on 1988 speech at a Practicing Law Institute conference on the New Trade Law, New York.

Butler, Nicholas. 1983. "The Ploughshares War between Europe and America." *Foreign Affairs* 62 (Fall): 105–22.

Calder, Kent. 1988. *Crisis and Compensation.* Princeton: Princeton University Press.

Caplan, Lois. 1993. "The 1988 Beef and Citrus Agreement: Impact on US Exports." In *International Agriculture and Trade Reports: Asia and Pacific Rim.* Washington: US Department of Agriculture Economic Research Service (September).

Caves, Richard E., and Ronald W. Jones. 1977. *World Trade and Payments.* Rev. ed. Boston: Little, Brown and Company.

Chayes, Abram, and Antonia H. Chayes. 1993. "On Compliance." *International Organization* 47, no. 2 (Spring): 175–205.

Cho Soon. 1994. *The Dynamics of Korean Economic Development.* Washington: Institute for International Economics.

Cline, William R. 1982. *"Reciprocity": A New Approach to World Trade Policy?* POLICY ANALYSES IN INTERNATIONAL ECONOMICS 2. Washington: Institute for International Economics.

Cline, William R. 1987. *Informatics and Development.* Washington: Economics International, Inc.

Cline, William R. 1994. *International Debt Reexamined.* Washington: Institute for International Economics. Forthcoming.

Colchester, Nicholas, and David Buchan. 1990. *Europe Relaunched.* London: The Economist Books.

Commission of the European Communities. 1985. *Completing the Internal Market.* Luxembourg: Office for Official Publications of the European Communities (June).

Competitiveness Policy Council. 1992. *Building a Competitive America: First Annual Report to the President and Congress.* Washington: US Government Printing Office (March).

Cooke, Peter. 1989. "Recent Developments in the Prudential Regulation of Banks and the Evolution of International Banking Supervision." Remarks at the Joint Universities Conference on Regulating Commercial Banks, Canberra, Australia (1–2 August).

Council for Economic Planning and Development, Taiwan. 1989. *Detailed Action Plan for Strengthening Economic and Trade Ties with the United States.* Taipei (March).

Coyle, William, and Dyck, John. 1989. "It Will Benefit American Agriculture." *Choices,* fourth quarter: 27.

Cray Research, Inc. 1990. "The Japanese Public Sector: Problems and Prospects for US Supercomputer Vendors." Minneapolis, May.

Dasgupta, P. and Joseph Stiglitz. 1980. "Uncertainty, Industrial Structure and the Speed of R&D." *Bell Journal of Economics* (Spring): 1–28.

Davis, Theodore H. 1991. "Combatting Piracy of Intellectual Property in International Markets: A Proposed Modification of the Special 301 Action." *Vanderbilt Journal of Transnational Law* 24, no. 3: 505–33.

Deardorff, Alan V. 1990. "Should Patent Protection Be Extended to All Developing Countries?" *The World Economy* 13 (December): 497–507.

Deardorff, Alan V. 1992. "Welfare Effects of Global Patent Protection." *Economica* 59 (February): 35–51.

Desai, Ashok V. 1989a. "The Politics of India's Trade Policy." In Henry R. Nau, *Domestic Trade Politics and the Uruguay Round.* New York: Columbia University Press.

Desai, Ashok V. 1989b. "India in the Uruguay Round." *Journal of World Trade* 26 (December): 33–58.

Destler, I. M. 1989. "United States Trade Policymaking in the Uruguay Round." In Henry R. Nau, *Domestic Trade Politics and the Uruguay Round*. New York: Columbia University Press.

Destler, I. M. 1992. *American Trade Politics*. Rev. ed. Washington: Institute for International Economics.

Destler, I. M., and C. Randall Henning. 1989. *Dollar Politics: Exchange Rate Policymaking in the United States*. Washington: Institute for International Economics.

Destler, I. M., and John Odell. 1987. *Anti-Protection: Changing Forces in United States Trade Politics*. Washington: Institute for International Economics.

Destler, I. M., and Hideo Sato, eds. 1983. *Coping with US-Japan Conflicts*. Lexington, MA: Lexington Books, D. C. Heath and Co.

Diwan, Ishac, and Dani Rodrik. 1991. "Patents, Appropriability and North-South Trade." *Journal of International Economics* 30 (February): 1–27.

Dixit, Avinash. 1986. "Trade Policy: An Agenda for Research." In Paul R. Krugman, *Strategic Trade Policy and the New International Economics*. Cambridge, MA: MIT Press.

Dixit, Avinash. 1987. "How Should the United States Respond to Other Countries' Trade Policies?" In Robert Stern, *US Trade Policies in a Changing World Economy*. Cambridge, MA: MIT Press.

Dyck, John, Shwu-Eng Webb, and Felix Spinelli. 1993. "Livestock Markets Flourish, Benefitting US Agriculture." In *International Agriculture and Trade Reports: Asia and Pacific Rim*. US Department of Agriculture Economic Research Service (September).

Economic Planning Board, Korea. 1989. *Korea-U.S. Economic Relationship—Issues and Prospects*. Seoul (November).

Eglin, Richard. 1987. "Surveillance of Balance of Payments Measures in the GATT." *The World Economy* 10, no. 1 (March): 1–26.

Elliott, Kimberly Ann, and Peter P. Uimonen. 1993. "The effectiveness of economic sanctions with application to the case of Iraq." *Japan and the World Economy* 5: 403–09.

Elwell, Craig, and Alfred Reifman. 1994. "U.S.-Japan Trade Confrontation: Economic Perspective and Policy Options." CRS Report 94-526E. Washington: Congressional Research Service, Library of Congress.

Ethier, Wilfred. 1979. "Internationally Decreasing Costs and World Trade." *Journal of International Economics* 9: 1–24.

Ethier, Wilfred. 1982. "National and International Returns to Scale in the Modern Theory of International Trade." *American Economic Review* 72: 389–405.

Evans, Peter B. 1993. "Building an Integrative Approach to International and Domestic Politics: Reflections and Projections." In Peter B. Evans, Harold K. Jacobson, and Robert D. Putnam, *Double-Edged Diplomacy: International Bargaining and Domestic Politics*. Berkeley: University of California Press.

Evans, Peter B., Harold K. Jacobson, and Robert D. Putnam. 1993. *Double-Edged Diplomacy: International Bargaining and Domestic Politics*. Berkeley: University of California Press.

Fallows, James. 1994. *Looking at the Sun: The Rise of the New East Asian Economic and Political System*. New York: Pantheon.

Farren, J. Michael. 1989. Testimony before the Senate Commerce Committee on the Japanese space industry (4 October).

Feketekuty, Geza. 1990. "US Policy on 301 and Super 301." In Jagdish Bhagwati and Hugh T. Patrick, *Aggressive Unilateralism: America's 301 Trade Policy and the World Trading System*. Ann Arbor: University of Michigan Press.

Finger, J. Michael. 1991. "That Old GATT Magic No More Casts Its Spell (How the Uruguay Round Failed)." *Journal of World Trade* 25 (April): 19–22.

Finger, J. Michael, and Julio Nogues. 1987. "International Control of Subsidies and Countervailing Duties." *World Bank Economic Review* 1, no. 4 (September): 707–25.

Fisher, Bart S., and Ralph G. Steinhardt III. 1982. "Section 301 of the Trade Act of 1974: Protection for U.S. Exporters of Goods, Services, and Capital." *Law and Policy in International Business* 14, no. 3: 569–690.

Fitchett, Delbert A. 1988. *Agricultural Trade Protectionism in Japan: A Survey.* World Bank Discussion Paper No. 28. Washington: World Bank.

Flamm, Kenneth. 1991. "Making New Rules: High-Tech Trade Friction and the Semiconductor Industry." *The Brookings Review* (Spring): 22–29.

Frank, Isaiah. 1987. *The GATT, Quantitative Restrictions and the Balance of Payments.* Development Policy Issues Series, Report No. VPERS 10. Washington: World Bank (March).

Frankel, Jeffrey A. 1984. *The Yen/Dollar Agreement: Liberalizing Japanese Capital Markets.* POLICY ANALYSES IN INTERNATIONAL ECONOMICS 9. Washington: Institute for International Economics.

Franklin, Michael. 1988. *Rich Man's Farming: The Crisis in Agriculture.* London and New York: Royal Institute for International Affairs/Routledge (Chatham House Papers).

Fritsch, Winston, and Gustavo Franco. 1991a. "Brazil and the World Economy in the 1990s." In Fritsch, *Latin America's Integration into the World Economy.* Forthcoming.

Fritsch, Winston, and Gustavo Franco. 1991b. *Foreign Direct Investment in Brazil.* Paris: Organization for Economic Cooperation and Development.

Funabashi, Yoichi. 1986. "Kome kuronikuru" (Rice chronicles). *Sekai* (November): 282–305.

Funabashi, Yoichi. 1989. *Managing the Dollar: From the Plaza to the Louvre.* 2d ed. Washington: Institute for International Economics.

Gadbaw, R. Michael, and Timothy J. Richard, eds. 1988. *Intellectual Property Rights: Global Consensus, Global Conflict?* Boulder, CO: Westview Press.

General Accounting Office (GAO). 1982. *International Insurance Trade—U.S. Market Open: Impact of Foreign Barriers Unknown.* ID-82-39. Washington, 23 August.

General Accounting Office (GAO). 1987. *Combating Unfair Foreign Trade Practices.* NSIAD-87-100. Washington (March).

General Accounting Office (GAO). 1988. *US-Japan Trade: Evaluation of the Market-Oriented Sector-Specific Talks.* NSIAD-88-205. Washington (July).

General Accounting Office (GAO). 1991. *High Performance Computing: Industry Uses of Supercomputers and High-Speed Networks.* IMTEC-91-58. Washington (July).

General Accounting Office (GAO). 1993. *Agricultural Marketing: Export Opportunities for Wood Products in Japan Call for Customer Focus.* RCED-93-137. Washington (May).

General Agreement on Tariffs and Trade (GATT). 1979. "Understanding on Notification, Consultation, Dispute Settlement and Surveillance." Document L/4907, adopted on 28 November 1979, reprinted in GATT, *Basic Instruments and Selected Documents, Twenty-Sixth Supplement* 1980, 210–18.

General Agreement on Tariffs and Trade (GATT). 1988. "Japan—Restrictions on Imports of Certain Agricultural Products." Document L/6253, reprinted in GATT, *Basic Instruments and Selected Documents, Thirty-Fifth Supplement* 1989, 163–245. Also reprinted in *International Legal Materials* 27:1539 (November 1988).

General Agreement on Tariffs and Trade (GATT). 1992. "Follow-up on the Panel Report 'European Economic Community–Payments and Subsidies Paid to Processors and Producers of Oilseeds and Related Animal-Feed Proteins.' " DS28/R, 31. Geneva (March).

General Agreement on Tariffs and Trade (GATT). 1993a. *Trade Policy Review of Brazil.* Geneva (March).

General Agreement on Tariffs and Trade (GATT). 1993b. *Final Act Embodying the Results of the Uruguay Round of Multilateral Trade Negotiations.* MTN/FA; UR-93-0246. Geneva (15 December).

General Agreement on Tariffs and Trade (GATT). 1994a. *Analytical Index: Guide to GATT Law and Practice.* 6th ed. Geneva.

General Agreement on Tariffs and Trade (GATT). 1994b. "Increases in Market Access Resulting from the Uruguay Round." Geneva: Information and Media Relations Division (12 April).

George, Aurelia. 1986. "The politics of agricultural protection in Japan." In Kym Anderson and Yujiro Hayami, *The Political Economy of Agricultural Protection: East Asia in International Perspective.* Sydney, London, and Boston: Allen and Unwin.

Gold, Peter L., and Dick K. Nanto. 1991. *Japan-US Trade: US Exports of Negotiated Products, 1985–90."* CRS Report 91-891E. Washington: Congressional Research Service, Library of Congress (26 November).

Golub, Stephen S. 1994. *The United States–Japan Current Account Imbalance: A Review.* IMF Paper on Policy Analysis and Assessment 94/8 (March).

Graham, Edward M. 1993. "Liberalizing of Policies Affecting Inward FDI into Korea." Unpublished paper. Washington: Institute for International Economics.

Graham, Edward M., and Paul Krugman. 1991. *Foreign Direct Investment in the United States.* Rev. ed. Washington: Institute for International Economics.

Graham, Edward M., and J. David Richardson. N.d. *Global Competition Policy.* Washington: Institute for International Economics. Forthcoming.

Greaney, Theresa M. 1993. "Import Now! An Analysis of Voluntary Import Expansions to Increase US Market Shares in Japan." Unpublished working paper. University of Michigan, Department of Economics (November).

Grier, Jean Heilman. 1992. "The Use of Section 301 to Open Japanese Markets to Foreign Firms." *North Carolina Journal of International Law* 17: 1–44.

Haggard, Stephan. 1988. "Policy Challenges for Newly Industrializing Asia." In *East Asia: Challenges for U.S. Economic and Security Interests in the 1990's.* Committee Print No. 100-40. Washington: Committee on Ways and Means, US House of Representatives (26 September).

Haggard, Stephan. 1990. *Pathways from the Periphery: The Politics of Growth in the Newly Industrializing Countries.* Ithaca, NY: Cornell University Press.

Haley, John O. 1986. "Administrative Guidance versus Formal Regulation: Resolving the Paradox of Industrial Policy." In Saxonhouse and Yamamura, *Law and Trade Issues of the Japanese Economy.* Seattle: University of Washington Press.

Hartmann, Monika. 1991. "Old Wine in New Bottles: Agricultural Protectionism in the EC." *Intereconomics* (March/April): 58–63.

Hathaway, Dale. 1987. *Agriculture and the GATT: Rewriting the Rules.* POLICY ANALYSES IN INTERNATIONAL ECONOMICS 20. Washington: Institute for International Economics.

Hathaway, Dale. 1990. "Agriculture." In Jeffrey J. Schott, *Completing the Uruguay Round.* Washington: Institute for International Economics.

Hayami, Yujiro. 1987. *Japanese Agriculture Under Siege: The Political Economy of Agricultural Policies.* New York: St. Martin's Press.

Helpman, Elhanan. 1993. "Innovation, Imitation and Intellectual Property Rights." *Econometrica* 61 (November): 1247–80.

Hemmi, Kenzo. 1982. "Agriculture and Politics in Japan." In Emery N. Castle and Kenzo Hemmi, *US-Japan Agricultural Trade Relations.* Washington: Resources for the Future.

Hillman, Jimmye. 1983. "U.S. and EC Agricultural Trade Policies: Confrontation or Negotiation?" *Intereconomics* (March/April): 72–77.

Hillman, Jimmye S., and Robert A. Rothenberg. 1988. *Agricultural Trade and Protection in Japan.* London: Gower Publishing Company for the Trade Policy Research Centre.

Hills, Carla. 1989. Statement before the House of Representatives, Committee on Ways and Means, Subcommittee on Trade. Washington (8 June).

Hindley, Brian. 1987. "Different and More Favorable Treatment—and Graduation." In J. M. Finger and A. Olechowski, *The Uruguay Round: A Handbook for the Multilateral Trade Negotiations.* Washington: World Bank.

Houpt, James V. 1986. *International Trends for US Banks and Banking Markets.* Board of Governors of the Federal Reserve System Staff Study No. 156 (May).

Hudec, Robert E. 1975. "Retaliation Against Unreasonable Foreign Trade Practices: The New Section 301 and GATT Nullification and Impairment." *Minnesota Law Review* 59: 461–539.

Hudec, Robert E. 1987. *Developing Countries in the GATT Trading System*. Aldershot: Gower Publishing Company for the Trade Policy Research Centre.

Hudec, Robert E. 1988. "Legal Issues in US Trade Policy." In Robert E. Baldwin, Carl B. Hamilton, and André Sapir, *Issues in US-EC Trade Relations*. Chicago: University of Chicago Press.

Hudec, Robert E. 1990a. "Mirror, Mirror on the Wall: The Concept of Fairness in United States Trade Policy." Proceedings of the Canadian Council of International Law, Ottawa, Ontario.

Hudec, Robert E. 1990b. "Thinking About the New Section 301: Beyond Good and Evil." In J. Bhagwati and H. Patrick, *Aggressive Unilateralism*. Ann Arbor: University of Michigan Press.

Hudec, Robert E. 1992. "The Judicialization of GATT Dispute Settlement." In Michael Hart and Debra Steger, *In Whose Interest? Due Process and Transparency in International Trade*. Ottawa: Center for Trade Policy and Law, Carleton University.

Hudec, Robert E. 1993. *Enforcing International Trade Law*. Salem, NH: Butterworth Legal Publishers.

Hudec, Robert E. 1994. "Dispute Settlement." OECD Workshop on the New World Trading System, Paris, 25–26 April.

Hudec, Robert, Daniel Kennedy, and Mark Sgarbossa. 1993. "A Statistical Profile of GATT Dispute Settlement Cases: 1948–1989." *Minnesota Journal of Global Trade 2* (Winter): 1–113.

Hufbauer, Gary Clyde, Diane T. Berliner, and Kimberly Ann Elliott. 1986. *Trade Protection in the United States: 31 Case Studies*. Washington: Institute for International Economics.

Hufbauer, Gary Clyde, and Kimberly Ann Elliott. 1994. *Measuring the Costs of Protection in the United States*. Washington: Institute for International Economics.

Hufbauer, Gary Clyde, Jeffrey J. Schott, and Kimberly Ann Elliott. 1990. *Economic Sanctions Reconsidered*. 2nd ed., rev. Washington: Institute for International Economics.

Iguchi, Tomohito. 1988. "Takeshita hōbei! Sono kyakkō no kage ni sansei suru shōkadai" (Takeshita visits the US! The issues piling up behind the footlights). *Kankai* (March): 104–14.

Imai, Hisao. 1988. "Kokkai no budaiura o nozoku" (Peeping behind the scenes at the Diet). *Kankai* (June): 19–29.

Industrial Bank of Japan. 1990. "Data Relating to the Japanese Bond Market." Unpublished paper (November).

Jackson, John. 1989. *The World Trading System*. Cambridge, MA: MIT Press.

Jackson, John. 1994. Testimony before the Senate Finance Committee, 23 March.

Japanese Ministry of Finance–US Department of the Treasury Working Group. 1984. *Report on Yen/Dollar Exchange Rate Issues*. Washington: US Department of the Treasury (May).

Johnson, D. Gale, ed. 1987. *Agricultural Reform Efforts in the United States and Japan*. New York: New York University Press.

Johnson, Chalmers. 1982. *MITI and the Japanese Economic Miracle: The Growth of Industrial Policy, 1925–1975*. Stanford, CA: Stanford University Press.

Kankai, Japan. 1987. "Shin zoku no kōzu: nōrinsuisansho" [Composition of the *zoku* (new series): Ministry of Agriculture, Forestry and Fisheries]. *Kankai* (September), 112–123.

Kankai, Japan. 1988a. "Kankai jinmyaku chiri: Nōrinsuisansho no maku" (Geography of the bureaucratic network: Ministry of Agriculture, Forestry and Fisheries). *Kankai* (January): 38–48.

Kankai, Japan. 1988b. "Ketsudan serareru! Gyuuniku-orenji jiyuka" (Pressed to resolution! Beef-orange liberalization). *Kankai* (June): 92–98.

Keidanren, Japan. 1988. *Shokuhin Kōgyō Hakusho* (White Paper on the Food Industry). Keidanren Nōsei Mondai Kondankai (Keidanren Agricultural Problems Roundtable), June.

Keizai, Shingikai. 1987. "Policy Recommendations of the Economic Council—Action for Economic Restructuring." Tokyo: Economic Council (14 May).

Key, Sydney J. 1989a. "Mutual Recognition: Integration of the Financial Sector in the European Community." *Federal Reserve Bulletin* (September).

Key, Sydney J. 1989b. *Financial Integration in the European Community*. Board of Governors of the Federal Reserve System International Finance Discussion, Paper No. 349 (April).

Key, Sydney J. 1992. "Is National Treatment Still Viable? US Policy in Theory and Practice." Proceedings of a Conference on World Banking and Securities Markets After 1992. Geneva: International Center for Monetary Affairs.

Key, Sydney J., and Hal S. Scott. 1991. *International Trade in Banking Services: A Conceptual Framework*. Occasional Paper No. 35. Washington: Group of Thirty.

Kim Chulsu. 1990. "Super 301 and the World Trading System: A Korean View." In Jagdish Bhagwati and Hugh T. Patrick, *Aggressive Unilateralism: America's 301 Trade Policy and the World Trading System*. Ann Arbor: University of Michigan Press.

Kim Kihwan, and Chung Hwa Soo. 1989. "Korea's Domestic Trade Politics and the Uruguay Round." In Henry R. Nau, *Domestic Trade Politics and the Uruguay Round*. New York: Columbia University Press.

Kobayashi, Shōichi. 1988. "Orenji to mikan wa kyōgō shinai" (Oranges and mikan do not compete). *Sekai* (November): 301–09.

Kozmetsky, George. 1987. "Supercomputers and National Policy: Maintaining US Preeminence in an Emerging Industry." In J. R. Kirkland and J. H. Poore, *Supercomputers: A Key to US Scientific, Technological, and Industrial Preeminence*. New York: Praeger.

Krauss, Ellis S. 1993. "U.S.-Japan Negotiations on Construction and Semiconductors, 1985–87: Building Friction and Relation-Chips." In Peter Evans, Harold Jacobson, and Robert Putnam, *Double-Edged Diplomacy: International Bargaining and Domestic Politics*. Berkeley: University of California Press.

Krauss, Ellis S., and Simon Reich. 1992. "Ideology, Interests and the American Executive: Toward a Theory of Foreign Competition and Manufacturing Trade Policy." *International Organization* 46, no. 4, (Autumn): 857–97.

Krueger, Anne O. 1974. "The Political Economy of the Rent-Seeking Society." *American Economic Review* 64: 291–303.

Krueger, Anne O. 1978. *Liberalization Attempts and Consequences*. Cambridge, MA: Ballinger Publishing Co.

Krugman, Paul. 1984a. "Import Protection as Export Promotion: International Competition in the Presence of Oligopoly and Economies of Scale." In H. Kierzkowski, *Monopolistic Competition and International Trade*. Oxford: Clarendon Press.

Krugman, Paul. 1984b. *The US Response to Foreign Industrial Targeting*. Brookings Papers on Economic Activity, no. 1: 77–131.

Krugman, Paul, ed. 1986. *Strategic Trade Policy and the New International Economics*. Cambridge, MA: The MIT Press.

Krugman, Paul. 1987a. "Market Access and Competition in High Technology Industries: A Simulation Exercise." In Henry K. Kierzkowski, *Protection and Competition in International Trade*. London: Blackwell.

Krugman, Paul. 1987b. "Strategic Sectors and International Competition." In Robert M. Stern, *US Trade Policies in a Changing World Economy*. Cambridge, MA: MIT Press.

Krugman, Paul. 1991. *Geography and Trade*. Cambridge, MA: MIT Press.

Kupfer, Andrew. 1989. "Smith to Japan: Here's the Beef." *Fortune* (2 January): 53.

Kusano, Atsushi. 1983. *Nichibei Orenji Kōshō* (The Japan-US Orange Negotiations). Tokyo: Nihon Keizai Shimbunsha.

Lardy, Nicholas R. 1994. *China in the World Economy*. Washington: Institute for International Economics.

Lawrence, Robert Z. 1987. *Imports in Japan: Closed Markets or Minds?* Brookings Papers on Economic Activity, no. 2: 517–54.

Lawrence, Robert Z. 1990. "Discussion." In Robert Z. Lawrence and Charles L. Schultze, *An American Trade Strategy: Options for the 1990s*. Washington: Brookings Institution.

Lawrence, Robert Z. 1991a. "How Open Is Japan?" In Paul Krugman, *Trade with Japan: Has the Door Opened Wider?* Chicago: University of Chicago Press.

Lawrence, Robert Z. 1991b. *Efficient or Exclusionist? The Import Behavior of Japanese Corporate Groups.* Brookings Papers on Economic Activity, no. 1: 311–41.

Lawrence, Robert Z. 1993. "Japan's Different Trade Regime: An Analysis with Particular Reference to Keiretsu." *Journal of Economic Perspectives* 7 (Summer): 3–20.

Leutwiler, F., et al. 1985. *Trade Policies for a Better Future.* Geneva: General Agreement on Tariffs and Trade.

Lichtenberg, Frank R. 1992. *R&D Investment and International Productivity Differences.* NBER Working Paper No. 4161. Cambridge, MA: National Bureau of Economic Research.

Logsdon, John M. 1992. "US-Japanese Space Relations at a Crossroads." *Science* 255 (17 January): 294–300.

Long, O., et al. 1989. *Public Scrutiny of Protection: Domestic Policy Transparency and Trade Liberalization.* London: Gower Publishing Company for the Trade Policy Research Centre.

Longworth, John W. 1983. *Beef in Japan: Politics, Production, Marketing and Trade.* St. Lucia, Queensland: University of Queensland Press.

Low, Patrick. 1993. *Trading Free: The GATT and US Trade Policy.* New York: The Twentieth Century Fund Press.

Madison, Christopher. 1983. "If It Can't Beat Europe's Farm Export Subsidies, U.S. May Opt to Join Them." *National Journal* (15 January).

Maki, Hidero. 1987. "Bōeki masatsu kaishō ni tōkaiseisō" (All efforts to resolve trade friction). Interview in *Kankai* (August): 140–47.

Makinson, Larry. 1990. *Open Secrets: The Dollar Power of PACs in the Congress.* Washington: The Congressional Quarterly, Inc.

Mann, Catherine L. 1987. *Protection and Retaliation: Changing the 'Rules of the Game.'* Brookings Papers on Economic Activity, no. 1: 311–48.

Mansfield, Edwin. 1994. *Intellectual Property Protection, Foreign Direct Investment, and Technology Transfer.* Washington: International Finance Corporation Discussion Paper 19 (February).

Maskus, Keith. 1990. "Normative Concerns in the International Protection of Intellectual Property Rights." *The World Economy* (September): 387–409.

Maskus, Keith. 1993. "Intellectual Property Rights and the Uruguay Round." Federal Reserve Bank of Kansas City. *Economic Review* 78, no. 1: 11–25.

Maskus, Keith, and Denise Eby Konan. 1994. "Trade Related Intellectual Property Rights: Issues and Exploratory Results." In Robert Stein and Alan Deardorff, *Analytical and Negotiating Issues in the Global Trading System.* Ann Arbor: University of Michigan Press.

Mastanduno, Michael. 1991. "Do Relative Gains Matter?" *International Security* 16, no. 1 (Summer): 73–113.

Mastanduno, Michael. 1992. "Setting Market Access Priorities: The Use of Super 301 in US Trade with Japan." *The World Economy* 15, no. 6 (November): 729–53.

Mayer, Frederick W. 1992. "Managing domestic differences in international negotiations: the strategic use of internal side-payments." *International Organization* 46, no. 4 (Autumn): 793–818.

McMillan, John. 1990. "Strategic Bargaining and Section 301." In Jagdish Bhagwati and Hugh T. Patrick, *Aggressive Unilateralism: America's 301 Trade Policy and the World Trading System.* Ann Arbor: University of Michigan Press.

McPherson, M. Peter. 1988. "It's Time to Rethink the Role of GATT in Economic Development Strategies." US Department of the Treasury news release. Remarks before the American Enterprise Institute, Washington (14 September).

Mesevage, Thomas. 1991. "The Carrot and the Stick: Protecting US Intellectual Property in Developing Countries." *Rutgers Computer and Technology Law Journal* 17, no. 2: 421–50.

Ministry of Agriculture, Forestry, and Fisheries (MAFF), Japan. 1986. Planning Division, Minister's Secretariat, *Nijuisseiki e mukete no Nōsei no Kihon Hōkō* (Fundamental Direction of Agricultural Policy toward the Twenty-first Century). Tokyo: Sōzō Shōbō.

Ministry of Agriculture, Forestry, and Fisheries (MAFF), Japan. 1987a. "Basic Direction of Agricultural Policy Toward the 21st Century." *Japan's Agricultural Review* 15 (March), published by Japan International Agricultural Council for MAFF.

Ministry of Agriculture, Forestry, and Fisheries (MAFF), Japan. 1987b. Planning Division, Minister's Secretariat, *Zusetsu 21 seiki e no Nosei no Tenkai* (Development of Agricultural Policy for the 21st Century Illustrated). Tokyo: Chikyuusha.

Miyashita, Hiroyuki. 1987. "'Kenshiki aru giin' zukuri o mezasu nyuu nōrinzoku no riidaa" (New leader of the farm *zoku* who aims to make 'Dietmen with insight') (interview with Hata), *Seikai ōrai* (October): 70–81.

Moffett, Jeffrey, and Thomas Waggener. 1992. *The Development of the Japanese Wood Trade: Historical Perspective and Current Trends.* Center for International Trade in Forest Products Working Paper 38. Seattle: University of Washington (March).

Muramatsu, Michio. 1981. *Sengo Nihon no Kanryōsei* (The Bureaucracy in Postwar Japan). Tokyo: Tokyo Keizai Shimposha.

Muramatsu, Michio. 1987. "In Search of National Identity: The Politics and Policies of the Nakasone Administration." In Kenneth Pyle, *The Trade Crisis: How Will Japan Respond?* Seattle: Society for Japanese Studies.

Muramatsu, Michio, and Ellis Krauss. 1984. "Bureaucrats and Politicians in Policymaking: the Case of Japan." *American Political Science Review* 78, no. 1 (March): 126–46.

Muramatsu, Michio, and Ellis Krauss. 1987. "The Conservative Policy Line and the Development of Patterned Pluralism." In Yamamura Kozo and Yasuba Yasukichi, *The Political Economy of Japan: Volume 1: The Domestic Transformation.* Stanford: Stanford University Press.

Nanto, Dick K. 1991. *Unfair Foreign Trade Practices and Extension of Super 301.* CRS Report 91-546E. Washington: Congressional Research Service, Library of Congress (25 June).

National Academy of Sciences. 1992. *The Government Role in Civilian Technology.* Washington: National Academy Press.

Nihon Keizai Shimbunsha. 1983. *Jiminto Seichokai* (LDP Policy Affairs Research Council). Tokyo: Nihon Keizai Shimbunsha.

Nihon Nōgyo Shimbun. 1987. "Pawaa wa batsugun giin shuudan" (Diet groups with unrivaled power). 16 April.

Niskanen, William A. 1988. *Reaganomics: An Insider's Account of the Politics and the People.* New York: Oxford University Press.

Nivola, Pietro S. 1993. *Regulating Unfair Trade.* Washington: Brookings Institution.

Nogues, Julio. 1990. "Patents and Pharmaceutical Drugs: Understanding the Pressures on Developing Countries." *Journal of World Trade* 24, no. 6 (December): 81–103.

Noland, Marcus. 1992a. "Protectionism in Japan." Unpublished working paper. Washington: Institute for International Economics.

Noland, Marcus. 1992b. "Public Policy, Private Preferences, and the Japanese Trade Pattern." Unpublished working paper. Washington: Institute for International Economics.

Odell, John S. 1993. "International Threats and Internal Politics: Brazil, the European Community, and the United States, 1985–87." In Peter Evans, Harold K. Jacobson, and Robert D. Putnam, *Double-Edged Diplomacy: International Bargaining and Domestic Politics.* Berkeley: University of California Press.

Odell, John S., and Anne Dibble. 1988. *Brazilian Informatics and the United States: Defending Infant Industry Versus Opening Foreign Markets.* Pew Case Studies Center Case No. 128. Washington: Institute for the Study of Diplomacy, Georgetown University.

Odell, John S., and Margaret Matzinger-Tchakerian. 1988. *European Community Enlargement and the United States.* Pew Case Studies Center Case No. 130. Washington: Institute for the Study of Diplomacy, Georgetown University.

Office of Technology Assessment. 1991. *Competing Economies: America, Europe and the Pacific Rim.* OTA-ITE-498. Washington: US Government Printing Office (October).

Ohdake, Hideo. 1980. *Gendai Nihon no Seijikenryoku Keizaikenryoku* (Political and Economic Power in Modern Japan). Tokyo: Sanichi Shobo.

Organization for Economic Cooperation and Development (OECD). 1991. *Agricultural Policies, Markets and Trade: Monitoring and Outlook 1991*. Paris: OECD.

Oxley, Alan. 1990. *The Challenge of Free Trade*. New York: St. Martin's Press.

Oye, Kenneth A. 1992. *Economic Discrimination and Political Exchange: World Political Economy in the 1930s and 1980s*. Princeton, NJ: Princeton University Press.

Paarlberg, Robert L. 1986. "Responding to the CAP: Alternative Strategies for the USA." *Food Policy* 11 (May): 157–73.

Perez-Garcia, John. 1991. *An Assessment of the Impacts of Recent Environmental and Trade Restrictions on Timber Harvest and Exports*. Center for International Trade in Forest Products Working Papers 133 (April). Seattle: University of Washington.

Petri, Peter A. 1987. "Japan, Korea, and United States–Korean Trade Relations." In *Managing United States–Korean Trade Conflict*. Committee Print no. 100-24. Washington: Committee on Ways and Means, US House of Representatives (21 September).

Petri, Peter A. 1991. "Japanese Trade in Transition: Hypotheses and Recent Evidence." In Paul Krugman, *Trade with Japan: Has the Door Opened Wider?* Chicago: University of Chicago Press.

Pindyck, R. S., and D. L. Rubinfeld. 1981. *Econometric Models and Economic Forecasts*. New York: McGraw-Hill Book Co.

Porges, Amelia. 1989. Casenote on GATT panel decision on Japanese semiconductor trade measures. *American Journal of International Law* 83: 388.

Porges, Amelia. 1991. "U.S.-Japan Trade Negotiations: Paradigm's Lost." In Paul Krugman, *Trade with Japan: Has the Door Opened Wider?* Chicago: University of Chicago Press.

Prestowitz, Clyde V. 1988. *Trading Places: How We Allowed Japan to Take the Lead*. New York: Basic Books.

Putnam, Robert. 1988. "Diplomacy and Domestic Politics: The Logic of Two-Level Games." *International Organization* 42 (Summer): 427–60.

Putnam, Robert D. 1993. "Diplomacy and Domestic Politics: The Logic of Two-Level Games." In Peter Evans, Harold K. Jacobson, and Robert D. Putnam, *Double-Edged Diplomacy: International Bargaining and Domestic Politics*. Berkeley: University of California Press.

Pyle, Kenneth B., ed. 1987. *The Trade Crisis: How Will Japan Respond?* Seattle: University of Washington, The Society for Japanese Studies.

Reich, Robert B. 1991. *The Work of Nations*. New York: Alfred A. Knopf.

Reich, Michael, Yoshio Endo, and Peter Timmer. 1986. "Agriculture: The Political Economy of Structural Change." In Thomas McCraw, *America versus Japan*. Cambridge, MA: Harvard University Press.

Reichhardt, Tony. 1992. *US Commercial Space Activities*. CRS Report 92-125 SPR. Washington: Congressional Research Service, Library of Congress (1 February).

Richardson, J. David. 1983. "US International Trade Policies in a World of Industrial Change." In Federal Reserve Bank of Kansas City, *Industrial Change and Public Policy*. Kansas City: Federal Reserve Bank of Kansas City.

Richardson, J. David. 1989. "Empirical Research on Trade Liberalization Under Imperfect Competition: A Survey." *OECD Economic Studies*, no. 12 (Spring): 8–50.

Richardson, J. David. 1991. *U.S. Trade Policy in the 1980s: Turns—and Roads Not Taken*. NBER Working Paper No. 3725. Cambridge, MA: National Bureau of Economic Research.

Richardson, J. David. 1993. *Sizing Up US Export Disincentives*. Washington: Institute for International Economics.

Rohrer, Karl A., and Marcia S. Smith. 1989. *Space Commercialization in China and Japan*. CRS Report 89-367 SPR. Washington: Congressional Research Service, Library of Congress (9 June).

Ryan, Michael P. 1990. "Leveling the Playing Field: Settling Pacific Basin Disputes Regarding Unfair East Asian Trade Practices." Ph.D. dissertation, Department of Political Science, University of Michigan.

SaKong, Il. 1993. *Korea in the World Economy*. Washington: Institute for International Economics.

Sato, Hideo, and Timothy Curran. 1982. "Agricultural Trade: The Case of Beef and Citrus." In Destler and Sato, *Coping with US-Japan Conflicts*. Lexington, MA: Lexington Books, D. C. Heath and Co.

Saxonhouse, Gary R. 1993. "What Does Japanese Trade Structure Tell Us About Japanese Trade Policy?" *Journal of Economic Perspectives* 7 (Summer): 21–43.

Schelling, Thomas. 1960. *The Strategy of Conflict*. Cambridge, MA: Harvard University Press.

Schoppa, Leonard J. 1993. "Two Level Games and Outcomes: Why Gaiatsu Succeeds in Japan in Some Cases but Not in Others." *International Organization* 47 (Summer): 353–86.

Schott, Jeffrey J. 1989. *Free Trade Areas and U.S. Trade Policy*. Washington: Institute for International Economics.

Schott, Jeffrey J. 1994. *The Uruguay Round: An Assessment*. Washington: Institute for International Economics. Forthcoming.

Schott, Jeffrey J., and Murray G. Smith, eds. 1988. *The Canada–United States Free Trade Agreement: The Global Impact*. Washington: Institute for International Economics.

Sell, Susan K. 1989. "Intellectual Property as a Trade Issue: From the Paris Convention to the GATT." *Legal Studies Forum* 13, no. 4: 407–22.

Siebeck, Wolfgang E., ed. 1990. *Strengthening Protection of Intellectual Property in Developing Countries: A Survey of the Literature*. World Bank Discussion Paper 112. Washington: World Bank (December).

Smith, Marcia S. 1992. *Space Activities of the United States and Other Launching Countries/ Organizations: 1957–1991*. CRS Report 92-427 SPR. Washington: Library of Congress, Congressional Research Service (11 May).

Space Activities Commission, Japan. 1987. "Towards the New Age of Space Development." Long Range Policy Study Group, 26 May.

Srinivasan, T. N., and Koichi Hamada. 1989. "The US-Japan Trade Problem." Unpublished paper, Yale University.

Subramanian, Arvind. 1990. "TRIPS and the Paradigm of the GATT: A Tropical Temperate View." *The World Economy* 13 (December): 509–21.

Subramanian, Arvind. 1991. "The International Economics of Intellectual Property Rights Protection: A Welfare-Theoretic Trade Policy Analysis." *World Development* 19 (August): 945–56.

Sykes, Alan O. 1990. " 'Mandatory' Retaliation for Breach of Trade Agreements: Some Thoughts on the Strategic Design of Section 301." *Boston University International Law Journal* 8, no. 2 (Fall): 301–24.

Sykes, Alan O. 1992. "Constructive Unilateral Threats in International Commercial Relations: The Limited Case for Section 301." *Law and Policy in International Business* 23 (June): 263–330.

Tahara, Takafumi. 1993. "Beef Trade Liberalization and Its Impacts on Production and Trade in Japan." Presentation before International Agribusiness Management Association Symposium III. Photocopy.

Talbot, Ross B. 1978. *The Chicken War: An International Trade Conflict between the United States and the European Economic Community, 1961–64*. Ames, IA: Iowa State University Press.

Tsuchiya, Keizo. 1989. "Agricultural Import Liberalization and Its Impact on the Domestic Market for Beef." Paper presented at US-Japan Economic Agenda session on agricultural trade, Washington (22 March).

Tyson, Laura D'Andrea. 1992. *Who's Bashing Whom? Trade Conflict in High-Technology Industries*. Washington: Institute for International Economics.

US Department of Agriculture, Economic Research Service. 1992. *Western Europe Agriculture and Trade Report*. RS-92-4 (December). Washington.

US Department of Agriculture, Economic Research Service. 1993a. *Europe International Agriculture and Trade Reports*. RS-93-5 (September). Washington.

US Department of Agriculture, Economic Research Service. 1993b. *International Agriculture and Trade Reports: Asia and Pacific Rim*. September. Washington.

US Department of Commerce. 1989. *The Japanese Solid Wood Products Market*. Washington: US Government Printing Office.

US Department of Commerce. 1992. *Global Markets for Supercomputers: The Impact of the US-Japan Supercomputer Procurement Agreement*. Washington (October).

US Department of the Treasury. 1986. *National Treatment Study: Report to Congress on Foreign Government Treatment of US Commercial Banking and Securities Organizations*. Washington.

US Department of the Treasury. 1990. *National Treatment Study: Report to Congress on Foreign Government Treatment of US Commercial Banking and Securities Organizations*. Washington.

US Federal Reserve System, Board of Governors. 1989. *Report on Implementation of the Primary Dealers Act* (Schumer Amendment Report). Washington (15 August).

US Government Task Force on the EC Internal Market. 1990. "An Assessment of Economic Policy Issues Raised by the European Community's Single Market Program." Washington: US Trade Representative (May).

US House of Representatives. 1988. Omnibus Trade and Competitiveness Act of 1988, Conference Report to Accompany HR3. Report 100-576, 100th Congress, 2nd session (20 April).

US House of Representatives, Committee on Agriculture. 1993. Joint hearing of the Subcommittee on Foreign Agriculture and Hunger and Subcommittee on General Farm Commodities. Washington (29 July).

US House of Representatives, Committee on Energy and Commerce. 1986. "Unfair Foreign Trade Practices: Barriers to U.S. Exports." Report by the Subcommittee on Oversight and Investigations. 99th Congress, 2nd Session. Washington: Congressional Research Service (May).

US House of Representatives, Committee on Energy and Commerce. 1987. Hearing on Informatics Trade Problems with Brazil before the Subcommittee on Commerce, Consumer Protection, and Competitiveness, Committee Serial No. 100-90, 15 July.

US House of Representatives, Committee on Government Operations. 1992. "Is the Administration Giving Away the US Supercomputer Industry?" Washington: US Government Printing Office.

US House of Representatives, Committee on Ways and Means. 1973. Hearings, 93rd Congress, 1st Session, H.R. 6767 (9 May).

US House of Representatives, Committee on Ways and Means. 1982. "Reciprocal Trade and Market Access Legislation." Hearing before the Subcommittee on Trade, Committee Serial No. 97-77, 26 July.

US House of Representatives, Committee on Ways and Means. 1989. Hearing before the Subcommittee on Trade, Committee Serial No. 101-28, 8 June.

US International Trade Commission. 1985. *Review of the Effectiveness of Trade Dispute Settlement Under the GATT and Tokyo Round Agreements*. USITC Publication 1793 (December). Washington.

US International Trade Commission. 1987. *U.S. Global Competitiveness: Oilseeds and Oilseed Products*. Report to the US Senate Committee on Finance, USITC Publication 2045 (December). Washington.

US International Trade Commission. 1988. *Foreign Protection of Intellectual Property Rights and the Effects on US Industry and Trade*. USITC Publication 2065 (February). Washington.

US Senate, Committee on Agriculture, Nutrition, and Forestry, Subcommittee on Domestic and Foreign Marketing and Product Promotion. 1987. Statement of the National Broiler Council. S. Hrg. 100-218. Washington (10 March).

US Senate, Committee on Banking. 1990. "Fair Trade in Financial Services Act of 1990: Report to Accompany S. 2028." 101st Congress, 2nd Session, Report 101-367 (13 July).

US Senate, Committee on Finance. 1986. Hearing on Presidential Authority to Respond to Unfair Trade Practices. 99th Congress, 2nd Session (22 July).

US Senate, Committee on Finance. 1987. Hearing on Improving Enforcement of Trade Agreements. 100th Congress, 1st Session (17 March).

US Senate, Committee on Finance. 1989a. Hearing on Trip Report on Congressional Delegation headed by Bentsen, 101st Congress, 1st Session, S. Report 101-40 (July).

US Senate, Committee on Finance. 1989b. *Oversight of the Trade Act of 1988.* 100th Congress, 1st Session, Washington (1 March).

US Trade Representative (USTR). 1989. Statement of Ambassador Carla Hills. Washington (25 May).

US Trade Representative (USTR). 1993. *Section 301 Table of Cases.* Washington (1 September).

Wade, Robert. 1990. *Governing the Market: Economic Theory and the Role of Government in East Asian Industrialization.* Princeton: Princeton University Press.

Wallach, Lori. 1993. "Hidden Dangers of GATT and NAFTA." In *The Case Against Free Trade: GATT, NAFTA, and the Globalization of Corporate Power.* San Francisco: Earth Island Press.

Weiss, Frank D. 1989. "Domestic Dimensions of the Uruguay Round: The Case of West Germany in the European Communities." In Henry R. Nau, *Domestic Trade Politics and the Uruguay Round.* New York: Columbia University Press.

Whalley, John. 1989. *The Uruguay Round and Beyond.* London: Macmillan.

Williams, S. Linn. 1989. Testimony before the Senate Commerce Committee, hearings on the Japanese Space Industry (4 and 5 October).

Williams, S. Linn. 1991. "The Case Against Gephardt II." *International Economic Insights* (November/December): 24–28.

Williamson, John, ed. 1990. *Latin American Adjustment.* Washington: Institute for International Economics.

Winham, Gilbert R. 1986. *International Trade and The Tokyo Round Negotiations.* Princeton: Princeton University Press.

Wolf, Martin. 1994. *The Resistable Appeal of Fortress Europe.* Washington: American Enterprise Institute for the Center for Policy Studies.

Wolferen, Karel van. 1989. *The Enigma of Japanese Power.* London: Macmillan.

Woolcock, Stephen. 1991. *Market Access Issues in EC-US Relations: Trading Partners or Trading Blows?* London: Pinter Publishers for the Royal Institute of International Affairs.

Wray, William D. 1991. "Japanese Space Enterprise: The Problem of Autonomous Development." *Pacific Affairs* 64, no. 4 (Winter): 463–88.

Yabunaka, Mitoji. 1993. *Taibei keizai kosho: Masatsu no jitsuzo* (In search of new US-Japan economic relations: Views from the negotiating table). Tokyo: Simul Shuppankai.

Yamaguchi, Asao. 1987a. "Kachuu no kuri o hirotta 'Zeisei yuigadokuson kōji' " (Tax policy's super parishioner who snatched the chestnuts from the fire). *Seikai Orai* (January): 54–63.

Yamaguchi, Asao. 1987b. "Nōkyō: Sōno Hikari to Kage" (Nokyo: its light and shadow). *Kankai* (April): 114–23.

Yoshikuni, Takashi. 1988. "Nōsanbutsu Jiyuka Jidai no Nōgyō Seisaku no Tenkai" (Prospects for Agricultural Policy in the Era of Agricultural Products Liberalization). *Kankai* (November): 114–122.

Young, Soogil. 1989. "Korean Trade Policy—Implications for Korean-US Cooperation." In Thomas O. Bayard and Soogil Young, *Economic Relations Between the United States and Korea: Conflict or Cooperation?* Special Report 8. Washington: Institute for International Economics (January).

Yu Xiaoming, and Frank McCormick. 1992. "Environmental and Economic Policy Coordination: An Analysis of Forest Products Trade Between Japan and the United States." Reports submitted under grant 91-61 from the Japan–United States Friendship Commission. Washington.

Index

481

BIS. *See* Bank for International Settlements
Blair House agreement, 209–10, 222, 222*n*, 223–30, 224*n*, 226*n*, 347
Block, John, 138, 214
Bond markets. *See* Government bond markets
BOP. *See* Balance of payments
BOP Committee. *See* Balance of Payments Restrictions Committee
Border broadcasting case, Canadian, 71
Border measures. *See also specific measure*
  negotiations on, success of, 258
  traditional, and likelihood of market opening, 85
Brady Plan, 347
Brazil
  agricultural subsidies, 212
  balance of payments position, 159–60, 162–64
  citrus production, 260*b*
  Code of Industrial Property, 196
  debt servicing, disputes over, 159–60
  economic indicators, 150, 157, 158*t*
  economic reforms in, 161, 202, 315–16
  economic relations with US, 150, 151*t*, 197, 202
  foreign exchange allocation system, 156, 162
  foreign investment in, 150
  import licensing system, 156–57
    elimination of, 62
  import substitution policy, 197, 202
  industrial policy, 156–57
  Informatics Law, 156, 162
  Informatics Market Reserve policy, 163, 197
  informatics policies, 18, 93, 95–96, 150, 150*n*, 161, 193*n*, 197, 203
  IPR protection, 59*n*, 73, 150, 187–208, 350
    301 case, 189*t*, 196–207
  Law of Similars, 156, 156*n*, 160–61
  national treatment claims, 273
  pharmaceutical patent protection, 19, 71, 96–97, 150, 150*n*, 187–208
    301 case, 196–207
  priority designation of, 172, 187, 198–99
    motivation for, 150, 168–69
  section 301 targeting of, 58*t*, 60*t*, 67*t*, 150
  special 301 case, 332
  super 301 case, 39, 41–42, 43*t*, 62, 149, 155–64, 171, 198, 316–17, 326–27, 336, 350
    motivation for, 150–52
    results of, 162–64, 315
  trade dependence, 166
  trade liberalization in, 95, 155, 157–63, 170, 198, 315
  US trade with, 150, 151*t*
Brazilian Association of Fine Chemicals, 199
Brazilian Office of Patents and Trademarks, 203
Bretton Woods system, collapse of, 12

Britain
  agricultural policy, 224, 226, 231–32
  Banking Act of 1987, Article 91, 288*n*
  Financial Services Act of 1986, Part X, 288*n*
  and financial services case, 287–88, 295–96, 298–300, 304–05
  government bond market, Federal Reserve assessment of, 282
  IPR protection cases, 206*n*
  universal banking system, and mirror-image reciprocity, 270
British Aerospace, 119
British Bankers' Association, 288
Brittan, Leon, 175, 226, 226*n*, 227, 291–94, 299–300
Brock, William E., 15, 52, 138, 236, 242, 324
Brooks-Murkowski sanctions, on Japanese construction, 262
Buchan, David, 209–10
Building Experts Committee, 144–45
Bulgaria, IPR protection, 196*n*
Bush administration
  Brazilian IPR dispute, 198, 202
  China super 301 case, 318*b*
  Korean dispute, 180
  satellite dispute, 113, 116
  section 301 investigations, 57
  special and differential treatment for developing countries, 171–72
  supercomputer dispute, 111
  trade policy, 40*b*, 52
  wood products dispute, 140
Buy American Act of 1988, Title VII, 22

CACEX, 156, 160
Cairns Group, 226, 228, 231
Calf price deficiency payment scheme, 256
California citrus industry, and Japanese citrus dispute, 244, 249
Canada
  beef exports, 236*n*
  beer case, 70*n*, 214*n*
  border broadcasting case, 71
  and Brazilian import restrictions, 160
  cattle and meat import restrictions, 26
  counterretaliation to section 301 case, 66
  IPR protection, 190*n*, 196*n*
  priority designation of, 150
  1992 *Register of United States Barriers to Trade*, 28*b*
  retaliation by, 83
  section 301 targeting of, 58*t*, 67*t*
  subway railcar subsidies, 59*n*
  wood products dispute, 57*n*, 59*n*, 146–47, 147*n*–148*n*
Canada-US Free Trade Agreement, 17, 18, 280, 307*n*–308*n*, 307–08, 339
Canned fruit subsidies, EC, 18, 62, 92*n*, 211, 215–16
CAP. *See* Common Agricultural Policy
Capital adequacy requirements, 308

financial liberalization in, US encouragement of, 273–86

financial services negotiations, 95, 188, 273–86, 342, 350. *See also* Schumer amendment

government bond market. *See* Government bond markets, Japanese

government ministries. *See specific ministry*

government procurement practices, 39, 40*b*–41*b*, 41–42, 43*t*, 96, 165, 315
  and satellite dispute, 101–2, 115, 119–22
  and supercomputer dispute, 101–2, 105–12, 119–22

housing trends/codes, 135*n*, 138–39, 138*n*–139*n*, 142–44, 146

import barriers, cigarettes, 18, 62, 68, 147*n*, 241, 334

imports, 315*n*
  agricultural, 238
  beef, 234*t*, 243, 256–58
  citrus, 234*t*
  wood products, 134–35, 135*n*, 136*t*, 138, 140

industrial policy, 101*n*, 101–3

interest rate controls, 301*n*

IPR protection, 190*n*

nontariff barriers, 10*n*
  for tobacco exports, 147*n*
  for wood products, 134, 137–39, 141, 143–45

offshore food processing companies, 257–58

pork quotas, 251

price differentials, monitoring of, 41*b*

priority designation of, 110–11, 143, 150, 172

producer subsidy equivalents, 10*n*

quantitative import restrictions, elimination of, 235

reluctance to retaliate, 83

results-oriented amendment targeting of, 32–36, 38–40, 40*b*

rice policy, 56, 238–41, 254, 258*n*, 262, 264–66

satellite case. *See* Satellites

saving-investment gap, reduction of, 40*b*–41*b*

section 301 targeting of, 57, 58*t*, 60*t*, 67*t*, 90, 91*t*

securities affiliates, 270*n*, 278*n*

semiconductor case, 63, 63*n*, 68, 71, 73, 95–97, 101, 109*n*, 109, 315, 334, 341

space program, organizational structure of, 114*b*

starch-potato quotas, 248–49

steel arrangement with EC, 59*n*

subsidies, as proportion of national income, 10*n*

super 301 cases, 101–48, 315. *See also* Satellites; Supercomputers; Wood products

supercomputer market, 107*n*, 110*t*, 110–11
  US shares of, 108, 109*n*, 110–11

tariffs, for wood products, 135–37, 141, 143–46

trade barriers, 23. *See also specific barrier*
  structural nature of, 33–34, 39–40, 106*b*, 134, 341–42

trade dependence, 336

transportation machinery protection, 106*b*

US policy toward, worldwide condemnation of, 77

US trade imbalance with, 53, 338

wood industry in, decline of, 142, 142*n*

wood products case. *See* Wood products

Japan Agricultural Standards (JAS), 139, 145
  Technical Committee, 144

Japan Communications Satellite (JC-SAT), 115

Japan Economic Institute (JEI), 114*b*, 143*n*, 146*n*

The Japanese Solid Wood Products Market (Department of Commerce), 140

Japan Federation of Employers' Associations, 242

Japan Housewives Association. *See* Shufuren

"Japan problem," 33–35, 35*n*, 42, 53

Johnson, Manuel H., 287*n*

Juppe, Alain, 224, 227, 229

Justified disobedience, 53–54, 68–70, 72

Kaifu, Toshiki, 117

Kantor, Mickey, 44, 122*n*, 194*b*, 199–200, 223, 226*n*, 227, 323

Kato, Koichi, 241, 245, 249, 251–54

Keidanren, 242

keiretsu, 41*b*, 106*b*, 107*n*

Kemp, Jack, 37

Kennedy administration, agriculture policy, 210–11

Key, Sydney, 302*n*, 309*n*, 343*n*

Kim Chulsu, 178

Kim Young Sam, 175, 186

Kohl, Helmut, 227–28

Korea
  agricultural liberalization in, 178–80
  austerity campaign, 180, 186
  beef dispute, 66, 68, 171, 176–77, 181, 243
  beef exports, 236*n*
  Economic Planning Board, 180
  economic reforms in, 173–76
  financial services, 303*n*
  foreign investment barriers, 177–81, 186
  GSP eligibility for, termination of, 177
  heavy-industry effort, 173–74
  import restrictions
    beef, 66, 68, 171, 176
    beer, 176–77
    tobacco, 176
    wine, 176
  insurance market, barriers to, 18, 66, 176
  IPR protection, 18, 66, 176–77, 189*t*, 193, 194*b*, 196*n*
  localization laws, elimination of, 178–79
  market opening in, forces for, 173–85

unconditional, 339
  definition of, 10
  nondiscrimination based on, 9
MPA. *See* Major Projects Arrangement
MPP. *See* Massively parallel processing
MPT. *See* Ministry of Post and
  Telecommunications
Mulford, David C., 162, 267, 269, 278, 281,
  292*n*, 294, 305, 306*n*
Multilateralism, 9
  aggressive. *See* Aggressive multilateralism
  contingent, 18
Multilateral liberalization, 75
Multilateral negotiations, 79–80
  in financial services, 272, 307–08
  under GATT, 51–52
  internal US politics of, 74–75
  by Reagan administration, 14–18, 74
  US pressure for, 53
Multilateral trading system
  impact of beef/citrus agreement on, 259–62
  impact of IPR dispute on, 207–08
Murata, Ryohei, 111, 118, 118*n*, 132, 143*n*
Mutual recognition, of different national
  regulations, 343, 343*n*

NAFTA. *See* North American Free Trade
  Agreement
Nakagawa, Ichiro, 236, 239
Nakao, Eiichi, 249*n*
Nakasone, Yasuhiro, 138, 236, 241–42, 242*n*,
  247, 276
NASDA. *See* National Space Development
  Agency
National Aeronautics and Space
  Administration (NASA), 112, 115, 131–32,
  132*n*
National Cattlemen's Association, 237, 243,
  243*n*
National Farmers Union, 249
National Forest Products Association, 134*n*,
  140–41, 144
National Institute of Fusion Science, 122*n*
National Oilseeds Processors Association, 222
National Pork Producers Council, 243*n*
National security, and strategic industries,
  102–3, 131*n*, 132–33, 133*n*, 134
National Space Development Agency, 114*b*,
  117–19
National Sunflower Association, 229
National Trade Estimate Reports, 16, 28*b*,
  28–29
  1989, 110, 150, 160, 164, 166
  1993, 145–46
  1994, 181
  and satellite dispute, 115, 117*n*
  special 301 provisions, 194*b*
  and super 301 evolution, 32, 42*n*, 48
National treatment, 331, 337–40
  assessment of, 269, 269*n*

EC, 281–83
  Federal Reserve, 281–83
  de facto, 268*n*, 281, 299*n*–302*n*
  definition of, 268, 337, 337*n*
  de jure, 268*n*, 281
  reciprocal (conditional). *See* Reciprocal
    national treatment
  unconditional. *See* Unconditional national
    treatment
NAVSTAR Global Positioning System, 113
NEC, 103–4, 104*b*, 105, 111, 119, 122*n*, 132–33
Netherlands, and financial services case, 296
Newly industrializing economies, 171
Newman, Barry S., 305*n*
New Zealand
  beef exports, 236*n*
  producer subsidy equivalents, 10*n*
NFPA. *See* National Forest Products
  Association
NHK, 116–19
Nicaragua, and US sugar quota, 73
NIEs. *See* Newly industrializing economies
Nihon Keizei Shimbun, 122*n*
Nijuisseiki e mukete no Nosei no Kihon Hoko,
  239–40, 242*n*
Nikkeiren, 242
Nippon Telephone and Telegraph (NIT), 103,
  107–08, 115, 117–18
Nisseikyo, 244
Nokyo, 238, 240–41, 264
  insurance arm. *See* Zenkyoren
  political arm. *See* Zenchu
  savings scheme. *See* Norin Chukin
  trading arm. *See* Zennoh
Noland, Marcus, 35*n*, 36*n*, 53, 54, 340, 342*n*,
  343
Nomura Securities, 275, 277, 280
Nonaligned Movement, 165
Noncompliance
  and GATT, 85
  retaliation for, 325–26
Nondiscrimination, 331, 337
  based on unconditional MFN treatment, 9
  definition of, 337
Nonpecuniary externalities, 124*n*, 124–25, 130
Nonreciprocity, special and differential
  treatment for developing countries and,
  154
Nontariff barriers, 10*n*, 338
  Japanese, 10*n*
  for tobacco exports, 147*n*
  for wood products, 134, 137–39, 141,
    143–45
Norin Chukin, 240
North American Free Trade Agreement, 44, 80,
  196*n*, 205, 227–28, 273, 307–08, 339, 347
Northwest Cherry Growers, 179
Nosanbutsu jiyuka taisaku shoiinkai
  (Subcommittee on Agricultural Products
  Liberalization), 241, 247

Subsidies. *See also specific subsidy*
  and likelihood of market opening, 85
  to offset foreign dumping, 9
  as proportion of national income, 10*n*
Subsidies Code, 213–14
Subway railcar, Canadian subsidies for, 59*n*
Sugar, EC export subsidies for, 62, 212*n*,
  213–14
Sugar quota, 73, 212*n*, 212–14, 324
Summers, Lawrence H., 305*n*
Sunflower seed, diesel fuel based on, French
  subsidies for, 223
Sunkist Foods, 244, 244*n*, 257
Super 301, 1, 19, 23–49. *See also specific case*
  agreements, monitoring of, 145
  agricultural disputes, 314
  alternatives to, 323–26
  under Clinton administration, 42–49, 313,
    321, 321*n*, 323, 327
  counterretaliation to, 167–68, 318*b*, 321, 321*n*
  and creative minilateralism, 349
  criticism of, 313, 317–22
  definition of, 29
  effectiveness of, 171–72, 185–86, 313, 317,
    336–37
  evolution of, 24*t*, 32–38
  failure of, 316–17, 321
  foreign hostility to, 322, 337
  mandatory retaliation under, 29, 31–32, 37,
    37*n*
  and market opening, 316, 327
  renewal of, 42–45
  requirements under, 37
  results of, 40–42, 43*t*, 49, 313–27
    in 1989–90, 314–17
    and political pressures, 317
  versus section 301 and Gephardt
    amendment, 37*n*, 37–38, 45–49, 46*t*–47*t*,
    314, 318*b*–319*b*, 332, 336–37
  and strengthening of GATT, 145
  success rate, 316, 327
    factors that affect, 320
  target selection under, 38–40
  and Uruguay Round, 69
Supercomputer Procurement Review board,
  122, 122*n*
Supercomputers
  agreements on
    1987, 105–10, 129
    1990, 110–12, 129, 131–32, 132*n*
    assessment of, 119–34
  commercial use of, 102*n*, 103–05, 129*n*
  definition of, 104*b*
  development of, 103
  export subsidies for, 130, 130*n*
  externalities, 124–28, 130
  global market for, 104*b*
  history of, 103*n*, 103–4
  Japanese market for, 107*n*, 121*n*

Japanese policies, 103–5
Japanese sales of, 110*t*, 110–11, 131
large-scale, 104*b*
producers of, 103–5, 104*b*
profitability of, 123–24
as strategic industry, 122–28
super 301 case involving, 39, 41–42, 43*t*, 96,
  101–12, 315–16, 327
  policy implications of, 128–29
  role of reciprocity in, 130–34
  role of retaliation in, 129–30
US policies, 103–05
US sales of, 110*t*, 110–11
  in Japan, 108, 109*n*, 110–11
Supply-control schemes, domestic, enforcement
  of, GATT exemption for, 246
Sutherland, Peter, 227, 341
Switzerland
  government bond market, Federal Reserve
    assessment of, 282*n*
  product marking standards, 59*n*

TAC. *See* Trade Assessment Commission
TACA. *See* Trade Agreement Compliance Act
Taiwan
  agricultural liberalization in, 181–85
  beer import barriers, 176–77
  Council for Economic Planning and
    Development, 175
  detailed action plan, 181
  economic reforms in, 173–76
  GSP eligibility for, termination of, 177
  IPR protection, 59*n*, 185, 189*t*, 194*b*, 196*n*, 200
  Japanese colonial domination of, 173
  manufacturing liberalization program, 185
  market opening in, forces for, 173–85
  Ministry of Economic Affairs, Industrial
    Development Bureau, 175
  national treatment claims, 273
  political status of, 175
  priority designation of, 185
  section 301 targeting of, 58*t*, 60*t*, 68, 90, 91*t*,
    177
  special 301 investigation, 332
  super 301 agreements with, 171–77, 181–85,
    316–17, 326–27
    assessment of, 181, 184*t*, 314–15
    political issues in, 186
  trade dependence, 166, 176–77, 185, 186*f*,
    336–37
  trade discrimination by, 66
  trade liberalization agreements with, 39–40,
    42, 43*t*
  trade liberalization in, 173, 175–76, 181–86,
    315–17
  US trade with, 173, 173*n*
Takeshita, Noboru, 238, 242, 247–54
Tangerines, 251*n*
Target country
  conditions in

and bargaining strategy, 84
and likelihood of trade agreement, 82
political balance in, and section 301 case
  outcome, 88t, 89, 232, 317, 350
pro-change constituency in
  importance of, 82, 93, 95, 231–32, 264, 303
  lack of, 82, 96
vulnerability of, and section 301 case
  outcome, 86
Tariff Act of 1930, 25, 208n. See also Smoot-
  Hawley debacle
Tariffication
  Uruguay Round goal of, 258
  without exception, 266
Tariffs. See also specific tariff
  average, on industrial goods, 2
  bargaining, 25, 25n
  GATT reduction of, 25, 336
  and likelihood of market opening, 85
  presidential authority to set, 25
  versus quantitative restrictions, 164
  reduction
    GATT success with, 336
    trade gains from, 334
Technical assistance, to developing countries,
  for structural and
regulatory harmonization, 350
Technical committees, to monitor wood
  products agreement, 144–46
Technical standards, and likelihood of market
  opening, 85
Technological externalities, 124–26
  examples of, 126–27
  verification of, 127–28
Technology drivers, 124
Technology transfer, 202, 205
Telecommunications. See also Satellites
  GATT role in, 12
  Japanese protection of, 106b
Telecommunications Trade Act of 1988, 22
Terpstra, Ellen, 245
Thailand
  IPR protection, 189t, 194b, 195, 200, 205
  section 301 targeting of, 58t, 61t, 62, 67t, 71
Thinking Machines, 104b, 120
Third-country markets, EC export subsidies in,
  211–12, 286
Threats
  defiance of, direct economic costs of, 80, 85
  implicit, 84, 92
  and negotiator's credibility, 85
  public, 84–85, 92
    definition of, 333n
  retaliatory. See Retaliatory threats
  and section 301 case outcome, 88t, 89, 330
Tobacco. See Cigarettes
Tohoku University, 111
Tokyo, as global financial center, 284
Tokyo Institute of Technology, 108

Tokyo Round, 13–15, 27, 138, 147, 192, 213,
  235–36
Tokyo Stock Exchange, membership in,
  barriers to, 274, 276–78
Tomato concentrates, EC import price system
  for, abolition of, 213
Toronto summit, 264
Toshiba, 104, 119
Toward Renewed Growth in Latin America
  (Balassa et al.), 157n
TPAP. See Trade Policy Action Plan (1985)
Trade Act of 1974, 12, 24t, 31, 65, 290, 320n
  section 181, 28b
  section 301, 210. See also Section 301
  ection 305, 105–07
Trade Act of 1988. See Omnibus Trade and
  Competitiveness Act of 1988
Trade Agreement Compliance Act, 323, 325–26
Trade agreements. See also specific agreement
  compliance with, monitoring of, 29, 46t–47t
  discriminatory, 335
  foreign compliance with, monitoring of, 29,
    46t–47t
  international, enforcement of, 73
  likelihood of, and conditions in target
    country, 82
  on MFN basis, 66, 263, 339–40
  monitoring and enforcement of, 325–26
Trade Agreements Act of 1979, 24t, 27, 31, 65.
  See also Section 301
Trade and Tariff Act of 1984, 16, 24t, 27–29, 31,
  65, 193, 196. See also Section 301
Trade Assessment Commission, 349–50
Trade balance
  ability of trade policy to correct, 53–54
  and bargaining strategy, 84
  and 301 case outcome, 89
  import side of, 9
  US, deterioration of, 13–14
  US-Japan, 53
Trade barriers. See also specific barrier
  aggressive attack on, 9
  impact of aggressive unilateralism on, 2–3
  systemic nature of, and trade agreement
    success, 336
  transparency of, and section 301 case results,
    332
  type of
    and likelihood of market opening, 85
    and section 301 case outcome, 87t–88t, 89
    and US trade imbalance, 14
Trade bills, protectionist, 16n
Trade dependence. See also specific country
  level of, and section 301 case results, 333
Trade Expansion Act of 1962, 210
  section 252, 24t, 25–26, 212
Trade gains, from section 301 agreements, 68,
  334
Trade liberalization. See Liberalization

National Trade Estimate Reports. *See*
National Trade Estimate Reports
and oilseeds dispute, 218, 220–21, 231
priority practices/countries identification, 29,
35–36, 38–40, 40*b*, 42*n*, 45, 46*t*–47*t*, 48–49,
172, 194*b*, 194–95, 314, 317, 320, 323, 332
private petitions to, 26–27, 27*n*
public investigation files, 56, 59
retaliation by
limitations on, 47*t*, 49
mandatory, 29, 31–32, 36, 36*n*, 47*t*, 49
retaliation for noncompliance, 325–26
screening of prospective 301 cases, 92
section 301 cases initiated by, 27, 57, 59, 327,
332–33, 333*n*. *See also specific case*
success rate, 88*t*, 89–90
special 301 cases, 196*n*
supercomputer investigation, 105–06, 110–11,
120–21
super 301 policy, 37, 45, 101*n*, 317
and wood products case, 141–43, 145
Universal banking systems, and mirror-image
reciprocity, 270–71, 279, 286, 303
Unjustifiable practices, 27
definition of, 29–31
Unjustified disobedience, 346–47
Unreasonable practices, 27
definition of, 29–31, 31*n*
Uruguay Round, 1–3, 17, 29*n*, 38, 41, 49, 79–80,
350
and aggressive unilateralism, 330–31, 335,
337, 347
agricultural disputes, 209–16, 224, 234, 237,
243, 252–55, 258, 260*b*, 263, 265–66, 347
completion of, 59, 343
agriculture and, 225–29
and domestic politics, 73–77, 234, 237
expansion of Government Procurement Code
during, 103
financial services negotiations, 272, 296,
307–8
impact on effectiveness of US retaliatory
threats, 343, 344*b*
India's position in, 167
IPR protection, 187–88, 190–92, 192*n*, 194*b*,
195–97, 199–200, 202, 204–5, 207, 347
and Korean dispute, 180
launch of, 55, 68–69, 72, 74, 76
new negotiation areas, 57, 68–69, 72, 89, 149,
151–52, 154, 166, 192, 322, 345. *See also*
Foreign investment; Intellectual property
rights; Services
oilseeds dispute, 219–20, 222, 230, 230*n*
tariff liberalization, 258, 336
trade gains from, 334
Understanding on the Balance of Payments
Provisions of the GATT 1994, 164
US objectives in, Brazilian and Indian
opposition to, 150–51, 154–55, 168–70, 317

US trade gains from, 68
and wood products dispute, 140, 143–46,
146*n*, 316
US Agency for International Development, 350
Ushiba, Nobuhiko, 137
US Meat Export Federation (USMEF), 243,
243*n*, 258, 264–65
Tokyo representative. *See* Seng, Philip
USSR, US grain embargo, 212
Utsumi, Makoto, 278, 306, 306*n*

Variable import fees, 211, 211*n*, 213, 252
Vector processors, 104*b*
Vegetable oils
EC tax on, 218
US exports of, 229
Vegetable producers, EC support for, 62
Very large-scale integrated circuits (VLSI),
103–04
Volcker, Paul, 13
Voluntary export restraints (VERs), 9, 57*n*
Voluntary import expansion (VIE), 340–41

Wagyu beef production, 257
Walnuts, US exports of, 214
Watanabe, Michio, 239, 248
Watch lists, for IPR protection, 194*b*, 195, 200
Weingarten, Fred W., 104*b*
Wheat flour, EC export subsidies for, 62, 70,
213–14
Wheat gluten, EC imports of, 221
Williams, Linn, 116
Wilson, Bruce, 306*n*
Wilson, Michael, 28*b*
Wine, import restrictions on, 176–77, 221
Win set
in beef and citrus case, 237, 264–65
definition of, 237
factors that determine, 259
WIPO. *See* World Intellectual Property
Organization
Wolf, Martin, 343*n*
Wolff, Alan Wm., 347
Wood construction, Japanese, limitations on,
135*n*, 138–39, 138*n*–139*n*, 142–44, 250, 262
Wood products
1990 agreement on, 144, 326, 342
evaluation of, 144–48
Canadian subsidies for, 57*n*, 59*n*
foreign performance-based test results for,
141
Japanese imports of, 134–35, 135*n*, 136*t*, 140,
145–48
ratio of raw to finished products, 135, 137
Japanese industry, decline of, 142, 142*n*
Japanese nontariff barriers to, 134, 137–39,
141, 143–45, 350
Japanese subsidies for, 142, 144
Japanese tariff structure for, 135–37, 141,
143–46

Japanese technical barriers to, 39, 41, 43*t*, 68,
 96, 106*b*, 134–48, 155
 super 301 case involving, 139–44, 241,
 315–16, 326, 342
 US exports, 134–35, 135*n*, 136*t*, 138, 140
 US industry, 140, 140*n*–141*n*
Wood Products Subcommittee (US-Japan Trade
 Committee), 144
Workman, Willard, 165
World Bank, 152, 159–60
World Intellectual Property Organization, 169*n*,
 193*n*, 197
World Trade Organization (WTO), 3, 266, 331,
 337, 343
 counterretaliation approved by, 347
 dispute settlement mechanism, 29*n*, 204, 208,
 208*n*, 326, 332, 335, 343–45, 345*n*, 348, 351
 potential US violations of, 346–48
 IPR agreement, 204–6
 legal/economic analytic capacity, 348–50,
 349*n*
 reciprocal liberalization in, 322
 retaliation approved by, 343–50
 trade rules, enforcement of, 345

Wyden, Ron, 148*n*

Yamamura, Agricultural Minister, 236–37
Yamanaka, Sadanori, 238, 247, 249, 249*n*, 253,
 265
Yen
 appreciation of, 23, 146, 148
 depreciation of, 138*n*
Yen-dollar negotiations, and Japanese financial
 liberalization, 274–75, 278, 305, 309
Yerxa, Rufus, 220–21
Yeutter, Clayton, 18–19, 32, 74, 108, 108*n*, 111,
 193, 197, 237, 242, 245, 248–50, 252, 254,
 260*b*, 263–65
Yoshikuni, Takashi, 240*n*

Zenchu (Zenkoku Nogyo Dantai Chuo
 Rengokai), 238, 240–41, 247,
249, 252, 265
Zenkoku Nogyo Kumiai Rengokai. *See* Nokyo
Zenkyoren, 240
Zennoh, 240–41, 247*n*
Zero tariff bindings, EEC, 209, 211–12, 230
zoku, 239–40, 250–54, 264

Other Publications from the
Institute for International Economics

POLICY ANALYSES IN INTERNATIONAL ECONOMICS Series

BOOKS

Economic Sanctions Reconsidered (in two volumes)
  Economic Sanctions Reconsidered: Supplemental Case Histories
  Gary Clyde Hufbauer, Jeffrey J. Schott, and Kimberly Ann Elliott/*1985, 2d ed.*
    December 1990

ISBN cloth 0-88132-115-X	928 pp.
ISBN paper 0-88132-105-2	928 pp.

  Economic Sanctions Reconsidered: History and Current Policy
  Gary Clyde Hufbauer, Jeffrey J. Schott, and Kimberly Ann Elliott/*December 1990*

ISBN cloth 0-88132-136-2	288 pp.
ISBN paper 0-88132-140-0	288 pp.

Pacific Basin Developing Countries: Prospects for the Future
Marcus Noland/*January 1991*

ISBN cloth 0-88132-141-9	250 pp.
ISBN paper 0-88132-081-1	250 pp.

Currency Convertibility in Eastern Europe
John Williamson, editor/*October 1991*

ISBN cloth 0-88132-144-3	396 pp.
ISBN paper 0-88132-128-1	396 pp.

Foreign Direct Investment in the United States
Edward M. Graham and Paul R. Krugman/*1989, 2d ed. October 1991*

ISBN paper 0-88132-139-7	200 pp.

International Adjustment and Financing: The Lessons of 1985-1991
C. Fred Bergsten, editor/*January 1992*

ISBN paper 0-88132-112-5	336 pp.

North American Free Trade: Issues and Recommendations
Gary Clyde Hufbauer and Jeffrey J. Schott/*April 1992*

ISBN cloth 0-88132-145-1	392 pp.
ISBN paper 0-88132-120-6	392 pp.

American Trade Politics
I. M. Destler/*1986, 2d ed. June 1992*

ISBN cloth 0-88132-164-8	400 pp.
ISBN paper 0-88132-188-5	400 pp.

Narrowing the U.S. Current Account Deficit
Allen J. Lenz/*June 1992*

ISBN cloth 0-88132-148-6	640 pp.
ISBN paper 0-88132-103-6	640 pp.

The Economics of Global Warming
William R. Cline/*June 1992*

ISBN cloth 0-88132-150-8	416 pp.
ISBN paper 0-88132-132-X	416 pp.

U.S. Taxation of International Income: Blueprint for Reform
Gary Clyde Hufbauer, assisted by Joanna M. van Rooij/*October 1992*

ISBN cloth 0-88132-178-8	304 pp.
ISBN paper 0-88132-134-6	304 pp.

Who's Bashing Whom? Trade Conflict in High-Technology Industries
Laura D'Andrea Tyson/*November 1992*

ISBN cloth 0-88132-151-6	352 pp.
ISBN paper 0-88132-106-0	352 pp.

Currencies and Politics in the United States, Germany, and Japan
C. Randall Henning/*September 1994*
                    ISBN paper 0-88132-127-3   432 pp.

Estimating Equilibrium Exchange Rates
John Williamson, editor/*September 1994*
                    ISBN paper 0-88132-076-5   320 pp.

Managing the World Economy: Fifty Years After Bretton Woods
Peter B. Kenen, editor/*September 1994*
                    ISBN paper 0-88132-212-1   448 pp.

Reciprocity and Retaliation in U.S. Trade Policy
Thomas O. Bayard and Kimberly Ann Elliott/*September 1994*
                    ISBN paper 0-88132-084-6   528 pp.

SPECIAL REPORTS

1   Promoting World Recovery: A Statement on Global Economic Strategy
    by Twenty-six Economists from Fourteen Countries/*December 1982*
    (out of print)   ISBN paper 0-88132-013-7   45 pp.

2   Prospects for Adjustment in Argentina, Brazil, and Mexico:
    Responding to the Debt Crisis
    John Williamson, editor/*June 1983*
    (out of print)   ISBN paper 0-88132-016-1   71 pp.

3   Inflation and Indexation: Argentina, Brazil, and Israel
    John Williamson, editor/*March 1985*
                           ISBN paper 0-88132-037-4   191 pp.

4   Global Economic Imbalances
    C. Fred Bergsten, editor/*March 1986*
                           ISBN cloth 0-88132-038-2   126 pp.
                           ISBN paper 0-88132-042-0   126 pp.

5   African Debt and Financing
    Carol Lancaster and John Williamson, editors/*May 1986*
    (out of print)   ISBN paper 0-88132-044-7   229 pp.

6   Resolving the Global Economic Crisis: After Wall Street
    Thirty-three Economists from Thirteen Countries/*December 1987*
                           ISBN paper 0-88132-070-6   30 pp.

7   World Economic Problems
    Kimberly Ann Elliott and John Williamson, editors/*April 1988*
                           ISBN paper 0-88132-055-2   298 pp.

    Reforming World Agricultural Trade
    Twenty-nine Professionals from Seventeen Countries/*1988*
                           ISBN paper 0-88132-088-9   42 pp.

8   Economic Relations Between the United States and Korea:
    Conflict or Cooperation?
    Thomas O. Bayard and Soo-Gil Young, editors/*January 1989*
                           ISBN paper 0-88132-068-4   192 pp.

FORTHCOMING

The Globalization of Industry and National Governments
C. Fred Bergsten and Edward M. Graham

The Political Economy of Korea–United States Cooperation
C. Fred Bergsten and Il SaKong, editors

International Debt Reexamined
William R. Cline

Trade, Jobs, and Income Distribution
William R. Cline

Overseeing Global Capital Markets
Morris Goldstein and Peter Garber

Foreign Direct Investment in the United States, Third Edition
Edward M. Graham and Paul R. Krugman

Global Competition Policy
Edward M. Graham and J. David Richardson

Toward a Pacific Economic Community?
Gary Clyde Hufbauer and Jeffrey J. Schott

Measuring the Costs of Protection in Japan
Yoko Sazanami, Shujiro Urata, and Hiroki Kawai

The Uruguay Round: An Assessment
Jeffrey J. Schott

The Case for Trade: A Modern Reconsideration
J. David Richardson

The Future of the World Trading System
John Whalley, in collaboration with Colleen Hamilton

For orders outside the US and Canada please contact:

Longman Group UK Ltd.
PO Box 88
Harlow, Essex CM 19 5SR
UK

Telephone Orders: 0279 623923
Fax: 0279 414130
Telex: 81259

Canadian customers can order from the Institute or from either:

RENOUF BOOKSTORE
1294 Algoma Road
Ottawa, Ontario K1B 3W8
Telephone: (613) 741-4333
Fax: (613) 741-5439

LA LIBERTÉ
3020 chemin Sainte-Foy
Quebec G1X 3V6
Telephone: (418) 658-3763
Fax: (800) 567-5449